BedandPet.Com Guide to

California Pet Friendly Hotels

By Milo Maxwell
as told to Laurence A. Canter

Bed & Pet® Publications
Host Milo Corporation

Published in the United States by Bed & Pet® Publications,
an imprint of Host Milo Corporation
www.bedandpet.com

This publication is designed to provide accurate information in regard to the subject matter covered, as of the time this was written. It is sold with the understanding that the information concerning hotel pet policies, fees, and descriptions is subject to change at any time. This book is intended only as a reference.

ISBN 978-0-615-49904-8

How to use this guide

Sample Listing

Milo's Favorite Hotel B&B
1234 First Street
Pet City CA 95814
(619) 123-4567
$119 - $309
Bed & Pet Discount Offered

Pet Policy: Dogs only, up to 80 lbs. Daily pet fee of $10 per pet. Pet amenities include personalized dog dish and dog room service menu with tasty canine treats prepared by our chefs.

Features: Number of rooms: 15, Number of floors: 3, Business services, Free wireless Internet, Free breakfast, Multilingual staff, Complimentary newspapers in lobby, Concierge desk, Smoke-Free property, Porter/bellhop, Security guard, Limo or Town Car service available, Tennis courts, Free parking, Full service Health Club.

Note the following details within each hotel listing:

Special Feature Icons

 Bed & Breakfast

 Golf Course

 Tennis Courts

 Marina

 Romantic

Star Ratings

 1 to 5 stars (higher is better)

Nothing negative should be implied to those shown as *Not Rated.* This means only that insufficient reviews were available for a reliable rating.

Rates & Discounts

Rates listed are the hotel's standard published rates. If ***Bed & Pet Discount Offered*** appears below the rate, Bed & Pet has negotiated discounted rates and last minute specials for the property. To get the best rate you must either book online at BedAndPet.com or by telephone,

Using promo code 102350:
U.S. and Canada: 1-800-780-5733
Europe: 00-800-11-20-11-40

Pet Policies

Pet policies listed are the most current information available, however policies and fees do change. You may wish to verify the current policy directly with the hotel.

Adelanto

Also see the following nearby communities that have pet friendly properties:
Victorville - 8 miles

Days Inn Adelanto
11628 Bartlett Ave
Adelanto CA 92301
(760) 246-8777
$47 - $99
Bed & Pet Discount Offered

Pet Policy: Dogs allowed in some rooms, $10 per night. Limit of 2 dogs.

Features: Free breakfast, Business services, Parking (free), Complimentary newspapers in lobby, Swimming pool - outdoor seasonal, Guest laundry, Free wireless Internet.

Alameda

Also see the following nearby communities that have pet friendly properties:
Oakland - 3 mile, Emeryville - 5 miles, Berkeley - 7 miles, Brisbane - 9 miles, San Francisco - 9 miles

Extended Stay America Oakland - Alameda
1350 Marina Village Pkwy
Alameda CA 94501
(510) 864-1333
$71 - $99
Bed & Pet Discount Offered

Pet Policy: One pet is allowed in each guest room. A $25 per day non-refundable cleaning fee (not to exceed $150) will be charged the first night of your stay.

Features: Guest laundry, Elevator, Number of rooms: 121, Number of floors: 4, Parking Free, Free wireless Internet.

Extended Stay Deluxe Oakland - Alameda Airport
1260 S Loop Rd
Alameda CA 94502
$64 - $129
Bed & Pet Discount Offered

Pet Policy: One pet is allowed in each guest room. A $25 per day non-refundable cleaning fee (not to exceed $150) will be charged the first night of your stay.

Features: Guest laundry, Elevator, Number of rooms: 88, Number of floors: 3, Barbecue grill(s), Free breakfast, Parking (free), Front desk (limited hours), Internet access, Use of nearby fitness center (discount).

Alpine

Ayres Inn Alpine
1251 Tavern Rd
Alpine CA 91901
(619) 445-5800
$109 - $139
Bed & Pet Discount Offered

Pet Policy: Pets accepted, $45 additional charge.

Features: Number of rooms: 97, Number of floors: 2, Business services, Barbecue grill(s), Coffee in lobby, Guest laundry, Free breakfast, Nearby fitness center (free), Swimming pool - outdoor.

Alturas

Best Western Trailside Inn
343 North Main St.
Alturas CA 96101
(530) 233-4111
$73 - $91

Pet policy: Dogs only. Must declare pets. No cats please and one dog maximum, additional charge $10, undeclared pets $100.00 additional charge

Features: Cable satellite television, Free wireless Internet, Outdoor heated swimming pool, Business services, Free continental breakfast.

Essex Motel
1216 North Main Street
Alturas CA 96101
(530) 233-2821
From $62
Bed & Pet Discount Offered

Pet policy: Pets accepted, $10 per pet per stay.

Features: Business services, Guest laundry, Parking (free), Free wireless Internet.

Super 8 Motel - Alturas
511 N Main St U.S. 395
Alturas CA 96101
(530) 233-3545
$55 - $174
Bed & Pet Discount Offered

Pet policy: Pets accepted.

Features: Free breakfast, Wheelchair accessible, Number of floors: 2, Business services, Parking (free),

Amador City

Also see the following nearby communities with pet friendly lodging:
Sutter Creek - 2 miles, Jackson - 5 miles

Imperial Hotel
14202 Hwy 49
Amador City CA 95601
(209) 267-9172
$105 - $134
Bed & Pet Discount Offered

Pet policy: Small dogs allowed. $35 per night per dog, limit of 2 per room. Please do not leave unattended in room and keep leashed when outside. Pets are not allowed in dining or living room, but are welcome on the verandah or in the court yard. Pets are not allowed on the furniture in the guest room or in the public areas. If your pet does sleep on the bed with you, ask us for a sheet to put over the duvet cover.

Features: Free wireless Internet, Number of rooms: 9, Free breakfast, Parking (free).

American Canyon

Also see the following nearby communities having pet friendly lodging:
Vallejo - 5 miles - Napa - 8 miles

Holiday Inn Express & Suites Napa American Canyon
5001 Main Street
American Canyon CA 94503
(707) 552-8100
$89 - $229
Bed & Pet Discount Offered

Pet Policy: Pets accepted, $50 per stay. First floor guestrooms are near exits for your convenience.

Features: Accessible bathroom, In-room accessibility equipment for the deaf, Braille or raised signage, Swimming pool – outdoor. Business services, Free breakfast, Concierge desk, Grocery/convenience store, Wireless Internet, Fitness facilities.

Anaheim

Also see the following nearby communities that have pet friendly properties:: Garden Grove - 4 miles, Orange - 4 miles, Fullerton - 4 miles, Placentia - 5 miles, Buena Park - 6 miles, Cypress - 6 miles, Brea - 6 miles, La Palma - 7 miles, Santa Ana - 7 mile, La Mirada - 8 miles, Fountain Valley - 8 miles, Cerritos - 8 miles, Los Alamitos - 8 miles, Yorba Linda - 9 miles, Hawaiian Gardens - 9 miles

Anaheim Plaza Hotel
1700 S Harbor Blvd
Anaheim CA 92802
(714) 772-5900
$50 - $333
Anaheim Plaza Hotel
Bed & Pet Discount Offered

Pet Policy: Pets allowed in smoking rooms only. A non-refundable pet fee of $10 per night is charged. Pet owners agree to not leave their pet unattended at any time during their stay at the hotel. Pets are not permitted in any of the food & beverage areas or at the pool. Pets must always be on a leash or in a cage while they are in any public or common place within the hotel. Maid service will be provided only if the pet is removed from the room during the service. Pet owner will be fully responsible for any injuries to the hotel employee or other hotel guest caused by their pets. Pet owners must pick up after their pets or a $150.00 clean up fee will be added to their room account.

Features: Business Center, Swimming pool – outdoor, Bar/lounge, Pool table, Concierge services, Restaurant(s), Gift shops or newsstand, Internet (additional charge), Parking fee $14/24 Hours In/Out, Dry cleaning/laundry service, Breakfast available additional charge.

Not rated
Best Western Anaheim Hills
5710 E La Palma Ave
Anaheim CA 92807
(714) 779-0252
$72 - $109

Pet Policy: Pets allowed, Domestic small animals, $15.00 per pet per night, only in QQ rooms.

Features: HBO, Free wireless Internet, Continental breakfast (free), Swimming pools (indoor and outdoor), Fitness Center, Business center.

Clarion Hotel Anaheim Resort
616 W Convention Way
Anaheim CA 92802
(714) 750-3131
$109 - $139
Bed & Pet Discount Offered

Pet Policy: Pets less than 40 lbs, $10 per pet per day additional charge plus $25 refundable deposit.

Features: Poolside bar, Business Center, ATM/Banking, Security guard, Swimming pool-outdoor, Concierge services, Guest laundry, Bar/lounge, Room service, Restaurant(s), Gift shop, Airport transportation additional charge, Complimentary newspapers in lobby, Porter/bellhop Internet (free), Use of nearby fitness center (discount), Area shuttle additional charge, Theme park shuttle additional charge.

★★★

Clarion Hotel Anaheim Resort
616 W Convention Way
Anaheim CA 92802
(714) 750-3131
$109 - $139
Bed & Pet Discount Offered

Pet Policy: Pets less than 40 lbs, $10 per pet per day additional charge plus $25 refundable deposit.

Features: Poolside bar, Business Center, ATM/Banking, Security guard, Swimming pool-outdoor, Concierge services, Guest laundry, Bar/lounge, Room service, Restaurant(s), Gift shop, Airport transportation additional charge, Complimentary newspapers in lobby, Porter/bellhop Internet (free), Use of nearby fitness center (discount) Area shuttle additional charge, Theme park shuttle additional charge.

★★

Days Inn Anaheim Maingate
2200 S Harbor Blvd
Anaheim CA 92802
(714) 750-5211
$50 - $99
Bed & Pet Discount Offered

Pet Policy: Accepts dogs only, up to 25 lbs, $25 per night. Limit 2 per room.

Features: Swimming pool - outdoor, RV & Truck parking, Business services, Guest laundry, Parking (free), Complimentary newspapers in lobby, Wireless Internet, Free Breakfast.

★★★½

Embassy Suites Hotel Anaheim-North
3100 E Frontera St
Anaheim CA 92806
(714) 632-1221
$116 - $214
Bed & Pet Discount Offered

Pet Policy: Pets up to 50 lbs. $35 per day.

Features: Free Breakfast, Bar, Restaurant(s), Room service (limited hours), ATM/banking, Gift shops or newsstand, Number of rooms: 222, Suitable for children, Pool table, Parking (free), Multilingual staff, Business center, Porter/bellhop, Security guard, Wireless Internet, Dry cleaning/laundry service, Swimming pool - indoor, Fitness facilities .

★★
Extended Stay America - Anaheim Convention Center
1742 S Clementine St
Anaheim CA 92802
(714) 502-9988
$58- $81
Bed & Pet Discount Offered

Pet Policy: One pet is allowed in each guest room. A $25 per day non-refundable cleaning fee (not to exceed $150) will be charged the first night of your stay. Weight, size and breed restrictions may apply. Please contact the hotel directly with inquiries.

Features: Guest laundry, Swimming pool - outdoor, Elevator, Parking (free), Security guard, Wireless Internet, Use of nearby fitness center (discount).

★★
Extended Stay America Orange County - Anaheim Hill
1031 N Pacificenter Dr
Anaheim CA 92806
(714) 630-4006
$54- $104
Bed & Pet Discount Offered

Pet Policy: One pet up to 50 lbs is allowed in each guest room. A $25 per day non-refundable cleaning fee (not to exceed $150) will be charged.

Features: Guest laundry, Elevator, Number of rooms: 116, Number of floors: 3, Parking (free), Wireless Internet.

★★★½
Hilton Anaheim
777 W Convention Way
Anaheim CA 92802
(714) 750-4321
$88- $419
Bed & Pet Discount Offered

Pet Policy: Well behaved pets up to 75 lbs welcome, limit of 2 per room. The hotel will charge $50 service additional charge per stay for guests with pets. Pets may not be left unattended in the hotel room. Pets are not allowed in any food service area. Pets must be kept on a leash and you must clean up after your pet. Cell phone # must be provided at check in. Housekeeping may not service rooms with unattended pets. Private in-room pet care service available.

Features: Dry cleaning/laundry service, Indoor & outdoor pools, Bar/lounge, Restaurant(s), Gift shops or newsstand, Room Service, Hair salon, Steam room, Number of rooms: 1,572, Number of floors: 14, Pool table, Safe-deposit box, Spa services on site, Multilingual staff, 24-hour front desk, Porter/bellhop Security guard, Wireless Internet, Massage - treatment rooms. Concierge desk, Fitness facilities, ATM/Banking, Health Club, Business Center, Self and valet parking (additional charge).

★★★½
Hotel Menage Anaheim Boutique Hotel
1221 S Harbor Blvd
Anaheim CA 92805
(714) 758-0900
$127- $427
Bed & Pet Discount Offered

Pet Policy: Dogs only, up to 25 lbs., $25 per night. Limit 2 per room.

Features: ATM/Banking, Swimming pool - outdoor, Elevator, Poolside bar, Business center, Room Service, Security guard, Guest laundry, Concierge services, ***Continued on next page***

Hotel Menage Anaheim Boutique Hotel
Continued from previous page

Restaurant(s). Breakfast available additional charge. Complimentary newspapers in lobby, 24-hour front desk Porter/bellhop, Free wireless Internet. Smoke-Free property, Parking (valet) $12/24 Hours In/Out, Self- Parking fee $10/24 Hours In/Out, Fitness facilities, Theme park shuttle additional charge.

★★★
Hotel Pepper Tree
2375 West Lincoln Ave
Anaheim CA 92801
(714) 774-7370
$118 - $162

Pet Policy: Pets accepted, $15 per night per pet plus $150 deposit.

Features: Fitness center, Heated outdoor BBQ facilities, Restaurant, Kitchens in all rooms, Private balconies or fountain patios.

★★½
La Quinta Inn & Suites Anaheim
1752 S Clementine St
Anaheim CA 92802
(714) 635-5000
$99- $179
Bed & Pet Discount Offered

Pet Policy: Cats and dogs up to 50 pounds are accepted in all guest rooms. Housekeeping services for rooms with pets require pet owner be present or pet must be crated. No additional charges or deposits are required.

Features: Elevator, Business services, Suitable for children, Accessible bathroom, Swimming pool - outdoor, Gift shops or newsstand, Free breakfast. Parking (free), Multilingual staff, Complimentary newspapers in lobby, Wireless Internet, Dry cleaning/laundry service, Fitness facilities .

Not rated
Lemon Tree Hotel Suites
1600 East Lincoln Avenue
Anaheim CA 92805
(714) 772-0200
$80 - $129

Pet Policy: Limited accommodations for guest pets - small dogs only. Must have bedding & be on lead at all times. Pet fee: $15 per pet per night.

Features: Number of rooms: 30, Number of furnished apartments: 57, Fitness center, Guest laundry, BBQ, Business center, Non-smoking property, Swimming pool – outdoor – heated, Free wireless Internet.

★★
Motel 6 Anaheim Main Gate
100 W Disney Way
Anaheim CA 92802
(714) 520-9696
$99- $179
Bed & Pet Discount Offered

Pet Policy: Well-behaved pets stay Free. Animals that pose a health or safety risk may not remain onsite, and include those that, in our manager's discretion, are too numerous for any one room, cause damage to our property or that of other guests, are too disruptive, are not properly attended, or demonstrate undue aggression. All pets must be declared at check-in. In consideration of all guests, pets must be attended to and under control at all times. If unavoidable circumstances require a pet to remain in a room while the owner is offsite, the pet must be secured in a crate or travel carrier on your service day to avoid injury or damage. Pets must be on a leash or securely carried outside of guest rooms and under control at all times.

Features: Swimming pool - outdoor, Elevator, Guest laundry, ATM/banking, Gift shops or newsstand, Parking (free), Multilingual staff, Accessible bathroom, Roll-in shower, Accessibility equipment for the deaf, Braille or raised signage, Wireless Internet (additional charge), Business Center.

★★★½
Red Lion Hotel Anaheim
1850 S Harbor Blvd
Anaheim CA 92802
(714) 750-2801
$95- $259
Bed & Pet Discount Offered

Pet Policy: Pets welcome, $20 per stay.

Features: ATM/banking, Elevator, Business center, Bar/lounge, Restaurant(s), Swimming pool - outdoor, Concierge services, Gift shops or newsstand, Number of rooms: 310, Number of floors: 8, Breakfast available additional charge, Multilingual staff, Complimentary newspapers in lobby, Porter/bellhop, Security guard. Smoke-Free property, Dry cleaning/laundry service, Free wireless Internet, Fitness facilities, Parking (additional charge).

★★★
Residence Inn Anaheim Hills Yorba Linda
125 S Festival Dr
Anaheim CA 92806
(714) 974-8880
$119- $124
Bed & Pet Discount Offered

Pet Policy: Pets allowed, $75 per stay.

Features: Babysitting or child care, Elevator, Swimming pool - outdoor, Hair salon, Number of rooms: 128, Number of suites: 128. Parking (free), Complimentary newspapers in lobby, Business center, Internet access, Smoke-Free property, Fitness facilities .

★★★

Residence Inn by Marriott Anaheim Maingate
1700 S Clementine St
Anaheim CA 92802
(714) 533-3555
$139- $359
Bed & Pet Discount Offered

Pet Policy: Pets up to 75 lbs allowed, $100 per stay.

Features: Business Center, Barbecue Grill(s), Coffee in lobby, Swimming pool - outdoor, Children's swimming pool, Free breakfast, Concierge, Security guard, Gift shops or newsstand, Parking (free), Multilingual staff, Complimentary newspapers in lobby, Limo or Town Car service available, Internet access (free), Smoke-Free property, Dry cleaning/laundry service, Tennis on site, Fitness facilities, Theme park shuttle additional charge, Beach/pool umbrellas, Designated smoking areas, Free reception, Grocery/convenience store.

★★

Rodeway Inn & Suites Anaheim
2145 S Harbor Blvd
Anaheim CA 92802
(714) 251-6262
$49 - $129
Bed & Pet Discount Offered

Pet Policy: Rodeway Inns charge an additional $10 per night per pet and require a $50 damage deposit, which is refunded if the room is in order at check out. Max of 2 pets per room. A veterinarian certificate that the pet is on a flea and parasite program and that they are Free from parasites is required. Pets may not be left alone in the room unless in a cage.

Features: Swimming pool - outdoor, Business services, Number of rooms: 58, Number of floors: 2, Coffee in lobby, Guest laundry, Free breakfast, Parking (free), Multilingual staff, Complimentary newspapers in lobby, Free wireless Internet.

★★

Rodeway Inn Maingate
1211 S West Place
Anaheim CA 92802
(714) 533-2500
$45 - $61
Bed & Pet Discount Offered

Pet Policy: Rodeway Inns charge an additional $10 per night per pet and require a $50 damage deposit, which is refunded if the room is in order at check out. Max of 2 pets per room. A veterinarian certificate that the pet is on a flea and parasite program and that they are Free from parasites is required. Pets may not be left alone in the room unless in a cage.

Features: Number of floors: 2, Coffee in lobby, Guest laundry, Free breakfast, Parking (free), Complimentary newspapers in lobby, Free wireless Internet.

★★★½

Sheraton Anaheim Hotel
900 S Disneyland Dr
Anaheim CA 92802
(714) 778-1700
$129 - $396
Bed & Pet Discount Offered

Pet Policy: Dogs (50 pounds and under) and cats are allowed. There is a $25 plus tax per stay cleaning fee. Service animals are exempt from the weight restriction and cleaning charge. Pets must be accompanied in the guest rooms at all times.
Continued on next page

Sheraton Anaheim Hotel
Continued from previous page

Features: Restaurant(s), Swimming pool - outdoor, Gift shops or newsstand, Internet (additional charge), Safe-deposit, Multilingual staff, Porter/bellhop, Bar/lounge, Arcade/game room, Currency exchange, Suitable for children, Pool table, ATM/banking, Business services, Room service, Security guard, Concierge services, Parking fee $10/24 Hours, Accessible bathroom, Roll-in shower, In-room accessibility equipment for the deaf, Braille or raised signage, Dry cleaning/laundry service, Fitness facilities.

★★★½

Sheraton Park Hotel at the Anaheim Resort
1855 S Harbor Blvd
Anaheim CA 92802
(714) 750-1811
$114 - $995
Bed & Pet Discount Offered

Pet Policy: Pets up to 80 pounds are allowed. There is a limit of one pet per room and pet rooms are restricted to the first floor. A $50 cleaning fee will be charged.

Features: Suitable for children, Room service (limited hours), Poolside bar, ATM/Banking, Bar/lounge, Business center, Restaurant(s), Concierge services, Gift shops or newsstand, Number of rooms: 490, Internet (additional charge), Currency exchange, Multilingual staff Complimentary newspapers in lobby, Porter/bellhop, Smoke-Free property, Dry cleaning/laundry service, Swimming pool - outdoor, Fitness facilities, Self-parking fee, Valet Parking fee.

★★★

Staybridge Suites Anaheim Resort
1855 S Manchester Ave
Anaheim CA 92802
(714) 748-7700
$95 - $260
Bed & Pet Discount Offered

Pet Policy: Pets up to 80 lbs, $15 first night, $10 thereafter not to exceed $150. Must have vaccination records with you.

Features: Accessible bathroom, Roll-in shower, In-room accessibility equipment for the deaf, Braille or raised signage .

★★½

TownePlace Suites Anaheim Maingate
1730 S State College Blvd
Anaheim CA 92806
(714) 939-9700
$139 - $279
Bed & Pet Discount Offered

Pet Policy: Pets allowed with $100 sanitation additional charge.

Features: Swimming pool – outdoor, Hair salon, Number of suites: 140, Number of floors: 4, Parking (free), Complimentary newspapers in lobby, Business center, Free wireless Internet, Fitness facilities .

Anderson

Also the following nearby communities that have pet friendly lodging: Redding - 10 miles

Baymont Inn & Suites Anderson
2040 Factory Outlets Dr
Anderson CA 9600
(530) 365-6100
$55 - $139
Bed & Pet Discount Offered

Pet Policy: Pet friendly, $10 per pet per night.

Features: Swimming pool - indoor, Business services, Coffee in lobby, Free breakfast, Parking (free), Complimentary newspapers in lobby, high speed, Internet (free), Sauna, Fitness facilities, Guest laundry.

Not rated
Best Western Anderson Inn
2688 Gateway Dr
Anderson CA 96007
(530) 365-2753
$80 - $94

Pet Policy: Pets allowed. $15 per pet per night.

Features: Cable TV with HBO, Coffee maker, Hair drier, Iron & ironing board.

★★★½

Gaia Shasta Hotel
4125 Riverside Place
Anderson CA 96007
(530) 365-7077
$79 - $110
Bed & Pet Discount Offered

Pet Policy: Pets accepted, $25 per stay. Limit 2. Pets must be on leash at all times.

Features: Bar/lounge, Outdoor pool, Library, Full-service health spa, Restaurant(s), Coffee in lobby, 24-hour business center, Complimentary newspapers, Porter/bellhop, Limo or Town Car service available, Concierge, Massage - treatment room(s), Smoke-Free property, Dry cleaning/laundry, Fitness facilities, Free wireless Internet.

Angels Camp

Angels Inn Motel
600 North Main Street
Angels Camp CA 95221
(209) 736-4242
$63 - $79

Pet Policy: Pet rooms are available at a charge of $10 per pet per night, plus a deposit of $50.

Features: Free espresso drinks, Oreo cookies and vacation packages, Free continental breakfast, Free wireless Internet, Swimming pool – outdoor (seasonal), Laundry facilities, Microwaves.

Not rated
BW Plus Cedar Inn & Suites
444 South Main
Angels Camp CA 95222
(209) 736-4000
$107 - $179

Pet Policy: Dogs, at least 1 year old allowed. $15 per day.

Features: Fireplaces available, two room suite with spa available, HBO, Free wireless Internet, Free continental breakfast, Mini refrigerator, Heated swimming pool, Exercise facilities.

Antioch

★★
Best Western Heritage Inn
3210 Delta Fair Blvd
Antioch CA 94509
(925) 778-2000
From $79
Bed & Pet Discount Offered

Pet Policy: Pets accepted with additional charge.

Features: Swimming pool - outdoor, Elevator, Number of rooms: 72, Number of floors: 2, Coffee in lobby, Parking (free), Complimentary newspapers in lobby, Use of nearby fitness center (free), Free wireless Internet, Dry cleaning/laundry service, Free breakfast.

★★
Ramada Inn
2436 Mahogany Way
Antioch CA 94509
(925) 754-6600
$55- $109
Bed & Pet Discount Offered

Pet Policy: Pets allowed, $50 per stay.

Features: Free Breakfast, Swimming pool - outdoor, Elevator, Parking (free), Multilingual staff, Complimentary newspapers in lobby, Security guard, Internet (free), Number of rooms: 116, Dry cleaning/laundry service, Restaurant(s), Accessible bathroom, Roll-in shower, Use of nearby fitness center (free), Accessibility equipment for the deaf.

Arcadia

Also see the following nearby communities that have pet friendly lodging: Monrovia - 2 miles, El Monte - 4 miles, Pasadena - 5 miles, Rosemead - 5 miles, San Gabriel - 5 miles, South El Monte - 7 miles, South Pasadena - 7 miles, Monterey Park - 8 miles, City Of Industry - 10 miles

Extended Stay America Los Angeles - Arcadia
401 E Santa Clara St
Arcadia CA 91006
(626) 446-6422
$64- $94
Bed & Pet Discount Offered

Pet Policy: One medium-size pet is allowed in each guest room. A $25 per day non-refundable cleaning fee (not to exceed $150) will be charged the first night of your stay.

Features: Elevator, Number of rooms: 122, Number of floors: 3, Barbecue grill(s), Internet (additional charge), Parking (free), Multilingual staff, Use of nearby fitness center (free), Front desk (limited hours), Dry cleaning/laundry service.

★★★
Residence Inn by Marriott Arcadia
321 E Huntington Dr
Arcadia CA 91006
(626) 446-6500
From $119
Bed & Pet Discount Offered

Pet Policy: Pets allowed, $100 per stay.

Features: Swimming pool - outdoor, Business services, Barbecue grill(s), Coffee in lobby, Grocery, Parking (free), Complimentary newspapers in lobby, Smoke-Free property, Free Breakfast, Dry cleaning/laundry service, Number of rooms: 120, Number of floors: 2, Tennis on site, Fitness facilities.

Arcata

Also see the following nearby communities that have pet friendly lodging: Eureka - 7 miles

Best Western Arcata Inn
4827 Valley West Blvd
Arcata CA 95521
(707) 826-0313
$71 - $119

Pet Policy: Allows dogs only. $20 per stay. No cats.

Features: Cable TV with HBO, Free wireless Internet, Free continental breakfast, Heated indoor outdoor swimming pool, Hot tub, Business services.

Comfort Inn Arcata
4701 Valley West Blvd
Arcata CA 95521
(707) 826-2827
$74- $129
Bed & Pet Discount Offered

Pet Policy: Pet charge of 15.00/night per pet, limit two pets per room, maximum 25 pounds. No cats. Refundable pet deposit of 20.00

Features: Coffee in lobby, Swimming pool - indoor, Number of rooms: 57, Number of floors: 2, Free breakfast, Parking (free), High speed, Internet (free).

Days Inn Arcata CA
4975 Valley West Blvd
Arcata CA 95521
(707) 822-4861
$79 - $89
Bed & Pet Discount Offered

Pet Policy: Pet friendly rooms available, $35 additional charge.

Features: Bar/lounge, Airport transportation (free), Indoor pool, Restaurant(s), Room service (limited hours), Number of rooms: 76, Number of floors: 2, Computer rental, Internet (additional charge), Guest laundry, Business center, Smoke-Free property, Use of nearby fitness center (discount).

Quality Inn Arcata
3535 Janes Rd
Arcata CA 95521
(707) 822-0409
$72- $134
Bed & Pet Discount Offered

Pet Policy: Quality Inns charge an additional $10 per night per pet. They may require a $50 damage deposit, which is refunded if the room is in order at check out. Quality Inns accept any well-behaved pets with a maximum of 3 per room, but dogs are limited to 50 pounds. They do not currently require a veterinarian certificate. Pets may not be left alone in the room unless in a cage.

Features: Coffee in lobby, Number of rooms: 64, Number of floors: 2, Free breakfast, Parking (free), Accessible bathroom, In-room accessibility equipment for the deaf, Outdoor pool – seasonal..

Super 8 Motel - Arcata
4887 Valley West Blvd
Arcata CA 95521
(707) 822-8888
$45- $79
Bed & Pet Discount Offered

Pet Policy: Pets accepted, $25 per pet per night.

Features: Free breakfast, Parking (free).

Atascadero

Also see the following nearby communities that have pet friendly lodging: Paso Robles - 10 miles

Super 8 Motel - Atascadero
6505 Morro Rd
1 Block From 101
Atascadero CA 93422
(805) 466-0794
$53- $124
Bed & Pet Discount Offered

Pet Policy: Pets accepted, $10 per night per pet.

Features: Number of floors: 2, Free breakfast, Accessible bathroom, In-room accessibility equipment for the deaf, Braille or raised signage.

Auburn

Best Western Golden Key
13450 Lincoln Way
Auburn CA 95603
(530) 885-8611
$78- $109

Pet Policy: Pet allowed, no restrictions. $20 per pet. Limited number of pet rooms.

Features: Number of rooms: 68, Microwave, Refrigerator, Cable TV, Free wireless Internet, Free continental breakfast, Year round heated swimming pool and hot tub.

Comfort Inn Central
1875 Auburn Ravine Rd
Auburn CA 95603
(530) 885-1800
$79 - $94
Bed & Pet Discount Offered

Pet Policy: Pets up to 30 lbs, $15 per night per pet. Limit 2 per room.

Features: Business services, Guest laundry, Swimming pool - outdoor, Number of rooms: 80, Number of floors: 2, Free breakfast, Parking (free), High speed Internet (free), Fitness facilities.

Holiday Inn Auburn
120 Grass Valley Hwy
Auburn CA 95603
(530) 887-8787
$115 - $130
Bed & Pet Discount Offered

Pet Policy: Dogs less than 30 lbs. $20 per day plus $20 deposit. Limit 1 dog per room.

Features: Bar/lounge, Restaurant, Room service, Outdoor pool, Number of floors: 3, Multilingual staff, Business center, Fitness facilities, Accessible bathroom, In-room accessibility equipment for the deaf, Braille or raised signage, Dry cleaning/laundry.

Motel 6 Auburn
1819 Auburn Ravine Rd
Auburn CA 95603
(530) 888-7829
$59 - $62
Bed & Pet Discount Offered

Pet Policy: Well-behaved pets stay free. Animals that pose a health or safety risk may not remain onsite, and include those that, in our manager's discretion, are too numerous for any one room, cause damage to our property or that of other guests, are too disruptive, are not properly attended, or demonstrate undue aggression. All pets must be declared at check-in. In consideration of all guests, pets must be attended to and under control at all times. If unavoidable circumstances require a pet to remain in a room while the owner is offsite, the pet must be secured in a crate or travel carrier. Pets must be on a leash or securely carried outside of guest rooms and under control at all times.

Features: Coffee in lobby, Swimming pool - outdoor, Wheelchair accessible, Business services, Accessible bathroom, Free wireless Internet, Area shuttle (free).

★★

Quality Inn Auburn
13490 Lincoln Way
Auburn CA 95603
(530) 885-7025
From $84
Bed & Pet Discount Offered

Pet Policy: Quality Inns charge an additional $10 per night per pet. They may require a $50 damage deposit, which is refunded if the room is in order at check out. Quality Inns accept any well-behaved pets with a maximum of 3 per room, but dogs are limited to 50 pounds. They do not currently require a veterinarian certificate. Pets may not be left alone in the room unless in a cage.

Features: Elevator, Shopping on site, Parking (free), Multilingual staff, Complimentary newspapers in lobby, Business center, Wireless Internet, Casino, Swimming pool - outdoor seasonal, Number of floors: 3, Number of rooms: 75.

★★

Super 8 Auburn CA
140 E Hillcrest Dr
Auburn CA 95603
(530) 888-8808
$54 - $78

Pet Policy: Pets accepted but must call hotel directly for details and reservations.

Features: Business services, Guest laundry, Parking (free), Complimentary newspapers in lobby, Business center, Internet (free), Swimming pool - outdoor seasonal, Free breakfast.

Avalon

Catalina Canyon Resort and Spa
888 Country Club Dr
Avalon CA 90704
(310) 510-0325
$89 - $369
Bed & Pet Discount Offered

Pet Policy: Pet Friendly: a $50 pet fee will be charged at arrival

Features: Elevator, Full-service health spa, Restaurant(s), Bar/lounge, Swimming pool - outdoor, Number of rooms: 74, Number of floors: 4, Massage - treatment room(s), Smoke-Free property, Spa services on site, Fitness facilities, Free wireless Internet.

Bakersfield

Americas Best Value Inn Oak Street
889 Oak Street
Bakersfield CA 93304
(661) 336-0475
$49 - $55

Pet Policy: Small pets only, $10 per night per pet

Features: Number of rooms: 42, Microwave and mini fridge, Wireless Internet (free), HBO, Free breakfast, Swimming pool, Guest laundry.

Best Western Crystal Palace Inn & Suites
2620 Buck Owens Blvd
Bakersfield CA 93308
(661) 327-9651
$65 - $75

Pet Policy: Pets less than 50 pounds. $10. Limited pet rooms.

Features: Number of rooms: 190, HBO, Free wireless Internet, Free full breakfast, Swimming pool and hot tub – outdoor, Fitness center, Airport shuttle (free), Restaurant, Bar/lounge, Business center.

Not rated
Best Western Heritage Inn
253 Trask Street
Bakersfield CA 93312
(661) 764-6268
$76 - $106

Pet Policy: Small pets only.

Features: Free continental breakfast, Wireless Internet(fee), Swimming pool – outdoor, Complimentary newspaper.

Best Western Plus Hill House
700 Truxtun Ave
Bakersfield CA 93301
(661) 327-4064
$70 - $96
Bed & Pet Discount Offered

Pet Policy: Pets up to 50 lbs allowed. $10 per pet per night.

Features: Swimming pool - outdoor, Bar/lounge, Restaurant(s), Number of rooms: 97 Number of floors: 2, Business services, Free breakfast, Parking (free), Multilingual staff, Complimentary newspapers in lobby, Fitness facilities, Free wireless Internet, Wheelchair accessible.

Days Inn Bakersfield
818 Real Rd
Bakersfield CA 93309
(661) 324-6666
$50 - $62
Bed & Pet Discount Offered

Pet Policy: Pets welcome, $20 per pet per stay. No size restrictions.

Features: Coffee in lobby, Free breakfast, Parking (free), Complimentary newspapers in lobby, Internet (free), Swimming pool - outdoor seasonal, Business services.

Doubletree Hotel Bakersfield
3100 Camino Del Rio Ct
Bakersfield CA 93308
(661) 323-7111
$74 - $159
Bed & Pet Discount Offered

Pet Policy: Pets accepted, $50 per stay per pet. Limit 2 pets.

Features: Swimming pool - outdoor, Bar/lounge, Airport transportation (free), Restaurant(s), Room service, ATM/banking, Gift shops or newsstand, Number of rooms: 262, Number of floors: 3, Breakfast available additional charge, Nightclub, Parking (free), Multilingual staff, Complimentary newspapers in lobby, Porter/bellhop, Internet (free), Poolside bar, Dry cleaning/laundry service, Fitness facilities.

Econo Lodge Bakersfield
5200 Olive Tree Ct
Bakersfield CA 93308
(661) 392-1511
$44 - $54
Bed & Pet Discount Offered

Pet Policy: Pet Accommodation: $10 per pet per stay. Pet Limit: 2 small pets under 20 lbs.

Features: Free breakfast, Guest laundry, Business services, Swimming pool - outdoor, Number of rooms: 101, Number of floors: 2, Coffee in lobby, Parking (free), Free wireless Internet.

Extended Stay America Bakersfield - California Ave
3318 California Ave
Bakersfield CA 93304
(661) 322-6888
$44- $54
Bed & Pet Discount Offered

Pet Policy: One pet is allowed in each guest room. A $25 per day non-refundable cleaning fee (not to exceed $150) will be charged the first night of your stay. "Signature" rooms do not currently accommodate pets.

Features: Guest laundry, Elevator, Number of rooms: 120, Number of floors: 3, Parking (free), Front desk (limited hours), Wireless Internet.

Extended Stay Deluxe
3600 Chester Ln
Bakersfield CA 93309
(661) 328-8181
$86 - $136
Bed & Pet Discount Offered

Pet Policy: One medium-size pet is allowed in each guest room. A $25 per day non-refundable cleaning fee (not to exceed $150) will be charged the first night of your stay.

Features: Guest laundry, Elevator, Number of rooms: 80, Number of floors: 4, Barbecue grill(s), Internet (additional charge), Free breakfast, Parking (free), Front desk (limited hours), Fitness facilities.

Holiday Inn Hotel and Suites North
3927 Marriott Drive
Bakersfield CA 93308
(661) 377-8000
$75 - $139
Bed & Pet Discount Offered

Pet Policy: Pets up to 25 lbs, $25 per night additional charge plus $50 per stay deposit. May not leave unattended in room.

Features: Accessible bathroom, In-room accessibility equipment for the deaf, Braille or raised signage, Swimming pool - indoor, Business center, Bar/lounge, Restaurant(s), Room service (limited hours), Number of rooms: 120, Number of suites: 26, Number of floors: 4, Complimentary newspapers in lobby, Porter/bellhop, Free wireless Internet, Dry cleaning/laundry service, Fitness facilities.

Homewood Suites by Hilton Bakersfield
1505 Millrock Way
Bakersfield CA 93311
(661) 664-0400
$124 - $149
Bed & Pet Discount Offered

Pet Policy: Pets up to 50 lbs accepted, $75 per stay.

Features: Bar/lounge, Airport transportation (free), Swimming pool - outdoor, Wheelchair accessible, Shopping on site, Number of suites: 57, Number of floors: 4, Parking (free), Room service, Business center, Fitness facilities.

Hotel Rosedale
2400 Camino Del Rio Crt
Bakersfield CA 93308
(800) 430-7627
$95 - $235
Bed & Pet Discount Offered

Pet Policy: Pets accepted, $20 additional charge. Large grassy area for dogs.

Features: Swimming pool - outdoor, Bar/Lounge, Airport transportation (free), Restaurant(s), Room service, Number of rooms: 167, Number of floors: 2, Parking (free), Dry cleaning/laundry service, Wheelchair accessible, ATM/banking, suitable for children, Coffee in lobby, Free breakfast, Multilingual staff, Free wireless Internet, 24-hour business center, Smoke-Free property, Roll-in shower, Fitness facilities.

La Quinta Inn & Suites Bakersfield North
8858 Spectrum Pkwy
Bakersfield CA 93308
(661) 393-7775
$82 - $87
Bed & Pet Discount Offered

Pet Policy: Pets up to 25 lbs, no additional charge. Limit 2 per room. Must not be left unattended and must be leashed when outside the room

Features: Suitable for children, Business center, Elevator, Guest laundry, Use of nearby fitness center (free), Coffee in lobby, Accessible bathroom, Number of rooms: 65, Number of floors: 3, Free breakfast, Parking (free), Complimentary newspapers in lobby, Internet (free), Swimming pool - indoor, Fitness facilities.

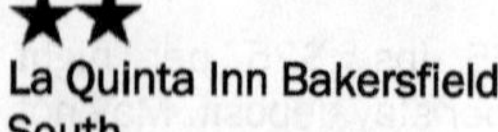

La Quinta Inn Bakersfield South
3232 Riverside Dr
Bakersfield CA 93308
(661) 325-7400
$59 - $69
Bed & Pet Discount Offered

Pet Policy: Cats and dogs up to 50 pounds are accepted in all guest rooms. Housekeeping services for rooms with pets require pet owner be present or pet must be crated. No additional charges or deposits are required.

Features: Swimming pool - outdoor, Accessible bathroom, Elevator, Number of rooms: 129, Number of floors: 3, Business services, Coffee in lobby, Free breakfast, Parking (free), Multilingual staff, Complimentary newspapers in lobby, Use of nearby fitness center (discount), Dry cleaning/laundry service, Internet (free).

★★

Ramada Limited Central
830 Wible Rd
Bakersfield CA 93304
(661) 831-1922
$99 - $145
Bed & Pet Discount Offered

Pet Policy: Pets Accepted, $10 per night per pet.

Features: Free breakfast, Parking (free), Complimentary newspapers in lobby, Swimming pool - outdoor seasonal.

★★★

Residence Inn by Marriott Bakersfield
4241 Chester Ln
Bakersfield CA 93309
(661) 321-9800
$169 - $170
Bed & Pet Discount Offered

Pet Policy: Pets allowed, $100 cleaning fee per stay.

Features: Business services, Swimming pool - outdoor, Airport transportation (free), Number of rooms: 114, Number of floors: 2, Barbecue grill(s), Coffee in lobby, Free breakfast, Parking (free), Complimentary newspapers in lobby, Free wireless Internet, Dry cleaning/laundry service, Tennis on site, Fitness facilities.

★★

Rodeway Inn & Suites Bakersfield
3400 Chester Lane
Bakersfield CA 93309
(661) 328-1100
$54 - $69
Bed & Pet Discount Offered

Pet Policy: Rodeway Inns charge an additional $10 per night per pet and require a $50 damage deposit, which is refunded if the room is in order at check out. Max of 2 pets per room. A veterinarian certificate that the pet is on a flea and parasite program and that they are Free from parasites is required. Pets may not be left alone in the room unless in a cage.

Features: Free Breakfast, Sauna, Swimming pool - outdoor, Elevator, Gift shops or newsstand, Number of rooms: 74, Number of floors: 3, Business services, Coffee in lobby, Guest laundry, Parking (free), Free wireless Internet.

Rodeway Inn Near I-5
200 Trask St
Bakersfield CA 93314
(661) 764-5221
$59 - $69
Bed & Pet Discount Offered

Pet Policy: Rodeway Inns charge an additional $10 per night per pet and require a $50 damage deposit, which is refunded if the room is in order at check out. Max of 2 pets per room. A veterinarian certificate that the pet is on a flea and parasite is required. Pets may not be left alone in the room unless in a cage.

Features: Coffee in lobby, Swimming pool - outdoor, Number of rooms: 53, Number of floors: 2, Free breakfast, Parking (free), Complimentary newspapers in lobby, Wireless Internet, Accessible bathroom, Braille or raised signage.

6257 Knudsen Dr
Bakersfield CA 93308
(661) 399-210
$59 - $79
Bed & Pet Discount Offered

Pet Policy: Pets accepted, $10 per night per pet.

Features: Free breakfast, Coffee in lobby, Business center, Number of rooms: 46, Number of floors: 2, Business services, Guest laundry, Complimentary newspapers, Wheelchair accessible, Multilingual staff, Free wireless Internet, Accessible bathroom, Fitness facilities.

Studio 6 Bakersfield

6141 Knudsen Dr
Bakersfield CA 93308
(661) 393-1277
$65 - $85
Bed & Pet Discount Offered

Pet Policy: Well-behaved pets are permitted with a fee of $10 per day to a maximum of $50 per stay. Pets must be under owners control at all times and not left unattended in room unless in a crate. Please declare the pet at check-in.

Features: Free wireless Internet, Elevator, Swimming pool - outdoor, Wheelchair accessible, Business services, Coffee in lobby, Guest laundry, Parking (free), Multilingual staff, Technology support staff.

Super 8 Bakersfield CA
3620 Wible Rd
Bakersfield CA 93309
(661) 833-1000
$42 - $89
Bed & Pet Discount Offered

Pet Policy: Pets accepted, $5 per day

Features: Coffee in lobby, Guest laundry, Parking (free), Complimentary newspapers in lobby, Swimming pool - outdoor seasonal, Free breakfast, Business services.

Super 8 Bakersfield Central
901 Real Rd
Bakersfield CA 93309
(661) 322-1012
$54 - $70
Bed & Pet Discount Offered

Pet Policy: Pets accepted, $10 per pet per night.

Features: Number of floors: 3, Parking (free), 24 - hour front desk, Swimming pool, Free wireless Internet, Free breakfast.

★★★½

The Padre Hotel
1702 18th St
Bakersfield CA 93301
(661) 427-4900
$89 - $169
Bed & Pet Discount Offered

Pet Policy: Pets up to 25 lbs, $100 per stay. Limit 1 pet per room.

Features: Number of rooms: 112, Number of suites: 13, Number of floors: 9, Nightclub, Technology support staff, Elevator, Smoke-Free property, Porter/bellhop, Restaurants: 3, Complimentary newspapers in lobby, Bar/lounge, Dry cleaning/laundry service, Translation services, Accessible bathroom, Spa services on site, Security guard, Business services, Wheelchair accessible, Suitable for children, Parking garage (fee), Multilingual staff, Roll-in shower, Free wireless Internet, Billiards, Braille or raised signage, Room service (24 hours), Accessibility equipment for the deaf.

★★

Travelodge Inn & Suites Bakersfield
1011 Oak Street
Bakersfield CA 93304
(661) 325-0772
$43 - $64
Bed & Pet Discount Offered

Pet Policy: Pets accepted, $10 per pet per night.

Features: Swimming pool - outdoor, Guest laundry, Free breakfast, Free wireless Internet.

★★

Vagabond Inn Bakersfield North
6100 Knudsen Dr
Bakersfield CA 93308
(661) 392-1800
$50 - $55
Bed & Pet Discount Offered

Pet Policy: Pets accepted, $20 plus $5 per night per pet.

Features: Airport transportation (free), Restaurant(s), Swimming pool - outdoor, Number of rooms: 154, Number of floors: 2, Business services, Coffee in lobby, Guest laundry coin-op, Free breakfast, Parking (free), Complimentary newspapers in lobby, Security guard, Bar/lounge.

★★

Vagabond Inn Bakersfield South
6501 Colony Rd
Bakersfield CA 93307
(661) 831-9200
$50 - $79
Bed & Pet Discount Offered

Pet Policy: Pets accepted, $5 per night per pet.

Features: Business services, Airport transportation (free), Swimming pool - outdoor, Number of rooms: 134, Number of floors: 2, Coffee in lobby, Guest laundry, Free breakfast, Parking (free), Complimentary newspapers in lobby, Security guard, Free wireless Internet.

Banning

Also see the following nearby communities that have pet friendly lodging: Beaumont - 5 miles

Days Inn Banning
2320 W Ramsey Street
Banning CA 92220
(951) 849-0092
$89 - $163
Bed & Pet Discount Offered

Pet Policy: Pets welcome, $10 per night.

Features: Business services, Internet (additional charge), Parking (free), Multilingual staff, Complimentary newspapers in lobby, Swimming pool - outdoor seasonal, Free breakfast.

Super 8 Banning Casino
1690 W Ramsey St
Banning CA 92220
(951) 849-8888
$46 - $75
Bed & Pet Discount Offered

Pet Policy: Dogs only. $10 additional charge.

Features: Restaurant(s), Number of rooms: 50, Number of suites: 10, Number of floors: 2, Free breakfast, Parking (free), Multilingual staff, Complimentary newspapers in lobby, Business center, Swimming pool - outdoor seasonal, Internet (free).

Travelodge Banning Casino and Outlet Mall
1700 W Ramsey St
Banning CA 92220
(951) 849-1000
$40 - $94
Bed & Pet Discount Offered

Pet Policy: Small pets accepted, $10 per day per pet. May also require deposit.

Features: Fitness facilities, Restaurant(s), Swimming pool - outdoor, Number of rooms: 42, Number of floors: 2, Guest laundry, Free breakfast, Parking (free), Complimentary newspapers in lobby, Business center, Casino, Internet (free).

Barstow

Also see the following nearby communities that have pet friendly lodging: Yermo - 10 miles

Best Western Desert Villa Inn
1984 E Main St
Barstow CA 92311
(760) 256-1781
$76 - $104
Bed & Pet Discount Offered

Pet Policy: Pets accepted with small additional charge at check in.

Features: Business services, Swimming pool - outdoor, Number of rooms: 95, Number of floors: 2, Free breakfast, Multilingual staff, Free wireless Internet, Fitness facilities.

Comfort Suites Barstow
2571 Fisher Blvd
Barstow CA 92311
(760) 253-3600
$109 - $124
Bed & Pet Discount Offered

Pet Policy: Pet accommodation: $25/night per pet. Pet deposit: $150 Pet limit: 2 pets per room, up to 40 pounds.

Features: Business center, Swimming pool - outdoor, Guest laundry, Elevator, Fitness facilities, Number of rooms: 83.

Country Inn & Suites
2812 Lenwood Road
Barstow CA 92311
(760) 307-3121
$81 - $154
Bed & Pet Discount Offered

Pet Policy: $20 additional charge per pet, per night. Refundable, one-time deposit of $50 required at check-in.

Features: Health club, Complimentary newspapers, Business center, Indoor pool, Wheelchair accessible, Number of suites: 41, Number of floors: 4, Free wireless Internet, Guest laundry, Smoke-Free.

Days Inn Barstow CA
1590 Coolwater Ln
Barstow CA 92311
(760) 256-1737
$36 - $62
Bed & Pet Discount Offered

Pet Policy: Pets welcome, $10 per night

Features: Coffee in lobby, Free breakfast, Complimentary newspapers in lobby, Swimming pool, Number of rooms: 111, Number of floors: 2, Guest laundry, Free wireless Internet.

Days Inn South Lenwood
2551 Commerce Pkwy
Barstow CA 92311
(760) 253-2121
$55 - $79
Bed & Pet Discount Offered

Pet Policy: Pets allowed, $5 per night per pet.

Features: Guest laundry, Swimming pool - outdoor, Number of floors: 3, Business services, Coffee in lobby, Arcade/game room, Parking (free), Multilingual staff.

Econo Lodge Barstow
1230 E Main St
Barstow CA 92311
(760) 256-2133
$55 - $59
Bed & Pet Discount Offered

Pet Policy: Dogs only, $10 per night. Must declare pets at check in. Limited rooms.

Features: Business services, Swimming pool - outdoor, Number of rooms: 50, Number of floors: 2, Free breakfast, Parking (free), Multilingual staff.

Economy Inn Barstow
1243 E Main St
Barstow CA 92311
(877) 747-8713
$45 - $50
Bed & Pet Discount Offered

Pet Policy: Pets allowed, $!0 per night per pet.

Features: Parking (free), Number of rooms: 30, Number of floors: 2, Free wireless Internet, RV and truck parking, Room service, Coffee in lobby.

Hampton Inn and Suites
2710 Lenwood Road
Barstow CA 92311
(760) 253-2600
$139 - $179
Bed & Pet Discount Offered

Pet Policy: Large pets, up to 150 lbs accepted.

Features: Business Center, Gift shops or newsstand, Number of rooms: 90, Number of suites: 26, Free breakfast, Children's swimming pool, Multilingual staff, Roll-in shower, In-room accessibility equipment for the deaf, Braille or raised signage, Dry cleaning/laundry, Free wireless Internet, Outdoor pool, Wheelchair accessible, Fitness facilities.

Holiday Inn Express Barstow-Historic Route 66
1861 W Main St
Barstow CA 92311
(760) 256-1300
$94 - $103
Bed & Pet Discount Offered

Pet Policy: Pets allowed, $25 per stay additional charge plus $50 refundable deposit.

Features: Swimming pool – outdoor, Business center, Gift shops or newsstand, Number of rooms: 65, Number of floors: 3, Barbecue grill(s), Video library, Free breakfast, Multilingual staff, Complimentary newspapers in lobby, Free wireless Internet, Nearby fitness center (discount), Accessible bathroom, In-room accessibility equipment for the deaf, Braille or raised signage, Dry cleaning/laundry service, Fitness facilities.

Holiday Inn Express Hotel & Suites Barstow
2700 Lenwood Rd
Barstow CA 92311
(760) 253-9200
$130 - $166
Bed & Pet Discount Offered

Pet Policy: Pets accepted. $25 refundable deposit. No additional charge.

Features: Swimming pool - outdoor, Business center, Accessible bathroom, In-room accessibility equipment for the deaf, Braille or raised signage, Gift shops or newsstand, Number of rooms: 110, Number of floors: 3, Coffee in lobby, Free breakfast, Multilingual staff, Complimentary newspapers in lobby, Wireless Internet, Nearby fitness center (discount), Dry cleaning/laundry service.

Quality Inn Barstow
1520 E Main St
Barstow CA 92311
(760) 256-6891
$79 - $109
Bed & Pet Discount Offered

Pet Policy: Pets welcome for an additional $10 per night per pet plus a $50 damage deposit, which is refunded if the room is in order at check out. Quality Inns accept any well-behaved pets with a maximum of 3 per room, but dogs are limited to 50 pounds. Pets may not be left alone in the room unless in a cage.

Features: Swimming pool - outdoor, Free breakfast, Restaurant(s), Number of rooms: 100, Number of floors: 2, Parking (free), Fitness facilities.

Ramada Inn Barstow
1511 E Main St
Barstow CA 92311
(760) 256-5673
$63 - $79
Bed & Pet Discount Offered

Pet Policy: Small pets allowed, $20 per stay.

Features: Room service (limited hours), Business services, Parking (free), Full-service health spa, Swimming pool - outdoor seasonal, Dry cleaning/laundry service, Free breakfast.

Rodeway Inn Barstow
1261 East Main Street
Barstow CA 92311
(760) 256-7581
$62 - $75

Pet Policy: Rodeway Inns charge an additional $10 per night per pet and require a $50 damage deposit, which is refunded if the room is in order at check out. Max of 2 pets per room. A veterinarian certificate that the pet is Free from parasites is required. Pets may not be left alone in the room unless in a cage.

Features: Free continental breakfast, Free wireless Internet, Heated swimming pool.

Super 8 Barstow
170 Coolwater Ln
Barstow CA 92311
(760) 256-8443
$55 - $71

Pet Policy: Pets allowed, $10 per night

Features: Swimming pool - outdoor, Free breakfast, Free wireless Internet, RV and truck parking.

Travelodge Barstow
1630 E Main St
Barstow CA 92311
(760) 256-8931
$33- $54
Bed & Pet Discount Offered

Pet Policy: Pets accepted, $8 per day.

Features: Free breakfast, Complimentary newspapers in lobby, RV and truck parking, Free wireless Internet, Swimming pool - outdoor, Parking (free).

Bass Lake

Also see the following nearby communities that have pet friendly lodging: Oakhurst - 4 miles

★★★

Pines Resort & Conference Center
54432 North Shore Road
Bass Lake CA 93604
(559) 642-3121
$99 - $149

Pet Policy: Pets permitted in 6 of the condos, $75 per pet per stay. Limit 2 pets.

Features: Number of Chalets: 84, Number of suites with fireplaces: 20, Full kitchens, Free breakfast vouchers.

Beaumont

Also see the following nearby communities that have pet friendly lodging: Banning - 5 miles

Americas Best Value Inn
625 East Fifth Street
Beaumont CA 92223
(888) 315-2378
$47 - $68

Pet Policy": Pets less than 50 lbs, $10 per night per pet. Limit 2 per room.

Features: Number of rooms: 22, Number of floors: 2, Free continental breakfast, Swimming pool.

Not Rated
Best Western El Rancho Motor Inn
480 East 5th Street
Beaumont CA 92223
(951) 845-2176
$71 - $129

Pet Policy: Pets accepted on advance approval. Please contact hotel directly for reservations.

Features: Refrigerators, Microwaves, Free wireless Internet.

Rodeway Inn Beaumont
1265 E 6th St
Beaumont CA 92223
(951) 845-1436
$54 - $69
Bed & Pet Discount Offered

Pet Policy: Pets accepted with a fee of $10 per night per pet plus a $50 deposit which is refunded if the room is in order at check out. Max of 2 pets per room. A veterinarian certificate that the pet is on a flea and parasite. Pets may not be left alone in the room unless in a cage.

Free wireless Internet, Swimming pool - outdoor, Guest laundry, Free breakfast, Parking (free), Number of rooms: 16.

Bell Gardens

Also see the following nearby communities that have pet friendly lodging: Commerce - 2 miles, Downey - 2 miles, Pico Rivera - 3 miles, Huntington Park - 5 miles, Norwalk - 5 miles, Whittier - 6 miles, Monterey Park - 6 miles, Rosemead - 8 miles, Cerritos - 8 miles, La Mirada - 9 miles, South El Monte - 9 miles, San Gabriel - 9 miles, Hawaiian Gardens - 10 miles

Comfort Inn & Suites Bell Gardens
7330 Eastern Ave
Bell Gardens CA 90201
(562) 928-3452
$74 - $90
Bed & Pet Discount Offered

Pet Policy: Pets accepted with management approval. Cleaning fee of $50 will be assessed for housing a pet without management approval.

Features: Swimming pool - outdoor, Number of floors: 3, Multilingual staff, Fitness facilities, Number of rooms: 115.

Motel 6 - Los Angeles
6344 Eastern Avenue
Bell Gardens CA 90201
(323) 560-8221
$61 - $62
Bed & Pet Discount Offered

Pet Policy: Pets welcome, no additional charge. Must declare at check-in. Must not leave alone in room. Must be leashed or crated.

Features: Elevator, Guest laundry, Business services, Parking (free), Free wireless Internet.

Belmont

Also see the following nearby communities that have pet friendly lodging: San Carlos - 2 miles, San Mateo - 3 miles, Redwood City - 4 miles, Burlingame - 5 miles, Millbrae - 7 miles, Menlo Park - 8 miles, San Bruno - 10 miles

Extended Stay America
120 Sem Ln
Belmont CA 94002
(650) 654-0344
$86 - $121
Bed & Pet Discount Offered

Pet Policy: One pet is allowed per room. A $25 per day non-refundable cleaning fee (not to exceed $150) will be charged the first night of your stay.

Features: Guest laundry, Number of rooms: 108, Number of floors: 5, Internet (additional charge), Parking (free), Nearby fitness center (discount).

Hyatt Summerfield Suites Belmont/Redwood Shores
400 Concourse Dr
Belmont CA 94002
(650) 591-8600
$118 - $129
Bed & Pet Discount Offered

Pet Policy: Accepts 2 pets per suite, only one pet can be a dog weighing no more than 50 lbs. Cats must be declawed and housebroken. $100 fee per stay.

Outdoor pool, Gift shops or newsstand, Number of rooms: 132, Number of floors: 3, BBQ area, Coffee in lobby, Video library, Free breakfast, Multilingual staff, Complimentary newspapers, Smoke-Free, Dry cleaning/laundry service, Grocery/convenience store, Free wireless Internet, Fitness facilities.

Ben Lomond

Also see the following nearby communities that have pet friendly lodging: Scotts Valley - 5 miles, Santa Cruz - 8 miles

Quality Inn & Suites, Santa Cruz Mountains
9733 Highway 9
Ben Lomond CA 95005
(831) 336-2292
$99 - $109
Bed & Pet Discount Offered

Pet Policy: Pets up to 25 lbs, $25 per night. Limit 1 pet per room. Must reserve in advance.

Features: Smoke-Free property, Roll-in shower, Concierge , Number of rooms: 23, Number of floors: 2, Business services, Coffee in lobby, Free breakfast, Complimentary newspapers, Dry cleaning/laundry service, Free wireless Internet, Swimming pool.

Berkeley

Also see the following nearby communities that have pet friendly lodging: Emeryville - 2 miles, Richmond - 7 miles, Alameda - 7 miles, Oakland - 8 miles

Americas Best Value Inn-Berkeley / San Francisco
1620 San Pablo Ave
Berkeley CA 94702
(510) 525-6770
$78 - $120
Bed & Pet Discount Offered

Pet Policy: Accepts pets, $10 per night per pet.

Features: Restaurant(s), Number of rooms: 39, Number of floors: 2, Airport transportation additional charge, Coffee in lobby, Complimentary newspapers, Free wireless Internet.

Beau Sky Hotel
2520 Durant Ave
Berkeley CA 94704
(510) 540-7688
$109 - $119
Bed & Pet Discount Offered

Pet Policy: Accepts dogs, any size, no additional charge.

Features: Coffee in lobby, Business services, Restaurant(s), Room service (limited hours), Concierge services, Number of rooms: 20, Number of floors: 3, Parking (additional charge), Free breakfast, Smoke-Free property.

★★★½

DoubleTree by Hilton Berkeley Marina
200 Marina Blvd
Berkeley CA 94710
(510) 548-7920
$107 - $174
Bed & Pet Discount Offered

Pet Policy: Dogs less than 50 lbs allowed, $75 per stay. Limit of 2 dogs per room.

Features: Swimming pool - indoor, Bar/lounge, Restaurant(s), Room service (limited hours), Gift shops or newsstand, Number of rooms: 378, Business services, Multilingual staff, Porter/bellhop, Free wireless Internet, Marina on site, Sauna, Smoke-Free property, Roll-in shower, In-room accessibility equipment for the deaf, Braille or raised signage, Complimentary newspapers in lobby, Health club, Dry cleaning/laundry service.

★★★½

Hotel Durant, a Joie de Vivre Boutique Hotel
2600 Durant Ave
Berkeley CA 94704
(510) 845-8981
$145 - $239
Bed & Pet Discount Offered

Pet Policy: Pets accepted with additional charge at check-in. We offer organic treats and toy footballs for our four-legged guests.

Features: Nearby fitness center (discount), Coffee in lobby, Bar/Lounge, Elevator, Concierge, Restaurant(s), Room service (limited hours), Number of rooms: 143, Number of suites: 5, Number of floors: 6, Airport transportation additional charge, Breakfast available additional charge, Nightclub, Multilingual staff, Complimentary newspapers in lobby, Business center, Porter/bellhop, Security guard, Limo or Town Car service available, Floor butler, Internet (free), Smoke-Free property, Poolside bar, Dry cleaning/laundry service, Parking fee.

★★

La Quinta Inn Berkeley
920 University Ave
Berkeley CA 94710
(510) 849-1121
$79 - $94
Bed & Pet Discount Offered

Pet Policy: Two dogs, any size, allowed in each room with no additional charge. Pets should be crated when left alone in the room, and pets are not allowed in the pool and the breakfast area.

Features: Free Breakfast, Elevator, Number of rooms: 112, Number of floors: 3, Business services, Parking (free), Internet (free), Swimming pool - outdoor seasonal, Accessible bathroom, Guest laundry, Fitness facilities.

★★
Rodeway Inn Berkeley
1461 University Ave
Berkeley CA 94702
(510) 848-3840
$74 - $89
Bed & Pet Discount Offered

Pet Policy: Rodeway Inns charge an additional $10 per night per pet and require a $50 damage deposit, which is refunded if the room is in order at check out. Max of 2 pets per room. A veterinarian certificate that the pet is on a flea and parasite program and that they are Free from parasites is required. Pets may not be left alone in the room unless in a cage.

Features: Guest laundry, Number of rooms: 43, Number of floors: 1, Free breakfast, Parking (free), Free wireless Internet.

The Claremont Hotel & Spa
41 Tunnel Road
Berkeley CA 94705
(510) 843-3000
$169 - $254
Bed & Pet Discount Offered

Pet Policy: Pets allowed, $300 refundable deposit per pet, limit 2 pets, less than 35 lbs.

Features: Business Center, Health Club, Sauna, Steam Room, Currency Exchange, Wheelchair Accessible, Swimming pool - outdoor, Elevator, Concierge desk, Full-service health spa, Multilingual staff, Porter/bellhop, Security guard, Wireless Internet, Beauty services, Massage - treatment room(s), Smoke-Free property, Technology helpdesk, Accessible bathroom, Bar/lounge, Restaurant(s), Supervised child care/activities, Shopping on site, Number of rooms: 279, Computer rental, Breakfast available additional charge, Parking (valet) $24 Daily, Dry cleaning/laundry service, Babysitting or child care, Gift shops or newsstand, Children's swimming pool, Shoe shine, Room service, Medical assistance available, Children's club, Designated smoking areas, Beach/pool umbrellas, Creche (nursery), Number of outdoor swimming pools 3, Smoke-Free property, tennis courts 10.

Beverly Hills

Also see the following nearby communities that have pet friendly lodging: West Hollywood - 2 miles, Culver City - 4 miles, Los Angeles - 5 miles, Universal City - 5 miles, Hollywood - 5 miles, Studio City - 6 miles, Santa Monica - 6 miles, Venice - 7 miles, Marina Del Rey - 7 miles, Sherman Oaks - 7 miles, Inglewood - 8 miles, Burbank - 9 miles, Glendale - 9 miles

★★★★
Avalon Hotel Beverly Hills
9400 W Olympic Blvd
Beverly Hills CA 90212
(310) 277-5221
$239- $399
Bed & Pet Discount Offered

Pet Policy: Pets allowed. $100 per stay.

Features: Swimming pool - outdoor, Cell phone/mobile rental, Spa services on site, Shoe shine, Concierge services, Bar/lounge, Business services, Restaurant(s), Number of rooms: 88, Internet (additional charge), Multilingual staff, Room service, Parking (valet) $30 Daily, Babysitting or child care, Fitness facilities.

Beverly Wilshire - Beverly Hills, A Four Seasons Hotel
9500 Wilshire Blvd
Beverly Hills CA 90212
(310) 275-5200
$454 - $1,600
Bed & Pet Discount Offered

Pet Policy: Guests can bring one pet per room at no extra charge. Pet beds are available. Guests checking in with their pet must sign a waiver saying they will not leave the animal alone in the room.

Features: Bar/lounge, Babysitting or child care, Elevator, Swimming pool - outdoor, Wheelchair accessible, Gift shops or newsstand, Shopping on site, Number of rooms: 395, Number of suites: 252, Number of floors: 14, Coffee in lobby, Poolside bar, Currency exchange, Room service (24 hours), Spa services on site, Multilingual staff, Porter/bellhop, Security guard, Dry cleaning/laundry service, Beauty services, Concierge desk, Massage - treatment room(s), Smoke-Free property, Technology support staff, Media library, Wireless Internet (additional charge), Accessible bathroom, 24-hour business center, Fitness facilities, 2 Restaurants, Valet Parking (additional charge).

L'Ermitage Beverly Hills
9291 Burton Way
Beverly Hills CA 90210
(310) 278-3344
$425 - $565
Bed & Pet Discount Offered

Pet Policy: Pets up to 40 lbs, $150 per stay. Limit 2 pets per room.

Features: Parking (valet), Swimming pool – outdoor, Room service (24 hours), Security guard, Bar/lounge, Wheelchair accessible, Spa services on site, Parking (valet) $32/24 Hours In/Out, Elevator, Restaurant(s), Number of rooms: 119, Number of floors: 8, Breakfast available additional charge, Multilingual staff, Complimentary newspapers in lobby, Porter/bellhop, Limo or Town Car service available, Concierge desk, Dry cleaning/laundry service, Fitness facilities, Free wireless Internet, Massage - treatment room(s), Technology support staff, 24-hour business center, Smoke-Free property.

★★★♥

Maison 140
140 S Lasky Dr
Beverly Hills CA 90212
(310) 281-4000
$195 - $360
Bed & Pet Discount Offered

Per Policy: Dogs less than 50 lbs accepted, $100 per stay.

Features: Business center, Elevator, Bar/lounge, On-site car rental, Number of rooms: 43, Number of floors: 3, Airport transportation additional charge, Parking fee, Breakfast available additional charge, Multilingual staff, Complimentary newspapers in lobby, Porter/bellhop, Free wireless Internet, Smoke-Free property, Concierge services, Nearby fitness center (discount), Room service (limited hours), Dry cleaning/laundry service.

Montage Beverly Hills
225 N Canon Dr
Beverly Hills CA 90210
(310) 860-7800
$474 - $7,470
Bed & Pet Discount Offered

Pet Policy: Montage Beverly Hills looks forward to providing the best accommodations and service for your pet. There is a $30 daily charge for our animal guests. Many amenities will be provided for pets to enjoy during their stay. Comfy beds, bowls and treats will be left in your guestroom or suite. Pets should be leashed in all public areas. Special services, including sitting, walking and grooming, are available through our concierge.

Features: Wireless Internet (additional charge), Bar/lounge, Swimming pools – indoor & outdoor, Hair salon, Concierge services, Number of rooms: 201, Number of suites: 55, Room service (24 hours), Dry cleaning/laundry service, Limo or Town Car service available, Full-service health spa, Parking garage, Children's club, Number of restaurants 2.

The Beverly Hilton
9876 Wilshire Blvd
Beverly Hills CA 90210
(310) 274-7777
$199 - $445
Bed & Pet Discount Offered

Pet Policy: Pets up to 75 lbs, $25 per day, to a maximum of $75 per stay

Features: Business Center, Elevator, Swimming pool - outdoor, Shoe shine, Wheelchair accessible, Poolside bar, Coffee in lobby, Concierge desk, Beauty services, Room service (24 hours), Technology helpdesk, Shopping on site, Spa services on site, Currency exchange, Bar/lounge, Medical assistance available, ATM/banking, Restaurant(s), Number of rooms: 570, Internet (additional charge), Breakfast available additional charge, Multilingual staff, Porter/bellhop, Security guard, Limo or Town Car service available, Massage - treatment room(s), Dry cleaning/laundry service, Fitness facilities, Billiards, Parking (additional charge).

The Mosaic Hotel - Beverly Hills
125 S Spalding Dr
Beverly Hills CA 90212
(310) 278-0303
$281- $700
Bed & Pet Discount Offered

Pet Policy: Pets less than 30 lbs accepted, $150 additional charge per stay. Limit 1 pet per room.

Features: Business Center, Sauna, Bar/Lounge, Swimming pool - outdoor, Parking (valet) $25/24 Hours In/Out, Security guard, Room service (24 hours), Concierge services, Restaurant(s), Number of rooms: 49, Airport transportation additional charge, Poolside bar, Complimentary newspapers in lobby, Porter/bellhop, Limo or Town Car service available, Internet (free), Smoke-Free property, Dry cleaning/laundry service, Fitness facilities.

The Peninsula Beverly Hills
9882 Santa Monica Blvd
Beverly Hills CA 90212
(310) 551-2888
$434 - $6,250
Bed & Pet Discount Offered

Pet policy: Pets welcome, $35 per pet per night. No size restrictions.

Features: Parking (valet) $34/night, Bar/lounge, Shopping on site, Business center, Restaurant(s), Swimming pool - outdoor, Gift shops or newsstand, Number of rooms: 193, Number of floors: 5, Airport transportation (fee), Cell phone rental, Translation services, Computer rental, Coffee in lobby, Breakfast available additional charge, Poolside bar, Currency exchange, Health club, Shoe shine, Multilingual staff, Complimentary newspapers in lobby, Porter/bellhop, Security guard, Limo or Town Car service available, Medical assistance available, Free wireless Internet, Beauty services, Concierge desk, Massage - treatment room(s), Steam room, Sauna, Smoke-Free property, Full-service health spa, Room service (24 hours), Babysitting or child care, Accessible bathroom, Braille or raised signage.

Big Bear Lake

Bear Creek Resort
40210 Big Bear Blvd
Big Bear Lake CA 92315
(909) 878-0220
$89 - $323
Bed & Pet Discount Offered

Pet Policy: Pet friendly cabins available

Features: Restaurant(s), Self-parking (free), Swimming pool - outdoor seasonal, Massage - treatment room(s).

Best Western Big Bear Chateau
42200 Moon Ridge Rd
Big Bear Lake CA 92315
(909) 866-6666
$84 - $285
Bed & Pet Discount Offered

Pet Policy: Pets allowed.$25 cleaning fee first night and $5 each additional.

Features: Free breakfast, Parking (free), Free wireless Internet, Fitness facilities, Restaurant(s), Number of rooms: 80, Number of floors: 3. Swimming pool – outdoor.

★★½

Big Bear Frontier
40472 Big Bear Blvd
Big Bear Lake CA 92315
(909) 866-5888
$69 - $299
Bed & Pet Discount Offered

Pet Policy: Pets are welcome for an additional charge of $15 per pet per night.

Features: Free wireless Internet, Swimming pool - outdoor, Pool table, Private beach, Business services, Barbecue grill(s), Coffee in lobby, Number of rooms: 57,Multilingual staff, In-room accessibility.

Big Bear Lakefront Lodge
40360 Lakeview Dr
Big Bear Lake CA 92315
(909) 866-8271
$67 - $425
Bed & Pet Discount Offered

Pet Policy: Pet Designated Rooms · Pets under 25 lbs. only · $10 charge per night for pets · 1 pet per room.

Features: Business services, Barbecue grill(s), Video library, Parking (free), Spa services on site, Free wireless Internet, Marina on site.

Not Rated
Knights Inn Big Bear Lake
573 Lynn Rd
Big Bear Lake CA 92315
(909) 878-0115
$62 - $89

Pet Policy: Pets allowed in certain rooms only, $15 per night.

Features: Bar/lounge, Parking (free), Multilingual staff, Free breakfast, Front desk (limited hours, Free wireless Internet.

The Timberline Lodge
39921 Big Bear Blvd
Big Bear Lake CA 92315
(909) 866-4141
$45 - $195
Bed & Pet Discount Offered

Pet Policy: There is a pet charge of $20 for the first night and $10 for each additional night per pet.

Featured: Barbecue grill(s), Video library Number of rooms: 15, Number of floors: 2, Suitable for children, Parking (free), Multilingual staff, Front desk (limited hours), Internet Free wireless Internet.

Bishop

Not rated
Americas Best Value Inn
192 Short Street
Bishop CA 93514
(760) 873-4912
$71 - $89

Pet Policy: Pets, any size, $7 per night pet. Limit 2 per room.

Features: Free continental breakfast, Free wireless Internet, Microwave and mini fridge, Coffee maker, Swimming pool – outdoor (seasonal), Guest laundry, BBQ area.

Not rated
BW Plus Bishop Holiday Spa
1025 N Main Street
Bishop CA 93514
(760) 873-3543
$84 - $129

Pet Policy: Pets allowed, $25 per night. Limited number of pet rooms.

Features: Wide screen TV, Coffee maker, Refrigerator, Microwave.

Comfort Inn
805 N Main St
Bishop CA 93514
(760) 873-4284
$84 - $89
Bed & Pet Discount Offered

Pet Policy: Pet accommodation: 15.00/night, per pet (limit 2 pets/room).

Features: Guest laundry, Number of rooms: 54, Number of floors: 2, Business services, Free breakfast, Swimming pool - outdoor seasonal.

Days Inn Bishop
724 W Line St
Bishop CA 93514
(760) 872-1095
$57 - $96
Bed & Pet Discount Offered

Pet Policy: Pets welcome, $10 per night

Features: Swimming pool, Wireless Internet, Number of floors: 2.

★★½

Holiday Inn Express Hotel & Suites Bishop
636 N Main St
Bishop CA 93514
(760) 872-2423
$85 - $133
Bed & Pet Discount Offered

Pet Policy: Pet allowed, $25 per night per pet. First floor only. Undeclared pets result in $250 charge.

Features: Free breakfast, Accessible bathroom, In-room accessibility equipment for the deaf, Braille or raised signage, Swimming pool - indoor, Business services, Coffee in lobby, Multilingual staff, Number of rooms: 66, Number of suites: 17, Number of floors: 2, Complimentary newspapers in lobby, Free wireless Internet, Sauna, Dry cleaning/laundry service, Fitness facilities.

★★½

La Quinta Inn Bishop-Mammoth Lakes
651 N. Main Street
Bishop CA 93514
(760) 873-6380
$89 - $100
Bed & Pet Discount Offered

Pet Policy: Pets up to 50 lbs, no additional charge. Limit of 2. Must be leashed or crated in all public areas.

Features: Suitable for children, Free breakfast, Accessible bathroom, Gift shops or newsstand, Airport transportation additional charge, Restaurant, Complimentary newspapers in lobby, Smoke-Free property, Free wireless Internet, Business center.

★★

Ramada Limited Bishop CA
155 E Elm St
Bishop CA 93514
(760) 872-1771
$68 - $90
Bed & Pet Discount Offered

Pet Policy: Pets permitted, $15 per night. Limit of 2 per room, no size restriction.

Features: Barbecue grill(s), Free breakfast, Parking (free), Multilingual staff, Complimentary newspapers in lobby, Swimming pool - outdoor seasonal, Business Center.

Super 8 Bishop
535 S Main St.
Bishop CA 93514
(760) 872-1386
$53 - $85

Pet Policy: Pets allowed, $10 per night.

Features: Swimming Pool – outdoor, Guest laundry, Free breakfast, Free wireless Internet Coffee maker, refrigerator, hair dryer.

Vagabond Inn Bishop
1030 N Main St
Bishop CA 93514
(760) 873-6351
$74 - $78
Bed & Pet Discount Offered

Pet Policy: Pets, any size, $15 per night per pet.

Features: Guest laundry, Free wireless Internet, Restaurant(s), Concierge services, Number of rooms: 80, Free breakfast, Sauna, Swimming pool - outdoor seasonal.

Blythe

Americas Best Value Inn
850 West Hobson
Blythe CA 92225-1416
(760) 922-5145
$59 - $89

Pet Policy: Pets allowed, any size, $5 per night. Limit 2 pets per room.

Features: Free continental breakfast, Number of Floors: 1, Swimming pool, BBQ area, Free wireless Internet, Microwave, Mini refrigerator, Coffee maker, Suites with kitchenettes available, Handicap accessible rooms available.

★

Best Western Sahara Motel
825 W Hobson Way
Blythe CA 92225
(760) 922-7105
$74 - $95

Pet Policy: Small pets allowed, $10 per night.

Features: Free continental, Swimming pool – outdoor – year round.

Capital Suites Hotel
545 E Hobson Way
Blythe CA 92225
(760) 922-9209
$79 - $89

Pet Policy: Pets accepted, $15 per night.

Features: Coffee maker, Refrigerator, Microwave, Iron and ironing board, Hair dryer, HBO, Free continental breakfast, Complimentary USA Today, Outdoor pool and spa. Free wireless Internet.

★★

Days Inn Blythe
1673 East Hobson Way
Blythe CA 92225
(760) 922-5101
$55- $79
Bed & Pet Discount Offered

Pet Policy: Pets welcome, $10 per night

Business services, Barbecue grill(s), Coffee in lobby, Free breakfast, Parking (free), Complimentary newspapers in lobby, Full-service health spa, Internet Free wireless Internet, Swimming pool - outdoor seasonal.

Knights Inn Blythe
1127 East Hobson Way
Blythe CA 92225
(760) 922-4126
$60 - $65
Bed & Pet Discount Offered

Pet Policy: Pets allowed, $5 per night.

Features: Business services, Number of floors: 2, Free breakfast, Parking (free), Swimming pool - outdoor seasonal, Internet (free).

Quality Inn
600 W Donlon St
Blythe CA 92225
(760) 921-2300
$89 - $125
Bed & Pet Discount Offered

Pet Policy: Pets accepted. Contact hotel directly for details and reservations.

Features: Accessible bathroom, In-room accessibility equipment for the deaf, Braille or raised signage, Business center, Indoor pool, Number of floors: 2, Coffee in lobby, Free breakfast, Multilingual staff, Free wireless Internet, Dry cleaning/laundry service, Fitness facilities.

★★
Regency Inn and Suites - Blythe
903 W Hobsonway
Blythe CA 92225
(760) 922-4146
$65 - $75
Bed & Pet Discount Offered

Pet Policy: Pets allowed, $10 per pet per night.

Features: Free wireless Internet, Number of rooms: 49, Free breakfast, Parking (free), Business center, Swimming pool - outdoor seasonal.

★★
Rodeway Inn & Suites
1781 E Hobsonway
Blythe CA 92225
(760) 922-3334
$59 - $89
Bed & Pet Discount Offered

Pet Policy: Rodeway Inns charge an additional $10 per night per pet and require a $50 damage deposit, which is refunded if the room is in order at check out. Max of 2 pets per room. A veterinarian certificate that the pet is on a flea and parasite is required. Pets may not be left alone in the room unless in a cage.

Features: Wheelchair accessible, Barbecue grill(s), Braille or raised signage, Restaurant, Swimming pool - outdoor, Number of rooms: 34, Free breakfast, Free wireless Internet, RV and truck parking, Accessible bathroom, Complimentary newspapers in lobby.

★
Super 8 Blythe
550 W Donlon St..
Blythe CA 92225
(760) 922-8881
$59 - $69

Pet Policy: Pets allowed, any size, $10 per night. Limit 4 pets per room.

Features: Free breakfast, Swimming pool – outdoor, Free wireless Internet, Microwave, Refrigerator, HBO.

Bodega

Also see the following nearby communities that have pet friendly lodging: Valley Ford - 1 mile, Occidental - 5 miles, Sebastopol - 8 miles

Sonoma Coast Villa & Spa
16702 Highway 1
Bodega CA 94922

Pet Policy: Accepts domesticated dogs up to 50 lbs. Maximum of 2 per room. There is a $50 nonrefundable service additional charge per night per pet . Pets must not be left alone in the room and must be leashed outside of room. Pets are not

Continued on next page

Sonoma Coast Villa & Spa
Continued from previous page

(707) 876-9818
$135 - $325

allowed in food service areas. You are responsible for any damage your pet causes to the resort, any litter associated with the pet and any noise made by the pet during your stay. Guests must inform the front office of any pets in room and must sign a copy of the pet policy at time of check in.

Features: Private patios, Swimming pool and indoor spa, Wood burning fireplaces, Free Internet, Restaurant, Spa facilities, Free full breakfast.

Borrego Springs

Not Rated
Stanlunds Resort Inn & Suites
2771 Borrego Springs Road
Borrego Springs CA 92204
(760) 767-5501
$135 - $150

Pet Policy: Pets welcome, $10 per pet per night additional charge.

Features: Free wireless Internet, Microwave/fridge combination or kitchenette in each room.

Boyes Hot Springs

Also see the following nearby communities that have pet friendly lodging: Sonoma - 6 miles, Petaluma - 9 miles, Yountville - 9 miles, Napa - 10 miles

★★★★
Fairmont Sonoma Mission Inn
100 Boyes Blvd
Boyes Hot Springs CA 95416
(707) 938-9000
$299 - $709

Pet Policy: Pets accepted, $25 per night, limit 2 per room. Please contact the hotel directly and ask for the Guest Service Supervisor, at 707 939 2467 to make the necessary arrangements for your pet. Pets must not be left alone in room, and are not permitted in food or pool areas.

Features: Spa, Golf course, Number of rooms: 226.

Brea

Also see the following nearby communities that have pet friendly lodging: Placentia - 3 miles, Fullerton - 3 miles, Anaheim - 6 miles, Walnut - 7 miles, Yorba Linda - 7 miles, Diamond Bar - 8 miles, City Of Industry - 8 miles, La Mirada - 8 miles, Orange - 8 miles, Buena Park - 9 miles, Whittier - 9 miles, La Palma - 10 miles

★★★
Chase Suite Hotel Brea
3100 E Imperial Hwy
Brea CA 92821
(714) 579-3200
$89 - $219
Bed & Pet Discount Offered

Pet Policy: Pets are always welcome. Our apartment-style accommodations and gracious grounds give your pet's easy access to the outdoors and lots of room to explore. Pet fee is $10 per day, per pet but not to exceed $150 per stay.

Features: Outdoor pool, On-site car rental, Number of suites: 98, Number of floors: 2, Coffee in lobby, Free breakfast, Grocery, Nearby fitness center (free), Free wireless Internet, Dry cleaning/laundry service, Smoke-Free property, 24-hour business center, Free reception, Smoke-Free property, Area shuttle (free).

Embassy Suites Hotel Brea-North Orange County
900 E Birch St
Brea CA 92821
(714) 990-6000
$119 - $599
Bed & Pet Discount Offered

Pet Policy: Pets up to 50 lbs., $40 per day per pet. Must book pet friendly room in advance.

Features: Bar/lounge, Room service (limited hours), Free breakfast, Elevator, Restaurant(s), ATM/banking, Concierge services, Gift shops or newsstand, Number of floors: 7, Parking (free), Multilingual staff, Business center, Porter/bellhop, Wireless Internet, Dry cleaning/laundry service, Swimming pool - outdoor, Fitness facilities.

Homestead Orange County - Brea
3050 E Imperial Hwy
Brea CA 92821
(714) 528-2500
$62- $72
Bed & Pet Discount Offered

Pet Policy: Pets allowed, no size restriction, $25 per day to a maximum of $150 per stay. Limit of 1 pet per room.

Features: Guest laundry, Elevator, Number of rooms: 133, Number of floors: 3, Parking (free), Wireless Internet, Nearby fitness center (discount).

Bridgeport

Ruby Inn
333 Main Street
Bridgeport CA 93517
(877) 747-8713
$117 - $150

Pet Policy: Pets welcome, must be attended at all times, grassy fenced pet area, advance notification required (some rooms are pet-Free).

Features: Number of rooms: 30, Non-smoking property, Free wireless Internet, Free continental breakfast, BBQ area, Microwave, Refrigerators, Coffee makers.

Brisbane

Also see the following nearby communities that have pet friendly lodging: South San Francisco - 2 miles, San Bruno - 4 miles, Millbrae - 6 miles, San Francisco - 6 miles, Burlingame - 7 miles, Alameda - 9 miles

Homewood Suites by Hilton San Francisco Airport No
2000 Shoreline Ct
Brisbane CA 94005
(650) 589-1600
$109 - $194
Bed & Pet Discount Offered

Pet Policy: Pets up to 50 lbs, $75 per stay. Limit of 2 pets per room.

Features: Elevator, Airport transportation (free), Swimming pool - indoor, Gift shops or newsstand, Coffee in lobby, Free breakfast, Parking (free), Multilingual staff, Complimentary newspapers in lobby, Accessible bathroom, In-room accessibility equipment for the deaf, Dry cleaning/laundry service, Wheelchair Accessible, Fitness facilities, Restaurant(s) ATM/banking, Free reception, 24-hour business center, Free wireless Internet.

Buellton

Also see the following nearby communities that have pet friendly lodging: Solvang - 4 miles

★★

Holiday Inn Express Hotel & Suites Bishop 630 Avenue Of The Flags
Buellton CA 93427
(805) 688-0022
$119 - $139
Bed & Pet Discount Offered

Pet Policy: Quality Inns charge an additional $10 per night per pet. They may require a $50 damage deposit, which is refunded if the room is in order at check out. Quality Inns accept any well-behaved pets with a maximum of 3 per room, but dogs are limited to 50 pounds. Pets may not be left alone in the room unless in a cage.

Features: Coffee in lobby, Free breakfast, Parking (free), High speed, Internet access Free, Accessible bathroom, Roll-in shower, In-room accessibility.

★★★½

Santa Ynez Valley Marriott
555 Mcmurray Rd
Buellton CA 93427
(805) 688-1000
$135 - $319
Bed & Pet Discount Offered

Pet Policy: Pets allowed, $80 cleaning fee per stay.

Features: Bar/lounge, Room service (limited hours), On-site car rental, Restaurant(s), Swimming pool - outdoor, Gift shops or newsstand, Number of rooms: 149, Number of floors: 4, Airport transportation additional charge, Suitable for children, Breakfast available additional charge, Pool table, Parking (free), Spa services on site, Porter/bellhop, Beauty services, Massage - treatment room(s), Sauna, Dry cleaning/laundry service, ATM/banking, Tennis on site, Fitness facilities, Multilingual staff, Wheelchair accessible, 24-hour business center, Casino shuttle (free), Free wireless Internet, Smoke-Free property.

Buena Park

Also see the following nearby communities that have pet friendly lodging: La Palma - 1 mile, Cypress - 2 miles, Cerritos - 3 miles, La Mirada - 4 miles, Hawaiian Gardens - 4 miles, Los Alamitos - 4 miles, Fullerton - 5 miles, Anaheim - 6 miles, Norwalk - 6 miles, Garden Grove - 7 miles, Whittier - 8 miles, Seal Beach - 8 miles, Brea - 9 miles, Placentia - 9 miles, Downey - 9 miles, Orange - 9 miles, Signal Hill - 9 miles, Long Beach - 10 miles, Fountain Valley - 10 miles

★★

InnSuites Hotel & Suites
7555 Beach Blvd
Buena Park CA 90620
(714) 523-2883
$30 - $119
Bed & Pet Discount Offered

Pet Policy: Dogs and cats, up to 30 lbs, $25 per pet per stay.

Features: Swimming pool - outdoor, Arcade/game room, Gift shops or newsstand, Number of rooms: 175, Number of floors: 2, Internet access - additional charge, Free breakfast, Free parking, Dry cleaning/laundry service.

Red Roof Inn Buena Park
7121 Beach Blvd
Buena Park CA 90620
(714) 670-9000
$59- $136
Bed & Pet Discount Offered

Pet Policy: One well-behaved family pet is permitted. Pets must be declared during guest registration. In consideration of all Red Roof guests, pets must never be left unattended in the guestroom.

Features: Free wireless Internet, Elevator, Guest laundry, Swimming pool - outdoor, ATM/banking, Number of rooms: 131, Number of floors: 4, Coffee in lobby, Free breakfast, Parking (free), Multilingual staff, Complimentary newspapers in lobby, Accessible bathroom, Braille or raised signage.

Rodeway Inn Near Maingate Knott's
7930 Beach Blvd
Buena Park CA 90620
(714) 994-6480
$59 - $139
Bed & Pet Discount Offered

Pet Policy: Rodeway Inns charge an additional $10 per night per pet and require a $50 damage deposit, which is refunded if the room is in order at check out. Max of 2 pets per room. A veterinarian certificate that the pet is on a flea and parasite program and that they are Free from parasites is required. Pets may not be left alone in the room unless in a cage.

Features: Free breakfast, Guest laundry, Swimming pool - outdoor, Number of rooms: 76.

Super 8 Buena Park/Knotts Berry Farm
7800 Crescent Ave
Buena Park CA 90620
(714) 527-2201
$55 - $146
Bed & Pet Discount Offered

Pet Policy: Pets allowed. Additional charge of $15 per day per pet.

Features: Free breakfast, Coffee in lobby, Swimming pool - outdoor, Number of rooms: 90, Number of floors: 2, Parking (free), Complimentary newspapers in lobby, Dry cleaning/laundry service.

Burbank

Also see the following nearby communities that have pet friendly lodging: Universal City - 4 miles, Studio City - 4 miles, Glendale - 4 miles, Hollywood - 5 miles, West Hollywood - 7 miles, Sherman Oaks - 7 miles, Van Nuys - 8 miles, Beverly Hills - 9 miles

Burbank Extended Stay Apartments
2021 West Olive Avenue
Burbank CA 91506
(818) 848-9048
$116 - $132
Bed & Pet Discount Offered

Pet Policy: Pets accepted, $100 deposit per stay.

Features: Barbecue grill(s), Swimming pool - outdoor, Number of rooms: 77, Number of floors: 2, Guest laundry, Parking (free), Front desk (limited hours), Number of outdoor swimming pools 2, Free wireless Internet.

★★
Extended Stay America Los Angeles - Burbank Airport
2200 W Empire Ave
Burbank CA 91504
(818) 567-0952
$89- $104
Bed & Pet Discount Offered

Pet Policy: One medium-size pet is allowed in each guest room. A $25 per day non-refundable cleaning fee (not to exceed $150) will be charged the first night of your stay.

Features: Elevator, Number of rooms: 140, Number of floors: 4, Internet (additional charge), Parking (free), Front desk (limited hours).

★★★
Holiday Inn Burbank-Media Center
150 E Angeleno Ave
Burbank CA 91502
(818) 841-4770
$129 - $209
Bed & Pet Discount Offered

Pet Policy: Pets accepted, $50 per stay. Lower floors only, not available in suites.

Features: Business services, Bar/lounge, Restaurant(s), Room service (limited hours), Swimming pool - outdoor, Concierge services, Gift shops or newsstand, Number of rooms: 485, Number of suites: 102, Number of floors: 20, Parking (free), Free wireless Internet, Steam room, Sauna, Accessible bathroom, In-room accessibility equipment for the deaf, Braille or raised signage, Dry cleaning/laundry service.

★★★★
Hotel Amarano Burbank -
322 N Pass Ave
Burbank CA 91505
(818) 842-8887
$256 - $585
Bed & Pet Discount Offered

Pet Policy: Pets welcome, $75 per stay. No size restrictions.

Features: Sauna, Computer rental, Business center, Beauty services, Health club, Elevator, Medical assistance available, Bar/lounge, Shoe shine, Coffee in lobby, Currency exchange, Room service (24 hours), Parking (valet) $26/day, Airport transportation (free), Restaurant(s), Number of rooms: 99, Number of floors: 4, Cell phone/mobile rental, Breakfast available additional charge, Multilingual staff, Complimentary newspapers, Porter/bellhop, Security guard, Limo or Town Car service available, Wireless, Internet (free), Massage - treatment room(s), Smoke-Free property, Concierge, Babysitting or child care, Accessible bathroom, Braille or raised signage, Dry cleaning/laundry.

★★★½
Los Angeles Marriott Burbank Airport
2500 N Hollywood Way
Burbank CA 91505
(818) 843-6000
$139 - $199
Bed & Pet Discount Offered

Pet Policy: Pets permitted with $75 per stay cleaning fee.

Features: Business Center, Security guard, Restaurant(s), Concierge services, Gift shops or newsstand, Business services, Parking fee, Pool table, Currency exchange, Multilingual staff, Porter/bellhop, ***Continued on next page***

Los Angeles Marriott Burbank
Continued from previous page

Room service (24 hours), Airport transportation (free), Bar/lounge, ATM/banking, Suitable for children, Dry cleaning/laundry service, Free wireless Internet, Swimming pool - outdoor, Number of rooms: 409, Number of suites: 79, Smoke-Free property, Area shuttle (free), Fitness facilities.

★★★
Residence Inn by Marriott Burbank Downtown
321 S 1st St
Burbank CA 91502
(818) 260-8787
$149 - $259
Bed & Pet Discount Offered

Pet Policy: Pets welcome, $100 per stay fee.

Features: Barbecue grill(s), Free breakfast, ATM/banking, Business center, Multilingual staff, Complimentary newspapers in lobby, Free wireless Internet, Elevator, Swimming pool - outdoor, Concierge services, Number of rooms: 166, Number of floors: 5, Library, Parking fee $15/24 Hours In/Out, Grocery/convenience store, Dry cleaning/laundry service, Fitness facilities.

★★★½
Safari Inn, a Coast Hotel
1911 W Olive Ave
Burbank CA 91506
(818) 845-8586
$109 - $129
Bed & Pet Discount Offered

Pet Policy: Pets welcome, $25 per stay plus $200 refundable deposit. Limit 2 pets per room. Must not leave unattended in room, and must be leashed when outside the room.

Features: Guest laundry, Room service (limited hours), Swimming pool - outdoor, Concierge services, Number of rooms: 55, Number of floors: 2, Parking (free), Multilingual staff, Complimentary newspapers in lobby, Wireless, Internet (free), Fitness facilities.

Burlingame

Also see the following nearby communities that have pet friendly lodging: Millbrae - 2 miles, San Mateo - 3 miles, San Bruno - 4 miles, South San Francisco - 5 miles, Belmont - 5 miles, Brisbane - 7 miles, San Carlos - 8 miles, Montara - 9 miles, Moss Beach - 9 miles, Redwood City - 10 mile

★★★½
Crowne Plaza San Francisco International Airport
1177 Airport Blvd
Burlingame CA 94010
(650) 342-9200
$68 - $224
Bed & Pet Discount Offered

Pet Policy: Surrounded by beautiful parkland green space, our pet friendly hotel presents spacious, pet friendly rooms. The hotel requires $125 pet deposit, $25 of which is non-refundable.

Features: Wheelchair accessible, Number of rooms: 309, Number of floors: 10, Parking fee, Coffee in lobby, Breakfast available additional charge, Dry cleaning/laundry, Nearby fitness center (discount), Wireless Internet (additional charge), Business center, Bar/lounge, Concierge, Room service, Airport transportation (free), Indoor pool, Restaurant(s), Hair salon, Gift shops or newsstand, Multilingual staff, Complimentary newspapers in lobby, Porter/bellhop, Accessible bathroom, In-room accessibility equipment for the deaf, Braille or raised signage.

★★★½

Doubletree Hotel San Francisco Airport
835 Airport Blvd
Burlingame CA 94010
(650) 344-5500
$76 - $379
Bed & Pet Discount Offered

Pet Policy: Pets up to 50 lbs, $40 additional charge.

Features: Business Center, ATM/Banking, Elevator, Security guard, Bar/lounge, Restaurant(s), Room service (limited hours), Gift shops or newsstand, Number of rooms: 388, Number of floors: 8, Computer rental, Breakfast available additional charge, Library, Video library, Multilingual staff, Complimentary newspapers in lobby, Porter/bellhop, Free wireless Internet, Dry cleaning/laundry service, Fitness facilities, Accessible bathroom, Braille or raised signage, Accessibility equipment for the deaf, Parking – fee.

★★★½

Embassy Suites San Francisco Airport - Burlingame
150 Anza Blvd
Burlingame CA 94010
(650) 342-4600
$119 - $229
Bed & Pet Discount Offered

Pet Policy: Pets up to 75 lbs. $50 additional charge per pet per stay.

Features: Elevator, Sauna, Business services, Parking fee $15 Per Night, Bar/lounge, Swimming pool - indoor, Restaurant(s), Gift shops or newsstand, Number of suites: 340, Internet (additional charge), Free breakfast, Nightclub, Multilingual staff, Complimentary newspapers in lobby, Porter/bellhop, Security guard, Room service (limited hours), ATM/banking, Dry cleaning/laundry service, Fitness facilities, Airport transportation (free).

★★★★

Hilton San Francisco Airport
600 Airport Blvd
Burlingame CA 94010
(650) 340-8500
$101 - $319
Bed & Pet Discount Offered

Pet Policy: Pets up to 60 lbs. Pet fee: $75.

Features: Bar/lounge, Elevator, swimming pool - indoor, Airport transportation (free) available 24 hours, Room service (24 hours), 24-hour business center, Shopping center shuttle (free), Restaurant(s), ATM/banking, Concierge services, Number of rooms: 402, Number of floors: 15, Computer rental, Internet (additional charge), Breakfast available additional charge, Currency exchange, Multilingual staff, Complimentary newspapers in lobby, Porter/bellhop, Security guard, Medical assistance available, Parking garage additional charge, Smoke-Free property, Nearby fitness center (discount), Dry cleaning/laundry service, Accessible bathroom, In-room accessibility equipment for the deaf, Braille or raised signage.

Red Roof Inn San Francisco Airport
777 Airport Blvd
Burlingame CA 94010
(650) 342-7772
$59 - $89
Bed & Pet Discount Offered

Pet Policy: One well-behaved family pet is permitted. Pets must be declared during guest registration. In consideration of all Red Roof guests, pets must never be left unattended in the guestroom.

Features: Restaurant, Number of rooms: 213, Number of floors: 5, Coffee in lobby, Breakfast available additional charge, Parking (free), Complimentary newspapers, Outdoor pool - seasonal, Nearby fitness center (free), Business center, Airport transportation (free), Accessible bathroom, In-room accessibility equipment for the deaf, Braille or raised signage, Free wireless Internet.

San Francisco Airport Marriott Waterfront
1800 Old Bayshore Hwy
Burlingame CA 94010
(650) 692-9100
$119 - $249
Bed & Pet Discount Offered

Pet Policy: Pets allowed. $75 per stay cleaning fee.

Features: Concierge, Shoe shine, Sauna, Room service (limited hours), Business Center, Breakfast available additional charge, Coffee shop or cafe, Health club, Multilingual staff, Complimentary newspapers, Porter/bellhop, Security guard, Indoor pool, Bar/lounge, Gift shop, Number of rooms: 661, Number of floors: 11, Internet (additional charge), Parking $18/day, Airport transportation (free) available 24 hours, Accessible bathroom, Handicapped parking. In-room accessibility equipment for the deaf, Braille or raised signage, Dry cleaning/laundry service.

Buttonwillow

Econo Lodge Inn And Suites
20688 Tracy Ave
Buttonwillow CA 93206
(661) 764-5207
$58 - $59
Bed & Pet Discount Offered

Pet Policy: Pet accommodation: $5 per pet, per stay. Pet limit: maximum 2 pets per room, up to 100 lbs.

Features: Swimming pool - outdoor, Wheelchair accessible, Number of floors: 2, Multilingual staff.

Motel 6 Buttonwillow Central
20645 Tracy Ave
Buttonwillow CA 93206
(661) 764-5121
$68 - $69
Bed & Pet Discount Offered

Pet Policy: Pets welcome, no additional charge. Must declare at check-in. Must not leave alone in room. Must be leashed or crated.

Features: Guest laundry, BBQ area, Business center, Outdoor pool, Free wireless Internet, RV and truck parking, Coffee in lobby.

Pet Policy: Pets welcome, $10 per night per pet. Limit 2 per room.

Super 8 Buttonwillow
20681 Tracy Ave
Buttonwillow CA 93206
(661) 764-5117
$55 - $60

Features: Swimming pool & hot tub– outdoor, Free breakfast, Free wireless Internet, Microwaves, refrigerators, Coffee makers, Hair dryers, HBO.

Calabasas

Also see the following nearby communities that have pet friendly lodging: Woodland Hills - 5 miles, Canoga Park - 6 miles, Topanga - 7 miles, Westlake Village - 8 miles, Tarzana - 8 miles, Chatsworth - 9 miles, Simi Valley - 9 miles

Country Inn & Suites By Carlson Calabasas
23627 Calabasas Rd
Calabasas CA 91302
(818) 222-5300
$104 - $105
Bed & Pet Discount Offered

Pet Policy: Pets under 15 pounds, $35 first night, $15 each additional

Features: Free Breakfast, Business services, Swimming pool - outdoor, Elevator, Room service, Dry cleaning/laundry service, Smoke-Free property, Free wireless Internet, Bar/lounge, Number of rooms: 122, Number of suites: 2, Number of floors: 3, Coffee in lobby, Complimentary newspapers in lobby, Parking garage(free), Fitness facilities.

Calexico

Also see the following nearby communities that have pet friendly lodging: El Centro - 8 miles

Best Western John Jay Inn
2421 Scaroni Rd
Calexico CA 92231
(760) 768-0442
$84 - $89
Bed & Pet Discount Offered

Pet Policy: Pets accepted on advance approval. Please contact hotel directly for reservations.

Features: Fitness facilities, Swimming pool - outdoor, Wheelchair accessible, Free breakfast, Complimentary newspapers in lobby, Front desk (limited hours), Free wireless Internet, RV and truck parking, Parking (free).

Quality Inn Calexico
801 S Imperial Avenue
Calexico CA 92231
(760) 357-3271
$69 - $89
Bed & Pet Discount Offered

Pet Policy: Pets accepted, $10 per night.

Features: Business Center, Outdoor Swimming pool, Restaurant(s), Complimentary newspapers in lobby, Smoke-Free property, Multilingual staff, Elevator, Guest laundry, Free breakfast, Free wireless Internet, Number of rooms: 41.

Quality Inn Calexico
801 South Imperial Avenue
Calexico CA 92231
(760) 357-3271
$79- $130

Pet Policy: Pets welcome, $10 per night.

Features: Free breakfast, Free wireless Internet, Coffee maker, Complimentary daily newspaper, Restaurant, Outdoor pool, Guest laundry, Microwave and refrigerators available in upgraded rooms.

Calistoga

Also see the following nearby communities that have pet friendly lodging: St Helena - 7 miles

Brannan Cottage Inn
109 Wapoo Avenue
Calistoga CA 94515-
(707) 942-4200
$195 - $270

Pet Policy: Pets allowed, $25 per day per pet plus $100 refundable deposit.

Features: Full Breakfast, Private baths, Number of rooms :6, Fireplaces in 5 of the rooms, Front desk (limited hours), Smoke-Free property, Free wireless Internet.

Not rated
Calistoga Village Inn
1880 Lincoln Ave.
Calistoga CA 94515
(707) 942-0991
From $79

Pet Policy: Pet friendly rooms are $35 in addition to room charge. A refundable $50 deposit is taken in case of any pet damage. Guests will be charged a $150 additional charge for taking pets into non-pet friendly rooms.

Features: Spa onsite, Naturally heated mineral pools, Coffee in lobby, Air-conditioning, Cable TV, Hair dryers.

Chelsea Garden Inn
1443 2nd Street
Calistoga CA 94515-1419
(707) 942-0948
$197 - $253
Bed & Pet Discount Offered

Pet Policy: Pets are accepted but you must call the property directly for details and booking.

Features: Swimming pool - outdoor, Number of rooms: 5, Number of floors: 2, Business services, Library, Free breakfast, Parking (free), Internet (free).

Solage Calistoga
755 Silverado Trl
Calistoga CA 94515
(866) 942-7442
$315 - $915
Bed & Pet Discount Offered

Pet Policy: Dogs welcome, $100 additional charge per stay. At Solage Calistoga we welcome your canine companions. We'll provide a plush dog bed, water and food bowls, as well as all-natural doggie treats.

Continued on next page

Solage Calistoga
Continued from previous page

Features: Bar/lounge, Beauty services, Children's swimming pool, Full-service health spa, Babysitting or child care, Restaurant(s), Swimming pool - outdoor, Concierge services, Number of rooms: 89, Number of floors: 1, Business services, Poolside bar, Complimentary newspapers in lobby, Use of nearby fitness center (free), Room service, Limo or Town Car service available, Massage - treatment room(s), Steam room, Dry cleaning/laundry service, Parking (free), Free wireless Internet.

Camarillo

Also see the following nearby communities that have pet friendly lodging: Oxnard - 7 miles, Port Hueneme - 8 miles, Thousand Oaks - 9 miles, Santa Paula - 9 miles

Residence Inn by Marriott Camarillo
2912 Petit Street
Camarillo CA 93012
(805)-388-7997
From $139

Pet Policy: Pets allowed, $100 cleaning fee per stay.

Features: Number of rooms: 128, Free breakfast, Dry cleaning/laundry service, Free wireless Internet, Smoke-Free, Fitness facilities, Full kitchens.

Cambria

Also see the following nearby communities that have pet friendly lodging: San Simeon - 4 miles

Not rated
Cambria Palms Motel
2662 Main Street
Cambria CA 93428
(805) 927-4485
$99 - $109

Pet Policy: If you plan to bring a pet(s), you must notify us at the time you make your reservation, as pets are allowed in designated Pet Friendly rooms only. We charge $19 for one pet.

Features: Number of rooms: 18, Free wireless Internet, In room coffee, Cable TV, Free wine tasting at nearby Moonstone Cellars.

★★★

Cambria Pines Lodge
2905 Burton Dr
Cambria CA 93428
(800) 966-6490
$119 - $319
Bed & Pet Discount Offered

Pet Policy: Well-behaved pets accepted for $25 per night per pet, limit of two. Pets may not be left unattended in room.

Features: Gift shops or newsstand, Free wireless Internet, Restaurant(s), Number of rooms: 152, Number of floors: 2, Free breakfast, Complimentary newspapers in lobby, Business center, Swimming pool - outdoor, Bar/lounge, Library, Spa services on site, Suitable for children, Room service (limited hours), Massage - treatment room(s).

Not rated
Cambria Shores Inn
6276 Moonstone Beach Drive
Cambria CA 93428
(805) 927-8644
$249 - $250

Pet Policy: Dogs welcome, no size limits. $15 per night per dog.

Features: Non-smoking property, Free continental breakfast brought to room, Refrigerator and Microwave in all rooms, Flat screen TV, Free wireless Internet, DVD library.

El Colibri Boutique Hotel & Spa
5620 Moonstone Beach Dr
Cambria CA 93428
(805) 924-3003
$149 - $259
Bed & Pet Discount Offered

Pet Policy: Accepts dogs under 20 lbs, $25 per stay.

Features: Parking (free), Free wireless Internet, Free breakfast, Business services, Number of rooms: 34, Front desk hours, Smoke-Free property, Bar/lounge, Full--service health spa, Accessible bathroom.

★★★
FogCatcher Inn
6400 Moonstone Beach Dr
Cambria CA 93428
(805) 927-1400
$159 - $369
Bed & Pet Discount Offered

Pet Policy: Dogs allowed, any size, $25 per night per dog. Limit of 2 per room.

Features: Free wireless Internet, Swimming pool - outdoor, Number of rooms: 60, Business services, Free breakfast, Parking (free), Complimentary newspapers in lobby, 24-hour front desk.

Mariner's Inn by the Sea
6180 Moonstone Beach Dr
Cambria CA 93428
(805) 927-4621
$99 - $129
Bed & Pet Discount Offered

Pet Policy: Pets accepted, $15 per pet per night.

Features: Business services, Coffee in lobby, Free wireless Internet, Number of rooms: 26, Parking (free), 24-hour front desk.

Sea Otter Inn
6656 Moonstone Beach Dr
Cambria CA 93428
(805) 927-5888
$129 - $179
Bed & Pet Discount Offered

Pet Policy: Accepts well-behaved pets, $25 per night. Must arrange directly with hotel at 805-927-5888.

Features: Gift shops or newsstand, Number of rooms: 25, Number of floors: 1, Parking (free), Front desk (limited hours), Free wireless Internet, Concierge services, Coffee in lobby, Swimming pool - outdoor.

The Pickford House B&B
2555 Macleod Way
Cambria CA 93428
(805) 927-8619
$195 - $195
Bed & Pet Discount Offered

Pet Policy: Pets are allowed on a case-by-case basis and the decision is at the discretion of the property owner. Please contact the property directly to get approval. An additional security deposit could be required.
Continued on next page

The Pickford House B&B
Continued from previous page

Any reports by our on-site caretaker or Complaints of neighbors that pets are causing problems or are left alone anywhere on property (barking, etc.) can result in eviction without refund. When pets are let outside to do their business, guests shall immediately clean up after them and ensure that they are Free of dirt, mud, etc. prior to re-entering the house. Please keep pets off of the beds. Pets should be clean and treated with Frontline or Advantix prior to arriving.

Features: Free Breakfast, Number of rooms: 8, Parking (free), Smoke-Free property.

Cameron Park

Also see the following nearby communities that have pet friendly lodging: Placerville - 9 miles, Folsom - 10 miles

Quality Inn & Suites Cameron Park
3361 Coach Ln
Cameron Park CA 95682
(530) 677-2203
$64- $89
Bed & Pet Discount Offered

Pet Policy: Pets up to 100 lbs permitted, $15 per pet per night. Limit of 3 pets per room.

Features: Number of rooms: 63, Parking (free), Accessible bathroom, In-room accessibility equipment for the deaf, Braille or raised signage, Internet (free).

Campbell

Also see the following nearby communities that have pet friendly lodging: Los Gatos - 4 miles, San Jose - 5 miles, Cupertino - 5 miles, Santa Clara - 8 miles, Sunnyvale - 8 miles

Campbell Inn
675 E Campbell Ave
Campbell CA 95008
(408) 374-4300
$108 - $269
Bed & Pet Discount Offered

Pet Policy: Pets allowed with additional charge.

Features: Free breakfast, Airport transportation (free), Tennis on site, Elevator, Number of rooms: 95, Number of floors: 2, Complimentary newspapers in lobby, Use of nearby fitness center (free), 24-hour front desk Free wireless Internet, Swimming pool - outdoor seasonal, Accessible bathroom, Dry cleaning/laundry service.

★★★½

Larkspur Landing Campbell
550 W Hamilton Ave
Campbell CA 95008
(408) 364-1514
$88 - $169
Bed & Pet Discount Offered

Pet Policy: Pets welcome, $75 plus $10 per day additional charge.

Features: Concierge services, Number of rooms: 116, Number of floors: 4, Library, Video library,

Continued on next page

Larkspur Landing Campbell Continued from previous page

Free breakfast, Business Center, Coffee in lobby, Grocery, Parking (free), Multilingual staff, Complimentary newspapers in lobby, Limo or Town Car service available, Free wireless Internet, Dry cleaning/laundry service, Smoke-Free property, Fitness facilities.

★★★

Residence Inn by Marriott San Jose
2761 S Bascom Ave
Campbell CA 95008
(408) 559-1551
$108- $159
Bed & Pet Discount Offered

Pet Policy: Pets allowed, $100 per stay cleaning fee.

Features: Free Breakfast, Swimming pool - outdoor, Business services, Airport transportation (free), Number of rooms: 80, Number of floors: 2, Barbecue grill(s), Coffee in lobby, Parking (free), Complimentary newspapers in lobby, Use of nearby fitness center (free), Free wireless Internet, Smoke-Free property, Dry cleaning/laundry service.

★★½

TownePlace Suites by Marriott San Jose Campbell
700 E Campbell Ave
Campbell CA 95008
(408) 370-4510
$89 - $199
Bed & Pet Discount Offered

Pet Policy: Pets allowed. $75 cleaning fee.

Features: Parking (free), Barbecue grill(s), Guest laundry, Number of rooms: 95, Number of floors: 4, Nearby fitness center (discount), Coffee in lobby, Free breakfast, Complimentary newspapers in lobby, Smoke-Free property, Grocery/convenience store, Free wireless Internet, 24-hour business center.

Canoga Park

Also see the following nearby communities that have pet friendly lodging: Woodland Hills - 2 miles, Tarzana - 4 miles, Chatsworth - 4 miles, Northridge - 4 miles, Calabasas - 6 miles, Van Nuys - 7 miles, Topanga - 8 miles, Sherman Oaks - 9 miles, Simi Valley - 9 miles

★★

Motel 6 Canoga Park
7132 De Soto Avenue
Canoga Park CA 91303
(818) 883-6666
$62 - $68
Bed & Pet Discount Offered

Pet Policy: Well-behaved pets stay Free. Animals that pose a health or safety risk may not remain onsite, and include those that, in our manager's discretion, are too numerous for any one room, cause damage to our property or that of other guests, are too disruptive, are not properly attended, or demonstrate undue aggression. All pets must be declared at check-in. Pets must be attended to and under control at all times. If unavoidable circumstances require a pet to remain in a room while the owner is offsite, the pet must be secured in a crate or travel carrier. Pets must be on a leash or securely carried outside of guest rooms.

Features: Swimming pool - outdoor, Number of rooms: 64, Number of floors: 2, Free wireless Internet, Restaurant(s), Coffee in lobby, Guest laundry, Parking (free).

Canyon Lake

Also see the following nearby communities that have pet friendly lodging: Sun City - 4 miles, Lake Elsinore - 6 miles

Rodeway Inn & Suites Canyon Lake
31820 Railroad Canyon Rd
Canyon Lake CA 92587
(951) 244-1164
$49- $59
Bed & Pet Discount Offered

Pet Policy: Rodeway Inns charge an additional $10 per night per pet and require a $50 damage deposit, which is refunded if the room is in order at check out. Max of 2 pets per room. A veterinarian certificate that the pet is on a flea and parasite program and that they are Free from parasites is required. Pets may not be left alone in the room unless in a cage.

Features:) Number of rooms: 34, Business services, Restaurant(s), Free breakfast, Parking (free), Complimentary newspapers in lobby, Room service, Free wireless Internet.

Capistrano Beach

Also see the following nearby communities that have pet friendly lodging: Dana Point - 2 miles, San Clemente - 3 miles, San Juan Capistrano - 5 miles, Laguna Beach - 9 miles

Capistrano Seaside Inn
34862 Pacific Coast Hwy
Capistrano Beach CA 92624
(949) 496-1399
$89 - $129
Bed & Pet Discount Offered

Pet Policy: Small pets only.

Features: Free Breakfast, Business services, Number of rooms: 28, Number of floors: 2, Barbecue grill(s), Parking (free), Internet (free).

Carlsbad

Also see the following nearby communities that have pet friendly lodging: Oceanside - 5 miles, Vista - 6 miles, Encinitas - 6 miles, San Marcos - 7 miles

Extended Stay America San Diego - Carlsbad Village
1050 Grand Ave
Carlsbad CA 92008
(760) 729-9380
$74 - $94
Bed & Pet Discount Offered

Pet Policy: One pet is allowed in each guest room. A $25 per day non-refundable cleaning fee (not to exceed $150) will be charged the first night of your stay.

Features: Guest laundry, Swimming pool - outdoor, Elevator, Number of rooms: 106, Number of floors: 3, Barbecue grill(s), Parking (free), Front desk (limited hours).

Not Rated
Four Seasons Residences Aviara
7210 Blue Heron Place
Carlsbad CA 92011
(760) 268-1200
$325 - $595

Pet Policy: Pets welcome under the following additional charge schedule: $75.00 for Villa Guest Room; $100.00 for One Bedroom Villa; $175.00 for Two Bedroom Villa. Please let us know prior to your arrival that you will be bringing your pet. While in residence, please contact Housekeeping to arrange for a convenient time for Villa servicing. We regret that pets are not allowed in any food and beverage outlet, health clubs, spa, or pool areas. (This exclusion does not apply to guide dogs.) Please keep pets on a leash when on property outside your Villa.

Features: Health club, Swimming pool, Golf course, Tennis courts, Full service spa, Restaurants.

★★★
Homewood Suites Carlsbad North
2223 Palomar Airport Rd
Carlsbad CA 92011
(760) 431-2266
$143 - $179
Bed & Pet Discount Offered

Pet Policy: Pets up to 25 lbs, $75 per stay.

Features: Swimming pool - outdoor, Concierge services, Gift shops or newsstand, Number of rooms: 145, Suitable for children, Free breakfast, Parking (free), Dry cleaning/laundry service, Multilingual staff, Free reception, Smoke-Free property, Grocery/convenience store, Free wireless Internet, 24-hour business center, Fitness facilities.

★★½
Hyatt Summerfield Suites San Diego
5010 Avenida Encinas
Carlsbad CA 92008
(760) 929 8200
$116 - $159
Bed & Pet Discount Offered

Pet Policy: Accepts two pets per room, only one of which may be a dog. Pets must not exceed 25 lbs and must be house broken. The hotel may charge up to a $200 non-refundable cleaning fee that will be assessed to the guest. Cleaning fee cannot exceed $200. With the exception of service animals, pets are not allowed in the Guest House or food service areas and must be on a leash when.

Features: BBQ area, Wheelchair accessible, Suitable for children, Multilingual staff, Limo or Town Car service available, Technology support staff, Designated smoking areas, Pick up service from train station, Area shuttle (free), 24-hour business center, Theme park shuttle (free), Smoke-Free property, Free reception, Swimming pool - outdoor, Free breakfast, Number of rooms: 98, Parking (free), Complimentary newspapers in lobby, Swimming pool - outdoor (heated), Coffee in lobby, Smoke-Free property, Dry cleaning/laundry service, Free wireless Internet, Fitness facilities, Accessible bathroom, In-room accessibility equipment for the deaf, Braille or raised signage.

★★½

La Quinta Inn San Diego-Carlsbad
760 Macadamia Dr
Carlsbad CA 92009
(760) 438-2828
$79 - $149
Bed & Pet Discount Offered

Pet Policy: Pets up to 40 lbs allowed, no additional charge. Must not leave unattended and must clean up after.

Features: Business center, Elevator, Swimming pool - outdoor, Accessible bathroom, Number of rooms: 111, Number of floors: 3, Free breakfast, Parking (free), Complimentary newspapers in lobby, Internet (free), Smoke-Free property, Dry cleaning/laundry service, Fitness facilities.

Not rated

Oakwood Carlsbad
6610 Ambrosia Lane
Carlsbad CA 92009
(602) 687-3322
$137 - $204

Pet Policy: Pets accepted with limitations and additional charge. Contact hotel directly for more information and to make reservations.

Features: Fully furnished apartments, Fully equipped kitchens, Linens, VCR, TV, Housewares, Cable TV, Weekly housekeeping.. 30 day minimum stay may be required.

★★★★★

Park Hyatt Aviara Resort
7100 Four Seasons
Carlsbad CA 92009
(760) 448-1234
$349 - $660
Bed & Pet Discount Offered

Pet Policy: 1 pet per room, up to 15 lbs.

Features: Technology support staff, Number of rooms: 329, Number of floors: 5, Number of suites: 44, Massage - treatment room(s), Steam room, Concierge desk, Tennis on site, Shopping on site, Golf course on site, Beauty services, Designated smoking areas, Wireless Internet (additional charge), Number of outdoor swimming pools 2, Fitness facilities, Elevator, Poolside bar, Computer rental, Cell phone/mobile rental, Restaurants: 3, Complimentary newspapers in lobby, 24-hour business center, Full-service health spa, Porter/bellhop, Swimming pool - outdoor, Accessibility equipment for the deaf, Gift shops or newsstand, Dry cleaning/laundry service, Translation services, Arcade/game room, ATM/banking, Media library, Accessible bathroom, Children's club, Coffee in lobby, Wheelchair accessible, Health club, Currency exchange, Suitable for children, Bar/lounge, Children's swimming pool, Babysitting or child care, Multilingual staff, Billiards, Room service (24 hours), Security guard, Spa services on site, Valet Parking (additional charge).

Quality Inn & Suites North Legoland Area Carlsbad
751 Raintree Drive
Carlsbad CA 92009
(760) 931-1185
$80- $174
Bed & Pet Discount Offered

Pet Policy: Quality Inns charge an additional $10 per night per pet. They may require a $50 damage deposit, which is refunded if the room is in order at check out. Quality Inns accept any well-behaved pets with a maximum of 3 per room, but dogs are limited to 80 pounds. Pets may not be left alone in the room unless in a cage.

Features: Guest laundry, Business center, Swimming pool - outdoor, Elevator, Concierge services, Number of rooms: 113, Number of floors: 3, Free breakfast, Parking (free), Multilingual staff, Restaurant(s), Free wireless Internet, Fitness facilities.

Ramada Carlsbad by the Sea
751 Macadamia Dr
Carlsbad CA 92011
(760) 438-2285
$45 - $300
Bed & Pet Discount Offered

Pet Policy: Pet friendly, no charge.

Features: Swimming pool – outdoor, Business center, Elevator, Parking (free), Complimentary newspapers in lobby, Free breakfast, Internet (free).

Residence Inn by Marriott Carlsbad
2000 Faraday Ave
Carlsbad CA 92008
(760) 431-9999
$119 - $199
Bed & Pet Discount Offered

Pet Policy: Pets allowed, $75 cleaning fee per stay.

Features: Free wireless Internet, Business services, Concierge services, Number of rooms: 121, Number of floors: 3, Suitable for children, Barbecue grill(s), Coffee in lobby, Free breakfast, Parking (free), Complimentary newspapers in lobby, Smoke-Free property, Swimming pool, Pick up service from train station, Accessible bathroom, In-room accessibility equipment for the deaf, Braille or raised signage, Dry cleaning/laundry service, Fitness facilities.

Rodeway Inn Legoland
3570 Pio Pico Dr
Carlsbad CA 92008
(760) 729-2383
$55 - $69
Bed & Pet Discount Offered

Pet Policy: Rodeway Inns charge an additional $10 per night per pet and require a $50 damage deposit, which is refunded if the room is in order at check out. Max of 2 pets per room. A veterinarian certificate that the pet is on a flea and parasite program and that they are Free from parasites is required. Pets may not be left alone in the room unless in a cage.

Features: Coffee in lobby, Swimming pool - outdoor, Business center, Number of rooms: 67, Number of floors: 2, Suitable for children, Free breakfast, Complimentary newspapers in lobby, Free wireless Internet.

★★★★

Sheraton Carlsbad Resort & Spa
5480 Grand Pacific Dr
Carlsbad CA 92008
(760) 827-2400
$138 - $239
Bed & Pet Discount Offered

Pet Policy: The Sheraton Carlsbad Resort & Spa accepts dogs only up to 80 lbs. No more than one dog per room. Please be advised that dogs must be accompanied by owners at all times. Hotel has the option to charge a cleaning fee after the room has been evaluated upon guest departure. Guests must sign pet-waiver upon check-in and will be charged a pet fee of $35 per day.

Features: Bar/lounge, Spa services on site, ATM/banking, Room service, Security guard, Business center, Restaurant(s) 1, On-site car rental, Steam room, Sauna, Swimming pool - outdoor, Gift shops or newsstand, Number of rooms: 250, Number of floors: 3, Translation services, Suitable for children, Breakfast available additional charge, Multilingual staff, Complimentary newspapers in lobby, Limo or Town Car service available, Full-service health spa, Internet (free), Massage - treatment room(s), Parking (valet) $16 per night, Dry cleaning/laundry service, Elevator, Concierge desk, Wheelchair accessible, Tennis on site.

Carmel

Also see the following nearby communities that have pet friendly lodging: Monterey - 5 miles, Pacific Grove - 7 miles, Seaside - 7 miles, Carmel Valley - 9 miles

Carmel Crystal Bay Inn
24815 Carpenter
Carmel CA 93923
(831) 624-6400
$99 - $149
Bed & Pet Discount Offered

Pet Policy: Small pets welcome, $20 per night.

Features: Business services, Guest laundry, Free breakfast, Media library, Video library, Parking (free), Complimentary newspapers in lobby, Wireless Internet, Smoke-Free property, Accessible bathroom, In-room accessibility equipment for the deaf.

★★★

Carmel Lodge
San Carlos St at 5th Ave
Carmel CA 93921
(831) 624-1255
$133 - $194
Bed & Pet Discount Offered

Pet Policy: Dogs welcome, $35 per day. Does not include Cottage Suite.

Features: Smoke-Free property, Technology helpdesk, Swimming pool - outdoor, Number of rooms: 42, Number of floors: 2, Suitable for children, Coffee in lobby, Multilingual staff, Complimentary newspapers in lobby, Parking fee $10 Daily, Free wireless Internet, Free breakfast.

Carmel Mission Inn
3665 Rio Rd
Carmel CA 93923
(831) 624-1841
$155 - $234
Bed & Pet Discount Offered

Pet Policy: Dogs up to 50 lbs welcome, $35 per stay. Must reserve in advance.

Features: Swimming pool - outdoor, Smoke-Free property, Bar/lounge, Elevator, Restaurant(s), Room service , ATM/banking, Concierge services, Business services, Breakfast available additional charge, Parking (free), Multilingual staff, Complimentary newspapers in lobby, Porter/bellhop, Internet (free), Massage - treatment room(s), Accessible bathroom, In-room accessibility, Braille or raised signage, Dry cleaning/laundry service, Fitness center.

Carmel Resort Inn
Carpenter St, between First and Second
Carmel CA 93921
(831) 624-3113
$115 - $171
Bed & Pet Discount Offered

Pet Policy: Well behaved pets always welcome. $20 per pet per night. Our community proudly encourages pets to roam Freely on Carmel Beach.

Features: Sauna, Number of rooms: 31, Number of floors: 1, Barbecue grill(s), Free breakfast, Parking (free), Multilingual staff, Complimentary newspapers in lobby, Front desk (limited hours), Smoke-Free property, Accessible bathroom, Free wireless Internet.

Carmel River Inn
26600 Oliver Rd
Carmel CA 93923
(831) 624-1575
$105 - $135
Bed & Pet Discount Offered

Pet Policy: Pets are accepted in designated cottages. We charge a nightly additional charge of $20 per night per pet for up to two well-behaved pets per cottage. Carmel River Inn is a pet-friendly hotel. Not only are we a pet friendly hotel, but we are also pleased to recommend some fun activities for a pet friendly vacation.

Features: Suitable for children, Barbecue grill(s), Parking (free), Multilingual staff, Complimentary newspapers in lobby, Internet (free), Massage - treatment room(s), Smoke-Free property, Swimming pool - outdoor seasonal.

Carmel Valley Ranch
One Old Ranch Road
Carmel CA 93923
(831) 625-9500
$325 - $455
Bed & Pet Discount Offered

Pet Policy: Pets allowed, $50 per stay.

Features: Swimming pool - outdoor, Security guard, Concierge services, Golf course on site, Tennis on site (9 courts), Bar/lounge, Dry cleaning/laundry service, Children's swimming pool, Beauty services, Number of outdoor swimming pools 2, RV and truck parking, Full-service health spa, Massage - spa treatment room(s), *Continued on next page*

Caramel Valley Ranch
Continued from previous page

Steam room, Children's club, Restaurant(s), Room service, Gift shops or newsstand, Number of rooms: 144, Number of floors: 1, Breakfast available additional charge, Parking (free), Multilingual staff, Complimentary newspapers in lobby, Porter/bellhop, Accessible bathroom, In-room accessibility equipment for the deaf, Braille or raised signage, Supervised child care/activities, Wheelchair accessible, Shopping on site, Library, Medical assistance available, Smoke-Free property, Media library, 24-hour business center, Fitness facilities, Coffee in lobby, Free Internet access .

Not Rated
Casa de Carmel
Monte Verde Ave at Ocean Ave
Carmel CA 93921
(831) 624-2429
$135 - $136

Pet Policy: Pets welcome, $20 per pet per night.

Features: Number of rooms: 7, Free continental breakfast.

★
Hofsas House Hotel
3rd and 4th Street at San Carlos
Carmel CA 93921
(831) 624-2745
$105 - $269

Pet Policy: Dogs welcome, $25 per night.

Features: Number of rooms: 38, Fireplaces in most rooms, Wet bars or kitchens, Free continental breakfast, Heated swimming pool, Sauna, Free wireless Internet.

★★
Monte Verde Inn
On Monte Verde
between Ocean and 7th
Carmel CA 93921
(831) 624-6046
$140 - $180
Bed & Pet Discount Offered

Pet Policy: Pets welcome, $20 per pet per night.

Features: Number of rooms: 15, Number of suites: 2, Free breakfast, Parking (free), Front desk (limited hours), Smoke-Free property, Free wireless Internet, Accessible bathroom.

★★★★
Quail Lodge Resort
8205 Valley Greens Dr
Carmel CA 93923
(831) 624-2888
$219 - $219
Bed & Pet Discount Offered

Pet Policy: Pets accepted, $25 per day. Doggie treat and other amenities provided.

Features: Swimming pool - outdoor, Business services, Restaurant(s), Number of rooms: 97 Guest laundry, Free breakfast, Spa services on site, Accessible bathroom, In-room accessibility equipment for the deaf, Braille or raised signage Golf course on site, Tennis on site, Fitness facilities.

Svendsgaard's Inn
San Carlos St And 4th Ave
Carmel CA 93921
(831) 624-1511
$127 - $259
Bed & Pet Discount Offered

Pet Policy: Quiet, non-aggressive pets are welcome, $25 per night per pet, limit 2 per room.. A pet bed, pet blanket, food & water dish will be provided for the use of your pet during your stay on request. Pets must not be left unattended in room and should be leashed when outside the room. Pets are not allowed on beds or furniture.

Features: Number of rooms: 35, Number of floors: 2, Complimentary breakfast, Parking (free), Front desk (limited hours), Coffee in lobby, Swimming pool, Concierge services, Complimentary newspapers in lobby.

Carmel Valley

Also see the following nearby communities that have pet friendly lodging: Carmel - 9 miles

Not Rated
Carmel Valley Lodge
8 Ford Rd At Carmel Valley Rd
Carmel Valley CA 93924
(831) 659-2261
$198 - $227
Bed & Pet Discount Offered

Pet Policy: Dogs only, $25 per day - limit 2 per room. Must stay in dog friendly designated rooms. Dogs get treats when they arrive. They have plenty of space on the grounds and a leash post on each patio. Just minutes away is Carmel-By-The-Sea, one of the most dog friendly cities in the country. And on the Carmel Beach, your dog can run Free without a leash.

Features: Coffee in lobby, Free breakfast, Free wireless Internet, Number of rooms: 31, Parking (free).

Carpinteria

Holiday Inn Express Hotel & Suites Carpinteria
5606 Carpinteria Ave
Carpinteria CA 93013
(805) 566-9499
$89 - $163

Pet Policy: Pet friendly hotel. Charge of $10 per pet per day. Size limitations. Specific Room Restrictions. Must reserve room directly with hotel.

Features: Free Breakfast, Swimming pool - outdoor, Number of rooms: 108, Number of floors: 2, Business services, Parking (free), Multilingual staff, Complimentary newspapers in lobby, Internet (free), Accessible bathroom, In-room accessibility equipment for the deaf, Braille or raised signage, Dry cleaning/laundry service, Fitness facilities.

Carson

Also see the following nearby communities that have pet friendly lodging: Torrance - 4 miles, Gardena - 4 miles, Harbor City - 4 miles, Long Beach - 6 miles, Redondo Beach - 7 miles, Signal Hill - 7 miles, Hermosa Beach - 8 miles, Hawthorne - 8 miles, San Pedro - 8 miles, Manhattan Beach - 9 miles, Downey - 10 miles, Huntington Park - 10 miles, El Segundo - 10 mile

Doubletree Hotel Carson
2 Civic Plaza Drive
Carson CA 90745
(310) 830-9200
$101- $184
Bed & Pet Discount Offered

Pet Policy: Pets permitted with $50 per stay additional charge.

Features: Bar/lounge, Elevator, Restaurant(s), Room service, ATM/banking, Gift shops or newsstand, Number of rooms: 221, Business services, Breakfast available additional charge, Parking (free), Multilingual staff, Complimentary newspapers in lobby, Concierge desk, Free wireless Internet, Accessible bathroom, Dry cleaning/laundry service, Swimming pool - outdoor, Fitness facilities.

Extended Stay America Los Angeles - Carson
401 E Albertoni St
Carson CA 90746
(310) 323-2080
$66 - $86
Bed & Pet Discount Offered

Pet Policy: One pet up to 25 lbs is allowed in each guest room. A $25 per day non-refundable cleaning fee (not to exceed $150) will be charged the first night of your stay. May not book a signature room if you bring pets.

Features: Guest laundry, Number of rooms: 107, Number of floors: 3, Wireless Internet (additional charge), Front desk (limited hours), Security guard.

Castaic

Also see the following nearby communities that have pet friendly lodging: Valencia - 6 miles, Santa Clarita - 8 miles, Stevenson Ranch - 8 miles

Not rated
Castaic Inn
31411 Ridge Route Rd
Castaic CA 91384
(661) 257-0229
$57 - $79

Pet Policy: Pet friendly

Features: Free continental breakfast, Free wireless Internet.

Rodeway Inn Magic Mountain Area
31558 Castaic Rd
Castaic CA 91384
(661) 295-1100
$64 - $79
Bed & Pet Discount Offered

Pet Policy: Rodeway Inns charge an additional $10 per night per pet and require a $50 damage deposit, which is refunded if the room is in order at check out. Max of 2 pets per room. A veterinarian certificate that the pet is on a flea and parasite program and that they are Free from parasites is required. Pets may not be left alone in the room unless in a cage.

Continued on next page

Rodeway Inn – Magic Mountain
Continued from previous page

Features: Swimming pool – outdoor, Gift shops or newsstand, rooms: 120, Number of floors: 2, Business services, Coffee in lobby, Parking (free), Complimentary newspapers in lobby, Free breakfast, Guest laundry.

Castro Valley

Also see the following nearby communities that have pet friendly lodging: Hayward - 5 miles, Union City - 8 miles, San Ramon - 8 miles, Dublin - 8 miles, Danville - 9 miles, Oakland - 10 miles, Pleasanton - 10 miles

Quality Inn Castro Valley
2532 Castro Valley Blvd
Castro Valley CA 94546
(510) 538-9501
$80 - $100
Bed & Pet Discount Offered

Pet Policy: Pets accepted for additional charge of $10 night under 10 lbs, $20 per night over 10 lbs per pet. Pet limit: 4 pets per room.

Features: Elevator, Restaurant(s), Swimming pool - outdoor, Number of rooms: 60, Number of floors: 3, Free breakfast, Parking (free), Multilingual staff, Business center, Concierge desk, Free wireless Internet, Accessible bathroom, In-room accessibility equipment for the deaf, Braille or raised signage, Dry cleaning/laundry service, Fitness facilities.

Cathedral City

Also see the following nearby communities that have pet friendly lodging: Rancho Mirage - 4 miles, Palm Springs - 4 miles, Thousand Palms - 6 miles, Palm Desert - 8 miles

Cathedral City Travelodge
67495 E Us Highway 111
Cathedral City CA 92234
(760) 328-2616
$63 - $127
Bed & Pet Discount Offered

Pet Policy: Pets permitted, $10 per pet per day. Limit 2 per room.

Features: Business services, Barbecue grill(s), Parking (free), Smoke-Free property, Swimming pool - outdoor seasonal, RV and truck parking, Free wireless Internet, Free breakfast.

Doral Desert Princess Resort
67967 Vista Chino
Cathedral City CA 92234
(760) 322-7000
$166- $443
Bed & Pet Discount Offered

Pet Policy: Dogs up to 25 lbs allowed, $75 per stay each, limit of 2 per room. Must book in first floor rooms only.

Features: Swimming pool - outdoor, Elevator, Security guard, Spa services on site, Bar/lounge, Room Service, Airport transportation (free), Concierge services, ATM/banking, Poolside bar, Restaurant(s), Gift shops or newsstand, Shopping on site, Number of rooms: 285, Business services,

Continued on next page

Doral Desert Princess Resort
Continued from previous page

Computer rental, Internet (additional charge), Breakfast available additional charge, Health club, Parking (free), Multilingual staff, Complimentary newspapers in lobby, Porter/bellhop, Medical assistance available, Beauty services, Massage - treatment room(s), Sauna, Technology helpdesk, Dry cleaning/laundry service, Golf course on site, Tennis on site, Fitness facilities.

★★

Quality Inn & Suites Date Palm
69151 E Palm Canyon Dr
Cathedral City CA 92234
(760) 324-5939
$79 - $199
Bed & Pet Discount Offered

Pet Policy: Quality Inns charge an additional $10 per night per pet plus a $50 damage deposit, which is refunded if the room is in order at check out. Quality Inns accept any well-behaved pets up to 40 pounds with a maximum of 2 per room.

Features: Swimming pool – outdoor, Guest laundry, Number of suites: 97, Free breakfast, Parking (free), Smoke-Free property, Accessible bathroom, In-room accessibility equipment for the deaf, Braille or raised signage, Elevator, Barbecue grill(s), Use of nearby fitness center (free), Business center, Free wireless Internet.

Cayucos

Also see the following nearby communities that have pet friendly lodging: Morro Bay - 5 miles

Cayucos Beach Inn
333 South Ocean Avenue
Cayucos CA 93430
(805) 995-2828
$110 - $155
Bed & Pet Discount Offered

Pet Policy: Pets welcome, $10 per pet per night.

Features: Accessible bathroom, Free wireless Internet, Wheelchair accessible, ATM/banking, Number of rooms: 30, Number of suites: 6, Number of floors: 2, Suitable for children, Coffee in lobby, Free breakfast, Parking (free), Multilingual staff, Smoke-Free property.

Not rated:
Cayucos Pier View Suites
14 N Ocean Ave
Cayucos CA 93430
(805) 995-0014
$195 - $240

Pet Policy: Pets are welcome and are counted as a "person" occupant. If more than 4 occupants, there is an additional $25 per occupant additional charge. Otherwise, no pet fee. In other words, pets are considered the same as your children.

Features: Furnished apartments, Fully equipped gourmet kitchens, Cable television, Free wireless Internet, Jacuzzi tubs , Weekly rates available.

Ceres

Also see the following nearby communities that have pet friendly lodging: Modesto - 4 miles, Turlock - 9 miles, Salida - 10 miles

Microtel Inn And Suites Modesto Ceres
1760 Herndon Road
Ceres CA 95307
(209) 538-6466
$54 - $78
Bed & Pet Discount Offered

Pet Policy: Accepts small pets less than 10 lbs, no additional charge.

Features: Swimming pool - outdoor, Number of floors: 3, Coffee in lobby, Free breakfast, Parking (free), Multilingual staff, Business center, Dry cleaning/laundry service, Internet (free), Fitness facilities.

Cerritos

Also see the following nearby communities that have pet friendly lodging: La Palma - 3 miles, Hawaiian Gardens - 3 miles, La Mirada - 3 miles, Buena Park - 3 miles, Norwalk - 3 miles, Cypress - 4 miles, Los Alamitos - 4 miles, Whittier - 6 miles, Downey - 6 miles, Fullerton - 7 miles, Pico Rivera - 8 miles, Signal Hill - 8 miles, Anaheim - 8 miles, Seal Beach - 8 miles, Bell Gardens - 8 miles, Long Beach - 9 miles, Garden Grove - 10 miles, Commerce - 10 miles

Sheraton Cerritos Hotel at Towne Center
12725 Center Court Dr S
Cerritos CA 90703
(562) 809-1500
$88 - $178
Bed & Pet Discount Offered

Pet Policy: Two pets up to 50 pounds each are allowed per room. A non-refundable deposit of $25 per stay is required. Pets cannot be left unattended in the guest room. The hotel reserves the right to charge for additional cleaning or damage caused by the pet. If damage is found after checkout, credit card on record will be charged.

Features: Swimming pool - outdoor, Business center, Bar/lounge, Restaurant(s), Room service (limited hours), Concierge services, Gift shops or newsstand, Number of rooms: 203, Number of floors: 8, Internet (additional charge), Breakfast available additional charge, Parking (free), Complimentary newspapers in lobby, Fitness facilities.

Chatsworth

Also see the following nearby communities that have pet friendly lodging: Canoga Park - 4 miles, Northridge - 4 miles, Woodland Hills - 6 miles, Tarzana - 7 miles, Simi Valley - 7 miles, Van Nuys - 8 miles, Stevenson Ranch - 9 miles, Calabasas - 9 miles

Ramada Inn Chatsworth
21340 Devonshire St
Chatsworth CA 91311
(818) 998-5289
$75 - $94
Bed & Pet Discount Offered

Pet Policy: Pets up to 15 lbs, $10 per pet per night.

Features: Free Breakfast, Bar/lounge, Elevator, Restaurant(s), Parking (free), Internet (free), Business center, Swimming pool - outdoor, Room service, Accessible bathroom, In-room accessibility equipment for the deaf, Braille or raised signage.

Staybridge Suites Chatsworth
21902 Lassen St
Chatsworth CA 91311
(818) 773-0707
$95 - $190
Bed & Pet Discount Offered

Pet Policy: Pets up to 60 lbs, $75 for up to 6 nights, $150 for 7 or longer. 2 pets permitted but together must not exceed 60 lbs. Must have proof of current vaccinations.

Features: Accessible bathroom, In-room accessibility equipment for the deaf, Braille or raised signage, Swimming pool - outdoor, Gift shops or newsstand, Number of suites: 114, Number of floors: 3, Free breakfast, Business center, Internet (free), Dry cleaning/laundry service, Fitness facilities.

Chester

Not Rated
Best Western Rose Quartz Inn
306 Main Street
Chester CA 96020
(530) 258-2002
$77 - $139

Pet Policy: Pets accepted with approval of management. Please contact hotel directly for booking and details.

Features: Outdoor spa, Business center, Free continental breakfast, Free wireless Internet.

Chico

Best Western Heritage Inn – Chico
Best Western Heritage Inn
25 Heritage Ln
Chico CA 95926
(530) 894-8600
$89 - $90
Bed & Pet Discount Offered

Pet Policy: Pets accepted on advance approval. Please contact hotel directly for reservations.

Features: Complimentary newspapers in lobby, Swimming pool - outdoor seasonal, RV and truck parking, Free breakfast, Free wireless Internet, Parking (free), Business center.

Not rated
Budget Inn
1717 Park Ave
Chico CA 95928
(530) 342-9472
$65 - $75

Pet Policy: Pets accepted with additional charge at check-in.

Features: Free wireless Internet, Microwave and mini fridge in each room, Cable TV.

Heritage Inn Express Chico
725 Broadway St
Chico CA 95928
(530) 343-4527
$74 - $75
Bed & Pet Discount Offered

Pet Policy: All pets accepted, $20 per pet per stay.

Features: Swimming pool - outdoor, Guest laundry, Free breakfast, Parking (free).

Holiday Inn Chico
685 Manzanita Ct
Chico CA 95926
(530) 345-2491
$85.9932 - $175
Bed & Pet Discount Offered

Pet Policy: We have pet friendly rooms available with an additional charge of $30. Pets are not to be left unattended in rooms. Please use pet carriers or leashes when out of guestroom. No pets in pool area, lounge or restaurant.

Features: Bar/lounge, Airport transportation (free), Restaurant(s), Room service (limited hours), Swimming pool - outdoor, ATM/banking, Gift shops or newsstand, Number of rooms: 172, Number of suites: 9, Number of floors: 5, Coffee in lobby, Free breakfast, Parking (free), Business center, Elevator, Multilingual staff, Complimentary newspapers in lobby, Concierge desk, Internet (free), Accessible bathroom, In-room accessibility equipment for the deaf, Braille or raised signage, Dry cleaning/laundry service, Fitness facilities.

★★★

Oxford Suites Chico
2035 Business Ln
Chico CA 95928
(530) 899-9090
$98 - $129
Bed & Pet Discount Offered

Pet Policy: Accepts medium size dogs, $35 per stay.

Features: Internet (free), Airport transportation (free), Business center, Security guard, Coffee in lobby, Nearby fitness center (discount), Steam room, Sauna, Swimming pool - outdoor, Free breakfast, Gift shops or newsstand, Number of rooms: 183, Number of floors: 4, Suitable for children, Video library, Parking (free), Complimentary newspapers in lobby, 24-hour front desk Dry cleaning/laundry service.

★★

Quality Inn Chico
715 Main Street
Chico CA 95928
(530) 343-7911
$85 - $160
Bed & Pet Discount Offered

Pet Policy: Quality Inns charge an additional $10 per night per pet. They may require a $50 damage deposit, which is refunded if the room is in order at check out. Quality Inns accept any well-behaved pets with a maximum of 3 per room, but dogs are limited to 50 pounds. Pets may not be left alone in the room unless in a cage.

Features; Number of rooms: 51, Number of floors: 2, Parking (free), Restaurant(s), Swimming pool - outdoor, Free wireless Internet.

★★★

Residence Inn by Marriott Chico
2485 Carmichael Drive
Chico CA 95928

Pet Policy: Pets welcome, no size limits. $75 per stay.

Features: Business services, Free breakfast,
Continued on next page

Residence Inn Chico
Continued from previous page

(530) 894-5500
$134 - $135
Bed & Pet Discount Offered

Grocery, Dry cleaning/laundry service, Free wireless Internet, Swimming pool - outdoor, Complimentary newspapers in lobby, Smoke-Free property, Free reception

Not rated
Safari Inn
2352 Esplande
Chico CA 95926
(530) 343-3201
$35 - $55

Pet Policy: Dogs allowed, any size, smoking rooms only, $15 per night. Limit of 2 dogs per room.

Features: Free indoor parking., local calls, Coffee & tea.

Super 8 Chico CA
655 Manzanita Ct
Chico CA 95926
(530) 345-2533
$55 - $85
Bed & Pet Discount Offered

Pet Policy: Pets permitted, $10 per night. Limit of 2 per room.

Features: Free breakfast, Business services, Parking (free), Swimming pool - outdoor seasonal.

Vagabond Inn Chico
630 Main St
Chico CA 95928
(530) 895-1323
$61 - $100
Bed & Pet Discount Offered

Pet Policy: Pets permitted, no size limit. $10 per night per pet. Maximum of 2 pets per room.

Features: Free Breakfast, Number of rooms:43, Number of suites: 2, Number of floors: 2, Coffee in lobby, Parking (free), Multilingual staff, Complimentary newspapers in lobby, Swimming pool - outdoor seasonal, Free wireless Internet.

Chino

Also see the following nearby communities that have pet friendly lodging: Chino Hills - 2 miles, Pomona - 6 miles, Ontario - 6 miles, Claremont - 6 miles, Diamond Bar - 6 miles, Upland - 7 miles, Walnut - 9 miles, San Dimas - 9 miles, Rancho Cucamonga - 9 miles, Yorba Linda - 10 miles

Extended Stay America Los Angeles - Chino Valley
4325 Corporate Center Ave
Chino CA 91710
(909) 597-8675
$64 - $69
Bed & Pet Discount Offered

Pet Policy: One pet is allowed in each guest room. A $25 per day non-refundable cleaning fee (not to exceed $150) will be charged the first night of your stay.

Features: Guest laundry, Elevator, Number of rooms: 102, Number of floors: 3, Suitable for children, Parking (free), Multilingual staff, Use of nearby fitness center (free), Wireless Internet.

Chino Hills

Also see the following nearby communities that have pet friendly lodging: Chino - 2 miles, Diamond Bar - 5 miles, Pomona - 6 miles, Yorba Linda - 7 miles, Walnut - 8 miles, Claremont - 8 miles, Ontario - 8 miles, Upland - 9 miles, San Dimas - 10 miles

Holiday Inn Express Hotel & Suites Chino Hills
15433 Fairfield Ranch Rd
Chino Hills CA 91709
(877) 863-4780
$90 - $123
Bed & Pet Discount Offered

Pet Policy: Pets accepted. Additional charge charged.

Features: Fitness facilities, Swimming pool - indoor, Free breakfast, Business center, Dry cleaning/laundry service, Free wireless Internet, Accessible bathroom, In-room accessibility equipment for the deaf, Braille or raised signage.

Chowchilla

Chowchilla Days Inn Gateway to Yosemite
220 E Robertson Blvd
Chowchilla CA 93610
(559) 665-4821
$59 - $78
Bed & Pet Discount Offered

Pet Policy: Pets accepted, $10 per day.

Features: Internet (free), Wheelchair accessible, Number of floors: 2, Business services, Complimentary newspapers in lobby, Swimming pool - outdoor seasonal.

Holiday Inn Express & Suites Gateway to Yosemite
309 Prosperity Ave
Chowchilla CA 93610
(559) 665-3300
$77 - $106
Bed & Pet Discount Offered

Pet Policy: Pets up to 75 lbs. $25 per pet per night

Features: Swimming pool - outdoor, ATM/banking, Gift shops or newsstand, Number of floors: 3, Business center, Concierge desk, Wireless Internet, Accessible bathroom, In-room accessibility equipment for the deaf, Braille or raised signage, Fitness facilities.

Chula Vista

Also see the following nearby communities that have pet friendly lodging: National City - 4 miles, San Ysidro - 5 miles, Coronado - 6 miles

Comfort Inn & Suites Chula Vista
632 E Street
Chula Vista CA 91910
(619) 426-2500
$94 - $129
Bed & Pet Discount Offered

Pet Policy: Pet Accommodation: 25.00 per stay, up to 15 lbs. Pet Limit: 2 pets per room.

Features: Elevator, Guest laundry, Free breakfast, Swimming pool - outdoor, Number of rooms: 88, Number of floors: 4, Internet (free), Business center, Fitness facilities.

La Quinta Inn San Diego Chula Vista
150 Bonita Rd
Chula Vista CA 91910
(619) 691-1211
$85 - $86
Bed & Pet Discount Offered

Pet Policy: Pets up to 50 lbs, accepted, no additional charge. Limit 2 per room.

Features: Swimming pool - outdoor, Accessible bathroom, Room service (limited hours), Number of rooms: 142, Business services, Free breakfast, Parking (free), Multilingual staff, Dry cleaning/laundry service, Internet access (free), Fitness facilities.

★★

Vagabond Inn Chula Vista
230 Broadway
Chula Vista CA 91910
(619) 422-8305
$59 - $76
Bed & Pet Discount Offered

Pet Policy: Pet friendly rooms available with additional charge.

Features: Free Breakfast, Guest laundry, Swimming pool - outdoor, Concierge services, Airport transportation additional charge, Internet (free), Coffee in lobby.

City Of Industry

Also see the following nearby communities that have pet friendly lodging: Walnut - 4 miles, South El Monte - 6 miles, El Monte - 7 miles, Diamond Bar - 7 miles, Whittier - 8 miles, Brea - 8 miles, Glendora - 9 miles, Rosemead - 9 miles, Fullerton - 9 miles, Pomona - 9 miles, Monrovia - 10 miles, La Mirada - 10 miles, Pico Rivera - 10 miles, Arcadia - 10 miles, San Dimas - 10 miles.

Pacific Palms Resort
1 Industry Hills Pkwy
City Of Industry CA 91744
(626) 854-2496
$159 - $160
Bed & Pet Discount Offered

Pet Policy: Pets accepted, $35 per night.

Features: Sauna, Business Center, Security guard, Swimming pool - outdoor, Bar/lounge, Elevator, Restaurants: 3, Room service (limited hours), ATM/banking, Gift shops or newsstand, Number of rooms: 292, Number of floors: 11, Computer rental, Breakfast available additional charge, Guest laundry, Currency exchange, Health club, Shoe shine, Multilingual staff, Complimentary newspapers in lobby, Porter/bellhop, Technology helpdesk, Dry cleaning/laundry service, Golf course on site, Concierge services, Smoke-Free property, Free wireless Internet, Full-service health spa, Valet Parking fee.

Claremont

Also see the following nearby communities that have pet friendly lodging: Upland - 4 miles, Pomona - 4 miles, San Dimas - 4 miles, Chino - 6 miles, Ontario - 8 miles, Glendora - 8 miles, Chino Hills - 8 miles, Diamond Bar - 8 miles, Rancho Cucamonga - 8 miles, Walnut - 10 miles

Hotel Casa 425
425 W 1st St
Claremont CA 91711
(909) 624-2272
$145 - $172
Bed & Pet Discount Offered

Pet Policy: Pets less than 40 lbs, $65 per pet per stay. Limit 2 per room. Must not be left unattended in room and must be leashed when outside room.

Features: Business center, Bar/lounge, Free breakfast, Concierge services, Elevator, Video library, Dry cleaning/laundry service, Number of rooms: 28, Number of floors: 3, Suitable for children, Coffee in lobby, Parking (free), Complimentary newspapers in lobby, Parking garage, Smoke-Free property, Fitness facilities, Free wireless Internet.

Not rated
Hotel Claremont
840 S Indian Hill Blvd
Claremont CA 91711
(909) 621-4831
$99 - $114
Bed & Pet Discount Offered

Pet Policy: Pets accepted with additional charge.

Features: Free Breakfast, Restaurant(s), Wheelchair accessible, Shopping on site, Business services, Parking (free), Multilingual staff, Swimming pool - outdoor, Free wireless Internet.

Clearlake

Not rated
Americas Best Value Inn
13865 Lakeshore Drive
Clearlake CA 95422
(707) 995-1555
$62 - $99

Pet Policy: Limited pets accepted with additional charge. Please contact hotel directly for booking and more details.

Features: Number of rooms:20, Fishing dock, Pier, Jet ski and boat rentals nearby, Free continental breakfast, Complimentary daily newspaper, Swimming pool – outdoor – seasonal, Wireless Internet (free), Microwave and mini fridge, Coffee maker.

Clear Lake Cottages & Marina
13885 Lakeshore Drive
Clearlake CA 95422
(707) 995-5253
$119 - $159
Bed & Pet Discount Offered

Pet Policy: Pets welcome, $20 per night per pet, maximum of 3 pets per room. There is an additional $100 cleaning fee if it is necessary to remove pet hair from furniture. We welcome our furry, four-footed guests with their own "Pet Package" including a bed, food and water bowls, a pet towel, waste bags and a welcome treat!

Features: Barbecue grill(s), Front desk (limited hours), Front desk hours, Swimming pool – outdoor.

Cloverdale

Also see the following nearby communities that have pet friendly lodging: Geyserville - 8 miles

Not rated
Cloverdale Oaks Inn
123 South Cloverdale Blvd
Cloverdale CA 95425
(707) 894-2404
$60 - $65

Pet Policy: Medium size pets accepted, $15 per night per pet.

Features: Free Continental breakfast, Data ports, Non-smoking property, Free tour pickup, Coffee makers, Microwaves and refrigerators available, Cable TV, Cribs available.

Not rated 
Old Crocker Inn
1126 Old Crocker Inn Rd
Cloverdale CA 95425
(707) 894-4000
$139 - $235

Pet Policy: Pets welcome, no additional charge. Limit of 3 per room.

Features: Number of rooms: 10, Private baths, Gas fireplace, Free wireless Internet, Bathrobes, Whirlpool baths in some rooms, Full breakfast, In-room massage available.

★★
Super 8 Cloverdale
1147 S Cloverdale Blvd
Cloverdale CA 95425
(707) 894-9288
$55 - $179
Bed & Pet Discount Offered

Pet Policy: Pets accepted with advanced booking.

Features: Free breakfast, Business center, Number of rooms: 43, Number of floors: 2, Guest laundry, Parking (free), Swimming pool - outdoor seasonal, Internet (free), Fitness facilities.

Clovis

Also see the following nearby communities that have pet friendly lodging: Fresno - 8 miles

★★½
Hampton Inn Suites Clovis
855 Gettysburg Ave
Clovis CA 93612
(559) 348-0000
$113 - $144
Bed & Pet Discount Offered

Pet Policy: Pets up to 40 lbs, $50 per stay

Features: Bar/lounge, Swimming pool - outdoor, Wheelchair accessible, Number of suites: 30, Number of floors: 4, Parking (free), Business center, Smoke-Free property, Fitness facilities, Free breakfast.

★★★
Homewood Suites Clovis
835 Gettysburg Ave
Clovis CA 93612
(559) 292-4004
$104- $169

Pet Policy: Pets up to 40 lbs, $75 per stay.

Features: Airport transportation (free), Swimming pool - outdoor heated, Wheelchair accessible, Number of suites: 83, Number of floors: 4, Suitable for children, Fitness facilities, Barbecue grill(s), Free breakfast, ***Continued on next page***

Homewood Suites Clovis
Continued from previous page

Bed & Pet Discount Offered

Grocery, Parking (free), Multilingual staff, Complimentary newspapers in lobby, Dry cleaning/laundry service, Designated smoking areas, Free wireless Internet, Accessible bathroom, In-room accessibility equipment for the deaf, Braille or raised signage, Area shuttle (free), 24-hour business center, Free reception.

Coalinga

Not rated
Best Western Big Country Inn
25020 W Dorris Ave
Coalinga CA 93210
(559) 935-0866
$89 - $109

Pet Policy: Allows pets under 50 pounds. $20 additional charge.

Features: Free full breakfast, Microwave and refrigerator, Cable TV.

Coalinga Travelodge
25278 W Dorris Ave
South I-5, Exit Hwy 198
Coalinga CA 93210
(559) 935-2063
$48 - $60
Bed & Pet Discount Offered

Pet Policy: Pets accepted, $5 per night.

Features: Free breakfast, Parking (free), Complimentary newspapers in lobby, Swimming pool - outdoor seasonal.

Colton

Also see the following nearby communities that have pet friendly lodging: Rialto - 4 miles, San Bernardino - 4 miles, Redlands - 8 miles, Riverside - 9 miles

Holiday Inn Express Colton
2830 S Iowa Ave
Colton CA 92324
(951) 788-9900
$81 - $98
Bed & Pet Discount Offered

Pet Policy: Pets allowed up to 75 lbs. $25 per night plus $25 deposit. Pets must be leashed or crated at all times when not in room.

Features: Business center, Suitable for children, Swimming pool - outdoor, ATM/banking, Number of rooms: 150, Number of suites: 2, Number of floors: 4, Free breakfast, Parking (free), Multilingual staff, Complimentary newspapers in lobby, Designated smoking areas, Accessible bathroom, In-room accessibility equipment for the deaf, Braille or raised signage, Dry cleaning/laundry service, Free wireless Internet, Fitness facilities.

Commerce

Also see the following nearby communities that have pet friendly lodging: Bell Gardens - 2 miles, Pico Rivera - 3 miles, Downey - 4 miles, Huntington Park - 5 miles, Monterey Park - 5 miles, Norwalk - 7 miles, Whittier - 7 miles, Rosemead - 7 miles, San Gabriel - 7 miles, South El Monte - 8 miles, South Pasadena - 9 miles, El Monte - 9 miles, La Mirada - 10 miles, Cerritos - 10 miles

Doubletree Hotel Los Angeles/Commerce
5757 Telegraph Rd
Commerce CA 90040
(323) 887-8100
$98 - $119
Bed & Pet Discount Offered

Pet Policy: Pets up to 20 lbs accepted, $25 additional charge.

Features: ATM/Banking, Business Services, Elevator, Swimming pool - outdoor, Bar/lounge, Restaurant(s), Room service (limited hours), Concierge services, Number of rooms: 201, Number of floors: 7, Breakfast available additional charge, Parking (free), Multilingual staff, Complimentary newspapers in lobby, Wireless Internet, Accessible bathroom, Braille or raised signage, Dry cleaning/laundry service, Fitness facilities.

Concord

Also see the following nearby communities that have pet friendly lodging: Pleasant Hill - 4 miles, Walnut Creek - 6 miles, Martinez - 7 mile

Concord Inn & Suites
1370 Monument Blvd
Concord CA 94520
(925) 827-8998
$50 - $127
Bed & Pet Discount Offered

Pet Policy: Pets accepted with additional charge.

Features: Coffee in lobby, Guest laundry, Business center, Number of rooms: 42, Number of floors: 3, Parking (free), Internet (free), Fitness facilities.

Crowne Plaza Concord-Walnut Creek
45 John Glenn Dr
Concord CA 94520
(925) 825-7700
$86 - $209
Bed & Pet Discount Offered

Pet Policy: We are a dog friendly hotel. We accept two dogs up to 35 pounds. Several rooms have been designated as pet rooms. Close to an area where your pets can walk and exercise. Pet Deposit: $50 (USD) per stay. Pet fee: $35.00 (USD) per night.

Features: Room service (limited hours), Swimming pool - indoor, Restaurant(s), Gift shops or newsstand, Breakfast available additional charge, Parking (free), Multilingual staff, Porter/bellhop, Number of rooms: 324, Number of floors: 3, Business center, Bar/lounge, Accessible bathroom, In-room accessibility equipment for the deaf, Braille or raised signage, Dry cleaning/laundry service, Fitness facilities, Free wireless Internet.

Days Inn Concord
5370 Clayton Rd
Concord CA 94521
(925) 674-9400
$71 - $99
Bed & Pet Discount Offered

Pet Policy: Pets allowed. Small daily additional charge may be required. Limit of 2 pets per room.

Features: Business services, Coffee in lobby, Free breakfast, Gift shops or newsstand, Number of rooms: 33, Parking (free), Complimentary newspapers in lobby.

★★★½
Hilton Concord
1970 Diamond Blvd
Concord CA 94520
(800) 850-9327
$68 - $219
Bed & Pet Discount Offered

Pet Policy: Up to two pets less than 70 pounds in total are allowed for an additional charge of $75 per night and a $250 refundable additional charge.

Features: Swimming pool - outdoor, Bar/lounge, Elevator, Restaurant(s), ATM/banking, Gift shops or newsstand, Number of rooms: 329, Number of floors: 11, Breakfast available additional charge, Parking (free), Multilingual staff, Complimentary newspapers in lobby, Business center, Porter/bellhop, Wireless Internet, Accessible bathroom, Braille or raised signage, Dry cleaning/laundry service, Fitness facilities.

★★★
Red Lion Hotel Concord - Walnut Creek
1050 Burnett Ave
Concord CA 94520
(925) 687-5500
$79 - $89
Bed & Pet Discount Offered

Pet Policy: Pets welcome, $10 per stay.

Features: Accessible bathroom, In-room accessibility equipment for the deaf, Braille or raised signage, Bar/lounge, Airport transportation (free), Restaurant(s), Swimming pool - outdoor, ATM/banking, Number of rooms: 189, Number of floors: 6, Parking (free), Multilingual staff, Complimentary newspapers in lobby, Room service, Business center, Internet (free), Dry cleaning/laundry service, Fitness facilities.

Corning

Not rated
Best Western Corning
2165 Solano Street
Corning CA 96021
(530) 824-2468
$67- $94

Pet Policy: Pets allowed in designated pet rooms. $10 per night per pet.

Features: Indoor heated swimming pool & spa, Fitness room, Business center, Free wireless Internet, Free breakfast.

Not Rated
Days Inn Corning
3475 Hwy 99 West/I-5
Corning CA 96021
(530) 824-2000
$55 - $84

Pet Policy: Pets welcome, $10 per night

Features: Free deluxe breakfast, Free local calls, Free HBO. All rooms newly renovated include refrigerators, hairdryers, AM/FM alarm clock. RV truck parking. 24 hour wet bar.

Holiday Inn Express Hotel & Suites Corning
3350 Sunrise Way
Corning CA 96021
(530) 824-6400
$98 - $185
Bed & Pet Discount Offered

Pet Policy: We welcome pets! A non-refundable pet fee of $10 will be applied, per night, per pet. 125 lb. weight limit. No nearby kennel. Pet bowls and treats are available at the front desk.

Features: Guest laundry, Swimming pool - outdoor, Business center, Accessible bathroom, In-room accessibility equipment for the deaf, Braille or raised signage, Number of floors: 4, Complimentary newspapers in lobby, Use of nearby fitness center (free), Concierge desk, Wireless Internet, Sauna.

Corona

Ayres Suites Corona West
1900 Frontage Road
Corona CA 92882
(951) 738-9113
$85 - $99
Bed & Pet Discount Offered

Pet Policy: Pets accepted, $45 additional charge.

Features: Fitness facilities, Swimming pool - outdoor, Room service (limited hours), Number of suites: 113, Number of floors: 2, Business services, Barbecue grill(s), Coffee in lobby, Free breakfast, Parking (free), Multilingual staff, Complimentary newspapers in lobby, Use of nearby fitness center (free), Security guard, Internet (free), Dry cleaning/laundry service.

Best Western Kings Inn
1084 Pomona Rd
Corona CA 92882
(951) 734-4241
$84 - $89
Bed & Pet Discount Offered

Pet Policy: Up to 2 dogs per room with an 80 pound weight limit. Additional pet types (cats, birds, etc.) may be accepted at the hotel's discretion. Pet rate is $10 per day with a $100 per week maximum. A refundable cleaning & damage deposit of $50 is required upon check-in. If damage occurs or excessive cleaning is needed, the deposit can become non-refundable and the hotel may charge additionally to cover the costs.

Features: Swimming pool - outdoor, Free breakfast, Parking (free), Multilingual staff, Accessible bathroom, In-room accessibility equipment for the deaf, Free wireless Internet, Business services.

Not Rated
Hotel Paseo
1805 West Sixth Street
Corona CA 92882
(951) 371-7185
$89 - $299

Pet Policy: Dogs and cats under 25 lbs accepted. $75 cleaning fee.

Features: Large desks, Direct TV, Free wireless Internet, Breakfast, Nearby fitness center (complimentary vouchers), Concierge desk.

Knights Inn Corona
13689 Magnolia Ave
Corona CA 92879
(951) 279-5620
$39 - $69
Bed & Pet Discount Offered

Pet Policy: Pets accepted, $20 per night per pet.

Features: Free wireless Internet, Smoke-Free property.

Residence Inn by Marriott Corona Riverside
1015 Montecito Dr
Corona CA 92879
(951) 371-0107
$110 - $179
Bed & Pet Discount Offered

Pet Policy: Pets allowed, $75 per stay cleaning fee

Features: Accessible bathroom, Braille or raised signage, Dry cleaning/laundry service, Free wireless Internet, 24-hour business center, Elevator, Swimming pool - indoor, Wheelchair accessible, Number of suites: 95, Free breakfast, Grocery, Parking (free), Multilingual staff, Smoke-Free property, Tennis on site, Fitness facilities, Free reception.

Not rated
Scottish Inns & Suites Carona
210 South Lincoln Avenue
Corona CA 92882
(951) 272-4800
$49 - $90

Pet Policy: All pets allowed, $5 per pet per night.

Features: Number of rooms: 60, non-smoking, Jacuzzi, Free wireless Internet, Microwave, Mini fridge.

Coronado

Also see the following nearby communities that have pet friendly lodging: National City - 4 miles, Chula Vista - 6 miles, San Ysidro - 10 miles

Coronado Inn
266 Orange Avenue
Coronado CA 92118
(619) 435-4121
$89 - $109

Pet Policy: Pets Allowed, $15 additional charge.

Features: Free wireless Internet, Swimming pool, Free continental breakfast.

Loews Coronado Bay Resort & Spa
4000 Coronado Bay Rd
Coronado CA 92118
(619) 424-4000
$189 - $519
Bed & Pet Discount Offered

Pet Policy: No pet restrictions. Loews Hotels offer a standardized *Loews Loves Pets* program at the chain's 16 hotels across the US and in Canada. Well behaved pets of all types (except some aggressive breeds) are welcome. The Loews program offers specialized services and first-class amenities designed to make pets and their owners feel at home when traveling together. Amenities: Personal welcoming note from the hotel general manager with a listing of pet services available at the hotel, including dog-walking routes, veterinarian information, pet shop and grooming locations, pet attractions, pet-sitters, pet-friendly restaurants, and other resources. Specialized bedding for dogs and cats. Free bag of pet treats and a pet toy. Special pet place mats with food and water bowls, and a special *Do Not Disturb*: sign. Room Service Menu: Menu items include dishes such as grilled lamb or chicken with rice for dogs, grilled liver or salmon with rice for cats, and for health conscious cats and dogs Loews also offers a vegetarian entrée. Additional Pet Services: Pet-walking and sitting services can be arranged through the concierge desk. The Loews *Did You Forget Closet* includes: dog and cat beds in different sizes, leashes and collars, and pet videos; guests can also purchase essential items through the *Did You Forget Closet* including: kitty litter boxes, pooper-scoopers, and pet toys. Rooms for guests staying with pets undergo special cleaning procedures including the use of specially-filtered vacuums to remove pet allergens in preparation for subsequent guests.

Features: ATM/Banking, Poolside bar, Business services, Children's swimming pool, Swimming pool – outdoor Arcade/game room, Room service (24 hours), Bar/lounge, Computer rental, Supervised child care/activities, Spa services on site, Parking (valet) $28 per day (in/out), Multilingual staff, Complimentary newspapers in lobby, Wireless Internet, Babysitting or child care, Hair salon, Concierge services, Gift shops or newsstand Number of rooms: 440, Cell phone/mobile rental, Translation services, Suitable for children, Pool table, Coffee shop or cafe, Accessible bathroom, In-room accessibility equipment for the deaf, Braille or raised signage, Fitness facilities.

Not rated 
SuiteAmerica Coronado Shores
1515 Second Street
Coronado CA 92118
(888) 444-8650
$120 - $134

Pet Policy: Pets are accepted, a significant additional charge may be charged. Please contact hotel directly for reservations.

Features: Furnished apartments with fully equipped kitchens, Free wireless Internet, coffee maker, Iron ironing board, Hair dryer, Mini bar, Tennis courts on site, Fitness center, 3 Swimming pools, Business center, BBQ area, 18 seat movie theater.

Corte Madera

Also see the following nearby communities that have pet friendly lodging: Mill Valley - 2 miles, San Rafael - 4 miles, Sausalito - 5 miles, Richmond - 9 miles

★★½
Marin Suites Hotel
45 Tamal Vista Blvd
Corte Madera CA 94925
(415) 924-3608
$91 - $158
Bed & Pet Discount Offered

Pet Policy: Pets allowed, $20 per pet per night, limit of 2 per room. Marin Suites Hotel provides 2 cover sheets, a pet towel, waste bags and welcome treats.

Features: Swimming pool - outdoor, Concierge services, Number of suites: 100, Business services, Internet access - additional charge, Guest laundry, Free breakfast, Parking (free), Fitness facilities.

Costa Mesa

Also see the following nearby communities that have pet friendly lodging: Newport Beach - 3 miles, Fountain Valley - 5 miles, Santa Ana - 5 miles, Huntington Beach - 6 miles, Garden Grove - 8 miles, Irvine - 10 miles, Orange - 10 miles

★★★½
Costa Mesa Marriott
500 Anton Blvd
Costa Mesa CA 92626
(714) 957-1100
$119 - $249
Bed & Pet Discount Offered

Pet Policy: Pets allowed, $75 per stay.

Features: Swimming pool - outdoor, Bar/lounge, Elevator, Airport transportation (free), Restaurant(s), Room service (limited hours), Gift shops or newsstand, Number of suites: 253, Number of floors: 11, Coffee in lobby, Complimentary newspapers in lobby, Business center, Wireless Internet, Parking garage additional charge, Smoke-Free property, Dry cleaning/laundry service, Fitness facilities.

★★★½
Hilton Orange County / Costa Mesa
3050 Bristol St
Costa Mesa CA 92626
(714) 540-7000

Pet Policy: Pets up to 35 lbs, $75 per stay. The following are provided: Dog treat upon check-in, In-room pet bed, In-room pet bowl, Clean up bags, Designated pet potty area.

Continued on next page

Hilton Orange County / Costa Mesa
Continued from previous page

$116 - $219
Bed & Pet Discount Offered

Features: Swimming pool - outdoor, Bar/lounge, Airport transportation (free), Restaurant(s), Hair salon, ATM/banking, Concierge services, Gift shops or newsstand, Number of rooms: 484, Computer rental, Suitable for children, Internet (additional charge), Currency exchange, Room service (24 hours), Shoe shine, Multilingual staff, Porter/bellhop, Security guard, Limo or Town Car service available, Parking (valet) $27/day, Accessible bathroom, Braille or raised signage, Dry cleaning/laundry service, Fitness facilities, Designated smoking areas, 24-hour business center, Shopping center shuttle (free).

★★
La Quinta Inn John Wayne/Orange County Airport
1515 S Coast Dr
Costa Mesa CA 92626
(714) 957-5841
$55 - $70
Bed & Pet Discount Offered

Pet Policy: Cats and dogs up to 50 pounds are accepted in all guest rooms. Housekeeping services for rooms with pets require pet owner be present or pet must be crated. No additional charges or deposits are required.

Features: Elevator, Swimming pool - outdoor, Accessible bathroom, Airport transportation (free), Number of rooms: 160, Number of floors: 3, Business services, Coffee in lobby, Free breakfast, Health club, Parking (free), Multilingual staff, Wireless Internet, Dry cleaning/laundry service.

★★
Motel 6 Newport Beach
2274 Newport Blvd
Costa Mesa CA 92627
(949) 646-7445
$56 - $74
Bed & Pet Discount Offered

Pet Policy: Well-behaved pets stay Free. Animals that pose a health or safety risk may not remain onsite, and include those that, in our manager's discretion, are too numerous for any one room, cause damage to our property or that of other guests, are too disruptive, are not properly attended, or demonstrate undue aggression. All pets must be declared at check-in. In consideration of all guests, pets must be attended to and under control at all times. If unavoidable circumstances require a pet to remain in a room while the owner is offsite, the pet must be secured in a crate or travel carrier. Pets must be on a leash or securely carried outside of guest rooms and under control at all times.

Features: Accessible bathroom, In-room accessibility equipment for the deaf, Braille or raised signage, Free wireless Internet, Swimming pool - outdoor, Number of rooms: 94, Number of floors: 3, Parking (free).

Not rated 
Oakwood Costa Mesa
3400 Ave of the Arts
Costa Mesa CA 92626
(866) 836-9330
$141 - $187

Pet Policy: Pets accepted with limitations and additional charge. Contact hotel directly for more information and to make reservations.

Features: Furnished apartments, Fitness center, Pool and spa, a fitness center and sauna, indoor racquetball, lighted tennis courts, library, and conference center. Minimum stay of 30 days may be required.

Ramada Inn and Suites
1680 Superior Avenue
Costa Mesa CA 92627
(949) 645-2221
$89 - $129
Bed & Pet Discount Offered

Pet Policy: Pets accepted up to 15 lbs, $5 per night plus $100 refundable deposit. Limited to pet-friendly designated rooms.

Features: Swimming pool - outdoor, Airport transportation (free), Full-service health spa, Complimentary newspapers in lobby, Airport transportation (free) during limited hours, Bar/lounge, Restaurant(s), Free wireless Internet.

★★★
Residence Inn By Marriott Costa Mesa
881 Baker St
Costa Mesa CA 92626
(714) 241-8800
$169 - $200
Bed & Pet Discount Offered

Pet Policy: Pets allowed, $100 cleaning fee per stay.

Features: Free breakfast, Swimming pool - outdoor, Airport transportation (free) during limited hours, Number of rooms: 144, Number of floors: 2, Barbecue grill(s), Coffee in lobby, Coffee shop or cafe, Grocery, Parking (free), Complimentary newspapers in lobby, Business center, Free wireless Internet, Smoke-Free property, Swimming pool - outdoor (heated), Dry cleaning/laundry service, Fitness facilities.

The Hotel Hanford
3131 Bristol St
Costa Mesa CA 92626
(714) 557-3000
$119 - $199
Bed & Pet Discount Offered

Pet Policy: Pets up to 30 lbs accepted, $50 per stay additional charge.

Features: ATM/Banking, Swimming pool - outdoor, Elevator, Wheelchair accessible, Shopping center shuttle (free), Bar/lounge, Airport transportation (free), Restaurant(s), Concierge services, Number of rooms: 230, Number of floors: 5, Breakfast available additional charge, Parking (free), Multilingual staff, Porter/bellhop, Smoke-Free property, Accessible bathroom, In-room accessibility equipment for the deaf, Braille or raised signage, Dry cleaning/laundry service, Coffee in lobby, Complimentary newspapers in lobby, Fitness facilities, Room service, Free wireless Internet, area shuttle (free), 24-hour business center.

★★★★

The Westin South Coast Plaza
686 Anton Blvd
Costa Mesa CA 92626
(714) 540-2500
$159 - $309
Bed & Pet Discount Offered

Pet Policy: Dogs weighing 40 pounds or less are welcome at The Westin South Coast Plaza. Dogs over 40 pounds may be permitted, but require advanced, written permission directly from hotel.

A heavenly experience awaits you and your Dog. Book the Pampered Pooch package and receive: A signature Westin Heavenly Dog Bed, A food bowl and mat, Heavenly Dog tag and one Aqua Pure Breed portable, disposable mineral water dish. An official "Dog in Room" privacy sign. Guests Traveling with Dogs Dog owners must sign a liability waiver at check-in. Cleaning fees may apply. Dogs may not be left unattended in guest rooms. Designated Dog Area. There is a park conveniently located across the street from The Westin South Coast Plaza.

Features: Nearby fitness center (discount), Swimming pool - outdoor, Bar/lounge, Airport transportation (free), Elevator, Restaurant(s), ATM/banking, Concierge services, Shopping on site, Number of rooms: 390, Number of floors: 16, Breakfast available additional charge, Poolside bar, Room service (24 hours), Shoe shine, Multilingual staff, Complimentary newspapers in lobby, Business center, Porter/bellhop, Security guard, Limo or Town Car service available, Wireless Internet (additional charge), Parking garage (fee), Smoke-Free property, Dry cleaning/laundry service, Tennis on site.

★★

Travelodge Orange County Airport
1400 SE Bristol St
Costa Mesa CA 92707
(800) 578-7878
$55 - $79
Bed & Pet Discount Offered

Pet Policy: Some pets are permitted. Please contact hotel directly for approval and booking.

Features: Guest laundry, Restaurant(s), Swimming pool - outdoor, Number of rooms: 120, Number of floors: 2, Free breakfast, Parking (free), Complimentary newspapers in lobby, Free wireless Internet, Fitness facilities, Business center.

★★

Vagabond Inn Costa Mesa
3205 Harbor Blvd
Costa Mesa CA 92626
(714) 557-8360
$53 - $63
Bed & Pet Discount Offered

Pet Policy: Small pets only, $10 per night.

Features: Area shuttle (free), Barbecue grill(s), Swimming pool - outdoor, Number of rooms: 125, Number of floors: 2, Business services, Coffee in lobby, Free breakfast, Parking (free), Complimentary newspapers in lobby, Airport transportation (free), Multilingual staff, Free wireless Internet.

Wyndham Orange County
3350 Avenue Of The Arts
Costa Mesa CA 92626
(714) 751-5100
$89 - $179
Bed & Pet Discount Offered

Pet Policy: Dogs up to 40 lbs accepted, $50 per stay. Outdoor patio at the Terra nova Restaurant is also dog friendly.

Features: Swimming pool - outdoor, Bar/lounge, Airport transportation (free), Restaurant(s), Room service, ATM/banking, Number of rooms: 238, Business services, Parking fee, Internet (additional charge), Multilingual staff, Complimentary newspapers in lobby, Accessible bathroom, In-room accessibility equipment for the deaf, Braille or raised signage, Dry cleaning/laundry service, Fitness facilities.

Crescent City

Also see the following nearby communities that have pet friendly lodging: Castle Rock - 4 miles

Americas Best Value Inn Crescent City
440 Highway 101 N
Crescent City CA 95531
(707) 464-4141
$52 - $65
Bed & Pet Discount Offered

Pet Policy: Accepts small pets.

Features: Number of floors: 2, Number of rooms: 61, Accessible bathroom, Free breakfast, Coffee in lobby, Accessibility equipment for the deaf, Free wireless Internet, Wheelchair accessible, Parking (free), Front desk (limited hours).

Not Rated
Front Street Inn
102 L Street
Crescent City CA 95531
(707) 464-4113
$54 - $85

Pet Policy: Small pets allowed, $15 per night plus deposit. Must book by phone directly with hotel.

Features: Free wireless Internet, Coffee maker, Microwave and mini fridge in all rooms.

Not Rated
Gardenia Motel Crescent City
119 L Street
Crescent City CA 95531
(707) 464-2181
$49 - $64

Pet Policy: Small pets allowed.

Free wireless Internet, Guest laundry.

Quality Inn And Suites Redwood
100 Walton St
Crescent City CA 95531
(707) 464-3885
$89 - $99
Bed & Pet Discount Offered

Pet Policy: Pets accepted, $15 per pet per stay. Limit 2 per room.

Features: Business services, Coffee in lobby, Guest laundry, Number of rooms: 46, Free breakfast.

Super 8 Crescent City
685 Hwy 101 S
Crescent City CA 95531
(707) 464-4111
$38 - $75
Bed & Pet Discount Offered

Pet Policy: Pets less than 50 lbs, $12 per night per pet.

Features: Free breakfast, Business services, Parking (free).

Culver City

Also see the following nearby communities that have pet friendly lodging: Los Angeles - 2 miles, Marina Del Rey - 4 miles, Beverly Hills - 4 miles, Inglewood - 4 miles, Venice - 4 miles, Santa Monica - 5 miles, West Hollywood - 6 miles, El Segundo - 6 miles, Hawthorne - 7 miles, Hollywood - 8 miles, Manhattan Beach - 9 miles, Universal City - 9 miles, Studio City - 9 miles

Four Points by Sheraton Los Angeles Westside
5990 Green Valley Cir
Culver City CA 90230
(310) 641-7740
$118 - $169
Bed & Pet Discount Offered

Pet Policy: Pets up to 50 pounds are allowed. A $25 non-refundable cleaning fee is required at check-in. Guests with pets are limited to rooms on first level.

Features: Dry cleaning/laundry service, Security guard, Swimming pool - outdoor, Bar/lounge, Restaurant(s), Number of rooms: 195, Number of floors: 8, Parking fee, Breakfast available additional charge, Multilingual staff, Complimentary newspapers in lobby, Porter/bellhop, Free wireless Internet, Elevator, Accessible bathroom, In-room accessibility equipment for the deaf, Braille or raised signage, Room service (limited hours), ATM/banking, Wheelchair accessible, Library, 24-hour business center, Fitness facilities, Smoke-Free property.

★★★

Radisson Hotel Los Angeles Westside
6161 W Centinela Ave
Culver City CA 90230
(310) 649-1776
$81- $213
Bed & Pet Discount Offered

Pet Policy: Pets allowed, $50 per stay plus $100 refundable deposit. Pet rooms on first floor only.

Features: On-site car rental, ATM/Banking, Currency Exchange, Shoe Shine, Security guard, Airport transportation (free), Parking fee $14/24 Hours In/Out, Wireless Internet (additional charge), Restaurant(s), Swimming pool - outdoor, Concierge services, Gift shops or newsstand, Number of rooms: 371, Number of floors: 12, Suitable for children, Multilingual staff, Porter/bellhop, Limo or Town Car service available, Dry cleaning/laundry service, 24-hour business center, Bar/lounge, Room service (limited hours Accessible bathroom, Fitness facilities.

Cupertino

Also see the following nearby communities that have pet friendly lodging: Sunnyvale - 4 miles, Santa Clara - 5 miles, Campbell - 5 miles, Mountain View - 6 miles, Los Gatos - 7 miles, Los Altos - 8 miles, San Jose - 8 miles, Milpitas - 9 miles, Palo Alto - 10 miles

Cypress Hotel - a Kimpton Hotel
10050 S De Anza Blvd
Cupertino CA 95014
(408) 253-8900
$98 - $219
Bed & Pet Discount Offered

Pet Policy: Pets welcome. No size restriction. No Additional charges. Special pet amenities include treats, bowls, tags with hotel info, and even pet packages with special food, dog walking, and toys.

Features: Business Center, Bar/lounge, Airport transportation (free), Restaurant(s), Concierge services, Number of rooms: 224, Number of floors: 9, Translation services, Suitable for children, Breakfast available additional charge, Shoe shine, Multilingual staff, Complimentary newspapers in lobby, Room service, Porter/bellhop, Limo or Town Car service available, Free wireless Internet, Smoke-Free property, Accessible bathroom, In-room accessibility equipment for the deaf, Braille or raised signage, Dry cleaning/laundry service, Security guard, Fitness facilities, Valet Parking fee.

Cypress

Also see the following nearby communities that have pet friendly lodging: La Palma - 2 miles, Los Alamitos - 2 miles, Buena Park - 2 miles, Hawaiian Gardens - 3 miles, Cerritos - 4 miles, Seal Beach - 6 miles, La Mirada - 6 miles, Garden Grove - 6 miles, Anaheim - 6 miles, Fullerton - 7 miles, Norwalk - 8 miles, Signal Hill - 8 miles, Huntington Beach - 8 miles, Fountain Valley - 8 miles, Long Beach - 8 miles, Orange - 9 miles, Whittier - 10 miles

Homestead Orange County - Cypress
5990 Corporate Ave
Cypress CA 90630
(714) 761-2766
$66- $89
Bed & Pet Discount Offered

Pet Policy: Pets allowed, no size restriction, $25 per day to a maximum of $150 per stay. Limit of 1 pet per room.

Features: Elevator, Number of rooms: 104, Number of floors: 3, Business services, Internet (additional charge), Parking (free) Bar/lounge.

Rodeway Inn Cypress
5311 Lincoln Avenue
Cypress CA 90630
(714) 952-9388
$59- $69
Bed & Pet Discount Offered

Pet Policy: Rodeway Inns charge an additional $10 per night per pet and require a $50 damage deposit, which is refunded if the room is in order at check out. Max of 2 pets per room. A veterinarian certificate that the pet is on a flea and parasite program is required. Pets may not be left alone in the room unless in a cage

Features: Number of rooms: 42, Number of floors: 3, Business services, Guest laundry, Free breakfast, Parking (free), On-site medical assistance available.

Woodfin Suite Hotel Cypress
5905 Corporate Ave
Cypress CA 90630
(714) 828-4000
$104 - $239
Bed & Pet Discount Offered

Pet Policy: Pets up to 25 lbs accepted, $10 per day.

Features: Elevator, Swimming pool - outdoor, Free breakfast, Parking (free), Smoke-Free property, Bar/lounge, Wheelchair accessible, ATM/banking, Gift shops or newsstand, Number of rooms: 142, Suitable for children, Multilingual staff, Dry cleaning/laundry service, Grocery/convenience store, Free wireless Internet, Accessible bathroom, Braille or raised signage, Area shuttle (free), Shopping center shuttle (free), Theme park shuttle (free), Smoke-Free property, Business center, Fitness facilities.

Dana Point

Also see the following nearby communities that have pet friendly lodging: Capistrano Beach - 2 miles, San Juan Capistrano - 4 miles, San Clemente - 5 miles, Laguna Beach - 6 miles, Laguna Hills - 9 miles

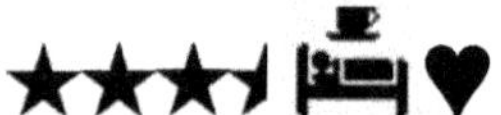

Blue Lantern Inn, A Four Sisters Inn
34343 Street Of The Blue Lantern
Dana Point CA 92629
(949) 661-1304
$195 - $245
Bed & Pet Discount Offered

Pet Policy: Dogs only, up to 40 lbs, $65 per stay, limit of 2 (just one additional charge). Dogs must not be left unattended in rooms, must be leashed outside of room, and must be quiet so as to not disturb others. Limited number of pet rooms and must be booked in advance.

Features: Concierge services, Free breakfast, Free wireless Internet, Elevator, Wheelchair accessible, Suitable for children, Coffee in lobby, Garden, Library, Video library, Complimentary newspapers in lobby, Porter/bellhop, Dry cleaning/laundry service, Massage - treatment room(s), Smoke-Free property, Parking (free), Spa services on site, Business center, Media library, Fitness facilities, Free reception.

★★★½

Doubletree Guest Suites Doheny Beach
34402 Pacific Coast Hwy
Dana Point CA 92629
(949) 661-1100
$111 - $259
Bed & Pet Discount Offered

Pet Policy: Pets up to 50 lbs accepted, $30 per night per pet.

Features: Swimming pool - outdoor, Security guard, Bar/lounge, ATM/banking, Suitable for children, Room service (limited hours), Restaurant(s), Gift shops or newsstand, Number of rooms: 195, Internet (additional charge), Multilingual staff, Complimentary newspapers in lobby, Porter/bellhop, Dry cleaning/laundry service, Fitness facilities, Self or Valet Parking fee.

Holiday Inn Express Hotel & Suites Dana Point
34280 Pacific Coast Hwy
Dana Point CA 92629
(949) 248-1000
$107 - $152
Bed & Pet Discount Offered

Pet Policy: Pets accepted, $75 per night. Pets may not be left unattended in room at any time.

Features: Accessible bathroom, In-room accessibility equipment for the deaf, Braille or raised signage, Swimming pool - outdoor, Number of rooms: 86, Number of suites: 50, Number of floors: 4, Business center, Multilingual staff, Complimentary newspapers in lobby, Internet (free), Nearby fitness center (discount), Dry cleaning/laundry service.

★★★★★♥
The Ritz-Carlton, Laguna Niguel
1 Ritz Carlton Dr
Dana Point CA 92629
(949) 240-2000
$374- $755
Bed & Pet Discount Offered

Pet Policy: Pets are welcome at The Ritz-Carlton, Laguna Niguel. There is a $150 one-time non-refundable pet cleaning fee per stay, as well as a $50 per night boarding additional charge. We welcome all well-mannered, disease Free dogs and cats. No more than two pets may occupy each guestroom. Pets must be leashed or held in arms in all common areas of the Resort. We regret that pets are not allowed in the hotel's restaurants, the Bar, the Fitness Center and Spa, the Pool Areas or The Ritz Carlton Club Level lounge.

Features: Restaurant(s), Swimming pool - outdoor, Concierge services, Gift shops or newsstand, Shopping on site, Number of rooms: 393, Computer rental, Accessible bathroom, In-room accessibility equipment for the deaf, Security guard, Babysitting or child care, Barbecue grill(s), ATM/banking, Shoe shine, Bar/lounge, Medical assistance available, Translation services, Business center, Currency exchange, Hair salon, Breakfast available additional charge, Poolside bar, Health club, Room service (24 hours), Spa services on site, Multilingual staff, Porter/bellhop, Wireless Internet, Full-service health spa, Dry cleaning/laundry service, Suitable for children, Valet Parking fee.

★★★★★♥
The St. Regis Monarch Beach Resort
1 Monarch Beach Resort
Dana Point CA 92629
(949) 234-3200
$388 - $420
Bed & Pet Discount Offered

Pet Policy: Pets up to 30 lbs accepted with $150 per stay additional charge. Must not leave in room unattended and not permitted in public eating areas. The following pet amenities are offered: Dog bed ; 1 bark street journal; 1 l paw; 1 pooch bag.

Features: Full-service health spa, Video library, Medical assistance available, ATM/banking, Security guard, Shopping on site, Supervised child care/activities, ***Continued on next page***

The St. Regis Monarch Beach Resort ***Continued from previous page***	Steam room, Health club, Room service (24 hours), Swimming pool - outdoor, Beauty services, Concierge, Sauna, Computer rental Technology helpdesk, Bar/lounge, Cell phone/mobile rental, Private beach, Restaurant(s), Gift shops or newsstand, Number of rooms: 400, Breakfast available additional charge, Poolside bar, Parking (free), Children's swimming pool, Complimentary newspapers, Business center, Porter/bellhop, Massage treatment room(s), Dry cleaning/laundry service, Golf course on site, Tennis on site.

Danville

Also see the following nearby communities that have pet friendly lodging: San Ramon - 4 miles, Walnut Creek - 6 miles, Dublin - 9 miles, Castro Valley - 9 miles, Pleasant Hill - 10 miles

Best Western Danville Sycamore
803 Camino Ramon
Danville CA 94526
(925) 855-8888
$67 - $85
Bed & Pet Discount Offered

Pet Policy: Up to 2 dogs per room with an 80 pound weight limit. Additional pet types (cats, birds, etc.) may be accepted at the hotel's discretion. Pet rate is $15.00 per day with a $100 per week maximum.

Features: Number of rooms: 62, Number of floors: 2, Coffee in lobby, Guest laundry, Multilingual staff, 24-hour business center, Restaurant(s), Wheelchair accessible, Free breakfast, Health club, Swimming pool - outdoor seasonal, Designated smoking areas, Free wireless Internet, Accessible bathroom, equipment for the deaf, Braille or raised signage.

Davis

Also see the following nearby communities that have pet friendly lodging: Dixon - 8 miles

Days Inn UC Davis
4100 Chiles Rd
Davis CA 95616
(530) 792-0800
$75 - $102
Bed & Pet Discount Offered

Pet Policy: Pets allowed, $10 per night

Features: Coffee in lobby, Business center, Number of rooms: 79, Number of floors: 2, Accessible bathroom, Smoke-Free property, Arcade/game room, Pool table, Health club, Outdoor pool – seasonal.

Econo Lodge Davis
221 D St
Davis CA 95616
(530) 756-1040
$70 - $94
Bed & Pet Discount Offered

Pet Policy: Pets accepted, $5 per night.

Features: Number of rooms: 26, Number of floors: 2, Business services, Coffee in lobby, Free breakfast, Dry cleaning/laundry service.

Hallmark Inn Davis
110 F St
Davis CA 95616
(530) 753-3600
$134 - $155
Bed & Pet Discount Offered

Pet Policy: Pets up to 25 lbs, $75 additional charge. Very limited number of pet rooms so must book in advance.

Features: Free wireless Internet, Bar/lounge, Fitness facilities, Restaurant(s), Swimming pool - outdoor, Number of rooms: 134, Poolside bar, Free breakfast, Complimentary newspapers in lobby, Business center, Dry cleaning/laundry service, Free reception.

La Quinta Inn & Suites Davis
1771 Research Park Dr
Davis CA 95616
(530) 758-2600
$89 - $119
Bed & Pet Discount Offered

Pet Policy: Pets allowed without additional charge. Must not leave unattended in room.

Features: Accessible bathroom, Number of rooms: 50, Number of floors: 3, Airport transportation additional charge, Free breakfast, Multilingual staff, Nearby fitness center (free), Business center, Internet (free), Smoke-Free property, Outdoor pool - seasonal, Dry cleaning/laundry service.

University Park Inn & Suites
1111 Richards Blvd
Davis CA 95616
(530) 756-0910
$90 - $101
Bed & Pet Discount Offered

Pet Policy: Pets accepted, $10 per pet per night. Our spacious, pet friendly guestrooms offer plenty of space for you and your four-legged friend to stretch out and relax, and our hotel is located within easy access of local parks, walking paths and pet shops. Special pet friendly package available - please call hotel directly at 530-756-0910 for details.

Features: Business services, Elevator, Number of floors: 2, Restaurant(s), Wheelchair accessible, Swimming pool - outdoor, Free breakfast, Wireless Internet (additional charge), RV and truck parking.

Del Mar

Also see the following nearby communities that have pet friendly lodging: Rancho Santa Fe - 5 miles, La Jolla - 6 miles, Encinitas - 7 mile

Best Western Stratford Inn
710 Camino Del Mar
Del Mar CA 92014
(858) 755-1501
$108 - $169
Bed & Pet Discount Offered

Pet Policy: Pets accepted with small additional charge at check-in.

Features: Free breakfast, Business services, Swimming pools – 2 outdoor, Number of rooms: 94, Number of floors: 2, Coffee in lobby, Parking (free), Multilingual staff, Complimentary newspapers in lobby, Massage - treatment room(s), Smoke-Free property, Dry cleaning/laundry service, Beauty services, Full-service health spa, Wireless Internet.

★★★½

Hilton San Diego Del Mar
15575 Jimmy Durante Blvd
Del Mar CA 92014
(858) 792-5200
$95 - $204
Bed & Pet Discount Offered

Pet Policy: Pets up to 75 lbs accepted, $50 per stay.

Features: Business center, Swimming pool - outdoor, ATM/banking, Concierge services, Gift shops or newsstand, Number of rooms: 257, Number of floors: 3, Breakfast available additional charge, Room service (24 hours), Wireless Internet, Smoke-Free property, Parking (valet) $17 Per Day, Bar/lounge, Restaurant(s), Accessible bathroom, Braille or raised signage, Dry cleaning/laundry service, Fitness facilities.

★★★★

Villa LAuberge
1540 Camino Del Mar
Del Mar CA 92014
(800) 245-9757
$143 - $359

Pet Policy: Pets welcome, $75 per stay for one pet, $125 for two, plus $75 deposit.

Features: Flat screen TV, Fitness center, Swimming pool, Sauna/ Jacuzzi, Tennis courts.

Delano

★★

Rodeway Inn Delano
2211 Girard St
Delano CA 93215
(661) 725-1022
$63 - $75
Bed & Pet Discount Offered

Pet Policy: Rodeway Inns charge an additional $10 per night per pet and require a $50 damage deposit, which is refunded if the room is in order at check out. Max of 2 pets per room. A veterinarian certificate that the pet is on a flea and parasite program and that they are Free from parasites is required. Pets may not be left alone in the room unless in a cage.

Features: Number of rooms: 45, Free breakfast, Parking (free), Swimming pool - outdoor seasonal, Airport transportation (free), Self-parking.

Desert Hot Springs

Also see the following nearby communities that have pet friendly lodging: Palm Springs - 8 miles

★★

Tuscan Springs Hotel & Spa
68187 Club Circle Dr
Desert Hot Springs CA 92240
(760) 251-0189
$165 - $245

Pet Policy: Pets accepted. Contact hotel directly for details and booking.

Features: Sauna, Swimming pool - outdoor, Number of rooms: 18, Parking (free), Spa services on site, Internet (free), Massage - treatment room(s), Free breakfast.

Diamond Bar

Also see the following nearby communities that have pet friendly lodging: Walnut - 2 miles, Pomona - 4 miles, Chino Hills - 5 miles, Chino - 6 miles, City Of Industry - 7 miles, San Dimas - 7 miles, Brea - 8 miles, Claremont - 8 miles, Glendora - 9 miles, Yorba Linda - 9 miles, Placentia - 9 miles

Ayres Suites Diamond Bar
21951 Golden Springs Dr
Diamond Bar CA 91765
(909) 860-6290
$99 - $109
Bed & Pet Discount Offered

Pet Policy: Pets accepted, $45 per stay. Limit 2 per room. Doggie beds, bowl and biscuits provided.

Features: Swimming pool – outdoor, Security guard, Room service (limited hours), Concierge services, Elevator, Restaurant(s), Number of rooms: 101, Number of floors: 3, Free breakfast, Parking (free), Complimentary newspapers in lobby, Dry cleaning/laundry service, Free wireless Internet, Suitable for children, Multilingual staff, Designated smoking areas, Area shuttle (free), 24-hour business center, Free reception, Designated smoking areas, Fitness facilities.

Dinuba

Also see the following nearby communities that have pet friendly lodging: Kingsburg - 8 miles

Holiday Inn Express Hotel & Suites Dinuba
375 S Alta Ave
Dinuba CA 93618
(559) 595-1500
$75 - $103
Bed & Pet Discount Offered

Pet Policy: Pets accepted, $50 per night plus $100 refundable deposit.

Features: Accessible bathroom, In-room accessibility equipment for the deaf, Braille or raised signage, Free breakfast, Complimentary newspapers in lobby, Business center, Internet (free), Fitness facilities.

Dixon

Also see the following nearby communities that have pet friendly lodging: Davis - 8 miles, Vacaville - 10 miles

Best Western Plus Inn Dixon
1345 Commercial Way
Dixon CA 95620
(707) 678-1400
$67 - $75
Bed & Pet Discount Offered

Pet Policy: Up to 2 dogs per room with an 80 pound weight limit. Additional pet types (cats, birds, etc.) may be accepted at the hotel's discretion. Pet rate is $15.00 per day with a $100 per week maximum.

Features: Business center, Sauna, Swimming pool - outdoor, Free breakfast, Coffee in lobby, Steam room, Number of rooms: 105, Number of floors: 2, Guest laundry, Parking (free), Complimentary newspapers in lobby, Wireless, Internet (free), Use of nearby fitness center (discount).

Comfort Suites West of UC Davis
155 Dorset Dr.
Dorsett Dr & N First St
Dixon CA 95620
(707) 676-5000
$74 - $89
Bed & Pet Discount Offered

Pet Policy: Pet Accommodation: $15.00 for pets under 25 pounds. For pets over 25 pounds, $$25.

Features: Free wireless Internet, Business center, Number of rooms: 85, Elevator, Fitness facilities, Free breakfast, Swimming pool - outdoor, Smoke-Free property, Roll-in shower, Swimming pool - outdoor heated, Accessible bathroom.

★★
Red Roof Inn Dixon
1480 Ary Lane
Dixon CA 95020
(707) 693-0606
$58 - $78
Bed & Pet Discount Offered

Pet Policy: One well-behaved family pet is permitted. Pets must be declared during guest registration. In consideration of all Red Roof guests, pets must never be left unattended in the guestroom.

Features: Free Breakfast, Wheelchair accessible, Free wireless Internet, Number of rooms: 60, Number of suites: 13, Number of floors: 3, Guest laundry, Complimentary newspapers, Outdoor pool – seasonal. Nearby fitness center (discount), Accessible bathroom, In-room accessibility equipment for the deaf, Braille or raised signage, Coffee in lobby.

★★
Super 8 Dixon / UC Davis
2500 Plaza Ct
Dixon CA 95620
(707) 678-3399
$45 - $65
Bed & Pet Discount Offered

Pet Policy: Small pets only. Deposit required.

Features: Elevator, Swimming pool - outdoor, Free wireless Internet, Free breakfast, Guest laundry, Fitness facilities.

Downey

Also see the following nearby communities that have pet friendly lodging: Bell Gardens - 2 miles, Norwalk - 3 miles, Pico Rivera - 4 miles, Commerce - 4 miles, Whittier - 6 miles, Huntington Park - 6 miles, Cerritos - 6 miles, La Mirada - 7 miles, Hawaiian Gardens - 7 miles, La Palma - 9 miles, Monterey Park - 9 miles, Buena Park - 9 miles, Carson - 10 miles, Long Beach - 10 miles, Los Alamitos - 10 miles, Signal Hill - 10 miles, South El Monte - 10 miles

★★★½
Embassy Suites Hotel - Downey
8425 Firestone Blvd
Downey CA 90241
(562) 861-1900
$121 - $214
Bed & Pet Discount Offered

Pet Policy: Pets up to 75 lbs accepted. Additional charge $25 per day.

Features: Business center, Bar/lounge, Restaurant(s), Room service (limited hours), Concierge, Gift shops or newsstand, Number of suites: 219, Number of floors: 8, Free breakfast, Wireless Internet (additional charge), Security guard, Dry cleaning/laundry, Sauna, Fitness facilities.

Dublin

Also see the following nearby communities that have pet friendly lodging: Pleasanton - 4 miles, San Ramon - 5 miles, Castro Valley - 8 miles, Danville - 9 miles, Livermore - 9 miles

Extended Stay America Dublin - Hacienda Dr.
4500 Dublin Blvd
Dublin CA 94568
(925) 875-9556
$64 - $99
Bed & Pet Discount Offered

Pet Policy: One pet is allowed in each guest room. A $25 per day non-refundable cleaning fee (not to exceed $150) will be charged the first night of your stay. Weight, size and breed restrictions may apply. Please contact the hotel directly with inquiries. Please Note: "Signature" rooms do not currently accommodate pets, with the exception of handicap accessible rooms.

Features: Guest laundry, Elevator, Number of rooms: 122, Number of floors: 3, Parking (free), Wireless Internet additional charge.

Holiday Inn Dublin
6680 Regional Street
Dublin CA 94568
(925) 828-7750
$69 - $146
Bed & Pet Discount Offered

Pet Policy: Pets welcome, $35 per stay. Please notify desk of pet at check-in.

Features: Sauna, Business Center, Indoor pool, Accessible bathroom, In-room accessibility equipment for the deaf, Braille or raised signage, Bar/lounge, Restaurant(s), Room service Number of rooms: 234, Breakfast available additional charge, Spa services on site, Multilingual staff, Complimentary newspapers, Beauty services, Free wireless Internet, Massage - treatment room(s), Dry cleaning/laundry, Fitness facilities, Wheelchair accessible, Pick up service from train station.

La Quinta Inn & Suites Dublin-Pleasanton
6275 Dublin Blvd
Dublin CA 94568
(925) 828-9393
$125 - $140
Bed & Pet Discount Offered

Pet Policy: Dogs and cats, up to 50 lbs accepted without additional charge. Must be crated or out of room for housekeeping.

Features: Accessible bathroom, Wheelchair accessible, Free breakfast, Outdoor pool, Business center, Number of suites: 34, Number of floors: 3, Smoke-Free, Internet (free), Fitness facilities.

Not Rated:
Oakwood At Archstone Emerald Pk
5095 Haven Place
Dublin CA 94568
(925) 560-1600
$138 - $173

Pet Policy: Pets accepted with limitations and additional charge. Contact hotel directly for more information and to make reservations.

Features: Furnished apartments, Fitness center, Swimming pool & spa, Fully equipped kitchens, VCR, TV, Housewares, Weekly housekeeping.

Not Rated:
Oakwood At Dublin Waterford Pl
4800 Tassajara Road
Dublin CA 94568
(602) 687-3322
$129 - $177

Pet Policy: Pets accepted with limitations and additional charge. Contact hotel directly for more information and to make reservations.

Features: Furnished apartments, Fitness center, Swimming pool & spa, Washer & dryer, Fully equipped kitchens, VCR, TV, Housewares, Weekly housekeeping.

Not Rated:
Oakwood at Emerald Park
5050 Hacienda Drive
Dublin CA 94568
(925) 875-0500
$250 - $251

Pet Policy: Pets accepted with limitations and additional charge. Contact hotel directly for more information and to make reservations.

Features: Furnished apartments, Fitness center, Swimming pool & spa, Fully equipped kitchens, VCR, TV, Housewares, Weekly housekeeping.

Dunnigan

Americas Best Value Inn
3930 County Road 89
Dunnigan CA 95937
(530) 724-3333
$50 - $61

Pet Policy: Pets up to 40 lbs accepted, $10 per pet per night.

Features: Number of rooms: 37, Number of floors: 2, Swimming pool – outdoor, HBO, Mini fridge, Free continental breakfast.

Dunsmuir

Also see the following nearby communities that have pet friendly lodging: Mount Shasta - 7 miles

★★

Best Choice Inn Dunsmuir
4221 Siskiyou Ave
Dunsmuir CA 96025
(530) 235-4010
$67 - $72
Bed & Pet Discount Offered

Pet Policy: Pets allowed with $10 per day additional charge.

Features: Number of rooms: 30, Business services, Room service (24 hours), RV and truck parking (free), Accessible bathroom, In-room accessibility for the deaf, Free wireless Internet.

★★

Oak Tree Inn Dunsmuir
4000 Siskiyou Ave
Dunsmuir CA 96025
(530) 235-4100
$89 - $109
Bed & Pet Discount Offered

Pet Policy: Pets welcome, $10 per pet per night plus $150 refundable deposit. No size restrictions.

Free breakfast, Parking (free), Free wireless Internet, RV and truck parking, Restaurant(s), Fitness facilities, Guest laundry.

El Cajon

Also see the following nearby communities that have pet friendly lodging: La Mesa - 6 miles

Best Western Courtesy Inn
1355 E Main St
El Cajon CA 92021
(619) 440-7378
$80 - $140

Pet Policy: Pets accepted on advance approval. Please contact hotel directly for reservations.

Features: Number of Rooms: 47, Free wireless Internet, Cable TV, Free hot breakfast.

Quality Inn & Suites San Diego East County
1250 El Cajon Blvd
El Cajon CA 92020
(619) 588-8808
$64 - $85
Bed & Pet Discount Offered

Pet Policy: Pets accepted, $10 per night

Features: Free breakfast, Elevator, Number of rooms: 96, Number of floors: 3, Parking (free), Complimentary newspapers in lobby, Swimming pool - outdoor seasonal, Roll-in shower, Business services, Coffee in lobby, Free wireless Internet.

Relax Inn And Suites
1220 W Main St
El Cajon CA 92020
(619) 442-2576
$57 - $67
Bed & Pet Discount Offered

Pet Policy: Small pets allowed, $20 per night per pet.

Features: Restaurant(s), Room service (limited hours), Swimming pool - outdoor, Number of rooms: 38, Number of floors: 2, Business services, Parking (free), Free breakfast, Free wireless Internet.

Super 8 El Cajon, CA
471 N Magnolia Ave
El Cajon CA 92020
(619) 447-3999
$47 - $79
Bed & Pet Discount Offered

Pet Policy: Rodeway Inns charge an additional $10 per night per pet and require a $50 damage deposit, which is refunded if the room is in order at check out. Max of 2 pets per room. A veterinarian certificate that the pet is on a flea and parasite program and that they are Free from parasites is required. Pets may not be left alone in the room unless in a cage.

Features: Swimming pool - outdoor, Number of rooms: 47, Number of floors: 3, Guest laundry, Parking (free), Wireless, Internet (free), Free Breakfast, Elevator.

Travelodge El Cajon
425 West Main St
El Cajon CA 92020
(619) 441-8250
$39 - $79
Bed & Pet Discount Offered

Pet Policy: Pets allowed, $10 per day per pet.

Features: Free breakfast, Swimming pool - outdoor, Number of rooms: 43, Number of floors: 2, Coffee in lobby, Parking (free), Complimentary newspapers in lobby, Business center, Free wireless Internet.

Not rated
Villa Serena Motel El Cajon
771 El Cajon Blvd
El Cajon CA 92020
(877) 747-8713
$38 - $52

Pet Policy: Medium sized pets allowed, $10 per pet per night.

Features: Coffee service from 7 10 am, Free high speed Wireless Internet, Free parking, cable TV.

El Centro

Also see the following nearby communities that have pet friendly lodging: Calexico - 8 miles

★★
Brunner's Inn & Suites
215 N Imperial Ave
El Centro CA 92243
(760) 337-5550
$55- $80
Bed & Pet Discount Offered

Pet Policy: Pet Friendly

Features: Bar/lounge, Restaurant(s), Swimming pool - outdoor, Number of rooms: 88, Number of floors: 2, Suitable for children Barbecue grill(s), Coffee in lobby, Pool table, Free breakfast, Parking (free), Complimentary newspapers in lobby, Use of nearby fitness center (free), Beauty services, Wireless Internet, Dry cleaning/laundry service.

Not rated
Budget Inn & Suites El Centro
1212 Adams Avenue
El Centro CA 92243
(877) 747-8713
$37 - $43

Pet Policy: Up to two well-behaved pets are allowed for an additional charge of $5 per pet per night. Please note that pets should not be left unattended and that pets are not allowed in the pool or the restaurant.

Features: Swimming pool - outdoor, Parking (free), Business center, Guest laundry, Free breakfast, Free wireless Internet.

Clarion Inn El Centro
1455 Ocotillo Dr
El Centro CA 92243
(760) 352-5152
$75 - $109
Bed & Pet Discount Offered

Pet Policy: Pets up to 20 lbs. $10 per night.

Features: Bar/lounge, Room service (limited hours), Number of rooms: 147, Number of floors: 2, Guest laundry, Parking (free), Complimentary newspapers in lobby, Wireless Internet, Swimming pool - outdoor, Multilingual staff, Fitness facilities.

Comfort Inn & Suites
2354 S 4th St
El Centro CA 92243
(760) 335-3502
$79 - $129
Bed & Pet Discount Offered

Pet Policy: Pets accepted, $10 per night. Limit of 1 pet per room. Must not leave unattended.

Features: Elevator, Business services, Bar/lounge, Swimming pool - outdoor, Number of rooms: 110, Number of floors: 3, Internet (additional charge), Free breakfast, Complimentary newspapers in lobby, Sauna, Fitness facilities.

Rodeway Inn & Suites
455 Wake Ave
El Centro CA 92243
(760) 352-6620
$46 - $54
Bed & Pet Discount Offered

Pet Policy: Accepts dogs of any size, $5 per night per dog.

Features: Wheelchair accessible, Coffee in lobby, Swimming pool - outdoor, Number of rooms: 49, Number of floors: 1, Free breakfast, Parking (free), Multilingual staff, Complimentary newspapers in lobby, Business center, Dry cleaning/laundry service, Free wireless Internet, RV and truck parking.

Sun Valley Inn & Suites
1425 Adams Ave
El Centro CA 92243
(760) 352-5511
$60 - $70
Bed & Pet Discount Offered

Pet Policy: Pets Allowed.

Features: Swimming pool - outdoor, Free breakfast, Business services, Free wireless Internet, Number of rooms: 50, Number of floors: 2, Suitable for children, Barbecue grill(s), Coffee in lobby, Guest laundry, Parking (free), Multilingual staff.

TownePlace Suites Marriott El Centro
3003 S Dogwood Ave
El Centro CA 92243
(760) 370-3800
$124 - $144
Bed & Pet Discount Offered

Pet Policy: Pets allowed, $100 per stay.

Features: Elevator, Restaurant(s), Number of floors: 4, Parking (free), Swimming pool, Wireless Internet, Smoke-Free property.

★★

Value Inn El Centro
2030 Cottonwood Circle
El Centro CA 92243
(760) 353-7750
$40 - $55
Bed & Pet Discount Offered

Pet Policy: Pets accepted.

Features: Free breakfast, Internet (free), Number of floors: 2, Business services, Parking (free), 24-hour front desk.

El Monte

Also see the following nearby communities that have pet friendly lodging: South El Monte - 2 miles, Rosemead - 3 miles, Arcadia - 4 miles, San Gabriel - 5 miles, Monrovia - 5 miles, Pasadena - 7 miles, Monterey Park - 7 miles, City Of Industry - 7 miles, South Pasadena - 8 miles, Pico Rivera - 8 miles, Whittier - 8 miles, Commerce - 9 miles

Americas Best Value Inn
12040 Garvey Ave
El Monte CA 91734
(626) 442-8354
$63 - $120

Pet Policy: Pets allowed, $15 per night. Limit of 1 pet per room.

Features: Number of rooms: 51, Number of suites: 10, Number of Floors: 3, Free continental breakfast, Free wireless Internet, Microwave & micro fridge, Coffee maker, HBO.

El Portal

★★★
Yosemite View Lodge
11136 Highway 140
El Portal CA 95318
(888) 742-4371
$120 - $319
Bed & Pet Discount Offered

Pet Policy: Pets, any size, $10 per pet per night.

Features: ATM/Banking, Swimming pool - indoor, Elevator, Swimming pool - outdoor, Restaurant(s), Gift shops or newsstand, Number of rooms: 278, Business services, Guest laundry, Grocery, Parking (free), Multilingual staff, Bar/Lounge.

El Segundo

Also see the following nearby communities that have pet friendly lodging: Hawthorne - 2 miles, Manhattan Beach - 2 miles, Inglewood - 3 miles, Hermosa Beach - 4 miles, Marina Del Rey - 5 miles, Redondo Beach - 6 miles, Gardena - 6 miles, Los Angeles - 6 miles, Culver City - 6 miles, Venice - 7 miles, Torrance - 8 miles, Santa Monica - 9 miles, Carson - 10 mile

★★★½
Embassy Suites LAX International Airport South
1440 E Imperial Ave
El Segundo CA 90245
(310) 640-3600
$110 - $189
Bed & Pet Discount Offered

Pet Policy: Pets up to 35 lbs allowed. $35 per day.

Features: Indoor pool, Airport transportation (free), Free Breakfast, Parking $21/day, Business center, Number of rooms: 349, Number of floors: 5, Wireless Internet (additional charge), Room service (limited hours), Security guard, Bar/lounge, Elevator, ATM/banking, Concierge services, Restaurant(s), Gift shops or newsstand, Multilingual staff, Complimentary newspapers in lobby, Porter/bellhop, Airport transportation (free) available 24 hours, dry cleaning/laundry service, Area shuttle (free), Fitness facilities, Free reception.

★★
Homestead Los Angeles - LAX Airport - El Segundo
1910 E Mariposa Ave
El Segundo CA 90245
(310) 607-4000
$79 - $99
Bed & Pet Discount Offered

Pet Policy: Pets allowed, $25 per day, up to $150 per stay.

Features: Nearby fitness center (discount), ATM/banking, Number of rooms: 151, Number of floors: 2, Business services, Barbecue grill(s), Front desk (limited hours), Wireless Internet additional charge, Dry cleaning/laundry service.

★★★
Hyatt Summerfield Suites Los Angeles LAX/El Segundo
810 S Douglas St
El Segundo CA 90245
(310) 725-0100
$124 - $209
Bed & Pet Discount Offered

Pet Policy: A maximum of two pets per suite. Dogs not allowed if over 50 lbs; cats must be declawed; all pets must be housebroken. We reserve the right to refuse certain pets. One-time additional charge of $150 (one-bedroom suite) or $200 (two-bedroom suite) and a daily charge of $10. Pet policy must be signed at check-in. ***Continued on next page***

Hyatt Summerfield Suites Los Angeles LAX/El Segundo Continued from previous page

Features: Business services, Barbecue grill(s), Concierge services, Swimming pool - outdoor, Gift shops or newsstand, Number of rooms: 122, Coffee in lobby, Video library, Free breakfast, Parking (free), Multilingual staff, Complimentary newspapers in lobby, Use of nearby fitness center (free), Free wireless Internet, Smoke-Free property, Dry cleaning/laundry service.

★★★

Residence Inn By Marriott El Segundo
2135 E El Segundo Blvd
El Segundo CA 90245
(310) 333-0888
$119 - $219
Bed & Pet Discount Offered

Pet Policy: Pets allowed, $100 cleaning fee per stay.

Features: Free Breakfast, Business services, Swimming pool - outdoor, Coffee in lobby, Airport transportation (free), Elevator, Number of rooms: 150, Number of floors: 4, Barbecue grill(s), Breakfast available additional charge, Video library, Parking (free), Complimentary newspapers in lobby, Free wireless Internet, Accessible bathroom, In-room accessibility equipment for the deaf, Braille or raised signage, Dry cleaning/laundry service, Tennis on site, Fitness facilities.

★★★

Summerfield LAX-El Segundo
810 S DOUGLAS AVE
El Segundo CA 90245
(310) 725-0100
$139 - $169

Pet Policy: A maximum of two pets per suite. Dogs not allowed if over 50lbs; cats must be declawed; all pets must be housebroken. We reserve the right to refuse certain pets. One-time additional charge of $150 (one-bedroom suite) or $200 (two-bedroom suite) and a daily charge of $10. Pet policy must be signed at check-in.

Features: Free breakfast buffet, Free parking, Wireless Internet (free), BBQ, Pool, Jacuzzi, Sport court, Full kitchens in 1 and 2 bedroom suites.

Elk Grove

Extended Stay America Sacramento - Elk Grove
2201 Long Port Ct
Elk Grove CA 95758
(916) 683-3753
$64 - $89
Bed & Pet Discount Offered

Pet Policy: One pet is allowed in each guest room. A $25 per day non-refundable cleaning fee (not to exceed $150) will be charged the first night of your stay.

Features: Guest laundry, Elevator, Number of rooms: 92, Number of floors: 3, Coffee in lobby, Parking (free), Use of nearby fitness center (free), Front desk (limited hours), Wireless Internet – additional charge.

★★½
Fairfield Inn and Suites by Marriott Sacramento El
8058 Orchard Loop
Elk Grove CA 95624
(916) 681-5400
$89 - $154
Bed & Pet Discount Offered

Pet Policy: Pets allowed with $35 cleaning fee.

Features: Swimming pool - indoor, Coffee in lobby, Free breakfast, Parking (free), Technology support staff, Number of rooms: 76, Number of floors: 3, Guest laundry, Complimentary newspapers in lobby, Fitness facilities, Wheelchair accessible, Free wireless Internet, Smoke-Free property, 24-hour business center.

★★½
Holiday Inn Express Hotel & Suites Elk Grove
2460 Maritime Drive
Elk Grove CA 95758
(916) 478-4000
$90 - $124
Bed & Pet Discount Offered

Pet Policy: Pets less than 50 lbs accepted, $30 per stay.

Features: Free breakfast, Elevator, Swimming pool - outdoor, Gift shops or newsstand, Number of rooms: 65, Number of floors: 3, Parking (free), Free wireless Internet, Accessible bathroom, In-room accessibility equipment for the deaf, Braille or raised signage, Dry cleaning/laundry service, Business Center, Fitness facilities.

★★½
Holiday Inn Express Hotel & Suites Elk Grove
9175 W Stockton Blvd
Elk Grove CA 95758
(916) 478-9000
$110 - $143
Bed & Pet Discount Offered

Pet Policy: Pets less than 50 lbs accepted, $30 per stay.

Features: Swimming pool - outdoor, Gift shops or newsstand, Number of rooms: 116, Number of floors: 3, Free breakfast, Parking (free), Multilingual staff, Front desk (limited hours), Business center, Free wireless Internet, Accessible bathroom, In-room accessibility equipment for the deaf, Braille or raised signage, Dry cleaning/laundry service, Fitness facilities.

Emeryville

Also see the following nearby communities that have pet friendly lodging: Berkeley - 2 miles, Alameda - 5 miles, Oakland - 6 miles, Richmond - 8 miles, San Francisco - 10 miles

★★
ESA Oakland Emeryville
3650 Mandela Parkway
Emeryville CA 94608
(510) 923-1481
$90 - $124

Pet Policy: One pet is allowed in each guest room. A $25 per day non-refundable cleaning fee (not to exceed $150) will be charged the first night of your stay.

Features: Studio suites, Full kitchen, Movie channels, 2 line phone with data port, Guest laundry, Weekly housekeeping. Minimum stay of 30 days may be required.

Woodfin Suite Hotel Emeryville
5800 Shellmound St
Emeryville CA 94608
(510) 601-5880
$109 - $206
Bed & Pet Discount Offered

Pet Policy: Accepts dogs and cats, up to 50 lbs, $10 per day per pet, maximum of $250 per stay. Limit of 2 pets per room.

Features: Outdoor pool, Bar/lounge, Smoke-Free property, Free wireless Internet, 24-hour business center, Restaurant(s), Number of rooms: 202, Number of floors: 12, Coffee in lobby, Video library, Grocery, Multilingual staff, Security guard, Room service, Dry cleaning/laundry, Fitness facilities.

Encinitas

Also see the following nearby communities that have pet friendly lodging: Rancho Santa Fe - 5 miles, Carlsbad - 6 miles, Del Mar - 7 miles, San Marcos - 8 miles, Vista - 9 miles

Best Western Encinitas Inn
85 Encinitas Blvd
Encinitas CA 92024
(760) 942-7455
$107- $375

Pet Policy: Allows pets under 30 pounds. $50 additional charge.

Features: HBO, Free wireless Internet, Jacuzzi tub and kitchenette in suites, Free continental breakfast, Outdoor heated pool and hot tub, Business services.

Econo Lodge Encinitas
410 N Coast Hwy 101
Encinitas CA 92024
(760) 436-4999
$74 - $84
Bed & Pet Discount Offered

Pet Policy: Pet Accommodation: 25.00/night Pet Limit: 1 pet/room, 40 pounds and under

Features: Swimming pool - outdoor, Number of rooms: 30, Number of floors: 2, Free breakfast, Smoke-Free property, Free wireless Internet

Howard Johnson Encinitas
607 Leucadia Blvd
Encinitas CA 92024
(760) 944-3800
$59 - $75
Bed & Pet Discount Offered

Pet Policy: Pets accepted for $25 per night. Only 8 pet friendly rooms available, all smoking.

Features: Swimming pool - outdoor, Business services, Shopping on site, Coffee in lobby, Parking (free), Complimentary newspapers in lobby, Wireless Internet.

Leucadia Beach Inn
1322 N Coast Hwy 101
Encinitas CA 92024
(760) 943-7461
$69 - $79
Bed & Pet Discount Offered

Pet Policy: Pet Friendly upon approval. Please contact property directly for details.

Features: Barbecue grill(s), Number of rooms: 23, Number of floors: 2, Suitable for children, Parking (free), Front desk (limited hours), Accessible bathroom, In-room accessibility.

Quality Inn & Suites Moonlight Beach / Lego Land /
186 N Coast Highway 101
Encinitas CA 92024
(760) 944-0301
$69 - $99
Bed & Pet Discount Offered

Pet Policy: Quality Inns charge an additional $10 per night per pet. They may require a $50 damage deposit, which is refunded if the room is in order at check out. Quality Inns accept any well-behaved pets with a maximum of 3 per room, but dogs are limited to 50 pounds. Pets may not be left alone in the room unless in a cage.

Features: Guest laundry, Business services, Free breakfast, Number of rooms: 45 Parking (free), Multilingual staff, Complimentary newspapers in lobby, Front desk (limited hours).

Escondido

Also see the following nearby communities that have pet friendly lodging: San Marcos - 5 miles, Vista - 7 miles

Not rated
Best Western Escondido Hotel
1700 Seven Oakes road
Escondido CA 92026
(760) 740-1700
$93 - $179

Pet Policy: Pets up to 30 pounds allowed, $25 additional charge. Clerk must approve on check in.

Features: 2 room suites and family suites available, Free wireless Internet, Microwave, Refrigerator, HBO, Free continental breakfast. Business center, Swimming pool – outdoor – heated center, outdoor heated pool and whirlpool.

★★★
Castle Creek Inn Resort Spa
29850 Circle R Way
Escondido CA 92026
(760) 751-8800
$89 - $495
Bed & Pet Discount Offered

Pet Policy: Pets accepted, $35 per pet per night.

Features: Free Wireless, Sauna, Full-service health spa, Swimming pool – outdoor, Dry cleaning/laundry service, Business services, Suitable for children, Coffee in lobby, Parking (free), Multilingual staff, Concierge desk, Fitness facilities, Number of rooms: 33, Golf course on site, Accessible bathroom, Tennis on site.

★★
Comfort Inn Escondido
1290 W Valley Pkwy
Escondido CA 92029
(760) 489-1010
$79 - $109
Bed & Pet Discount Offered

Pet Policy: Pet Accommodation: 1$0.00 per night . Pet Limit: One pet per room, up to 25 lbs.

Features: Swimming pool - outdoor, Business center, Elevator, Coffee in lobby, Free breakfast, Parking (free), Multilingual staff, Complimentary newspapers in lobby, Free wireless Internet, Dry cleaning/laundry service, Fitness facilities, Number of rooms: 93

Rodeway Inn Escondido
250 W El Norte Pkwy
Escondido CA 92026
(760) 746-0441
$58 - $88
Bed & Pet Discount Offered

Pet Policy: Rodeway Inns charge an additional $10 per night per pet and require a $50 damage deposit, which is refunded if the room is in order at check out. Max of 2 pets per room. A veterinarian certificate that the pet is on a flea and parasite program and that they are Free from parasites is required Pets may not be left alone in the room unless in a cage.

Features: Coffee in lobby, Number of rooms: 25, Number of floors: 2, Business services, Free breakfast, Parking (free), 24-hour front desk.

Eureka

Also see the following nearby communities that have pet friendly lodging: Arcata - 7 miles

Best Western Plus Bayshore Inn
3500 Broadway
Eureka CA 95503
(707) 268-8005
$80 - $179

Pet Policy: Pets accepted with advance approval. $40 additional charge per stay.

Features: Free full breakfast, fresh cookies upon arrival, HBO, Nintendo 64, Microwave, Refrigerator, Free wireless Internet, Indoor and outdoor heated swimming pool, Cocktail lounge, Business center.

Carter House Inns
301 L St
Eureka CA 95501
(707) 444-8062
$165 - $185
Bed & Pet Discount Offered

Pet Policy: Pets welcome, $50 additional charge. Please let us know when you are checking in if you are travelling with your dog. They will receive a special keepsake blanket and water bowl.

Features: Free Breakfast, Babysitting or child care, Porter/bellhop, Wheelchair accessible, Parking (free), Concierge desk, Massage treatment room(s), Smoke-Free property, Media library, Dry cleaning/laundry service, Free wireless Internet.

Clarion Resort Eureka
2223 4th St
Eureka CA 95501
(707) 442-3261
$94 - $129
Bed & Pet Discount Offered

Pet Policy: Pets up to 20 lbs, $10 per night. Limit 1 pet per room.

Features: Business center, Free breakfast, Swimming pool - indoor, Elevator, Coffee in lobby, Number of rooms: 63, Number of floors: 3, Guest laundry, Parking (free), Complimentary newspapers in lobby, Free wireless Internet, Accessible bathroom, In-room accessibility equipment for the deaf, Braille or raised signage, Fitness facilities.

Comfort Inn Eureka
4260 Broadway St
Eureka CA 95503
(707) 444-2019
$94 - $105
Bed & Pet Discount Offered

Pet Policy: Pets accepted, $25 pet stay for non-smoking room, no charge for smoking room.

Features: Airport transportation additional charge, Business center, Smoke-Free property, Swimming pool - indoor, Number of rooms: 48, Number of floors: 2, Free breakfast, Parking (free), Coffee in lobby, Dry cleaning/laundry service, Free wireless Internet, Fitness facilities.

Econo Lodge
1630 4th St
Eureka CA 95501
(707) 443-8041
$54 - $69
Bed & Pet Discount Offered

Pet Policy: Dogs only, less than 30 lbs. $8 per night.

Features: Business services, Swimming pool - indoor, Number of rooms: 41, Number of floors: 2, Free breakfast, Parking (free), Complimentary newspapers in lobby, Beauty services.

Eureka Travelodge
4 4th St
Eureka CA 95501
(707) 443-6345
$53 - $65
Bed & Pet Discount Offered

Pet Policy: 1 small dog allowed, $10 per night.

Features: Business services, Free breakfast, Parking (free), Multilingual staff, Complimentary newspapers in lobby, Wireless Internet.

Quality Inn Eureka
1209 4th St
Eureka CA 95501
(707) 443-1601
$84 - $106
Bed & Pet Discount Offered

Pet Policy: Pets up to 50 lbs accepted, $10 per stay. Limit of 2 pets per room.

Features: Business services, Swimming pool - outdoor, Free breakfast, Gift shops or newsstand, Number of rooms: 60, Number of floors: 2, Parking (free), Sauna.

Red Lion Hotel Eureka
1929 4th St
Eureka CA 95501
(707) 445-0844
$85- $165
Bed & Pet Discount Offered

Pet Policy: Pets welcome, $20 per stay.

Features: ATM/Banking, Bar/Lounge, Swimming pool - outdoor, Elevator, Airport transportation (free), Restaurant(s), Room service (limited hours), Gift shops or newsstand, Number of rooms: 175, Number of floors: 3, Pool table, Parking (free), Multilingual staff, Complimentary newspapers in lobby, Business center, Free wireless Internet, Dry cleaning/laundry service, Fitness facilities

Rodeway Inn -eureka
2014 4th St
Eureka CA 95501
(707) 444-0401
$54 - $79
Bed & Pet Discount Offered

Pet Policy: Rodeway Inns charge an additional $10 per night per pet and require a $50 damage deposit, which is refunded if the room is in order at check out. Max of 2 pets per room. A veterinarian certificate that the pet is on a flea and parasite program and that they are Free from parasites is required. Pets may not be left alone in the room unless in a cage.

Features: Accessible bathroom, In-room accessibility equipment for the deaf, Number of rooms: 27, Number of floors: 2, Business services, Free breakfast, Parking (free), Wireless, Internet (free)

Fairfield

Also see the following nearby communities that have pet friendly lodging: Suisun City - 1 mile, Vacaville - 9 miles

Americas Best Value Inn
3331 N Texas Street
Fairfield CA 94533
(707) 426-6161
$45 - $62
Bed & Pet Discount Offered

Pet Policy: Small pets welcome for $10 per pet per night.

Features: Elevator, Swimming pool - outdoor, Number of rooms: 101, Number of floors: 3, Coffee in lobby, Guest laundry, Parking (free), Swimming pool - outdoor seasonal, Free wireless Internet.

★★★
Courtyard by Marriott
1350 Holiday Lane
Napa Valley Area
Fairfield CA 94533
(707) 422-4111
$124 - $125
Bed & Pet Discount Offered

Pet Policy: Pets allowed $25 per night per pet. Limit of 2 pets. May not be left alone in room.

Features: Business services, Coffee in lobby, Free Internet, Massage - treatment room(s), Smoke-Free property, Bar/lounge, Outdoor pool, Business center, Restaurant(s), Number of rooms: 133, Number of floors: 4, Breakfast available additional charge, Parking (free), Complimentary newspapers in lobby, Security guard, Beauty services, Full-service health spa, Dry cleaning/laundry service, Wheelchair accessible, Multilingual staff, Pick up service from train station, Accessible bathroom, Accessibility equipment for the deaf, Area shuttle (free).

★★
Extended Stay America Fairfield - Napa Valley
1019 Oliver Rd
Fairfield CA 94534
(707) 438-0932
$69 - $104

Pet Policy: One pet is allowed in each guest room. A $25 per day non-refundable cleaning fee (not to exceed $150) will be charged the first night of your stay. Weight, size and breed restrictions may apply. Please contact the hotel directly with inquiries. Please Note: "Signature" rooms do not currently accommodate pets. ***Continued on next page.***

Extended Stay America Fairfield
Continued from previous page

Features: Guest laundry, Coffee in lobby, Number of rooms: 104, Number of floors: 3, Business services, Suitable for children, Wireless Internet.

Not Rated
Gateway Inn Fairfield
2100 N Texas Street
Fairfield CA 94533
(707) 425-1051
$54 - $64

Pet Policy: Pet friendly, specific details not provided by hotel.

Features: Microwave & mini fridge, Coffee maker, Hair dryer, Iron & ironing board, Free wireless Internet, Swimming pool – outdoor, Guest laundry.

★★★
Homewood Suites by Hilton Fairfield-Napa Valley
4755 Business Center Drive
Fairfield CA 94534
(707) 863-0300
$92 - $219
Bed & Pet Discount Offered

Pet Policy: Pets up to 50 lbs, $100 per stay. Pets not allowed in lodge, may never be left alone.

Features: Restaurant(s), Gift shops or newsstand, Number of floors: 4, Parking (free), Complimentary newspapers in lobby, Free wireless Internet, Grocery/convenience store, Free breakfast, Swimming pool - indoor, Business center, Dry cleaning/laundry service, Fitness facilities.

★★★
Staybridge Suites Fairfield Napa Valley Area
4775 Business Center Dr
Fairfield CA 94534
(707) 863-0900
$111 - $174
Bed & Pet Discount Offered

Pet Policy: Pets up to 40 lbs, $75 for up to 6 nights, $150 for 7 or longer. Must have proof of current vaccinations.

Features: Accessible bathroom, In-room accessibility equipment for the deaf, Braille or raised signage, Swimming pool - indoor, Number of suites: 82, Number of floors: 3, Airport transportation additional charge, Barbecue grill(s), Library, Free breakfast, Grocery, Parking (free), Multilingual staff, Business center, Free wireless Internet, Dry cleaning/laundry services, Fitness facilities.

Fallbrook

Also see the following nearby communities that have pet friendly lodging: Temecula - 9 mile

Econo Lodge Inn & Suites Fallbrook
1608 S Mission Road
Fallbrook CA 92028
(888) 365-4113
$54 - $79
Bed & Pet Discount Offered

Pet Policy: Pets accepted, $10 per night.

Features: Parking (free), Smoke-Free property, Coffee in lobby, Number of rooms: 35, Number of floors: 2, Free breakfast, Business center, Free wireless Internet.

Oak Creek Manor
4735 Olive Hill Road
Fallbrook CA 92028
(760) 451-2468
$199 - $275
Bed & Pet Discount Offered

Pet Policy: Pets less than 50 lbs accepted, $40 per stay.

Features: Free breakfast, Number of rooms: 4, Private dock, Gardens.

Pala Mesa Golf Resort - Temecula
2001 Old Highway 395
Fallbrook CA 92028
(760) 728-5881
$172 - $270
Bed & Pet Discount Offered

Pet Policy: Pets accepted, $50 per pet per stay

Features: Business Center, Bar/Lounge Wheelchair Accessible, Swimming pool - outdoor, Golf course on site, Tennis on site. Room service, Restaurant(s), ATM/banking, Concierge services, Gift shops or newsstand, Number of rooms: 133, Number of floors: 2, Breakfast available additional charge, Parking (free), Multilingual staff, Complimentary newspapers in lobby, Porter/bellhop, Security guard, Dry cleaning/laundry service, Free wireless Internet, Fitness facilities.

★★
Rodeway Inn Fallbrook
1635 S Mission Rd
Fallbrook CA 92028
(760) 728-6174
$59 - $89
Bed & Pet Discount Offered

Pet Policy: Rodeway Inns charge an additional $10 per night per pet and require a $50 damage deposit, which is refunded if the room is in order at check out. Max of 2 pets per room. A veterinarian certificate that the pet is on a flea and parasite program is required. Pets may not be left alone in the room unless in a cage.

Features: Number of rooms: 50, Number of floors: 2, Guest laundry, Free breakfast, Parking (free), Complimentary newspapers in lobby, Free wireless Internet, Coffee in lobby, Swimming pool – outdoor.

Fillmore

Also see the following nearby communities that have pet friendly lodging: Santa Paula - 10 miles

Not rated
Best Western La Posada Motel
827 VENTURA ST
Fillmore CA 93015
(805) 524-0440
$75 - $110

Pet Policy: Pets, any size allowed, $15 per day per pet.

Features: Free wireless Internet, Free continental breakfast, Outdoor swimming pool and hot tub.

Fish Camp

★★★★

Tenaya Lodge at Yosemite
1122 Highway 41
Fish Camp CA 93623
(559) 683-6555
$129 - $199
Bed & Pet Discount Offered

Pet Policy: A non-refundable additional charge of $75 will be charged for any dog, any size. No other pets accepted. Two well-behaved canines per room are permitted for the $75 additional charge. Guests may have a third dog in the room for an additional charge of $25. Service animals are always allowed. Pet owners will be liable for any additional cleaning bills or repairs, should they be required.

Features: Concierge desk, Business Center, Sauna, Bar/Lounge, Swimming pool - indoor, Arcade/game room, Restaurant(s), Gift shops or newsstand, Shopping on site, Number of rooms: 244, Number of floors: 4, Ski storage, Breakfast available additional charge, Pool table, Health club, Spa services on site, Complimentary newspapers in lobby, Porter/bellhop, Security guard, Wireless Internet additional charge, Massage - treatment room(s), Swimming pool - outdoor seasonal, Children's club, Accessible bathroom, Dry cleaning/laundry service.

Folsom

Also see the following nearby communities that have pet friendly lodging: Rancho Cordova - 7 miles, Cameron Park - 10 miles, Rocklin - 10 miles

Lake Natoma Inn
702 Gold Lake Dr
Folsom CA 95630
(916) 351-1500
$89 - $249
Bed & Pet Discount Offered

Pet Policy: All pets welcome, $15 per pet per night plus $45 cleaning fee per stay.

Features: Sauna, Business Center, Restaurant(s), Room service (limited hours), Concierge services, Number of rooms: 120, Number of suites: 18, Number of floors: 4, Airport transportation additional charge, Breakfast available additional charge, Smoke-Free property, Swimming pool - outdoor seasonal, Dry cleaning/laundry service, Fitness facilities, Bar/lounge, Free wireless Internet.

★★★♥

Larkspur Landing Folsom
121 Iron Point Rd
Folsom CA 95630
(916) 355-1616
$89 - $179
Bed & Pet Discount Offered

Pet Policy: Pets welcome, $75 per stay.

Features: Free wireless Internet, 24-hour business center, Smoke-Free property, Free Breakfast, Coffee in lobby, Room service (limited hours), Concierge services, Number of rooms: 84, Number of floors: 4, Video library, Grocery, Multilingual staff, Complimentary newspapers in lobby, Use of nearby fitness center (free), Dry cleaning/laundry service.

Not rated
Oakwood at Iron Point
1550 Iron Point Rd
Folsom CA 95630
(916) 985-8949
$124 - $157

Pet Policy: Pets accepted with limitations and additional charge. Contact hotel directly for more information and to make reservations.

Features: Fully furnished apartments, Swimming pool and spa, Business center, Concierge services. Minimum stay of 30 days may be required.

★★★
Residence Inn by Marriott Folsom Sacramento
2555 Iron Point Rd
Folsom CA 95630
(916) 983-7289
$150 - $190
Bed & Pet Discount Offered

Pet Policy: Pets allowed, $100 cleaning fee per stay.

Features: Elevator, Swimming pool - indoor, Wheelchair accessible, Number of suites: 107, Number of floors: 3, Parking (free), Complimentary newspapers in lobby, High speed Internet, Smoke-Free property, Fitness facilities

Not rated
Synergy Willow Springs
250 McAdoo Drive
Folsom CA 95630
(800) 372-2496
$83 - $89

Pet Policy: Dogs or cats up to 25 lbs. $20 per month plus $200 refundable deposit for cats, $400 refundable deposit for dogs. Limit of 1 pet per unit.

Features: Fully furnished apartments including housewares, Heated lap pool, Fitness center, Racquetball court, telephone/answering machine. Minimum stay of 30 days may be required.

Fort Bragg

Also see the following nearby communities that have pet friendly lodging: Mendocino - 7 miles

★★
Americas Best Value Inn Seabird
191 South St.
Fort Bragg CA 95437-5508
(707) 964-4731
$63 - $95

Pet Policy: Small pets only, $10 per night per pet.

Features: Free wireless Internet, Number of rooms: 65, Refrigerator, Coffee maker, Swimming pool and spa indoor.

Atrium - Garden Inn by the Sea
700 N Main St
Fort Bragg CA 95437
(707) 964-9440
$96 - $116
Bed & Pet Discount Offered

Pet Policy: Your well behaved dog is welcome to accompany you for a $35 additional charge per visit. Choose from one of our three pet-friendly rooms: The Quilt, Rendezvous or Garden.

Features: Free breakfast, Number of rooms: 10, Parking (free), Smoke-Free property, Free wireless Internet.

Not rated
Coast Inn and Spa Fort Bragg
18661 North Highway 1
Fort Bragg CA 95437
(707) 964-2852
$69 - $199

Pet Policy: Pets welcome, $10 per night per pet. Limit 2. Must not be left unattended in room.

Features: Outdoor hot tub, BBQ, Outside fireplace, Natural healing center.

Glass Beach Inn
726 N Main St
Fort Bragg CA 95437
(707) 964-6774
$106 - $107
Bed & Pet Discount Offered

Pet Policy: Pets welcome, $25 per pet per night.

Features: Concierge services, Number of rooms: 9, Free breakfast.

Pine Beach Inn
16801 N Highway 1
Fort Bragg CA 95437
(707) 964-5603
$69 - $133
Bed & Pet Discount Offered

Pet Policy: Dogs permitted, $10 per day, only in the Whaler building.

Features: Free breakfast, Free wireless Internet, Accessible bathroom, Bar/lounge, Restaurant, Number of rooms: 50, Business services, Coffee in lobby, Private beach, Smoke-Free, Tennis courts.

★
Super 8 Fort Bragg
Fort Bragg CA 95437
(707) 964-4003
$73 - $95

Pet Policy: Pets accepted, $10 per night additional charge. Limited number of pet rooms so please confirm directly with hotel before arrival.

Features: Free breakfast, Free wireless Internet.

Fortuna

Holiday Inn Express Fortuna
1859 Alamar Way
Fortuna CA 95540
(707) 725-5500
$80 - $116
Bed & Pet Discount Offered

Pet Policy: All pets allowed, $20 per night. Please keep dog on a leash at all times and use designated dog walking area. Pets allowed in downstairs only, not in suites. There are a limited number of pet rooms available.

Features: Accessible bathroom, In-room accessibility equipment for the deaf, Braille or raised signage, Coffee in lobby, Video library, Free breakfast, Multilingual staff, Nearby fitness center (free), Business center, Free wireless Internet, Indoor pool, Bar/lounge, Concierge, Gift shops or newsstand, Number of rooms: 46, Number of suites: 2, Number of floors: 2, Dry cleaning/laundry service.

Fountain Valley

Also see the following nearby communities that have pet friendly lodging: Huntington Beach - 3 miles, Santa Ana - 5 miles, Garden Grove - 5 miles, Costa Mesa - 5 miles, Newport Beach - 8 miles, Orange - 8 miles, Cypress - 8 miles, Anaheim - 8 miles, Seal Beach - 8 miles, Los Alamitos - 9 miles, La Palma - 10 miles, Buena Park - 10 miles

Residence Inn by Marriott Huntington Beach-
9930 Slater Ave
Fountain Valley CA 92708
(714) 965-8000
$159 - $160
Bed & Pet Discount Offered

Pet Policy: Pets allowed, $100 cleaning fee per stay

Features: Swimming pool - outdoor, Number of rooms: 122, Number of floors: 2, Business services, Barbecue grill(s), Coffee in lobby, Free breakfast, Parking (free), Complimentary newspapers in lobby, Free wireless Internet, Smoke-Free property, Grocery/convenience store, Dry cleaning/laundry service, Fitness facilities.

Fowler

Also see the following nearby communities that have pet friendly lodging: Selma - 4 miles

La Quinta Inn & Suites Fowler
190 N 10th St
Fowler CA 93625
(559) 834-6300
$79 - $89
Bed & Pet Discount Offered

Pet Policy: Pets under 25 lbs allowed, $100 additional charge per stay.

Features: Fitness facilities, Swimming pool - outdoor, Wheelchair accessible, Number of rooms: 70, Number of suites: 26, Number of floors: 3, Coffee in lobby, Free breakfast, Parking (free), Multilingual staff, Complimentary newspapers. Smoke-Free property, Free wireless Internet, Accessible bathroom, In-room accessibility equipment for the deaf, Braille or raised signage, Business center.

Freedom

Also see the following nearby communities that have pet friendly lodging: Watsonville - 2 miles

Comfort Inn Watsonville
112 Airport Blvd
Freedom CA 95019
(831) 728-2300
$80 - $109
Bed & Pet Discount Offered

Pet Policy: Dogs only, $15 per day. Must be at least 1 year old. Our pet friendly hotel offers comfortable accommodations and convenient central location near the top dog friendly beaches and parks, fun area attractions and exciting outdoor activities in the Monterey and Santa Cruz areas.

Features: Elevator, Coffee in lobby, Free breakfast, Coffee shop or cafe, Parking (free), Multilingual staff, Wireless Internet, Number of rooms: 41, Number of floors: 3, Business center.

Fremont

Also see the following nearby communities that have pet friendly lodging: Newark - 2 miles, Union City - 6 miles, Milpitas - 8 miles, Santa Clara - 9 miles, Hayward - 10 miles

★★★
Best Western Garden Court Inn
5400 Mowry Ave
Fremont CA 94538
(510) 792-4300
$69 - $129
Bed & Pet Discount Offered

Pet Policy: Pets under 20 lbs, $15 per pet per night.

Features: Free Breakfast, Elevator, Swimming pool - outdoor, Room service (limited hours), Number of rooms: 125, Number of floors: 3, Coffee in lobby, Parking (free), Complimentary newspapers in lobby, Security guard, Free wireless Internet, Accessible bathroom, Accessibility equipment for the deaf, Braille or raised signage.

★★½
Comfort Inn
47031 Kato Road
Fremont CA 94538
(510) 490-2900
$60 - $89
Bed & Pet Discount Offered

Pet Policy: Pet Accommodation: $25.00 per night., Limit of 2 pets, per room, 40 lbs. and under. If booking directly online, please advise hotel of accompanying pets in our Special Request Section or call us directly for reservations.

Features: Swimming pool - outdoor, Elevator, Number of rooms: 114, Number of suites: 8, Number of floors: 3, Coffee in lobby, Free breakfast, Parking (free), Multilingual staff, Complimentary newspapers in lobby, Business center, Free wireless Internet, Accessible bathroom, In-room accessibility equipment for the deaf, Braille or raised signage, Dry cleaning/laundry service, Fitness facilities.

★★
Days Inn Fremont/Milpitas
46101 Warm Springs Blvd
Fremont CA 94539
(510) 656-2800
$43 - $124
Bed & Pet Discount Offered

Pet Policy: Pets allowed but additional charge not disclosed. Please contact hotel before booking.

Features: Parking (free), Coffee in lobby, Free breakfast, Elevator, Number of rooms: 49, Number of floors: 3, Complimentary newspapers in lobby, Business center, Free wireless Internet.

★★
Extended Stay America Fremont - Newark
5355 Farwell Pl
Fremont CA 94536
(510) 794-8040
$54 - $79
Bed & Pet Discount Offered

Pet Policy: One pet is allowed in each guest room. A $25 per day non-refundable cleaning fee (not to exceed $150) will be charged the first night of your stay. Weight, size and breed restrictions may apply. Please contact the hotel directly with inquiries. Please Note: "Signature" rooms do not currently accommodate pets.

Features: Elevator, Number of rooms: 119, Number of floors: 3, Business services, Internet - additional charge, Front desk (limited hours).

Extended Stay America Fremont - Warm Springs
46312 Mission Blvd
Fremont CA 94539
(510) 979-1222
$57- $87
Bed & Pet Discount Offered

Pet Policy: One pet is allowed in each guest room. A $25 per day non-refundable cleaning fee (not to exceed $150) will be charged the first night of your stay.

Features: Guest laundry, Elevator, Number of rooms: 101, Number of floors: 4, Internet - additional charge, Parking (free), Front desk (limited hours).

Extended Stay Deluxe Fremont - Newark
5375 Farwell Pl
Fremont CA 94536
(510) 794-9693
$79 - $84
Bed & Pet Discount Offered

Pet Policy: One small pet is allowed in each guest room. A $25 per day non-refundable cleaning fee (not to exceed $150) will be charged the first night.

Features: Guest laundry, Swimming pool - outdoor, Number of rooms: 81, Number of floors: 3, Internet - additional charge, Free breakfast, Parking (free), Front desk (limited hours), Fitness facilities.

Homestead Fremont -
46080 Fremont Blvd
Fremont CA 94538
(510) 353-1664
$61 - $81
Bed & Pet Discount Offered

Pet Policy: Pets allowed, no size restriction, $25 per day to a maximum of $150 per stay. Limit of 1 pet per room.

Features: Guest laundry, Elevator, Number of rooms: 128, Number of floors: 3, Barbecue grill(s), Internet - additional charge, Parking (free), Multilingual staff, Nearby fitness center (discount), Business services.

La Quinta Inn and Suites Fremont
46200 Landing Pkwy
Fremont CA 94538
(510) 445-0808
$55 - $99
Bed & Pet Discount Offered

Pet Policy: Cats and dogs up to 50 pounds are accepted in all guest rooms. Housekeeping services for rooms with pets require pet owner be present or pet must be crated. No additional charges or deposits are required.

Features: Accessible bathroom, Outdoor pool, Concierge, Number of rooms: 144, Number of floors: 5, Video library, Health club, Multilingual staff, Complimentary newspapers, Wireless Internet, Dry cleaning/laundry, Free breakfast.

Residence Inn by Marriott Fremont Silicon Valley
5400 Farwell Pl
Fremont CA 94536
(510) 794-5900
$99 - $129
Bed & Pet Discount Offered

Pet Policy: Pets allowed, $100 cleaning fee per stay.

Features: Swimming pool - outdoor, Business services, Free breakfast, Number of rooms: 80, Number of floors: 2, Barbecue grill(s), Coffee in lobby, Multilingual staff, Complimentary newspapers in lobby, Free wireless Internet, Smoke-Free property, Dry cleaning/laundry, Fitness facilities.

Fresno

Also see the following nearby communities that have pet friendly lodging: Clovis - 8 miles

Ambassador Inn and Suites
1804 W Olive Ave
Fresno CA 93728
(559) 442-1082
$59 - $99
Bed & Pet Discount Offered

Pet Policy: Pets under 20 lbs allowed with nightly additional charge.

Features: Swimming pool - outdoor, Guest laundry, Number of rooms: 54, Number of floors: 2, Pool table, Business center, Free wireless Internet.

Americas Best Value Water Tree Inn
4141 N Blackstone Ave
Fresno CA 93726
(559) 222-4445
$64 - $84
Bed & Pet Discount Offered

Pet Policy: Pets welcome. $75 cleaning fee per stay.

Features: Free wireless Internet, Restaurant, Outdoor pool, Number of rooms: 134, Number of floors: 2, Business services, Coffee in lobby, Free breakfast, Parking (free), Multilingual staff, Complimentary newspapers in lobby, Porter/bellhop.

Best Western Plus Village Inn
3110 N Blackstone Ave
Fresno CA 93703
(559) 226-2110
$80 - $92
Bed & Pet Discount Offered

Pet Policy: Pets accepted with prior approval. Contact hotel directly

Features: Multilingual staff, Smoke-Free property, Free wireless Internet, Business services, Outdoor pool, Number of rooms: 151, Number of floors: 2, Free breakfast, Complimentary newspapers in lobby.

Crossland Fresno-West
3460 W Shaw Ave
Fresno CA 93711
(559) 277-8700
$39 - $54
Bed & Pet Discount Offered

Pet Policy: One pet is allowed in each guest room. A $25 per day non-refundable cleaning fee (not to exceed $150) will be charged the first night of your stay. Weight, size and breed restrictions may apply.

Features: Guest laundry, Elevator, Number of rooms: 129, Number of floors: 3, Suitable for children, Parking (free), Front desk (limited hours), Wireless Internet.

Days Inn Fresno CA
4061 N Blackstone Ave
Fwy 41 Ashlan Ave
Fresno CA 93726
(559) 222-5641
$47 - $65
Bed & Pet Discount Offered

Pet Policy: Small pets allowed, $20 per night.

Features: Coffee in lobby, Free breakfast, Parking (free), Complimentary newspapers in lobby, Business center, Wireless Internet, Swimming pool - outdoor seasonal.

Days Inn Fresno South
2640 S 2nd St
Fresno CA 93706
(559) 237-6644
$51 - $84
Bed & Pet Discount Offered

Pet Policy: Small Pets Allowed $20 per pet per night. Based on availability and prior reservations.

Features: Free breakfast, Parking (free), Complimentary newspapers in lobby, Business center, Free internet, Swimming pool - outdoor seasonal

Econo Lodge Fresno
6309 N Blackstone Ave
Fresno CA 93710
(559) 439-0320
$59 - $69
Bed & Pet Discount Offered

Pet Policy: Dogs under 30 lbs accepted, $30 per stay per pet. Limit of 2 per room.

Features: Coffee in lobby, Business services, Guest laundry, Free breakfast, Number of rooms: 35, Number of floors: 1, Parking (free), Swimming pool - outdoor seasonal.

Econo Lodge Fresno
445 N Parkway Dr
Fresno CA 93706
(559) 485-5019
$49- $54
Bed & Pet Discount Offered

Pet Policy: Dogs up to 30 lbs, $30 each per stay. Limit of 2 per room

Features: Free wireless Internet, Swimming pool - outdoor, Wheelchair accessible, Gift shops or newsstand, Number of rooms: 60, Number of floors: 2, Business services, Coffee in lobby, Free breakfast, Self-parking

Extended Stay America Fresno - North
7135 N Fresno St
Fresno CA 93720
(559) 438-7105
$64 - $79
Bed & Pet Discount Offered

Pet Policy: One pet is allowed in each guest room. A $25 per day non-refundable cleaning fee (not to exceed $150) will be charged the first night of your stay. Please Note: "Signature" rooms do not currently accommodate pets, with the exception of handicap accessible rooms.

Features: Room service (limited hours), Number of rooms: 120, Number of floors: 3, Business services, Suitable for children, Internet - additional charge, Parking (free), Multilingual staff, 24-hour front desk.

La Quinta Inn & Suites Fresno North West
5077 N Cornelia Ave
Fresno CA 93722
(559) 275-3700
$84 - $100
Bed & Pet Discount Offered

Pet Policy: Pets accepted no extra charge

Features: Accessible bathroom, Fitness facilities, Number of rooms: 72, Number of suites: 22, Number of floors: 3, Free breakfast, Currency exchange, Parking (free), Complimentary newspapers in lobby, Business center, Internet (free), Swimming pool – outdoor.

La Quinta Inn & Suites Fresno Riverpark
330 E Fir Avenue
Fresno CA 93720
(559) 449-0928
$102 - $132
Bed & Pet Discount Offered

Pet Policy: Cats and dogs up to 50 pounds are accepted in all guest rooms. Housekeeping services for rooms with pets require pet owner be present or pet must be crated. No additional charges or deposits are required.

Features: Outdoor pool, Free breakfast, Business center, Accessible bathroom, Number of rooms: 56, Number of floors: 4, Nearby fitness center (free), Free wireless Internet, Smoke-Free, Guest laundry.

La Quinta Inn Fresno/Yosemite
2926 Tulare St
Fresno CA 93721
(559) 442-1110
$52 - $85
Bed & Pet Discount Offered

Pet Policy: Cats and dogs up to 50 pounds are accepted in all guest rooms. Housekeeping services for rooms with pets require pet owner be present or pet must be crated. No additional charges or deposits are required.

Features: Outdoor pool, Accessible bathroom, Number of rooms: 130, Business services, Coffee in lobby, Free breakfast, Health club, Multilingual staff, Free wireless Internet, Dry cleaning/laundry service.

La Quinta Inn & Suites Fresno North
5079 N Cornelia Drive
Fresno CA 93722
(559) 275-3700
$67 - $109

Pet Policy: Pets any size allowed, no additional charge. Must not leave unattended and must clean up after.

Features: Number of rooms:72, number of floors: 3, Free wireless Internet, Free breakfast, Free newspaper, Business center, Fitness center, Guest laundry.

★★

Motel 6 Shaw Ave & Hwy 99
5021 N Barcus Ave
Fresno CA 93722
(559) 276-1910
$55- $64
Bed & Pet Discount Offered

Pet Policy: Well-behaved pets stay Free. Animals that pose a health or safety risk may not remain onsite, and include those that, in our manager's discretion, are too numerous for any one room, cause damage to our property or that of other guests, are too disruptive, are not properly attended, or demonstrate undue aggression. All pets must be declared at check-in. Pets must be attended to and under control at all times. If unavoidable circumstances require a pet to remain in a room while the owner is offsite, the pet must be secured in a crate or travel carrier. Pets must be on a leash or securely carried outside of guest rooms

Features: Coffee in lobby, Number of rooms: 86, Number of floors: 2, Swimming pool - outdoor seasonal.

Park Lawn Hotel
3093 N Parkway Drive Fresno
Fresno CA 93722
(559) 276-7745
$55 - $60
Bed & Pet Discount Offered

Pet Policy: Pets accepted. Please contact hotel directly for pet policy details.

Business services, Coffee in lobby, Internet - additional charge, Multilingual staff, Complimentary newspapers in lobby, Swimming pool - outdoor seasonal.

Quality Inn Fresno
4278 W Ashlan Ave
Fresno CA 93722
(559) 275-2727
$75 - $83
Bed & Pet Discount Offered

Pet Policy: Pets up to 30 lbs allowed, $30 per stay, limit of 2. May not be left unattended in room.

Features: Security guard, Bar/lounge, Elevator, Restaurant(s), Concierge services, Gift shops or newsstand, Business services, Coffee in lobby, Breakfast available additional charge, Pool table on site, Parking (free), Multilingual staff, Complimentary newspapers in lobby, Porter/bellhop, Swimming pool - outdoor seasonal, Dry cleaning/laundry service, Number of rooms: 122.

Ramada Fresno
5046 N Barcus Avenue
Fresno CA 93722
(559) 277-5700
$99 - $129
Bed & Pet Discount Offered

Pet Policy: Pet friendly, $20 per stay.

Features: Smoke-Free property, Swimming pool - outdoor, Wheelchair accessible, Cell phone/mobile rental, Business services, Coffee in lobby,

Multilingual staff, Elevator, Fitness facilities, Free breakfast, Parking (free), Complimentary newspapers in lobby, Dry cleaning/laundry service, Free wireless Internet.

Residence Inn By Marriott Fresno
5322 N Diana St
Fresno CA 93710
(559) 222-8900
$135 - $189
Bed & Pet Discount Offered

Pet Policy: Dogs accepted, $75 per stay. Limit of 2.

Features: Swimming pool - outdoor, Free Breakfast, Elevator, Number of rooms: 120, Number of floors: 3, Business services, Barbecue grill(s), Coffee in lobby, Parking (free), Complimentary newspapers in lobby, Dry cleaning/laundry service, Tennis on site, Fitness facilities.

Rodeway Inn Fresno
959 N Parkway Dr
Fresno CA 93728
(559) 445-0322
$44 - $79
Bed & Pet Discount Offered

Pet Policy: Rodeway Inns charge an additional $10 per night per pet and require a $50 damage deposit, which is refunded if the room is in order at check out. Max of 2 pets per room. A veterinarian certificate that the pet is on a flea and parasite program is required. ***Continued on next page***

Rodeway Inn Fresno
Continued from previous page

Pets may not be left alone in the room unless in a cage.

Features: Number of rooms: 67, Number of floors: 2, Guest laundry, Free breakfast, Free wireless Internet.

★★
Rodeway Inn Fresno
6730 N Blackstone Ave
Fresno CA 93710
(559) 431-3557
$69 - $89
Bed & Pet Discount Offered

Pet Policy: Rodeway Inns charge an additional $10 per night per pet and require a $50 damage deposit, which is refunded if the room is in order at check out. Max of 2 pets per room. A veterinarian certificate that the pet is on a flea and parasite program and that they are Free from parasites is required. Pets may not be left alone in the room unless in a cage.

Features: Business services, Free breakfast, Elevator, Number of rooms: 133, Number of floors: 3, Guest laundry, Parking (free), Multilingual staff, Free wireless Internet, Swimming pool - outdoor seasonal.

★★
San Joaquin Hotel
1309 W Shaw Ave
Fresno CA 93711
(559) 225-1309
$75 - $145
Bed & Pet Discount Offered

Pet Policy: Pets accepted, $50 per pet per stay.

Features: Swimming pool - outdoor, Free breakfast, Business center, Elevator, Number of rooms: 69, Number of floors: 3, Coffee in lobby, Parking (free), Suitable for children, Designated smoking areas, Braille or raised signage, Dry cleaning/laundry service, Free wireless Internet, Fitness facilities.

★★
Super 8 Fresno Convention Center Area
2127 Inyo St
Fresno CA 93721
(559) 268-0621
$59 - $119
Bed & Pet Discount Offered

Pet Policy: Allows dogs up go $30 lbs, $15 per night per pet. Limit of 2.

Features: Free breakfast, Business center, Free wireless Internet, Parking (free), Swimming pool - outdoor seasonal.

Super 8 Fresno North
6051 North Thesta Ave
Fresno CA 93710
(559) 435-6593
$68 - $69

Pet Policy: Up to 2 well-behaved pets accepted, $10 per night per pet. Pets may not be left in room unattended.

Features: Free breakfast, Parking (free), Swimming pool - outdoor seasonal, Number of floors: 2.

Super 8 Motel - Fresno Hwy 99
1087 N Parkway Dr
Fresno CA 93728
(559) 268-0741
$40 - $60
Bed & Pet Discount Offered

Pet Policy: Pets allowed, $10 per pet per night.

Features: Free breakfast, Business services, Parking (free), Swimming pool - outdoor seasonal.

TownePlace by Marriott Suites
7127 N Fresno St
Fresno CA 93720
(559) 435-4600
$99 - $100
Bed & Pet Discount Offered

Pet Policy: Pets accepted, $100 cleaning fee per stay.

Features: Business services, Barbecue grill(s), Coffee in lobby, Swimming pool - outdoor, Number of rooms: 92, Number of floors: 3, Free breakfast, Grocery, Dry cleaning/laundry service, Fitness facilities.

University Inn
2655 E Shaw Ave
Fresno CA 93710
(559) 294-0224
$79 - $80
Bed & Pet Discount Offered

Pet Policy: Pet friendly. No additional charge or size limit.

Features: Number of floors: 2, Swimming pool - outdoor, Free breakfast, Room service.

Vagabond Inn Fresno
2570 S East Ave
Fresno CA 93706
(559) 486-1188
$59 - $69
Bed & Pet Discount Offered

Pet Policy: Allows dogs any size, $10 per night.

Features: Free Breakfast, Restaurant(s), Number of rooms: 121, Number of floors: 2, Coffee in lobby, Parking (free), Multilingual staff, Free wireless Internet, Swimming pool - outdoor seasonal.

Fullerton

Also see the following nearby communities that have pet friendly lodging: Brea - 3 miles, Placentia - 4 miles, Anaheim - 4 miles, La Mirada - 5 miles, Buena Park - 5 miles, La Palma - 7 miles, Cerritos - 7 miles, Cypress - 7 miles, Orange - 7 miles, Whittier - 8 miles, Garden Grove - 8 miles, Yorba Linda - 9 miles, Hawaiian Gardens - 9 miles, Norwalk - 9 miles, City Of Industry - 9 miles, Walnut - 9 miles, Los Alamitos - 9 miles

Marriott Fullerton - By California State University
2701 Nutwood Ave
Fullerton CA 92831
(714) 738-7800
$89 - $183
Bed & Pet Discount Offered

Pet Policy: Pets accepted with $100 additional charge plus $100 refundable deposit.

Features: Outdoor pool, Sauna, Number of rooms: 224, Number of floors: 6, Accessible bathroom, Accessibility equipment for the deaf, Smoke-Free property, Bar/lounge, Restaurant(s), ATM/banking, Gift shop, Complimentary newspapers, Room service, Business center, Free wireless Internet, Parking garage, Dry cleaning/laundry service, Fitness facilities.

Garden Grove

Also see the following nearby communities that have pet friendly lodging: Anaheim - 4 miles, Orange - 4 miles, Santa Ana - 4 miles, Fountain Valley - 5 miles, Cypress - 6 miles, Huntington Beach - 7 miles, Buena Park - 7 miles, La Palma - 7 miles, Los Alamitos - 8 miles, Fullerton - 8 miles, Placentia - 8 miles, Costa Mesa - 8 miles, Hawaiian Gardens - 9 miles, Seal Beach - 10 miles, Cerritos - 10 miles, La Mirada - 10 miles

★★★½

Anaheim Marriott Suites
12015 Harbor Blvd
Garden Grove CA 92840
(714) 750-1000
$129 - $199
Bed & Pet Discount Offered

Pet Policy: Pets allowed - $35 cleaning fee.

Features: Business center, Swimming pool - outdoor, Multilingual staff, Porter/bellhop, Wireless Internet additional charge, Bar/lounge, Elevator, Restaurant(s), ATM/banking, Gift shops or newsstand, Number of rooms: 371, Number of floors: 14, Breakfast available (additional charge), Arcade/game room, Parking (valet) $18/Day, Accessible bathroom, In-room accessibility equipment for the deaf, Braille or raised signage, Dry cleaning/laundry service, Room service, Fitness facilities, Smoke-Free.

★★

Candlewood Suites North Orange County
12901 Garden Grove Blvd
Garden Grove CA 92843
(714) 539-4200
$64 - $126
Bed & Pet Discount Offered

Pet Policy: Pets allowed with a nonrefundable additional charge of $15 for the first night and $10 for each additional night up to a $150. Weight limit is 80 lbs. Pet agreement must be signed at check-in. Vaccination record may be required.

Features: Business services, Fitness facilities, Accessible bathroom, In-room accessibility for the deaf, Braille or raised signage, Gift shops or newsstand, Number of rooms: 133, Number of suites: 133, Number of floors: 4, Airport transportation additional charge, Parking (free), Multilingual staff, Free Internet access, Dry cleaning/laundry service

★★★

Homewood Suites by Hilton Anaheim Resort
12005 Harbor Blvd
Garden Grove CA 92840
(714) 740-1800
$109 - $259
Bed & Pet Discount Offered

Pet Policy: Pets up to 75 lbs accepted, $50 pet stay, limit of 2 pets per room. Pets may not be left unattended in the hotel room. Pets are not allowed in any food service area. Pets must be kept on a leash in public areas and you must clean up after your pet. Cell phone # must be provided at check in.

Features: Swimming pool - outdoor, Gift shops or newsstand, Number of rooms: 166, Number of floors: 7, Suitable for children, Free breakfast, Grocery, Business center, Security guard, Dry cleaning/laundry service, Fitness facilities, Parking fee.

Residence Inn By Marriott Anaheim Resort Area
11931 Harbor Blvd
Garden Grove CA 92840
(714) 591-4000
$188 - $289
Bed & Pet Discount Offered

Pet Policy: Pets allowed, $100 per stay.

Features: Elevator, Parking fee, Swimming pool - outdoor, Business Center, Children's swimming pool, Airport transportation additional charge, ATM/banking, Concierge services, Gift shops or newsstand, Number of rooms: 200, Number of floors: 8, Barbecue grill(s), Arcade/game room, Free breakfast, Multilingual staff, Security guard, Limo or Town Car service available, Free wireless Internet, Accessible bathroom, In-room accessibility equipment for the deaf, Braille or raised signage, Dry cleaning/laundry service, Fitness facilities.

★★★½

Sheraton Garden Grove-Anaheim South
12221 Harbor Blvd
Garden Grove CA 92840
(714) 703-8400
$109- $149
Bed & Pet Discount Offered

Pet Policy: One dog up to 60 pounds is allowed per room. A cleaning charge of $150 per room per stay will apply. Pets are not allowed in the public areas. Pets must be accompanied by owner at all times on a leash or in a crate. Pets cannot be left unattended in the guest room, unless pet is crated. Guests must sign a waiver regarding the pet regulations at check-in. No other pets, including cats, are allowed.

Features: Room service (limited hours), Bar/lounge, Business center, Currency exchange, Restaurant(s), Gift shops or newsstand, Number of rooms: 285, Number of floors: 7, Breakfast available additional charge, Multilingual staff, Complimentary newspapers in lobby, Security guard, Wireless Internet, Concierge desk, Smoke-Free property, Swimming pool - outdoor seasonal, Parking fee $12 Per Night, Dry cleaning/laundry service, Fitness facilities.

Gardena

Also see the following nearby communities that have pet friendly lodging: Carson - 4 miles, Hawthorne - 4 miles, Torrance - 4 miles, Redondo Beach - 5 miles, Hermosa Beach - 5 miles, Manhattan Beach - 6 miles, El Segundo - 6 miles, Inglewood - 6 miles, Harbor City - 6 miles, Huntington Park - 8 miles, Los Angeles - 9 miles

★★

Carson Plaza Hotel
111 W Albertoni Street
Gardena CA 90248
(310) 329-0651
$63- $94
Bed & Pet Discount Offered

Pet Policy: Pets allowed, $5 per night per pet plus $50 deposit.

Features: Fitness facilities, Swimming pool - outdoor, Concierge services, Number of rooms: 60, Number of floors: 3, Business services, Free breakfast, Parking (free), Complimentary newspapers in lobby, Free wireless Internet, Accessible bathroom.

Extended Stay America Economy Los Angeles - South
18602 S Vermont Ave
Gardena CA 90248
(310) 515-5139
$56 - $81
Bed & Pet Discount Offered

Pet Policy: One pet is allowed in each guest room. A $25 per day non-refundable cleaning fee (not to exceed $150) will be charged the first night of your stay. Weight, size and breed restrictions may apply. Please contact the hotel directly with inquiries. Please Note: "Signature" rooms do not currently accommodate pets, with the exception of handicap accessible rooms.

Features: Guest laundry, Number of rooms: 137, Number of floors: 3, Internet (additional charge), Front desk (limited hours), Security guard.

★★

Rodeway Inn Gardena
15607 S Normandie Ave
Gardena CA 90247
(310) 516-8701
$79 - $95
Bed & Pet Discount Offered

Pet Policy: Rodeway Inns charge an additional $10 per night per pet and require a $50 damage deposit, which is refunded if the room is in order at check out. Max of 2 pets per room. A veterinarian certificate that the pet is on a flea and parasite program is required. Pets may not be left alone in the room unless in a cage.

Features: Free breakfast, Outdoor pool, Dry cleaning/laundry service. Free Internet, Number of rooms: 50.

Geyserville

Also see the following nearby communities that have pet friendly lodging: Healdsburg - 6 miles, Cloverdale - 8 miles

Geyserville Inn
21714 Geyserville Ave
Geyserville CA 95441
(707) 857-4343
$78- $105
Bed & Pet Discount Offered

Pet Policy: Pets allowed, $20 per pet per night.

Features: Outdoor pool, Accessible bathroom, Braille or raised signage, Concierge, Number of rooms: 41, Number of suites: 5, Number of floors: 2, Coffee in lobby, Breakfast available additional charge, Coffee shop or cafe, Multilingual staff, Complimentary newspapers, Free wireless Internet, Smoke-Free.

Gilroy

Also see the following nearby communities that have pet friendly lodging: San Martin - 5 miles

Quality Inn And Suites Gilroy
8430 Murray Ave
Gilroy CA 95020
(408) 847-5500
$79 - $89
Bed & Pet Discount Offered

Pet Policy: Pets allowed, $10 per pet per night. Limit 2 per room.

Features: Swimming pool - outdoor, Free breakfast, Restaurant(s), Number of rooms: 47, Number of floors: 2, Business services, Coffee in lobby, Guest laundry, Wireless Internet, Restaurant.

Glendale

Also see the following nearby communities that have pet friendly lodging: Hollywood - 4 miles, Burbank - 4 miles, Universal City - 5 miles, South Pasadena - 7 miles, West Hollywood - 7 miles, Studio City - 7 miles, Pasadena - 9 miles, Beverly Hills - 9 miles, Monterey Park - 10 miles

Days Inn Glendale
600 N Pacific Ave
Glendale CA 91203
(818) 956-0202
$75 - $93
Bed & Pet Discount Offered

Pet Policy: Pets are allowed, Cats & Dogs only up to 50 lbs, must be supervised at all times, owner must be present during housekeeping services, only in smoking rooms, $50 refundable deposit per pet per room.

Features: Swimming pool - outdoor, Restaurant(s), Free wireless Internet, Bar/lounge, Elevator, ATM/banking, Business services, Coffee in lobby, Parking (free), Multilingual staff, Complimentary newspapers in lobby, Dry cleaning/laundry service.

Hilton Los Angeles North/Glendale
100 W Glenoaks Blvd
Glendale CA 91202
(818) 956-5466
$109 - $199
Bed & Pet Discount Offered

Pet Policy: Pets up to 75 lbs accepted, $75 per stay additional charge. Limit 2 pets per room.

Features: ATM/Banking, Elevator, Sauna, Parking garage additional charge, Airport transportation (free), Room service (24 hours), Bar/lounge, Security guard, Health club, Restaurant(s), Swimming pool - outdoor, Gift shops or newsstand, Number of rooms: 351, Number of floors: 19, Breakfast available additional charge, Multilingual staff, Complimentary newspapers in lobby, Porter/bellhop, Wireless Internet additional charge, Concierge desk, Technology helpdesk, Accessible bathroom, In-room accessibility equipment for the deaf, Braille or raised signage, Dry cleaning/laundry service, 24-hour business center, On-site car rental.

Homestead Los Angeles - Glendale
1377 West Glenoaks Blvd
Glendale CA 91206
(818) 956-6665
$76 - $116
Bed & Pet Discount Offered

Pet Policy: Pets allowed, no size restriction, $25 per day to a maximum of $150 per stay. Limit of 1 pet per room.

Features: Guest laundry, Nearby fitness center (discount), Elevator, Number of rooms: 86, Number of floors: 3, Coffee in lobby, Parking (free), Multilingual staff, Front desk (limited hours), Wireless Internet.

Rodeway Inn Regalodge
2oo West Colorado Street
Glendale CA 91204
(818) 246-7331
$62 - $90

Pet Policy: Rodeway Inns charge an additional $10 per night per pet and require a $50 damage deposit, which is refunded if the room is in order at check out. Max of 2 pets per room. A veterinarian certificate that the pet is on a flea and parasite program is required. Pets may not be left alone in the room unless in a cage.

Features: Wireless Internet, Swimming pool – outdoor, Coffee in lobby, HBO.

★★

Vagabond Inn Glendale
120 W Colorado St
Glendale CA 91204
(818) 240-1700
$79 - $104
Bed & Pet Discount Offered

Pet Policy: Pets accepted in designated pet friendly rooms, $10 per pet per night.

Features: Free Breakfast, Outdoor pool, Business services, Number of rooms: 52, Coffee in lobby, Multilingual staff, Complimentary newspapers.

Glendora

Also see the following nearby communities that have pet friendly lodging: San Dimas - 4 miles, Pomona - 6 miles, Claremont - 8 miles, Monrovia - 8 miles, Walnut - 8 miles, Diamond Bar - 9 miles, City Of Industry - 9 miles

Garden Inn and Suites Glendora
606 W Route 66
Glendora CA 91740
(626) 963-9361
$89 - $1,000
Bed & Pet Discount Offered

Pet Policy: One pet per room accepted with a $25 additional charge per night in select rooms only.

Features: Business services, Guest laundry, Complimentary newspapers in lobby, Number of rooms: 38, Coffee in lobby, Free breakfast, Front desk (limited hours), Nearby fitness center (discount), Free wireless Internet.

Goleta

Bacara Resort & Spa
8301 Hollister Ave
Goleta CA 93117
(805) 968-0100
$289 - $1,900
Bed & Pet Discount Offered

Pet Policy: Pets accepted. $150 per pet per stay.

Features: Bar/lounge, Babysitting or child care, Fitness facilities, 3 Swimming pools - outdoor heated, Wheelchair accessible, Supervised child care/activities, ATM/banking, Gift shops or newsstand, Shopping on site, Number of rooms: 360, Number of suites: 49, Cell phone/mobile rental, Translation services, Computer rental, Coffee in lobby, Arcade/game room, Pool table, Poolside bar, Currency exchange, Health club, Room service (24 hours), Multilingual staff, Complimentary newspapers in lobby, ***Continued on next page***

Bacara Resort & Spa
Continued from previous page

Porter/bellhop, Security guard, Dry cleaning/laundry service, Beauty services, Concierge desk, Full-service health spa, Massage - spa treatment room(s), Steam room, Sauna, Smoke-Free property, Technology helpdesk, Children's club, On-site medical assistance available, Free wireless Internet, Accessible bathroom, In-room accessibility equipment for the deaf, Braille or raised signage, 3 Restaurants, 24-hour business center, Free reception, Golf course on site, Tennis on site, Valet Parking fee.

Grass Valley

Also see the following nearby communities that have pet friendly lodging: Nevada City - 8 miles

Best Western Gold Country Inn
11972 Sutton Way
Grass Valley CA 95945
(530) 273-1393
$79 - $94
Bed & Pet Discount Offered

Pet Policy: Pets Allowed Based On The Availability Of Pet Friendly Rooms. Up To 2 Dogs Per Room With An 80 Pound Weight Limit. Additional Pet Types Cats, Birds, Etc. May Be Accepted At The Hotel's Discretion. Pet Rate Is $20 Per Day With A $100 Per Week Maximum. A Refundable Cleaning And Damage Deposit Of $50 Is Required Upon Check-in. If Damage Occurs Or Excessive Cleaning Is Needed, The Deposit Can Become Non-refundable And The Hotel May Charge Additionally To Cover The Costs Of Repair-cleaning.property.

Features: Barbecue grill(s), Beach/pool umbrellas, Guest laundry, Business center, Free breakfast, Parking (free), Swimming pool - outdoor seasonal, Free wireless Internet, Fitness facilities, Accessible bathroom.

Best Western Gold Country Inn
972 Sutton Way
Grass Valley CA 95945
(530) 273-1393
$94 - $129

Pet Policy: Small pets only. $20 additional charge.

Features: Number of rooms: 84, Number of floors: 2, Swimming pool – outdoor, Free wireless Internet, Business center, Fitness Center, Free breakfast, Coffee in lobby, Complimentary newspaper.

Coach N' Four Motel
628 S Auburn St
Grass Valley CA 95945
(530) 273-8009
$52 - $70
Bed & Pet Discount Offered

Pet Policy: Pet friendly.

Features: Parking (free), Free wireless Internet, Number of rooms: 17, Free breakfast, Front desk (limited hours.

Golden Chain Resort Motel
13413 State Highway 49
Grass Valley CA 95949
(530) 273-7279
$52 - $79
Bed & Pet Discount Offered

Pet Policy: Up to two pets are welcome for an additional $10 per stay per pet. There is no size restriction.

Features: Barbecue grill(s), Swimming pool - outdoor seasonal, RV and truck parking.

Holiday Inn Express Hotel & Stes Gold Miners Inn-G
121 Bank Street
Grass Valley CA 95945
(530) 477-1700
$109 - $149
Bed & Pet Discount Offered

Pet Policy: Pets accepted, $50 per stay. No charge for service animals.

Features: Accessible bathroom, Accessibility equipment for the deaf Braille or raised signage, Number of rooms: 80, Number of floors: 2, Free breakfast, Multilingual staff, Front desk (limited hours), Business center, Free wireless Internet, Nearby fitness center (discount), Dry cleaning/laundry service.

Not rated
Holiday Lodge Grass Valley
1221 East Main Street
Grass Valley CA 95945
(530) 273-4406
$99 - $100

Pet Policy: Up to two pets are allowed for an additional charge of $25 per stay per pet. The pet owner should clean up any mess.

Features: Swimming pool – outdoor seasonal, Free continental breakfast, Fitness equipment, Free wireless Internet.

Not rated
Sierra Mountain Inn
816 West Main Street
Grass Valley CA 95945
(800) 377-8133
$99 - $159

Pet Policy: Dog friendly, $25 or $35 per night additional charge, depending on room selected. Poofy pooch pads and food & water bowls are included.

Features: Non-smoking property, Free wireless Internet, Coffee maker, Kitchenettes in some room.

Stagecoach Motel
405 S Auburn St
Grass Valley CA 95945
(530) 272-3701
$49 - $50
Bed & Pet Discount Offered

Pet Policy: Small and medium size pets welcome, $10 per night. No limit to number of pets.

Features: Number of rooms: 16, Free breakfast, Front desk (limited hours).

Groveland

★★

Americas Best Value Inn
7633 Highway 120 Buck Meadows
Groveland CA 95321
(209) 962-5281
$89 - $110

Pet Policy: Pets allowed, $15 per night per pet.

Features: Free wireless Internet, HBO, Coffee maker, Hair dryer, Iron & ironing board, Microwave and refrigerator in some rooms.

Hotel Charlotte B&B
18736 Main Street
Groveland CA 95321
(209) 962-6455
$159 - $339
Bed & Pet Discount Offered

Pet Policy: Pets under 25 lbs, $25 per stay additional charge. Only one pet friendly room so book in advance.

Features: Free Breakfast, Suitable for children, Bar/lounge, Restaurant(s), Number of rooms: 10, Number of floors: 2, Free wireless Internet, Smoke-Free property.

The Groveland Hotel at Yosemite National
18767 Main Street
Groveland CA 95321
(209) 962-4000
$145 - $285
Bed & Pet Discount Offered

Pet Policy: Pets welcome, $15 per pet per night. To ensure your pet is well fed and properly pampered, we provide a comfy granny quilt for napping and a good night's sleep, a two-bowl pet dish and a delicious bedtime treat personally paw-selected by our own pets Rusty or Miss Kitty. Please do not leave pets in room unattended.

Features: Free Breakfast, Video library, Suitable for children, Bar/lounge, Number of rooms: 17, Spa services, Restaurant(s), Garden, Concierge services, Free wireless Internet, Parking (free).

Gualala

Also see the following nearby communities that have pet friendly lodging: The Sea Ranch - 9 miles

Not rated

Gualala Country Inn
47955 Center St
Gualala CA 95445
(707) 884-4343
$135 - $190

Pet Policy: Pets allowed, $10 per pet per stay. Must not leave unattended in room, and must be leashed when on hotel grounds. Do not bring pets into food area.

Features: Private bath, fireplace, 2 line phone, Internet (free), Cable TV, Hair dryer, Iron and ironing board, Coffee maker, Free continental breakfast.

Surf Inn
39170 South Highway 1
Gualala CA 95445
(707) 884-3571
$98 - $170
Bed & Pet Discount Offered

Pet Policy: Pets welcome, $10 per day per pet.

Features: Free wireless Internet, Number of rooms: 20, Number of floors: 1, Barbecue grill(s), Parking (free), Smoke-Free property, Coffee in lobby.

Guerneville

Also see the following nearby communities that have pet friendly lodging: Occidental - 7 miles

Dawn Ranch Lodge & Roadhouse Restaurant
16467 River Rd
Guerneville CA 95446
(707) 869-0656
$179 - $325
Bed & Pet Discount Offered

Pet Policy: Dog Friendly. $50 additional charge.

Features: Coffee in lobby, Swimming pool - outdoor, Bar/lounge, Restaurant(s), Number of rooms: 53, Wireless Internet.

Sonoma Orchid Inn formerly Ridenhour Inn
12850 River Road
Guerneville CA 95446
(707) 869-4466
$149 - $229
Bed & Pet Discount Offered

Pet Policy: Dogs are allowed in several rooms, if available. There are several pet-free rooms as well which never allow pets. No pets are allowed in the main house (yes, that includes our own). An additional charge of $30 per night applies.

Features: Bar/lounge, Number of rooms: 10, Suitable for children, Barbecue grill(s), Video library, Free breakfast, Free wireless Internet.

Half Moon Bay

Also see the following nearby communities that have pet friendly lodging: Moss Beach - 6 miles, Montara - 6 miles.

Coastside Inn
230 Cabrillo Hwy S
Half Moon Bay CA 94019
(650) 726-3400
$97 - $124
Bed & Pet Discount Offered

Pet Policy: Small pets, $15 per night per pet. Ground floor units only.

Features: Accessible bathroom, Accessibility equipment for the deaf, Braille or raised signage, Number of rooms: 52, Number of suites: 1, Number of floors: 2, Coffee in lobby, Business center, Nearby fitness center (discount), Free wireless Internet, Free breakfast.

Comfort Inn Half Moon Bay
2930 Cabrillo Hwy N
Half Moon Bay CA 94019
(650) 712-1999
$104 - $134
Bed & Pet Discount Offered

Pet Policy: Pet Accommodation: $10 per night per pet. Pet Limit: 2 pets per room under 85 pounds

Features: Coffee in lobby, Free breakfast, Business services, Number of rooms: 54, Number of floors: 2, Accessible bathroom, In-room accessibility equipment for the deaf, Braille or raised signage, Fitness facilities

Days Inn Half Moon Bay
3020 Cabrillo Hwy N
Half Moon Bay CA 94019
(650) 726-9700
$71 - $109
Bed & Pet Discount Offered

Pet Policy: Pets allowed, $15 per day. No cats.

Features: Business services, Free breakfast, Parking (free), Complimentary newspapers in lobby.

★★

Harbor View Inn
51 Ave. Alhambra
Half Moon Bay CA 94018
(650) 726-2329
$86 - $96
Bed & Pet Discount Offered

Pet Policy: Dogs only, under 35 lbs. $10 per day per pet. Limit 2 per room.

Features: Free breakfast, Coffee shop or cafe, Number of rooms: 17, Number of floors: 2, Coffee in lobby, Parking (free), Smoke-Free property.

The Ritz-Carlton, Half Moon Bay
1 Miramontes Point Rd
Half Moon Bay CA 94019
(650) 712-7000
$385 - $845
Bed & Pet Discount Offered

Pet Policy: Dogs welcome, $125 cleaning fee.

Features: Valet Parking fee, Breakfast available additional charge, Health club, Room service (24 hours), Spa services on site, Shoe shine, Multilingual staff, Complimentary newspapers in lobby, Porter/bellhop, Security guard, Limo or Town Car service available, Concierge desk, Sauna, Children's club, Bar/lounge, Babysitting or child care, Swimming pool - indoor, Beauty services, Full-service health spa, Restaurants: 2, Supervised child care/activities, Gift shops or newsstand, Shopping on site, Number of rooms: 261, Dry cleaning/laundry service, Accessible bathroom, In-room accessibility equipment for the deaf, Braille or raised signage, Fitness facilities, Free Internet access, ATM/banking, Golf course on site, Smoke-Free property, Massage - treatment room(s), Tennis on site, Steam room, Wheelchair accessible, Elevator.

Zaballa House
324 Main St
Half Moon Bay CA 94019
(650) 726-9123
$129 - $234
Bed & Pet Discount Offered

Pet Policy: Please let us know if you plan to bring your pet with you when you make your reservation. Dog lover rooms are based upon availability. Please contact us at (650) 726-9123 for confirmation of your request. Nightly additional charges will be charged upon arrival.

Features: Free breakfast, Business services, Library, Complimentary newspapers in lobby.

Hanford

Also see the following nearby communities that have pet friendly lodging: Lemoore - 7 miles

Irwin Street Inn
522 N Irwin St
Hanford CA 93230
(559) 583-8000
$89 - $90
Bed & Pet Discount Offered

Pet Policy: Pets accepted, $50 per pet per stay.

Features: Free wireless Internet, LCD TV, Microwaves on request, Refrigerator, Irons & ironing boards, Hair dryers, Separate sitting and dining areas.

★★

Super 8 Hanford
918 E Lacey Blvd
Hanford CA 93230
(559) 582-1736
$44 - $65
Bed & Pet Discount Offered

Pet Policy: Pets accepted, $20 per night additional charge.

Features: Swimming pool - outdoor, Number of floors: 2, Free breakfast, Business center, Free wireless Internet, Parking (free), Swimming pool - outdoor seasonal.

Harbor City

Also see the following nearby communities that have pet friendly lodging: Torrance - 2 miles, Carson - 4 miles, San Pedro - 5 miles, Redondo Beach - 5 miles, Gardena - 6 miles, Hermosa Beach - 7 miles, Long Beach - 8 miles, Manhattan Beach - 8 miles, Signal Hill - 8 miles, Hawthorne - 9 miles

Rodeway Inn & Suites Pacific Coast Highway
1665 Pacific Coast Hwy
Harbor City CA 90710
(310) 326-9026
$64 - $84
Bed & Pet Discount Offered

Pet Policy: Rodeway Inns charge an additional $10 per night per pet and require a $50 damage deposit, which is refunded if the room is in order at check out. Max of 2 pets per room. A veterinarian certificate that the pet is on a flea and parasite program. Pets may not be left alone in the room unless in a cage.

Features: Number of rooms: 33, Number of floors: 2, Business services, Coffee in lobby, Complimentary newspapers in lobby, Free Internet access.

Hawaiian Gardens

Also see the following nearby communities that have pet friendly lodging: Los Alamitos - 2 miles, La Palma - 3 miles, Cerritos - 3 miles, Cypress - 3 miles, Buena Park - 4 miles, Norwalk - 5 miles, La Mirada - 5 miles, Signal Hill - 6 miles, Seal Beach - 6 miles, Long Beach - 6 miles, Downey - 7 miles, Whittier - 8 miles, Fullerton - 9 miles, Anaheim - 9 miles, Garden Grove - 9 miles, Bell Gardens - 10 miles, Pico Rivera - 10 miles

La Quinta Inn & Suites Hawaiian Gardens
12441 Carson St
Hawaiian Gardens CA 90716
(562) 860-2500
$82 - $104
Bed & Pet Discount Offered

Pet Policy: Pets accepted no extra charge

Features: Accessible bathroom, Number of rooms: 53, Free breakfast, Free wireless Internet, Number of suites: 7, Number of floors: 4, Parking (free), Fitness facilities, Smoke-Free property.

Hawthorne

Also see the following nearby communities that have pet friendly lodging: El Segundo - 2 miles, Manhattan Beach - 3 miles, Inglewood - 3 miles, Hermosa Beach - 4 miles, Gardena - 4 miles, Redondo Beach - 5 miles, Los Angeles - 6 miles, Torrance - 7 miles, Marina Del Rey - 7 miles, Culver City - 7 miles, Carson - 8 miles, Venice - 8 miles, Harbor City - 9 miles, Huntington Park - 9 miles

Candlewood Suites LAX Hawthorne
11410 Hawthorne Blvd.
Hawthorne CA 90250
(310) 722-2707
$89 - $117
Bed & Pet Discount Offered

Pet Policy: Pets under 40 lbs accepted $75 per pet night for first 6 nights, $150 per night for 7 and more. Pets must have current vaccination records.

Features: Accessible bathroom, In-room accessibility equipment for the deaf, Braille or raised signage, Number of floors: 4, Number of suites: 96, Fitness facilities, Barbecue grill(s), Business center, Area shuttle (free), Grocery/convenience store.

★★½

TownePlace Suites-Hawthorne/LAX by Marriott
14400 Aviation Blvd
Hawthorne CA 90250
(310) 725-9696
$79 - $155
Bed & Pet Discount Offered

Pet Policy: Pets allowed. $100 cleaning fee.

Features: Swimming pool - outdoor, Elevator, Number of rooms: 144, Number of floors: 4, Business services, Barbecue grill(s), Coffee in lobby, Parking (free), Dry cleaning/laundry service, Free Internet access, Fitness facilities.

Hayward

Also see the following nearby communities that have pet friendly lodging: Union City - 4 miles, Castro Valley - 5 miles, Newark - 9 miles, Fremont - 10 miles

Americas Best Value Inn
2460 Whipple Rd
Hayward CA 94544
(510) 489-3888
$70 - $71

Pet Policy: Pets allowed with approval, $50 deposit. Please contact hotel directly to book with pets.

Features: Business services, Free breakfast, Guest laundry, Number of rooms: 76, Number of floors: 2, Parking (free).

Comfort Inn Hayward
24997 Mission Blvd
Hayward CA 94544
(510) 538-4466
$55 - $85
Bed & Pet Discount Offered

Pet Policy: Pet accommodation: $15/night (up to 2 pets/room 25 lbs. or under). Refundable Pet Deposit: $100.

Features: Business Center, Free breakfast, Sauna, Number of rooms: 62, Number of floors: 2, Guest laundry, Parking (free), Complimentary newspapers in lobby, Free Internet access.

Heritage Inn Express
410 W A St
Hayward CA 94541
(510) 785-0260
$36 - $45
Bed & Pet Discount Offered

Pet Policy: Pets accepted, $10 per night, maximum of $50 per stay.

Features: Elevator, Number of rooms: 60, Number of floors: 3, Parking (free), Swimming pool - outdoor seasonal, Internet (additional charge.

La Quinta Inn & Suites Hayward / Oakland Airport
20777 Hesperian Blvd
Hayward CA 94541
(510) 732-6300
$65 - $115
Bed & Pet Discount Offered

Pet Policy: Pets up to 50 lbs accepted, no additional charge. Owner must be present or pet crated for housekeeping services.

Features: Swimming pool – outdoor, Accessible bathroom, Elevator, Airport transportation (free), Number of rooms: 146, Number of floors: 3, Coffee in lobby, Free breakfast, Parking (free), Multilingual staff, Complimentary newspapers in lobby, Business center, Free wireless Internet, Dry cleaning/laundry service, Fitness facilities, Smoke-Free property.

Healdsburg

Also see the following nearby communities that have pet friendly lodging: Geyserville - 6 miles, Windsor - 6 miles

Dry Creek Inn
198 Dry Creek Rd
Healdsburg CA 95448
(707) 433-0300
$69 - $199
Bed & Pet Discount Offered

Pet Policy: The Best Western Dry Creek Inn is a family-friendly, pet-friendly hotel, with excellent facilities dedicated to pets. Our special amenities are designed to make your family visit easy and enjoyable, especially when you bring along your furry loved ones. At the Best Western Dry Creek Inn, you can avoid expensive pet-boarding additional charges by asking for one of our special "pets-only" pet-friendly rooms. When you check in, we will add a nominal $30 additional charge per night (limited to two animals per room). We also offer help finding local pet-supply stores, groomers, veterinarians, dog parks. Sorry, but no pets are allowed in our Luxury Tuscan rooms (only service animals)

Continued on next page

Dry Creek Inn
Continued from previous page

Features: Elevator, Outdoor pool, Restaurant(s), Number of rooms: 103, Business services, Guest laundry, Free breakfast, Multilingual staff, Complimentary newspapers, Free wireless Internet, Accessible bathroom, In-room accessibility equipment for the deaf, Braille or raised signage, Fitness facilities.

★★★½

Healdsburg Inn on the Plaza, A Four Sisters Inn
112 Matheson
Healdsburg CA 95448
(707) 433-6991
$196 - $197
Bed & Pet Discount Offered

Pet Policy: Dogs only, up to 40 lbs, $65 additional charge, limit 2 per room. Pet owners will be liable for any additional cleaning bills or repairs, should they be required. All pets must be vaccinated and licensed and you agree to obtain and provide current records from a licensed veterinarian regarding this. The inn may request this information from you at any time.

Features: Elevator, Wheelchair accessible, Concierge, Number of rooms: 12, Number of floors: 2, Business services, Coffee in lobby, Parking nearby, Complimentary newspapers, Accessible bathroom, Smoke-Free property, Free reception, Free wireless Internet, Free breakfast.

★★★★ ♥

The Grape Leaf Inn
539 Johnson Street
Healdsburg CA 95448
(707) 433-8140
$280 - $567

Pet Policy: Pet friendly. Please contact property directly for restrictions and additional charges.

Features: Business services, Concierge, Gift shops or newsstand, Free breakfast, Multilingual staff, Complimentary newspapers, Porter/bellhop, Limo or Town Car service available, Free wireless Internet.

Hemet

★★

Americas Best Value Inn and Suites, Hemet
800 W Florida Ave
Hemet CA 92543
(951) 929-6366
$58 - $73
Bed & Pet Discount Offered

Pet Policy: Small pets allowed with advance approval directly from hotel.

Features: Wheelchair accessible, Number of rooms: 64, Guest laundry, Free breakfast, Multilingual staff, Swimming pool, Designated smoking areas, Accessible bathroom, Free wireless Internet.

Not rated

Best Western of Hemet
2625 W Florida Ave
Hemet CA 92343
(951) 925-6605
$71 - $89

Pet Policy: Pets accepted on advance approval. Please contact hotel directly for reservations.

Features: Number of rooms :87, Kitchenettes available in limited rooms, Restaurant, Pool & Spa – outdoor, Free wireless Internet.

Quality Inn Hemet
1201 W Florida Ave
Hemet CA 92543
(951) 766-1902
$89 - $139
Bed & Pet Discount Offered

Pet Policy: Quality Inns charge an additional $10 per night per pet. They may require a $50 damage deposit, which is refunded if the room is in order at check out. Quality Inns accept any well-behaved pets with a maximum of 3 per room, but dogs are limited to 50 pounds. Pets may not be left alone in the room unless in a cage

Features: Outdoor pool, Business services, Coffee in lobby, Number of rooms: 54, Number of floors: 2, Free breakfast, Multilingual staff.

Super 8 Hemet
3510 W Florida Ave
Hemet CA 92545
(951) 658-2281
$50 - $73
Bed & Pet Discount Offered

Pet Policy: Pets welcome, $5 per day per pet.

Features: Coffee in lobby, Elevator, Business services, Free breakfast, Parking (free), Complimentary newspapers in lobby, Swimming pool - outdoor seasonal.

★★

Vagabond Inn Hemet
2688 East Florida Ave
Hemet CA 92544
(800) 522-1555
$50 - $65
Bed & Pet Discount Offered

Pet Policy: Pets accepted, $10 per night.

Features: Coffee in lobby, Restaurant(s), Number of rooms: 27, Number of floors: 2, Suitable for children, Parking (free), Multilingual staff, Free wireless Internet

Hermosa Beach

Also see the following nearby communities that have pet friendly lodging: Manhattan Beach - 2 miles, Redondo Beach - 2 miles, Hawthorne - 4 miles, El Segundo - 4 miles, Torrance - 5 miles, Gardena - 5 miles, Inglewood - 7 miles, Harbor City - 7 miles, Carson - 8 miles, Marina Del Rey - 9 miles, Los Angeles - 10 miles

Quality Inn and Suites Hermosa Beach
901 Aviation Blvd
Hermosa Beach CA 90254
(310) 374-2666
$99 - $189
Bed & Pet Discount Offered

Pet Policy: Pets allowed, $20 per night plus $100 refundable deposit.

Features: Elevator, ATM/banking, Number of rooms: 68, Number of floors: 3, Coffee in lobby, Free breakfast, Parking garage (free), Multilingual staff, Complimentary newspapers in lobby, Business center, Free wireless Internet, Dry cleaning/laundry service, Fitness facilities

Hesperia

Also see the following nearby communities that have pet friendly lodging: Victorville - 8 miles

Econo Lodge Hesperia
11976 Mariposa Rd
Hesperia CA 92345
(760) 949-1515
$54- $64
Bed & Pet Discount Offered

Pet Policy: Pet Accommodation:$10 per pet/night. Pet Limit: 1 pet per room. 25 pounds or under.

Features: Number of rooms: 54, Number of floors: 2, Coffee in lobby, Guest laundry, Free breakfast, Parking (free), Complimentary newspapers in lobby, Multilingual staff.

Holiday Inn Express Hotel & Suites Hesperia
9750 Key Point Ave
Hesperia CA 92345
(760) 949-1515
$81 - $130
Bed & Pet Discount Offered

Pet Policy: Small pets allowed, $25 per night. Pets may not be left alone at any time.

Features: Swimming pool - indoor, Restaurant(s), Number of floors: 3, Cell phone/mobile rental, Guest laundry, Multilingual staff, Complimentary newspapers in lobby, Business center, Wireless Internet, Accessible bathroom, In-room accessibility equipment for the deaf, Braille or raised signage, Fitness facilities.

La Quinta Inn & Suites Hesperia Victorville
12000 Mariposa Rd
Hesperia CA 92345
(760) 949-9900
$84- $104
Bed & Pet Discount Offered

Pet Policy: Cats and dogs up to 50 pounds are accepted in all guest rooms. Housekeeping services for rooms with pets require pet owner be present or pet must be crated. No additional charges or deposits are required.

Features: Indoor pool, Coffee in lobby, Free breakfast, Complimentary newspapers, Accessible bathroom, Business Center, Free Internet, Fitness facilities.

Motel 6 Hesperia Victorville
9757 Cataba Road
Hesperia CA 92345
(760) 947-0094
$49 - $59
Bed & Pet Discount Offered

Pet Policy: Well-behaved pets stay Free. Animals that pose a health or safety risk may not remain onsite, and include those that, in our manager's discretion, are too numerous for any one room, cause damage to our property or that of other guests, are too disruptive, are not properly attended, or demonstrate undue aggression. All pets must be declared at check-in. Pets must be attended to and under control at all times. If unavoidable circumstances require a pet to remain in a room while the owner is offsite, the pet must be secured in a crate or travel carrier. Pets must be on a leash or securely carried outside of guest rooms.

Continued on next page

Motel 6 Hesperia Victorville
Continued from previous page

Features: Free wireless Internet,, Outdoor pool, Number of rooms: 99, Number of floors: 3, Coffee in lobby, Guest laundry, Multilingual staff, Business center, RV and truck parking, Designated smoking areas, Accessible bathroom, Wheelchair accessible.

Super 8 Hesperia Victorville
12033 Oakwood Ave
Hesperia CA 92345
(760) 949-3231
$46 - $61
Bed & Pet Discount Offered

Pet Policy: Pets accepted, $10 per night.

Features: Free breakfast

Hollister

Not rated
Best Western San Benito Inn
660 San Felipe Road
Hollister CA 95023
(831) 637-9248
$76 - $134

Pet Policy: Pets accepted, $35 per night per pet. Pets should not be left alone in room, must be leashed in public areas, and are not permitted in food or pool areas.

Features: Free continental breakfast, Outdoor pool, Free wireless Internet, HBO, Refrigerator & microwave, Hair dryer, Coffee maker, Iron & ironing board.

Hollywood

Also see the following nearby communities that have pet friendly lodging: Universal City - 3 miles, West Hollywood - 3 miles, Glendale - 4 miles, Beverly Hills - 5 miles, Studio City - 5 miles, Burbank - 5 miles, Los Angeles - 7 miles, Culver City - 8 miles, Sherman Oaks - 9 miles, South Pasadena - 10 miles

Best Western Hollywood Hills
6141 Franklin Ave
Hollywood CA 90028
(323) 464-5181
$118 - $199
Bed & Pet Discount Offered

Pet Policy: Pets up to 10 lbs, $75 per night per pet. Maximum of 2 pets per room.

Features: Valet parking, Parking fee, Bar/lounge, Business services, Guest laundry, Swimming pool - outdoor, Number of rooms: 86, Coffee shop or cafe, Multilingual staff, Elevator, Free wireless Internet.

Highland Gardens Hotel
7047 Franklin Ave
Hollywood CA 90028
(323) 850-0536
$118 - $158
Bed & Pet Discount Offered

Pet Policy: Pets under 25 lbs, $25 per night. Limit 1 per room.

Features: Nearby fitness center (free), Multilingual staff, Security guard, Parking garage (free), Wireless Internet – additional charge, Free Breakfast, Swimming pool - outdoor, Concierge services, Suitable for children, Coffee in lobby ATM/banking, Number of rooms: 72, Number of floors: 2, Airport transportation additional charge, Business services, Complimentary newspapers in lobby, Smoke-Free property, Dry cleaning/laundry service.

★★★

Hollywood Heights Hotel
2005 N Highland Ave
Hollywood CA 90068
(888) 726-8580
$134 - $179
Bed & Pet Discount Offered

Pet Policy: Pets up to 75 lbs, $75 per stay. May have two pets provided total weight does not exceed 75 lbs. May not leave unattended in room. Must have proof of current vaccinations for pets. Must be leashed when outside of room.

Features: Swimming pool - outdoor, Elevator, Business center, Parking (valet) $22/24 Hours In/Out, Dry cleaning/laundry service, Bar/lounge, Restaurant(s), Room service (limited hours), ATM/banking, Gift shops or newsstand, Number of rooms: 160, Number of floors: 6, Breakfast available additional charge, Multilingual staff, Complimentary newspapers in lobby, Porter/bellhop, Limo or Town Car service available, Concierge desk, Smoke-Free property, Free wireless Internet, Fitness facilities.

★★

Motel 6 Hollywood
1738 Whitley Ave
Hollywood CA 90028
(323) 464-6006
$98- $100
Bed & Pet Discount Offered

Pet Policy: Well-behaved pets stay free. Animals that pose a health or safety risk may not remain onsite, and include those that, in our manager's discretion, are too numerous for any one room, cause damage to our property or that of other guests, are too disruptive, are not properly attended, or demonstrate undue aggression. All pets must be declared at check-in. Pets must be attended to and under control at all times. If unavoidable circumstances require a pet to remain in a room while the owner is offsite, the pet must be secured in a crate or travel carrier. Pets must be on a leash or securely carried outside of guest'

Features: Smoke-Free property, Guest laundry, Parking fee, Accessible bathroom, Free wireless Internet, Business center.

Rodeway Inn Hollywood
6826 West Sunset Boulevard
Hollywood CA 90028
(323) 465-7186
$69 - $109
Bed & Pet Discount Offered

Pet Policy: Rodeway Inns charge an additional $10 per night per pet and require a $50 damage deposit, which is refunded if the room is in order at check out. Max of 2 pets per room. A veterinarian certificate that the pet is on a flea and parasite is required. Pets may not be left alone in the room unless in a cage.

Features: Business services, Parking (free), Coffee in lobby, Swimming pool - outdoor, Free breakfast, Number of rooms: 28, Number of floors: 2, Airport transportation additional charge, Multilingual staff.

★★★★

The Redbury @ Hollywood and Vine
1717 Vine St
Hollywood CA 90028
(323) 962-1717
$255 - $742
Bed & Pet Discount Offered

Pet Policy: Pets up to 30 lbs, $!00 per stay. May not leave pets alone in room.

Features: Bar/lounge, Babysitting or child care, Elevator, Restaurant(s), Wheelchair accessible, Parking (valet - additional charge), Concierge services, Number of rooms: 57, Number of floors: 5, Suitable for children, Currency exchange, Coffee shop or cafe, Grocery, Room service (24 hours), Complimentary newspapers in lobby, Use of nearby fitness center (free), Porter/bellhop, Security guard, Dry cleaning/laundry service, Limo or Town Car service available, Beauty services, Massage - spa treatment room(s), Smoke-Free property, Wireless Internet – additional charge, Accessible bathroom, 24-hour business center.

★★★★

W Hollywood
6250 Hollywood Blvd
Hollywood CA 90028
(323) 798-1300
$258- $399
Bed & Pet Discount Offered

Pet Policy: We welcome cats and dogs 40 pounds or less. Guests must sign a waiver upon check-in and will be charged $25 per pet per day above the room rate. There is also a non-refundable $100 cleaning fee regardless of length of stay

Features: Valet Parking fee, Multilingual staff, Elevator, Beauty services, Business center, Wheelchair accessible, Steam room, Area shuttle (free), Porter/bellhop, Outdoor pool, Massage - treatment room(s), Concierge, Smoke-Free, Health club, 2 Restaurants, Bar/lounge, Number of rooms: 305, Free wireless Internet, Full-service health spa, Currency exchange, Room service (24 hours), Dry cleaning/laundry, Gift shops or newsstand.

Huntington Beach

Also see the following nearby communities that have pet friendly lodging: Fountain Valley - 3 miles, Costa Mesa - 6 miles, Seal Beach - 7 miles, Garden Grove - 7 miles, Santa Ana - 7 miles, Cypress - 8 miles, Los Alamitos - 8 miles, Newport Beach - 9 miles, La Palma - 10 miles

Extended Stay America Orange County - Huntington B
5050 Skylab Rd
Huntington Beach CA 92647
(714) 799-4887
$67 - $87
Bed & Pet Discount Offered

Pet Policy: One medium-size pet is allowed in each guest room. A $25 per day non-refundable cleaning fee (not to exceed $150) will be charged the first night of your stay.

Features: Guest laundry, Number of rooms: 104, Number of floors: 3, Business services, Parking (free), Wireless Internet – additional charge.

Shorebreak Hotel a Joie De Vivre Hotel
500 Pacific Coast Hwy
Huntington Beach CA 92648
(714) 861-4470
$188 - $549
Bed & Pet Discount Offered

Pet Policy: Dogs welcome, no size limit or additional charges. Shorebreak Hotel in Huntington Beach has a Pet-a-Potty - a 4 x 8 lawn specifically for dogs that is located on the second floor deck and other pet amenities on request.

Features: Valet Parking fee, Gift shops or newsstand, Bar/lounge, Breakfast available additional charge, Porter/bellhop, Concierge , Music library, Beach/pool umbrellas, Media library, Restaurants: 2, Room service (24 hours), Multilingual staff, Limo or Town Car service available, Technology helpdesk, Number of rooms: 157, Number of floors: 4, Shopping on site, Complimentary newspapers in lobby, Smoke-Free property, Accessible bathroom, In-room accessibility equipment for the deaf, Braille or raised signage, Dry cleaning/laundry service, Free wireless Internet, Fitness facilities, Wheelchair accessible, 24-hour business center.

The Waterfront Beach Resort, A Hilton Hotel
21100 Pacific Coast Hwy
Huntington Beach CA 92648
(714) 845-8000
$203 - $317
Bed & Pet Discount Offered

Pet Policy: Pets up to 75 lbs, $75 per day deep cleaning fee.

Features: Business center, Room service, Bar/lounge, Outdoor pool, Concierge, Restaurant(s), Gift shops or newsstand, Number of rooms: 290, Number of floors: 12, Translation services, Wireless Internet – additional charge, Breakfast available additional charge, Multilingual staff, Complimentary newspapers, Porter/bellhop, Limo or Town Car service available, Smoke-Free property, Children's club, Dry cleaning/laundry service, Tennis courts, Fitness facilities, Valet Parking fee.

Huntington Park

Also see the following nearby communities that have pet friendly lodging: Commerce - 5 miles, Bell Gardens - 5 miles, Downey - 6 miles, Monterey Park - 7 miles, Pico Rivera - 7 miles, Gardena - 8 miles, Los Angeles - 9 miles, Inglewood - 9 miles, Norwalk - 9 miles, Hawthorne - 9 miles, Carson - 10 miles

Rodeway Inn Near L.A. Live
6340 Santa Fe Ave
Huntington Park CA 90255
(323) 589-5971
$49 - $84
Bed & Pet Discount Offered

Pet Policy: Rodeway Inns charge an additional $10 per night per pet and require a $50 damage deposit, which is refunded if the room is in order at check out. Max of 2 pets per room. A veterinarian certificate that the pet is on a flea and parasite program is required. Pets may not be left alone in the room unless in a cage.

Features: Restaurant, Number of rooms: 47, Number of floors: 2.

Idyllwild

Always Inn Idyllwild Cottages
53785 Country Club Dr.
Idyllwild CA 92549
(949) 374-6165
$209 - $229
Bed & Pet Discount Offered

Pet Policy: Pets allowed, $25 per night.

Features: Number of rooms: 3, Number of floors: 2, Parking (free), Wireless Internet, Suitable for children, Barbecue grill(s)

Not rated
Idyllwild Inn
54300 Village Center Road
Idyllwild CA 92549
(888) 659-2552
$96 - $120

Pet Policy: 2 dogs allowed in most cabins. Idyllwild is a very pet friendly town with several restaurants that allow pet owners to eat on the deck with their animals.

Features: Fireplaces in some cabins..

Not rated ♥
Quiet Creek Inn
26345 Delano Drive
Idyllwild CA 92549
(951) 659-6110
$130 - $165

Pet Policy: Pets allowed, $35 cleaning fee plus deposit if not paying by credit card. Limit of 2 pets per room. You MAY NOT leave your pet(s) alone in room or cabin. Please do not allow your pets on the furniture, including the bed, unless you provide your own cover for the furniture. You must clean up after your pet while on the property, even if in a wooded area

Features: Cabins with Wood burning fireplaces, Refrigerators and microwaves, Wireless Internet, Cable TV, DVD players,.

The Tahquitz Inn at Idyllwild
25840 State Hwy 243
Idyllwild CA 92549
(877) 659-4554
$94 - $129
Bed & Pet Discount Offered

Pet Policy: Dogs only, $10 per pet per night. No size restriction.

Features: Parking (free), Dial-up Internet access (free), Front desk (limited hours).

Indio

Also see the following nearby communities that have pet friendly lodging: La Quinta - 4 miles, Palm Desert - 7 miles

★★
Best Western Date Tree Hotel
81909 Indio Blvd
Indio CA 92201
(760) 347-3421
$99- $225
Bed & Pet Discount Offered

Pet Policy: Pets allowed, $10 per pet per night.

Features: Swimming pool - outdoor, Number of rooms: 118, Number of floors: 2, Free breakfast, Parking (free), Smoke-Free property, Business services, Dry cleaning/laundry service, Free wireless Internet, Fitness facilities.

Clarion Inn
84096 Indio Springs Dr
Indio CA 92201
(760) 342-6344
$84- $129
Bed & Pet Discount Offered

Pet Policy: Pet accommodation: $25 per stay, per pet. Pet limit: maximum of 2 pets per room.

Features: Elevator, Number of floors: 2, Swimming pool - outdoor, Wheelchair accessible, Self-parking

★★★
Indian Palms Country Club and Resort
48630 Monroe St
Indio CA 92201
(760) 775-4444
$118 - $179
Bed & Pet Discount Offered

Pet Policy: Pets accepted, $15 per night per pet

Features: Free wireless Internet, RV and truck parking, Swimming pool - outdoor, Bar/lounge, Business services, Coffee in lobby, Parking (free), Complimentary newspapers in lobby, Use of nearby fitness center (free), Front desk (limited hours), Security guard, Restaurant(s), Concierge services, Gift shops or newsstand, Number of rooms: 59, Number of floors: 2, Golf course on site, Tennis on site.

Quality Inn Indio
43505 Monroe St
Indio CA 92201
(760) 347-4044
$84 - $159
Bed & Pet Discount Offered

Pet Policy: Quality Inns charge an additional $10 per night per pet. They may require a $50 damage deposit, which is refunded if the room is in order at check out. Quality Inns accept any well-behaved pets with a maximum of 3 per room, but dogs are limited to 50 pounds. Pets may not be left alone in the room unless in a cage.

Features: Swimming pool - outdoor, Gift shops or newsstand, Number of rooms: 62, Number of floors: 2, Free breakfast, Coffee in lobby, Business services.

Royal Plaza Inn
82347 US Highway 111
Indio CA 92201
(760) 347-0911
$59 - $113
Bed & Pet Discount Offered

Pet Policy: Dogs and cats accepted, $!0 per night plus $50 per stay. Up to 3 pets allowed in a room.

Features: Coffee in lobby, RV and truck parking, Number of rooms: 99, Accessible bathroom, Smoke-Free property, Bar/lounge, Shopping center shuttle (free), Restaurant, Free wireless Internet, Guest laundry, Wheelchair accessible, Concierge, Multilingual staff, Braille or raised signage, Heated Swimming pool, Airport transportation (free)

Super 8 Motel Indio
81753 Highway 111
Indio CA 92201
(760) 342-0264
$52 - $189
Bed & Pet Discount Offered

Pet Policy: Pets welcome, $15 per pet per night.

Features: Barbecue grill(s), Babysitting or child care, Guest laundry, Free breakfast, Parking (free), Security guard, Swimming pool - outdoor seasonal, Business services.

Inglewood

Also see the following nearby communities that have pet friendly lodging: El Segundo - 3 miles, Hawthorne - 3 miles, Los Angeles - 3 miles, Culver City - 4 miles, Marina Del Rey - 5 miles, Manhattan Beach - 5 miles, Venice - 6 miles, Gardena - 6 miles, Hermosa Beach - 7 miles, Beverly Hills - 8 miles, Redondo Beach - 8 miles, Santa Monica - 8 miles, Huntington Park - 9 miles, West Hollywood - 9 miles, Torrance - 10 miles

Rodeway Inn & Suites Inglewood
3940 W Century Blvd
Inglewood CA 90303
(310) 672-4570
$55 - $71
Bed & Pet Discount Offered

Pet Policy: Rodeway Inns charge an additional $10 per night per pet and require a $50 damage deposit, which is refunded if the room is in order at check out. Max of 2 pets per room. A veterinarian certificate that the pet is on a flea and parasite program is required. Pets may not be left alone in the room unless in a cage.

Features: Number of rooms: 36, Business services, Coffee in lobby, Free breakfast, Parking (free), Complimentary newspapers, RV and truck parking.

Irvine

Also see the following nearby communities that have pet friendly lodging: Lake Forest - 2 miles, Laguna Hills - 4 miles, Newport Beach - 9 miles, Laguna Beach - 9 miles, Santa Ana - 10 miles, Costa Mesa - 10 miles

★★
Candlewood Suites Irvine
16150 Sand Canyon Ave
Irvine CA 92618
(949) 788-0500
$64 - $120
Bed & Pet Discount Offered

Pet Policy: Pets allowed with a nonrefundable additional charge of $15 for the first night and $10 for every additional night up to $150. Pet must weigh less than 80 lbs. Pet agreement must be signed at check-in. A record of complete and up-to-date vaccinations may be required.

Features: Business services, Fitness center, Guest laundry, Accessible bathroom, In-room accessibility equipment for the deaf, Braille or raised signage, Gift shops or newsstand, Free Wireless Internet.

★★★½
Embassy Suites Irvine-Orange County Airport
2120 Main St
Irvine CA 92614
(949) 553-8332
$109 - $134
Bed & Pet Discount Offered

Pet Policy: Pets welcome, $100 per pet per stay.

Features: Swimming pool - indoor, Airport transportation (free), Bar/lounge, Free breakfast, Elevator, Restaurant(s), Room service (limited hours), Gift shops or newsstand, Number of suites: 293, Coffee in lobby, Complimentary newspapers in lobby, Wireless Internet– additional charge, Accessible bathroom, In-room accessibility equipment for the deaf, Dry cleaning/laundry service, Wheelchair accessible, Business center, Free reception, Fitness facilities, Parking (fee).

★★★½
Hilton Irvine Orange County Airport
18800 Macarthur Blvd
Irvine CA 92612
(866) 763-3059
$95 - $180
Bed & Pet Discount Offered

Pet Policy: The Hilton Irvine charges a $50 non-refundable additional charge for pets. No pet will be allowed stay at the Hilton Irvine unless the additional charge is paid. (Service animals are not considered pets and therefore are not subject to any charge).

Features: Parking (valet) $12, Room service (limited hours), Bar/lounge, Airport transportation (free), Restaurant(s), ATM/banking, Concierge services, Gift shops or newsstand, Number of rooms: 292, Suitable for children, Currency exchange, Multilingual staff, Porter/bellhop, Dry cleaning/laundry service, Wheelchair accessible, Breakfast available additional charge, Health club, Complimentary newspapers in lobby, Technology support staff, Designated smoking areas, Wireless Internet (additional charge), 24-hour business center, Area shuttle (free), Tennis on site, Swimming pool – outdoor.

Homestead Orange County - Irvine Spectrum
30 Technology Dr
Irvine CA 92618
(949) 727-4228
$64 - $89
Bed & Pet Discount Offered

Pet Policy: Pets allowed, no size restriction, $25 per day to a maximum of $150 per stay. Limit of 1 pet per room.

Features: Number of rooms: 149, Number of floors: 2, Barbecue grill(s), Wireless Internet - additional charge, Parking (free), Front desk (limited hours), Dry cleaning/laundry service

La Quinta Inn & Suites Irvine Spectrum
14972 Sand Canyon Ave
Irvine CA 92618
(949) 551-0909
$69 - $89
Bed & Pet Discount Offered

Pet Policy: Cats and dogs up to 50 pounds are accepted in all guest rooms. Housekeeping services for rooms with pets require pet owner be present or pet must be crated. No additional charges or deposits are required.

Features: Elevator, Free breakfast, Health club, Parking (free), Multilingual staff, Free wireless Internet, Airport transportation (free), Swimming pool - outdoor, Number of rooms: 147, Number of floors: 4, Accessible bathroom, In-room accessibility equipment for the deaf, Braille or raised signage, Dry cleaning/laundry service.

Not rated
Marriott Executay Camden Main
2801 Main St
Irvine CA 92614
(888) 526-0566
$154 - $162

Pet Policy: Pets up to 40 lbs accepted, $500 deposit, $250 is non-refundable. No aggressive breeds permitted.

Features: Furnished apartments, Kitchens with dishwasher and microwave, Washer/Dryer in each unit, Fireplace, Free wireless Internet, Cable TV, Swimming Pool, Sauna, Steam room, Fitness center. Minimum stay of 30 days may be required.

Not rated
Oakwood Irvine
2750 Kelvin Avenue
Irvine CA 92614
(877) 902-0832
$128 - $156

Pet Policy: Pets accepted with limitations and additional charge. Contact hotel directly for more information and to make reservations.

Features: Furnished apartments, Concierge services, Swimming pool. Fitness center, Business center. Minimum stay of 30 days .

Residence Inn by Marriott Irvine John Wayne Airport
2855 Main St
Irvine CA 92614
(949) 261-2020
$119 - $229
Bed & Pet Discount Offered

Pet Policy: Pets allowed, $100 cleaning fee per stay.

Features: Business services, Outdoor pool, Gift shops or newsstand, Number of rooms: 174, Number of floors: 8, BBQ area, Coffee in lobby, Free breakfast, Parking (free), Complimentary newspapers, Airport transportation (free), Dry cleaning/laundry, Tennis courts, Fitness center.

★★★

Residence Inn by Marriott Irvine Spectrum
10 Morgan
Irvine CA 92618
(949) 380-3000
$93 - $200
Bed & Pet Discount Offered

Pet Policy: Pets allowed, $100 fee per stay.

Features: Business services, Outdoor pool, Number of rooms: 112, Number of floors: 2,BBQ area, Coffee in lobby, Free breakfast, Grocery, Parking (free), Complimentary newspapers, Free wireless Internet, Dry cleaning/laundry, Tennis courts, Fitness center..

Jackson

Also see the following nearby communities that have pet friendly lodging: Sutter Creek - 3 miles, Amador City - 5 miles

Best Western Amador Inn
200 S Hwy 49
Jackson CA 95642
(209) 223-0211
$71 - $119

Pet Policy: Pets allowed. $15 per night.

Features: Fireplace in some rooms, Swimming pool – outdoor, Restaurant.

Jamestown

Also see the following nearby communities that have pet friendly lodging: Sonora - 4 miles

Country Inn Sonora
18730 Highway 108
Jamestown CA 95327
(209) 984-0315
$89 - $279

Pet Policy: Some pet friendly rooms.

Features: Number of rooms: 61, Free wireless Internet, Swimming pool.

Julian

Not rated.

2 Lilac Acres Guest Home
2848 Three Peaks Lane
Julian CA 92036
(858) 205-2797
$166 - $185

Pet Policy: Dogs under 35 pounds welcome with $200 security deposit paid upon booking, and dog must be on flea prevention. You are expected to clean up after your pet. Must book with hotel.

Features: Kitchen fully stocked, Free wireless Internet, Deck, Fireplace, Pellet stove.

Kettleman City

Not rated
Best Western Kettleman City Inn
33410 Powers Dr
Kettleman City CA 93239
(559) 386-0804
$84 - $138

Pet Policy: Pets accepted on advance approval. Please contact hotel directly for reservations.

Features: Free continental breakfast, Coffee maker, Guest laundry, HBO, Jacuzzi rooms available, Refrigerators available, Wireless Internet.

Super 8 Kettleman City
I-5 Hwy 41 E to Bernard Drive
Kettleman City CA 93239
(559) 386-9530
$58 - $81

Pet Policy: Pets accepted, $10 per night.

Features: Free super start breakfast. Outdoor pool 6am 10pm. Cable with HBO. Smoking and nonsmoking rooms available. Coffee available in lobby 24 hours. Free high speed internet.

King City

Courtesy Inn
4 Broadway Circle
King City CA 93930
(831) 385-4646
$72 - $98
Bed & Pet Discount Offered

Pet Policy: Pet friendly, $10 per day per pet.

Features: Business Center, Free Breakfast, Swimming pool - outdoor, RV and truck parking, Restaurant(s), Parking (free), Number of rooms: 63, Coffee in lobby, Guest laundry, Use of nearby fitness center (free), Private beach, Free wireless Internet, Accessible bathroom, Smoke-Free property.

Days Inn King City CA
1130 Broadway St
King City CA 93930
(831) 385-5921
$47 - $120
Bed & Pet Discount Offered

Pet Policy: Pets allowed, $5 per night per pet.

Features: Business services, Barbecue grill(s), Free breakfast, Parking (free), Complimentary newspapers in lobby, Free Internet access, Swimming pool - outdoor seasonal

Kingsburg

Also see the following nearby communities that have pet friendly lodging: Selma - 8 miles, Dinuba - 8 miles

Quality Inn Kingsburg
401 Sierra St
Kingsburg CA 93631
(559) 897-1022
$70 - $85
Bed & Pet Discount Offered

Pet Policy: Pets accepted $15 per night, plus $100 refundable deposit. Limit of 1 pet per room.

Features: Number of rooms: 47, Swimming pool - outdoor, Wheelchair accessible, Number of floors: 2, Business services, Parking (free), Wireless Internet.

La Jolla

Also see the following nearby communities that have pet friendly lodging: Del Mar - 6 miles, San Diego - 9 miles

Hilton La Jolla Torrey Pines
10950 N Torrey Pines Rd
La Jolla CA 92037
(858) 558-1500
$164 - $239
Bed & Pet Discount Offered

Pet Policy: Pets up to 75 lbs, $75 per stay.

Features: Bar/lounge, Concierge services, Room service (24 hours), Shoe shine, Nearby fitness center (discount), Swimming pool - outdoor, Parking (valet) $25 Per Day, Tennis on site, Elevator, Restaurant(s), Gift shops or newsstand, Number of rooms: 394, Multilingual staff, Complimentary newspapers in lobby, Business center, Porter/bellhop, Wireless Internet, Smoke-Free property, Accessible bathroom, In-room accessibility equipment for the deaf, Braille or raised signage, Dry cleaning service.

La Jolla Inn
1110 Prospect St
La Jolla CA 92037
(858) 454-0133
$189 - $250
Bed & Pet Discount Offered

Pet Policy: 1 Dog, up to 35 lbs permitted with a $50 per night additional charge plus $200 refundable deposit. No cats. Pets must never be left unattended in the guest rooms or on the premises and are not allowed in the dining room or the interior public areas of the Inn. We will provide a comfy area in the garden for your pets while you are enjoying your breakfast. We provide your pet with food and water bowls, a comfy pet bed, Pet Sheets to protect the furniture and plastic disposal bags that must be disposed of in the trash containers in the park or other public disposal areas.

Features: Suitable for children, Room service (limited hours), Free breakfast, Number of rooms: 23, Number of suites: 2, Smoke-Free property, Dry cleaning/laundry service, Coffee in lobby, Complimentary newspapers in lobby, Free wireless Internet, Front desk (limited hours), Snack bar/deli, Parking garage.

La Valencia Hotel
1132 Prospect St
La Jolla CA 92037
(858) 454-0771
$263 - $1,250
Bed & Pet Discount Offered

Pet Policy: Pets up to 75 lbs, $25 per pet per night additional charge.

Features: Business Center, Concierge desk, Swimming pool - outdoor, Poolside bar, Coffee in lobby, Restaurant(s), Number of rooms: 115, Number of floors: 11, Airport transportation additional charge, Breakfast available additional charge, Currency exchange, Multilingual staff, Complimentary newspapers in lobby, Porter/bellhop, Free wireless Internet, ***Continued on next page***

La Valencia Hotel
Continued from previous page

Massage - treatment room(s), Parking (valet) $22 Daily, Accessible bathroom, In-room accessibility equipment for the deaf, Dry cleaning/laundry service, Elevator attendant, Video library, Room service (24 hours), Spa services, Bar/lounge, Shoe shine, Security guard, Fitness facilities.

Not rated
Marriott Executstay Regents
9253 Regents Road
La Jolla CA 92037
(888) 526-0566
From $146 per night

Pet Policy: Pets accepted up to 50 lbs. $500 deposit, $250 non-refundable. Limit 2 pets per apartment, no aggressive breeds.

Features: Furnished apartments, Full kitchens with dishwasher & microwave, Fireplace, Washer & Dryer in each unit, Business Center, Swimming Pool & Spa, Fitness center, Free wireless Internet. Minimum stay of 30 days required.

Not rated
Oakwood La Jolla UTC North
9253 Regents Road
La Jolla CA 92037
(858) 274-5276
$137 - $163

Pet Policy: Pets accepted with restrictions and fee. Contact hotel directly for details and reservations.

Features: Furnished apartments, Concierge, Swimming pool, Fitness center, Business center, Full kitchens, Minimum stay of 30 days may be required..

★★★
Residence Inn By Marriott La Jolla
8901 Gilman Dr
La Jolla CA 92037
(858) 587-1770
$149 - $249
Bed & Pet Discount Offered

Pet Policy: Pets allowed, $100 cleaning fee per stay.

Features: Gift shops or newsstand, Number of rooms: 288, Number of floors: 2, Business services, Free breakfast, Grocery, Parking (free), Multilingual staff, Complimentary newspapers, Porter/bellhop, Outdoor pool, Barbecue grill(s), Coffee in lobby, Airport transportation (free), Security guard, Free wireless Internet, Accessible bathroom, Braille or raised signage, Dry cleaning/laundry service, Fitness facilities, Restaurant, Area shuttle (free).

★★★½
San Diego Marriott La Jolla
4240 La Jolla Village Dr
La Jolla CA 92037
(858) 587-1414
$139 - $198
Bed & Pet Discount Offered

Pet Policy: Pets accepted, $75 per stay cleaning fee.

Features: Outdoor & Indoor pools, Concierge, Business Center, Room service, Nightclub, Bar/lounge, Restaurant(s), Gift shop, Number of rooms: 365, Number of floors: 15, Computer rental, Coffee in lobby, Breakfast available additional charge, Arcade/game room, Health club, Shoe shine, Multilingual staff, Free newspapers, Porter/bellhop, Security guard, Limo or Town Car service available, Wireless Internet – additional charge, Parking fee, Smoke-Free property, Dry cleaning/laundry .

Scripps Inn La Jolla
555 Coast Blvd South
La Jolla CA 92037
(858) 454-3391
$265 - $266
Bed & Pet Discount Offered

Pet Policy: Pets allowed, in designated pet friendly rooms only, $50 additional charge per stay. Your pet will be greeted with their very own additional charging place mat and bag of treats. We ask that you not leave your pet in your guest room or vehicle unattended. If there is a time you will not have your pet with you, let us know so that we can give you phone numbers for pet friendly restaurants, pet sitter or other options. You are responsible for your pets behavior. Pets must remain on leash or under owner command at all times while on Scripps Inn property.

Features: Self-parking fee, Wheelchair accessible, Airport transportation additional charge, Free breakfast, Multilingual staff, Concierge desk, Smoke-Free property, Technology helpdesk, Accessible bathroom, Dry cleaning/laundry service, Free wireless Internet.

★★★½

Sheraton La Jolla Hotel
3299 Holiday Ct
La Jolla CA 92037
(858) 453-5500
$108 - $189
Bed & Pet Discount Offered

Pet Policy: Dogs less than 80 pounds are allowed. Dogs cannot be left alone in the guest room. Cats are not allowed. Guest must sign a waiver at check-in before dog is allowed in any guest room or public area. Dogs are not allowed in any food and beverage or pool area. A pet cleaning fee of $40 per stay will be charged to your room.

Features: Business Center, Bar/lounge, Elevator, Restaurant(s), ATM/banking, Concierge services, Number of rooms: 252, Number of floors: 4, Multilingual staff, Complimentary newspapers in lobby, Room service, Porter/bellhop, Security guard, Wireless Internet, Accessible bathroom, In-room accessibility equipment for the deaf, Braille or raised signage, On-site car rental, Suitable for children, Parking fee, Fitness facilities, Swimming pool - outdoor.

The Bed and Breakfast Inn at La Jolla
7753 Draper Ave
La Jolla CA 92037
(858) 456-2066
$189 - $369

Pet Policy: Only 1 designated pet room which requires advanced approval. Please contact property directly for reservation.

Features: Year built 1913. Number of rooms: 13, Number of suites: 2, Non-smoking property, Full breakfast, Limited parking (compacts only), Wireless Internet (free - in library/den), Complimentary newspapers and coffee in lobby, private baths.

La Mesa

Also see the following nearby communities that have pet friendly lodging: El Cajon - 6 miles, San Diego - 6 miles, National City - 7 miles

Heritage Inn La Mesa
7851 Fletcher Pkwy
La Mesa CA 91942
(619) 698-9444
$49 - $64
Bed & Pet Discount Offered

Pet Policy: Small pets only, $10 per night per pet.

Features: Parking (free), Multilingual staff, Swimming pool - outdoor seasonal, Elevator, Wheelchair accessible, Number of rooms: 105, Number of floors: 4, Coffee in lobby, Guest laundry, Free breakfast, Security guard, Wireless (high-speed) Internet access (free), Accessible bathroom.

★★

Rodeway Inn La Mesa
4210 Spring St
La Mesa CA 91941
(619) 589-7288
$64 - $74
Bed & Pet Discount Offered

Pet Policy: Rodeway Inns charge an additional $10 per night per pet and require a $50 damage deposit, which is refunded if the room is in order at check out. Max of 2 pets per room. A veterinarian certificate that the pet is on a flea and parasite program and that they are Free from parasites is required. Pets may not be left alone in the room unless in a cage.

Features: Guest laundry, Number of rooms: 44, Number of floors: 2, Free breakfast, Parking (free), 24-hour front desk.

La Mirada

Also see the following nearby communities that have pet friendly lodging: Cerritos - 3 miles, Buena Park - 4 miles, Norwalk - 4 miles, La Palma - 4 miles, Whittier - 4 miles, Fullerton - 5 miles, Hawaiian Gardens - 5 miles, Cypress - 6 miles, Los Alamitos - 7 miles, Downey - 7 miles, Pico Rivera - 7 miles, Anaheim - 8 miles, Brea - 8 miles, Bell Gardens - 9 miles, Placentia - 9 miles, Commerce - 10 miles, City Of Industry - 10 miles, Garden Grove - 10 miles, South El Monte - 10 miles

Extended Stay America Los Angeles - La Mirada
14775 Firestone Blvd
La Mirada CA 90638
(714) 670-8579
$59 - $83
Bed & Pet Discount Offered

Pet Policy: One medium-size pet is allowed in each guest room. A $25 per day non-refundable cleaning fee (not to exceed $150) will be charged the first night of your stay.

Features: Guest laundry, Elevator, Number of rooms: 104, Number of floors: 3, Parking (free), Multilingual staff, Front desk (limited hours), Wireless Internet, Use of nearby fitness center (discount), Bar/lounge.

Residence Inn by Marriott La Mirada
14419 Firestone Blvd
La Mirada CA 90638
(714) 523-2800
$138 - $139
Bed & Pet Discount Offered

Pet Policy: Pets allowed, $100 per stay cleaning fee.

Features: Number of suites: 147, Number of floors: 2, Barbecue grill(s), Free breakfast, Parking (free), Complimentary newspapers in lobby, Free wireless Internet, Smoke-Free property, Guest laundry, Business services, Concierge desk Coffee in lobby, Accessible bathroom, In-room accessibility equipment for the deaf, Fitness facilities

La Palma

Also see the following nearby communities that have pet friendly lodging: Buena Park - 1 mile, Cypress - 2 miles, Cerritos - 3 miles, Hawaiian Gardens - 3 miles, Los Alamitos - 3 miles, La Mirada - 4 miles, Norwalk - 6 miles, Fullerton - 7 miles, Anaheim - 7 miles, Seal Beach - 7 miles, Garden Grove - 7 miles, Whittier - 8 miles, Signal Hill - 8 miles, Long Beach - 9 miles, Downey - 9 miles, Fountain Valley - 10 miles, Huntington Beach - 10 miles, Brea - 10 miles

La Quinta Inn and Suites Buena Park
3 Centerpointe Dr
La Palma CA 90623
(714) 670-1400
$72 - $105
Bed & Pet Discount Offered

Pet Policy: Cats and dogs up to 50 pounds are accepted in all guest rooms. Housekeeping services for rooms with pets require pet owner be present or pet must be crated. No additional charges or deposits are required.

Features: Elevator, Accessible bathroom, Swimming pool - outdoor, Number of rooms: 157, Coffee in lobby, Free breakfast, Parking (free), Multilingual staff, Complimentary newspapers in lobby, Business center, Dry cleaning/laundry service, Free wireless Internet, Fitness facilities

La Quinta

Also see the following nearby communities that have pet friendly lodging: Indio - 4 miles, Palm Desert - 5 miles, Rancho Mirage - 10 miles

Embassy Suites La Quinta Hotel & Spa
50-777 Santa Rosa Plaza
La Quinta CA 92253
(760) 777-1711
$111 - $639
Bed & Pet Discount Offered

Pet Policy: Pets up to 25 lbs, $50 additional charge. Must book pet friendly room in advance.

Features: Free breakfast, Swimming pool - outdoor, Bar/lounge, Elevator, Restaurant(s), Parking (free), Multilingual staff, Porter/bellhop, Wireless Internet, Concierge desk, Full-service health spa, Massage - treatment room(s), Dry cleaning/laundry service, Business center.

La Quinta Resort & Club - A Waldorf Astoria Resort
49 - 499 Eisenhower Drive
La Quinta CA 92253
(760) 564-4111
$315 - $629
Bed & Pet Discount Offered

Pet Policy: Cats and dogs up to 50 pounds are accepted in all guest rooms. Housekeeping services for rooms with pets require pet owner be present or pet must be crated. No additional charges or deposits are required.

Features: Sauna, Concierge desk, Floor butler, Supervised child care/activities, ATM/banking, Currency exchange, Security guard, Bar/lounge, Shopping on site, Business center, Room service (limited hours), Health club, Technology helpdesk, Translation services, Beauty services, Children's swimming pool, Swimming pool - outdoor, Restaurant(s), Gift shops or newsstand, Number of rooms: 796, Number of floors: 2, Breakfast available additional charge, Poolside bar, Multilingual staff, Porter/bellhop, Limo or Town Car service available, Wireless Internet, Full-service health spa, Massage - treatment room(s), Dry cleaning/laundry service, Tennis on site.

Laguna Beach

Also see the following nearby communities that have pet friendly lodging: Dana Point - 6 miles, Laguna Hills - 7 miles, San Juan Capistrano - 7 miles, Lake Forest - 8 miles, Capistrano Beach - 9 miles, Newport Beach - 9 miles, Irvine - 9 miles

Holiday Inn Laguna Beach
696 S Coast Hwy
Laguna Beach CA 92651
(949) 494-1001
$132 - $299
Bed & Pet Discount Offered

Pet Policy: Pets under 20 lbs, $75 per stay. No additional charge for reptiles, fish, or service animals.

Features: Accessible bathroom, In-room accessibility equipment for the deaf, Braille or raised signage, Bar/lounge, Restaurant(s), Room service, Outdoor pool, Concierge, Number of rooms: 54, Number of floors: 3, Coffee in lobby, Breakfast available additional charge, Multilingual staff, Complimentary newspapers, Business center, Wireless Internet, Dry cleaning/laundry service, Fitness center, Parking fee.

Laguna Beach Inn
2020 South Coast Hwy
Laguna Beach CA 92651
(949) 494-5450
$125 - $219
Bed & Pet Discount Offered

Pet Policy: Dogs up to 35 lbs allowed, $35 per night additional charge.

Features: Number of rooms: 23, Number of floors: 2, BBQ area, Coffee in lobby, Parking (free), Nearby fitness center (free), Free breakfast, Business services, Concierge, Dry cleaning/laundry service, Swimming pool - outdoor, Smoke-Free property, Free wireless Internet, Beach/pool umbrellas.

Laguna Cliffs Inn
475 N Coast Hwy
Laguna Beach CA 92651
(949) 497-6645
$148 - $219
Bed & Pet Discount Offered

Pet Policy: Pets up to 80 lbs, $20 per night plus refundable $100 deposit. Maximum of 2 per room. Must be registered at check-in. Sorry, pit bulls and Rottweiler breeds are not allowed.

Features: Swimming pool - outdoor, Sauna, Elevator, Number of rooms: 36, Number of floors: 2, Coffee in lobby, Complimentary newspapers in lobby, Wireless Internet, Concierge desk, Parking garage (free), Smoke-Free property, Beach/pool umbrellas, Accessible bathroom, 24-hour business center

Montage Laguna Beach
30801 Coast Hwy
Laguna Beach CA 92651
(866) 271-6953
$475 - $1,095
Bed & Pet Discount Offered

Pet Policy: Pets up to 25 lbs accepted, $100 per stay. Limit 2 per room. Pets allowed in ground floor rooms only.

Features: Bar/lounge, Babysitting or child care, Elevator, Fitness facilities, Swimming pool - outdoor heated, Wheelchair accessible, Valet parking – additional charge, Supervised child care/activities, Gift shops or newsstand, Shopping on site, Number of rooms: 250, Number of suites: 60, Number of floors: 5, Airport transportation additional charge, Cell phone/mobile rental, Translation services, Computer rental, Coffee in lobby, Poolside bar, Currency exchange, Health club, Room service (24 hours), Multilingual staff, Complimentary newspapers in lobby, Porter/bellhop, Security guard, Dry cleaning/laundry service, Limo or Town Car service available, Beauty services, Concierge, Full-service health spa, Massage - spa treatment room(s), Steam room, Sauna, Smoke-Free property, Technology helpdesk, Children's club, Technology support staff, On-site medical assistance available, Free Internet access, Pick up service from train station, Accessible bathroom, In-room accessibility equipment for the deaf, Braille or raised signage, Area shuttle (free), Number of restaurants 3, Business center, 3 outdoor swimming pools..

★★★

Pacific Edge Hotel on Laguna Beach, a Joie de Vivre
647 South Coast Hwy
Laguna Beach CA 92651
(949) 281-5709
$129 - $319
Bed & Pet Discount Offered

Pet Policy: Dogs Only. Fido-friendly packages, amenities and a progressive pet policy designed to make hotel stays hospitable for dogs and their owners alike. Unlike many hotels, Joie de Vivre's properties do not impose weight restrictions on dogs and do not charge pet fees (provided there is no damage to a guestroom and dog owners abide by pet policy rules).
Continued on next page

Pacific Edge Hotel on Laguna Beach
Continued from previous page

Features: Swimming pool - outdoor, Arcade/game room, Coffee in lobby, Bar/lounge, Parking (valet - additional charge), Concierge services, Multilingual staff, Use of nearby fitness center (free), Room service, Dry cleaning/laundry service, Designated smoking areas, Beach/pool umbrellas, Free wireless Internet, 24-hour business center, Number of outdoor swimming pools 2, Number of rooms: 130, Number of floors: 5, Complimentary newspapers in lobby, Restaurant(s), Smoke-Free property

★★
The Tides Laguna Beach
460 N. Coast Hwy
Laguna Beach CA 92651
(949) 494-2494
$142 - $173
Bed & Pet Discount Offered

Pet Policy: Pets welcome, $25 per pet per night.

Features: Barbecue Grill(s), Swimming pool - outdoor, Number of rooms: 11, Number of suites: 10, Number of floors: 2, Coffee in lobby, Parking (free), Free wireless Internet, Smoke-Free property

★★½
Travelodge Laguna Beach
30806 South Coast Highway
Laguna Beach CA 92651
(949) 499-2227
$55 - $140
Bed & Pet Discount Offered

Pet Policy: Small pets (fit in carrier) accepted, $10 per pet.

Features: Swimming pool - outdoor, Sauna, Number of rooms: 43, Number of floors: 2, Video library, Parking (free), Complimentary newspapers in lobby, Business center, Free wireless Internet, Smoke-Free property, Coffee in lobby

Laguna Hills

Also see the following nearby communities that have pet friendly lodging: Lake Forest - 2 miles, Irvine - 4 miles, San Juan Capistrano - 6 miles, Laguna Beach - 7 miles, Dana Point - 9 miles

★★★
The Hills Hotel
25205 La Paz Rd
Laguna Hills CA 92653
(949) 586-5000
$141 - $142
Bed & Pet Discount Offered

Pet Policy: Pets welcome, $30 per pet per night. We offer a few grass areas with a Doggy Station on the south end of the hotel.

Features: Concierge services, Bar/lounge, Elevator, Restaurant(s), Room service (limited hours), ATM/banking, Number of rooms: 147, Number of floors: 4, Breakfast available additional charge, Parking (free), Multilingual staff, Complimentary newspapers in lobby, Smoke-Free property, Dry cleaning/laundry service, Fitness facilities, Free wireless Internet, Wheelchair accessible, Nearby fitness center (discount), Accessible bathroom, RV and truck parking, 24-hour business center, Translation services, Swimming pool - outdoor

Lake Arrowhead

Lake Arrowhead Resort
27984 Highway 189
Lake Arrowhead CA 92382
(909) 336-1511
$171 - $211
Bed & Pet Discount Offered

Pet Policy: Your pet is also our guest. Please register your pet at the Front Desk upon arrival and display a pet door sign on your guestroom doorknob at all times. Acceptable pets include cats and dogs weighing no more than 25 pounds and at least one year old. Service animals are welcome at any time. Weight limits and pet fee do not apply. Your pet should be fully trained. Your pets must be leashed at all times outside your guest room. Proper clean-up and disposal of pet waste is your responsibility Pets are not permitted in anywhere food and beverages are served, at the outdoor pool or at Spa of the Pines. Pets should not be left alone in your guestroom for any length of time. Should your pet become the unlikely subject of another guest's complaint, you likely will be asked to have a sitter with your pet at all times or board it elsewhere. Credits and rebates given to other guests because of your pet's disturbance or poor behavior will be charged to your account. You will be charged a $20 per pet, room rate for each night of your stay. Included are pet concierge services, loaner pet supplies, a pet room service menu and special deep cleaning of your room upon departure.

***Features*:** Concierge, Babysitting or child care, Bar/lounge, Restaurant(s), Number of rooms: 173, Number of floors: 3, Full-service health spa, Private beach, Accessible bathroom, In-room accessibility equipment for the deaf, Braille or raised signage, Free wireless Internet, Wheelchair accessible, Beach/pool umbrellas, Security guard, Massage - treatment room(s), Beauty services, Multilingual staff, 24-hour business center, Gift shops or newsstand, Smoke-Free property, Poolside bar, Health club, Outdoor pool - seasonal, Room service (24 hours), Dry cleaning/laundry service.

Saddleback Inn
300 S. State HWY 173
Lake Arrowhead CA 92352
(909) 336-3571
$127 - $249
Bed & Pet Discount Offered

Pet Policy: Pets welcome in some cottages, no additional charge.

Features: Bar/lounge, Room service, Wheelchair accessible, Coffee in lobby, Free breakfast, Multilingual staff, Complimentary newspapers, Private beach, Smoke-Free, Grocery/convenience store, Accessible bathroom, Free wireless Internet.

Lake Elsinore

Also see the following nearby communities that have pet friendly lodging: Canyon Lake - 6 miles, Sun City - 10 miles

Quality Inn Lake Elsinore
31808 Casino Dr
Lake Elsinore CA 92530
(951) 674-9694
$59 - $66
Bed & Pet Discount Offered

Pet Policy: Pets allowed, $20 per pet per night plus $75 refundable deposit.

Features: Coffee in lobby, Free breakfast, Number of rooms: 55, Number of floors: 2, Guest laundry, Parking (free), Multilingual staff, Wireless Internet, Swimming pool - outdoor seasonal

Lake Forest

Also see the following nearby communities that have pet friendly lodging: Laguna Hills - 2 miles, Irvine - 2 miles, Laguna Beach - 8 miles, San Juan Capistrano - 8 miles, Newport Beach - 10 mile

Candlewood Suites Irvine East
3 S Pointe Dr
Lake Forest CA 92630
(949) 598-9105
$61 - $106
Bed & Pet Discount Offered

Pet Policy: Pets up to 80 lbs allowed with additional charge. $15 the first night per pet. Each additional night is $10 per each pet, not to exceed $150 per pet. Pet agreement must be signed at check-in.

Features: Fitness facilities, Accessible bathroom, In-room accessibility equipment for the deaf, Braille or raised signage, Number of floors: 3, Business services, Multilingual staff.

Extended Stay America Orange County - Lake Forest
20251 Lake Forest Dr
Lake Forest CA 92630
(949) 598-1898
$59 - $87
Bed & Pet Discount Offered

Pet Policy: One pet is allowed in each guest room. A $25 per day non-refundable cleaning fee (not to exceed $150) will be charged the first night.

Features: Guest laundry, Number of rooms: 119, Number of floors: 3, BBQ area, Coffee in lobby, Wireless Internet – additional charge, Nearby fitness center (discount).

★★½

Quality Inn & Suites Lake Forest
23702 Rockfield Blvd
Lake Forest CA 92630
(949) 458-1900
$79 - $85
Bed & Pet Discount Offered

Pet Policy: Quality Inns charge an additional $10 per night per pet. They may require a $50 damage deposit, which is refunded if the room is in order at check out. Quality Inns accept any well-behaved pets with a maximum of 3 per room, but dogs are limited to 50 pounds. Pets may not be left alone in the room unless in a cage

Features: Number of rooms: 112, Guest laundry, Free breakfast, Complimentary newspapers in, Free wireless Internet, Bar/lounge, Outdoor pool, Business center, Fitness facilities.

Staybridge Suites Lake Forest
2 Orchard
Lake Forest CA 92630
(949) 462-9500
$96 - $240
Bed & Pet Discount Offered

Pet Policy: Pets up to 80 lbs, $75 for up to 6 nights, $150 for 7 or longer. 2 pets permitted but together must not exceed 60 lbs. Must have proof of current vaccinations.

Features: Business services, Accessible bathroom, In-room accessibility equipment for the deaf, Braille or raised signage, Swimming pool - outdoor, Free breakfast, Grocery, Parking (free), Multilingual staff, Free wireless Internet, Dry cleaning/laundry service, Area shuttle (free), Fitness facilities.

The Prominence Hotel and Suites
20768 Lake Forest Drive
Lake Forest CA 92630
(949) 900-1288
$89 - $128
Bed & Pet Discount Offered

Pet Policy: Pets allowed, $20 per pet per night. Must stay in first floor specially designed pet rooms.

Features: Coffee in lobby, Guest laundry, Swimming pool - outdoor, Business center, Number of rooms: 60, Number of floors: 3, Free breakfast, Smoke-Free property Roll-in shower, Wheelchair accessible, Computer rental, Barbecue grill(s), Multilingual staff, Complimentary newspapers, Technology helpdesk, Fitness center, Free wireless Internet.

Lakeport

Also see the following nearby communities that have pet friendly lodging: Nice - 7 miles, Upper Lake - 8 miles

Clear Lake Bed and Breakfast
2 Sixteenth Street
Lakeport CA 95453
(707) 263-9071
$165 - $167
Bed & Pet Discount Offered

Pet Policy: Pets allowed, $25 per pet per stay. Only 1 pet friendly room available.

Features: Library, Number of rooms: 3, Business services, Barbecue grill(s), Guest laundry, Free breakfast, Wireless Internet

Lancaster

Also see the following nearby communities that have pet friendly lodging: Palmdale - 7 miles

Comfort Inn & Suites Lancaster
1825 W Avenue J12
Lancaster CA 93534
(661) 723-2001
$119 - $139
Bed & Pet Discount Offered

Pet Policy: Pet accommodation: $30 per night/pet. Pet limit: max 3 per room, up to 25 lbs.

Features: Sauna, Swimming pool – outdoor, Elevator, Number of rooms: 58, Number of floors: 3, Free breakfast, Parking (free), Dry cleaning/laundry service, Fitness facilities, Free wireless Internet.

Holiday Inn Express Lancaster
43719 17th St W
Lancaster CA 93534
(661) 951-8848
$100 - $171
Bed & Pet Discount Offered

Pet Policy: Dogs welcome in designated pet friendly rooms, $10 per night plus $100 refundable deposit.

Features: Outdoor pool, Number of rooms: 88, Number of floors: 3, Complimentary newspapers, Business center, Accessible bathroom, In-room accessibility equipment for the deaf, Braille or raised signage, Dry cleaning/laundry, Free wireless Internet, Fitness center.

★★★
Oxford Inn & Suites Lancaster
1651 W Avenue K
Lancaster CA 93534
(661) 949-3423
$79 - $146
Bed & Pet Discount Offered

Pet Policy: Medium size cats and dogs accepted for $25 per pet per 7 days with a two pet limit. The charge is assessed at check out. Aggressive breeds not allowed. Pets must not be left unattended in room, must be leashed when in public areas, and are not permitted in dining, pool or spa areas.

Features: Outdoor pool, BBQ area, Business center, Video library, Nearby fitness center (free), Bar/lounge, Room service, Shoe shine, Airport transportation (free), Security guard, Free breakfast, Coffee in lobby, Gift shops or newsstand, Number of rooms: 173, Number of floors: 4, Complimentary newspapers, Free wireless Internet, Dry cleaning/laundry.

Lathrop

Not rated
Days Inn Lathrop
14851 S Harlan Rd
Lathrop CA 95376
(209) 982-1959
$55 - $79

Pet Policy: Pets accepted, $10 per pet per night.

Features: Free continental breakfast, Sauna and steam room, In room Jacuzzi, Outdoor swimming pool, Guest laundry, Microwave, Refrigerator, VCR, Cable TV and pay per view.

Holiday Inn Express Hotel & Suites Lathrop - South
15688 S Harlan Rd
Lathrop CA 95330
(209) 373-2700
$89 - $113
Bed & Pet Discount Offered

Pet Policy: Pets allowed in select rooms only. $200 deposit required.

Features: Accessible bathroom, in-room accessibility equipment for the deaf, Braille or raised signage, Bar/lounge, Elevator, Fitness facilities, Swimming pool - indoor, ATM/banking, Number of rooms: 81, Number of suites: 24, Number of floors: 3, Parking (free), Business center, Dry cleaning/laundry service, Internet access, Smoke-Free property, Grocery/convenience store.

Quality Inn & Suites Lathrop
16855 Old Harlan Rd I 5 Louise Ave Exit
Lathrop CA 95330
(209) 858-1234
$64 - $69
Bed & Pet Discount Offered

Pet Policy: Pets up to 30 lbs, $20 per night. Limit 1 pet per room.

Features: Swimming pool - outdoor, Number of rooms: 65, Number of floors: 2, Business services, Guest laundry, Parking (free), Multilingual staff, Free wireless Internet, Steam room, Sauna, Fitness facilities.

Lebec

Econo Lodge Gorman
49713 Gorman Post Rd
Lebec CA 93243
(661) 248-6411
$59 - $69
Bed & Pet Discount Offered

Pet Policy: Pet accommodation:$10/night per pet. Pet Deposit: $20/stay.

Features: Room service (limited hours), Airport transportation (free), Bar/lounge, Restaurant(s), Number of rooms: 58, Number of floors: 2, Parking (free).

Holiday Inn Express Hotel & Suites Frazier Park
612 Wainwright Ct
Lebec CA 93243
(661) 248-1600
$76 - $112
Bed & Pet Discount Offered

Pet Policy: Pets allowed, $20 per night, first floor only. Must reserve in advance. Lots of running room around the hotel for your pet to enjoy.

Features: Accessible bathroom, Accessibility equipment for the deaf, Braille or raised signage, Swimming pool - outdoor, Business center, Fitness facilities, Concierge services, Number of rooms: 77, Free breakfast.

Lemoore

Also see the following nearby communities that have pet friendly lodging: Hanford - 7 miles

Days Inn Lemoore CA
877 E D Street And Bush
Lemoore CA 93245
(559) 924-1261
$64 - $90
Bed & Pet Discount Offered

Pet Policy: Pets allowed, $15 per day, per pet.

Features: Parking (free), Barbecue grill(s), Complimentary newspapers in lobby, Wireless Internet, additional charge, Swimming pool - outdoor seasonal

Lincoln

Also see the following nearby communities that have pet friendly lodging: Rocklin - 7 miles, Roseville - 8 miles

Holiday Inn Express Hotel & Suites Lincoln
155 Ferrari Ranch Rd
Lincoln CA 95648
(916) 644-3440
$90 - $132
Bed & Pet Discount Offered

Pet Policy: Pets up to 40 lbs, $35 per night. No aggressive breeds. For extended stays, discount may be offered on the pet fee.

Features: Swimming pool - indoor, Number of floors: 3, Business center, Wireless Internet, Sauna, Accessible bathroom, In-room accessibility equipment for the deaf, Braille or raised signage, Fitness facilities.

Lindsay

Super 8 Lindsay CA
390 N Highway 65
Lindsay CA 93247
(559) 562-5188
$75 - $80
Bed & Pet Discount Offered

Pet Policy: Pets under 35 lbs accepted, $10 per night.

Features: Business services, Guest laundry, Free breakfast, Parking (free), Wireless Internet.

Little River

Also see the following nearby communities that have pet friendly lodging: Mendocino - 4 mile

Cottages at Little River Cove
7533 N Highway 1
Little River CA 95456
(707) 937-5339
$179 - $239
Bed & Pet Discount Offered

Pet Policy: Dogs welcome, $25 per pet. At the Cottages we know that pets need vacations, too! We are the premier pet friendly lodging location in Mendocino, with private cottages and beautiful gardens and lawns for taking walks. In our designated pet friendly cottages we allow up to three dogs to accompany you. We welcome our furry, four-footed guests with their own "Pet Package" including a bed, food and water bowls, a beach towel, waste bags and a welcome treat!

Features: Concierge services, Number of rooms: 9.

Little River Inn
7751 N Hwy 1
Little River CA 95456
(707) 937-5942
$145 - $290
Bed & Pet Discount Offered

Pet Policy: Pets welcome, $25 per pet per night. Limit 2 per room. Must not leave unattended in room. Must keep leashed outside of room.

Features: Video library, Suitable for children, Bar/lounge, Full-service health spa, Restaurant(s), Gift shops or newsstand, Number of rooms: 64, Breakfast available additional charge, Golf course on site, Tennis on site.

★★★

Stevenswood Lodge
8211 N Highway One
Little River CA 95456
(707) 937-2810
From $225
Bed & Pet Discount Offered

Pet Policy: Pets welcome, $25 per pet per stay. Should be leashed when outside of room. No allowed in food service or spa areas.

Features: Concierge, Full-service health spa, Bar/lounge, Restaurant(s), Wheelchair accessible, Gift shops or newsstand, Number of floors: 2, Arcade/game room, Health club, Business center.

Not rated

The Anderson Sea Side Inn
6051 N HIGHWAY ONE
Little River CA 95456
(707) 937-1543
$114 - $264

Pet Policy: Pets welcome, $20 per pet per night.

Features: Number of cabins: 12, Private bathrooms, BBQs, TV with DVD, Free wireless Internet, Fireplaces and Kitchenettes in some rooms.

★★★

The Inn at Schoolhouse Creek
7051 N Highway 1
Little River CA 95456
(800) 731-5525
$196 - $400
Bed & Pet Discount Offered

Pet Policy: Dogs welcome. $50 cleaning fee per stay. They give you a doggie care bag when you check in, most units have a pet chest full of towels, bowls and deodorizer. Very popular place with dog owners.

Features: Restaurant(s), Massage - spa treatment room(s.)

Livermore

Also see the following nearby communities that have pet friendly lodging: Pleasanton - 7 miles, Dublin - 9 mile

Extended Stay America Livermore - Airway Boulevard
2380 Nissen Dr
Livermore CA 94550
(925) 373-1700
$54 - $79
Bed & Pet Discount Offered

Pet Policy: One medium-size pet is allowed in each guest room. A $25 per day non-refundable cleaning fee (not to exceed $150) will be charged the first night of your stay.

Features: Guest laundry, Elevator, Number of rooms: 122, Number of floors: 3, Wireless Internet (additional charge), Parking (free), Multilingual staff, Front desk (limited hours), Bar/lounge.

Holiday Inn Express Hotel & Suites Livermore
3000 Constitution Dr
Livermore CA 94551
(925) 961-9600
$80 - $118
Bed & Pet Discount Offered

Pet Policy: Pets up to 30 lbs, $30 per night.

Features: Accessible bathroom, In-room accessibility equipment for the deaf, Braille or raised signage, Outdoor pool, Gift shops or newsstand, Number of rooms: 92, Number of suites: 15, Number of floors: 3, Barbecue grill(s), Free breakfast, Multilingual staff, Complimentary newspapers in lobby, Business center, Free wireless Internet, Dry cleaning/laundry service, Fitness facilities.

★★
La Quinta Inn Livermore
7700 S Front Rd
Exit Greenville
Livermore CA 94551
(925) 373-9600
$79 - $130
Bed & Pet Discount Offered

Pet Policy: Cats and dogs up to 50 pounds are accepted in all guest rooms. Housekeeping services for rooms with pets require pet owner be present or pet must be crated. No additional charges or deposits are required.

Features: Free Breakfast, Sauna, Business Center, Coffee in lobby, Swimming pool - indoor, Elevator, Accessible bathroom, Number of rooms: 58, Number of suites: 12, Number of floors: 3, Parking (free), Multilingual staff, Complimentary newspapers in lobby, Designated smoking areas, RV and truck parking, Free Internet, Fitness facilities

★★★
Residence Inn by Marriott Livermore
1000 Airway Blvd
Livermore CA 94551
(925) 373-1800
$99 - $100
Bed & Pet Discount Offered

Pet Policy: Pets allowed with $75 one-time cleaning fee.

Features: Swimming pool - outdoor, Number of rooms: 96, Number of floors: 2, Barbecue grill(s), Coffee in lobby, Free breakfast, Parking (free), Complimentary newspapers in lobby, Smoke-Free property, Dry cleaning/laundry service, Tennis on site, Fitness facilities, Wheelchair accessible, Accessible bathroom, 24-hour business center, Free reception, Suitable for children, Free wireless Internet.

★★
Studio Inn Livermore
1321 Portola Ave
Livermore CA 94551
(925) 447-1515
$56 - $57
Bed & Pet Discount Offered

Pet Policy: Accepts dogs and cats up to 100 lbs, $15 per night to a maximum of $300 per stay, plus $25 deposit. Limit 2 per room.

Features: Number of rooms: 15, Number of floors: 1, Free wireless Internet

Lodi

Also see the following nearby communities that have pet friendly lodging: Stockton - 9 miles

★
Best Western Royal Host Inn
710 S Cherokee Lane
Lodi CA 95240
(209) 369-8484
$53 - $119

Pet Policy: Pets under 45 lbs accepted, $15 per stay.

Features: Sitting area and working desk, Jacuzzi in suites, Free full hot breakfast, Swimming pool – outdoor, Free wireless Internet.

Microtel Inn And Suites -
6428 W Banner Rd
Lodi CA 95242
(209) 367-9700
$39- $89
Bed & Pet Discount Offered

Pet Policy: Pets all sizes welcome with additional charge at check-in.

Features: Number of floors: 3, Business services, Parking (free), Multilingual staff, Swimming pool.

Motel 6 Lodi
1140 S Cherokee Ln
Lodi CA 95240
(209) 334-6422
$56 - $68
Bed & Pet Discount Offered

Pet Policy: Well behaved pets and service animals are welcome with no additional charge. Must not leave unattended and must be leashed when in public areas.

Features: Business center, Free wireless Internet, RV and truck parking, Swimming pool - outdoor

Lompoc

Americas Best Value Inn
1200 North H Street
Lompoc CA 93436
(805) 735-3737
$40 - $84

Pet Policy: Pets allowed, $25 per night per pet. Limit 2 per room, no size restriction.

Features: Free continental breakfast, Guest Laundry, BBQ area, Number of rooms: 54, Free wireless Internet, Cable TV, Coffee maker.

Comfort Inn & Suites
1621 North H Street
Lompoc CA 93436
(805) 735-8555
$89 - $99
Bed & Pet Discount Offered

Pet Policy: Quality Inns charge an additional $10 per night per pet. They may require a $50 damage deposit, which is refunded if the room is in order at check out. Quality Inns accept any well-behaved pets with a maximum of 3 per room, but dogs are limited to 50 pounds. Pets may not be left alone in the room unless in a cage.

Features: Swimming pool - outdoor, Elevator, Fitness facilities, Business services, Parking (free), Multilingual staff, Wireless Internet, Free Breakfast, Dry cleaning/laundry service, Number of rooms: 218

★★

Days Inn Lompoc
1122 North H Street
Lompoc CA 93436
(805) 735-7744
$63 - $99
Bed & Pet Discount Offered

Pet Policy: Pets allowed, $25 per stay.

Features: Swimming pool - indoor, Business services, Guest laundry, Free breakfast, Parking (free), Multilingual staff, Fitness facilities.

Embassy Suites Lompoc - Central Coast
1117 North H Street
Lompoc CA 93436
(805) 735-8311
$109 - $160
Bed & Pet Discount Offered

Pet Policy: Pets up to 35 lbs, $25 additional charge.

Features: Free breakfast, Free reception Business center, Outdoor pool, Gift shops or newsstand, Number of floors: 3, Multilingual staff, Wireless Internet, Accessible bathroom, In-room accessibility equipment for the deaf, Braille or raised signage, Dry cleaning/laundry service, Fitness facilities.

Travelodge Lompoc California
1415 E Ocean Ave
Lompoc CA 93436
(805) 736-6514
$48 - $119
Bed & Pet Discount Offered

Pet Policy: Pets accepted, $15 per pet per day.

Features: Business services, Barbecue grill(s), Free breakfast, Guest laundry, Swimming pool - outdoor, Number of rooms: 50, Number of floors: 2, Parking (free), Free wireless Internet.

Not rated
White Oaks Hotel
3955 Apollo Way
Lompoc CA 93436
(805) 733-5000
$49 - $79

Pet Policy: Pets accepted, $10 per pet per night

Features: Pool closed as of this writing, Microwave, Refrigerator, Coffee maker, Data ports.

Lone Pine

Not rated
BW Plus Frontier Motel
1008 S Main
Lone Pine CA 93545
(760) 876-5571
$81 - $110

Pet Policy: Pets allowed, no restrictions.

Features: Number of rooms: 73, Wireless Internet, Cable TV, Free continental breakfast, Heated swimming pool, Laundry facilities, Airport shuttle (free).

Comfort Inn Lone Pine
1920 S Main St
Lone Pine CA 93545
(760) 876-8700
$99 - $109
Bed & Pet Discount Offered

Pet Policy: Pet accommodation: $20 per night/per pet. Pet Limit: 2 pets per room, limited availability of pet friendly rooms.

Features: Business services, Coffee in lobby, Swimming pool - outdoor, Number of rooms: 58, Number of floors: 2, Free breakfast, Parking (free), Free wireless Internet

Long Beach

Also see the following nearby communities that have pet friendly lodging: Signal Hill - 0 miles, Seal Beach - 5 miles, Hawaiian Gardens - 6 miles, Carson - 6 miles, Los Alamitos - 6 miles, Harbor City - 8 miles, Cypress - 8 miles, Cerritos - 9 miles, La Palma - 9 miles, San Pedro - 9 miles, Torrance - 9 miles, Norwalk - 9 miles, Downey - 10 miles, Buena Park - 10 miles

Carlton Motel Long Beach
4034 Long Beach Blvd
Long Beach CA 90807
(562) 965-7765
$54 - $99
Bed & Pet Discount Offered

Pet Policy: Pet friendly

Features: Number of rooms: 35, Number of floors: 1, Free breakfast, Parking (free), Front desk (limited hours), Free Internet.

Colonial Pool and Spa Motel
802 E Pacific Coast Hwy
Long Beach CA 90806
(877) 747-8713
$65 - $80
Bed & Pet Discount Offered

Pet Policy: Pets welcome

Features: Free breakfast, Swimming pool - outdoor, Number of rooms: 60, Number of floors: 2, Coffee in lobby, Parking (free), Complimentary newspapers in lobby, Free wireless Internet

Doubletree Hotel Maya, a Doubletree Hotel
700 Queensway Drive
Long Beach CA 90802
(562) 435-7676
$152 - $249
Bed & Pet Discount Offered

Pet Policy: Pets allowed, $100 refundable deposit. No aggressive dog breeds allowed.

Features: Outdoor pool, Restaurant(s), Gift shops or newsstand, Number of rooms: 195, Number of floors: 5, Parking - fee, Multilingual staff, Complimentary newspapers, Porter/bellhop, Fitness facilities, Business center, Concierge, Security guard, Room service (limited hours), Bar/lounge, Dry cleaning/laundry service, Free wireless Internet

Extended Stay America Los Angeles - Long Beach Air
4105 E Willow St
Long Beach CA 90815
(562) 989-4601
$74 - $89
Bed & Pet Discount Offered

Pet Policy: One pet is allowed in each guest room. A $25 per day non-refundable cleaning fee (not to exceed $150) will be charged the first night of your stay.

Features: Guest laundry, Number of rooms: 134, Number of floors: 3, Parking (free), Front desk (limited hours), Wireless Internet (additional charge).

Hilton Long Beach
701 W Ocean Blvd
Long Beach CA 90831
(562) 983-3400
$116 - $234
Bed & Pet Discount Offered

Pet Policy: Pets up to 75 lbs, $75 additional charge.

Features: Business center, Concierge, Bar/lounge, Outdoor pool, Restaurant(s), Number of rooms: 397, Number of floors: 15, Internet (additional charge), Breakfast available additional charge, Multilingual staff, Complimentary newspapers, Porter/bellhop, Smoke-Free property, Parking (valet) $19/day, Accessible bathroom, In-room accessibility equipment for the deaf, Braille or raised signage, Dry cleaning/laundry service, Gift shop, Grocery/convenience store, Fitness facilities, Area shuttle (free), Billiards, Room service (24 hours).

Holiday Inn Long Beach Airport Hotel and Conference
2640 N Lakewood Blvd
Long Beach CA 90815
(562) 597-4401
$103 - $200
Bed & Pet Discount Offered

Pet Policy: Pets under 25 lbs, $25 per stay.

Features: Bar/lounge, Restaurant(s), Room service (limited hours), Concierge, Number of rooms: 222, Number of floors: 13, Breakfast available additional charge, Parking (free), Multilingual staff, Porter/bellhop, ATM/Banking, Outdoor pool, Business services, Airport transportation (free), Accessible bathroom, In-room accessibility equipment for the deaf, Braille or raised signage, Dry cleaning/laundry service, Free wireless Internet, Area shuttle (free), Fitness facilities

Hotel Current
5325 E Pacific Coast Hwy
Long Beach CA 90804
(562) 597-1341
$84- $139
Bed & Pet Discount Offered

Pet Policy: Small pets welcome, $10 per night. Offers a fun Doggie Gift Bag with pet friendly items.

Features: Cruise terminal shuttle (free), Smoke-Free property, Airport transportation (free), Restaurant(s), Swimming pool - outdoor, Number of rooms: 143, Number of floors: 2, Business services, Suitable for children, Guest laundry, Free breakfast, Parking (free), Multilingual staff, Complimentary newspapers in lobby, Use of nearby fitness center (free), Free wireless Internet, Bar/lounge, Area shuttle (free), Accessible bathroom.

Renaissance Long Beach Hotel
111 E Ocean Blvd
Long Beach CA 90802
(562) 437-5900
$138- $289
Bed & Pet Discount Offered

Pet Policy: Pets allowed, $75 cleaning fee per stay.

Features: Business Center, Sauna, Concierge desk, Swimming pool - outdoor, Bar/lounge, Restaurant(s), Gift shops or newsstand, Number of rooms: 374, Number of floors: 12, Computer rental, Coffee in lobby, Breakfast available additional charge, Room service (24 hours), Complimentary newspapers in lobby, Porter/bellhop, Security guard, Wireless Internet (additional charge), Massage - treatment room(s), Smoke-Free property, Dry cleaning/laundry service, Fitness facilities, Parking fee.

Residence Inn by Marriott Downtown Long Beach
600 Queensway Drive
Long Beach CA 90802
(562) 495-0700
$138 - $229
Bed & Pet Discount Offered

Pet Policy: Pets allowed, $100 cleaning fee per stay.

Features: Number of suites: 178, Number of floors: 11, Smoke-Free property, Parking fee, Coffee in lobby, Free breakfast, Spa services on site, Dry cleaning/laundry service, Free wireless Internet.

Residence Inn By Marriott
4111 E Willow St
Long Beach CA 90815
(562) 595-0909
$129 - $180
Bed & Pet Discount Offered

Pet Policy: Pets allowed, $100 per stay cleaning fee.

Features: Business services, Outdoor pool, Airport transportation (free), Number of rooms: 216, Number of floors: 2,BBQ area, Coffee in lobby, Parking (free), Complimentary newspapers, Dry cleaning/laundry, Free Breakfast, Tennis courts, Fitness facilities.

Rodeway Inn Long Beach
50 Atlantic Ave
Long Beach CA 90802
(562) 435-8369
$81 - $128
Bed & Pet Discount Offered

Pet Policy: Rodeway Inns charge an additional $10 per night per pet plus a $50 damage deposit, which is refunded if the room is in order at check out. Max of 2 pets per room. A veterinarian certificate that the pet is on a flea and parasite program is required. Pets may not be left alone in the room unless crated.

Features: Coffee in lobby, Concierge, Number of rooms: 34, Free breakfast, Parking (free), Multilingual staff, Complimentary, Free wireless Internet, Dry cleaning/laundry service

Super 8 Long Beach
4201 E Pacific Coast Hwy
Long Beach CA 90804
(562) 597-7701
$63 - $87
Bed & Pet Discount Offered

Pet Policy: Pets accepted, $10 per night.

Features: Parking (free), Sauna, Number of floors: 2, Business services, High speed Internet.

Not rated 

The Turret House Inn
556 Chestnut Avenue
Long Beach CA 90802
(562) 624-1991
$84 - $107

Pet Policy: Pets with advanced approval. Must contact hotel directly for reservations and pet information.

Features: Number of rooms: 5, Private baths, Free wireless Internet, Direct TV, Free continental breakfast.

★★★½

The Westin Long Beach
333 E Ocean Blvd
Long Beach CA 90802
(562) 436-3000
$119 - $189
Bed & Pet Discount Offered

Pet Policy: Dogs only, up to 40 lbs, no fee.

Features: Outdoor pool, Sauna, Bar/Lounge, Concierge, Dry cleaning/laundry, Restaurant(s), Supervised child care/activities, Gift shop, Number of rooms: 460, Business services, Computer rental, Breakfast available additional charge, Room service (24 hours), Shoe shine, Multilingual staff, Complimentary newspapers, Porter/bellhop, Limo or Town Car service available, Technology helpdesk, Nearby fitness center (discount), Parking fee.

Vagabond Inn Convention Center Long Beach
150 Alamitos Ave
Long Beach CA 90802
(562) 435-7621
$65 - $79
Bed & Pet Discount Offered

Pet Policy: Pets allowed, $10 per night for small pets, $15 for large pets. Limit 2 pets per room.

Features: Elevator, Coffee in lobby, Business services, Number of rooms: 60, Number of floors: 3, Free breakfast, Parking (free), Multilingual staff, Complimentary newspapers in lobby.

Los Alamitos

Also see the following nearby communities that have pet friendly lodging: Cypress - 2 miles, Hawaiian Gardens - 2 miles, La Palma - 3 miles, Buena Park - 4 miles, Seal Beach - 4 miles, Cerritos - 4 miles, Signal Hill - 6 miles, Long Beach - 6 miles, La Mirada - 7 miles, Norwalk - 7 miles, Garden Grove - 8 miles, Huntington Beach - 8 miles, Anaheim - 8 miles, Fountain Valley - 9 miles, Fullerton - 9 miles, Downey - 10 mile

Residence Inn by Marriott
4931 Katella Ave
Los Alamitos CA 90720
(714) 484-5700
$124 - $189
Bed & Pet Discount Offered

Pet Policy: Pets allowed, $100 cleaning fee per stay.

Features: Outdoor pool, Free breakfast, Number of suites: 155, Number of floors: 4, Complimentary newspapers, Wireless Internet (additional charge), Grocery/convenience store, Dry cleaning/laundry.

Los Altos

Also see the following nearby communities that have pet friendly lodging: Mountain View - 2 miles, Palo Alto - 3 miles, Menlo Park - 5 miles, Sunnyvale - 6 miles, Cupertino - 8 miles, Santa Clara - 8 miles, Redwood City - 9 miles

Residence Inn Marriott Palo Alto - Los Altos
4460 El Camino Real
Los Altos CA 94022
(650) 559-7890
$128 - $260
Bed & Pet Discount Offered

Pet Policy: Pets allowed, $100 per stay cleaning fee.

Features: Outdoor pool, Free breakfast, Business center, Number of rooms: 156, Number of floors: 3, Suitable for children, BBQ area, Coffee in lobby, Grocery, Multilingual staff, Complimentary newspapers, Free wireless Internet, Dry cleaning/laundry, Tennis courts, Fitness facilities.

Los Angeles

Also see the following nearby communities that have pet friendly lodging: Culver City - 2 miles, Inglewood - 3 miles, Beverly Hills - 5 miles, Marina Del Rey - 5 miles, Venice - 6 miles, West Hollywood - 6 miles, El Segundo - 6 miles, Hawthorne - 6 miles, Santa Monica - 7 miles, Hollywood - 7 miles, Manhattan Beach - 8 miles, Huntington Park - 9 miles, Universal City - 9 miles, Gardena - 9 miles, Studio City - 10 miles, Hermosa Beach - 10 miles

Baxter 5 - Apartments
1549 Baxter Street
Los Angeles CA 90026
(323) 660-2111
From $200
Bed & Pet Discount Offered

Pet Policy: We accept pets, all sizes, our primary concerns are noise (Big dog? Big bark.) and due to concern for the Hardwood flooring in most of our apartments - weight. Pet clean additional charge of $50 per pet.

Continued on next page

Baxter 5 – Apartments
Continued from previous page

Features: Number of rooms: 6, Number of floors: 1, Business services, Internet (additional charge), Guest laundry, Parking (free), Video library, Smoke-Free property, Breakfast.

★★★
Custom Hotel LAX
8639 Lincoln Blvd
Los Angeles CA 90045
(310) 645-0400
$141 - $241
Bed & Pet Discount Offered

Pet Policy: Pet Friendly. Additional charge.

Features: Poolside bar, Concierge desk, Bar/lounge, Elevator, Swimming pool - outdoor, Number of rooms: 259, Number of floors: 12, Multilingual staff, Parking (valet) $20 Per Night, Accessible bathroom, In-room accessibility equipment for the deaf, Braille or raised signage, Dry cleaning/laundry service, Airport transportation (free), Complimentary newspapers in lobby, Restaurant, Smoke-Free property, Billiards or pool table, Free wireless Internet, 24-hour business center, Fitness facilities.

★
ESA Los Angeles South
18602 S Vermont Ave
Los Angeles CA 90248
(310) 515-5139
$53 - $91

Pet Policy: One pet is allowed in each guest room. A $25 per day non-refundable cleaning fee (not to exceed $150) will be charged the first night of your stay.

Features: Furnished apartments, Full kitchen, Data port, Guest laundry, Weekly housekeeping. Minimum stay of 30 days may be required.

★★
Extended Stay America Los Angeles - LAX Airport
6531 S Sepulveda Blvd
Los Angeles CA 90045
(310) 568-9337
$74 - $114

Pet Policy: One pet is allowed in each guest room. A $25 per day non-refundable cleaning fee (not to exceed $150) will be charged the first night of your stay. Weight, size and breed restrictions may apply. Please contact the hotel directly for booking.
Features: Guest laundry, Elevator, Number of rooms: 133, Number of floors: 4, Business services, Parking (free), Front desk (limited hours), Security guard, Wireless Internet.

★★★
Farmer's Daughter
115 S Fairfax Ave
Los Angeles CA 90036
(323) 937-3930
$168 - $239
Bed & Pet Discount Offered

Pet Policy: Dogs only, under 20 lbs. $50 per pet.

Features: Restaurant(s), Complimentary newspapers, Free wireless Internet, 24-hour business center, Smoke-Free property, Coffee in lobby, Outdoor pool, Concierge, Nearby fitness center (discount), Parking (valet) $18.70/Day, Room service, Number of rooms: 66, Number of floors: 3, Video library, Multilingual staff, Smoke-Free property

Four Seasons Los Angeles
300 S Doheny Dr
Los Angeles CA 90048
(310) 273-2222
$434 - $1,350
Bed & Pet Discount Offered

Pet Policy: Dogs and cats, under 15 lbs, are welcome. Limit one pet per room.

Features: Bar/lounge, Restaurants: 2, Outdoor pool, Number of rooms: 285, Limo or Town Car service available, Full-service health spa, Business center, Area shuttle (free), Gift shops or newsstand, Coffee in lobby, Poolside bar, Currency exchange, Health club, Room service, Shoe shine, Multilingual staff, Complimentary newspapers, Porter/bellhop, Dry cleaning/laundry, Medical assistance available, Concierge , Technology support staff, Wireless Internet (additional charge), Valet Parking fee.

Hilton Checkers
535 South Grand Avenue
Los Angeles CA 90071
(213) 624-0000
$127 - $339
Bed & Pet Discount Offered

Pet Policy: Pets up to 75 lbs accepted, $75 per stay.

Features: Outdoor pool, Parking fee, Room service (24 hours), Wheelchair accessible, Security guard, Full-service health spa, Bar/lounge, Coffee in lobby, Restaurant(s), Concierge, Number of rooms: 188, Number of floors: 15, Multilingual staff, Complimentary newspapers, Porter/bellhop, Dry cleaning/laundry, Breakfast available additional charge, Wireless Internet (additional charge), Business center, Accessible bathroom.

Hilton Los Angeles Airport And Towers
5711 W Century Blvd
Los Angeles CA 90045
(310) 410-4000
$84 - $274
Bed & Pet Discount Offered

Pet Policy: Pets up to 75 lbs accepted, $50 per stay.

Features: Outdoor pool, ATM/Banking, Concierge, Security guard, Business Center, Currency Exchange, Airport transportation (free), Room service (24 hours), Bar/lounge, Restaurant(s), Gift shops or newsstand, Number of rooms: 1,234, Number of floors: 17, Computer rental, Wireless Internet (additional charge), Parking - fee, Multilingual staff, Limo or Town Car service available, Airport transportation (free), Dry cleaning/laundry, Fitness center.

Hollywood Historic Hotel
5162 Melrose Avenue
Los Angeles CA 90038
(323) 378-6312
$65 - $72
Bed & Pet Discount Offered

Pet Policy: Pets up to 40 lbs accepted, $35 per night.

Features: Number of rooms: 62, Number of floors: 3, Parking (free), Front desk (limited hours),

Hollywood Hotel
1160 North Vermont Avenue
Los Angeles CA 90029
(323) 315-1800
$118 - $300
Bed & Pet Discount Offered

Pet Policy: Dogs and cats up to 35 lbs, $35 per night per pet, to a maximum of $245 per stay.

Features: Sauna, Security guard, Outdoor pool,, Bar/Lounge, Wheelchair accessible, Restaurant(s), Concierge, Translation services, Limo or Town Car service available, Smoke-Free, Technology helpdesk, Technology support staff, Grocery/convenience store, Free wireless Internet, RV and truck parking, Theme park shuttle additional charge, Gift shops, Number of rooms: 128, Number of floors: 4, Free breakfast, Multilingual staff, Complimentary newspapers, Business center, Porter/bellhop, Accessible bathroom, In-room accessibility equipment for the deaf, Braille or raised signage, Dry cleaning/laundry, Fitness facilities, Self-parking fee.

Not rated
Hotel Bel Air
701 Stone Canyon Road
Los Angeles CA 90077
(310) 472-1211
$536 - $653

Pet Policy: Dogs and cats welcome. Free pet basket (for cats and dogs) available, Custom-designed bowl with the name of the pet can be easily arranged in advance, Name tag with the name of the pet, Specific menus and food options available, The grooms are pleased to walk dogs in the Tuileries Garden.

Features: Boutique full service hotel is undergoing extensive renovations at the time of this writing, will not reopen until the latter half of 2011.

★★★★
Hotel Palomar Los Angeles Westwood - a Kimpton Hot
10740 Wilshire Blvd
Los Angeles CA 90024
(310) 475-8711
$203 - $549
Bed & Pet Discount Offered

Pet Policy: Pets welcome. No size restriction. No Additional charges. Special pet amenities include treats, bowls, tags with hotel info, and even pet packages with special food, dog walking, and toys

Features: Swimming pool - outdoor, Business Center, Bar/lounge, Room service (24 hours), Restaurant(s), Number of rooms: 238, Number of suites: 26, Breakfast available additional charge, Spa services on site, Porter/bellhop, Free wireless Internet, Dry cleaning/laundry service, Valet Parking fee

★★★★

Hyatt Regency Century Plaza
2025 Avenue Of The Stars
Los Angeles CA 90067
(310) 228-1234
$152 - $499
Bed & Pet Discount Offered

Pet Policy: Dogs welcome, $35 per night service charge. Hyatt Regency Century Plaza's Executive Chef, Manfred Lassahn, created an in-room doggie menu guaranteed to make even the most well-trained dog sit up and beg. Each tail-wagging item is prepared to order and will be served only when entrees and treats are cooled at a temperature safe for doggie's palettes (pet owners should plan on 60 minutes delivery time). Menu items cost $5 and are made with all-natural ingredients, edible by humans. Menu items include "Bark-fest" Grrrrrrr-nola and Bower's Bacon Pancakes; "Yappi-tizers" Buddy Burger and K-9 Green Bean Casserole; and "Tail-Waggin" Treats Barkin' Biscotti; Snicker-Poodles; Chef's Biscuit and Cold Nose Bark Bar.Perfect for rest and play, the hotel's backyard grounds include grassy gardens and a designated "barking lot" complete with disposal bags and trash bin. Hyatt Gold Passport members accompanied by their pet receive a welcome kit, and a Hyatt Gold Pawsport that includes the dog's name, birthday, owner information, Hyatt Gold Passport number and Pawsport stamp boxes to track visits.Hyatt Gold Passport members earn 500 Hyatt Gold Passport points with each qualifying stay, while pampered pooches enjoy special canine amenities that include: Classic, plush - round 28" doggie bed Stainless steel double diner serving bowl in room upon arrival Home-made, all-natural welcome treat Specially designed in room haute-dog menu Annual birthday card

Features: Swimming pool - outdoor, Beauty services, Health club, Business center, Steam room, Bar/lounge, Room service (24 hours), ATM/banking, Elevator, Full-service health spa, Shoe shine, Concierge desk, Security guard, Hair salon, Restaurant(s), Gift shops or newsstand, Translation services, Coffee in lobby, Breakfast available additional charge, Multilingual staff, Porter/bellhop, Limo or Town Car service available, Wireless Internet, Massage - treatment room(s), Parking (valet) $31/24 Hours In/Out, Accessible bathroom, In-room accessibility equipment for the deaf, Braille or raised signage, Dry cleaning/laundry service.

InterContinental Century City
2151 Avenue Of The Stars
Los Angeles CA 90067
(310) 284-6500
$219 - $574
Bed & Pet Discount Offered

Pet Policy: Pets up to 25 lbs, $100 per stay cleaning fee.

Features: Bar/Lounge, Concierge, Fitness Facilities, Restaurant(s), Gift shops or newsstand, Number of rooms: 363, Number of suites: 180, Number of floors: 14, Cell phone/mobile rental, Computer rental, Multilingual staff, Complimentary newspapers in lobby, Porter/bellhop, Security guard, Limo or Town Car service available, Wireless Internet (additional charge), Shoe shine, Outdoor pool, Room service (24 hours), ATM/banking, Parking (valet) $32/day, Accessible bathroom, In-room accessibility equipment for the deaf, Braille or raised signage, Dry cleaning/laundry service, Babysitting or child care, Business center, Currency exchange, Sauna.

★★★★
JW Marriott Los Angeles
900 W Olympic Blvd
Los Angeles CA 90015
(213) 765-8600
$199 - $429
Bed & Pet Discount Offered

Pet Policy: Pets accepted with $125 per stay cleaning fee.

Features: Beauty services, Restaurant(s), Full-service health spa, Swimming pool - outdoor, Bar/lounge, Fitness facilities, Accessibility equipment for the deaf, Accessible bathroom, Braille or raised signage.

★★★
La Quinta Inn & Suites LAX
5249 W Century Blvd
Los Angeles CA 90045
(310) 645-2200
$83 - $105
Bed & Pet Discount Offered

Pet Policy: Cats and dogs up to 50 pounds are accepted in all guest rooms. Housekeeping services for rooms with pets require pet owner be present or pet must be crated. No additional charges or deposits are required.

Features: Free breakfast, ATM/Banking, Elevator, Business center, Accessible bathroom, Bar/lounge, Airport transportation (free), Restaurant(s), Room service (limited hours), Swimming pool - outdoor, Concierge services, Gift shops or newsstand, Number of rooms: 278, Number of floors: 10, Coffee in lobby, Guest laundry, Free wireless Internet, Airport transportation (free) available 24 hours, Fitness facilities, Self-parking fee.

★★★★
Luxe Hotel Sunset Boulevard
11461 W Sunset Blvd
Los Angeles CA 90049
(310) 476-6571
$186 - $1,540
Bed & Pet Discount Offered

Pet Policy: Pet Policy: Pets under 50 lbs accepted, $250 per stay cleaning fee. Limit 2 per suite. Must not leave pets unattended and must clean up after them.

Continued on next page

Luxe Hotel Sunset Boulevard
Continued from previous page

Features: Bar/Lounge, Outdoor pool, Business Services, Babysitting or child care, Restaurant(s), Room service, Number of rooms: 160, Multilingual staff, Porter/bellhop, Security guard, Free wireless Internet, Spa services, Parking (valet) $24 Per Day, Accessible bathroom, In-room accessibility equipment for the deaf, Braille or raised signage, Dry cleaning/laundry service, Smoke-Free, Fitness center.

Not rated
Maison Blanche Homes
135 North Doheny Drive 105
Los Angeles CA 90048
(800) 230-4134
From $315

Pet Policy: Dogs and cats accepted, $300 refundable pet deposit.

Features: Furnished apartments, both long and short-term stays available.

Not rated
Marriott Execustay Palazzo Park
6220 West Third Street
Los Angeles CA 90036
(888) 526-0566
From $199

Pet Policy: Pets accepted up to 50 lbs. $500 deposit, $250 non-refundable. Limit 2 pets per apartment, no aggressive breeds.

Features: Furnished apartments, Full kitchens, Gas fireplaces, Business center, Concierge, Fitness Center, Pool and spa, Massage treatment rooms.

Not Rated
Oakwood at 1010 Wilshire
1010 Wilshire Blvd
Suite 1
Los Angeles CA 90017
(866) 245-4137
From $121

Pet Policy: Pets up to 35 lbs welcome, $10 per day, plus repair of any damages.

Features: Fully furnished apartments, Business Center, Lounge. Minimum stay of 30 days may be required.

Not Rated
Oakwood at Metro 417
417 S HILL ST
Los Angeles CA 90013
(213) 620-0095
$136 - $151

Pet Policy: Pets accepted with limitations and additional charge. Contact hotel directly for more information and to make reservations.

Features: Furnished apartments, billiard room. Minimum stay of 30 days may be required.

Not rated
Oakwood at Palazzo East
348 S Hauser Blvd
Los Angeles CA 90036
(682) 687-3385
$139 - $218

Pet Policy: Pets accepted with limitations and additional charge. Contact hotel directly for more information and to make reservations.

Features: Fully furnished apartments, Health spa, Swimming pool – Olympic size, Concierge . Minimum stay of 30 days may be required.

Not Rated
Oakwood Toluca Hills
3600 Barham Blvd
Los Angeles CA 90068
(323) 851-3450
$87 - $177

Pet Policy: Pets accepted with limitations and additional charge Contact hotel directly for more information and to make reservations.

Features: Fully furnished apartments, Fireplaces, BBQ area, Fitness Center, Spa, Steam Room, Swimming Pool.

★★★★
Omni Los Angeles Hotel at California Plaza
251 S Olive St
Los Angeles CA 90012
(213) 617-3300
$135 - $399
Bed & Pet Discount Offered

Pet Policy: Pets under 25 lbs, $75 per stay.

Features: Bar/lounge, Room service (24 hours), ATM/banking, Parking (valet) $30/24 Hours In/Out, Security guard, Concierge desk, Swimming pool - outdoor, Restaurant(s), Gift shops or newsstand, Number of rooms: 453, Number of floors: 17, Accessible bathroom, In-room accessibility equipment for the deaf, Dry cleaning/laundry service, Business Center, Free Internet, Breakfast available additional charge, Multilingual staff, Porter/bellhop, Limo or Town Car service available, Full-service health spa.

★★½
Radisson at USC, Los Angeles
3540 S Figueroa Street
Los Angeles CA 90007
(213) 748-4141
$134 - $249
Bed & Pet Discount Offered

Pet Policy: Pets allowed, $50 per stay.

Features: Elevator, Restaurant(s), Room service (limited hours), Concierge services, Gift shops or newsstand, Number of floors: 11, Breakfast available additional charge, Coffee in lobby, Bar/lounge, Swimming pool – outdoor, Health club, Multilingual staff.

★★★½
Radisson Hotel Los Angeles Airport
6225 W Century Blvd
Los Angeles CA 90045
(310) 670-9000
$89 - $249
Bed & Pet Discount Offered

Pet Policy: Pets allowed with an additional charge.

Features: Bar/Lounge, Concierge Desk, Elevator, ATM/Banking, Airport transportation (free) available 24 hours, Restaurant(s), Swimming pool - outdoor, Parking (valet - fee), Gift shops or newsstand, Number of rooms: 600, Number of floors: 12, Breakfast available additional charge, Room service (24 hours), Spa services on site, Complimentary newspapers in lobby, Porter/bellhop, Security guard, Limo or Town Car service available, Free wireless Internet, Massage - treatment room(s), Technology helpdesk, Dry cleaning/laundry service, Fitness facilities

Residence Inn by Marriott Beverly Hills
1177 S Beverly Dr
Los Angeles CA 90035
(310) 228-4100
$169 - $429
Bed & Pet Discount Offered

Pet Policy: Pets allowed, $100 cleaning fee per stay.

Features: Elevator, Free Breakfast, Wheelchair accessible, Concierge services, Number of rooms: 186, Suitable for children, Grocery, Smoke-Free property, Free wireless Internet, Area shuttle (free), 24-hour business center, Free reception, ATM/banking, Business services, Coffee in lobby, Room service, Accessible bathroom, In-room accessibility equipment for the deaf, Braille or raised signage, Dry cleaning/laundry service, Fitness facilities, Self & Valet parking – additional charge.

★★

Rodeway Inn Convention Center
1904 W Olympic Blvd
Los Angeles CA 90006
(213) 380-9393
$79 - $95
Bed & Pet Discount Offered

Pet Policy: Rodeway Inns charge an additional $10 per night per pet and require a $50 damage deposit, which is refunded if the room is in order at check out. Max of 2 pets per room. A veterinarian certificate that the pet is on a flea and parasite program and that they are Free from parasites is required. Pets may not be left alone in the room unless in a cage.

Features: Swimming pool - outdoor, Elevator, Number of rooms: 54, Business services, Pool table, Free breakfast, Parking (free), Complimentary newspapers in lobby, Limo or Town Car service available, Multilingual staff.

★★

Rodeway Inn Culver City
11933 W Washington Blvd
Los Angeles CA 90066
(310) 398-1651
$87- $94
Bed & Pet Discount Offered

Pet Policy: Rodeway Inns charge an additional $10 per night per pet and require a $50 damage deposit, which is refunded if the room is in order at check out. Max of 2 pets per room. A veterinarian certificate that the pet is on a flea and parasite program and that they are Free from parasites is required. Pets may not be left alone in the room unless in a cage.

Features: Free breakfast, Number of rooms: 32, Number of floors: 2, Parking (free).

★★★

Shelter Hotels Los Angeles
457 S Mariposa Ave
Los Angeles CA 90020
(323) 380-6910
$108 - $119
Bed & Pet Discount Offered

Pet Policy: Pet friendly rooms available. No additional charge indicated but you may wish to confirm before arrival.

Features: Swimming pool - outdoor, Number of rooms: 47, Business services, Parking (free), Smoke-Free property, Concierge services, Multilingual staff, Free wireless Internet

★★★½

Sheraton Gateway Hotel Los Angeles Airport
6101 W Century Blvd
Los Angeles CA 90045
(310) 642-1111
$96 - $239
Bed & Pet Discount Offered

Pet Policy: Dogs only, $150 per stay

Features: Swimming pool - outdoor, Parking fee, Airport transportation (free), Business center, Bar/lounge, Concierge desk, Room service (24 hours), Elevator, Restaurant(s), Number of rooms: 804, Breakfast available additional charge, Smoke-Free property, Airport transportation (free) available 24 hours, Dry cleaning/laundry service, Fitness facilities, Accessible bathroom, Accessibility equipment for the deaf.

★★★½

Sheraton Los Angeles - Downtown
711 S Hope St
Los Angeles CA 90017
(213) 488-3500
$169 - $319
Bed & Pet Discount Offered

Pet Policy: Allows 1 pet, up to 80 lbs, $35 per stay.

Features: Business Center, Concierge desk, Bar/lounge, Room service (limited hours), Shoe shine, Elevator, Gift shops or newsstand, Number of rooms: 485, Number of floors: 24, Wireless Internet (additional charge), Breakfast available additional charge, Multilingual staff, Complimentary newspapers in lobby, Use of nearby fitness center (free), Smoke-Free property, Parking (valet) $28 Per day, Dry cleaning/laundry service, Currency exchange.

★★★★½

Sofitel Los Angeles
8555 Beverly Blvd
Los Angeles CA 90048
(310) 278-5444
$234 - $445
Bed & Pet Discount Offered

Pet Policy: Pets accepted at no additional charge.

Features: Room service (24 hours), Currency Exchange, Security guard, Bar/lounge, Concierge Desk, Spa services on site, Swimming pool - outdoor, Coffee in lobby, Shoe shine, Multilingual staff, Complimentary newspapers in lobby, Business center, Porter/bellhop, Limo or Town Car service available, Medical assistance available, Free wireless Internet, Beauty services, Massage - treatment room(s), Sauna, Restaurant(s), Gift shops or newsstand, Shopping on site, Accessible bathroom, In-room accessibility equipment for the deaf, Dry cleaning/Laundry service, Health club, Smoke-Free property, Valet Parking fee

★★

Super 8 Los Angeles-Culver City
12664 W Washington Blvd
Los Angeles CA 90066
(310) 306-8243
$75 - $130
Bed & Pet Discount Offered

Pet Policy: Pets accepted, $20 per night additional charge in designated rooms only.

Features: Swimming pool - outdoor, Number of floors: 2, Parking (free), Free wireless Internet.

Super 8 Los Angeles Alhambra
5350 S Huntington Drive
Los Angeles CA 90032
(323) 225-2310
$47 - $84
Bed & Pet Discount Offered

Pet Policy: Pets accepted, $20 per night additional charge in designated rooms only.

Features: Business services, Free breakfast, Parking (free), 24-hour front desk

Not Rated
The Crescent At Legacy
10833 Wilshire Blvd
Los Angeles CA 90024
(310) 474-6336
$260 - $261

Pet Policy: Pets under 50 lbs accepted.

Features: Furnished 2 bedroom 2 bath apartments, Washer & dryer in each unit, Direct TV, Free Wireless Internet, Free parking.

★★★½

The Orlando
8384 W 3rd St
Los Angeles CA 90048
(323) 658-6600
$207 - $303
Bed & Pet Discount Offered

Pet Policy: Pets under 15 lbs, $50 per day. Limit 1 pet, and only in second floor standard rooms. Pets must be leashed outside of room, are not permitted in any public areas, and must not be left unattended in room unless crated.

Features: Business Services, Concierge services, Elevator, Restaurant(s), Number of rooms: 98, Number of floors: 5, Breakfast available additional charge, Library, Shoe shine, Multilingual staff, Porter/bellhop, Free wireless Internet, Massage - treatment room(s), Smoke-Free property, Parking (valet) $26/24 Hours In/Out, Dry cleaning/laundry service, Room service (24 hours), Fitness facilities.

The Ritz-Carlton, Los Angeles
900 W. Olympic Blvd
Los Angeles CA 90015
(213) 743-8800
$348 - $539
Bed & Pet Discount Offered

Pet Policy: Pets up to 20 lbs, $125 one-time cleaning fee.

Features: Valet Parking fee, Wheelchair accessible, Braille or raised signage, Room service (24 hours), Limo or Town Car service available, Concierge desk, Accessibility equipment for the deaf, Multilingual staff, Beauty services, Area shuttle (free), Suitable for children, Bar/lounge, Elevator, Fitness facilities, Swimming pool - outdoor, Wireless Internet (additional charge), ATM/banking, Gift shops or newsstand, Restaurant(s), Steam room, Porter/bellhop, Massage - treatment room(s), Smoke-Free property, Accessible bathroom, Poolside bar, Number of rooms: 123, Dry cleaning/laundry service, Full-service health spa.

★★★½
The Standard Downtown LA
550 S Flower St
Los Angeles CA 90071
(213) 892-8080
$164 - $495
Bed & Pet Discount Offered

Pet Policy: Pets up to 80 lbs accepted, $100 per stay.

Features: ATM/banking, Elevator, Room service (24 hours), Concierge desk, Poolside bar, Nightclub, Free wireless Internet, Hair salon, Medical assistance available, Bar/lounge, Shopping on site, Business center, Health club, Beauty services, Security guard, Restaurant(s), Swimming pool - outdoor, Gift shops or newsstand, Number of rooms: 207, Number of floors: 12, Translation services, Breakfast available additional charge, Pool table, Multilingual staff, Complimentary newspapers in lobby, Limo or Town Car service available, Dry cleaning/laundry service, Valet Parking fee.

★★★½
The Westin Bonaventure Hotel and Suites
404 S Figueroa St
Los Angeles CA 90071
(213) 624-1000
$149 - $349
Bed & Pet Discount Offered

Pet Policy: Dogs up to 40 pounds are allowed. No additional charge. Dogs must be accompanied by owner at all times and are restricted from food and beverage areas as well as other areas designated by the hotel. All ADA dogs are allowed.

Features: ATM/Banking, Bar/Lounge, Swimming pool - outdoor, Sauna, Concierge Desk, Room service (24 hours), Elevator, Restaurant(s), Gift shops or newsstand, Shopping on site, Number of rooms: 1,354, Number of floors: 35, Wireless Internet (additional charge), Breakfast available additional charge, Currency exchange, Shoe shine, Multilingual staff, Business center, Porter/bellhop, Security guard, Limo or Town Car service available, Beauty services, Full-service health spa, Smoke-Free property, Dry cleaning/laundry service, Accessibility equipment for the deaf, Braille or raised signage, Accessible bathroom, Valet Parking fee

★★★½
The Westin Los Angeles Airport
5400 W Century Blvd
Los Angeles CA 90045
(310) 216-5858
$100 - $325
Bed & Pet Discount Offered

Pet Policy: Dogs up to 40 pounds are allowed in guest rooms. Without additional charges, dogs will be provided a Westin Heavenly Dog Bed if desired, along with a welcome kit that provides information and supplies. No other pets are permitted. The hotel reserves the right to charge for additional cleaning or damage caused by the dog.

Features: Security guard, Health club, Business Center, Sauna, ATM/banking, Coffee in lobby, Elevator, Room service (24 hours), Restaurant(s), Swimming pool - outdoor, ***Continued on next page***

The Westin Los Angeles Airport
Continued from previous page

Concierge, Gift shop, Number of rooms: 740, Number of floors: 12, Breakfast available additional charge, Parking (valet) $28/day, Airport transportation (free), Bar/lounge, Accessible bathroom, In-room accessibility equipment for the deaf, Currency exchange, Multilingual staff, Complimentary newspapers, Porter/bellhop, Wireless Internet (additional charge), Massage - treatment room(s), Dry cleaning/laundry service.

★★
Travelodge Hotel at LAX Airport
5547 W Century Blvd
Los Angeles CA 90045
(310) 649-4000
$64 - $100
Bed & Pet Discount Offered

Pet Policy: Pets allowed, $10 per day per pet. Only allowed in designated pet friendly rooms.

Features: Free Breakfast, Concierge, Airport transportation (free), Restaurant(s), Room service (limited hours), Outdoor pool, Gift shops or newsstand, Parking (free), Multilingual staff, Complimentary newspapers, Porter/bellhop, Security guard, Dry cleaning/laundry service, Fitness facilities

★★★★
W Los Angeles - Westwood
930 Hilgard Avenue
Los Angeles CA 90024
(310) 208-8765
$268 - $864
Bed & Pet Discount Offered

Pet Policy: Accepts cats and dogs up to 40 lbs. Guests must sign a waiver.. Pet fee is $25 per pet per day plus a one-time $100 cleaning fee.

Features: Parking (valet - additional charge), Health club, Room service (24 hours), Concierge, Bar/lounge, Restaurant(s), Outdoor pool, Number of suites: 258, Number of floors: 16, Cell phone/mobile rental, Computer rental, Coffee in lobby, Breakfast available additional charge, Library, Poolside bar, Shoe shine, Multilingual staff, Business center, Porter/bellhop, Security guard, Limo or Town Car service available, Medical assistance available, Beauty services, Full-service health spa, Massage - treatment room(s), Technology helpdesk, Dry cleaning/laundry service, Wireless Internet (fee).

Los Banos

Also see the following nearby communities that have pet friendly lodging: Santa Nella - 10 miles

Not rated
Best Western Executive Inn
301 W Pacheco Blvd
Los Banos CA 93635
(209) 827-0954
$64 - $8
5

Pet Policy: Up to 2 dogs per room with a 80 pound weight limit. Additional pet types (cats, birds, etc.) may be accepted at the hotel's discretion. Pet rate is $20 per day with a $100 per week maximum.

Features: Free wireless Internet, Sauna, Free breakfast, Fitness center, Swimming pool, Complimentary newspaper, Microwave and mini fridge, Fireplace in suites.

Days Inn Los Banos
2169 E Pacheco Blvd
Los Banos CA 93635
(209) 826-9690
$51 - $133
Bed & Pet Discount Offered

Pet Policy: Pets allowed, $10 per night.

Features: Barbecue Grill(s), Business Center, Free wireless Internet, Free breakfast, Multilingual staff, Complimentary newspapers in lobby, Swimming pool - outdoor seasonal, Coffee in lobby

Knights Inn Los Banos
1621 E Pacheco Blvd
Los Banos CA 93635
(209) 827-4600
$52 - $80
Bed & Pet Discount Offered

Pet Policy: Small pets accepted, $10 per pet per night.

Features: Restaurant(s), Business services, Free breakfast, Parking (free), Free Internet.

Pacheco Pass Inn
349 W Pacheco Blvd
Los Banos CA 93635
(877) 747-8713
$44 - $59

Pet Policy: Pets accepted. Contact property directly for details and booking.

Features: Outdoor pool, Wheelchair accessible, Number of rooms: 35, Number of floors: 2, Coffee in lobby, Parking (free), Multilingual staff, Free wireless Internet, Accessible bathroom, RV and truck parking.

Vagabond Inn Exec Los Banos
20 W Pacheco Blvd
Los Banos CA 93635
(209) 827-4677
$107 - $143
Bed & Pet Discount Offered

Pet Policy: Pets accepted, $10 per night. Limited area to walk pets on property.

Features: Indoor pool, Coffee in lobby, Number of floors: 2, Free wireless Internet. Accessible bathroom, In-room accessibility equipment for the deaf, 24-hour business center, Number of rooms: 42, Guest laundry, Video library, Free breakfast, Parking (free), Complimentary newspapers in lobby, Smoke-Free property, Fitness facilities.

Los Gatos

Also see the following nearby communities that have pet friendly lodging: Campbell - 4 miles, Cupertino - 7 miles, San Jose - 8 miles

Hotel Los Gatos & Spa, a Joie de Vivre Boutique Ho
210 E Main St
Los Gatos CA 95030
(408) 335-1700
$178 - $329
Bed & Pet Discount Offered

Pet Policy: Pet friendly hotel offering a pet amenity bag including treats, lavender spray and much more. $25 per night plus $75 per stay cleaning fee.

Features: Bar/Lounge, Sauna, Spa services on site, Parking (free), Valet Parking (fee), Video library, Concierge services, Use of nearby fitness center (free), Shoe shine, Wheelchair accessible,
Continued on next page

Hotel Los Gatos & Spa
Continued from previous page

Translation services, Breakfast available additional charge, Health club, Limo or Town Car service available, Massage treatment room(s), Technology helpdesk, 24-hour business center, Restaurant(s), Number of rooms: 72, Number of floors: 2, Multilingual staff, Complimentary newspapers, Porter/bellhop, Wireless Internet, Beauty services, Full-service health spa, Smoke-Free property, Dry cleaning/laundry service, Outdoor pool.

Los Gatos Lodge
50 Los Gatos Saratoga Road
Los Gatos CA 95032
(408) 354-3300
$99 - $159
Bed & Pet Discount Offered

Pet Policy: All pets welcome, $30 per stay cleaning fee.

Features: Bar/lounge, Room service (limited hours), Restaurant(s), Wheelchair accessible, Parking (free), Business center, Outdoor pool, Shopping on site, Guest laundry, Free breakfast, Dry cleaning/laundry service, Free wireless Internet, Fitness facilities.

Los Osos

Also see the following nearby communities that have pet friendly lodging: Morro Bay - 5 miles, San Luis Obispo - 9 miles

Not rated
Sea Pines Golf Resort
1945 Solano Street
Los Osos CA 93402
(805) 528-5252
From $114

Pet Policy: Pet friendly rooms available. No additional charge indicated but you may wish to confirm before arrival.

Features: Golf course, HBO, Coffee maker.

Lost Hills

Days Inn Lost Hills
14684 Aloma St
Lost Hills CA 93249
(661) 797-2371
$55 - $84
Bed & Pet Discount Offered

Pet Policy: Pets allowed, $10 per night.

Features: Swimming pool – outdoor, Number of rooms: 76, Free breakfast, Parking (free), Free wireless Internet.

Madera

Days Inn Madera CA
25327 Avenue 16
Madera CA 93637
(559) 674-8817
$50 - $84
Bed & Pet Discount Offered

Pet Policy: Pets allowed, $10 per night.

Features: Free breakfast, Restaurant(s), Business services, Coffee in lobby, Complimentary newspaper, Free Internet, Swimming pool - outdoor seasonal.

Madera Valley Inn
317 N G St
Madera CA 93637
(559) 664-0100
$42 - $65
Bed & Pet Discount Offered

Pet Policy: Small pets allowed, $15 per pet per night with a maximum of $30 per stay.

Features: Coffee in lobby, Business Center, Bar/Lounge, Outdoor pool, Dry cleaning/laundry, Restaurant, Room service, Number of rooms: 92, Number of floors: 5, Airport transportation (additional charge), Free breakfast, F newspapers, Free Internet, Nearby fitness center (discount).

Super 8 Madera CA
1855 W Cleveland Ave
Madera CA 93637
(559) 661-1131
$47 - $69
Bed & Pet Discount Offered

Pet Policy: Pet friendly, $5 per day per pet.

Features: Business services, Free breakfast, Parking (free), Swimming pool - outdoor seasonal.

Mammoth Lakes

Econo Lodge Wildwood Inn
3626 Main St - A
Mammoth Lakes CA 93546
(760) 934-6855
$75 - $199
Bed & Pet Discount Offered

Pet Policy: Pet Friendly. Additional charge $10.

Features: Babysitting or child care, Outdoor pool – seasonal, Number of rooms: 32, Number of floors: 2, Free breakfast.

Mammoth Lakes Travelodge
54 Sierra Blvd
Mammoth Lakes CA 93546
(760) 934-8892
$103 - $179
Bed & Pet Discount Offered

Pet Policy: Pets accepted, $10 per night.

Features: Sauna, Free breakfast, Restaurant(s), Coffee in lobby, Pool table, Multilingual staff, Complimentary newspapers in lobby, Business center, Wireless Internet.

Mammoth Mountain Inn
1 Minaret Rd
Mammoth Lakes CA 93546
(760) 934-2581
$129 - $549
Bed & Pet Discount Offered

Pet Policy: Pet s accepted with $50 per pet per night plus $200 refundable deposit.

Features: Guest laundry, Arcade/game room, Ski-in/Ski-out, Bar/lounge, Babysitting or child care, Outdoor pool, Gift shop, Computer rental, Room service, 2 Restaurants, Wheelchair accessible, Supervised child care/activities, Concierge, Business services, Ski storage, Video library, Multilingual staff, Complimentary newspapers, Porter/bellhop, Medical assistance available, Sauna, Smoke-Free, Grocery/convenience store, Free wireless Internet, Fitness facilities, Airport transportation (free).

Shilo Inn Suites - Mammoth Lakes
2963 Main St
Mammoth Lakes CA 93546
(760) 934-4500
$249 - $250
Bed & Pet Discount Offered

Pet Policy: Pet friendly

Features: Sauna, Airport transportation (free), Steam room, Swimming pool - indoor, Number of suites: 71, Business services, Ski storage, Guest laundry, Free breakfast, Parking (free), Smoke-Free property, Airport transportation (free), Fitness facilities.

Sierra Lodge
3540 Main St
Mammoth Lakes CA 93546
(760) 934-8881
$105 - $185
Bed & Pet Discount Offered

Pet Policy: Dogs accepted, $20 per night. Limit 2 dogs. Dogs must not be left in room alone.

Features: Airport transportation (free), Number of rooms: 35, Number of floors: 3, Business services, Coffee in lobby, Internet access – additional charge, Ski storage, Free breakfast, Ski shuttle, Smoke-Free property, Accessible bathroom.

Sierra Nevada Lodge
164 Old Mammoth Road
Mammoth Lakes CA 93546
(760) 934-2515
$135 - $169
Bed & Pet Discount Offered

Pet Policy: Rodeway Inns charge an additional $10 per night per pet and require a $50 damage deposit, which is refunded if the room is in order at check out. Max of 2 pets per room . A veterinarian certificate that the pet is on a flea and parasite program is required. Pets may not be left alone in the room unless in a cage.

Features: Sauna, Coffee in lobby, Number of rooms: 156, Number of floors: 2, Barbecue grill(s), Free breakfast, Multilingual staff, Swimming pool - outdoor seasonal, Nearby fitness center (discount), Airport transportation (free), Restaurant(s), Pool table, Smoke-Free property, Free wireless Internet, Guest laundry, Bar/lounge, Room service (limited hours, Suitable for children, Ski storage, Complimentary newspapers in lobby, Ski shuttle, Accessible bathroom, RV and truck parking, Shopping on site, Nightclub.

Snowcreek Resort
1254 Old Mammoth Road
Mammoth Lakes CA 93546
(760) 934-3333
$184 - $676

Pet Policy: Pets are accepted in pet-friendly designated rooms only.

Features: Fully furnished apartments, 1 – 4 bedrooms available, Fully equipped kitchens, Cable TV, VCR/DVD player, Washer and dryer, Outdoor grill, Fireplace, Wireless Internet available, Nine hole golf course, Free access to Snowcreek Athletic Club..

Tamarack Lodge Resort
163 Twin Lakes Rd
Mammoth Lakes CA 93546
(760) 934-2442
$80 - $499
Bed & Pet Discount Offered

Pet Policy: Pets allowed in cabins only, $30 per night per pet. Please do NOT book anything other than a cabin.

Features: Number of rooms: 34, Wireless Internet (additional charge), Bar/lounge, Restaurant(s).

The Mammoth Creek Inn
663 Old Mammoth Rd
Mammoth Lakes CA 93546
(760) 934-6162
$190 - $359
Bed & Pet Discount Offered

Pet Policy: Pets under 100 lbs, $29 per pet per day. Limit 2 pets per room. Must stay in pet designated rooms.

Features: Airport transportation (free), Concierge, Number of rooms: 15, Number of suites: 11, Number of floors: 2, Ski storage, Parking (free), Complimentary newspapers, Limo or Town Car service available, Sauna, Ski shuttle, Smoke-Free property, Billiards, Free wireless Internet, Area shuttle (free), Smoke-Free property.

The Westin Monache Resort
50 Hillside Dr
Mammoth Lakes CA 93546
(760) 934-0400
$159 - $759
Bed & Pet Discount Offered

Pet Policy: The Westin Monache Resort, Mammoth graciously welcomes pets of most sizes. Owners must sign a waiver at check-in and are responsible for any damage or excessive cleaning needed. Pets are not permitted in the resort's food and beverage outlets and may not be left alone in your room. We are happy to provide a Free Westin Heavenly Dog Bed and food bowl with mat.

Features: Bar/lounge, Room service (limited hours), Business center, Elevator, Restaurant(s), Swimming pool - outdoor, ATM/banking, Number of rooms: 230, Number of floors: 7, Suitable for children, Barbecue grill(s), Ski storage, Breakfast available (not included), Currency exchange, Complimentary newspapers in lobby, Free wireless Internet, Porter/bellhop, Concierge desk, Ski shuttle, Smoke-Free property, Children's club, Accessible bathroom, In-room accessibility equipment for the deaf, Braille or raised signage, Fitness facilities.

Manhattan Beach

Also see the following nearby communities that have pet friendly lodging: Hermosa Beach - 2 miles, El Segundo - 2 miles, Hawthorne - 3 miles, Redondo Beach - 4 miles, Inglewood - 5 miles, Gardena - 6 miles, Torrance - 6 miles, Marina Del Rey - 7 miles, Harbor City - 8 miles, Los Angeles - 8 miles, Venice - 9 miles, Carson - 9 miles, Culver City - 9 miles

Residence Inn by Marriott Manhattan Beach
1700 N Sepulveda Blvd
Manhattan Beach CA 90266
(866) 580-5993
$119 - $179
Bed & Pet Discount Offered

Pet Policy: Pets allowed, $100 per stay cleaning fee.

Features: Business services, Swimming pool - outdoor, ATM/banking, smoke-Free property, Free reception, Room service (limited hours), Number of suites: 176, Barbecue grill(s), Coffee in lobby, Free breakfast, Parking (free), Multilingual staff, Complimentary newspapers in lobby, Dry cleaning/laundry service, Fitness facilities.

★★★½

The Belamar, a Larkspur Collection Hotel
3501 N Sepulveda Blvd
Manhattan Beach CA 90266
(310) 750-0300
$138 - $209
Bed & Pet Discount Offered

Pet Policy: Dogs and Cats, up to 60 lbs, $75 per stay. Limit 1 pet per room. Must be in crate if left in room alone.

Features: Parking (valet), Bar/Lounge, Elevator, Swimming pool - outdoor, Wheelchair accessible, Room service, Free wireless Internet, 24-hour business center, Restaurant(s), ATM/banking, Concierge services, Number of rooms: 127, Number of floors: 3, Breakfast available (not included), Shoe shine, Multilingual staff, Complimentary newspapers in lobby, Use of nearby fitness center (free), Porter/bellhop, Security guard, Limo or Town Car service available, Medical assistance available, Smoke-Free property, Accessible bathroom, In-room accessibility equipment for the deaf, Braille or raised signage, Dry cleaning/laundry service.

Manteca

Also see the following nearby communities that have pet friendly lodging: Lathrop - 5 miles, Ripon - 5 miles, Salida - 10 miles

Americas Best Value Inn
1920 E Yosemite Ave
Manteca CA 95336
(209) 239-6115
$78 - $180
Bed & Pet Discount Offered

Pet Policy: Pets welcome, no additional charge but requires damage deposit.

Features: Bar/lounge, Business services, Swimming pool - outdoor, Number of rooms: 58, Number of floors: 2, Guest laundry, Free breakfast, Parking (free), Complimentary newspapers in lobby, Steam room, Free wireless Internet, Health club.

Best Western Executive Inn & Suites
1415 E Yosemite Ave
Manteca CA 95336
(209) 825-1415
$74 - $95
Bed & Pet Discount Offered

Pet Policy: Pets accepted with small additional charge at check in.

Features: Elevator, Swimming pool - outdoor, Number of rooms: 101, Number of floors: 3, Coffee in lobby, Free breakfast, Parking (free), Complimentary newspapers in lobby, Business center, Smoke-Free property, RV and truck parking, Dry cleaning/laundry service, Free wireless Internet, Fitness facilities.

Marina

Also see the following nearby communities that have pet friendly lodging: Seaside - 5 miles, Monterey - 7 miles, Pacific Grove - 8 miles, Salinas - 9 miles

Sanctuary Beach Resort
3295 Dunes Rd
Marina CA 93933
(877) 944-3863
$135 - $289
Bed & Pet Discount Offered

Pet Policy: Pets allowed, $40 per night per pet. Limit 2 pets per room.

Features: Bar/lounge, Swimming pool - outdoor, Business services, Restaurant(s), Room service (limited hours), Concierge services, Number of rooms: 60, Parking (free), Spa services on site, Complimentary newspapers in lobby, Front desk (limited hours), Porter/bellhop, Massage - treatment room(s), Smoke-Free property, Coffee in lobby, Dry cleaning/laundry service, Free wireless Internet.

Marina Del Rey

Also see the following nearby communities that have pet friendly lodging: Venice - 2 miles, Culver City - 4 miles, Santa Monica - 4 miles, Inglewood - 5 miles, Los Angeles - 5 miles, El Segundo - 5 miles, Hawthorne - 7 miles, Beverly Hills - 7 miles, Manhattan Beach - 7 miles, Hermosa Beach - 9 miles, West Hollywood - 9 miles

Marina del Rey Hotel
13534 Bali Way
Marina Del Rey CA 90292
(310) 301-1000
$109 - $169
Bed & Pet Discount Offered

Pet Policy: Pets welcome, $50 cleaning fee per 7 day stay.

Features: Business Center, Bar/Lounge, Outdoor pool, Restaurant(s), Room service (limited hours), Concierge, Gift shops or newsstand, Number of rooms: 157, Number of floors: 3, Breakfast available (not included), Parking (free), Multilingual staff, Porter/bellhop, Security guard, Free wireless Internet, Marina on site, Accessible bathroom, In-room accessibility equipment for the deaf, Dry cleaning/laundry service.

Marina International Hotel
4200 Admiralty Way
Marina Del Rey CA 90292
(310) 301-2000
$99 - $159
Bed & Pet Discount Offered

Pet Policy: Pets up to 25 lbs are welcome for $50 per stay. Just steps from the hotel are miles of walking paths, perfect to stroll with your pet.

Features: Outdoor pool, Bar/Lounge, Elevator, Security guard, Business Services, Restaurant(s), Room service, Concierge, Gift shops or newsstand, Number of rooms: 135, Number of floors: 3, Breakfast available (not included), Parking (free), Multilingual staff, Smoke-Free property, Dry cleaning/laundry, Free wireless Internet.

Not rated
Oakwood Marina Del Rey
4111 South Via Marina
Marina Del Rey CA 90292
(602) 427-2752
$157 - $177

Pet Policy: Pets accepted with limitations and additional charge. Contact hotel directly for more information and to make reservations.

Features: Furnished apartments, Convenience store on site, Fitness center, Jacuzzi, Office center, Full kitchens. Minimum stay of 30 days may be required.

The Ritz-Carlton, Marina del Rey
4375 Admiralty Way
Marina Del Rey CA 90292
(310) 574-4296
$209 - $749
Bed & Pet Discount Offered

Pet Policy: Pets up to 30 lbs accepted. Pamper your pet with luxurious surroundings that include waterfront walking trails and uncompromising levels of service. Pet fee: Non-refundable $125 cleaning fee for each guestroom occupied with a pet.

Features: Shoe shine, Business center, Room service (24 hours), Currency exchange, Swimming pool - outdoor, Security guard, Bar/lounge, Health club, Shopping on site, Computer rental, Translation services, Babysitting or child care, Restaurant(s), Gift shops or newsstand, Number of rooms: 304, Poolside bar, Multilingual staff, Complimentary newspapers in lobby, Porter/bellhop, Limo or Town Car service available, Concierge desk, Accessible bathroom, In-room accessibility equipment for the deaf, Braille or raised signage, Dry cleaning/laundry service, Parking (valet - additional charge),

Mariposa

Americas Best Value Inn
5052 HIGHWAY 140
Mariposa CA 95338
(209) 966-3607
$53 - $69

Pet Policy: Pets allowed. Nominal additional charge may be required.

Features: Number of rooms: 45, Cable TV, Coffee maker, Accessible bathroom, Hair dryer, Iron & Ironing board, In room movies, Cribs available.

Comfort Inn Yosemite Valley Gateway
4994 Bullion St
Mariposa CA 95338
(209) 966-4344
$65 - $170
Bed & Pet Discount Offered

Pet Policy: Pets up to 20 lbs accepted, $15 per night. Limit 2 pets per room.

Features: Coffee in lobby, Swimming pool - outdoor, Business services, Number of rooms: 59, Number of floors: 3, Free breakfast, Parking (free), Complimentary newspapers in lobby, Free wireless Internet.

Miners Inn
5181 Highway 49 N
Mariposa CA 95338
(209) 742-7777
$69 - $160
Bed & Pet Discount Offered

Pet Policy: Pets allowed, $15 per pet per night, in pet-designated rooms only. There are two pet friendly single king rooms, and 2 double queen rooms.

Features: Free wireless Internet, Bar/lounge, Restaurant(s), ATM/banking, Gift shops or newsstand, Number of rooms: 78, Coffee in lobby, Free breakfast, Parking (free), Smoke-Free property, Swimming pool - outdoor seasonal.

Yosemite Bed and Breakfast
4501 Bridgeport Drive
Mariposa CA 95338
(209) 742-4018
$119 - $249
Bed & Pet Discount Offered

Pet Policy: Pets accepted with advanced permission, $25 per night plus $100 refundable deposit.

Features: Suitable for children, Barbecue grill(s), Free breakfast, Smoke-Free property, Free wireless Internet.

Martinez

Also see the following nearby communities that have pet friendly lodging: Pleasant Hill - 4 miles, Concord - 7 miles, Walnut Creek - 7 miles, Vallejo - 10 mile

Best Western John Muir Inn
445 Muir Station Rd
Martinez CA 94553
(925) 229-1010
$89 - $119
Bed & Pet Discount Offered

Pet Policy: Pets allowed, $50 per pet per stay.

Features: Free breakfast, Business services, Swimming pool - outdoor seasonal, Elevator, Number of rooms: 115, Number of floors: 3 Guest laundry, Parking (free), Multilingual staff, Wireless Internet.

Marysville

Also see the following nearby communities that have pet friendly lodging: Yuba City - 3 mile

★★
America's Best Value Inn Marysville
721 10th St
Marysville CA 95901
(530) 742-8586
$49 - $64
Bed & Pet Discount Offered

Pet Policy: Small dogs accepted, $10 per pet per night.

Features: Free breakfast, Number of rooms: 42, Number of floors: 2, Coffee in lobby, Parking (free), Accessible bathroom, Accessibility equipment for the deaf, Wheelchair accessible, Free wireless Internet, Fitness facilities.

★★½
Comfort Suites Marysville
1034 N Beale Rd
Marysville CA 95901
(530) 742-9200
$104 - $119
Bed & Pet Discount Offered

Pet Policy: Pet Accommodation:$10 per night/per pet. Pet deposit: $100 (refundable). Pet Limit: 2 pets per room/50 lbs or under

Features: Business center, Guest laundry, Coffee in lobby, Elevator, Swimming pool - indoor, Number of rooms: 65, Number of floors: 3, Free breakfast, Complimentary newspapers in lobby.

★★
Motel 6 Marysville CA
803 E St
Marysville CA 95901
(530) 743-5465
$45 - $49
Bed & Pet Discount Offered

Pet Policy: Pets welcome, no additional charge. Must declare at check-in. Must not leave alone in room. Must be leashed or crated in public areas.

Features: Concierge services, Number of rooms: 39, Number of floors: 2, Coffee in lobby, Guest laundry, Parking (free), Multilingual staff, Free wireless Internet, Accessible bathroom, Braille or raised signage.

McCloud

★★★★½
McCloud River Mercantile Inn
241 Main Street
McCloud CA 96057
(530) 964-2330
$129 - $250
Bed & Pet Discount Offered

Pet Policy: Small pets welcome. No additional charge. Must be crated when outside room.

Features: Free breakfast, Restaurant(s), Gift shops or newsstand, Number of rooms: 10.

Mendocino

Also see the following nearby communities that have pet friendly lodging: Little River - 4 miles, Fort Bragg - 7 miles

Agate Cove Inn
11201 N Lansing Street
Mendocino CA 95460
(707) 937-0552
$259 - $260
Bed & Pet Discount Offered

Pet Policy: Small pets accepted, $20 per night, but only have one pet friendly room. Book well in advance.

Features: Free breakfast, Suitable for children, Number of rooms: 10, Spa services on site, Free wireless Internet.

Hill House Inn
10701 Palette Dr
Mendocino CA 95460
(707) 937-0554
$141 - $165
Bed & Pet Discount Offered

Pet Policy: Pets welcome, $25 first night, $15 each additional.

Features: Spa services on site, Concierge services, Number of rooms: 40, Number of suites: 4, Number of floors: 2, Business services, Parking (free), Complimentary newspapers in lobby, Porter/bellhop, Suitable for children, Elevator, Wheelchair accessible, Free wireless Internet, Free breakfast, Accessible bathroom

MacCallum House Inn
45020 Albion Street
Mendocino CA 95460
(707) 937-0289
$161 - $349
Bed & Pet Discount Offered

Pet Policy: We allow pets in all of our rooms, except the rooms in the main house (1 - 6). Pet owners are charged a $40 additional charge per night. In an effort to protect our rooms and property we provide you with a pet bed, a blanket and a blue pet towel. We also provide a stainless steel water and food dish on a rubber mat in the room. Enclosed in this kit are several waste bags and dog treats for your friend! Must keep pets off of furniture, and leashed when out of room. $100 cleaning fee will be charged if excessive pet hair or stains need tending. Pets must be Free of ticks and fleas, and up to date in vaccinations.

Features: Suitable for children, Guest laundry, Library, Video library, Bar/lounge, Free breakfast, Use of nearby fitness center (free), Babysitting or child care, Restaurant(s), Number of rooms: 19, Parking (free), Spa services on site, Free Internet, Smoke-Free property

Mendocino Hotel-Garden Suites
45080 Main St
Mendocino CA 95460
(707) 937-0511
$80 - $283
Bed & Pet Discount Offered

Pet Policy: Pets allowed in designated cottages. $25 per stay. Many pet friendly activities nearby.

Features: Restaurants: 3, Room service (limited hours), Concierge services, Number of rooms: 46, Number of suites: 5, Parking (free), Complimentary newspapers in lobby, Business center, Wheelchair accessible, Free wireless Internet, Massage - treatment room(s), Porter/bellhop, Coffee in lobby, Accessible bathroom.

Nicholson House Inn
951 Ukiah St
Mendocino CA 95460
(707) 937-0934
$109 - $189
Bed & Pet Discount Offered

Pet Policy: Well behaved pets are allowed for an extra charge of $35/visit. Owners are responsible for any damage or clean up from their pets. Unruly or noisy pets should be placed in your vehicle or somewhere outside the inn. Always keep your dog on a leash. The pet owner is financially responsible for any and all damage caused by the pet including labor, replacement and materials.

Features: Free breakfast, Suitable for children, Number of rooms: 3, Year Built 1906.

Stanford Inn by the Sea
44850 Comptche Ukiah Road
Mendocino CA 95460
(707) 937-5615
$198 - $243

Pet Policy: All pets welcome, $45 per stay for 1 pet, plus $22 for each additional. Over the years we have had a variety of non-human guests: dogs and cats, of course, but also iguanas, parrots, Vietnamese pot belly pigs, and a tortoise. Dogs will find a welcoming treat, stainless steel food and water dishes, "dog sheets" to protect the furniture and Intelligent Products pick-up bags and more. Pets should not be left alone in rooms. Well behaved dogs are welcome in our lobby but not our dining room. We can serve breakfast or dinner in the lobby on request.

Features: Wood burning fireplaces, Organic breakfasts, Restaurant, Number of rooms: 41.

Menlo Park

Also see the following nearby communities that have pet friendly lodging: Palo Alto - 3 miles, Redwood City - 4 miles, Los Altos - 5 miles, San Carlos - 6 miles, Mountain View - 7 miles, Belmont - 8 miles, Newark - 9 miles

Rosewood Sand Hill
2825 Sand Hill Road
Menlo Park CA 94025
(650) 561-1500
$275 - $765
Bed & Pet Discount Offered

Pet Policy: Pets under 25 lbs welcome, $50 per night. Canine guests enjoy dog beds and bowls, pet snacks and bottled water, and dog walking service.

Continued on next page

Rosewood Sand Hill
Continued from previous page

Features: Swimming pool - outdoor, Hair salon, Gift shops or newsstand, Shopping on site, Barbecue grill(s), Currency exchange, Health club, Multilingual staff, Business center, Limo or Town Car service available, Concierge, Full-service health spa, Massage - treatment room(s), Steam room, Sauna, Smoke-Free property, Accessible bathroom, In-room accessibility equipment for the deaf, Braille or raised signage, Dry cleaning/laundry service, Wireless Internet (additional charge), Restaurant(s), Free breakfast, Room service, Porter/bellhop, Doorman/doorwoman, Babysitting or child care.

Merced

Comfort Inn Merced
730 Motel Dr
Merced CA 95340
(209) 383-0333
From $79
Bed & Pet Discount Offered

Pet Policy: Pet Accommodations: $50 deposit, refundable at check out $20 per pet per stay.

Features: Business services, Elevator, Restaurant(s), Swimming pool - outdoor, Number of rooms: 65, Number of floors: 3, Sauna.

Holiday Inn Express Hotel & Suites Merced
151 S Parsons Ave
Merced CA 95341
(209) 384-3700
$84 - $117
Bed & Pet Discount Offered

Pet Policy: Pets up to 75 lbs, $25 per pet per night.

Features: Fitness facilities, Swimming pool - outdoor, Number of floors: 3, Complimentary newspapers in lobby, Business center, Wireless Internet, Accessible bathroom, In-room accessibility equipment for the deaf, Braille or raised signage

Merced Yosemite Travelodge
1260 Yosemite Pkwy
Merced CA 95340
(209) 722-6224
$42 - $125
Bed & Pet Discount Offered

Pet Policy: Pets any size welcome, $10 per pet per night.

Features: Business services, Free breakfast, Parking (free), Complimentary newspapers in lobby, Swimming pool - outdoor seasonal.

Quality Inn Merced
1213 V St
Merced CA 95340
(209) 723-3711
$44 - $59
Bed & Pet Discount Offered

Pet Policy: Quality Inns charge an additional $10 per night per pet plus a $50 damage deposit, which is refunded if the room is in order at check out. Quality Inns accept any well-behaved pets with a maximum of 3 per room, but dogs are limited to 50 pounds. Pets may not be left alone in the room unless crated.

Continued on next page

Quality Inn Merced
Continued from previous page

Features: Number of rooms: 95, Number of floors: 2, Business services, Wireless Internet, Multilingual staff, Complimentary newspapers, Nearby fitness center (discount), RV and truck parking, Dry cleaning/laundry service, Airport transportation (free), Coffee in lobby, Outdoor pool - seasonal, Technology support staff, Pick up service from train station, Area shuttle (free).

★★½

Ramada Inn Merced
2000 E Childs Ave
Merced CA 95340
(209) 723-3121
$63 - $99
Bed & Pet Discount Offered

Pet Policy: Pets welcome, $30 per stay.

Features: Restaurant(s), Breakfast available (not included), Parking (free), Complimentary newspapers in lobby, Swimming pool - outdoor seasonal

★★

Vagabond Inn Merced
1215 R St
Merced CA 95340
(209) 722-2738
$38 - $44
Bed & Pet Discount Offered

Pet Policy: Pet friendly rooms, $10 per night additional charge.

Features: Guest laundry, Free breakfast, Complimentary newspapers, Free wireless Internet, Number of rooms: 76, Number of floors: 2, Coffee in lobby, Accessible bathroom, In-room accessibility equipment for the deaf, Braille or raised signage

Mill Valley

Also see the following nearby communities that have pet friendly lodging: Corte Madera - 2 miles, Sausalito - 4 miles, San Rafael - 6 miles

Acqua Hotel, Mill Valley, a Joie de Vivre Boutique
555 Redwood And Hwy
Mill Valley CA 94941
(415) 380-0400
$128 - $219
Bed & Pet Discount Offered

Pet Policy: Joie de Vivre has 14 pet-friendly properties in California, with Fido-friendly packages, amenities and a progressive pet policy designed to make hotel stays hospitable for dogs and their owners alike. Joie de Vivre's properties do not impose weight restrictions on dogs and typically do not charge pet fees (provided there is no damage).

Features: Free breakfast, Concierge, Number of rooms: 50, Number of floors: 3, Wireless Internet (additional charge), Video library, Multilingual staff, Complimentary newspapers, Nearby fitness center (free), Business center, Limo or Town Car service available, Smoke-Free, Dry cleaning/laundry.

Millbrae

Also see the following nearby communities that have pet friendly lodging: Burlingame - 2 miles, San Bruno - 3 miles, South San Francisco - 4 miles, San Mateo - 5 miles, Brisbane - 6 miles, Belmont - 7 miles, Montara - 9 miles, Moss Beach - 9 miles, San Carlos - 9 miles

Clarion Hotel San Francisco Airport
401 E Millbrae Ave
Millbrae CA 94030
(650) 692-6363
$69 - $79
Bed & Pet Discount Offered

Pet Policy: Pet Limit - 1 pet per room. Up to 35 lbs.

Features: Breakfast available (not included), Room service (24 hours), Multilingual staff, Concierge, Computer rental, Currency exchange, Airport transportation (free), Bar/lounge, Parking fee, Translation services, Business center, Restaurant(s), Outdoor pool, Number of rooms: 251, Number of floors: 6, Accessible bathroom, In-room accessibility equipment for the deaf, Braille or raised signage, Dry cleaning/laundry service.

The Westin San Francisco Airport
1 Old Bayshore Hwy
Millbrae CA 94030
(650) 692-3500
$119 - $608
Bed & Pet Discount Offered

Pet Policy: Dogs only, up to 50 lbs. Refundable deposit required.

Features: Parking (valet) $25 day, Restaurant(s), Airport transportation (free), Bar/Lounge, Indoor pool, Concierge, Gift shop, Number of rooms: 393, Computer rental, Breakfast available (not included), Room service, Shoe shine, Multilingual staff, Complimentary newspapers, Business center, Porter/bellhop, Security guard, Medical assistance available, Free wireless Internet, Technology helpdesk, Dry cleaning/laundry, Fitness center.

Milpitas

Also see the following nearby communities that have pet friendly lodging: Santa Clara - 5 miles, Sunnyvale - 7 miles, San Jose - 8 miles, Fremont - 8 miles, Cupertino - 9 miles, Newark - 10 miles

Americas Best Value Inn-San Jose Airport
485 S Main St
Milpitas CA 95035
(408) 946-8383
$42 - $65
Bed & Pet Discount Offered

Pet Policy: Pets accepted under 20 lbs, $10 per pet per night. Limit 2 per room.

Features: Business services, Number of rooms: 80, Coffee in lobby, Internet (additional charge), Guest laundry, Free breakfast, Parking (free).

Best Western Brookside Inn
400 Valley Way
Milpitas CA 95035
(408) 263-5566
$78 - $139
Bed & Pet Discount Offered

Pet Policy: Pet friendly. No additional charge.

Features: Swimming pool - outdoor, Number of rooms: 78, Number of floors: 2, Business services, Coffee in lobby, Free breakfast, Multilingual staff, Complimentary newspapers in lobby, Free wireless Internet, Parking (valet) Additional charge, Dry cleaning/laundry service, Sauna, Steam Room.

★★★½

Crowne Plaza Silicon Valley San Jose
777 Bellew Dr
Milpitas CA 95035
(408) 321-9500
$79 - $214
Bed & Pet Discount Offered

Pet Policy: Dogs and cats, up to 50 lbs accepted. Must stay in 4th floor pet designated rooms.

Features: Sauna, Concierge desk, Swimming pool - outdoor, Business services, Bar/lounge, Airport transportation (free), Restaurant(s), Gift shops or newsstand, Number of suites: 20, Number of floors: 12, Multilingual staff, Complimentary newspapers in lobby, Room service, Porter/bellhop, Accessible bathroom, In-room accessibility equipment for the deaf, Braille or raised signage, Wireless Internet (additional charge), Fitness facilities.

★★

Executive Inn Milpitas
95 Dempsey Rd
Milpitas CA 95035
(408) 945-9000
$47 - $83

Pet Policy: Lists as pet friendly but no details available. Please contact hotel directly before making a reservation.

Features: Free continental breakfast, Coffee maker, Free wireless Internet..

★★

Extended Stay America San Jose - Milpitas
1000 Hillview Ct
Milpitas CA 95035
(408) 941-9977
$54 - $79
Bed & Pet Discount Offered

Pet Policy: One pet is allowed in each guest room. A $25 per day non-refundable cleaning fee (not to exceed $150) will be charged the first night.

Features: Guest laundry, Elevator, Number of floors: 3, Wireless Internet (additional charge), Free parking, Front desk (limited hours), Use of nearby fitness center (discount).

★★

Homestead San Jose - Milpitas
330 Cypress Dr.
Milpitas CA 95035
(408) 433-9700
$64 - $84
Bed & Pet Discount Offered

Pet Policy: Pets allowed, no size restriction, $25 per day to a maximum of $150 per stay. Limit of 1 pet per room.

Features: Guest laundry, Elevator, Pets accepted, Number of rooms: 161, Number of floors: 3, Barbecue grill(s), Coffee in lobby, Wireless Internet – additional charge, Parking (free), Front desk (limited hours), Business center, Fitness facilities.

★★★

Larkspur Landing Milpitas
40 Ranch Dr
Milpitas CA 95035
(408) 719-1212
$79 - $229
Bed & Pet Discount Offered

Pet Policy: Pets welcome, $75 per stay charge.

Features: Free wireless Internet, Free Breakfast, Elevator, Airport transportation (free), Number of suites: 124, Number of floors: 4, Coffee in lobby, Video library, Parking (free), Multilingual staff, Complimentary newspapers, Business center, Dry cleaning/laundry service, Fitness facilities.

Residence Inn By Marriott Milpitas
1501 California Cir
Milpitas CA 95035
(408) 941-9222
$89 - $179
Bed & Pet Discount Offered

Pet Policy: Pets allowed, $75 per stay cleaning fee.

Features: Business Center, Swimming pool - outdoor, Room service (limited hours), Number of suites: 120, Number of floors: 3, Free breakfast, Parking (free), Complimentary newspapers in lobby, Free wireless Internet, Dry cleaning/laundry service, Area shuttle (free), Fitness facilities.

★★★½

Sheraton San Jose Hotel
1801 Barber Ln
Milpitas CA 95035
(408) 943-0600
$199 - $200
Bed & Pet Discount Offered

Pet Policy: Allowed 1 medium size pet, no fee.

Features: Airport transportation (free), Restaurant(s), Room service, Concierge services, Gift shops or newsstand, Number of rooms: 229, Number of floors: 9, Suitable for children, Breakfast available (not included), Parking (free), Multilingual staff, Complimentary newspapers in lobby, Porter/bellhop, Security guard, Limo or Town Car service available, Free wireless Internet, Bar/Lounge, Swimming pool - outdoor, Dry cleaning/laundry service, Wheelchair accessible, Smoke-Free property, 24-hour business center, Fitness facilities.

★★★

Staybridge Suites Silicon Valley
321 Cypress Drive
Milpitas CA 95035
(408) 383-9500
$111 - $162
Bed & Pet Discount Offered

Pet Policy: Pets up to 80 lbs, $75 for up to 6 nights, $150 for 7 or longer. Must have proof of current vaccinations.

Features: Swimming pool - outdoor, Accessible bathroom, In-room accessibility equipment for the deaf, Braille or raised signage, Hair salon, Number of floors: 4, Parking (free), Complimentary newspapers in lobby, Business center, Wireless Internet, Fitness facilities.

★★★½

The Beverly Heritage
1820 Barber Ln
Milpitas CA 95035
(408) 943-9080
$111 - $236
Bed & Pet Discount Offered

Pet Policy: Pets permitted on first floor only, $25 per pet per stay, limit 2 per room.

Features: Business Center, Elevator, Airport transportation (free), Restaurant(s), Room service (limited hours), Concierge services, Number of rooms: 237, Number of floors: 3, Pool table, Multilingual staff, Complimentary newspapers in lobby, Porter/bellhop, Limo or Town Car service available, Free wireless Internet, Swimming pool - outdoor, Children's swimming pool, Smoke-Free property, Dry cleaning/laundry service, Bar/Lounge, Fitness facilities.

Towneplace Suites By Marriott Milpitas
1428 Falcon Dr
Milpitas CA 95035
(408) 719-1959
$84 - $209
Bed & Pet Discount Offered

Pet Policy: Pets allowed. $100 sanitation additional charge.

Features: Business Center, Swimming pool - outdoor, Elevator, Number of rooms: 143, Number of floors: 4, Barbecue grill(s), Coffee in lobby, Free breakfast, Parking (free), Complimentary newspapers in lobby, Wireless Internet, Airport transportation (free), Dry cleaning/laundry service, Fitness facilities.

Modesto

Also see the following nearby communities that have pet friendly lodging: Ceres - 4 miles, Salida - 6 miles

America Best Value Inn
1525 Mchenry Ave
Modesto CA 95350
(888) 315-2378
$49 - $59
Bed & Pet Discount Offered

Pet Policy: Accepts small pets.

Features: Free Breakfast, Swimming pool - outdoor, Number of rooms: 99, Number of floors: 2, Business services, Coffee in lobby, Parking (free), Multilingual staff, Complimentary newspapers in lobby, Free wireless Internet.

Clarion Modesto
1612 Sisk Rd
Modesto CA 95350
(209) 521-1612
$62 - $107
Bed & Pet Discount Offered

Pet Policy: Pet accommodation: $25/stay Pet limit: 1 pets per room 40 lbs or less.

Features: Swimming pool - outdoor, Business center, Bar/lounge, Concierge services, ATM/banking, Arcade/game room, Swimming pool - indoor, Restaurant(s), Number of rooms: 185, Number of floors: 2, Pool table on site, Parking (free), Multilingual staff, Complimentary newspapers in lobby, Room service, Limo or Town Car service available, Swimming pool - outdoor seasonal, Dry cleaning/laundry service, Restaurants, Wireless Internet, Fitness facilities.

Courtyard by Marriott Modesto
1720 Sisk Rd
Modesto CA 95350
(209) 577-3825
$114 - $135
Bed & Pet Discount Offered

Pet Policy: Pets under 40 lbs, $50 per stay. Limit 1 pet per room.

Features: Business Center, Bar/Lounge, Nearby fitness center (free), Outdoor pool, Restaurant(s), Number of rooms: 126, Number of floors: 2, Coffee in lobby, Grocery, Complimentary, Free wireless Internet, Accessible bathroom, In-room accessibility equipment for the deaf, Braille or raised signage, Dry cleaning/laundry service.

Doubletree Hotel Modesto
1150 9th St
Modesto CA 95354
(209) 526-6000
$91 - $179
Bed & Pet Discount Offered

Pet Policy: Pets up to 40 lbs accepted, $25 per day per pet.

Features: Technology helpdesk, Full-service health spa, Business center, Room service, Outdoor pool, Airport transportation (free), Hair salon, Gift shop, Nightclub, Multilingual staff, Porter/bellhop, Concierge, Massage - treatment room(s), Smoke-Free, Dry cleaning/laundry, Wireless Internet, Restaurant.

Knights Inn Modesto
115 Downey Ave
Modesto CA 95354
(209) 529-4370
$40 - $60
Bed & Pet Discount Offered

Pet Policy: Accepts pets up to 40 lbs, $20 per stay.

Features: Business services, Number of floors: 2, Free breakfast, Parking (free), Swimming pool - outdoor seasonal, Free Internet access.

Modesto - Days Inn
1312 Mchenry Ave
Modesto CA 95350
(209) 527-1010
$50 - $69
Bed & Pet Discount Offered

Pet Policy: Pets under 80 lbs accepted, $10 per pet per night. Limit 3 per room. Must not leave in room unattended.

Features: Free breakfast, Number of rooms: 102, Number of floors: 2, Business services, Coffee in lobby, Multilingual staff, Complimentary newspapers, Free wireless Internet, Outdoor pool - seasonal, Dry cleaning/laundry service.

Quality Inn
500 Kansas Ave
Modesto CA 95351
(209) 578-5400
$63 - $69
Bed & Pet Discount Offered

Pet Policy: Pets permitted $20 per night per pet plus $50 deposit. Designated pet rooms only. Limit 2 pets, must book in advance.

Features: Number of rooms: 68, Free breakfast, Parking (free), Swimming pool - outdoor seasonal.

Rodeway Inn Modesto
936 Mchenry Ave
Modesto CA 95350
(209) 523-7701
$48 - $53
Bed & Pet Discount Offered

Pet Policy: Rodeway Inns charge an additional $10 per night per pet plus a $50 damage deposit, which is refunded if the room is in order at check out. Max of 2 pets per room. A veterinarian certificate that the pet is on a flea and parasite program is required. Pets may not be left alone in the room unless crated.

Features: Airport transportation (free), Free breakfast, Bar/lounge, Outdoor pool, Number of rooms: 58, Business services, Parking (free), Multilingual staff, Free wireless Internet.

Super 8 Modesto
4100 Salida Blvd
Modesto CA 95358
(209) 543-9000
$55 - $70
Bed & Pet Discount Offered

Pet Policy: Pets accepted, $25 per stay.

Features: Business center, Outdoor pool, Free breakfast, Parking (free), Multilingual staff, Wireless Internet, Accessible bathroom, Fitness facilities, Steam room, Sauna.

Mojave

Americas Best Value Inn
16352 Sierra Hwy
Mojave CA 93501
(661) 824-9317
$58 - $65

Pet Policy: Pets under 35 lbs, $10 per pet.

Features: Free wireless Internet, Restaurant next door (10% discount), Microwave, Coffee maker, Mini fridge, HBO.

Not rated
Best Western Plus Desert Winds
16200 Sierra Hwy
Mojave CA 93501
(661) 824-3601
$82 - $92

Pet Policy: Small pets allowed. $10 additional charge.

Features: Free wireless Internet, Flat screen TV, Free continental breakfast, Swimming pool & spa – outdoor, Business services.

Days Inn Mojave CA
16100 Sierra Hwy
Mojave CA 93501
(661) 824-2421
$59 - $119
Bed & Pet Discount Offered

Pet Policy: Pets allowed, $10 per night.

Features: Swimming pool - outdoor, Barbecue grill(s), Free breakfast, Business center, Free wireless Internet, Number of rooms: 50, Number of floors: 2, Parking (free).

Econo Lodge Mojave
2145 Highway 58
Mojave CA 93501
(661) 824-2463
$52 - $55
Bed & Pet Discount Offered

Pet Policy: Pets accepted, $5 per night per pet. Limit 2 per room.

Features: Gift shops or newsstand, Free breakfast, Guest laundry, Swimming pool - outdoor, Number of rooms: 33.

Mariah Country Inn & Suites
1385 Highway 58
Mojave CA 93501
(661) 824-4980
$89 - $139
Bed & Pet Discount Offered

Pet Policy: One small pet is allowed for an additional $10 per night.

Features: Coffee in lobby, Free breakfast, Free wireless Internet, Bar/lounge, Fitness facilities, Airport transportation (free), Restaurant(s), Outdoor pool, Number of rooms: 50, Number of suites: 9, Business services, Guest laundry, Limo or Town Car service available.

Monrovia

Also see the following nearby communities that have pet friendly lodging: Arcadia - 2 miles, El Monte - 5 miles, Pasadena - 7 miles, Rosemead - 7 miles, San Gabriel - 7 miles, South El Monte - 7 miles, Glendora - 8 miles, South Pasadena - 9 miles, City Of Industry - 10 miles

Doubletree Monrovia - Pasadena area
924 W Huntington Dr
Monrovia CA 91016
(626) 357-1900
$104 - $169
Bed & Pet Discount Offered

Pet Policy: Pets up to 30 lbs, $50 per stay.

Features: Bar/lounge, Concierge services, Business center, Room service (limited hours), Restaurant(s), Swimming pool - outdoor, Gift shops or newsstand, Number of rooms: 171, Number of floors: 10, Suitable for children, Breakfast available (not included), Parking (free), Multilingual staff, Complimentary newspapers, Security guard, Free wireless Internet, Dry cleaning/laundry service, Fitness facilities.

★★

Homestead Los Angeles - Monrovia
930 S 5th Ave
Monrovia CA 91016
(626) 256-6999
$64 - $90
Bed & Pet Discount Offered

Pet Policy: Pets allowed, no size restriction, $25 per day to a maximum of $150 per stay. Limit of 1 pet per room.

Features: Guest laundry, Elevator, Number of rooms: 122, Number of floors: 3, Coffee in lobby, Wireless Internet (additional charge), Parking (free), Use of nearby fitness center (free), Porter/bellhop.

Montara

Also see the following nearby communities that have pet friendly lodging: Moss Beach – 1 mile, Half Moon Bay - 6 miles, San Bruno - 8 miles, Millbrae - 9 miles, Burlingame - 9 miles, South San Francisco - 10 miles

Farallone Inn
1410 Main Street
Montara CA 94037
(650) 728-8200
$89 - $90
Bed & Pet Discount Offered

Pet Policy: Pet friendly limited rooms, $25 per pet and $25 deposit.

Features: Guest laundry, Free breakfast, Restaurant(s), Room service (limited hours), Number of rooms: 9, Number of floors: 3, Parking (free), Front desk (limited hours), Smoke-Free property, Year Built 1906.

Monterey

Also see the following nearby communities that have pet friendly lodging: Seaside - 3 miles, Pacific Grove - 3 miles, Carmel - 5 miles, Marina - 7 miles

★★★
Bay Park Hotel
1425 Munras Ave
Monterey CA 93940
(831) 649-1020
$89 - $149
Bed & Pet Discount Offered

Pet Policy: We accept pets in our hotel rooms. Pet not to be left unattended in the room at any time. A charge of $20+tax per night applies. Pets only allowed on 1st and 2nd floor.

Features: Business center, Swimming pool - outdoor seasonal, Bar/lounge, Fitness facilities, Restaurant(s), Breakfast available (not included), Parking (free), Free wireless Internet

★★★
Best Western Victorian Inn
487 Foam St
Monterey CA 93940
(831) 373-8000
$118 - $289

Pet Policy: Pets accepted with advanced approval of manager. Please contact property directly for booking and details.

Features: Free Breakfast, Parking (additional charge), Business services, Nearby fitness center (discount), Coffee in lobby, Video library, Security guard, Elevator, Concierge services, Number of rooms: 70, Number of floors: 3, Multilingual staff, Complimentary newspapers in lobby, Porter/bellhop, Free wireless Internet, Dry cleaning/laundry service.

★★★
BW Plus Beach Resort Monterey
2600 Sand Dunes Drive
Monterey CA 93940
(831) 394-3321
$107 - $189

Pet Policy: Pets allowed with additional charge of $25 daily in pet area/$50 daily outside of pet area

Features: Number of rooms: 196, Parking - $10 per day, Fitness center, Swimming Pool, Wireless Internet, Restaurant, Room Service.

★★★½
Casa Munras
700 Munras Ave
Monterey CA 93940
(800) 222-2446
$105 - $229
Bed & Pet Discount Offered

Pet Policy: Pets allowed in designated rooms, $50 charged first night.

Features: Concierge, Bar/lounge, Business center, Spa services on site, Accessible bathroom, Restaurant(s), Gift shops or newsstand, Number of rooms: 171, Number of floors: 2, Video library, Multilingual staff, Complimentary newspapers, Porter/bellhop, Free wireless Internet, Beauty services, Massage - treatment room(s), Smoke-Free , Dry cleaning/laundry, Outdoor pool, Coffee in lobby, Breakfast available (not included), Fitness center.

Comfort Inn Monterey
1200 Olmsted Road
Monterey CA 93940
(831) 372-2945
$82 - $119
Bed & Pet Discount Offered

Pet Policy: Pets up to 40 lbs, $25 per pet per day. Limit 1 pet per room.

Features: Free Breakfast, Parking (free), Front desk (limited hours), Free wireless Internet, Poolside bar, Number of rooms: 46.

Comfort Inn Monterey Bay
2050 North Fremont Street
Monterey CA 93940
(831) 373-3081
$52 - $149
Bed & Pet Discount Offered

Pet Policy: Pets up to 40 lbs, $25 per pet per day. Limit 1 pet per room.

Features: Sauna, Bar/lounge, Restaurant(s), Number of floors: 2, Parking (free), Internet access, Number of rooms: 47

Comfort Inn Monterey by the Sea
1252 Munras Ave
Monterey CA 93940
(831) 372-2908
$72 - $89
Bed & Pet Discount Offered

Pet Policy: Pets up to 40 lbs, $25 per pet per day, plus $175 refundable deposit. Limit 1 pet per room.

Features: Suitable for children, Coffee in lobby, Free breakfast, Parking (free), Complimentary newspapers, Number of floors: 2, Swimming pool – outdoor.

Hyatt Regency Monterey Hotel & Spa
1 Old Golf Course Rd
Monterey CA 93940
(831) 372-1234
$148 - $239
Bed & Pet Discount Offered

Pet Policy: Pets accepted, $75 per stay.

Features: Room service, Business center, Security guard, Currency exchange, Concierge, Bar/lounge, Restaurant, Gift shop, Number of rooms: 575, Wireless Internet (additional charge), Breakfast available (not included), Multilingual staff, Porter/bellhop, Dry cleaning/laundry, Outdoor pool, Golf course, Tennis courts, Airport transportation (free), Area shuttle (free), Full-service health spa.

Mariposa Inn & Suites
1386 Munras Avenue
Monterey CA 93940
(831) 649-1414
$62 - $359
Bed & Pet Discount Offered

Pet Policy: Pets welcome, $40 per night.

Features: Swimming pool - outdoor, Elevator, Concierge services, Airport transportation (additional charge), Free breakfast, Smoke-Free property, Wheelchair accessible, Number of rooms: 50, Number of floors: 3, Parking (free), Complimentary newspapers in lobby, Use of nearby fitness center (free), Business center, Free wireless Internet.

★★
Monterey Bay Travelodge
2030 North Fremont St
Monterey CA 93940
(831) 373-3381
$41 - $119
Bed & Pet Discount Offered

Pet Policy: Pets accepted, $20 per night. Must book only in standard, 2 queen non-smoking rooms.

Features: Business center, Swimming pool outdoor, Bar/lounge, Restaurant, Free breakfast, Free parking, Multilingual staff, Complimentary newspapers, Concierge, Wireless Internet, Dry cleaning/laundry.

★★
Monterey Downtown Travelodge
675 Munras Ave
Monterey CA 93940
(831) 373-1876
$48 - $125
Bed & Pet Discount Offered

Pet Policy: Pets accepted, $20 per night. Must book in standard 2 Queen non-smoking rooms only.

Features: Business center, Coffee in lobby, Free breakfast, Complimentary newspapers in lobby, Free wireless Internet, Parking garage, Smoke-Free property, Swimming pool - outdoor seasonal.

Not rated
Monterey Fireside Lodge
1131 Tenth Street
Monterey CA 93940
(831) 373-4172
$107 - $129

Pet Policy: Pets welcome, $20 per pet per night. Please confirm with hotel prior to arrival as there are a limited number of pet friendly rooms.

Features: Free breakfast, Gas fireplace, Free wireless Internet.

★★★★
Portola Hotel & Spa at Monterey Bay
Two Portola Plaza
Monterey CA 93940
(866) 711-1534
$199 - $329
Bed & Pet Discount Offered

Pet Policy: Dogs only are welcome, $50 cleaning fee per stay. No size restrictions.

Features: Steam Room, Sauna, Health Club, ATM/Banking, Concierge desk, Swimming pool - outdoor, Pool table, Beauty services, Spa services on site, Security guard, Coffee in lobby, Room service (limited hours), Bar/lounge, Shopping on site, Elevator, Gift shops or newsstand, Number of rooms: 379, Number of floors: 7, Breakfast available (not included), Multilingual staff, Complimentary newspapers in lobby, Porter/bellhop, Massage - treatment room(s), Smoke-Free property, Parking (valet) $18 Daily, 2 Restaurants, Business center, Babysitting or child care, Wheelchair accessible, Limo or Town Car service available, Medical assistance available, Technology support staff, Full-service health spa, Accessible bathroom, In-room accessibility equipment for the deaf, Braille or raised signage, Dry cleaning/laundry service, Wireless Internet- additional charge.

★★

Quality Inn Monterey
2075 Fremont St
Monterey CA 93940
(831) 373-5551
$60 - $80
Bed & Pet Discount Offered

Pet Policy: Pets accepted, $20 per night per pet.

Features: Number of rooms: 42, Number of floors: 2, Guest laundry, Parking (free), Swimming pool - outdoor seasonal, Free breakfast, Coffee in lobby

★★

Rodeway Inn Monterey
2041 Fremont St
Monterey CA 93940
(831) 373-2911
$37 - $95
Bed & Pet Discount Offered

Pet Policy: Rodeway Inns charge an additional $10 per night per pet plus a $50 damage deposit, which is refunded if the room is in order at check out. Max of 2 pets per room. A veterinarian certificate that the pet is on a flea and parasite program is required. Pets may not be left alone in the room unless in a cage.

Features: Number of rooms: 22, Number of floors: 2, Free breakfast, Multilingual staff, Wireless Internet

Monterey Park

Also see the following nearby communities that have pet friendly lodging: San Gabriel - 3 miles, Rosemead - 4 miles, South Pasadena - 4 miles, Commerce - 5 miles, Pasadena - 6 miles, Pico Rivera - 6 miles, South El Monte - 6 miles, Bell Gardens - 6 miles, El Monte - 7 miles, Huntington Park - 7 miles, Arcadia - 8 miles, Downey - 9 miles, Whittier - 9 miles, Glendale - 10 miles

Floral Inn
1560 Monterey Pass Rd
Monterey Park CA 91754
(323) 263-9888
$58 - $66
Bed & Pet Discount Offered

Pet Policy: Pets accepted $5 per pet per day, plus $50 refundable deposit.

Features: Outdoor pool, Concierge, Number of rooms: 54, Number of suites: 2, Number of floors: 3, Guest laundry, Free breakfast, Parking (free), Multilingual staff, Free wireless Internet, Braille or raised signage.

Not rated

Rodeway Inn Monterey Park
1560 Monterey Pass Road
Monterey Park CA 91754
(323) 263-9888
$54 - $74

Pet Policy: Pets up to 100 lbs accepted, $5 per pet per night plus $50 refundable deposit. Limit 2 per room.

Features: Car rental desk, Number of rooms: 54.

Moreno Valley

Also see the following nearby communities that have pet friendly lodging: Redlands - 10 miles, Riverside - 10 miles

Comfort Inn Moreno Valley
23330 Sunnymead Blvd
Moreno Valley CA 92553
(951) 242-0699
$69 - $94
Bed & Pet Discount Offered

Pet Policy: Pet accommodation:$10/night per pet plus $50 per pet refundable deposit. Pet Limit: 2 pets/room under 50lbs.

Features: Guest laundry, Outdoor pool, Number of rooms: 93, Free breakfast, Complimentary newspapers, Free wireless Internet, Fitness center.

Econo Lodge Moreno Valley
24412 Sunnymead Blvd
Moreno Valley CA 92553
(951) 247-6699
$59 - $94
Bed & Pet Discount Offered

Pet Policy: Pet accommodation:$10/pet, per night. $50 Deposit- Refundable. 2 pets, per room. 25lbs. and under maximum.

Features: Swimming pool - outdoor, Free breakfast, Sauna, Swimming pool - outdoor seasonal, Number of floors: 2, Number of rooms: 50

★★½

La Quinta Inn & Suites Moreno Valley
23090 Sunnymead Blvd
Moreno Valley CA 92553
(951) 486-9000
$88 - $99
Bed & Pet Discount Offered

Pet Policy: Pets welcome, no additional charge but owner responsible for any damage. Must not be left unattended at any time.

Features: Accessible bathroom, Business center, Free breakfast, Complimentary newspapers in lobby, Fitness center, Guest laundry, Number of rooms: 62, Number of floors: 3, Parking (free), Swimming pool - indoor, Free wireless Internet.

Not rated

Motel 7 Moreno Valley
23581 Alessandro Blvd
Moreno Valley CA 92553
(877) 747-8713
$49 - $60

Pet Policy: Small pets allowed, $10 per pet per night.

Features: Number of rooms: 60, Swimming pool - outdoor, Parking (free).

Regency Inn And Suites
24810 Sunnymead Blvd
Moreno Valley CA 92553
(951) 247-8582
$60 - $65
Bed & Pet Discount Offered

Pet Policy: Pets allowed, $10 per night per pet. Limit 2 per room.

Features: Free wireless Internet, Parking (free), Swimming pool - outdoor, Number of rooms: 35, Business services, Free breakfast

Morgan Hill

Also see the following nearby communities that have pet friendly lodging: San Martin - 6 mile

Extended Stay America San Jose - Morgan Hill
605 Jarvis Dr
Morgan Hill CA 95037
(408) 779-9660
$64 - $79
Bed & Pet Discount Offered

Pet Policy: One pet is allowed in each guest room. A $25 per day non-refundable cleaning fee (not to exceed $150) will be charged the first night of your stay.

Features: Guest laundry, Elevator, Number of rooms: 92, Number of floors: 3, Wireless Internet (additional charge), Parking (free), Multilingual staff, Front desk (limited hours), Use of nearby fitness center (discount).

Morgan Hill Residence Inn
18620 Madrone Pkwy
Morgan Hill CA 95037
(408) 782-8311
$125 - $170
Bed & Pet Discount Offered

Pet Policy: Pets allowed, $100 cleaning fee per stay.

Features: Elevator, Swimming pool - indoor, Business services, BBQ grill(s), Coffee in lobby, Free breakfast, Parking (free), Complimentary newspapers in lobby, Use of nearby fitness center (free), Free wireless Internet, Dry cleaning/laundry service, Tennis on site, Fitness facilities.

★★
Quality Inn Morgan Hill
16525 Condit Rd
Morgan Hill CA 95037
(408) 779-0447
$59 - $60
Bed & Pet Discount Offered

Pet Policy: Quality Inns charge an additional $10 per night per pet. They may require a $50 damage deposit, which is refunded if the room is in order at check out. Quality Inns accept any well-behaved pets with a maximum of 3 per room, but dogs are limited to 50 pounds. Pets may not be left alone in the room unless in a cage.

Features: Free Breakfast, Swimming pool - outdoor, Business services, Parking (free), Multilingual staff, Complimentary newspapers in lobby, Use of nearby fitness center (free), Free wireless Internet, Dry cleaning/laundry service

Morro Bay

Also see the following nearby communities that have pet friendly lodging: Los Osos - 5 miles, Cayucos - 5 miles

Anchor Inn Morro Bay
220 Beach Street
Morro Bay CA 93442
(805) 772-3333
$52 - $105
Bed & Pet Discount Offered

Pet Policy: Pets welcome. Additional charge charged at check-in.

Features: Number of rooms: 31, Number of floors: 2, Business services, Free breakfast, Parking (free), Front desk (limited hours), Free wireless Internet, Coffee in lobby.

Not rated
Bayfront Inn
1150 Embarcadero
Morro Bay CA 93442
(805) 772-5607
From $75

Pet Policy: Pets of all kinds accepted, $25 cleaning fee per stay. We do not have a weight limitation but we do have a 2 animal limit per room. Dogs must be on a leash at all times when on premises. Birds or other exotic type animals must be crated in room and on premises. Pets are not allowed to be left in a room unattended unless crated. Pet sitters are available. The front desk can refer you to a local pet sitter.

Features: Number of rooms: 16, Free breakfast, Coffee maker, HBO, Restaurant, Free wireless Internet, Refrigerator.

Not Rated
Beach Bungalow and Suites
1050 Morro Avenue
Morro Bay CA 93442
(805) 772-9700
$219 - $269

Pet Policy: Pets under 20 lbs welcome, $20 per night. Pet friendly blankets offered.

Features: Number of rooms: 12, Free wireless Internet, Chenille Robes, Complimentary newspaper, Refrigerator, Non-smoking property, Available packages offer free breakfast at nearby restaurants.

★
Best Western El Rancho
2460 N Main Street
Morro Bay CA 93442
(805) 772-2212
$56. - $99

Pet Policy: Pets allowed. $25 per pet per night.

Features: Free in room movies, Free Wireless Internet, Continental breakfast, Outdoor heated swimming pool.

★★
Days Inn Morro Bay CA
1095 Main St
Morro Bay CA 93442
(805) 772-2711
$69 - $89
Bed & Pet Discount Offered

Pet Policy: Pets allowed, $22 per pet per night.

Features: Restaurant, Business services, Coffee in lobby, Free wireless Internet, Free breakfast, Complimentary newspapers.

★★★½
Inn At Morro Bay
60 State Park Rd
Morro Bay CA 93442
(805) 772-5651
$59 - $139
Bed & Pet Discount Offered

Pet Policy: Pets allowed, $50 per night.

Features: Room service, Bar/lounge, Restaurant, Concierge, Number of rooms: 98, Number of floors: 2, Business services, Breakfast available (not included), Porter/bellhop, Smoke-Free, Outdoor pool - seasonal, Accessible bathroom, Dry cleaning/laundry service.

★★½
Morro Shores Inn And Suites
290 Atascadero Rd
Morro Bay CA 93442
(805) 772-0222
$58 - $185
Bed & Pet Discount Offered

Pet Policy: Up to 2 pet allowed in a room, $10 per night per pet.

Features: Concierge, Number of rooms: 30, Number of floors: 2, Business services, Guest laundry, Free breakfast, Parking (free), Wireless Internet, Smoke-Free property.

★½
Rodeway Inn Morro Bay
540 Main St.
Morro Bay CA 93442
(805) 772-7503
$39 - $69
Bed & Pet Discount Offered

Pet Policy: Rodeway Inns charge $10 per night per pet plus a refundable $50 damage deposit. Max of 2 pets per room. A veterinarian certificate that the pet is on a flea and parasite program is required. Pets may not be left alone in the room unless in a cage.

Features: Business services, Number of rooms: 18, Number of floors: 2, Free breakfast, Free Internet.

Moss Beach

Also see the following nearby communities that have pet friendly lodging: Montara - 0 miles, Half Moon Bay - 6 miles, San Bruno - 8 miles, Millbrae - 9 miles, Burlingame - 9 miles, South San Francisco - 10 miles

Seal Cove Inn, A Four Sisters Inn
221 Cypress Ave
Moss Beach CA 94038-9646
(650) 728-4114
$235 - $325
Bed & Pet Discount Offered

Pet Policy: Dogs only, up to 40 lbs, $65 additional charge, limit 2 per room. Pet owners will be liable for any additional cleaning bills or repairs, should they be required. All pets must be vaccinated and licensed and you agree to obtain and provide current records from a licensed veterinarian regarding this. The inn may request this information from you at any time.

Features: Coffee in lobby, Free breakfast, Free wireless Internet, Number of rooms: 10, Number of floors: 1, Smoke-Free property, Concierge, Media library, Free reception, Accessible bathroom.

Mount Shasta

Also see the following nearby communities that have pet friendly lodging: Dunsmuir - 7 miles, Weed - 8 miles

Best Western Plus Tree House
111 Morgan Way
Mount Shasta CA 96067
(530) 926-3101
$116 - $143

Pet Policy: Pets accepted with advance management approval. Please call property directly.

Features: Bar/lounge, Elevator, Indoor pool, Restaurant(s), Number of rooms: 98, Number of floors: 3, Suitable for children, Free breakfast, Business center, Free wireless Internet, Smoke-Free property, Accessible bathroom, In-room accessibility equipment for the deaf, Braille or raised signage, RV and truck parking.

Best Western Plus Tree House
I-5 and Lake St
Mount Shasta CA 96067
(530) 926-3101
$116 - $179

Pet Policy: Pets allowed, $15 per pet per night.

Features: Free wireless Internet, HBO, Microwave and refrigerator, Restaurant, Bar/Lounge, Indoor swimming pool and spa, Fitness center, Guest laundry, Free full hot breakfast buffet.

Strawberry Valley Inn
1142 S Mount Shasta Blvd
Mount Shasta CA 96067
(530) 926-2052
$139 - $212
Bed & Pet Discount Offered

Pet Policy: Pets under 20 lbs accepted, $15 per night. Limit of 2 per room.

Features: Concierge s, Number of rooms: 15, Number of floors: 1, Suitable for children, Barbecue grill(s), Coffee in lobby, Free breakfast, Front desk (limited hours), Smoke-Free property, Billiards, Free wireless Internet, Accessible bathroom, Health club.

Mountain View

Also see the following nearby communities that have pet friendly lodging: Los Altos - 2 miles, Palo Alto - 4 miles, Sunnyvale - 4 miles, Cupertino - 6 miles, Santa Clara - 6 miles, Menlo Park - 7 miles, Newark - 10 mile

Homestead San Jose - Mountain View
190 E El Camino Real
Mountain View CA 94040
(650) 962-1500
$79 - $114
Bed & Pet Discount Offered

Pet Policy: Pets allowed, no size restriction, $25 per day to a maximum of $150 per stay. Limit of 1 pet per room.

Features: Guest laundry, Number of rooms: 133, Number of floors: 2, Barbecue grill(s), Wireless Internet (additional charge), Parking (free), Use of nearby fitness center (discount).

Not rated
Oakwood Mountain View
555 West Middlefield Rd
Mountain View CA 94043
(602) 427-2752
$130 - $232

Pet Policy: Pets accepted with limitations and additional charge. Contact hotel directly for more information and to make reservations.

Features: Furnished apartments, Free continental breakfast, Weekly happy hour, Fitness center. Minimum stay of 30 days may be required.

★★★

Residence Inn by Marriott Palo Alto Mountain View
1854 W El Camino Real
Mountain View CA 94040
(650) 940-1300
$109 - $219
Bed & Pet Discount Offered

Pet Policy: Pets allowed, $75 per stay cleaning fee.

Features: Free Breakfast, Swimming pool - outdoor, Number of rooms: 112, Number of floors: 2, Barbecue grill(s), Parking (free), Complimentary newspapers in lobby, Use of nearby fitness center (free), Free wireless Internet, Dry cleaning/laundry service, Tennis on site, Free reception.

Napa

Also see the following nearby communities that have pet friendly lodging: Yountville - 8 miles, American Canyon - 8 miles, Sonoma - 9 miles, Boyes Hot Springs - 10 miles

★★★

Bel Abri A French Country Inn
837 California Blvd
Napa CA 94559
(877) 561-6000
$127 - $219
Bed & Pet Discount Offered

Pet Policy: We are pet friendly and we have designated two rooms, one Deluxe and one Queen Superior, for our furry little four-legged friends. Our pet fee is an additional $25. We welcome small (under 45 lbs.), well behaved dogs with the following expectations: Pets are not allowed on the beds or any of the furniture. No more than 2 dogs per room. Pets must not be left in your room in your absence. Any damages incurred because of your pet will be added to your bill. All pets must be on a leash while on our property. Pets are not allowed in the lobby except for passing through. All pets must be curbed off property. *Continued on next page*

Bel Abri A French Country Inn Continued from previous page

We have an empty lot on the Second St. side. Pets that disturb other guests will be asked to depart. We can provide Doggy Day Care for an additional fee

Features: Wheelchair accessible, Number of floors: 3, Concierge, Free breakfast, Smoke-Free, Multilingual staff, Dry cleaning/laundry service, Free wireless Internet.

★★★½

Blackbird Inn, A Four Sisters Inn
1755 1st St
Napa CA 94559
(707) 226-2450
$187- $288
Bed & Pet Discount Offered

Pet Policy: Well behaved dogs under 40 lbs accepted for $65 each per stay, limit of 2. Dogs cannot be left in the room unattended and must be crated (or out of the room) in order for the housekeepers to service your room.

Features: Free Breakfast, Concierge, Number of rooms: 8, Coffee in lobby, Complimentary newspapers, Free wireless Internet, Year Built 1901, Free reception

★★★

Chabli Inn Napa Valley
3360 Solano Ave
Napa CA 94558
(707) 257-1944
$89 - $129

Pet Policy: Dogs up to 50 lbs accepted, $15 per dog per night. Limit of 2 per room.

Features: Coffee maker, Wet bar with refrigerator, Iron & ironing board, Cable TV, Outdoor pool and hot tub, Smoke-free property.

★★

Discovery Inn
500 Silverado Trl
Napa CA 94559
(707) 253-0892
$69 - $115
Bed & Pet Discount Offered

Pet Policy: Pets welcome, $20 per pet per day. At the front of our property you will find grass where you can play with your pet in the shade under our large tree. And at the back of our property you will find a large open field perfect for your dog to run around in.

Features: Free breakfast, Parking (free), Free wireless Internet.

★★★½

Embassy Suites Hotel - Napa Valley-Wine Country
1075 California Blvd
Napa CA 94559
(707) 253-9540
$127 - $279
Bed & Pet Discount Offered

Pet Policy: Allows Dogs under 100 lbs. $75 per stay. Limit of 2 per room.

Features: Business Center, Free breakfast, Bar/lounge, Restaurant(s), Room service, Concierge, Gift shop, Number of suites: 205, Number of floors: 3, Spa services, Multilingual staff, Complimentary Newspapers, Nearby fitness center (free), Porter/bellhop, Outdoor pool – seasonal, Indoor pool, Accessible bathroom, In-room accessibility equipment for the deaf, Braille or raised signage, Dry cleaning/laundry, Wireless Internet (fee).

Napa Inn
1137 Warren St
Napa CA 94559
(707) 257-1444
$149 - $247
Bed & Pet Discount Offered

Pet Policy: Dogs accepted, $20 per night per dog, limit of 2. Dogs not allowed in breakfast area.

Features: Free breakfast, Spa services on site, Smoke-Free property

Napa River Inn
500 Main St
Napa CA 94559
(707) 251-8500
$209 - $529
Bed & Pet Discount Offered

Pet Policy: Pets welcome, $25 per night. The following are provided: A custom-designed pet blanket embroidered with Napa River Inn logo A color-coordinated logo place mat Stainless steel food and water bowls, Napa Valley-based Cab-Bone-Nay or Char-Dog-Nay dog biscuits (made with real wine), Individually wrapped plastic doggie walk bag, A welcome letter to you and your pet with a list of pet support services, including dog walkers, on-call veterinarian, and souvenirs (We recommend at least 72 hours' notice for pet sitters due to the high demand for this service. Please contact concierge).

Features: Bar/Lounge, Restaurant(s), Room service , Parking garage, Wheelchair accessible, Shopping on site, Nightclub, Porter/bellhop, Beauty services, Full-service health spa, Massage treatment room(s), Grocery/convenience store, Free wireless Internet, Area shuttle (free), Concierge, Number of rooms: 66, Business services, Complimentary newspaper, Smoke-Free property, Accessible bathroom, In-room accessibility equipment for the deaf, Braille or raised signage, Dry cleaning/laundry service.

★★

Napa Valley Redwood Inn
3380 Solano Avenue
Napa CA 94558
(707) 257-6111
$90 - $150
Bed & Pet Discount Offered

Pet Policy: Pets welcome for $10 per stay.

Features: Free Internet, Free breakfast, Parking (free), Swimming pool - outdoor seasonal

★★★★★

The Carneros Inn
4048 Sonoma Highway
Napa CA 94559
(707) 299-4900
$390 - $2,500

Pet Policy: Pets allowed, $150 per stay, limit of 1 per room. Must not leave unattended.

Features: Private garden and porch for each cottage, Wood burning fireplace, Flat screen TV, DVD player, Wireless Internet, Full health spa, 3 Restaurants, Adults only pool & hot tub, Family pool area, shops, Complimentary bicycles, Concierge.

The Meritage Resort and Spa
875 Bordeaux Way
Napa CA 94558
(707) 251-1900
$158 - $299
Bed & Pet Discount Offered

Pet Policy: Accepts up to three dogs under 80 lbs for $50 each per stay. Please note that pets are not allowed in the pool, spa and the restaurant.

Features: Free wireless Internet, Swimming pool - outdoor, Room service (24 hours), Concierge desk, Business center, Bar/lounge, Restaurant(s), Gift shops or newsstand, Number of rooms: 158, Number of floors: 3, Coffee in lobby, Breakfast available (not included), Shoe shine, Multilingual staff, Complimentary newspapers, Porter/bellhop, Limo or Town Car service available, Medical assistance available, Beauty services, Full-service health spa, Massage - treatment room(s), Media library, Dry cleaning/laundry service, Smoke-Free property, Pick up service from train station, Area shuttle, Valet parking (fee).

★★★★

Westin Verasa
1314 McKinstry Street
Napa CA 94559
(707) 257-1800
$168 - $509
Bed & Pet Discount Offered

Pet Policy: Pets Are Welcome!

Features: Bar/lounge, Outdoor pool, Restaurant, Concierge, Coffee in lobby, Complimentary newspapers, Business center, Porter/bellhop, Smoke-Free, Wireless Internet (fee), Number of rooms: 180, Number of floors: 3, Accessible bathroom, In-room accessibility equipment for the deaf, Room service, Fitness center.

National City

Also see the following nearby communities that have pet friendly lodging: Coronado - 4 miles, Chula Vista - 4 miles, La Mesa - 7 miles, San Ysidro - 9 miles, San Diego - 9 miles

★★★

Clarion South Bay
700 National City Blvd
National City CA 91950
(619) 474-2800
$139 - $149
Bed & Pet Discount Offered

Pet Policy: Pet friendly with nominal fee.

Features: Airport transportation (free), Number of floors: 9, Multilingual staff, Business center, Fitness facilities.

★★

Comfort Inn I-805 Naval Base
1645 E Plaza Blvd
National City CA 91950
(619) 474-2400
$69 - $99
Bed & Pet Discount Offered

Pet Policy: Pet Accommodation:$10 per night. Pet limit: 25 lbs. 2 pet per room.

Features: Outdoor pool, Number of rooms: 91, Number of floors: 4, Free breakfast, Complimentary newspapers, Business services, Smoke-Free, Free wireless Internet..

Rodeway Inn National City
607 Roosevelt Ave
National City CA 91950
(619) 474-7502
$43 - $64
Bed & Pet Discount Offered

Pet Policy: Rodeway Inns charge a fee of $10 per night per pet and require a $50 damage deposit, which is refunded if the room is in order at check out. Max of 2 pets per room. A veterinarian certificate that the pet is on a flea and parasite program is required. Pets may not be left alone in the room unless in a cage.

Features: Business services, Guest laundry, Number of rooms: 40, Number of floors: 2, Free breakfast, Multilingual staff, Free wireless Internet.

Needles

Not rated
Best Western Colorado River Inn
2371 W BROADWAY
Needles CA 92363
(760) 326-4552
$74 - $119

Pet Policy: All pets welcome for small fee and refundable deposit.

Features: Number of rooms : 63, Microwave & refrigerator in all rooms, Coffee maker, HBO, Free wireless Internet, Free breakfast, Outdoor swimming pool and spa, Sauna.

★★
Days Inn Needles
1215 Hospitality Ln
Needles CA 92363
(760) 326-5836
$44 - $82
Bed & Pet Discount Offered

Pet Policy: Pets allowed, $10 per pet.

Features: Business services, Free breakfast, Parking (free), Complimentary newspapers in lobby, Free wireless Internet, Swimming pool - outdoor seasonal.

★½
Travelers Inn Needles
1195 3rd Street
Needles CA 92363
(760) 326-4900
$55 - $56
Bed & Pet Discount Offered

Pet Policy: Pets allowed, $10 per pet per night.

Features: Guest laundry, Business services, Swimming pool - outdoor, Shopping on site, Number of rooms: 54, Number of floors: 3, Parking (free), Room service, Accessible bathroom.

Nevada City

Also see the following nearby communities that have pet friendly lodging: Grass Valley - 8 miles

★★
Nevada City Inn
760 Zion St
Nevada City CA 95959
(530) 265-2253
$49 - $60
Bed & Pet Discount Offered

Pet Policy: Pets permitted, $10 per pet per night. Must not be left alone in room.

Features: Business services, Coffee in lobby, Free breakfast, Complimentary newspapers in lobby, Smoke-Free property, Free wireless Internet.

Newark

Also see the following nearby communities that have pet friendly lodging: Fremont - 2 miles, Union City - 5 miles, Hayward - 9 miles, Palo Alto - 9 miles, Menlo Park - 9 miles, Milpitas - 10 miles, Santa Clara - 10 miles, Sunnyvale - 10 miles, Mountain View - 10 miles

Chase Suite Hotel Newark
39150 Cedar Blvd
Newark CA 94560
(510) 795-1200
From $129
Bed & Pet Discount Offered

Pet Policy: Pets welcome, $10 per pet per day plus $150 refundable deposit. Our apartment-style accommodations and gracious grounds give your pets easy access to the outdoors and lots of room to explore.

Features: Free Breakfast, Swimming pool - outdoor, Number of floors: 2, Coffee in lobby, Video library, Parking (free), Multilingual staff, Complimentary newspapers in lobby, Free wireless Internet, Smoke-Free property, Dry cleaning/laundry service, Wheelchair accessible, Gift shops or newsstand, Suitable for children, Grocery/convenience store, Area shuttle (free), 24-hour business center.

Hilton Newark Fremont
39900 Balentine Dr
Newark CA 94560
(510) 490-8390
$80 - $149
Bed & Pet Discount Offered

Pet Policy: Pets up to 70 lbs accepted, $50 per stay fee. Limit 2 pets per room.

Features: Business Center, Swimming pool - outdoor, Elevator, Bar/lounge, Restaurant(s), Room service (limited hours), ATM/banking, Number of rooms: 312, Number of floors: 7, Breakfast available (not included, Nightclub, Parking (free), Multilingual staff, Complimentary newspapers in lobby, Limo or Town Car service available, Wireless Internet, Dry cleaning/laundry service, Fitness facilities.

Homewood Suites by Hilton Newark/Fremont
39270 Cedar Blvd
Newark CA 94560
(510) 791-7700
$80 - $199
Bed & Pet Discount Offered

Pet Policy: Pets up to 40 lbs. $50 cleaning fee PLUS $10 per day per pet.

Features: Swimming pool - outdoor, Number of suites: 192, Free breakfast, Parking (free), Multilingual staff, Business center, Security guard, Dry cleaning/laundry service, Elevator, Wheelchair accessible, Number of rooms: 192, Number of floors: 4, Suitable for children, Complimentary newspapers in lobby, Grocery/convenience store, Free wireless Internet, Accessible bathroom, In-room accessibility equipment for the deaf, Braille or raised signage, Free reception, Fitness facilities.

★★★

Residence Inn by Marriott Newark Silicon Valley
35466 Dumbarton Ct
Newark CA 94560
(510) 739-6000
$129 - $139
Bed & Pet Discount Offered

Pet Policy: Pets allowed, $100 per stay cleaning fee.

Features: Wireless Internet (additional charge), Number of rooms: 168, Number of floors: 6, Business services (limited), Coffee in lobby, Free breakfast, Parking (free), Multilingual staff, Complimentary newspapers in lobby, Dry cleaning/laundry service, Elevator, Swimming pool - outdoor, Tennis on site, Fitness facilities.

★★

TownePlace Suites by Marriott Newark Silicon Valle
39802 Cedar Blvd
Newark CA 94560
(510) 657-4600
From $78
Bed & Pet Discount Offered

Pet Policy: Pets accepted, $100 cleaning fee per stay.

Features: Business Center, Swimming pool - outdoor, Elevator, Number of rooms: 127, Number of floors: 4, Coffee in lobby, Wireless Internet- additional charge, Parking (free), Multilingual staff, Complimentary newspapers in lobby, 24-hour front desk Accessible bathroom, In-room accessibility equipment for the deaf, Braille or raised signage, Dry cleaning/laundry service, Fitness facilities.

★★★★

W Silicon Valley
8200 Gateway Blvd
Newark CA 94560
(510) 494-8800
$103 - $228
Bed & Pet Discount Offered

Pet Policy: Dogs and Cats up to 40 lbs, $25 per night plus $100 per stay cleaning fee. Many pet amenities including toys, custom beds, and pet concierge services including walking and pet sitting.

Features: Bar/lounge, Restaurant(s), Number of rooms: 174, Business services, Suitable for children, Free wireless Internet, Breakfast available (not included), Video library, Health club, Parking (free), Complimentary newspapers in lobby, Room service, Dry cleaning/laundry service, Swimming pool - outdoor, Wheelchair accessible, Multilingual staff, Coffee in lobby, Porter/bellhop, Media library.

Newport Beach

Also see the following nearby communities that have pet friendly lodging: Costa Mesa - 3 miles, Fountain Valley - 8 miles, Santa Ana - 8 miles, Huntington Beach - 9 miles, Laguna Beach - 9 miles, Irvine - 9 miles, Lake Forest - 10 miles

Balboa Inn
105 Main St
Newport Beach CA 92661
(949) 675-3412
$249 - $550
Bed & Pet Discount Offered

Pet Policy: Small pets welcome, $50 per pet.

Features: Business services, Parking (additional charge), Bar/lounge, Restaurant(s), Outdoor pool, Number of floors: 2, Breakfast available (not included), Accessible bathroom, In-room accessibility equipment for the deaf, Wireless Internet, Elevator, Spa services, Concierge, Room service.

★★
Extended Stay America Orange County - John Wayne A
4881 Birch St
Newport Beach CA 92660
(949) 851-2711
$62 - $109
Bed & Pet Discount Offered

Pet Policy: One pet is allowed in each guest room. A $25 per day non-refundable cleaning fee (not to exceed $150) will be charged the first night of your stay.

Features: Elevator, Number of rooms: 164, Number of floors: 4, Parking (free), Front desk (limited hours), Guest laundry, Wireless Internet- additional charge.

★★★★
Fairmont Newport Beach
4500 Macarthur Blvd
Newport Beach CA 92660
(866) 840-8402
$128 - $333
Bed & Pet Discount Offered

Pet Policy: Pets up to 25 lbs accepted, $25 per pet per night.

Features: Bar/Lounge, Outdoor pool, Security guard, Spa services, Concierge, Gift shop, Number of rooms: 440, Shoe shine, Airport transportation (free), Room service (24 hours), Cell phone/mobile rental, Computer rental, Wireless Internet (additional charge), Multilingual staff, Porter/bellhop, Limo or Town Car service available, Accessible bathroom, In-room accessibility equipment for the deaf, Braille or raised signage, Dry cleaning/laundry service, Business Center, Fitness facilities, Currency Exchange, Valet parking (additional charge).

★★★½
Hyatt Regency Newport Beach
1107 Jamboree Rd
Newport Beach CA 92660
(949) 729-1234
$143 - $269
Bed & Pet Discount Offered

Pet Policy: Pets up to 40 lbs accepted, $10 per pet per night plus $75 refundable deposit.

Features: Swimming pool - outdoor, Currency exchange, Airport transportation (free), Business center, Suitable for children, Room service (limited hours), Concierge services, ATM/banking, Restaurant(s), Gift shops or newsstand, Number of rooms: 405, Pool table, Multilingual staff, Porter/bellhop, Security guard, Fitness facilities, Elevator, Health club, Technology support staff, Dry cleaning/laundry service, Wireless Internet (additional charge), Bar/Lounge, Parking (additional charge)

★★★½
Newport Beach Marriott Bayview
500 Bayview Cir
Newport Beach CA 92660
(949) 854-4500
$118 - $269
Bed & Pet Discount Offered

Pet Policy: Pets accepted. Contact hotel directly.

Features: Business Center, Indoor and Outdoor pools, Parking (valet) $18.00 per day, Bar/lounge, Airport transportation (free), Restaurant(s), Room service (limited hours), Gift shop, Number of rooms: 254, Number of floors: 9, Coffee in lobby, Wireless Internet- additional charge, Complimentary newspapers, Dry cleaning/laundry, Fitness facilities.

Nice

Also see the following nearby communities that have pet friendly lodging: Upper Lake - 4 miles, Lakeport - 7 miles

Gingerbread Cottages
4057 East Highway 20
Nice CA 95464
(707) 274-0200
$150 - $151
Bed & Pet Discount Offered

Pet Policy: We welcome small non-shedding dogs (10 lbs. or less). Guests must inquire if available, pre-register their dog and agree to pet policies. We are happy to provide towels, a blanket, dishes, treats, and a bed for your little one(s) while visiting us; $25 for one or $40 for two per day.

Features: Barbecue Grill(s), Swimming pool - outdoor, Video library, Free breakfast, Parking (free), Private beach, Wireless Internet.

North Highlands

Also see the following nearby communities that have pet friendly lodging: Roseville - 7 miles, Rancho Cordova - 8 miles, Sacramento - 9 miles

Days Inn Sacramento
3425 Orange Grove
North Highlands CA 95660
(916) 488-4100
$50 - $59
Bed & Pet Discount Offered

Pet Policy: Pets accepted, $30 per pet per day. Smoking rooms only.

Features: Business services, Security guard, Swimming pool - outdoor seasonal, Bar/lounge, Restaurant(s), Free breakfast, Parking (free)

Northridge

Also see the following nearby communities that have pet friendly lodging: Chatsworth - 4 miles, Canoga Park - 4 miles, Van Nuys - 5 miles, Tarzana - 5 miles, Woodland Hills - 6 miles, Sherman Oaks - 7 mile

Extended Stay America Los Angeles - Northridge
19325 Londelius St
Northridge CA 91324
(818) 734-1787
$79 - $104
Bed & Pet Discount Offered

Pet Policy: One medium-size pet is allowed in each guest room. A $25 per day non-refundable cleaning fee (not to exceed $150) will be charged the first night of your stay.

Features: Guest laundry, Elevator, Number of rooms: 117, Number of floors: 4, Wireless Internet (additional charge), Parking (free), Multilingual staff, Front desk (limited hours).

Norwalk

Also see the following nearby communities that have pet friendly lodging: Downey - 3 miles, Cerritos - 3 miles, La Mirada - 4 miles, Whittier - 4 miles, Pico Rivera - 5 miles, Bell Gardens - 5 miles, Hawaiian Gardens - 5 miles, La Palma - 6 miles, Buena Park - 6 miles, Commerce - 7 miles, Los Alamitos - 7 miles, Cypress - 8 miles, Fullerton - 9 miles, Huntington Park - 9 miles, Long Beach - 9 miles, Signal Hill - 9 miles, South El Monte - 10 miles

Rodeway Inn Norwalk
11734 Imperial Hwy
Norwalk CA 90650
(562) 868-3211
$59 - $78
Bed & Pet Discount Offered

Pet Policy: Rodeway Inns charge a fee of $10 per night per pet and require a $50 damage deposit, which is refunded if the room is in order at check out. Max of 2 pets per room. A veterinarian certificate that the pet is on a flea and parasite program and that they are Free from parasites is required. Pets may not be left alone in the room unless in a cage.

Features: Business center, Number of rooms: 42, Number of floors: 2, Parking (free), Free wireless Internet.

Novato

Also see the following nearby communities that have pet friendly lodging: San Rafael - 8 miles

Days Inn Novato-San Francisco
8141 Redwood Blvd
Novato CA 94945
(415) 897-7111
$55 - $85

Pet Policy: Pets allowed, $10 per night per pet.

Features: Free continental breakfast, Swimming pool. Cable TV and DVD.

Inn Marin
250 Entrada Dr
Novato CA 94949
(415) 883-5952
$101 - $299
Bed & Pet Discount Offered

Pet Policy: Pets allowed, $20 per pet per week. No size limits.

Features: Room service (limited hours), Barbecue grill(s), Concierge services, Bar/lounge, Free breakfast, Coffee in lobby, Nearby fitness center (discount), Technology support staff, Pick up service from train station, RV and truck parking, Gift shops or newsstand, Number of rooms: 64, Number of floors: 1, Complimentary newspapers in lobby, Wheelchair accessible, Suitable for children, Parking (free), Multilingual staff, Porter/bellhop, Beauty services, Massage - treatment room(s), Swimming pool - outdoor seasonal, Technology helpdesk, Accessible bathroom, In-room accessibility equipment for the deaf, Dry cleaning/laundry service, Free wireless Internet, 24-hour business center, Area shuttle (free), Fitness facilities.

Travelodge Novato
7600 Redwood Blvd
Novato CA 94945
(415) 892-7500
$44 - $101
Bed & Pet Discount Offered

Pet Policy: Pets up to 20 lbs accepted, $10 per night per pet. No limit to number of pets.

Features: Elevator, Free breakfast, Fitness facilities, Number of floors: 3, Business services, Guest laundry, Parking (free).

Oakhurst

Also see the following nearby communities that have pet friendly lodging: Bass Lake - 4 miles

A Bed of Roses at Yosemite
43547 Whispering Pines Dr
Oakhurst CA 93644
(559) 642-6975
$140 - $325
Bed & Pet Discount Offered

Pet Policy: Several rooms have been designated especially for guests visiting with pets. We welcome well-behaved pets. Guests planning to stay with a pet must make advance reservations for themselves and their pet via valid credit card. Reservations may be made toll Free at 877-624-7673. Rooms are limited; therefore we suggest pet reservations made in advance, depending on season. There is a $20 per night additional charge for each pet. We provide a throw blanket, extra towels, a comfortable sleeping pad, water bowl, and of course, pet treats!!!!. Pets cannot be allowed on the furniture in either the guest rooms or the common use areas. All pets must be on a leash or in a cage in the common use areas. Pets are not allowed in the dining area. Guests with a pet that causes damage will be charged a fee of up to $200 without further authorization.

Features: Free breakfast, Suitable for children, Number of rooms: 4, Parking (free), Free Internet access, Smoke-Free property.

Americas Best Value Inn
48800 Royal Oaks Drive
Oakhurst CA 93644
(559) 658-5500
$62 - $159

Pet Policy: Small pets only, Limit of 1 per room.

Features: Number of rooms: 69, Free wireless Internet, HBO, Coffee maker, Microwave & mini fridge on request, Free continental breakfast.

BW Plus Yosemite Gateway Inn
40530 HIGHWAY 41
Oakhurst CA 93644
(559) 683-2378
$56 - $190

Pet Policy: Up to 2 dogs per room with a 80 pound weight limit. Additional pet types (cats, birds, etc.) may be accepted at the hotel's discretion. Pet rate is $20 per day with a $100 per week maximum. A refundable cleaning & damage deposit of $50 is required upon check-in. If damage occurs or excessive cleaning is needed, the deposit can become non-refundable and the hotel may charge additionally to cover the costs of repair/cleaning.

Number of rooms: 122, Coffee maker, Free wireless Internet, HBO, Restaurant, Indoor & Outdoor pools and spas. Fitness facilities, Guest laundry.

Comfort Inn Yosemite Area
40489 State Route 41
Oakhurst CA 93644
(559) 683-8282
$69 - $70
Bed & Pet Discount Offered

Pet Policy: Pets accepted, $20 per night.

Features: Coffee in lobby, Swimming pool - outdoor, Business services, Elevator, Gift shops or newsstand, Number of rooms: 113, Number of floors: 2, Free breakfast, Parking (free), Complimentary newspapers in lobby, Free wireless Internet, Accessible bathroom, In-room accessibility equipment for the .

Shilo Inn Suites - Oakhurst
40644 Hwy 41
Oakhurst CA 93644
(559) 683-3555
$52 - $71
Bed & Pet Discount Offered

Pet Policy: Pets allowed, $25 per stay. Limit of 2 per room.

Features: Sauna, Free wireless Internet, Swimming pool - outdoor, Elevator, Number of rooms: 80, Number of floors: 4, Coffee in lobby, Guest Laundry, Free breakfast, Parking (free), Complimentary newspapers in lobby, Steam room, Smoke-Free property, Fitness facilities.

Oakland

Also see the following nearby communities that have pet friendly lodging: Alameda - 3 miles, Emeryville - 6 miles, Berkeley - 8 miles, Castro Valley - 10 miles

Clarion Hotel Airport
500 Hegenberger Road
Oakland CA 94621
(510) 635-6000
$79 - $89

Pet Policy: Pets accepted, $10 per night per pet.

Features: Free shuttle to from Oakland, Golf packages, Free hot breakfast bar 7 days, Dry clean valet service, Refrigerator and microwave on request, Business center, Fitness center, Seasonal outdoor pool. Free wireless Internet, In room coffee, Iron and board, Hairdryer, Premium cable TV channels, Group rates available.

Extended Stay America Oakland - Emeryville
3650 Mandela Pkwy
Oakland CA 94608
(510) 923-1481
$99 - $109
Bed & Pet Discount Offered

Pet Policy: One pet is allowed in each guest room. A $25 per day non-refundable cleaning fee (not to exceed $150) will be charged the first night of your stay.

Features: Guest laundry, Parking (free), Wireless Internet (additional charge), Elevator, Number of rooms: 149, Number of floors: 4, Business services, Tennis on site.

★★★
Hilton Oakland Airport
1 Hegenberger Rd
Oakland CA 94621
(510) 635-5000
$99 - $129
Bed & Pet Discount Offered

Pet Policy: Pets welcome up to 75 lbs, $50 fee. When you arrive in your spacious guest room, you have access to some fun pet amenities such as a pet bed, food bowl, water bowl and the mat to go underneath. Be sure to request "doggie" bag before your arrival. It is filled with disposable waste bags, disinfectant, a dog tag and treats.

Features: Business Center, Swimming pool - outdoor, Parking (additional charge) $10 Per Day, Dry cleaning/laundry service, Complimentary newspapers in lobby, Porter/bellhop, Technology support staff, Free wireless Internet, Number of restaurants 2, Airport transportation (free), Room service (limited hours), Bar/lounge, Elevator, ATM/banking, Gift shops or newsstand, Number of rooms: 363, Number of floors: 3, Breakfast available (not included), Arcade/game room, Pool table, Currency exchange, Multilingual staff, Security guard, Fitness facilities.

★★★
Homewood Suites by Hilton Oakland-Waterfront
1103 Embarcadero
Oakland CA 94606
(510) 663-2700
$119 - $239
Bed & Pet Discount Offered

Pet Policy: Pets up to 30 lbs, $75 per stay. Pooper scoopers and bags are available.

Features: Business center, Elevator, ATM/banking, Gift shops or newsstand Number of rooms: 132, Number of floors: 3, Suitable for children, Barbecue grill(s), Coffee in lobby, Free breakfast, Grocery, Parking (free), Complimentary newspapers in lobby, Security guard, Free wireless Internet, Marina on site, Swimming pool - outdoor seasonal, Dry cleaning/laundry service, Fitness facilities.

★★
La Quinta Inn Oakland Airport/Coliseum
8465 Enterprise Way
Oakland CA 94621
(510) 632-8900
$62 - $80
Bed & Pet Discount Offered

Pet Policy: Pets welcome with $35 deposit.

Features: Free Breakfast, Elevator, Accessible bathroom, Airport transportation (free), Swimming pool - outdoor, Number of rooms: 148, Number of floors: 3, Coffee in lobby, Guest laundry, Parking (free), Complimentary newspapers in lobby, Free wireless Internet, Airport transportation (free) available 24 hours, Fitness facilities.

★★
Quality Inn Oakland Airport
8471 Enterprise Way
Oakland CA 94621
(866) 223-3257
$56 - $74
Bed & Pet Discount Offered

Pet Policy: Quality Inns charge a fee of $10 per night per pet but do not charge any other fees. They may require a $50 damage deposit, which is refunded if the room is in order at check out. Quality Inns accept any well-behaved pets with a maximum of 3 per room, but dogs are limited to 50 pounds. Pets may not be left alone in the room unless in a cage

Features: Indoor pool, Airport transportation (free), Number of rooms: 98, Coffee in lobby, Free breakfast, Multilingual staff, Complimentary newspaper, Business center, Wireless Internet (additional charge), Dry cleaning/laundry..

Waterfront Hotel, a Joie de Vivre Boutique Hotel
10 Washington Street
Oakland CA 94607
(510) 836-3800
$149 - $229
Bed & Pet Discount Offered

Pet Policy: Joie de Vivre has Fido-friendly packages, amenities and a progressive pet policy designed to make hotel stays hospitable for dogs and their owners alike. Joie de Vivre's properties do not impose weight restrictions on dogs and do not charge pet fees (provided there is no damage to a guestroom and dog owners abide by pet rules.

Features: Bar/Lounge, Business Center, Concierge, Indoor pool, Restaurant, Number of rooms: 143, Number of suites: 15, Business services, Wireless Internet (additional charge), Breakfast available (not included), Multilingual staff, Complimentary newspapers, Room service, Porter/bellhop, Security guard, Marina on site, Sauna, Smoke-Free, Dry cleaning/laundry, Fitness center, Valet parking (fee).

Occidental

Also see the following nearby communities that have pet friendly lodging: Bodega - 5 miles, Sebastopol - 5 miles, Valley Ford - 6 miles, Guerneville - 7 mile

★★★½

Inn At Occidental Of Sonoma
3657 Church St
Occidental CA 95465
(707) 874-1047
$349 - $350
Bed & Pet Discount Offered

Pet Policy: Well-behaved, housebroken dogs are permitted in the Sonoma Cottage and in designated Courtyard Rooms. $40 per night per pet. Pets should not be left alone in the room at any time or be left unattended while on the property. While in the public areas of the Inn, pets must be on a leash. We ask that you do not bring your pet into the living room or the dining room. Pets are welcome in the courtyard or on the verandah. Pets are not allowed on the furniture in the guest room or in the public areas. If your pet does sleep on the bed with you, ask us for a sheet to put over the duvet cover.

Features: Free Breakfast, Library, Number of rooms: 16 Free wireless Internet.

Oceanside

Also see the following nearby communities that have pet friendly lodging: Carlsbad - 5 miles, Vista - 8 miles

Extended Stay America
3190 Vista Way
Oceanside CA 92056
(760) 439-1499
$74 - $89
Bed & Pet Discount Offered

Pet Policy: One medium-size pet is allowed in each guest room. A $25 per day cleaning fee (not to exceed $150) will be charged the first night.

Features: Elevator, Number of rooms: 101, Number of floors: 3, Internet access - additional charge, Parking (free).

★★

La Quinta Inn San Diego-Oceanside
937 N Coast Hwy
Oceanside CA 92054
(760) 450-0730
$69 - $114
Bed & Pet Discount Offered

Pet Policy: Pets any size allowed, no fee. Must not leave unattended and must clean up after.

Features: Accessible bathroom, Concierge, 24-hour business center, Number of rooms: 40, Number of floors: 4, Coffee in lobby, Guest laundry, Free breakfast, Multilingual staff, Free wireless Internet, Smoke-Free.

Not rated
Marriott Executay The Villages of Monterey
3901 Mesa Drive
Oceanside CA 92056
(888) 526-0566
Call for prices.

Pet Policy: Pets accepted up to 50 lbs. $500 deposit, $250 non-refundable. Limit 2 pets per apartment, no aggressive breeds.

Features: Furnished apartments, Eat in kitchen, Tennis courts, Swimming pool and spa, Fitness center, Business center. Minimum stay of 30 days is required

Motel 6 Oceanside Downtown
909 N Coast Hwy
Oceanside CA 92054
(760) 721-1543
$59 - $75
Bed & Pet Discount Offered

Pet Policy: Well-behaved pets stay Free. Animals that pose a health or safety risk may not remain onsite, and include those that, in our manager's discretion, are too numerous for any one room, cause damage to our property or that of other guests, are too disruptive, are not properly attended, or demonstrate undue aggression. All pets must be declared at check-in. Pets must be attended to and under control at all times. If unavoidable circumstances require a pet to remain in a room while the owner is offsite, the pet must be secured in a crate or travel carrier. Pets must be on a leash or securely carried outside of guest rooms

Features: Outdoor pool, Guest laundry, Number of rooms: 106, Number of floors: 3, Business services, Accessible bathroom, Wheelchair accessible, BBQ area, Coffee in lobby, Complimentary newspapers, Free wireless Internet, Concierge.

Oceanside Travelodge
1401 N Coast Hwy
Oceanside CA 92054
(760) 722-1244
$55 - $125
Bed & Pet Discount Offered

Pet Policy: Accepts small dogs only, $25 per stay.

Features: Business services, Free breakfast, Guest laundry, ATM/banking, Coffee in lobby, Parking (free), Complimentary newspapers in lobby, Free wireless Internet.

Ramada Oceanside
1440 Mission Avenue
Oceanside CA 92054
(760) 967-4100
$62 - $139
Bed & Pet Discount Offered

Pet Policy: Pet friendly, $10 per pet per day.

Features: Business center, Elevator, Number of rooms: 70, Number of floors: 4, Guest laundry, Parking (free), Free wireless Internet, Grocery/convenience store, Free breakfast, Fitness facilities.

Residence Inn Marriott Oceanside
3603 Ocean Ranch Blvd
Oceanside CA 92056
(760) 722-9600
$158 - $269
Bed & Pet Discount Offered

Pet Policy: Pets welcome, $100 per stay cleaning fee.

Features: Swimming pool - outdoor, Number of floors: 4, Parking (free), Complimentary newspapers in lobby, Grocery/convenience store, Accessible bathroom, In-room accessibility equipment for the deaf, Braille or raised signage, Fitness facilities.

Super 8 Oceanside
3240 Mission Ave
Oceanside CA 92058
(760) 757-7700
$52 - $84
Bed & Pet Discount Offered

Pet Policy: Small pets permitted, $10 per pet per day.

Features: Outdoor pool, Number of rooms: 107, Business services, Coffee in lobby, Free breakfast, Multilingual staff, Complimentary newspapers in lobby, Free wireless Internet, Fitness facilities.

Ojai

Also see the following nearby communities that have pet friendly lodging: Ventura - 10 miles

Blue Iguana Inn
11794 N Ventura Ave
Ojai CA 93023
(805) 646-5277
$129 - $249
Bed & Pet Discount Offered

Pet Policy: Guests can arrange to bring pets by contacting the property directly.

Features: Outdoor pool, Supervised child care/activities, Number of rooms: 4, Number of suites: 8, Number of floors: 2, Business services, Free breakfast, Multilingual staff, Complimentary newspapers, Free wireless Internet, Nearby fitness center (discount), Dry cleaning/laundry service, Accessible bathroom.

★★½
Casa Ojai Inn
1302 E Ojai Ave
Ojai CA 93023
(805) 646-8175
$110 - $199
Bed & Pet Discount Offered

Pet Policy: Pets allowed in double queen rooms only

Features: Free breakfast, Business center, Parking (free), Multilingual staff, Smoke-Free property, Swimming pool - outdoor seasonal, Accessible bathroom, In-room accessibility equipment for the deaf, Braille or raised signage, Free wireless Internet.

★★½
Chantico Inn
406 W Ojai Ave
Ojai CA 93023
(805) 646-8100
$199 - $228
Bed & Pet Discount Offered

Pet Policy: Pets under 25 lbs accepted, $60 per stay fee. Limit 1 pet per room.

Features: Swimming pool - outdoor, Number of rooms: 22, Number of floors: 2, Free breakfast, Parking (free), Wheelchair accessible, Suitable for children, Coffee in lobby, Multilingual staff, Complimentary newspapers in lobby, Front desk (limited hours), Massage - spa treatment room(s), Designated smoking areas, Accessible bathroom.

Not rated:
Hummingbird Inn
1208 E Ojai Avenue
Ojai CA 93023
(805) 646-4365
$146 - $173

Pet Policy: All pets welcome, $10 per pet per night. Dog park nearby.

Features: Heated swimming pool and spa, Free breakfast.

Ojai Valley Inn And Spa
905 Country Club Rd
Ojai CA 93023
(800) 422-6524
$300 - $450
Bed & Pet Discount Offered

Pet Policy: Dogs welcome, $100 per stay. Our doggie room service is strictly five diamond and includes: a gourmet pet menu; your name on the outside of the room; plenty of dog friendly areas to be walked and exercised; and a special turn down service every evening. What more could you ask for? Please do not leave pets alone in room. Pets not allowed in food, pool, golf or spa areas. Please keep leashed outside of room.

Features: Year Built 1923, Golf course on site, Tennis on site, Children's swimming pool, Beauty services, Free wireless Internet, Bar/lounge, Steam room, Security guard, Supervised child care/activities, Concierge, Outdoor pool, Full-service health spa, Shopping on site, Room service (24 hours), Business center, Restaurant(s), Number of rooms: 308, Breakfast available (not included), Multilingual staff, Porter/bellhop, Limo or Town Car service available, Massage - treatment room(s), Children's club, Sauna, ATM/banking, Shoe shine, Coffee in lobby, Dry cleaning/laundry service.

Olympic Valley

Also see the following nearby communities that have pet friendly lodging: Truckee - 8 miles, Tahoe Vista - 9 miles

Painted Rock Lodge
5048 River Road
Olympic Valley CA 96146
(530) 412-0610
$412 - $784

Pet Policy: Pets will be considered. Please call property directly.

Features: Number of suites: 5, Hot tub, half-mile from Squaw Valley entrance, Wood burning fireplace in master suite,

Ontario

Also see the following nearby communities that have pet friendly lodging: Rancho Cucamonga - 4 miles, Upland - 5 miles, Chino - 6 miles, Claremont - 8 miles, Chino Hills - 8 miles, Pomona - 10 miles

Ayres Boutique Suites Ontario Airport
204 N Vineyard Avenue
Ontario CA 91764
(909) 937-9700
$80 - $90
Bed & Pet Discount Offered

Pet Policy: Pets accepted, $45 fee.

Features: Swimming pool - outdoor, Restaurant(s), On-site car rental, ATM/banking, Concierge services, Suitable for children, Coffee in lobby, Multilingual staff, Nearby fitness center (discount), Free wireless Internet, Accessibility equipment for the deaf, Area shuttle (free), 24-hour business center, Free reception, Shopping center shuttle (free), Dry cleaning/laundry service, Airport transportation (free), Room service (limited hours), Number of rooms: 106, Number of floors: 2, Free breakfast, Parking (free), Complimentary newspapers in lobby, Porter/bellhop, Limo or Town Car service available, Pick up service from train station.

Not rated
Best Ontario Inn
1045 West Mission Blvd
Ontario CA 91762
(909) 391-6668
$48 - $75

Pet Policy: Pets allowed.

Features: Swimming pool - outdoor, Number of rooms: 42, Number of floors: 2, Parking (free), Free wireless Internet, Accessible bathroom.

★★★½

Doubletree Hotel Ontario Airport
222 N Vineyard Ave
Ontario CA 91764
(909) 937-0900
$118 - $174
Bed & Pet Discount Offered

Pet Policy: Pets up to 25 lbs, $50 fee per stay.

Features: Bar/Lounge, Business Center, Shoe shine, Shopping on site, Swimming pool - outdoor, Nightclub, Elevator, ATM/banking, Airport transportation (free), Restaurant(s), Number of rooms: 484, Wireless Internet (additional charge), Multilingual staff, Use of nearby fitness center (free), Dry cleaning/laundry service.

★★
Econo Lodge Ontario
1655 E 4th St
Ontario CA 91764
(909) 986-7000
$54 - $64
Bed & Pet Discount Offered

Pet Policy: Pets up to 75 lbs accepted, $25 per night. Limit 1 pet per room.

Features: Guest laundry, Swimming pool - outdoor, Elevator, Number of rooms: 80, Number of floors: 3, Coffee in lobby, Free breakfast, Parking (free), Complimentary newspapers in lobby, Use of nearby fitness center (free), Free wireless Internet.

★★
Extended Stay America Los Angeles - Ontario Airport
3990 Inland Empire Blvd
Ontario CA 91764
(909) 944-8900
$64 - $79
Bed & Pet Discount Offered

Pet Policy: One pet up to 35 lbs is allowed in each guest room. A $25 per day non-refundable cleaning fee (not to exceed $150) will be charged the first night of your stay.

Features: Guest laundry, Swimming pool - outdoor, Elevator, Number of rooms: 127, Number of floors: 3, Coffee in lobby, Internet access – additional charge, Parking (free), Front desk (limited hours), Security guard.

★★★½
Hilton Ontario Airport
700 N Haven Ave
Ontario CA 91764
(909) 980-0400
$81- $199
Bed & Pet Discount Offered

Pet Policy: Pets up to 25 lbs, $75 fee.

Features: Elevator, Restaurant(s), Swimming pool – outdoor, Concierge services, Gift shops or newsstand, Number of rooms: 309, Number of floors: 11, Breakfast available (not included), Multilingual staff, Complimentary newspapers in lobby, Porter/bellhop, Security guard, Limo or Town Car service available, Smoke-Free property, Airport transportation (free) available 24 hours, Coffee in lobby, Pick up service from train station, Bar/lounge, Parking (valet) $15 Per Day, Accessible bathroom, In-room accessibility equipment for the deaf, Braille or raised signage, Dry cleaning/laundry service, Wheelchair accessible, Room service (24 hours), Free wireless Internet, 24-hour business center, Area shuttle (free), Fitness facilities.

★½
Knights Inn Ontario
1120 E Holt Blvd
Ontario CA 91761
(909) 984-9655
$42 - $65
Bed & Pet Discount Offered

Pet Policy: Pets welcome, No additional fee.

Features: Swimming pool - outdoor, Number of floors: 2, Free breakfast.

La Quinta Inn and Suites Ontario Airport
3555 Inland Empire Blvd
Ontario CA 91764
(909) 476-1112
$69 - $89
Bed & Pet Discount Offered

Pet Policy: Cats and dogs up to 50 pounds are accepted in all guest rooms. Housekeeping services for rooms with pets require pet owner be present or pet must be crated. No fees or deposits are required.

Features: Swimming pool - outdoor, Elevator, Accessible bathroom, Airport transportation (free), Number of rooms: 144, Free breakfast, Parking (free), Complimentary newspapers in lobby, Free wireless Internet, Dry cleaning/laundry service, Fitness facilities.

★★

Quality Inn Ontario Airport
514 N Vineyard Ave
Ontario CA 91764
(909) 937-2999
$74- $94
Bed & Pet Discount Offered

Pet Policy: Pets accepted up to 40 lbs, $20 per night plus $100 cash deposit if not using credit card. Limit 1 pet per room.

Features: Airport transportation (free), Guest laundry, Swimming pool - outdoor, Elevator, Number of rooms: 129, Number of floors: 3, Coffee in lobby, Free breakfast, Parking (free), Multilingual staff, Free wireless Internet, Restaurant(s), Business center, Fitness facilities.

★★

Red Roof Inn Ontario Airport
1818 E Holt Blvd
Ontario CA 91761
(909) 988-8466
$69 - $104
Bed & Pet Discount Offered

Pet Policy: Red Roof's Pet Policy: One well-behaved family pet is permitted. Pets must be declared during guest registration. In consideration of all Red Roof guests, pets must never be left unattended in the guestroom.

Features: Parking (free), Complimentary newspapers in lobby, Number of rooms: 108, Number of floors: 3, Elevator, Airport transportation (free), Swimming pool - outdoor, Wheelchair accessible, Free wireless Internet, Translation services, Coffee in lobby, Technology helpdesk, Dry cleaning/laundry service, Technology support staff, Multilingual staff.

Residence Inn By Marriott Ontario
2025 E Convention Center Way
Ontario CA 91764
(909) 937-6788
$99 - $169
Bed & Pet Discount Offered

Pet Policy: Pets allowed, $100 per stay cleaning fee.

Features: Business Services, Coffee in Lobby, Free Breakfast, Swimming pool - outdoor, Dry cleaning/laundry service, Airport transportation (free), Number of rooms: 200, Number of floors: 2, Barbecue grill(s), Grocery, Parking (free), Complimentary newspapers in lobby, Free wireless Internet, Smoke-Free property, Tennis on site, Fitness facilities.

Rodeway Inn Ontario Airport
4075 E Guasti Rd
Ontario CA 91761
(909) 390-8886
$54 - $69
Bed & Pet Discount Offered

Pet Policy: Pets under 25 lbs, $10 per pet per night. Limit 2 per room.

Features: Free Breakfast, Swimming pool - outdoor, Number of rooms: 100, Number of floors: 2, Guest laundry, Parking (free), Complimentary newspapers in lobby, Free wireless Internet, Coffee in lobby.

★★★½

Sheraton Ontario Airport Hotel
429 N Vineyard Ave
Ontario CA 91764
(909) 937-8000
$98 - $144
Bed & Pet Discount Offered

Pet Policy: Pets up to 40 lbs accepted, no additional fee.

Features: Outdoor pool, Airport transportation (free) available 24 hours, Bar/lounge, Restaurant(s), Room service (limited hours), Concierge, Gift shop, Number of rooms: 164, Number of floors: 6, Coffee in lobby, Breakfast available (not included), Multilingual staff, Complimentary newspapers, Business center, Porter/bellhop, Security guard, Wireless Internet, Dry cleaning/laundry service, Fitness facilities.

Orange

Also see the following nearby communities that have pet friendly lodging: Anaheim - 4 miles, Garden Grove - 4 miles, Santa Ana - 5 miles, Placentia - 6 miles, Fullerton - 7 miles, Yorba Linda - 8 miles, Fountain Valley - 8 miles, Brea - 8 miles, Buena Park - 9 miles, Cypress - 9 miles, Costa Mesa - 10 miles

★★★

Ayres Inn Orange
3737 W Chapman Ave
Orange CA 92868
(714) 978-9168
$113 - $119
Bed & Pet Discount Offered

Pet Policy: Pets accepted, $45 per stay. Limit 2 per room. Doggie beds, bowl and biscuits provided

Features: Free Breakfast, Security guard, Outdoor pool, Room service (limited hours), Concierge, Number of rooms: 129, Number of suites: 6, Number of floors: 6, Airport transportation (additional charge), Coffee in lobby, Free wireless Internet, Multilingual staff, Complimentary newspapers, Smoke-Free, Parking (free), Accessible bathroom, In-room accessibility equipment for the deaf, Braille or raised signage, Dry cleaning/laundry, Business center, Area shuttle (free), Fitness facilities.

★★★½

Doubletree Hotel Anaheim Orange County
100 The City Dr S
Orange CA 92868
(714) 634-4500
$125 - $259
Bed & Pet Discount Offered

Pet Policy: Pets up to 75 lbs accepted, $75 per pet per stay.

Features: Business Center, Currency Exchange, Concierge, Outdoor pool, Bar/lounge, Restaurant, Gift shops or newsstand, Number of rooms: 454, Pool table, Multilingual staff, Porter/bellhop, Security guard, Free Internet access, Dry cleaning/laundry service, Fitness facilities, Valet parking (fee).

Extended Stay America Orange County - Katella Ave
1635 W Katella Ave
Orange CA 92867
(714) 639-8608
$62 - $92
Bed & Pet Discount Offered

Pet Policy: One medium-size pet is allowed in each guest room. A $25 per day non-refundable cleaning fee (not to exceed $150) will be charged the first night of your stay.

Features: Guest laundry, Elevator, Number of rooms: 124, Number of floors: 4, Parking (free), Front desk (limited hours), Wireless Internet, Bar/lounge.

Hilton Suites Anaheim/Orange
400 N State College Blvd
Orange CA 92868
(714) 938-1111
$135 - $179
Bed & Pet Discount Offered

Pet Policy: Pets up to 75 lbs, $50 pet stay fee.

Features: Business Center, Swimming pools – both indoor and outdoor, Restaurant(s), Room service (limited hours), Gift shops or newsstand, Number of rooms: 230, Number of floors: 10, Multilingual staff, Wireless Internet, Parking (valet) $14/Night, Dry cleaning/laundry service, Fitness facilities.

Oroville

Americas Best Value Inn
580 Oro Dam Blvd
Oroville CA 95965
(530) 533-7070
$68 - $185

Pet Policy: Our hotel is pet friendly. Declared pets permitted in Pet Rooms only. Pet charge $10 per day. Pet deposit $20.

Features: Coffee maker, Microwave, Mini fridge, Hair dryer, Iron/board, Satellite TV, Free continental breakfast, Guest laundry, Jacuzzi rooms are available.

Comfort Inn Central
1470 Feather River Blvd
Oroville CA 95965
(530) 533-9673
$89 - $99.
Bed & Pet Discount Offered

Pet Policy: Dogs only, $10 per night plus $100 refundable deposit.

Features: Elevator, Swimming pool – outdoor, Guest laundry, Free breakfast, Sauna, Fitness facilities, Number of rooms: 54, Number of floors: 3.

Not rated
Days Inn Oroville
1745 Feather River Blvd
Oroville CA 95965
(530) 533-3297
$52 - $75

Pet Policy: Pets allowed, $10 per pet per day.

Features: Free breakfast, Pool, Truck & RV parking.

Oxnard

Also see the following nearby communities that have pet friendly lodging: Port Hueneme - 3 miles, Camarillo - 7 miles

Comfort Inn Oxnard
1001 E Channel Islands Blvd
Oxnard CA 93033
(805) 201-6000
$89 - $114
Bed & Pet Discount Offered

Pet Policy: Pet accommodation: $35 per stay Pet limit: maximum 1 pet per room, up to 25 pounds.

Features: Sauna, Outdoor pool, Babysitting or child care, Number of rooms: 95, Number of floors: 2, Business services, Guest laundry, Free breakfast, Complimentary newspapers, Free wireless Internet, Fitness facilities.

GrandStay Residential
2211 E Gonzales Rd
Oxnard CA 93036
(805) 983-6808
$109 - $110
Bed & Pet Discount Offered

Pet Policy: Pets allowed, $50 fee at check in.

Features: Dry cleaning/laundry service, Swimming pool - outdoor, Elevator, Grocery, Gift shops or newsstand, Barbecue grill(s), Free breakfast, Multilingual staff, Limo or Town Car service available, Free wireless Internet, Fitness facilities.

Residence Inn By Marriott
2101 W Vineyard Ave
Oxnard CA 93030
(805) 278-2200
$119 - $168
Bed & Pet Discount Offered

Pet Policy: Pets allowed, $100 per stay cleaning fee.

Features: Business services, Outdoor pool, Airport transportation (free), Number of suites: 252, Number of floors: 2, Coffee in lobby, Free breakfast, Multilingual staff, Complimentary newspaper, Free wireless Internet, Dry cleaning/laundry, Fitness center..

★★

Vagabond Inn Oxnard
1245 N Oxnard Blvd
Oxnard CA 93030
(805) 983-0251
$68 - $79
Bed & Pet Discount Offered

Pet Policy: Pets welcome, $5 per pet per night. No size restriction.

Features: Business services, Restaurant(s), Swimming pool - outdoor, Coffee in lobby, Parking (free), Complimentary newspapers in lobby, Use of nearby fitness center (free), Free breakfast.

Pacific Grove

Also see the following nearby communities that have pet friendly lodging: Monterey - 3 miles, Seaside - 5 miles, Carmel - 7 miles, Marina - 8 miles

Butterfly Grove Inn
1073 Lighthouse Ave.
Pacific Grove CA 93950
(831) 373-4921
$69 - $159

Pet Policy: Pets allowed, any size, $20 per night.

Features: Number of suites: 9, Number of floors: 2, Year round heated pool and spa, Playing area for kids, Free continental breakfast, Free parking.

Centrella Inn
612 Central Ave
Pacific Grove CA 93950
(800) 233-3372
$204 - $300
Bed & Pet Discount Offered

Pet Policy: Dogs and Cats up to 50 lbs will be considered, with advanced approval. The property allows pets in specific rooms only and has other pet restrictions. Guests can arrange to bring pets by contacting the property directly.

Features: Coffee in lobby, Year Built 1889, Number of rooms: 14, Number of suites: 5, Number of floors: 3, Business services, Free breakfast, Parking (free), Complimentary newspapers in lobby, Front desk (limited hours), Smoke-Free property, Wheelchair accessible, Suitable for children, Garden, Video library, Multilingual staff, Accessible bathroom, Free wireless Internet.

Gosby House Inn, a Four Sisters Inn
643 Lighthouse Ave
Pacific Grove CA 93950
(831) 375-1287
$161 - $259
Bed & Pet Discount Offered

Pet Policy: Dogs only, up to 40 lbs, $65 additional fee, limit 2 per room. Pet owners will be liable for any additional cleaning bills or repairs, should they be required. All pets must be vaccinated and licensed. You agree to provide current records from a licensed which the inn may request from you at any time.

Features: Free Breakfast, Concierge desk, Coffee in lobby, Complimentary newspapers in lobby, Free wireless Internet, Suitable for children, Front desk (limited hours), Free reception Number of rooms: 22, Number of floors: 2, Year Built 1877.

Green Gables Inn, A Four Sisters Inn
301 Ocean View Blvd
Pacific Grove CA 93950-2903
(831) 375-2095
$215 - $280
Bed & Pet Discount Offered

Pet Policy: Pets up to 40 lbs, $65 per stay per pet. Must not be left in room unattended.

Features: Room service (limited hours), Coffee in lobby, Library, Free breakfast, Complimentary newspapers in lobby, Concierge desk, Media library, Free wireless Internet, Number of rooms: 11, Number of floors: 3, Accessible bathroom, Wheelchair accessible, Dry cleaning/laundry service, Free reception.

Lighthouse Lodge And Suites
1150 Lighthouse Ave
Pacific Grove CA 93950
(831) 655-2111
$105 - $266
Bed & Pet Discount Offered

Pet Policy: Pets are welcome in any Lodge accommodations with the exception of the Upper Lodge Suites. Fee of $25 per day, maximum of $50.

Features: Wireless Internet (additional charge), Swimming pool - outdoor, Free breakfast, Concierge services, Number of rooms: 64, Number of suites: 31, Number of floors: 2, Coffee in lobby, Parking (free), Front desk (limited hours),

Pacific Gardens Inn
701 Asilomar Blvd
Pacific Grove CA 93950
(831) 646-9414
$105 - $230
Bed & Pet Discount Offered

Pet Policy: Up to 3 pets per room allowed with no fee, no size restrictions. Short walk to dog friendly beach.

Features: Accessible bathroom, Babysitting or child care, BBQ area, Coffee in lobby, Free breakfast, Complimentary newspapers, Free reception, Concierge, Guest laundry, Limo or Town Car service available, Media library, Multilingual staff, Number of rooms: 28, Number of suites: 6, Security guard, Smoke-Free property, Translation services, Wheelchair accessible, Free wireless Internet.

Pacific Grove Inn
581 Pine Ave
Pacific Grove CA 93950
(831) 375-2825
$130 - $140
Bed & Pet Discount Offered

Pet Policy: Pets accepted, $25 per pet per night fee. Only 3 rooms are pet friendly so please book in advance.

Features: Free breakfast, Coffee in lobby, Number of rooms: 16, Number of floors: 3, Parking (free), Complimentary newspapers in lobby, Front desk (limited hours), Smoke-Free property, Concierge desk, Wheelchair accessible, Free wireless Internet, Accessible bathroom, Free reception, Video library.

Sea Breeze Lodge
1101 Lighthouse Avenue
Pacific Grove CA 93950
(831) 372-7771
$79 - $172

Pet Policy: Pets accepted but must contact hotel directly for permission and restrictions.

Features: Swimming pool - outdoor, Concierge services, Coffee in lobby, Number of rooms: 30, Number of floors: 1, Free breakfast, Parking (free), Internet access, Smoke-Free property.

Palm Desert

Also see the following nearby communities that have pet friendly lodging: Rancho Mirage - 4 miles, La Quinta - 5 miles, Thousand Palms - 5 miles, Indio - 7 miles, Cathedral City - 8 miles

Best Western Plus Palm Desert Resort
74695 Highway 111
Palm Desert CA 92260
(760) 340-4441
$89 - $184
Bed & Pet Discount Offered

Pet Policy: Pets allowed, $10 per day.

Features: Free wireless Internet, Free Breakfast, Swimming pool - outdoor, Elevator, Guest laundry, Tennis on site, ATM/banking, Concierge services, Wheelchair accessible, Number of floors: 3, Number of rooms: 150, Accessible bathroom, Braille or raised signage, 24-hour business center, Parking (free), Multilingual staff, Complimentary newspapers in lobby, Smoke-Free property, Fitness facilities.

Comfort Suites Palm Desert
39585 Washington St
Palm Desert CA 92211
(760) 360-3337
$189 - $229
Bed & Pet Discount Offered

Pet Policy: Pet accommodation: $20 per night. Pet limit: 2 pets per room, up to 40 lbs

Features: Swimming pool - outdoor, Bar/lounge, Babysitting or child care, Elevator, ATM/banking, Number of rooms: 72, Number of floors: 3, Coffee in lobby, Wireless Internet– additional charge, Guest laundry, Free breakfast, Parking (free), Complimentary newspapers in lobby, Fitness facilities.

Embassy Suites Hotel Palm Desert
74700 Highway 111
Palm Desert CA 92260
(760) 340-6600
$212 - $569
Bed & Pet Discount Offered

Pet Policy: Pets up to 50 lbs, $50. Must book for pet friendly room in advance.

Features: Free Breakfast, Swimming pool - outdoor, Bar/lounge, Elevator, Restaurant(s), Room service (limited hours), Concierge services, Gift shops or newsstand, Number of rooms: 188, Number of floors: 3, Parking (free), Multilingual staff, ATM/banking, Suitable for children, Arcade/game room, Pool table, Complimentary newspapers in lobby, Security guard, Beach/pool umbrellas, Wireless Internet (additional charge), 24-hour business center, Free reception, Dry cleaning/laundry service, Wheelchair accessible, Outdoor tennis courts 6, Fitness facilities.

Holiday Inn Express Palm-Desert-Rancho Mirage/Golf
74675 Highway 111
Palm Desert CA 92260
(760) 340-4303
$102 - $198
Bed & Pet Discount Offered

Pet Policy: Pets allowed, $50 per stay. First floor rooms only.

Features: Swimming pool - outdoor, Number of rooms: 129, Number of suites: 11, Number of floors: 3, Coffee in lobby, Free breakfast, Multilingual staff, Free wireless Internet, Accessible bathroom, In-room accessibility equipment for the deaf, Braille or raised signage, Dry cleaning/laundry service, Fitness facilities.

Homewood Suites by Hilton Palm Desert
36999 Cook St
Palm Desert CA 92211
(760) 568-1600
$129 - $209
Bed & Pet Discount Offered

Pet Policy: Pets up to 45 lbs, $75 per stay.

Features: Bar/lounge, Fitness facilities, Swimming pool - outdoor, Wheelchair accessible, Number of suites: 121, Number of floors: 3, Parking (free), Business center.

Inn at Deep Canyon
74470 Abronia Trl
Palm Desert CA 92260
(877) 747-8713
$81 - $83
Bed & Pet Discount Offered

Pet Policy: Pets up to 75 lbs accepted, $10 per night. Limited to designated pet friendly rooms.

Features: Free Breakfast, Swimming pool - outdoor Number of floors: 2, Coffee in lobby, Parking (free), Complimentary newspapers in lobby, Free wireless Internet, Smoke-Free property, Barbecue grill(s), Front desk (limited hours), Nearby fitness center (discount), Designated smoking areas, Beach/pool umbrellas, Accessible bathroom.

★★★

Residence Inn By Marriott Palm Desert
38305 Cook St
Palm Desert CA 92211
(760) 776-0050
$126 - $399
Bed & Pet Discount Offered

Pet Policy: Pets allowed, $75 per stay cleaning fee.

Features: Dry cleaning/laundry service, Swimming pool - outdoor, Smoke-Free property, Number of suites: 130, Number of floors: 2, Barbecue grill(s), Coffee in lobby, Guest laundry, Free breakfast, Parking (free), Complimentary newspapers in lobby, Free wireless Internet, Tennis on site, Fitness facilities.

Palm Springs

Also see the following nearby communities that have pet friendly lodging: Cathedral City - 4 miles, Rancho Mirage - 8 miles, Desert Hot Springs - 8 miles, Thousand Palms - 9 mile

Not rated

A Place in the Sun Garden Hotel
754 San Lorenzo Road
Palm Springs CA 92264
(760) 325-0254
$112 - $113

Pet Policy: A Place in the Sun is known for its pet-friendly attitude.

Features: Fully furnished apartments,

★★★

Andreas Hotel & Spa
227 N Indian Canyon Drive
Palm Springs CA 92262
(760) 327-5701
$174- $195
Bed & Pet Discount Offered

Pet Policy: There is a $20 per night pet fee of which $5 per night is donated to help build the new Palm Springs Animal Shelter. Detailed pet policy is sent with confirmation letter and must be followed by pet owner.

Features: Free wireless Internet, Full-service health spa, Swimming pool - outdoor, Number of rooms: 25, Number of floors: 2, Suitable for children, Coffee in lobby, Free breakfast, Parking (free), Massage - treatment room(s), Smoke-Free property, Accessible bathroom, Braille or raised signage, Fitness facilities

Caliente Tropics Hotel
411 E Palm Canyon Drive
Palm Springs CA 92264
(760) 327-1391
$75 - $229
Bed & Pet Discount Offered

Pet Policy: Pets under 60 lbs accepted. $25 per night per pet. Not only does the inside of Caliente provide Palm Springs pet-friendly hotel rooms, but the tropical property's outside pool area is also pet friendly. A retractable lawn is great for playing Frisbee with your best dog friend, play fetch, or hang out and practice tricks.

Features: Outdoor pool, Coffee in lobby, Concierge, Number of rooms: 90, Number of floors: 2, Business services, Spa services on site, Free wireless Internet.

Canyon Club Hotel, a Gay Men's Resort
960 N Palm Canyon Drive
Palm Springs CA 92262
(760) 778-8042
$67 - $159
Bed & Pet Discount Offered

Pet Policy: Pets accepted, $10 per night, maximum of $100 per stay.

Features: Barbecue grill(s), Coffee in lobby, Free wireless Internet, Sauna, Swimming pool - outdoor, Number of rooms: 32, Number of floors: 3, Business services, Free breakfast, Parking (free), Complimentary newspapers, Steam room.

Casa Cody Inn B&B
175 S Cahuillo Rd
Palm Springs CA 92262
(760) 320-9346
$111 - $716

Pet Policy: Pets allowed, $15 per night.

Features: Two pools and a hot tub, 28 units, Private patios and fireplaces in some units, Free wireless internet, Kitchens in most units, Breakfast.

Colony Palms Hotel
572 North Indian Canyon
Palm Springs CA 92262
(800) 557-2187
$179 - $429
Bed & Pet Discount Offered

Pet Policy: We warmly welcome dog under 40 pounds. A $100 fee will apply per stay. Must reserve a patio room in advance.

Features: Bar/lounge, Full-service health spa, Concierge, Restaurant(s), Outdoor pool, Number of rooms: 56, Number of floors: 2, Wireless Internet (additional charge), Steam room, Nearby fitness center (discount), Dry cleaning/laundry service.

Extended Stay America Palm Springs - Airport
1400 E Tahquitz Canyon Way
Palm Springs CA 92262
(760) 416-0084
$74 - $128
Bed & Pet Discount Offered

Pet Policy: One small pet is allowed in each guest room. A $25 per day non-refundable cleaning fee (not to exceed $150) will be charged the first night of your stay.

Features: Guest laundry, Outdoor pool, Number of rooms: 104, Number of floors: 3, Wireless Internet, additional charge.

★★★★

Hilton Palm Springs Resort
400 E Tahquitz Canyon Way
Palm Springs CA 92262
(760) 320-6868
$132 - $439
Bed & Pet Discount Offered

Pet Policy: Pets allowed up to 75 lbs, $75 per stay.

Features: Business center, Swimming pool - outdoor, Bar/lounge, Airport transportation (free), Concierge services, Poolside bar, Room service (limited hours), Restaurant(s), Gift shops or newsstand, Number of rooms: 260, Number of floors: 3, Business services, Breakfast available (additional charge), Pool table, Multilingual staff, Porter/bellhop, Security guard, Wireless Internet, Smoke-Free property, Dry cleaning/laundry service, Fitness facilities, Elevator, Parking (additional charge).

★★★

Holiday Inn Resort Palm Springs
1800 E Palm Canyon Dr
Palm Springs CA 92264
(760) 323-1711
$143 - $266
Bed & Pet Discount Offered

Pet Policy: Dogs only, under 40 lbs, $20 per night.

Features: Swimming pool - outdoor, Bar/lounge, Room service (limited hours), ATM/banking, Airport transportation, Number of rooms: 255, Number of floors: 3, Breakfast available (additional charge), Parking (free), Multilingual staff, Complimentary newspapers in lobby, Business center, Porter/bellhop, Limo or Town Car service available, Accessible bathroom, In-room accessibility equipment for the deaf, Braille or raised signage, Dry cleaning/laundry service, Free wireless Internet, Area shuttle (free) Y

Hotel Zoso
150 S Indian Canyon Dr
Palm Springs CA 92262
(760) 325-9676
$114 - $269
Bed & Pet Discount Offered

Pet Policy: All pets up to 40 lbs welcome, $50 fee.

Features: Wheelchair accessible, Business Center, Bar/Lounge, Swimming pool - outdoor, Elevator, Security guard, ATM/banking, Airport transportation (free), Poolside bar, Suitable for children, Pool table, Designated smoking areas, Beach/pool umbrellas, Free wireless Internet, Area shuttle (free), Concierge desk, Restaurant(s), Gift shops or newsstand, Number of rooms: 163, Number of floors: 3, Multilingual staff, Complimentary newspapers in lobby, Porter/bellhop, Room service (limited hours), Parking (valet) $20 Per Day, Accessible bathroom, In-room accessibility equipment for the deaf, Braille or raised signage, Dry cleaning/laundry service, Fitness facilities.

★★★½
Hyatt Regency Suites Palm Springs
285 N Palm Canyon Dr
Palm Springs CA 92262
(760) 322-9000
$135 - $500
Bed & Pet Discount Offered

Pet Policy: Pets allowed, $25 per night. All breeds and sizes of dog are now accepted in our guest suites. We are also very excited to announce a partnership with Fresh Fetch, a local provider of home-cooked and veterinarian recommended meals. Fresh Fetch believes strongly in making pet food with real products and no processing. The Hyatt Regency Suites Palm Springs now stocks Fresh Fetch products for a truly unique dining experience for your pet. Simply refer to your room service menu.

Features: Outdoor pool, Concierge, Security guard, Number of rooms: 197, Number of floors: 6, Currency exchange, Accessible bathroom, In-room accessibility equipment for the deaf, Braille or raised signage, RV and truck parking, Business center, Wheelchair accessible, Airport transportation (free), Room service, Multilingual staff, Complimentary newspapers, Porter/bellhop, Designated smoking areas, Pick up service from train station, 3 Restaurants, Coffee in lobby, Piano, Bar/lounge, Gift shop, Breakfast available (additional charge), Poolside bar, Sauna, Parking (valet) $16 Daily, Dry cleaning/laundry service, Wireless Internet (additional charge), Area shuttle (free), Fitness facilities.

★★
Palm Springs Travelodge
333 E Palm Canyon Dr
Palm Springs CA 92264
(760) 327-1211
$63- $160
Bed & Pet Discount Offered

Pet Policy: Dogs only, less than 35 lbs. $20 per day.

Features: Free Breakfast, 2 outdoor swimming pools, Business services, Barbecue grill(s), Coffee in lobby, Accessible bathroom, In-room accessibility equipment for the deaf, Braille or raised signage, Concierge, Guest laundry, Complimentary newspapers.

★★½
Quality Inn Palm Springs
1269 E Palm Canyon Dr
Palm Springs CA 92264
(760) 323-2775
$109 - $179
Bed & Pet Discount Offered

Pet Policy: Quality Inns charge a fee of $10 per night per pet but do not charge any other fees. They may require a $50 damage deposit, which is refunded if the room is in order at check out. Quality Inns accept any well-behaved pets with a maximum of 3 per room, but dogs are limited to 50 pounds. Pets may not be left alone in the room unless in a cage

Features: Outdoor pool,, Number of rooms: 144, Number of floors: 2, BBQ area, Complimentary newspapers, Free wireless Internet, Fitness facilities, Guest laundry, Children's swimming pool.

Ramada Palm Springs
2000 N Palm Canyon Dr
Palm Springs CA 92262
(760) 320-0555
$89 - $157
Bed & Pet Discount Offered

Pet Policy: Dogs only, up to 20 lbs. $25 per day. Limit 2 dogs per room.

Features: Concierge, Number of rooms: 96, Number of floors: 2, Coffee in lobby, Free breakfast, Parking (free), Complimentary Newspapers, Porter/bellhop, Free wireless Internet, Business center, Swimming pool - outdoor, Dry cleaning/laundry service, Fitness facilities.

Renaissance Palm Springs Hotel
888 East Tahquitz Canyon Way
Palm Springs CA 92262
(760) 322-6000
$198 - $309
Bed & Pet Discount Offered

Pet Policy: Small pets accepted, $50 per pet per stay cleaning fee.

Features: Children's swimming pool, Poolside bar, Swimming pool - outdoor, Business center, ATM/banking, Wheelchair accessible, Airport transportation (free), Room service (limited hours), Concierge desk, Elevator, Bar/lounge, 3 Restaurants, Gift shops or newsstand, Number of rooms: 410, Number of floors: 5, Wireless Internet (additional charge), Breakfast available (additional charge), Multilingual staff, Porter/bellhop, Security guard, Dry cleaning/laundry service, Fitness facilities, Smoke-Free property, Accessible bathroom, Area shuttle (free), In-room accessibility equipment for the deaf, Braille or raised signage, Parking (additional charge).

Shilo Inn Suites - Palm Springs
1875 N Palm Canyon Dr
Palm Springs CA 92262
(760) 320-7676
$89 - $194
Bed & Pet Discount Offered

Pet Policy: Pets accepted, $25 per stay fee.

Features: Sauna, Security guard, Business center, Guest laundry, Concierge services, Steam room, Children's swimming pool, Airport transportation (free), Swimming pool - outdoor, Number of rooms: 124, Number of floors: 2, Coffee in lobby, Free breakfast, Parking (free), Multilingual staff, Wireless Internet, Smoke-Free property, Fitness facilities.

Not Rated
Tuscany Manor Resort
350 West Chino Canyon Road
Palm Springs CA 92262
(760) 416-8916
$89 - $109

Pet Policy: Pet friendly rooms available for small pets (up to 10 pounds)., $35 per pet per night charge. Must book in advance.

Features: Furnished apartments, Gated community, Fully equipped kitchens, Heated pool and spa, Wireless internet, Cable TV.

Palmdale

Also see the following nearby communities that have pet friendly lodging: Lancaster - 7 miles

Holiday Inn Palmdale-Lancaster
38630 5th St W
Palmdale CA 93551
(661) 947-8055
$104 - $175
Bed & Pet Discount Offered

Pet Policy: Pets allowed, $75 per stay fee.

Features: Free breakfast, Accessible bathroom, In-room accessibility equipment for the deaf, Braille or raised signage, Bar/lounge, Business center, Restaurant(s), Swimming pool - outdoor, Number of floors: 5, Parking (free), Multilingual staff, Complimentary newspapers in lobby, Room service, Porter/bellhop, Free wireless Internet, Concierge desk, Dry cleaning/laundry service, Fitness facilities.

★★★

Residence Inn by Marriott Palmdale
514 W Avenue P
Palmdale CA 93551
(661) 947-4204
$130 - $181
Bed & Pet Discount Offered

Pet Policy: Pets allowed, $100 per stay cleaning fee.

Features: Elevator, Swimming pool - indoor, Hair salon, Number of rooms: 90, Number of suites: 90, Number of floors: 3, Parking (free), Complimentary newspapers in lobby, Business center, Concierge desk, Wireless Internet, Smoke-Free property, Barbecue grill(s), Coffee in lobby, Accessible bathroom, In-room accessibility equipment for the deaf, Braille or raised signage, Dry cleaning/laundry service, Fitness facilities

★★★

Staybridge Suites Palmdale
420 Westpark Drive
Palmdale CA 93551
(661) 947-9300
$129 - $159
Bed & Pet Discount Offered

Pet Policy: Pets up to 80 lbs, $75 for up to 6 nights, $150 for 7 or longer. Must have proof of current vaccinations.

Features: Free breakfast, Free wireless Internet, Accessible bathroom, In-room accessibility equipment for the deaf, Braille or raised signage, Swimming pool - outdoor, Gift shops or newsstand, Guest laundry Parking (free), Business center, Grocery/convenience store, Fitness facilities.

★★

Super 8 Motel - Palmdale
200 W Palmdale Blvd
Palmdale CA 93551
(661) 273-8000
$54 - $85
Bed & Pet Discount Offered

Pet Policy: Pets welcome, $10 per night per pet.

Features: Swimming pool - outdoor, Free breakfast, Parking (free), RV and truck parking, Number of floors: 2

Palo Alto

Also see the following nearby communities that have pet friendly lodging: Los Altos - 3 miles, Menlo Park - 3 miles, Mountain View - 4 miles, Redwood City - 7 miles, Sunnyvale - 7 miles, Newark - 9 miles, San Carlos - 9 miles, Santa Clara - 9 miles, Cupertino - 10 miles

★★
Comfort Inn Palo Alto Stanford University
3945 El Camino Real
Palo Alto CA 94306
(650) 493-3141
$90 - $105
Bed & Pet Discount Offered

Pet Policy: Pets welcome, $20 per pet per night.

Features: Number of rooms: 70, Coffee in lobby, Free breakfast, Parking (free), Multilingual staff, Complimentary newspapers in lobby, Use of nearby fitness center (free), Business center, Free wireless Internet, Dry cleaning/laundry service.

★★★½
Crowne Plaza Cabana, Palo Alto
4290 El Camino Real
Palo Alto CA 94306
(650) 857-0787
$95 - $169
Bed & Pet Discount Offered

Pet Policy: Dogs under 25 lbs accepted, $50 per stay. Must stay in designated pet rooms.

Features: Parking (valet) $15 per day, Accessible bathroom, In-room accessibility equipment for the deaf, Braille or raised signage, Bar/lounge, Restaurant(s), Outdoor pool, Concierge, Gift shops or newsstand, Number of rooms: 194, Number of floors: 8, Room service (24 hours), Multilingual staff, Complimentary newspapers, Porter/bellhop, Security guard, Limo or Town Car service available, Free wireless Internet, Dry cleaning/laundry service, Fitness facilities, Elevator, Business center.

★★★★★
Four Seasons Silicon Valley at East Palo Alto
2050 University Ave
Palo Alto CA 94303
(650) 566-1200
$234 - $850
Bed & Pet Discount Offered

Pet Policy: Pets welcome, no fee and no size restriction.

Features: Bar/lounge, Babysitting or child care, Wheelchair accessible, Gift shops, Number of rooms: 173, Number of suites: 27, Number of floors: 10, Translation services, Computer rental, Parking (additional charge), Coffee in lobby, Poolside bar, Currency exchange, Health club, Room service (24 hours), Multilingual staff, Complimentary newspapers, Porter/bellhop, Security guard, Dry cleaning/laundry service, Limo or Town Car service available, Beauty services, Full-service health spa, Massage - treatment room(s), Technology support staff, Designated smoking areas, On-site medical assistance available, Media library, Wireless Internet (additional charge), Pick up service from train station, Accessible bathroom, In-room accessibility equipment for the deaf, Braille or raised signage, 24-hour business center, RV and truck parking, Area shuttle (free), Number of outdoor swimming pools 2.

Garden Court Hotel
520 Cowper Street
Palo Alto CA 94301
(650) 322-9000
$189 - $549
Bed & Pet Discount Offered

Pet Policy: Pets welcome, $49 per stay. Deluxe accommodation of choice at our Best Available Rate, Welcome amenity for pet and guest, Use of pet bed, matt, water and food dishes, Walking map, Pet support - biodegradable cleanup bags, Luxury turn-down service for pet and guests, Walks by request

Features: Concierge desk, Bar/lounge, Wheelchair accessible, Elevator, Beauty services, Massage - spa treatment room(s), Accessible bathroom, In-room accessibility equipment for the deaf, Braille or raised signage, 24-hour business center, Restaurant, Translation services, Computer rental, Suitable for children, Video library, Piano, Room service (24 hours), Shoe shine, Multilingual staff, Complimentary newspapers in lobby, Security guard, Limo or Town Car service available, Technology helpdesk, Nearby fitness center (discount), Technology support staff, Designated smoking areas, Music library, Creche (nursery), Number of rooms: 62, Number of floors: 4, Parking (additional charge), Coffee in lobby, Free breakfast, Porter/bellhop, Dry cleaning/laundry service, Free wireless Internet, Free reception.

★★

Quality Inn Stanford/Silicon Valley
3901 El Camino Real
Palo Alto CA 94306
(650) 493-2760
$85 - $110
Bed & Pet Discount Offered

Pet Policy: Pets up to 25 lbs, $20 per night per pet. Limit 2 per room.

Features: Number of rooms: 52, Coffee in lobby, Free breakfast, Complimentary newspapers in lobby Free wireless Internet, Smoke-Free property, Business Center.

★★★½

Sheraton Palo Alto Hotel
625 El Camino Real
Palo Alto CA 94301
(650) 328-2800
$99 - $349
Bed & Pet Discount Offered

Pet Policy: Dogs only, up to 80 lbs, no fee charged.

Features: Business Center, Swimming pool - outdoor, Bar/lounge, Babysitting or child care, Restaurant(s), ATM/banking, Concierge services, Gift shops or newsstand, Shopping on site, Number of rooms: 346, Number of floors: 4, Suitable for children, Breakfast available (additional charge), Pool table, Poolside bar, Currency exchange, Multilingual staff, Complimentary newspapers in lobby, Room service, Porter/bellhop, Security guard, Limo or Town Car service available, Free wireless Internet, Parking (valet) $14.00 Per Day, Fitness facilities.

The Westin Palo Alto
675 El Camino Real
Palo Alto CA 94301
(650) 321-4422
$149 - $379
Bed & Pet Discount Offered

Pet Policy: Dogs only, up to 80 lbs, no fee charged. Guests will be asked to sign a waiver upon check-in.

Features: Fitness facilities, Babysitting or child care, Swimming pool - outdoor, Bar/lounge, Restaurant(s), ATM/banking, Concierge services, Gift shops or newsstand, Shopping on site, Number of rooms: 183, Number of floors: 5, Computer rental, Suitable for children, Coffee in lobby, Breakfast available (additional charge), Arcade/game room, Pool table, Poolside bar, Currency exchange, Room service, Spa services on site, Multilingual staff, Complimentary newspapers, Porter/bellhop, Security guard, Free wireless Internet, Business Center, Parking (valet) $14.00 Per Day, Accessible bathroom, Accessibility equipment for the deaf, Dry cleaning/laundry service.

Paradise

★★

Comfort Inn Central
5475 Clark Rd
Paradise CA 95969
(530) 876-0191
$84 - $85
Bed & Pet Discount Offered

Pet Policy: Dogs only, $10 per night plus $!00 refundable deposit

Features: Business center, Guest laundry, Elevator, Number of rooms: 62, Number of floors: 3, Free breakfast, Parking (free), Swimming pool - outdoor seasonal, Accessible bathroom, In-room accessibility equipment for the deaf, Braille or raised signage, Fitness facilities

Pasadena

Also see the following nearby communities that have pet friendly lodging: South Pasadena - 3 miles, San Gabriel - 4 miles, Arcadia - 5 miles, Rosemead - 5 miles, Monterey Park - 6 miles, El Monte - 7 miles, Monrovia - 7 miles, South El Monte - 8 miles, Glendale - 9 miles

★★★½

Hilton Pasadena
168 S Los Robles Ave
Pasadena CA 91101
(626) 577-1000
$109 - $199
Bed & Pet Discount Offered

Pet Policy: Pets up to 75 lbs, $75 per stay cleaning fee.

Features: Swimming pool - outdoor, Parking (valet) $21 Daily, Dry cleaning/laundry service, Bar/lounge, Restaurant(s), Room service, ATM/banking, Number of rooms: 296, Number of floors: 14, Wireless Internet (additional charge), Breakfast available (additional charge), Grocery, Multilingual staff, Complimentary newspapers, Business center, Porter/bellhop, Security guard, Concierge, Airport transportation (additional charge), Fitness facilities.

Not rated
Marriott Executstay Holly Street
151 East Holly Street
Pasadena CA 91103
(888) 526-0566
$159 - $160

Pet Policy: Cats and small dogs welcome. Maximum 2 pets per apartment. Cats: Additional $300 pet deposit and $35 monthly pet rent per cat. Dogs: Additional $500 pet deposit and $50 monthly pet rent per dog. Dogs must weigh less than 50 pounds.

Features: Newly renovated corporate apartment property offers a fully equipped gourmet kitchen walk in closets, and an in unit washer and dryer. Minimum stay may be required.

Not Rated
Oakway at Gateway Villas
290 N Hudson Ave
Pasadena CA 91101
(602) 427-2752
$144 - $198

Pet Policy: Pets accepted with limitations and fee. Contact hotel directly for more information and to make reservations.

Features: Furnished Apartments, Swimming pool, Spa, Full kitchens, Gas fireplaces. Minimum stay required.

★★
Quality Inn Pasadena
3321 E Colorado Blvd
Pasadena CA 91107
(626) 796-9291
$73 - $85
Bed & Pet Discount Offered

Pet Policy: Quality Inns charge a fee of $10 per night per pet but do not charge any other fees. They may require a $50 damage deposit, which is refunded if the room is in order at check out. Quality Inns accept any well-behaved pets with a maximum of 3 per room, but dogs are limited to 50 pounds. Pets may not be left alone in the room unless in a cage.

Features: Sauna, Free breakfast, Swimming pool - outdoor, Elevator, Parking (free), Business center, Wireless Internet, Number of rooms: 70, Number of floors: 3, Complimentary newspapers in lobby, Swimming pool - outdoor seasonal, Babysitting or child care, Dry cleaning/laundry service, Fitness facilities.

★★
Rodeway Inn And Suites Pasadena
2860 E Colorado Blvd
Pasadena CA 91107
(626) 792-3700
$59 - $75
Bed & Pet Discount Offered

Pet Policy: Rodeway Inns charge a fee of $10 per night per pet and require a $50 damage deposit, which is refunded if the room is in order at check out. Max of 2 pets per room. A veterinarian certificate that the pet is on a flea and parasite program and that they are Free from parasites is required. Pets may not be left alone in the room unless in a cage.

Features: Business services, Coffee in lobby, Free breakfast, Elevator, Number of rooms: 33, Number of suites: 7, Number of floors: 3, Parking (free).

★★★½

Sheraton Pasadena Hotel
303 Cordova St
Pasadena CA 91101
(626) 449-4000
$129 - $239
Bed & Pet Discount Offered

Pet Policy: Two dogs up to 80 pounds are allowed per room. The hotel provides Free bedding, food and water bowl. The hotel reserves the right to charge for additional cleaning or damage caused by the pet. If damage is found after checkout, credit card on record will be charged.

Features: Business Center, Concierge services, ATM/banking, Room service (limited hours), Bar/lounge, Parking garage – additional charge, Restaurant(s), Swimming pool - outdoor, Gift shops or newsstand, Number of rooms: 314, Number of floors: 5, Wireless Internet (additional charge), Breakfast available (additional charge), Multilingual staff, Complimentary newspapers in lobby, Porter/bellhop, Security guard, Smoke-Free property, Elevator, Fitness facilities.

★★

Super 8 Motel - Pasadena
2863 E Colorado Blvd
Pasadena CA 91107
(626) 449-3020
$62.- $73
Bed & Pet Discount Offered

Pet Policy: Pets welcome, $20 per night per pet.

Features: Business services, Coffee in lobby, Free breakfast, Elevator, Parking (free), Swimming pool - outdoor seasonal

★★

The Saga Motor Hotel
1633 E Colorado Blvd
Pasadena CA 91106
(626) 795-0431
$69 - $79

Pet Policy: Dogs only, up to 15 lbs. $35 per stay. Limited to ground floor rooms.

Features: Business hotel, Smoke Free, swimming pool

★★★★

The Westin Pasadena
191 N Los Robles Ave
Pasadena CA 91101
(626) 792-2727
$160 - $259
Bed & Pet Discount Offered

Pet Policy: Dogs up to 40 pounds are allowed. No other pets, including cats, are permitted. A cleaning fee will be charged if damage to room is found.

Features: Bar/lounge, Restaurant(s), Swimming pool - outdoor, Parking – additional charge, ATM/banking, Concierge services, Gift shops or newsstand, Number of rooms: 300, Number of floors: 12, Wireless Internet (additional charge), Room service (24 hours), Multilingual staff, Complimentary newspapers in lobby, Business center, Porter/bellhop, Security guard, Limo or Town Car service available, Dry cleaning/laundry service, Fitness facilities.

Vagabond Inn Executive Pasadena
1203 E Colorado Blvd
Pasadena CA 91106
(626) 449-3170
$105 - $106
Bed & Pet Discount Offered

Pet Policy: Pets welcome, $25 per pet.

Features: Elevator, Swimming pool - outdoor, Business services, Coffee in lobby, Free breakfast, Parking (free), Multilingual staff, Complimentary newspapers in lobby, Free wireless Internet, Accessible bathroom, In-room accessibility equipment for the deaf, Braille or raised signage.

Paso Robles

Also see the following nearby communities that have pet friendly lodging: Atascadero - 10 miles

Creekside Bed and Breakfast
5325 Vineyard Drive
Paso Robles CA 93446
(805) 227-6585
$199 - $200
Bed & Pet Discount Offered

Pet Policy: Pets accepted, $25 per stay. Must indicate bringing pets when make reservation. Pet owners agree to keep their pet on a leash or in a cage while the pet is in any public or common area within the Creekside ground. Pet owners agree to not leave the pet unattended at any time while the pet is at Creekside.

Features: Free breakfast, Parking (free), Spa services on site, Number of rooms: 2, Number of floors: 2, Barbecue grill(s), Guest laundry, Limo or Town Car service available, Free wireless Internet.

Hampton Inn and Suites Paso Robles
212 Alexa Ct
Paso Robles CA 93446
(805) 226-9988
$129 - $214
Bed & Pet Discount Offered

Pet Policy: Pets up to 25 lbs allowed. Fee $50.

Features: Bar/lounge, Swimming pool - outdoor, Wheelchair accessible, Shopping on site, Number of suites: 24, Number of floors: 3, Computer rental, Arcade/game room, Parking (free), Business center, Smoke-Free property, Fitness facilities, Free breakfast.

Holiday Inn Express Hotel & Suites Paso Robles
2455 Riverside Ave
Paso Robles CA 93446
(805) 238-6500
$120 - $319
Bed & Pet Discount Offered

Pet Policy: Dogs only permitted, $35 per night. Must stay on designated pet friendly floor.

Features: Swimming pool – indoor, Restaurant(s), Gift shops or newsstand, Number of suites: 18, Number of floors: 3, Suitable for children, Free breakfast, Parking (free), Multilingual staff, Complimentary newspapers in lobby, Business center, Free wireless Internet, Accessible bathroom, In-room accessibility equipment for the deaf, Braille or raised signage, Dry cleaning/laundry service, Fitness facilities

La Quinta Inn & Suites Paso Robles
2615 Buena Vista Drive
Paso Robles CA 93446
(805) 239-3004
$119 - $179
Bed & Pet Discount Offered

Pet Policy: Pets welcome, no extra fee but owner responsible for any damage. Must not be left unattended at any time.

Features: Swimming pool - outdoor, Free breakfast, Business center, Accessible bathroom, Babysitting or child care, Elevator, Gift shops or newsstand, Number of rooms: 70, Number of floors: 3, Airport transportation (additional charge), Coffee in lobby, Library, Parking (free), Complimentary newspapers in lobby, Free wireless Internet, Smoke-Free property, Dry cleaning/laundry service, Fitness facilities.

Paso Robles Travelodge
2701 Spring St
Paso Robles CA 93446
(805) 238-0078
$47 - $159
Bed & Pet Discount Offered

Pet Policy: Well behaved pets are welcome. We have a pet walk area. There is a$10 per night charge for your pet.

Features: Free breakfast, Parking (free), Wireless Internet, Swimming pool - outdoor seasonal.

Villa Valdemosa
2552 Old Grove Lane
Paso Robles CA 93446
(805) 237-0170
$265 - $325
Bed & Pet Discount Offered

Pet Policy: Dogs only, under 70 lbs, $35 per night fee. For dogs over 50 lbs, we reserve right to require a $150 cleaning deposit. Dogs should not be left unattended in room, should be leashed outside of room, and are not permitted in dining area (except service dogs).

Features: Number of rooms: 5, Free breakfast, Use of nearby fitness center (free), Media library.

Patterson

Also see the following nearby communities that have pet friendly lodging: Westley - 4 miles

Best Western Plus Villa Del Lago Inn
2959 Speno Drive
Patterson CA 95363
(866) 744-2358
$89 - $99
Bed & Pet Discount Offered

Pet Policy: Pets accepted with small fee at check-in.

Features: Elevator, Swimming pool - outdoor, Sauna, Bar/Lounge, Restaurant(s), Number of rooms: 82, Number of suites: 2, Number of floors: 3, Coffee in lobby, Multilingual staff, Complimentary newspapers in lobby, Free wireless Internet, Accessible bathroom, In-room accessibility equipment for the deaf, Braille or raised signage, Dry cleaning/laundry service, Parking (free), Fitness facilities.

Petaluma

Also see the following nearby communities that have pet friendly lodging: Rohnert Park - 8 miles, Boyes Hot Springs - 9 miles

Americas Best Value Inn & Suites
5135 Montero Way
Petaluma CA 94954
(707) 795-9000
$50 - $55
Bed & Pet Discount Offered

Pet Policy: Small pets welcome, $15 per pet per night.

Features: Swimming pool - outdoor, Parking (free), Free wireless Internet.

Best Western Petaluma Inn
200 S MCDOWELL BLVD
Petaluma CA 94954
(707) 763-0994
$71 - $129

Pet Policy: Pets under 50 pounds, $35 per night. Maximum of 2 pets.

Features: Restaurant, Outdoor heated swimming pool, Business services, Free continental breakfast, HBO, Free wireless Internet.

Quality Inn Petaluma
5100 Montero Way
Petaluma CA 94954
(707) 664-1155
$79 - $139
Bed & Pet Discount Offered

Pet Policy: Quality Inns charge a fee of $10 per night per pet but do not charge any other fees. They may require a $50 damage deposit, which is refunded if the room is in order at check out. Quality Inns accept any well-behaved pets with a maximum of 3 per room, but dogs are limited to 50 pounds. Pets may not be left alone in the room unless in a cage.

Features: Coffee in lobby, Free breakfast, Swimming pool - outdoor, Sauna, Number of rooms: 110, Number of floors: 2, Business services, Parking (free), Free wireless Internet, Fitness facilities

Sheraton Sonoma County - Petaluma
745 Baywood Dr
Petaluma CA 94954
(707) 283-2888
$139 - $218
Bed & Pet Discount Offered

Pet Policy: Dogs up to 70 lbs without charge. Other pets may be considered but you must contact the hotel directly for approval and conditions.

Features: Bar/lounge, Outdoor pool, Restaurant(s), Room service (limited hours), Gift shop, Number of rooms: 183, Number of floors: 4, Free wireless Internet, Breakfast available (additional charge), Multilingual staff, Complimentary newspapers, Porter/bellhop, Marina on site, Sauna, Dry cleaning/laundry service, Wheelchair accessible, Coffee in lobby, Limo or Town Car service available, Concierge, Massage - spa treatment room(s), 24-hour business center, Smoke-Free, Fitness center, Accessible bathroom, Braille or raised signage.

Phelan

Not rated
Best Western Cajon Pass
8317 US Hwy 138
Phelan CA 92371
(760) 249-6777
$62 - $69

Pet Policy: Pets allowed. No size restriction.

Features: Free wireless Internet, Free continental breakfast, Iron & ironing board, Coffee maker, Microwave and mini fridge, Outdoor swimming pool and spa.

Pico Rivera

Also see the following nearby communities that have pet friendly lodging: Commerce - 3 miles, Bell Gardens - 3 miles, Whittier - 4 miles, Downey - 4 miles, Norwalk - 5 miles, South El Monte - 6 miles, Monterey Park - 6 miles, Rosemead - 6 miles, La Mirada - 7 miles, San Gabriel - 7 miles, Huntington Park - 7 miles, Cerritos - 8 miles, El Monte - 8 miles, Hawaiian Gardens - 10 miles, City Of Industry - 10 miles

Knights Inn Pico Rivera
6540 Rosemead Blvd
Pico Rivera CA 90660
(562) 942-1003
$57- $99
Bed & Pet Discount Offered

Pet Policy: Pets welcome, $8 per night per pet.

Features: Business services, Wireless Internet, Free, Complimentary newspapers in lobby, Swimming pool - outdoor seasonal

Pismo Beach

Also see the following nearby communities that have pet friendly lodging: San Luis Obispo - 7 miles

Cottage Inn By The Sea
2351 Price St
Pismo Beach CA 93449
(805) 773-4617
$119 - $269
Bed & Pet Discount Offered

Pet Policy: Dogs permitted, $20 per night each. Limit 2 big dogs or 3 small ones.

Features: Coffee in lobby, Swimming pool - outdoor, Concierge services, Number of rooms: 80, Number of floors: 2, Free breakfast, Parking (free), Complimentary newspapers in lobby, Free wireless Internet, Smoke-Free property, Business center.

Dolphin Bay Resort And Spa
2727 Shell Beach Rd
Pismo Beach CA 93449
(800) 516-0112
$335 - $712
Bed & Pet Discount Offered

Pet Policy: Pet Friendly Villas available with a nightly $65 pet fee.

Features: Swimming pool - outdoor, Bar/lounge, Babysitting or child care, Elevator, Airport transportation (free), Restaurant(s), Room service (limited hours), Gift shops or newsstand, Number of rooms: 62, Number of floors: 4, Suitable for children, Barbecue grill(s), Coffee in lobby, Breakfast available (additional charge), Video library, Grocery, Parking (free),

Continued on next page

Dolphin Bay Resort And Spa
Continued from previous page

Spa services on site, Shoe shine, Multilingual staff, Complimentary newspapers in lobby, Use of nearby fitness center (free), Porter/bellhop, Limo or Town Car service available, Medical assistance available, Free wireless Internet, Massage - treatment room(s), Accessible bathroom, Braille or raised signage, Dry cleaning/laundry service, Wheelchair accessible, Supervised child care/activities, Concierge services, Beauty services, Children's club, Designated smoking areas, Area shuttle (free), Business center, Fitness facilities

★★
Edgewater Inn And Suites
280 Wadsworth Ave
Pismo Beach CA 93449
(805) 773-4811
$98 - $212
Bed & Pet Discount Offered

Pet Policy: Pet friendly rooms at no additional charge.

Features: Swimming pool - outdoor, Number of rooms: 99, Number of floors: 3, Coffee in lobby, Free breakfast, Parking (free), Free wireless Internet, Dry cleaning/laundry service, Smoke-Free property, Accessible bathroom, Handicapped parking.

★★½
Oxford Suites Pismo Beach
651 Five Cities Dr
Pismo Beach CA 93449
(805) 773-3773
$94 - $151
Bed & Pet Discount Offered

Pet Policy: Medium size cats and dogs accepted for $25 per pet per stay, for up to seven days, with a two pet limit. The charge is assessed at check out and not included in your room rate. Aggressive breeds not allowed. Pets must not be left unattended in room, must be leashed when in public areas, and are not permitted in dining, pool or spa areas (service animals excepted).

Features: Sauna, Children's swimming pool, Swimming pool - outdoor, Free breakfast, Business center, Gift shops or newsstand, Shopping on site, Parking (free), Multilingual staff, Designated smoking areas, Accessible bathroom, In-room accessibility equipment for the deaf, Braille or raised signage, Free wireless Internet, Dry cleaning/laundry service, Fitness facilities.

Sandcastle Inn
100 Stimson Ave
Pismo Beach CA 93449
(800) 822-6606
$109 - $249
Bed & Pet Discount Offered

Pet Policy: Dogs permitted, $20 per night. Limit of 2 per room.

Features: Wheelchair Accessible, Elevator, Number of floors: 3, Number of rooms: 75, Coffee in lobby, Free breakfast, Parking (free), Gift shops or newsstand, Smoke-Free property, Complimentary newspapers in lobby, Accessible bathroom, 24-hour business center, Free wireless Internet, Use of nearby fitness center (discount).

Spyglass Inn
2705 Spyglass Dr
Pismo Beach CA 93449
(805) 773-4855
$80 - $249
Bed & Pet Discount Offered

Pet Policy: Pets accepted, $20 per night per pet

Features: Swimming pool - outdoor, Bar/Lounge, Restaurant(s), Room service (limited hours), Number of rooms: 82, Number of floors: 2, Business services, Parking (free), Complimentary newspapers in lobby, Free wireless Internet, Smoke-Free property.

The Cliffs
2757 Shell Beach Road
Pismo Beach CA 93449
(805) 773-5000
$149 - $414
Bed & Pet Discount Offered

Pet Policy: We encourage guests to bring their dogs -- and welcome them with many amenities at our Pismo Beach vacation retreat. For a one-time $50 fee, they will enjoy a Cliffs Resort dog tag, luxurious sleeping accommodations, and plenty of water. Your guest room will be prepared with a dog bed and bowl, and we'll even walk Fido upon request. Enjoy a memorable Pismo Beach vacation with your four-legged friend, which can include: - Overnight accommodations for two, plus your loyal friend - Dog tag and Dog Bed - Specialty Dog Room Service Menu - Food and water bowl - Dog walking service, available upon request

Features: Free wireless Internet, Concierge Desk, Business center, Airport transportation (free), Swimming pool - outdoor, Parking (free), Bar/lounge, Restaurant(s), Gift shops or newsstand, Number of rooms: 165, Number of floors: 5, Elevator, Breakfast available (additional charge), Room service (limited hours), Smoke-Free property, Pick up service from train station, Spa services on site, Multilingual staff, Complimentary newspapers in lobby, Porter/bellhop, Massage - treatment room(s), Airport transportation (free) available on request, Accessible bathroom, Braille or raised signage, Dry cleaning/laundry service, Fitness facilities.

★★

The Palomar Inn
1601 Shell Beach Road
Pismo Beach CA 93449
(805) 773-4204
$50 - $85
Bed & Pet Discount Offered

Pet Policy: Pets welcome, $15 per pet per night.

Features: Guest laundry, Coffee in lobby, Smoke-Free property, Number of rooms: 12, Number of floors: 1, Smoke-Free property, Wheelchair accessible, Accessible bathroom, Parking (free), Free wireless Internet, Translation services, Multilingual staff, Barbecue grill(s).

Placentia

Also see the following nearby communities that have pet friendly lodging: Brea - 3 miles, Fullerton - 4 miles, Yorba Linda - 5 miles, Anaheim - 5 miles, Orange - 6 miles, Garden Grove - 8 miles, Buena Park - 9 miles, Walnut - 9 miles, La Mirada - 9 miles, Diamond Bar - 9 miles

Residence Inn by Marriott
700 W Kimberly Ave
Placentia CA 92870
(714) 996-0555
$118 - $189
Bed & Pet Discount Offered

Pet Policy: Pets allowed, 1 time $100 cleaning fee.

Features: Free Breakfast, Outdoor pool, Number of rooms: 114, Number of floors: 2, Business services, Barbecue grill(s), Coffee in lobby, Complimentary newspapers in lobby, Gift shops or newsstand, Dry cleaning/laundry service, Tennis on site

Placerville

Also see the following nearby communities that have pet friendly lodging: Cameron Park - 9 miles

Best Western Placerville Inn
6850 Green Leaf Dr
Placerville CA 95667
(530) 622-9100
$151 - $185
Bed & Pet Discount Offered

Pet Policy: Pets welcome with no size restrictions. $25 per pet per day.

Features: Business center, Accessible bathroom, Casino shuttle (additional charge), Coffee in lobby, Free breakfast, Complimentary newspapers, Designated smoking areas, Dry cleaning/laundry service, Fitness facilities, Multilingual staff, Number of floors: 3, Number of rooms: 107, Number of suites: 11, RV and truck parking, Ski storage, Outdoor pool – seasonal, Wheelchair accessible, Free wireless Internet.

Fleming Jones Homestead B&B
3170 Newton Rd.
Placerville CA 95667-8368
(530) 344-0943
$140 - $145
Bed & Pet Discount Offered

Pet Policy: All pets are welcome, $10 per pet per day. Dogs must be approved in advance (call property directly) and may stay in the woodshed and bunkhouse rooms of the B&B. Pets are not to be left in the room unattended (except during breakfast); should be well-behaved

Features: Guest laundry, Library, Video library, Free breakfast.

Pleasant Hill

Also see the following nearby communities that have pet friendly lodging: Walnut Creek - 3 miles, Concord - 4 miles, Martinez - 4 miles, Danville - 10 miles

Extended Stay America
3220 Buskirk Ave
Pleasant Hill CA 94523
(925) 945-6788
$64 - $89
Bed & Pet Discount Offered

Pet Policy: Pets accepted, $25 per day.

Features: Guest laundry, Number of rooms: 122, Number of floors: 3, Wireless Internet (additional charge), Parking (free), Front desk (limited hours),

Hyatt Summerfield Suites -
2611 Contra Costa Blvd
Pleasant Hill CA 94523
(925) 934-3343
$98 - $189
Bed & Pet Discount Offered

Pet Policy: Small pets allowed, $5 per pet per night plus $150 per stay cleaning fee. Limit 2 pets per room.

Features: Dry cleaning/laundry, Outdoor pool, Gift shop, Number of rooms: 142, Number of floors: 4, BBQ area, Grocery, Multilingual staff, Business center, Security guard, Wireless Internet, Smoke-Free property, Free Breakfast, Fitness facilities

Residence Inn by Marriott
700 Ellinwood Way
Pleasant Hill CA 94523
(925) 689-1010
$119 - $249
Bed & Pet Discount Offered

Pet Policy: Pets allowed, $100 per stay cleaning fee.

Features: Bar/lounge, Free Breakfast, Business services, Outdoor pool, Number of rooms: 126, BBQ area, Coffee in lobby, Multilingual staff, Free wireless Internet, Smoke-Free, Grocery/convenience store, Dry cleaning/laundry, Fitness facilities.

Summerfield Pleasant Hill
2611 Contra Costa Blvd
Pleasant Hill CA 94523
(925) 934-3343
$109 - $199

Pet Policy: Pets allowed, $5 per day plus $150 per stay cleaning fee. Limit 2 pets per room, only 1 can be a dog.

Features: All suite hotel, Free Internet, Full kitchens, Free breakfast, Business center, Fitness center.

Pleasanton

Also see the following nearby communities that have pet friendly lodging: Dublin - 4 miles, Livermore - 7 miles, San Ramon - 9 miles, Castro Valley - 10 miles

Best Western Pleasanton Inn
5375 Owens Ct
Pleasanton CA 94588
(925) 463-1300
$79 - $80
Bed & Pet Discount Offered

Pet Policy: Small pets allowed. Refundable damage deposit $100.00 max 2 pets. Pet fee $35/day per pet

Features: Wireless Internet, Outdoor pool, Business center, Number of rooms: 95, Free breakfast, Complimentary newspapers, Nearby fitness center (discount), Accessible bathroom.

Extended Stay Deluxe Pleasanton - Chabot Drive
4555 Chabot Dr
Pleasanton CA 94588
(925) 730-0000
$69 - $99
Bed & Pet Discount Offered

Pet Policy: One pet is allowed in each guest room. A $25 per day cleaning fee (not to exceed $150) will be charged the first night of your stay.

Features: BBQ area, Outdoor pool, Coffee in lobby, Elevator, Number of rooms: 112, Number of floors: 3, Wireless Internet, Free breakfast, Parking (free), Dry cleaning/laundry, Fitness facilities.

Hilton Pleasanton at the Club
7050 Johnson Dr
Pleasanton CA 94588
(925) 463-8000
$109 - $119
Bed & Pet Discount Offered

Pet Policy: Pets up to 75 lbs, $50 fee.

Features: Swimming pool - outdoor, Bar/lounge, Tennis on site, Elevator, Restaurant(s), Room service (limited hours), ATM/banking, Gift shops or newsstand, Number of rooms: 294, Number of floors: 5, Airport transportation (additional charge), Computer rental, Coffee in lobby, Wireless Internet (additional charge), Breakfast available (additional charge), Coffee shop or cafe, Health club, Parking (free), Children's swimming pool, Spa services on site, Multilingual staff, Complimentary newspapers in lobby, Use of nearby fitness center (free), Business center, Porter/bellhop, Security guard, Limo or Town Car service available, Beauty services, Concierge desk, Full-service health spa, Massage - treatment room(s), Steam room, Sauna, Dry cleaning/laundry service.

Hyatt Summerfield Suites - Pleasanton
4545 Chabot Dr
Pleasanton CA 94588
(925) 730-0070
$98 - $210
Bed & Pet Discount Offered

Pet Policy: Pets accepted only for stays of at least 30 days. Fee. Contact hotel directly for booking and details.

Features: Swimming pool - outdoor, Free breakfast, Barbecue grill(s), Gift shops or newsstand, Number of rooms: 127, Number of floors: 3, Coffee in lobby, Video library, Parking (free), Multilingual staff, Complimentary newspapers in lobby, Business center, Free wireless Internet, Smoke-Free property, Dry cleaning/laundry service, Tennis on site, Fitness facilities.

Larkspur Landing Pleasanton
5535 Johnson Ct
Pleasanton CA 94588
(925) 463-1212
$69 - $149
Bed & Pet Discount Offered

Pet Policy: Pets welcome, $10 per pet day plus $75 per pet per stay.

Features: Free Breakfast, Elevator, Business services, Dry cleaning/laundry service, Number of rooms: 126, Number of floors: 4, Barbecue grill(s),
Continued on next page

Larkspur Landing Pleasanton
Continued from previous page

Coffee in lobby, Guest laundry, Video library, Grocery, Parking (free), Multilingual staff, Complimentary newspapers in lobby, Limo or Town Car service available, Free wireless Internet, Airport transportation (free), Accessible bathroom, In-room accessibility equipment for the deaf, Braille or raised signage, Fitness facilities.

Not rated
Marriott Executay Archstone
5708 Owens Drive
Pleasanton CA 94588
(800) 500-5110
30 day minimum stay, please call for rates and availability

Pet Policy: Pets accepted, $500 refundable deposit, plus $50 per month rent.

Features: Furnished apartments, Full kitchen, Dishwasher, Washer & Dryer, Fitness Center, Swimming pools and hot tubs, BBQ area..

Not Rated:
Oakwood at Archstone Hacienda
5662 Owens Drive
Pleasanton CA 94558
(602) 427-2752
$188 - $241

Pet Policy: Pets accepted with limitations and fee. Contact hotel directly for more information and to make reservations.

Features: Furnished apartments, Cable TV, Washer & dryer, Full kitchen. Minimum stay of 30 days may be required.

:
Pleasanton Marriott
11950 Dublin Canyon Rd
Pleasanton CA 94588
(925) 847-6000
$84 - $229
Bed & Pet Discount Offered

Pet Policy: Pets allowed, contact hotel directly.

Features: Swimming pool - outdoor, Bar/lounge, Elevator, Restaurant(s), Room service (limited hours), ATM/banking, Concierge services, Gift shops or newsstand, Number of rooms: 242, Number of floors: 6, Breakfast available (additional charge), Business center, Security guard, Free wireless Internet, Smoke-Free property, Dry cleaning/laundry service, Fitness facilities.

★★★
Residence Inn By Marriott Pleasanton
11920 Dublin Canyon Rd
Pleasanton CA 94588
(925) 227-0500
$161 - $229
Bed & Pet Discount Offered

Pet Policy: Pets allowed, $100 per stay cleaning fee.

Features: Elevator, Swimming pool - outdoor, Number of rooms: 135, Number of floors: 3, Barbecue grill(s), Library, Video library, Free breakfast, Parking (free), Complimentary newspapers in lobby, Smoke-Free property, Accessible bathroom, In-room accessibility equipment for the deaf, Braille or raised signage, Wireless Internet (additional charge), Fitness facilities, Free reception, Area shuttle (free), 24-hour business center, Wheelchair accessible, Grocery/convenience store.

Sheraton Pleasanton
5990 Stoneridge Mall Rd
Pleasanton CA 94588
(925) 463-3330
$88 - $99
Bed & Pet Discount Offered

Pet Policy: Two dogs up to 80 pounds are allowed per room, first and second floor rooms only. The hotel reserves the right to charge for additional cleaning or damage caused by the pet. If damage is found after checkout, credit card on record will be charged.

Features: Security guard. Outdoor pool, Smoke-Free property, Wireless Internet (additional charge), Area shuttle (free), 24-hour business center, Smoke-Free property, Room service (limited hours), Bar/lounge, Wheelchair accessible, Restaurant(s), Gift shops or newsstand, Number of rooms: 170, Number of floors: 6, Breakfast available (additional charge), Parking (free), Multilingual staff, Complimentary newspapers in lobby, Porter/bellhop, Dry cleaning/laundry service, Accessible bathroom, Braille or raised signage, Fitness facilities.

★★★
Summerfield Pleasanton
4545 Chabot Drive
Pleasanton CA 94588
(925) 730-0070
$189 - $239

Pet Policy: Pets accepted only for stays of at least 30 days. Fee. Please contact hotel directly for more details and booking.

Features: Suite hotel, Full kitchens, Dishwasher, Free hot breakfast buffet, Fitness center, Outdoor swimming pool, Grocery/Convenience store, Complimentary daily newspaper, Free social hour.

Tri Valley Inn & Suites, Pleasanton
2025 Santa Rita Rd
Pleasanton CA 94566
(925) 846-2742
$73 - $115
Bed & Pet Discount Offered

Pet Policy: Pets accepted, $10 per night. Limit 2 pets per room. Should not be left unattended.

Features: Swimming pool - outdoor, Restaurant(s), Number of rooms: 34, Number of floors: 1, Free breakfast, Multilingual staff, Complimentary newspapers in lobby, Parking (additional charge), Beauty services, Barbecue grill(s), Coffee in lobby, Designated smoking areas, Free wireless Internet, Braille or raised signage, RV and truck parking.

Pollock Pines

Not rated
Best Western Stagecoach Inn
5940 Pony Express Trail
Pollock Pines CA 95726
(530) 644-2029
$92 - $239

Pet Policy: Pets allowed with Restrictions 15 pound limit, 1 kenneled pet, $7.00 fee per night

Features: Suites and Kitchenettes available, HBO, Wireless Internet, Free continental breakfast, Outdoor swimming pool, Business services.

Pomona

Also see the following nearby communities that have pet friendly lodging: San Dimas - 3 miles, Claremont - 4 miles, Diamond Bar - 4 miles, Chino - 6 miles, Walnut - 6 miles, Glendora - 6 miles, Chino Hills - 6 miles, Upland - 7 miles, City Of Industry - 9 miles, Ontario - 10 miles

Sheraton Fairplex Hotel & Conference Center
601 W Mckinley Ave
Pomona CA 91768
(909) 622-2220
$119 - $169
Bed & Pet Discount Offered

Pet Policy: Two dogs up to 80 pounds are allowed per room. The hotel reserves the right to charge for additional cleaning or damage caused by the pet. If damage is found after checkout, credit card on record will be charged.

Features: Outdoor pool, Room service (limited hours), Concierge, Number of suites: 247, Parking (additional charge), Wireless Internet, additional charge, Guest laundry, Accessible bathroom, In-room accessibility equipment for the deaf, Braille or raised signage, Business Center, Fitness facilities.

Shilo Inn Hotel - Pomona/Diamond Bar
3200 W Temple Ave
Pomona CA 91768
(909) 598-0073
$80 - $125
Bed & Pet Discount Offered

Pet Policy: Dogs only, $25 fee

Features: Free Breakfast, Swimming pool - outdoor, Elevator, Number of rooms: 160, Number of floors: 4, Coffee in lobby, Smoke-Free property, Bar/lounge, Airport transportation (free), Fitness facilities

Shilo Inn Suites Hotel - Pomona Hilltop
3101 W Temple Ave
Pomona CA 91768
(909) 598-7666
$80 - $119
Bed & Pet Discount Offered

Pet Policy: Dogs only, $25 per stay fee. Limit 2 per room.

Features: Swimming pool - outdoor, Sauna, Free Breakfast, Parking (free), Steam room, Smoke-Free property, Bar/lounge, Restaurant(s), Number of rooms: 130, Number of floors: 3, Business services, Dry cleaning/laundry service, Fitness facilities.

Port Hueneme

Also see the following nearby communities that have pet friendly lodging: Oxnard - 3 miles, Camarillo - 8 mile

Country Inn & Suites By Carlson Port Hueneme
350 E Hueneme Rd
Port Hueneme CA 93041
(805) 986-5353
$89 - $149
Bed & Pet Discount Offered

Pet Policy: Pets welcome, $25 per day.

Features: Free breakfast, Dry cleaning/laundry service, Bar/lounge, Room service (limited hours), Outdoor pool, Concierge, Number of rooms: 135, Number of floors: 3, Library, Multilingual staff, Complimentary newspapers, Use of nearby fitness center (free), Wireless Internet (additional charge), Wheelchair accessible, 24-hour business center.

Porterville

Best Western Porterville Inn
350 Montgomery Ave
Porterville CA 93257
(559) 781-7411
$83 - $91
Bed & Pet Discount Offered

Pet Policy: Small pets accepted, $35.

Features: Wheelchair accessible, Free wireless Internet, Accessible bathroom, In-room accessibility equipment for the deaf, Braille or raised signage, RV and truck parking, Free breakfast, Swimming pool - outdoor, Hair salon, Number of rooms: 115, Number of floors: 2, Parking (free), Smoke-Free property, 24-hour business center, Fitness facilities.

Poway

Also see the following nearby communities that have pet friendly lodging: Rancho Santa Fe - 10 miles

Best Western Plus Poway/San Diego Hotel
13845 Poway Rd
Poway CA 92064
(858) 748-6320
$64 - $169
Bed & Pet Discount Offered

Pet Policy: Up to 2 dogs per room with a 80 pound weight limit. Additional pet types (cats, birds, etc.) may be accepted at the hotel's discretion. Pet rate is $10 per day with a $100 per week maximum. A refundable cleaning & damage deposit of $50 is required upon check-in. If damage occurs or excessive cleaning is needed, the deposit can become non-refundable and the hotel may charge additionally to cover the costs of repair/cleaning.

Features: 24-hour business center, Number of rooms: 43, Number of floors: 2, Free wireless Internet, Accessible bathroom, In-room accessibility equipment for the deaf, Braille or raised signage, RV and truck parking, Outdoor pool, Free breakfast, Multilingual staff, Dry cleaning/laundry service.

Rancho Cordova

Also see the following nearby communities that have pet friendly lodging: Folsom - 7 miles, North Highlands - 8 miles

Comfort Inn and Suites Rancho Cordova
12249 Folsom Blvd
Rancho Cordova CA 95742
(916) 351-1213
$67 - $79
Bed & Pet Discount Offered

Pet Policy: Pet Accommodation :$10 USD Per Pet/Night Max 2 per room Max 60 lbs Refundable Deposit Required:$50.

Features: Coffee in lobby, Business services, Guest laundry, Elevator, Swimming pool - outdoor, Barbecue grill(s), Free breakfast, Parking (free), Complimentary newspapers in lobby, Limo or Town Car service available, Free wireless Internet, Number of rooms: 118, Number of floors: 3.

Crossland Sacramento - Point East Drive
11299 Point East Dr
Rancho Cordova CA 95742
(916) 859-0280
$39 - $54
Bed & Pet Discount Offered

Pet Policy: One pet is allowed in each guest room. A $25 per day non-refundable cleaning fee (not to exceed $150) will be charged the first night of your stay. Weight, size and breed restrictions may apply.

Features: Guest laundry, Elevator, Number of rooms: 129, Number of floors: 3, Wireless Internet, Parking (free), Front desk (limited hours).

★★

Days Inn and Suites - Rancho Cordova
3240 Mather Field Rd
Rancho Cordova CA 95670
(916) 363-3344
$36 - $65
Bed & Pet Discount Offered

Pet Policy: A room for you and your pet may be available upon request. Pet fee is $20 per night.

Features: Coffee maker, Refrigerator and Microwave, Heated swimming pool, Sauna, Free continental breakfast, Free wireless Internet.

★★

Extended Stay America Sacramento - White Rock Road
10721 White Rock Rd
Rancho Cordova CA 95670
(916) 635-2363
$54 - $89
Bed & Pet Discount Offered

Pet Policy: One pet is allowed in each guest room. A $25 per day non-refundable cleaning fee (not to exceed $150) will be charged the first night of your stay.

Features: Guest laundry, Elevator, Number of rooms: 132, Number of floors: 3, Business services, Wireless Internet (additional charge), Parking (free).

★★½

Fairfield Inn & Suites by Marriott Rancho Cordova
10745 Gold Center Dr
Rancho Cordova CA 95670
(916) 858-8680
$60 - $119
Bed & Pet Discount Offered

Pet Policy: Pets accepted with $75 per stay fee

Features: Elevator, Wireless Internet (additional charge), Free breakfast, Parking (free), Business center, Dry cleaning/laundry service.

★★½

Hawthorn Suites by Wyndham Rancho Cordova
12180 Tributary Point Drive
Rancho Cordova CA 95670
(916) 351-9192
$50 - $59
Bed & Pet Discount Offered

Pet Policy: Pets Accepted, $50 per stay fee.

Features: Guest laundry, Swimming pool - outdoor, Number of floors: 3, Free breakfast, Parking (free), Free wireless Internet, Fitness facilities.

Holiday Inn Rancho Cordova
11269 Point East Dr
Rancho Cordova CA 95742
(916) 635-4040
$69 - $149
Bed & Pet Discount Offered

Pet Policy: Pets welcome, $25 per pet per stay. Limit 2 pets per room.

Features: Sauna, Bar/lounge, Outdoor pool, Nearby fitness center (discount), Accessible bathroom, Accessibility equipment for the deaf, Braille or raised signage, Business center, Restaurant, Room service, Number of rooms: 122, Number of floors: 3, Multilingual staff, Free wireless Internet, Dry cleaning/laundry service.

Hyatt Place Rancho Cordova
10744 Gold Center Dr
Rancho Cordova CA 95670
(916) 635-4799
$88 - $118
Bed & Pet Discount Offered

Pet Policy: Pets under 30 lbs, $10 per pet per night.

Features: Business services, Bar/lounge, Concierge, Coffee shop or cafe, Complimentary newspapers, Free wireless Internet, Smoke-Free property, Free breakfast, Dry cleaning/laundry, Fitness facilities.

Knights Inn Rancho Cordova
10271 Folsom Blvd
Rancho Cordova CA 95670
(916) 362-5800
$43 - $56
Bed & Pet Discount Offered

Pet Policy: Pets accepted, $25 per pet per stay.

Features: Swimming pool - outdoor, Number of floors: 2, Free breakfast, Parking (free).

La Quinta Inn & Suites Rancho Cordova-Sacramento
11131 Folsom Blvd
Rancho Cordova CA 95670
(916) 638-1111
$65 - $95
Bed & Pet Discount Offered

Pet Policy: Pets up to 25 lbs allowed without fee. Must not leave unattended in room.

Features: Swimming pool - outdoor, Accessible bathroom, Elevator, ATM/banking, Number of rooms: 130, Number of floors: 5, Guest laundry, Free breakfast, Parking (free), Complimentary newspapers in lobby, Use of nearby fitness center (free), Free wireless Internet, Dry cleaning/laundry service.

Red Roof Inn Rancho Cordova - Sacramento
10800 Olson Drive
US Route 50 at Zinfandel Drive
Rancho Cordova CA 95670
(916) 638-2500
$49 - $59
Bed & Pet Discount Offered

Pet Policy: Red Roof's Pet Policy: One well-behaved family pet is permitted unless they are prohibited by state law or ordinance. Service animals are always welcome. Pets must be declared during guest registration. In consideration of all Red Roof guests, pets must never be left unattended in the guestroom.

Continued on next page

Red Roof Inn Rancho Cordova
Continued from previous page

Features: Business services, Coffee in lobby, Swimming pool - outdoor, Guest laundry, Complimentary newspapers in lobby, Accessible bathroom, Number of rooms: 122, Number of floors: 3, Parking (free), Free wireless Internet, Multilingual staff, Accessibility equipment for the deaf, RV and truck parking, Fitness facilities

★★★

Residence Inn by Marriott Rancho Cordova
2779 Prospect Park Drive
Rancho Cordova CA 95670
(916) 851-1550
$150 - $151
Bed & Pet Discount Offered

Pet Policy: Pets allowed, $50 per stay cleaning fee.

Features: Nearby fitness center (free), Security guard, Smoke-Free property, Swimming pool - indoor, Restaurant(s), Number of rooms: 90, Number of floors: 3, Free breakfast, Parking (free), Complimentary newspapers in lobby, Dry cleaning/laundry service, Concierge, BBQ area, Coffee in lobby, Arcade/game room, Multilingual staff, Accessible bathroom, Accessibility equipment for the deaf, Braille or raised signage, Free wireless Internet, 24-hour business center, Free reception.

Vagabond Inn Executive Rancho Cordova
10713 White Rock Rd
Rancho Cordova CA 95670
(916) 631-7500
$44- $79
Bed & Pet Discount Offered

Pet Policy: Pets accepted, $10 per night.

Features: Free breakfast, Concierge, Business center, Room service (limited hours), Swimming pool – outdoor, Number of rooms: 116, Number of floors: 3, Complimentary newspapers in lobby, Wireless Internet, Accessible bathroom, Accessibility equipment for the deaf, Braille or raised signage, Dry cleaning/laundry service.

Rancho Cucamonga

Also see the following nearby communities that have pet friendly lodging: Ontario - 4 miles, Upland - 5 miles, Claremont - 8 miles, Chino

Aloft Ontario-Rancho Cucamonga
10480 4th St
Rancho Cucamonga CA 91730
(909) 484-2018
$79 - $229
Bed & Pet Discount Offered

Pet Policy: Animals are family, too! That's why Aloft Ontario-Rancho Cucamonga welcomes dogs up to 40 pounds. Our pet-friendly arf(SM) program offers a special bed, bowl, and a doggie bag of woof-alicious treats and toys, all Free to use during your stay. Please make sure they're on their best behavior—we don't want to charge you extra for housekeeping! If your dog weighs more than 40 pounds, please contact the hotel directly to discuss a waiver.

Features: Bar/lounge, Swimming pool - outdoor, Children's club, Airport transportation (free), Number of rooms: 136,

Aloft Ontario-Rancho Cucamonga
Continued from previous page

Continued on next page
Number of floors: 5, Business services, Breakfast available (additional charge), Arcade/game room, Restaurant, Nightclub, Parking (free), Multilingual staff, Complimentary newspapers in lobby, Limo or Town Car service available, Medical assistance available, Free wireless Internet, Smoke-Free property, Accessible bathroom, Accessibility equipment for the deaf, Braille or raised signage, Dry cleaning/laundry service, Fitness facilities.

★★★

Four Points by Sheraton Ontario-Rancho Cucamonga
11960 Foothill Blvd
Rancho Cucamonga CA 91739
(909) 204-6100
$105 - $129
Bed & Pet Discount Offered

Pet Policy: Pets up to 25 lbs accepted, $75 fee.

Features: Breakfast available (additional charge), Swimming pool - outdoor, Guest laundry, Gift shops or newsstand, Number of rooms: 118, Number of floors: 4, Smoke-Free property, Restaurant(s), Coffee in lobby, Parking (free), Room service, Free wireless Internet, 24-hour business center, Fitness facilities,

Homewood Suites Ontario-Rancho Cucamonga
11433 Mission Vista Dr
Rancho Cucamonga CA 91730
(909) 481-6480
$89 - $119
Bed & Pet Discount Offered

Pet Policy: Pets up to 25 lbs, $75 per stay.

Features: Free breakfast, Elevator, Grocery, Coffee in lobby, Business services, Barbecue grill(s), Airport transportation (additional charge), Business center, Room service (limited hours), Swimming pool – outdoor, Number of suites: 103, Number of floors: 4, Multilingual staff, Complimentary newspapers in lobby, Free wireless Internet, Dry cleaning/laundry service, Self-parking (free), Fitness facilities

TownePlace Suites by Marriott Ontario Airport
9625 Milliken Ave
Rancho Cucamonga CA 91730
(909) 466-1100
$299 - $300
Bed & Pet Discount Offered

Pet Policy: Pets allowed. $100 cleaning fee.

Features: Swimming pool - outdoor, Barbecue grill(s), Guest laundry, Airport transportation (free), Number of rooms: 112, Number of floors: 4, Coffee in lobby, Free breakfast, Parking (free), Complimentary newspapers in lobby, Business center, Concierge desk, Accessible bathroom, Accessibility equipment for the deaf, Braille or raised signage.

Rancho Mirage

Also see the following nearby communities that have pet friendly lodging: Cathedral City - 4 miles, Thousand Palms - 4 miles, Palm Desert - 4 miles, Palm Springs - 8 miles, La Quinta - 10 mile

Westin Mission Hills Resort & Spa
71333 Dinah Shore Dr
Rancho Mirage CA 92270
(760) 328-5955
$211 - $730
Bed & Pet Discount Offered

Pet Policy: Dogs up to 40 pounds are allowed without fee. Guest must sign a waiver at check-in stating that the dog will not be left alone in the room at any time. Dogs are not allowed in outlets or on pool deck. Guest is responsible for cleanup and any extra cost associated with clean up. Please Note: Villas do not allow dogs at all.

Features: Business Center, Swimming pool - outdoor, Concierge desk, Dry cleaning/laundry service, Bar/lounge, Restaurant(s), Supervised child care/activities, Gift shops or newsstand, Shopping on site, Number of rooms: 512, Number of floors: 2, Wireless Internet (additional charge), Poolside bar, Room service (24 hours), Shoe shine, Multilingual staff, Complimentary Newspapers, Porter/bellhop, Doorman/doorwoman, Security guard, medical assistance available, Beauty services, Full-service health spa, Steam room, Golf course on site, Tennis on site, Valet parking (fee).

Rancho Santa Fe

Also see the following nearby communities that have pet friendly lodging: Del Mar - 5 miles, Encinitas - 5 miles, San Marcos - 9 miles, Poway - 10 miles

Rancho Valencia
5921 Valencia Circle
Rancho Santa Fe CA 92067
(858) 756-1123
$699- $1,025
Bed & Pet Discount Offered

Pet Policy: Pets up to 40 lbs accepted, $75 fee per stay. Pets may not be left alone in room, and are not permitted in food or pool areas.

Features: Sauna, Free breakfast, Free wireless Internet, Concierge desk, Business center, Beauty services, Room service (24 hours), Bar/lounge, Video library, Full-service health spa, Steam room, Swimming pool – outdoor, Shoe shine, Restaurant(s), Gift shops or newsstand, Number of rooms: 49, Number of floors: 1, Parking (free), Multilingual staff, Complimentary newspapers in lobby, Porter/bellhop, Security guard, Medical assistance available, Massage - treatment room(s), Accessible bathroom, Dry cleaning/laundry service, Tennis on site.

Red Bluff

Best Western Plus -Antelope Inn
203 Antelope Blvd
I 5 to Hwy 36 and 99 East
Red Bluff CA 96080-2901
(530) 527-8882
$77 - $93

Pet Policy: Pets allowed with small nightly charge per pet. Limited to pet designated rooms.

Features: Free breakfast, Free wireless Internet, Cable TV.

★★

Comfort Inn Red Bluff
90 Sale Ln
Red Bluff CA 96080
(530) 529-7060
$84 - $94
Bed & Pet Discount Offered

Pet Policy: Pets accepted, $15 per night per pet.

Features: Pets accepted, Number of rooms: 67, Number of floors: 3, Swimming pool - outdoor seasonal, Coffee in lobby, Free breakfast, Free wireless Internet, Guest laundry, Business center, Fitness facilities.

★★½

Days Inn Red Bluff
5 Sutter Street
Sutter and Main Street
Red Bluff CA 96080
(530) 527-6130
$56 - $80
Bed & Pet Discount Offered

Pet Policy: Pets allowed, $10 per pet per night

Features: Business services, Coffee in lobby, Parking (free), Multilingual staff, Free wireless Internet, Swimming pool - outdoor seasonal, Free breakfast.

★

Econo Lodge Red Bluff
1142 North Main St.
Red Bluff CA 96080
(530) 243-3336
$44 - $84

Pet Policy: Pets welcome, $5 per night per pet.

Features: Free continental breakfast, Swimming pool – outdoor – seasonal, Refrigerators and microwaves in some rooms, Coffee makers.

★★

M Star Hotel
210 S Main Street
Red Bluff CA 96080
(530) 527-1150
$25 - $68
Bed & Pet Discount Offered

Pet Policy: Dogs and cats only, up to 25 lbs. $5 per pet per night. Limit 2 per room.

Features: Airport transportation (free), Barbecue grill(s), Area shuttle (free), Restaurant 1, Number of rooms: 51, Number of floors: 2, Breakfast available (additional charge), Suitable for children, Nearby fitness center (discount), Free wireless Internet, RV and truck parking, Accessible bathroom, Accessibility equipment for the deaf, Wheelchair accessible, Parking (free), Concierge desk, Swimming pool - outdoor seasonal.

Sportsman Lodge
768 Antelope Blvd
Red Bluff CA 96080
(530) 527-2888
$75 - $90
Bed & Pet Discount Offered

Pet Policy: Pets are allowed for an additional pet fee of $7 per night for 1 dog and $10 per night for 2 pets. The fee may be higher for larger or heavily-haired dogs. Pets may not be left unattended in the rooms at any time, and they must be well behaved, leashed, and cleaned up after.

Features: Parking (free), Swimming pool – outdoor.

Super 8 Motel Red Bluff
30 Gilmore Rd
Red Bluff CA 96080
(530) 529-2028
$49 - $65
Bed & Pet Discount Offered

Pet Policy: Pets allowed, $!0 per night per pet.

Features: Free breakfast, Number of floors: 2, Business services, Coffee in lobby, Parking (free), Complimentary newspapers in lobby, Swimming pool - outdoor seasonal, Free wireless Internet.

Travelodge Red Bluff
38 Antelope Blvd
Red Bluff CA 96080
(530) 527-6020
$46 - $65
Bed & Pet Discount Offered

Pet Policy: Pets permitted $8 per night.

Features: Free breakfast, Number of rooms: 41, Shopping on site, Business services, Parking (free), Multilingual staff, Complimentary newspapers in lobby, Wireless Internet, Restaurants next door, Swimming pool - outdoor seasonal.

Redding

Also see the following nearby communities that have pet friendly lodging: Anderson - 10 mile

Americas Best Inns Redding
1835 Park Marina Dr
Redding CA 96001
(877) 784-6835
$50 - $105

Pet Policy: Pets accepted.

Features: All rooms at the hotel are spacious kings and queens. Rooms are also available on a private lagoon with balconies and in room Jacuzzis. Private lagoon and boat dock is available to the guest for boating, fishing, rafting and kayaking on the Sacramento River. The hotel also offers a huge outdoor seasonal swimming pool and hot tub, Free high speed Internet, cable TV, in room coffee, microwaves and refrigerators.

Baymont Inn and Suites
2600 Larkspur Lane
Redding CA 96002
(530) 722-9100
$75 - $204
Bed & Pet Discount Offered

Pet Policy: Pet friendly. $30 per pet per night.

Features: Fitness facilities, Complimentary newspapers in lobby, Wireless Internet (additional charge), Free breakfast, Swimming pool – indoor

Comfort Inn Redding
850 Mistletoe Ln
Redding CA 96002
(800) 530-3324
$91 - $109
Bed & Pet Discount Offered

Pet Policy: Pet accommodation:$10/night Pet limit: 1 pet per room 20 lbs or less

Features: Business services, Gift shops or newsstand, Number of rooms: 70, Number of floors: 3, Free breakfast, Free wireless Internet, Outdoor pool - seasonal, Dry cleaning/laundry, Fitness center.

Econo Lodge Redding
2010 Pine Street
Redding CA 96001
(530) 243-3336
$53 - $74

Pet Policy: Pets may be accepted but policy was not made available. Please contact hotel directly for booking and details.

Outdoor Pool. Rooms With Kitchenettes Available. Free Continental Breakfast. HBO.

Fairfield Inn & Suites by Marriott Redding
5164 Caterpillar Rd
Redding CA 96003
(530) 243-3200
$114 - $119
Bed & Pet Discount Offered

Pet Policy: Pets accepted, $25 cleaning fee. Please confirm with hotel before arriving,

Features: Guest laundry, Free breakfast, Smoke-Free property, Fitness facilities, Wireless Internet, Complimentary newspapers, Outdoor pool, Business services, Coffee in lobby, Wheelchair accessible.

Holiday Inn Redding
1900 Hilltop Dr
Redding CA 96002
(530) 221-7500
$106 - $156
Bed & Pet Discount Offered

Pet Policy: The hotel accepts dogs only. Dogs must be leashed when not in the guest room. Dogs are not to be left in the guest room unattended at any time. Deposit $ 100 per stay, Fee $10 per night

Features: Fitness facilities, Bar/lounge, Babysitting or child care, Airport transportation (free), Restaurant(s), Outdoor pool, Number of suites: 6, Number of floors: 2, Cell phone/mobile rental, Business services, Coffee in lobby, Guest laundry, Room service , Complimentary newspapers, Wireless Internet, Accessible bathroom, Accessibility equipment for the deaf, Braille or raised signage.

La Quinta Inn & Suites Redding
2180 Hilltop Dr
Redding CA 96002
(530) 221-8200
$69 - $109
Bed & Pet Discount Offered

Pet Policy: Cats and dogs up to 50 pounds are accepted in all guest rooms. Housekeeping services for rooms with pets require pet owner be present or pet must be crated. No fees or deposits are required.

Features: Accessible bathroom, Number of rooms: 141, Number of floors: 3, Business services, Coffee in lobby, Free breakfast, Health club, Parking (free) Dry cleaning/laundry. Outdoor pool, Free Internet.

Oxford Suites Redding
1967 Hilltop Drive
Redding CA 96002
(530) 221-0100
$99 - $129
Bed & Pet Discount Offered

Pet Policy: Medium size cats and dogs accepted for $25 per pet per stay, for up to seven days, with a two pet limit. The charge is assessed at check out and not included in your room rate. Aggressive breeds not allowed. Pets must not be left unattended in room, must be leashed when in public areas, and are not permitted in dining, pool or spa areas (service animals excepted).

Features: Bar/lounge, Airport transportation (free), Swimming pool - outdoor, Health club, Free breakfast, Coffee in lobby, Elevator, Business center, Gift shops or newsstand, Number of rooms: 139, Number of floors: 4, Suitable for children, Video library, Parking (free), Complimentary newspapers in lobby, Free wireless Internet, Dry cleaning/laundry service.

★½

Quality Inn
2059 Hilltop Dr
Redding CA 96002
(530) 221-6530
$84 - $94
Bed & Pet Discount Offered

Pet Policy: Quality Inns charge a fee of $10 per night per pet but do not charge any other fees. They may require a $50 damage deposit, which is refunded if the room is in order at check out. Quality Inns accept any well-behaved pets with a maximum of 3 per room, but dogs are limited to 50 pounds. Pets may not be left alone in the room unless in a cage.

Features: Free breakfast, Gift shops or newsstand, Number of rooms: 90, Number of floors: 3, Business services, Parking (free), Complimentary newspapers in lobby, Free wireless Internet, Swimming pool - outdoor seasonal.

★★

Ramada Limited Redding
1286 Twin View Blvd
Redding CA 96003
(530) 246-2222
$67 - $117
Bed & Pet Discount Offered

Pet Policy: Pets welcome, $20 per night

Features: Swimming pool - indoor, Complimentary newspapers in lobby, Business center, Security guard, Free Internet, Dry cleaning/laundry service.

★★★

Red Lion Hotel Redding
1830 Hilltop Drive
Redding CA 96002
(530) 221-8700
$109 - $145
Bed & Pet Discount Offered

Pet Policy: Pets welcome, $20 per stay.

Features: Bar/Lounge, Airport transportation (free), Number of rooms: 192, Business services, Complimentary newspapers in lobby, Swimming pool - outdoor seasonal, Dry cleaning/laundry service, Free wireless Internet, Fitness facilities, Breakfast available (additional charge).

Redding CA Travelodge
540 N Market St
Redding CA 96003
(530) 243-5291
$64 - $92
Bed & Pet Discount Offered

Pet Policy: Pets allowed, $8 per night per pet. Limited number of pet rooms so book in advance.

Features: Swimming pool – outdoor, Complimentary newspapers in lobby, Business center, Accessible bathroom, Accessibility equipment for the deaf, Braille or raised signage, Fitness facilities.

Rodeway Inn Redding
532 N Market St
Redding CA 96003
(530) 241-6464
$55 - $75
Bed & Pet Discount Offered

Pet Policy: Rodeway Inns charge a fee of $10 per night per pet and require a $50 damage deposit, which is refunded if the room is in order at check out. Max of 2 pets per room. A veterinarian certificate that the pet is on a flea and parasite program and that they are Free from parasites is required. Pets may not be left alone in the room unless in a cage.

Features: Business services, Guest laundry, Restaurant(s), Swimming pool - outdoor, Number of rooms: 62, Number of floors: 2, Free breakfast, Parking (free).

Not rated
Shasta Lodge Redding
1245 Pine St
Redding CA 96001
(877) 747-8713
$40 - $55

Pet Policy: Pets accepted, $5 per pet per night.

Features: Business services, Free parking, Coffee in lobby, Smoking rooms available.

Not rated
Stardust Motel Redding
1200 Pine St
Redding CA 96001
(877) 747-8713
$35 - $45

Pet Policy: Small pets only, $10 per pet per day.

Features: Located within walking distance of Turtle Bay Exploration Park.

Vagabond Inn Redding
536 E Cypress Ave
Redding CA 96002
(530) 223-1600
$61 - $68
Bed & Pet Discount Offered

Pet Policy: Pet friendly, $20 per pet per night. Limit 2 pets per room.

Features: Swimming pool - outdoor, Number of floors: 2, Free breakfast, Parking (free).

Redlands

Also see the following nearby communities that have pet friendly lodging: San Bernardino - 6 miles, Colton - 8 miles, Moreno Valley - 10 miles

Ayres Hotel Redlands
1015 W Colton Avenue
Redlands CA 92374
(909) 335-9024
$109 - $129
Bed & Pet Discount Offered

Pet Policy: Pets up to 20 lbs, $15 per night

Features: Coffee in lobby, Outdoor pool, Number of rooms: 107, Free breakfast, Free newspapers, Free Internet, Dry cleaning/laundry, Concierge, Multilingual staff, Porter/bellhop, Limo or Town Car service available, Accessible bathroom, Accessibility equipment for the deaf, Braille or raised signage, Area shuttle (free), Business Center, Free reception, Smoke-Free, Fitness Center.

Redondo Beach

Also see the following nearby communities that have pet friendly lodging: Hermosa Beach - 2 miles, Torrance - 3 miles, Manhattan Beach - 4 miles, Harbor City - 5 miles, Hawthorne - 5 miles, Gardena - 5 miles, El Segundo - 6 miles, Carson - 7 miles, Inglewood - 8 miles, San Pedro - 9 miles

Not rated
Marriott Executay Ocean Club
300 The Village Dr
Redondo Beach CA 90277
(888) 526-0566
$166 - $175

Pet Policy: 2 pets per apartment allowed, cats permitted on any floor, dogs up to 40lbs permitted in designated apartments only. $500 Pet fees/deposits are required, $250 is non-refundable.

Features: Fully furnished apartments. 30 day minimum stay required.

Redway

Not rated
Dean Creek Resort
4112 Redwood Drive
Redway CA 95560
(707) 923-2555
$90 - $110

Pet Policy: Pet friendly

Features: Combination motel, campground and RV park.

Redwood City

Also see the following nearby communities that have pet friendly lodging: San Carlos - 3 miles, Menlo Park - 4 miles, Belmont - 4 miles, San Mateo - 7 miles, Palo Alto - 7 miles, Los Altos - 9 miles, Burlingame - 10 miles

Days Inn Redwood City CA
2650 El Camino Real
Redwood City CA 94061
(650) 369-9200
$63 - $104
Bed & Pet Discount Offered

Pet Policy: Small pets accepted, $5 fee.

Features: Sauna, Business services, Coffee in lobby, Free breakfast, Multilingual staff, Complimentary newspapers, Free wireless Internet, Swimming pool - outdoor seasonal, Fitness facilities

Sofitel San Francisco Bay
223 Twin Dolphin Dr
Redwood City CA 94065
(650) 598-9000
$85 - $355
Bed & Pet Discount Offered

Pet Policy: Pets accepted without additional charge.

Features: Bar/lounge, Security guard, Multilingual staff, Complimentary newspapers, Porter/bellhop, Doorman/doorwoman, Wireless Internet (additional charge), Concierge, Technology helpdesk, Shopping on site, Shoe shine, Currency exchange, Airport transportation (free), Computer rental, Number of rooms: 421, Number of floors: 7, Restaurant(s), Breakfast available (additional charge), Dry cleaning/laundry service, Outdoor pool - seasonal, 24-hour business center, Suitable for children, Coffee in lobby, Library, Room service, Fitness facilities, Valet parking (additional charge)

TownePlace Suites by Marriott Redwood City Redwood
1000 Twin Dolphin Dr
Redwood City CA 94065
(650) 593-4100
$89 - $90
Bed & Pet Discount Offered

Pet Policy: Pets accepted, $75 cleaning fee per stay.

Features: Dry cleaning/laundry service, Free wireless Internet, Elevator, Number of rooms: 95, Number of floors: 5, Barbecue grill(s), Coffee in lobby, Guest laundry, Free breakfast, Parking (free), Complimentary newspapers in lobby, Business center, Fitness facilities.

Rialto

Also see the following nearby communities that have pet friendly lodging: Colton - 4 miles, San Bernardino - 5 miles

Days Inn Fontana / Rialto
475 W Valley Blvd
Rialto CA 92376
(909) 877-0690
$55 - $109
Bed & Pet Discount Offered

Pet Policy: Pets allowed but fee not disclosed. Please contact hotel before booking. Most Days Inn's charge around $10 per night.

Features: Swimming pool - outdoor, Business center, Guest laundry, Free breakfast, Free wireless Internet, RV and truck parking.

Super 8 Rialto
2042 West Valley Blvd
Rialto CA 92376
(909) 877-5880
$65 - $75

Pet Policy: Pets accepted, $15 per night per pet.

Features: Microwave, Refrigerator, Iron with board, Coffee maker, Free continental breakfast, Free Internet and Satellite TV with HBO.

Richmond

Also see the following nearby communities that have pet friendly lodging: Berkeley - 7 miles, Emeryville - 8 miles, Corte Madera - 9 miles, San Rafael - 10 miles

★★
Days Inn Point Richmond
915 W Cutting Blvd
Richmond CA 94804
(510) 237-3000
$59 - $85
Bed & Pet Discount Offered

Pet Policy: Pets allowed, $20 per pet per night, plus $50 refundable deposit if not paying by credit card.

Features: Outdoor pool, Number of rooms: 106, Number of floors: 2, Coffee in lobby, Guest laundry, Free breakfast, Complimentary newspapers, Business center, Free wireless Internet, Accessible bathroom, Braille or raised signage, Fitness facilities.

★★
Extended Stay America Richmond - Hilltop Mall
3170 Garrity Way
Richmond CA 94806
(510) 222-7383
$64 - $89
Bed & Pet Discount Offered

Pet Policy: One pet is allowed in each guest room. A $25 per day non-refundable cleaning fee (not to exceed $150) will be charged the first night of your stay.

Features: Guest laundry, Elevator, Number of rooms: 101, Number of floors: 3, Wireless Internet (additional charge), Parking (free), Front desk (limited hours), Security guard Bar/lounge

Ridgecrest

Carriage Inn
901 N China Lake Blvd
Ridgecrest CA 93555
(760) 446-7910
$129 - $141

Pet Policy: Small pets allowed with $75 fee per stay.

Features: Free high speed Internet, On site gym, Sauna, Therapy pool, Lap pool, Restaurant, Room service.

Comfort Inn Ridgecrest
507 South China Lake Blvd
Ridgecrest CA 93555
(760) 375-9732
$79 - $80
Bed & Pet Discount Offered

Pet Policy: Pets up to 30 lbs, $25 per night.

Features: Number of rooms: 58, Number of suites: 5, Number of floors: 2, Free breakfast, Complimentary newspapers in lobby, Smoke-Free property, Swimming pool - outdoor seasonal, Accessible bathroom, Accessibility equipment for the deaf, Braille or raised signage.

★★
Econo Lodge Inn & Suites
201 W Inyokern Rd
Ridgecrest CA 93555
(760) 446-2551
$86 - $112
Bed & Pet Discount Offered

Pet Policy: Pet friendly. Be sure to indicate bringing pet on your reservation.

Features: Business services, Coffee in lobby, Free breakfast, Wireless Internet, Outdoor pool - seasonal, Number of rooms: 86, Accessible bathroom, Accessibility equipment for the deaf.

Heritage Inn & Suites
1050 N Norma Street
Ridgecrest CA 93555
(760) 446-6543
$81 - $125

Pet Policy: Only 1 pet per room - pets allowed in 2 1st floor pet rooms, non-smoking only - no pet fee.

Features: Number of floors: 2, Refrigerator, Microwave, Iron & board, Coffee maker, Computer data port, Full American breakfast (free), 1 bedroom Apartments available with living and dining rooms.

Rodeway Ridgecrest
131 W Upjohn Avenue
Ridgecrest CA 93555
(760) 384-3575
$54 - $69

Pet Policy: Pets limited to 25 lbs and under, 1 per room, for a fee of $10 per night plus a $50 damage deposit, which is refunded if the room is in order at check out. A veterinarian certificate that the pet is on a flea and parasite is required. Pets may not be left alone in the room unless in a cage.

Features: Free continental breakfast, Mini fridge and microwave, Free coffee in lobby,

Vagabond Inn Ridgecrest
426 S China Lake Blvd
Ridgecrest CA 93555
(760) 375-2220
$75 - $76
Bed & Pet Discount Offered

Pet Policy: Pets allowed, $10 per stay.

Features: Number of rooms: 35, Number of floors: 2, Business services, Coffee in lobby, Guest laundry, Free breakfast, Parking (free), Free wireless Internet.

Rio Vista

Not rated
Vista Royal Inn
640 State Highway 12
Rio Vista CA 94571
(877) 747-8713
$44 - $69

Pet Policy: Pets accepted. Please contact property directly for fees and booking information.

Features: Number of rooms: 16, Cable TV, Coffee makers, Refrigerators and microwaves.

Ripon

Also see the following nearby communities that have pet friendly lodging: Salida - 5 miles, Manteca - 5 miles, Lathrop - 9 miles

La Quinta Inn & Suites

Manteca - Ripon
1524 Colony Road
Ripon CA 95366
(209) 599-8999
$89 - $90
Bed & Pet Discount Offered

Pet Policy: Cats and dogs up to 50 pounds are accepted in all guest rooms. Housekeeping services for rooms with pets require pet owner be present or pet must be crated. No fees or deposits are required.

Features: Free breakfast, Business center, Outdoor pool, Number of suites: 25, Number of floors: 4, Guest laundry, Complimentary newspapers, Free wireless Internet, Sauna, Smoke-Free, Fitness facilities.

Riverside

Also see the following nearby communities that have pet friendly lodging: Colton - 9 miles, Moreno Valley - 10 miles

Not rated
Budget Inn Riverside
1911 University Avenue
Riverside CA 92507
(951) 686-8888
$44 - $69

Pet Policy: Pets allowed, $10 per stay per pet.

Features: Rental car desk.

★★
Comfort Inn University
1590 University Ave
Riverside CA 92507
(951) 683-6000
$84 - $109
Bed & Pet Discount Offered

Pet Policy: Pet Accommodation: $15 per night. Pet Limit: 2 pets up to 30 lbs, per room.

Features: Gift shop, Number of rooms: 115, Number of floors: 2, Free breakfast, Complimentary newspapers, Wireless Internet, Outdoor pool, Coffee in lobby, Business center, Fitness facilities.

★½
Econo Lodge Riverside
10705 Magnolia Ave
Riverside CA 92505
(951) 351-2424
$57 - $64
Bed & Pet Discount Offered

Pet Policy: Dogs only, $10 per night. Must mention pets at check in.

Features: Outdoor pool, Business services, Gift shop, Number of rooms: 50, Number of floors: 2, Guest laundry, Video library, Free breakfast, Complimentary newspapers, Accessible bathroom, In-room accessibility equipment for the deaf.

★★½
Hampton Inn and Suites Riverside/Corona East
4250 Riverwalk Pkwy
Riverside CA 92505
(951) 352-5020
$84 - $119
Bed & Pet Discount Offered

Pet Policy: Pets up to 50 lbs, $35 fee.

Features: Outdoor pool, Wheelchair accessible, Number of rooms: 131, Number of suites: 37, Number of floors: 4, Business center, Fitness facilities, Coffee in lobby, Free breakfast, Dry cleaning/laundry service, Free wireless Internet, Accessible bathroom, In-room accessibility equipment for the deaf, Braille or raised signage.

★★
Rodeway Inn Riverside
10518 Magnolia Ave
Riverside CA 92505
(951) 359-0770
$60 - $79
Bed & Pet Discount Offered

Pet Policy: Rodeway Inns charge a fee of $10 per night per pet plus a $50 damage deposit, which is refunded if the room is in order at check out. Max of 2 pets per room. A veterinarian certificate that the pet is on a flea and parasite program is required.. Pets may not be left alone in the room unless crated.

Features: Outdoor pool, Number of rooms: 57, Number of floors: 2, Free breakfast, Free wireless Internet, Business center.

Rocklin

Also see the following nearby communities that have pet friendly lodging: Roseville - 4 miles, Lincoln - 7 miles, Folsom - 10 miles

Heritage Inn Express Rocklin
4480 Rocklin Rd
Rocklin CA 95677
(916) 632-3366
$49 - $59
Bed & Pet Discount Offered

Pet Policy: Pets accepted, $25 fee per stay.

Features: Coffee in lobby, Elevator, Free breakfast, Swimming pool - outdoor seasonal, Parking (free), Multilingual staff, Business center, Free wireless Internet, Dry cleaning/laundry service.

★★

Howard Johnson Express Inn - Rocklin Suites
4420 Rocklin Rd
Rocklin CA 95677
(916) 624-4500
$41 - $179
Bed & Pet Discount Offered

Pet Policy: Pets allowed, $50 per stay.

Features: Number of rooms: 124, Business Center, Elevator, Coffee in lobby, Wireless Internet (additional charge), Parking (free), Multilingual staff, Casino nearby, Swimming pool - outdoor seasonal, Dry cleaning/laundry service.

★★★

Staybridge Suites Rocklin
6664 Lonetree Blvd
Rocklin CA 95765
(916) 781-7500
$90 - $176
Bed & Pet Discount Offered

Pet Policy: Pets up to 60 lbs, $75 for up to 6 nights, $150 for 7 or longer. Must have proof of current vaccinations.

Features: Accessible bathroom, In-room accessibility equipment for the deaf, Braille or raised signage, Business services, Free breakfast, Fitness facilities.

Rohnert Park

Also see the following nearby communities that have pet friendly lodging: Santa Rosa - 8 miles, Petaluma - 8 miles, Sebastopol - 8 miles

Doubletree Sonoma Wine Country
1 Doubletree Dr
Rohnert Park CA 94928
(707) 584-5466
$149 - $150
Bed & Pet Discount Offered

Pet Policy: Pets up to 50 lbs, $50 per stay.

Features Swimming pool - outdoor, Bar/lounge, Room service, Gift shops or newsstand, Number of rooms: 245, Airport transportation (additional charge), Coffee in lobby, Library, Multilingual staff, Complimentary newspapers, Porter/bellhop, Limo or Town Car service available, Restaurant(s), Pool table, Free wireless Internet, Accessible bathroom, In-room accessibility equipment for the deaf, Braille or raised signage, 24-hour business center, Dry cleaning/laundry service, Golf course on site, Outdoor tennis courts 2, Health club.

Rodeway Inn Rohnert Park
6288 Redwood Dr
Rohnert Park CA 94928
(707) 584-1600
$34 - $47
Bed & Pet Discount Offered

Pet Policy: Rodeway Inns charge a fee of $10 per night per pet and require a $50 damage deposit, which is refunded if the room is in order at check out. Max of 2 pets per room. A veterinarian certificate that the pet is on a flea and parasite program is required. Pets may not be left alone in the room unless in a cage.

Features: Business services, Number of rooms: 130, Number of floors: 2, Coffee in lobby, Free breakfast, Complimentary Newspapers, Wireless Internet, Swimming pool - outdoor seasonal, Dry cleaning/laundry service.

Rosemead

Also see the following nearby communities that have pet friendly lodging: San Gabriel - 2 miles, El Monte - 3 miles, South El Monte - 3 miles, Monterey Park - 4 miles, Pasadena - 5 miles, Arcadia - 5 miles, South Pasadena - 5 miles, Pico Rivera - 6 miles, Commerce - 7 miles, Monrovia - 7 miles, Whittier - 8 miles, Bell Gardens - 8 miles, City Of Industry - 9 miles

Rodeway Inn And Suites
3327 N. Del Mar Ave
Rosemead CA 91770
(626) 572-7180
$55 - $64
Bed & Pet Discount Offered

Pet Policy: Rodeway Inns charge a fee of $10 per night per pet and require a $50 damage deposit, which is refunded if the room is in order at check out. Max of 2 pets per room. A veterinarian certificate that the pet is on a flea and parasite program is required. Pets may not be left alone in the room unless in a cage.

Features: Business services, Number of rooms: 30, Free breakfast, Free wireless Internet.

Roseville

Also see the following nearby communities that have pet friendly lodging: Rocklin - 4 miles, North Highlands - 7 miles, Lincoln - 8 miles

Extended Stay America Sacramento - Roseville
1000 Lead Hill Blvd
Roseville CA 95678
(916) 781-9001
$59- $84
Bed & Pet Discount Offered

Pet Policy: One medium-size pet is allowed in each guest room. A $25 per day non-refundable cleaning fee (not to exceed $150) will be charged the first night of your stay.

Features: Guest laundry, Number of rooms: 122, Number of floors: 3, Wireless Internet (additional charge), Parking (free).

Homewood Suites Sacramento Roseville
401 Creekside Ridge Ct
Roseville CA 95678
(916) 783-7455
$95 - $169
Bed & Pet Discount Offered

Pet Policy: Pets up to 25 lbs, $75 per stay.

Features: Elevator, Swimming pool - outdoor, Number of suites: 111, Number of floors: 4, Barbecue grill(s), Free breakfast, Parking (free), Multilingual staff, Designated smoking areas, Accessible bathroom, In-room accessibility equipment for the deaf, Braille or raised signage, Dry cleaning/laundry service, Free wireless Internet, 24-hour business center, Wheelchair accessible, Fitness facilities.

★★★

Larkspur Landing Roseville
1931 Taylor Rd
Roseville CA 95661
(916) 773-1717
$88 - $124
Bed & Pet Discount Offered

Pet Policy: Pets welcome, $75 per pet per stay.

Features: Business Center, Elevator, Room service (limited hours), Concierge services, Number of rooms: 90, Number of floors: 3, Coffee in lobby, Library, Video library, Grocery, Parking (free), Multilingual staff, Complimentary newspapers in lobby, Limo or Town Car service available, Free wireless Internet, Dry cleaning/laundry service, Fitness facilities.

★★½

Orchid Suites
130 N Sunrise Ave
Roseville CA 95661
(800) 882-7848
$71 - $89
Bed & Pet Discount Offered

Pet Policy: Pets up to 25 lbs, $50 per stay.

Features: Bar/lounge, Free breakfast, Elevator, Business services, Swimming pool - outdoor seasonal, 24-hour business center, Free reception, Casino shuttle (free), Shopping center shuttle (free), Number of rooms: 179, Number of floors: 3, Parking (free), Free wireless Internet, Accessible bathroom, In-room accessibility equipment for the deaf, Braille or raised signage, Fitness facilities.

★★★

Residence Inn by Marriott Roseville
1930 Taylor Road
Roseville CA 95661
(916) 772-5500
$144 - $200
Bed & Pet Discount Offered

Pet Policy: Pets allowed, $100 per stay cleaning fee.

Features: Indoor pool, Number of suites: 90, Number of floors: 3, BBQ area, Coffee in lobby, Free breakfast, Grocery, Children's swimming pool, Complimentary newspapers, Concierge, Smoke-Free, Free wireless Internet, Dry cleaning/laundry service, Fitness facilities

Towneplace Suites Marriott Roseville
10569 Fairway Dr
Roseville CA 95678
(916) 782-2232
$89 - $165
Bed & Pet Discount Offered

Pet Policy: Pets allowed, $100 per stay.

Features: Swimming pool - indoor, Coffee in lobby, Number of suites: 115, Number of floors: 4, Free breakfast, Parking (free), Accessible bathroom, In-room accessibility equipment for the deaf, Braille or raised signage, Dry cleaning/laundry service, Free wireless Internet, Business services, Guest laundry, Elevator, Fitness facilities.

Sacramento

Also see the following nearby communities that have pet friendly lodging: West Sacramento - 4 miles, North Highlands - 9 miles,

Not rated:
Adren Acres Executive Suites and Cottages
2421 Clay Street
Sacramento CA 95815
(916) 402-7732
$71 - $129

Pet Policy: We only have a few cottages available for pets. Our pet security deposit is a minimum of $500. If you have pets, it is the guest's responsibility to cover all furniture. (Please ask for the covers if they are not in the cottage). Otherwise, there is $150 furniture cleaning charge .Also, we use a black lite to examine the carpet for animal secretions. (Carpet replacement is $750) We are sorry for being so strict, but our cottages are almost all new and our next guests expect them to be clean.

Features: Fully stocked kitchen, Wireless Internet, Cable TV and DVD player, Business center.

Best Western Expo Inn
1413 Howe Ave
Sacramento CA 95825
(916) 922-9833
$89 - $109
Bed & Pet Discount Offered

Pet Policy: Pets allowed. $25 per day.

Features: Free breakfast, Airport transportation (additional charge), Outdoor pool, Number of rooms: 125, Number of floors: 2, Coffee in lobby, Multilingual staff, Complimentary newspapers, Security guard, Free wireless Internet, Dry cleaning/laundry service, Fitness facilities.

Not rated:
Best Western John Jay Inn
15 Massie Court
Sacramento CA 95823
(916) 689-4425
$62 - $118

Pet Policy: Pets accepted on advance approval. Please contact hotel directly for reservations.

Features: Free continental breakfast, Free wireless Internet, HBO, Outdoor pool, spa and sauna, Exercise equipment, Guest laundry.

Best Western Sandman Motel
236 Jibboom Street
Sacramento CA 95814
(916) 443-6515
$67 - $109

Pet Policy: Pets allowed, $25 per stay.

Features: Wireless Internet, HBO, Free continental breakfast, Outdoor swimming pool and hot tub, Airport shuttle, Restaurant.

Clarion Hotel Mansion Inn
700 16th St
Sacramento CA 95814
(916) 444-8000
$69 - $99
Bed & Pet Discount Offered

Pet Policy: Pet accommodation: $50 per stay. Pet limit: 2 pets per room maximum 50 pounds.

Features: Complimentary newspapers , Free wireless Internet, Business Center, Number of rooms: 103, Dry cleaning/laundry service, ATM/banking, Free breakfast, Outdoor pool.

Days Inn Downtown
228 Jibboom Street
Sacramento CA 95814
(916) 443-4811
$43 - $94
Bed & Pet Discount Offered

Pet Policy: Pets welcome, $10 per pet per night.

Features: Business center, Airport transportation (free), Guest laundry, Free breakfast, Parking (free), Multilingual staff, Complimentary newspapers in lobby, Free wireless Internet, Swimming pool - outdoor seasonal.

Doubletree Hotel Sacramento
2001 Point West Way
Sacramento CA 95815
(916) 929-8855
$89 - $109
Bed & Pet Discount Offered

Pet Policy: Pets up to 30 lbs, $50 fee per stay.

Features: Swimming pool - outdoor, Bar/Lounge, Room service (limited hours), ATM/banking, Pool table, Elevator, Restaurant(s), Gift shops or newsstand, Number of rooms: 448, Number of floors: 4, Business services, Dry cleaning/laundry service, Breakfast available (additional charge), Pool table on site, Nightclub, Multilingual staff, Complimentary newspapers in lobby, Porter/bellhop, Security guard, Limo or Town Car service available, Free wireless Internet, Parking (additional charge), Fitness facilities.

Econo Lodge Sacramento
711 16th St
Sacramento CA 95814
(916) 443-6631
$59 - $69
Bed & Pet Discount Offered

Pet Policy: Pets accepted, $6 per night per pet.

Features: Coffee in lobby, Elevator, Gift shops or newsstand, Number of rooms: 40, Number of floors: 3, Business services, Free breakfast, Parking (free) 24-hour front desk

Extended Stay America Sacramento - Arden Way
2100 Havard St
Sacramento CA 95815
(916) 921-9942
$54 - $69
Bed & Pet Discount Offered

Pet Policy: One pet is allowed in each guest room. A $25 per day non-refundable cleaning fee (not to exceed $150) will be charged the first night of your stay.

Features: Guest laundry, Elevator, Number of rooms: 120, Number of floors: 3, Wireless Internet (additional charge), Parking (free), Front desk (limited hours).

Extended Stay America Sacramento - Northgate
3825 Rosin Ct
Sacramento CA 95834
(916) 920-8199
$49 - $74
Bed & Pet Discount Offered

Pet Policy: One pet is allowed in each guest room. A $25 per day non-refundable cleaning fee (not to exceed $150) will be charged the first night of your stay.

Features: Guest laundry, Elevator, Number of rooms: 120, Number of floors: 3, Business services, Wireless Internet (additional charge), Parking (free) Front desk (limited hours), Security guard.

Hawthorn Suites by Wyndham Sacramento
321 Bercut Dr
Sacramento CA 95814
(916) 441-1200
$71 - $119
Bed & Pet Discount Offered

Pet Policy: Pets welcome, $25 per stay.

Features: Free Breakfast, Swimming pool - outdoor, Bar/lounge, Elevator, Airport transportation (free) upon availability, Number of rooms: 272, Number of floors: 3, Barbecue grill(s), Parking (free), Security guard, Free wireless Internet, Dry cleaning/laundry service, Fitness facilities

Hilton Sacramento Arden West
2200 Harvard St
Sacramento CA 95815
(916) 922-4700
$92 - $264
Bed & Pet Discount Offered

Pet Policy: Pets up to 75 lbs, $75 per stay cleaning fee.

Features: Business Center, Bar/Lounge, Swimming pool - outdoor, Parking (free), ATM/banking, Restaurant(s), Room service (limited hours), Concierge services, Gift shops or newsstand, Number of rooms: 331, Number of floors: 12, Wireless Internet (additional charge), Breakfast available (additional charge), Multilingual staff, Porter/bellhop, Limo or Town Car service available, Sauna, Smoke-Free property, Security guard, Accessible bathroom, Accessibility equipment for the deaf, Braille or raised signage, Dry cleaning/laundry service, Fitness facilities, Elevator

Holiday Inn Express Sacramento Convention Center
728 16th St
Sacramento CA 95814
(916) 444-4436
$70 - $160
Bed & Pet Discount Offered

Pet Policy: Pets allowed, $50 per stay.

Features: Accessible bathroom, Accessibility equipment for the deaf, Braille or raised signage, Room service, Number of rooms: 132, Number of floors: 4, Airport transportation (additional charge), Free breakfast, Parking (free) Multilingual staff, Complimentary, Business center, Free wireless Internet, Smoke-Free property, Nearby fitness center (discount), Dry cleaning/laundry.

Homestead Sacramento - South Natomas
2810-2830 Gateway Oaks Dr
Sacramento CA 95833
(916) 564-7500
$64 - $74
Bed & Pet Discount Offered

Pet Policy: Pets allowed, no size restriction, $25 per day to a maximum of $150 per stay. Limit of 1 pet per room.

Features: Guest laundry, Nearby fitness center (discount), Number of rooms: 144, Number of floors: 2, Suitable for children, Barbecue grill(s), Wireless Internet (additional charge), Parking (free).

La Quinta Inn Sacramento Downtown
200 Jibboom St
Sacramento CA 95814
(916) 448-8100
$42 - $60
Bed & Pet Discount Offered

Pet Policy: Cats and dogs up to 50 pounds are accepted in all guest rooms. Housekeeping services for rooms with pets require pet owner be present or pet must be crated. No fees or deposits are required.

Features: Elevator, Airport transportation (free), Number of rooms: 168, Number of floors: 3, Business services, Guest laundry, Parking (free) Accessible bathroom, Multilingual staff, Free wireless Internet, Free breakfast, Swimming pool - outdoor, Fitness facilities.

La Quinta Inn Sacramento North
4604 Madison Ave
Sacramento CA 95841
(916) 348-0900
$55 - $79
Bed & Pet Discount Offered

Pet Policy: Cats and dogs up to 50 pounds are accepted in all guest rooms. Housekeeping services for rooms with pets require pet owner be present or pet must be crated. No fees or deposits are required.

Features: Nearby fitness center (free), Elevator, Swimming pool - outdoor, Accessible bathroom, Number of rooms: 127, Business services, Coffee in lobby, Free breakfast, Parking (free) Multilingual staff, Dry cleaning/laundry service, Free Internet.

Larkspur Landing Sacramento
555 Howe Ave
Sacramento CA 95825
(916) 646-1212
$99 - $199
Bed & Pet Discount Offered

Pet Policy: Pets welcome, $75 per pet per stay.

Features: Coffee in lobby, Business services, Barbecue grill(s), Video library, Free breakfast, Grocery, Parking (free), Multilingual staff, Complimentary newspapers, Porter/bellhop, Security guard, Limo or Town Car service available, Smoke-Free property, Nearby fitness center (discount), Dry cleaning/laundry service.

Not rated
Marriott Exeustay Harbor Oaks
2227 River Plaza Drive
Sacramento CA 95833
(916) 641-7999
$109 - $110

Pet Policy: Pets up to 75 lbs, $250 additional per pet per stay. Limit 2.

Features: Furnished apartments, Free wireless Internet, Cable TV, Full kitchen. Minimum stay of 30 days required.

★★
Motel 6 Cal Expo Sacramento
2030 Arden Way
Sacramento CA 95825
(916) 929-5600
$54 - $64
Bed & Pet Discount Offered

Pet Policy: Well-behaved pets stay Free. Animals that pose a health or safety risk may not remain onsite, and include those that, in our manager's discretion, are too numerous for any one room, cause damage to our property or that of other guests, are too disruptive, are not properly attended, or demonstrate undue aggression. All pets must be declared at check-in. Pets must be attended to and under control at all times. If unavoidable circumstances require a pet to remain in a room while the owner is offsite, the pet must be secured in a crate or travel carrier. Pets must be on a leash or securely carried outside of guest rooms.

Features: Swimming pool - outdoor Coffee in lobby, Business center, Number of rooms: 191, Number of floors: 2, Business services, Parking (free), Multilingual staff, Accessible bathroom, Accessibility equipment for the deaf, Braille or raised signage, Dry cleaning/laundry service, Free wireless Internet.

Quality Inn Natomas
3796 Northgate Blvd
Sacramento CA 95834
(916) 927-7117
$44 - $64
Bed & Pet Discount Offered

Pet Policy: Quality Inns accept any well-behaved pets with a maximum of 3 per room, $10 per night per pet, 70 pound weight limit. Pets may not be left alone in the room unless in a cage

Features: Swimming pool - outdoor, Business services, Coffee in lobby, Free breakfast, Parking (free), Security guard, Wireless Internet, Airport transportation (free), Number of rooms: 132.

Radisson Sacramento
500 Leisure Ln
Sacramento CA 95815
(951) 729-8530
$70 - $204
Bed & Pet Discount Offered

Pet Policy: Pets allowed, $50 per stay. No cats.

Features: Bar/lounge, Business center, Room service, Airport transportation (additional charge), Restaurant(s), Gift shop, Number of rooms: 306, Number of floors: 2, Breakfast available (additional charge), Multilingual staff, Complimentary newspapers, Porter/bellhop, Security guard, Concierge, Outdoor pool - seasonal, Accessible bathroom, Accessibility equipment for the deaf, Dry cleaning/laundry service, Free wireless Internet, Fitness facilities.

Ramada Sacramento
2600 Auburn Blvd
Sacramento CA 95821
(916) 442-6971
$71 - $99
Bed & Pet Discount Offered

Pet Policy: Pets welcome, $20 per pet per day.

Features: Outdoor pool, Number of rooms: 174, Number of floors: 4, Free breakfast, Restaurant(s), Business services, Coffee in lobby, Multilingual staff, Complimentary newspapers, Security guard, Smoke-Free, Wheelchair accessible, On-site car rental, Free wireless Internet, Guest laundry, Bar/lounge.

Residence Inn By Marriott Sacramento
1530 Howe Ave
Sacramento CA 95825
(916) 920-9111
$84 - $179
Bed & Pet Discount Offered

Pet Policy: Pets allowed, $100 per stay cleaning fee.

Features: BBQ area, Coffee in lobby, Free breakfast, Grocery, Parking (free), Complimentary newspapers, Nearby fitness center (free), Free wireless Internet, Swimming pool - outdoor, Accessible bathroom, Accessibility equipment for the deaf, Braille or raised signage, Dry cleaning/laundry service.

Residence Inn by Marriott Sacramento at Capitol Pa
1121 15th Street
Sacramento CA 95814
(916) 443-0500
$109 - $249
Bed & Pet Discount Offered

Pet Policy: Pets allowed, $100 per stay cleaning fee.

Features: Free breakfast, Swimming pool - outdoor, ATM/banking, Number of rooms: 235, Number of floors: 15, Free Internet, Parking $17 Daily.

Residence Inn By Marriott Sacramento South Natomas
2410 W El Camino Ave
Sacramento CA 95833
(916) 649-1300
$89 - $169
Bed & Pet Discount Offered

Pet Policy: Pets allowed, $75 per stay cleaning fee.

Features: Babysitting or child care, Swimming pool - outdoor, Number of rooms: 126, Number of floors: 2, Free breakfast, Parking (free), Complimentary newspapers in lobby, Airport transportation (free), Free wireless Internet, Fitness facilities.

Sheraton Grand Sacramento Hotel
1230 J St
Sacramento CA 95814
(916) 447-1700
$119 - $309
Bed & Pet Discount Offered

Pet Policy: Pets accepted, $100 per stay. The Sheraton Sweet Sleeper Dog Bed Available

Features: ATM/Banking, Steam Room, Bar/Lounge, Restaurant(s), Room service (limited hours), Swimming pool - outdoor, Gift shops or newsstand, Number of rooms: 503, Number of floors: 26, Business services, Wireless Internet (additional charge), Breakfast available (additional charge), Multilingual staff, Complimentary newspapers in lobby, Concierge desk, Smoke-Free property, Porter/bellhop, Security guard, Limo or Town Car service available, Marina on site, Dry cleaning/laundry service, Parking garage (additional charge), Fitness facilities.

★★★
Staybridge Suites Natomas
104 Promenade Cir
Sacramento CA 95834
(916) 575-7907
$129 - $200
Bed & Pet Discount Offered

Pet Policy: Pets under 80 lbs accepted, $75 per stay. Must have proof of current vaccinations

Features: Swimming pool - outdoor, Accessible bathroom, Accessibility equipment for the deaf, Braille or raised signage, Elevator, Number of suites: 117, Number of floors: 4, Barbecue grill(s), Coffee in lobby, Free breakfast, Grocery, Parking (free) Business center, Free wireless Internet, Dry cleaning/laundry service, Fitness facilities.

★★
Super 8 Sacramento Florin CA
7216 55th St
Sacramento CA 95823
(916) 427-7925
$40 - $53
Bed & Pet Discount Offered

Pet Policy: Pets permitted, $10 per pet per night.

Features: Business services, Free breakfast, Coffee in lobby, Parking (free), Swimming pool - outdoor seasonal, Number of rooms: 61, Number of floors: 3, Free wireless Internet, Guest laundry.

The Citizen Hotel, a Joie de Vivre Boutique Hotel
926 J Street
Sacramento CA 95814
(916) 447-2700
$159 - $279
Bed & Pet Discount Offered

Pet Policy: Dogs only, $100 refundable deposit.

Features: Parking (valet) $25/Day, Restaurant(s), ATM/banking, Multilingual staff, Porter/bellhop, Limo or Town Car service available, Smoke-Free property, Media library, Room service, Accessible bathroom, Accessibility equipment for the deaf, Braille or raised signage, Dry cleaning/laundry service, Wireless Internet (additional charge), Business center, Free reception.

TownePlace Suites Marriott Cal Expo
1784 Tribute Rd
Sacramento CA 95815
(916) 920-5400
$89 - $124
Bed & Pet Discount Offered

Pet Policy: Pets allowed. $100 cleaning fee.

Features: Outdoor pool Number of rooms: 118, Number of floors: 4, Free breakfast, Complimentary newspapers, Business center, Security guard, Free wireless Internet, Dry cleaning/laundry service, BBQ area, Smoke-Free , Fitness facilities.

★★

Travelodge Sacramento
9646 Micron Ave
Sacramento CA 95827
(916) 361-3131
$32 - $111
Bed & Pet Discount Offered

Pet Policy: Pets allowed, $10 per pet per night.

Features: Coffee in lobby, Swimming pool - outdoor, Number of rooms: 94, Number of floors: 3, Wireless Internet (additional charge), Guest laundry, Parking (free).

★★

Vagabond Inn Executive Old Town
909 3rd St
Sacramento CA 95814
(916) 446-1481
$75 - $84
Bed & Pet Discount Offered

Pet Policy: Pets accepted in smoking rooms only. Nightly fee.

Features: Outdoor pool, Free wireless Internet, Free breakfast, Airport transportation (free), Elevator, Number of rooms: 108, Business services, Coffee in lobby, Multilingual staff, Complimentary newspapers, Security guard, Accessible bathroom, Accessibility equipment for the deaf, Braille or raised signage, Dry cleaning/laundry service, Fitness facilities.

Vagabond Inn Midtown
1319 30th St
Sacramento CA 95816
(916) 454-4400
$55 - $62
Bed & Pet Discount Offered

Pet Policy: Pets accepted, $10 per night.

Features: Free Breakfast, Number of rooms: 81, Number of floors: 3, Coffee in lobby, Guest laundry, Parking (free), Multilingual staff, Complimentary newspapers in lobby, Swimming pool – outdoor.

Salida

Also see the following nearby communities that have pet friendly lodging: Ripon - 5 miles, Modesto - 6 miles, Ceres - 10 miles, Manteca - 10 miles

La Quinta Inn & Suites
4909 Sisk Rd
Salida CA 95368
(209) 579-8723
$94 - $107
Bed & Pet Discount Offered

Pet Policy: Pets welcome, no extra fee but owner responsible for any damage.

Features: Outdoor pool, Free breakfast, Accessible bathroom, Gift shops or newsstand, Number of rooms: 67, Number of floors: 3, Coffee in lobby, Complimentary newspapers, Security guard, Free wireless Internet, Dry cleaning/laundry service, Business center, Fitness facilities.

Salinas

Also see the following nearby communities that have pet friendly lodging: Marina - 9 miles

Not rated
Inns of California Salinas
555 Airport Blvd
Salinas CA 93905
(831) 424-1741
$71 - $93

Pet Policy: Pet friendly.

Features: Number of rooms: 96, Free wireless Internet, Business center, Heated pool, Coffee maker.

★★★
Residence Inn by Marriott Salinas Monterey
17215 El Rancho Way
Salinas CA 93907
(831) 775-0410
$155 - $190
Bed & Pet Discount Offered

Pet Policy: Pets allowed, $100 per stay cleaning fee.

Features: Indoor pool, Free Breakfast, Concierge, Number of suites: 107, Number of floors: 3, BBQ area, Coffee in lobby, Health club, Multilingual staff, Complimentary newspapers, Business center, Security guard, Free wireless Internet, Dry cleaning/laundry service.

★★
Super 8 Salinas
131 Kern Street
Salinas CA 93905
(831) 758-4693
$59 - $209
Bed & Pet Discount Offered

Pet Policy: Pets accepted. $15 fee.

Features: Swimming pool - outdoor, Number of floors: 2.

San Bernardino

Also see the following nearby communities that have pet friendly lodging: Colton - 4 miles, Rialto - 5 miles, Redlands - 6 miles

Best Western Hospitality Lane
294 E Hospitality Ln
San Bernardino CA 92408
(909) 381-1681
$74 - $99
Bed & Pet Discount Offered

Pet Policy: Pets allowed, $10 per day.

Features: Swimming pool - outdoor, Number of rooms: 83, Number of floors: 2, Business services, Free breakfast, Parking (free) Complimentary newspapers in lobby, Free wireless Internet.

Days Inn San Bernardino/Hospitality Lane
1909 Business Center Dr
San Bernardino CA 92408
(909) 889-0090
$58 - $114
Bed & Pet Discount Offered

Pet Policy: Pets under 20 lbs, $25 per day. Limit of 1 pet per room.

Features: Swimming pool - outdoor, Gift shops or newsstand, Number of rooms: 55, Number of floors: 2, Business services, Coffee in lobby, Free breakfast, Parking (free), Multilingual staff, Complimentary newspapers in lobby, Use of nearby fitness center (free)..

Econo Lodge San Bernardino
450 N G Street
San Bernardino CA 92410
(909) 885-0055
$54 - $70
Bed & Pet Discount Offered

Pet Policy: Pets up to 25 lbs, $50 per stay.

Features: Bar/lounge, Number of rooms: 82, Number of floors: 3, Airport transportation (additional charge), Free breakfast, Multilingual staff, Business center, Free wireless Internet, Dry cleaning/laundry service, Fitness facilities.

Hilton San Bernardino
285 E Hospitality Ln
San Bernardino CA 92408
(909) 889-0133
$103 - $180
Bed & Pet Discount Offered

Pet Policy: Pets up to 75 lbs, $50 per stay.

Features: Outdoor pool, Bar/Lounge, Restaurant(s), Concierge, Gift shop, Number of rooms: 238, Number of suites: 13, Number of floors: 7, Breakfast available (additional charge), Multilingual staff, Porter/bellhop, Security guard, Medical assistance available, Free wireless Internet, Nearby fitness center (discount), Dry cleaning/laundry, Room service, Wheelchair accessible, Coffee in lobby, Accessible bathroom, Accessibility equipment for the deaf, Braille or raised signage, Business center.

La Quinta Inn San Bernardino
205 E Hospitality Ln
San Bernardino CA 92408
(909) 888-7571
$49 - $99
Bed & Pet Discount Offered

Pet Policy: Cats and dogs up to 50 pounds are accepted in all guest rooms. Housekeeping services for rooms with pets require pet owner be present or pet must be crated. No fees or deposits are required.

Features: Accessible bathroom, Number of rooms: 153, Number of floors: 3, Coffee in lobby, Free breakfast, Multilingual staff, Nearby fitness center (free), Free Internet, Swimming pool - outdoor.

Quality Inn San Bernardino
1750 S Waterman Ave
San Bernardino CA 92408
(909) 888-4827
$74 - $80
Bed & Pet Discount Offered

Pet Policy: Pets up to 20 lbs, $50 per stay. Limit 1 pet per room.

Features: Outdoor pool Free breakfast, Guest laundry, Business services, Gift shops or newsstand, Number of rooms: 118, Number of floors: 3, Multilingual staff.

Residence Inn by Marriott San Bernardino
1040 Harriman Pl
San Bernardino CA 92408
(909) 382-4564
$140 - $180
Bed & Pet Discount Offered

Pet Policy: Pets allowed, $75 per stay cleaning fee

Features: Free breakfast, Business services, Swimming pool - indoor, Restaurant(s), Concierge services, Coffee in lobby, Parking (free), Smoke-Free property, Accessible bathroom, Accessibility equipment for the deaf, Braille or raised signage, Free wireless Internet, Fitness facilities.

Rodeway Inn San Bernardino
607 W 5th St
San Bernardino CA 92410
(909) 383-1500
$54 - $69
Bed & Pet Discount Offered

Pet Policy: Rodeway Inns charge a fee of $10 per night per pet plus a $50 damage deposit. Max of 2 pets per room. A veterinarian certificate that the pet is on a flea and parasite program is required. Pets may not be left alone in the room unless in a cage.

Features: Business services, Swimming pool - outdoor, Number of rooms: 51, Number of floors: 2, Free breakfast, Multilingual staff, Free Internet.

★★

San Bernardino Days Inn
1386 E Highland Ave
San Bernardino CA 92404
(909) 881-1702
$43 - $64
Bed & Pet Discount Offered

Pet Policy: Pets accepted, $25 per pet per day. Limit 2 per room.

Features: Restaurant(s), Outdoor pool, Number of rooms: 44, Number of floors: 2, Complimentary newspapers in lobby, Front desk (limited hours)

Super 8 San Bernardino
225 E Hospitality Lane
San Bernardino CA 92408
(909) 888-6777
$44 - $74
Bed & Pet Discount Offered

Pet Policy: Pets allowed, $9 per pet per night.

Features: Free breakfast, Business services, Coffee in lobby, Parking (free), Swimming pool - outdoor seasonal.

San Bruno

Also see the following nearby communities that have pet friendly lodging: South San Francisco - 2 miles, Millbrae - 3 miles, Burlingame - 4 miles, Brisbane - 4 miles, San Mateo - 7 miles, Montara - 8 miles, Moss Beach - 8 miles, Belmont - 10 miles, San Francisco - 10 miles.

Regency Inn SFO Airport
411 E San Bruno Ave
San Bruno CA 94066
(650) 589-7535
$49 - $69
Bed & Pet Discount Offered

Pet Policy: Pets accepted with fee.

Features: Number of rooms: 30, Number of floors: 2, Free breakfast, Parking (free) Parking (additional charge), Free wireless Internet.

★★★

Staybridge Suites San Francisco Airport
1350 Huntington Ave
San Bruno CA 94066
(650) 588-0770
$105 - $220
Bed & Pet Discount Offered

Pet Policy: Pet policy standard- $15 fee for the first night and a $10 fee for every additional night with a cap of $150. No pets over 80 lbs accepted.

Features: Business services, Airport transportation (free), Outdoor pool, Gift shop, Number of rooms: 92, Number of floors: 3, BBQ area, Free breakfast, Grocery, Multilingual staff, Complimentary newspapers, Nearby fitness center (discount), Accessible bathroom, Accessibility equipment for the deaf, Braille or raised signage, Dry cleaning/laundry.

San Carlos

Also see the following nearby communities that have pet friendly lodging: Belmont - 2 miles, Redwood City - 3 miles, San Mateo - 5 miles, Menlo Park - 6 miles, Burlingame - 8 miles, Palo Alto - 9 miles, Millbrae - 9 miles

Homestead San Francisco/San Carlos
3 Circle Star Way
San Carlos CA 94070
(650) 368-2600
$59 - $84
Bed & Pet Discount Offered

Pet Policy: Pets allowed, no size restriction, $25 per day to a maximum of $150 per stay. Limit of 1 pet per room.

Features: Business services, Coffee in lobby, Guest laundry, Number of rooms: 116, BBQ area, Wireless Internet, Nearby fitness center (discount).

San Clemente

Also see the following nearby communities that have pet friendly lodging: Capistrano Beach - 3 miles, Dana Point - 5 miles, San Juan Capistrano - 7 miles

Always Inn San Clemente Bed & Breakfast
177 Avenida Cabrillo
San Clemente CA 92672
(949) 374-6165
$149 - $150
Bed & Pet Discount Offered

Pet Policy: Pet Friendly. $25 per pet per night.

Features: Business services, Free Breakfast, Guest laundry, Supervised child care/activities, Concierge services, Barbecue grill(s), Coffee in lobby, Video library, Parking (free), Complimentary newspapers in lobby, Smoke-Free property, Free wireless Internet.

Not rated.

BW Plus Casablanca Inn
1601 N El Camino Real
San Clemente CA 92672
(949) 361-1644
$80 - $134

Pet Policy: Pets accepted on advance approval. Please contact the hotel directly.

Features: Microwave and mini fridge, Free continental breakfast, Outdoor heated pool and hot tub, Fitness facility.

Not rated

Four Seasons Pacifica
326 Encino Lane
San Clemente CA 92672
(949) 492-6103
$250 - $300

Pet Policy: Pets under 25 lbs allowed, no fee. Pets must be leashed when out of room, may not be left in room alone, and are not permitted in food, pool or health club areas.

Features: 2 & 3 bedroom suites, Fully equipped kitchens, Jacuzzi tubs.

★★★

Holiday Inn San Clemente
111 S Ave De La Estrella
San Clemente CA 92672
(949) 361-3000
$109 - $184
Bed & Pet Discount Offered

Pet Policy: Pets welcome, $20 per night per pet.

Features: Bar/lounge, Restaurant(s), Room service (limited hours), Swimming pool - outdoor, Concierge services, Number of rooms: 72, Number of suites: 20, Number of floors: 3, Airport transportation (additional charge), ***Continued on next page***

Holiday Inn San Clemente
Continued from previous page

Coffee in lobby, Multilingual staff, Complimentary newspapers in lobby, Wireless Internet, Parking garage, Accessibility equipment for the deaf, Braille or raised signage, Business services, Accessible bathroom, Dry cleaning/laundry service, Fitness facilities.

Not rated
Sea Horse Resort
602 Avenida Victoria
San Clemente CA 92672
(949) 492-1720
$109 - $259

Pet Policy: Pets up to 50 lbs accepted, $200 refundable deposit. Limit 2 pets per room.

Features: Furnished apartments, Fully equipped kitchens, Free beach access, Beach umbrellas.

San Diego

Also see the following nearby communities that have pet friendly lodging: La Mesa - 6 miles, La Jolla - 9 miles, National City - 9 miles

Andaz San Diego - a Hyatt Hotel
600 F St
San Diego CA 92101
(619) 849-1234
$126 - $499
Bed & Pet Discount Offered

Pet Policy: Pets up to 40 lbs, $150 per stay. Larger pets will be considered if you contact the hotel directly in advance.

Features: Poolside bar, Outdoor pool, Bar/lounge, Shoe shine, Spa services, Business services, Parking (valet) $30 Daily, Restaurant(s), Shopping on site, Number of rooms: 159, Number of floors: 6, Breakfast available (additional charge), Health club, Room service (24 hours), Multilingual staff, Complimentary newspapers, Porter/bellhop, Doorman/doorwoman, Limo or Town Car service available, Medical assistance available, Concierge, Smoke-Free property, Technology helpdesk, Accessible bathroom, Accessibility equipment for the deaf, Braille or raised signage, Dry cleaning/laundry service, Wheelchair accessible, Security guard, Free wireless Internet, Area shuttle (free), Nightclub.

Not rated
Best Western Americanna Inn
815 West San Ysidro Blvd
San Diego CA 92173
(619) 428-5521
$62 - $69
Bed & Pet Discount Offered

Pet Policy: Pets up to 80 lbs accepted, $20 per night plus $50 refundable deposit.

Features: Wet bar and refrigerator, Free continental breakfast, Outdoor heated swimming pool and spa.

★★
Best Western Lamplighter Inn at SDSU
6474 EL CAJON BLVD
San Diego CA 92115-2645
(619) 582-3088
$80 - $164

Pet Policy: Pets allowed. $15 per pet per night.

Features: Free wireless Internet, HBO, Free movies, Coffee maker, Iron & board, Free continental breakfast, Heated outdoor swimming pool.

★★
Best Western Mission Bay
2575 Clairemont Dr
San Diego CA 92117
(619) 275-5700
$64 - $189
Bed & Pet Discount Offered

Pet Policy: Allows dogs only, under 25 pounds. $250 refundable damage deposit.

Features: Business services, Swimming pool - outdoor, Concierge services, Number of rooms: 101, Number of floors: 3, Coffee in lobby, Free breakfast, Parking (free) Multilingual staff, Complimentary newspapers in lobby, Free wireless Internet, Accessible bathroom, Accessibility equipment for the deaf, Braille or raised signage.

★★★½
Bristol Hotel
1055 1st Ave
San Diego CA 92101
(619) 232-6141
$110 - $289
Bed & Pet Discount Offered

Pet Policy: Welcome amenity upon arrival for your pet. Pet bowls and pet bed placed in your room for your pet's use throughout your stay. Nightly turndown service for you and your pet. No pet deposit required.

Features: Business services, Bar/lounge, Number of rooms: 102, Number of floors: 8, Pool table, Concierge services, Elevator, ATM/banking, Wheelchair accessible, Health club, Multilingual staff, Complimentary newspapers in lobby, Restaurant(s), Porter/bellhop, Doorman/doorwoman, Smoke-Free property, Parking (valet) $22 Daily, Accessible bathroom, Dry cleaning/laundry service, Free wireless Internet, Security guard, Technology support staff, Room service, Breakfast available (additional charge).

★★
Cabrillo Inn and Suites
1150 Rosecrans St
San Diego CA 92106
(619) 223-5544
$45 - $80
Bed & Pet Discount Offered

Pet Policy: Pet Friendly

Features: Elevator, Wheelchair accessible, Parking (free), Business services, Free breakfast, Free wireless Internet, Number of rooms: 18, Number of suites: 1, , Number of floors: 2, Complimentary newspapers in lobby, Designated smoking areas, Accessible bathroom, Braille or raised signage.

Comfort Inn Mission Bay SeaWorld Area
4540 Mission Bay Drive
San Diego CA 92109
(858) 274-7888
$59 - $119
Bed & Pet Discount Offered

Pet Policy: Pet Accommodation: $25 per day Pet Limit: 2 pets in room, up to 45 lbs.

Features: Elevator, Free breakfast, Parking (free), Multilingual staff, Complimentary newspapers in lobby, Wheelchair accessible, Coffee in lobby, Dry cleaning/laundry service, Smoke-Free property, Free wireless Internet, Accessible bathroom, Accessibility equipment for the deaf, Braille or raised signage, 24-hour business center, Swimming pool - outdoor, Number of rooms: 116, Number of floors: 3, Fitness facilities.

★★★½
Crowne Plaza Hanalei San Diego - Mission Valley
2270 Hotel Cir N
San Diego CA 92108
(619) 297-1101
$95 - $149
Bed & Pet Discount Offered

Pet Policy: Pets welcome, $75 per stay.

Features: Business Center, Swimming pool - outdoor, Number of rooms: 417, Number of suites: 12, Number of floors: 8, Wireless Internet (additional charge), Breakfast available (additional charge), Multilingual staff, Complimentary newspapers in lobby, Porter/bellhop, Massage - treatment room(s), Concierge desk, Hair salon, Nearby fitness center (discount), Parking (additional charge) $12 Per Day, ATM/banking, Bar/lounge, Security guard, Computer rental, Spa services on site, Room service (limited hours), Restaurant(s), Gift shops or newsstand, Shopping on site, Accessible bathroom, Accessibility equipment for the deaf, Braille or raised signage, Dry cleaning/laundry.

★★★½
Doubletree Golf Resort San Diego
14455 Penasquitos Drive
San Diego CA 92129
(858) 672-9100
$79 - $144
Bed & Pet Discount Offered

Pet Policy: Accepts pets up to 50 lbs, $30 per night.

Features: Fitness facilities, Children's swimming pool, Smoke-Free property, Golf course, 2 outdoor pools, Business Center, Guest laundry, Bar/lounge, Sauna, Steam room, ATM/Banking, Restaurant(s), Gift shops or newsstand, Number of rooms: 174, Number of floors: 3, Airport transportation (additional charge), Breakfast available (additional charge), Health club, Multilingual staff, Room service, Free wireless Internet, Massage - treatment room(s), Billiards, Parking (additional charge) $8/day, Outdoor tennis courts: 5.

★★★
Doubletree Hotel San Diego - Del Mar
11915 El Camino Real
San Diego CA 92130
(858) 481-5900
$111 - $198
Bed & Pet Discount Offered

Pet Policy: The Doubletree Hotel Del Mar's pet policy is very simple and it is only a one-time charge of $50 for your pet's stay! If you have more than one pet, the charge will still be $50!! Upon check-in you will be asked to register your pet to ensure your pet's safety and security. After checking in your pet, they will receive a dog tag that identifies your pet as a VIP (Very Important Pet).

Features: Outdoor pool, Bar/lounge, Concierge, Room service, Wheelchair accessible, Restaurant, Number of rooms: 224, Number of floors: 5, Grocery/convenience store, Gift shop, Free wireless Internet, Breakfast available (additional charge), Parking (free), Children's swimming pool, Multilingual staff, Complimentary newspapers, Porter/bellhop, Dry cleaning/laundry service, Business center, Accessible bathroom, Fitness center, Area shuttle (free), Designated smoking areas.

Doubletree Hotel San Diego Mission Valley
7450 Hazard Center Dr
San Diego CA 92108
(619) 297-5466
$119 - $189
Bed & Pet Discount Offered

Pet Policy: Pets up to 75 lbs, $75 per stay.

Features: Wireless Internet (additional charge), Accessible bathroom, Accessibility equipment for the deaf, Braille or raised signage, Tennis on site, Number of rooms: 300, Number of floors: 11, Breakfast available (additional charge) Multilingual staff, Complimentary newspapers, Porter/bellhop, Security guard, Massage - treatment room(2), Indoor & Outdoor pools, Concierge, Parking (valet) $18 Daily, Restaurant(s), Gift shop, Dry cleaning/laundry service, Room service (limited hours), Suitable for children, Sauna, Business center, Fitness facilities, Piano.

★★★½
Embassy Suites San Diego Bay
601 Pacific Hwy
San Diego CA 92101
(619) 239-2400
$119 - $175
Bed & Pet Discount Offered

Pet Policy: Pets up to 75 lbs, $75 fee.

Features: Free Breakfast, Bar/lounge, Babysitting or child care, Beauty services, Business center, Room service (limited hours), Shoe shine, Swimming pool - indoor, Concierge, 2 Restaurants, Wheelchair accessible, Shopping on site, Coffee in lobby, Number of suites: 337, Number of floors: 12, Wireless Internet (additional charge), Pool table, Multilingual staff, Complimentary newspapers in lobby, Porter/bellhop, Doorman/doorwoman, Security guard, Designated smoking areas, Grocery/convenience store, Accessible bathroom, Accessibility equipment for the deaf, Braille or raised signage, Dry cleaning/laundry service, Fitness facilities, Free reception.

★★
ESA San Diego Hotel Circle
2085 Hotel Circle South
San Diego CA 92108
(619) 296-5570
$71 - $96

Pet Policy: One pet is allowed in each guest room. A $25 per day non-refundable cleaning fee (not to exceed $150) will be charged the first night of your stay.

Features: Furnished studio suites, Recliner, Work desk, Kitchen, TV with movie channels, Free local phone, Voice mail, 2 line phones with data port, Laundry facility, Weekly housekeeping.

★★
Extended Stay America San Diego - Mission Valley -
3860 Murphy Canyon Rd
San Diego CA 92123
(858) 292-8927
$64 - $89
Bed & Pet Discount Offered

Pet Policy: One pet is allowed in each guest room. A $25 per day non-refundable cleaning fee (not to exceed $150) will be charged the first night of your stay.

Features: Guest laundry, Number of rooms: 135, Number of floors: 2, Barbecue grill(s), Free wireless Internet, Parking (free), Front desk (limited hours).

★★

Extended Stay America San Diego-Hotel Circle
2087 Hotel Cir S
San Diego CA 92108
(619) 296-5570
$79 - $89
Bed & Pet Discount Offered

Pet Policy: One pet is allowed in each guest room. A $25 per day non-refundable cleaning fee (not to exceed $150) will be charged the first night of your stay.

Features: Elevator, Number of rooms: 166, Number of floors: 3, Parking (free), Nearby fitness center (discount), Guest laundry.

★★★

Four Points by Sheraton San Diego
8110 Aero Dr
San Diego CA 92123
(858) 277-8888
$99 - $129
Bed & Pet Discount Offered

Pet Policy: Pets accepted, $25 per stay, plus $100 refundable deposit.

Swimming pool - outdoor, Golf course on site, Elevator, Airport transportation (free), Wheelchair accessible, Bar/lounge, ATM/banking, Concierge desk, Room service (limited hours), Restaurant(s), Gift shops or newsstand, Shopping on site, Number of rooms: 225, Number of floors: 3, Breakfast available (additional charge), Parking (free) Multilingual staff, Complimentary newspapers in lobby, Porter/bellhop, Free wireless Internet, Smoke-Free property, Dry cleaning/laundry service, Fitness facilities, Coffee in lobby, Piano, Nightclub, Limo or Town Car service available, Accessible bathroom, Braille or raised signage, Area shuttle (free), 24-hour business center, RV and truck parking, Shopping center shuttle (free), Theme park shuttle (free), Smoke-Free property, Snack bar/deli.

★★½

Hampton Inn San Diego Del Mar
11920 El Camino Real
San Diego CA 92130
(858) 792-5557
$84 - $214
Bed & Pet Discount Offered

Pet Policy: Pets up to 25 lbs, $50 per stay.

Features: Free Breakfast, Elevator, Swimming pool - outdoor, Number of rooms: 129, Number of floors: 4, Coffee in lobby, Parking (free), Multilingual staff, Complimentary newspapers in lobby, Free wireless Internet, Dry cleaning/laundry service, Business center, Fitness facilities

★★

Harborview Inn & Suites
550 W Grape St
San Diego CA 92101
(619) 233-7799
$52 - $140
Bed & Pet Discount Offered

Pet Policy: All pets welcome, $10 per pet.

Features: Elevator, Guest laundry, Number of rooms: 31, Number of floors: 3, Free breakfast, Parking (free) Multilingual staff, Free wireless Internet, Concierge services, Suitable for children, Computer rental, 24-hour business center

Hawthorn Suites by Wyndham
1335 Hotel Circle S
San Diego CA 92108
(619) 299-3501
$67 - $119
Bed & Pet Discount Offered

Pet Policy: Pets accepted, $75 per stay fee.

Features: Coffee in lobby, Gift shops or newsstand, Number of rooms: 50, Number of floors: 3, BBQ area, Free breakfast, Parking (free) Multilingual staff, Complimentary newspapers, Free wireless Internet, Dry cleaning/laundry service, Fitness facilities.

★★

Heritage Inn - Sea World
3333 Channel Way
San Diego CA 92110
(619) 223-9500
$49 - $64.
Bed & Pet Discount Offered

Pet Policy: All pets up to 50 lbs welcome, $10 per pet.

Features: Swimming pool - outdoor seasonal, Coffee in lobby, Free breakfast, Parking (free), Wireless Internet.

★★★

Hilton San Diego Airport/Harbor Island
1960 Harbor Island Dr
San Diego CA 92101
(619) 291-6700
$160 - $260
Bed & Pet Discount Offered

Pet Policy: Pets up to 75 lbs, $75 per stay cleaning fee.

Features: Swimming pool - outdoor, Concierge services, Bar/lounge, Airport transportation (free), Sauna, Business center, Restaurant(s), Gift shops or newsstand, Number of rooms: 211, Number of floors: 9, Accessible bathroom, Accessibility equipment for the deaf, Braille or raised signage, Breakfast available (additional charge) Room service (24 hours), Porter/bellhop, Doorman/doorwoman, Security guard, Free wireless Internet, Airport transportation (free) available 24 hours, Dry cleaning/laundry service, Fitness facilities, Parking fee.

★★★★

Hilton San Diego Bayfront
1 Park Blvd
San Diego CA 92101
(619) 564-3333
$108 - $379
Bed & Pet Discount Offered

Pet Policy: Pets allowed up to 75 lbs. $50 per stay.

Features: Concierge, Bar/lounge, Poolside bar, Currency exchange, Swimming pool - outdoor, Smoke-Free property, Shopping on site, Number of rooms: 1190, Number of suites: 30, Number of floors: 30, Multilingual staff, Limo or Town Car service available, Babysitting or child care, Restaurant(s), Gift shops or newsstand, Parking (valet) $32 Per Night, Accessible bathroom, Accessibility equipment for the deaf, Braille or raised signage, Dry cleaning/laundry service, 3 Restaurants, Breakfast available (additional charge), Porter/bellhop, Beauty services, Full-service health spa, Massage - treatment room(s), Wireless Internet (additional charge), 24-hour business center, Room service (limited hours), On-site car rental.

★★★½
Hilton San Diego Gaslamp Quarter
401 K St
San Diego CA 92101
(619) 231-4040
$107 - $449
Bed & Pet Discount Offered

Pet Policy: Pets up to 75 lbs, $75 per stay fee.

Features: Concierge, Outdoor pool, Babysitting or child care, Restaurant(s), Supervised child care/activities, Number of rooms: 282, Number of floors: 12, Breakfast available (additional charge), Multilingual staff, Complimentary newspapers, Room service, Doorman/doorwoman, Free wireless Internet, Parking (valet) $32/night, Accessible bathroom, Accessibility equipment for the deaf, Braille or raised signage, Dry cleaning/laundry service, Bar/lounge, Wheelchair accessible, Porter/bellhop, Security guard, Beauty services, Full-service health spa, Business center, Smoke-Free property.

★★★½
Hilton San Diego Mission Valley
901 Camino Del Rio S
San Diego CA 92108
(619) 543-9000
$101 - $175
Bed & Pet Discount Offered

Pet Policy: Pets up to 75 lbs accepted, $50 per stay.

Features: Outdoor pool, Business center, Restaurant(s), Supervised child care/activities, Number of rooms: 350, Breakfast available (additional charge), Doorman/doorwoman, Porter/bellhop, Free wireless Internet, Smoke-Free, Room service, Computer rental, Technology helpdesk, Concierge, Parking (valet) $18/Day, Accessible bathroom, Accessibility equipment for the deaf, Braille or raised signage, Dry cleaning/laundry, Fitness center, Gift shop.

★★★
Holiday Inn San Diego Mission Valley
3805 Murphy Canyon Rd
San Diego CA 92123
(858) 278-9300
$100 - $215
Bed & Pet Discount Offered

Pet Policy: Pets allowed, $50 per pet per stay fee.

Features: Swimming pool - outdoor, Business services, Bar/lounge, Restaurant(s), Room service, Gift shops or newsstand, Number of rooms: 175, Number of suites: 19, Number of floors: 4, Wireless Internet (additional charge), Breakfast available (additional charge), Parking (free), Multilingual staff, Accessible bathroom, Accessibility equipment for the deaf, Braille or raised signage, Dry cleaning/laundry service, Fitness center.

★★★
Holiday Inn San Diego-On The Bay
1355 N Harbor Dr
San Diego CA 92101
(619) 232-3861
$125 - $314
Bed & Pet Discount Offered

Pet Policy: Pets welcome, $25 per night. Maximum of 2 pets per room. Must be crated if left in room alone.

Features: Bar/lounge, Airport transportation (free), Restaurant(s), Gift shops or newsstand, Number of rooms: 600, Number of suites: 10, Number of floors: 14, Cell phone/mobile rental, Currency exchange, Multilingual staff, ***Continued on next page***

Holiday Inn San Diego-On The Bay
Continued from previous page

Complimentary newspapers in lobby, Room service, Porter/bellhop, Concierge desk, Wireless Internet, Swimming pool - outdoor, Elevator, Business services, Parking (valet) $26 Per Day, Accessible bathroom, Accessibility equipment for the deaf, Braille or raised signage, Dry cleaning/laundry service, Fitness facilities.

★★★
Holiday Inn San Diego-Rancho Bernardo
17065 W Bernardo Dr
San Diego CA 92127
(858) 485-6530
$78 - $198
Bed & Pet Discount Offered

Pet Policy: Pets allowed, $50 per pet per stay fee. Limited to pet friendly designated rooms. Must be crated if left alone in room.

Features: Restaurant(s), Swimming pool - outdoor, Number of rooms: 178, Number of suites: 25, Number of floors: 3, Parking (free) Multilingual staff, Porter/bellhop, Free wireless Internet, Bar/lounge, Business center, Room service (limited hours), Accessible bathroom, Accessibility equipment for the deaf, Braille or raised signage, Dry cleaning/laundry service, Fitness facilities

★★
Homestead San Diego - Mission Valley
7444 Mission Valley Rd
San Diego CA 92108
(619) 299-2292
$59 - $84
Bed & Pet Discount Offered

Pet Policy: Pets allowed, no size restriction, $25 per day to a maximum of $150 per stay. Limit of 1 pet per room.

Features: Business services, Suitable for children, Barbecue grill(s), Front desk (limited hours), Wireless Internet, Nearby fitness center (discount),

★★
Homestead San Diego - Sorrento Mesa
9880 Pacific Heights Blvd
San Diego CA 92121
(858) 623-0100
$74 - $138
Bed & Pet Discount Offered

Pet Policy: Pets allowed, no size restriction, $25 per day to a maximum of $150 per stay. Limit of 1 pet per room.

Features: Guest laundry, Business services, Number of rooms: 135, Number of floors: 2, Barbecue grill(s), Wireless Internet, Parking (free), Front desk (limited hours).

★★★½
Hotel Indigo Gaslamp Quarter
509 9th Ave
San Diego CA 92101
(619) 727-4000
$178 - $434
Bed & Pet Discount Offered

Pet Policy: Pets welcome, no extra charge.

Features: Valet parking (additional charge), Accessible bathroom, Accessibility equipment for the deaf, Braille or raised signage, Concierge services, Number of rooms: 210, Room service (24 hours), Free wireless Internet, Bar/lounge, Restaurant(s), Business center, Porter/bellhop, Smoke-Free property, Fitness facilities.

Hotel Solamar - a Kimpton Hotel
435 6th Ave
San Diego CA 92101
(619) 819-9500
$149 - $490
Bed & Pet Discount Offered

Pet Policy: Pets welcome. No size restriction. No Fees. Special pet amenities include treats, bowls, tags with hotel info, and even pet packages with special food, dog walking, and toys

Features: Poolside bar, Bar/Lounge, Swimming pool - outdoor, Concierge, Number of rooms: 235, Number of floors: 10, Parking (fee), Coffee in lobby, Breakfast available (additional charge), Video library, Currency exchange, Room service, Multilingual staff, Complimentary newspapers, Business center, Doorman/doorwoman, Security guard, 2 restaurants,, Health club, Shoe shine, Smoke-Free property, Accessible bathroom, Accessibility equipment for the deaf, Braille or raised signage, Dry cleaning/laundry service, Free wireless Internet, Free reception.

★★½

La Quinta Inn and Suites San Diego Mission Valley
641 Camino Del Rio S
San Diego CA 92108
(619) 295-6886
$84 - $124
Bed & Pet Discount Offered

Pet Policy: Pets welcome, no extra fee but owner responsible for any damage. Must not be left unattended at any time.

Features: Accessible bathroom, Outdoor pool, Number of rooms: 169, Number of suites: 58, Number of floors: 3, Coffee in lobby, Free breakfast, Parking (free) Multilingual staff, Complimentary newspapers, Dry cleaning/laundry service, Fitness facilities, Free wireless Internet, Wheelchair accessible, 24-hour business center, Smoke-Free property.

★★½

La Quinta Inn San Diego Old Town/Airport
2380 Moore Street
San Diego CA 92110
(619) 291-9100
$119 - $139
Bed & Pet Discount Offered

Pet Policy: Pets up to 30 lbs allowed, no fee. Must not leave unattended and must clean up after.

Features: Accessible bathroom, Swimming pool - outdoor, Airport transportation (free), Coffee in lobby, Number of rooms: 79, Number of floors: 3, Parking (fee), Free breakfast, Multilingual staff, Free wireless Internet, Smoke-Free property, Dry cleaning/laundry service, Braille or raised signage, Business center.

★★

La Quinta Inn San Diego Scripps Poway
10185 Paseo Montril
San Diego CA 92129
(858) 484-8800
$69 - $79
Bed & Pet Discount Offered

Pet Policy: Cats and dogs up to 50 pounds are accepted in all guest rooms. Housekeeping services for rooms with pets require pet owner be present or pet must be crated. No fees or deposits are required.

Features: Outdoor pool, Accessible bathroom, Restaurant(s), Number of rooms: 120, Free breakfast, Parking (free) Multilingual staff, Free wireless Internet.

Marina Inn and Suites
1943 Pacific Hwy
San Diego CA 92101
(619) 232-7551
$64 - $165
Bed & Pet Discount Offered

Pet Policy: Pets accepted, $20 per pet per day.

Features: Coffee in lobby, Free breakfast, Number of rooms: 29, Number of suites: 2, Number of floors: 2, Parking (free), Multilingual staff, Complimentary newspapers in lobby, Business services, Guest laundry, Concierge services, Free wireless Internet.

Not rated
Marriott ExecuStay Lofts at 707
707 Tenth Ave
San Diego CA 92101
(888) 526-0566
$147 - $195

Pet Policy: Dogs and cats up to 40 lbs. $500 deposit, $250 non-refundable. No aggressive breeds. Must reserve in advance.

Features: Fully furnished apartments. 30 day Minimum stay may be required.

Marriott San Diego Del Mar
11966 El Camino Real
San Diego CA 92130
(858) 523-1700
$139 - $189
Bed & Pet Discount Offered

Pet Policy: Pets accepted, $75 per stay cleaning fee.

Features: Fitness Center, Concierge, Business Center, Bar/lounge, Room service, Security guard, Limo or Town Car service available, Wireless Internet (fee), Technology helpdesk, Restaurant(s), Number of rooms: 284, Number of floors: 11, Breakfast available (additional charge), Currency exchange, Multilingual staff, Complimentary newspapers, Parking (valet) $22/night, Roll-in shower, Accessibility equipment for the deaf, Braille or raised signage, Dry cleaning/laundry, Outdoor pool.

Marriott San Diego Mission Valley
8757 Rio San Diego Dr
San Diego CA 92108
(619) 692-3800
$89 - $209
Bed & Pet Discount Offered

Pet Policy: Pets accepted, $75 per stay cleaning fee.

Features: Business Center, Room service (limited hours), Bar/lounge, Sauna, Restaurant(s), Gift shop, Number of rooms: 257, Number of floors: 17, Wireless Internet (additional charge), Breakfast available (additional charge), Multilingual staff, Complimentary newspapers, Porter/bellhop, Security guard, Concierge, Smoke-Free, Outdoor pool, Parking (valet) $17 Daily, Dry cleaning/laundry service, Fitness facilities.

Not rated.
Oakwood at Promenade Rio Vista
2185 Station Village Way
San Diego CA 92108
(602) 427-2752
$124 - $164

Pet Policy: Pets accepted with limitations and fee. Contact hotel directly for more information and to make reservations.

Features: Furnished apartments, Minimum stay required, Pool and spa, BBQ pits, Fitness center. Business Center, Concierge.

Not rated.

Oakwood Mission Valley East
6554 Ambrosia
San Diego CA 92124
(602) 427-2752
$126 - $170

Pet Policy: Pets accepted with limitations and fee. Contact hotel directly for info and reservations.

Features: Fully furnished apartments. Minimum stay required.

★★★★

Omni San Diego Hotel
675 L St
San Diego CA 92101
(619) 231-6664
$199 - $650
Bed & Pet Discount Offered

Pet Policy: Pets up to 40 lbs accepted, $50 per stay.

Features: Concierge, Outdoor pool, Security guard, Business center, Bar/lounge, Restaurant(s), Gift shop, Number of rooms: 511, Number of floors: 21, Breakfast available (additional charge), Poolside bar, Room service (24 hours), Shoe shine, Multilingual staff, Porter/bellhop, Doorman/doorwoman, Limo or Town Car service available, Free wireless Internet, Parking (valet) $30 Per Day, Dry cleaning/laundry, Fitness facilities.

★★

Pacific Inn and Suites
1655 Pacific Hwy
San Diego CA 92101
(619) 232-6391
$74 - $179
Bed & Pet Discount Offered

Pet Policy: Pets accepted, $20 per pet per night. Limit 2 pets per room.

Features: Free breakfast, Outdoor pool, Number of rooms: 34, Number of floors: 2, Business services, Coffee in lobby, Free parking, Wireless Internet.

Pacific Shores Inn on Pacific Beach
4802 Mission Blvd
San Diego CA 92109
(858) 519-7796
$99 - $169
Bed & Pet Discount Offered

Pet Policy: Pets accepted, $35 per stay.

Features: Free Breakfast, Swimming pool - outdoor, BBQ area, Number of rooms: 56, Number of floors: 2, Business services, Coffee in lobby, Guest laundry, Parking (free), Multilingual staff, Smoke-Free property, Wireless Internet (additional charge).

★

Point Loma Inn & Suites
2933 Fenelon St.
San Diego CA 92106
(619) 222-4704
$64 - $119
Bed & Pet Discount Offered

Pet Policy: Small pets allowed, $20 per pet per day.

Features: Guest laundry, Number of rooms: 7, Number of floors: 2, Free breakfast, Parking (free) Multilingual staff, Free wireless Internet.

Porto Vista Hotel
1835 Columbia St
San Diego CA 92101
(619) 544-0164
$111 - $202
Bed & Pet Discount Offered

Pet Policy: Pets up to 40 lbs. welcome, $25 per day.

Features: Bar/lounge, Coffee in lobby, Concierge , Restaurant, Multilingual staff, Dry cleaning/laundry, Free wireless Internet, Fitness facilities, Number of rooms: 209, Number of floors: 4, Accessible bathroom, Valet parking (fee), Room service, Wheelchair accessible, Smoke-Free, Business center.

Quality Inn Airport SeaWorld Area
2901 Nimitz Blvd
San Diego CA 92106
(619) 224-3655
$69 - $99
Bed & Pet Discount Offered

Pet Policy: Pets up to 50 lbs, $15 per night per pet plus $25 deposit. Limit 2 pets per room.

Features: Business Center, Guest laundry, Bar/lounge, Number of rooms: 110, Number of floors: 6, Free breakfast, Parking $7/day, Airport transportation (additional charge), Limo or Town Car service available, Smoke-Free property, Outdoor pool, Free wireless Internet.

Quality Inn San Diego
9350 Kearny Mesa Rd
San Diego CA 92126
(858) 578-4350
$84 - $94
Bed & Pet Discount Offered

Pet Policy: Pets up to 50 lbs, $15 per night per pet plus $25 deposit. Limit 2 pets per room.

Features: Fitness facilities, Swimming pool - outdoor, Number of rooms: 60, Business services, Coffee in lobby, Guest laundry, Free breakfast.

Radisson Suite Hotel Rancho Bernardo
11520 W Bernardo Ct
San Diego CA 92127
(858) 451-6600
$110 - $154
Bed & Pet Discount Offered

Pet Policy: Dogs only, fewer than 50 lbs accepted, $25 cleaning fee per stay.

Features: Room service, Bar/lounge, Outdoor pool, Number of suites: 180, Number of floors: 3, Multilingual staff, Complimentary newspapers, Free wireless Internet, Restaurant, Nearby fitness center (free), Porter/bellhop, Designated smoking areas, Beach/pool umbrellas, Grocery/convenience store, Dry cleaning/laundry, Business center,

Residence Inn by Marriott Rancho Bernardo Carmel M
11002 Rancho Carmel Dr
San Diego CA 92128
(858) 673-1900
$129 - $180
Bed & Pet Discount Offered

Pet Policy: Pets allowed, $100 per stay cleaning fee.

Features: Business services, Outdoor pool, Number of rooms: 124, Number of floors: 3, BBQ area, Coffee in lobby, Free breakfast, Complimentary newspapers, Nearby fitness center (free), Smoke-Free property, Accessible bathroom, Accessibility equipment for the deaf, Braille or raised signage, Dry cleaning/laundry, Tennis courts.

★★★
Residence Inn By Marriott San Diego Central
5400 Kearny Mesa Rd
San Diego CA 92111
(858) 278-2100
$93 - $199
Bed & Pet Discount Offered

Pet Policy: Pets allowed, $75 per stay cleaning fee.

Features: Business services, Swimming pool - outdoor, Number of suites: 144, Number of floors: 2, Coffee in lobby, Free breakfast, Complimentary newspapers in lobby, Parking (free), Accessible bathroom, Accessibility equipment for the deaf, Braille or raised signage, Dry cleaning/laundry, Fitness facilities.

★★★
Residence Inn By Marriott San Diego Downtown
1747 Pacific Hwy
San Diego CA 92101
(619) 338-8200
$139 - $298
Bed & Pet Discount Offered

Pet Policy: Pets allowed, $100 per stay cleaning fee.

Features: Free breakfast, Multilingual staff, Complimentary newspapers in lobby, Wireless Internet, Airport transportation (free), ATM/banking, Number of suites: 121, Number of floors: 4, Coffee in lobby, Parking $12 per night, Accessible bathroom, Accessibility equipment for the deaf, Braille or raised signage, Business services, Barbecue grill(s), Concierge desk, Swimming pool - outdoor, Elevator, Dry cleaning/laundry service, Fitness facilities.

★★★
Residence Inn by Marriott San Diego Gaslamp
356 6th Avenue
San Diego CA 92101
(619) 487-1200
$259 - $289
Bed & Pet Discount Offered

Pet Policy: Pets allowed, $100 per stay cleaning fee.

Features: Valet parking (additional charge), Bar/lounge, Swimming pool - outdoor, Wheelchair accessible, Concierge, Gift shops or newsstand, Number of suites: 240, Number of floors: 14, Barbecue grill(s), Coffee in lobby, Free breakfast, Grocery, Multilingual staff, Complimentary newspapers in lobby, Porter/bellhop, Security guard, Dry cleaning/laundry service, Limo or Town Car service available, Parking garage, Smoke-Free property, Nearby fitness center (discount), Technology support staff, Free wireless Internet, Accessible bathroom, Accessibility equipment for the deaf, Braille or raised signage, 24-hour business center, 2 Restaurants, Fitness facilities, Free reception

★★★
Residence Inn by Marriott San Diego Mission Valley
1865 Hotel Cir S
San Diego CA 92108
(619) 881-3600
$169 - $199
Bed & Pet Discount Offered

Pet Policy: Pets allowed, $100 per stay cleaning fee.

Features: Free breakfast, Library, Airport transportation (additional charge), Barbecue grill(s), Arcade/game room, Gift shops or newsstand, Number of rooms: 192, Parking fee, Health club, Multilingual staff, Complimentary newspapers in lobby, Business center, Free wireless Internet, Dry cleaning/laundry service, Children's swimming pool, Outdoor pool.

★★★

Residence Inn by Marriott Scripps Poway Parkway
12011 Scripps Highland Dr
San Diego CA 92131
(858) 635-5724
$179 - $204
Bed & Pet Discount Offered

Pet Policy: Pets allowed, $75 per stay cleaning fee.

Features: Coffee in lobby, Swimming pool - outdoor, Business services, Barbecue grill(s), Free breakfast, Parking (free), Complimentary newspapers in lobby, Free wireless Internet, Elevator, Number of rooms: 85, Number of floors: 4, Dry cleaning/laundry service, Tennis on site, Fitness facilities.

★★★

Residence Inn By Marriott Sorrento Mesa
5995 Pacific Mesa Ct
San Diego CA 92121
(858) 552-9100
$154 - $219
Bed & Pet Discount Offered

Pet Policy: Pets allowed, $100 per stay cleaning fee.

Features: Free Breakfast, Outdoor pool, Number of rooms: 150, Number of floors: 3, Barbecue grill(s), Coffee in lobby, Library, Parking (free) Complimentary newspapers, Business center, Free wireless Internet, Grocery/convenience store, Dry cleaning/laundry service, Tennis courts, Fitness facilities.

★★

Rodeway Inn
4345 Mission Bay Dr
San Diego CA 92109
(619) 232-2525
$59 - $74
Bed & Pet Discount Offered

Pet Policy: Pets under 35 lbs, $75 per stay. Limit 1 pet per room.

Features: Free wireless Internet, Wheelchair accessible, Computer rental, Coffee in lobby, Parking (free) Multilingual staff, Business center, Nearby fitness center (discount), RV and truck parking.

★★

Rodeway Inn & Suites Downtown
719 Ash St
San Diego CA 92101
(619) 232-2525
$54 - $189
Bed & Pet Discount Offered

Pet Policy: Rodeway Inns charge a fee of $10 per night per pet plus a $50 damage deposit, which is refunded if the room is in order at check out. Max of 2 pets per room. A veterinarian certificate that the pet is on a flea and parasite program is required. Pets may not be left alone in the room unless in a cage.

Features: Business services, Concierge, Number of rooms: 67, Number of floors: 3, Free breakfast Multilingual staff, Complimentary newspapers, Free wireless Internet, Dry cleaning/laundry, Parking fee.

San Diego Marriott Marquis & Marina
333 W Harbor Dr
San Diego CA 92101
(619) 234-1500
$198 - $334
Bed & Pet Discount Offered

Pet Policy: Pets accepted, $75 per stay.

Features: Concierge, Bar/lounge, Business Center, Room service (24 hours), Outdoor pool, Poolside bar, Restaurant(s), Gift shop, Number of rooms: 1,362, Number of floors: 25, Wireless Internet (additional charge), Breakfast available (additional charge), Shoe shine, Multilingual staff, Complimentary newspapers, Doorman/doorwoman, ***Continued on next page***

San Diego Marriott Marquis & Marina
Continued from previous page

Security guard, Limo or Town Car service available, Marina, Parking $20/day, Accessible bathroom, Accessibility equipment for the deaf, Braille or raised signage, Dry cleaning/laundry, Tennis courts, Fitness center, Smoke-Free.

Se San Diego
1047 5th Ave
San Diego CA 92101
(619) 515-3000
$194 - $575
Bed & Pet Discount Offered

Pet Policy: Pet friendly, $150 per stay.

Features: Business center, Full-service health spa, Bar/lounge, Babysitting or child care, Restaurant(s), Outdoor pool, Poolside bar, Gift shops or newsstand, Number of rooms: 184, Number of suites: 40, Number of floors: 23, Currency exchange, Room service (24 hours), Multilingual staff, Porter/bellhop, Doorman/doorwoman, Limo or Town Car service available, Concierge, Floor butler, Massage - treatment room(s), Smoke-Free, Technology helpdesk, On-site medical assistance available, Dry cleaning/laundry service, Wireless Internet (additional charge), Coffee in lobby, Parking (valet) $36 Daily.

Seacoast Palms Inn
4760 Mission Blvd
San Diego CA 92109
(858) 483-6780
$62 - $99
Bed & Pet Discount Offered

Pet Policy: Pets accepted, $35 per pet per stay. Maximum 2 per room.

Features: Number of rooms: 50, Number of floors: 2, Parking (free), Multilingual staff, Front desk (limited hours), Smoke-Free property

Sheraton San Diego Hotel and Marina
1380 Harbor Island Dr
San Diego CA 92101
(619) 291-2900
$109 - $504
Bed & Pet Discount Offered

Pet Policy: Dogs up to 50 pounds are allowed. Dogs cannot be left alone in the guest room. Dog bed and feeding bowl are provided.

Features: Outdoor pool, Children's swimming pool, Arcade/game room, Bar/lounge, Concierge services, Currency exchange, Airport transportation (free), Business center, Security guard, 5 Restaurants in hotel, Gift shops or newsstand, Computer rental, Pool table, Room service (24 hours), Multilingual staff, Complimentary newspapers in lobby, Porter/bellhop, Doorman/doorwoman, Number of rooms: 1,053, Dry cleaning/laundry service, Wireless Internet (additional charge), Fitness facilities, Parking fee.

Sheraton San Diego Hotel, Mission Valley
1433 Camino Del Rio S
San Diego CA 92108
(619) 260-0111
$99 - $179
Bed & Pet Discount Offered

Pet Policy: 1 dog, up to 75 lbs permitted. A deep cleaning fee will be charged.

Features: Business Center, Concierge desk, Swimming pool - outdoor, Bar/lounge, Elevator, Restaurant(s), Number of rooms: 260, Number of floors: 14 Multilingual staff, Complimentary newspapers in lobby, Porter/bellhop, Limo or Town Car service available, Wireless Internet (additional charge), Room service (limited hours), ATM/banking, Nearby fitness center (discount), Accessible bathroom, Accessibility equipment for the deaf, Braille or raised signage, Dry cleaning/laundry service, Poolside bar, Self-parking (additional charge).

★★★½

Sheraton Suites San Diego at Symphony Hall
701 A St
San Diego CA 92101
(619) 696-9800
$149 - $299
Bed & Pet Discount Offered

Pet Policy: Pets up to 80 pounds are allowed. Guest must sign a waiver at check-in before dog is allowed in any guest room or public area. The hotel will provide at Sweet Sleeper Dog Bed. Dogs are not allowed in any food and beverage or pool area.

Features: Business Center, Indoor pool, Concierge, Parking (valet) $28 Per Day, Bar/lounge, Restaurant(s), Number of suites: 264, Number of floors: 16, Room service (24 hours), Multilingual staff, Porter/bellhop, Doorman/doorwoman, Security guard, Elevator, Gift shops or newsstand Complimentary newspapers in lobby, Limo or Town Car service available, Free wireless Internet, Smoke-Free property, Nearby fitness center (discount), Accessible bathroom, Accessibility equipment for the deaf, Braille or raised signage, Dry cleaning/laundry service.

★★

Sommerset Suites Hotel
606 Washington St
San Diego CA 92103
(619) 692-5200
$133 - $169
Bed & Pet Discount Offered

Pet Policy: Pets up to 35 lbs accepted, $50 per stay. Limit 2 per room.

Features: Business center, Barbecue grill(s), Number of suites: 80, Free breakfast, Swimming pool, Dry cleaning/laundry service, Free wireless Internet, Self-parking (additional charge)

★★★

Staybridge Suites San Diego
11855 Avenue Of Industry
San Diego CA 92128
(888) 299-2208
$115 - $241
Bed & Pet Discount Offered

Pet Policy: Pets up to 80 lbs, $15 first night, $10 thereafter not to exceed $150. Must have vaccination records with you.

Business center, Free breakfast, Barbecue grill(s), Accessible bathroom, Accessibility equipment for the deaf, Braille or raised signage, ***Continued on next page***

Staybridge Suites San Diego
Continued from previous page

Swimming pool - outdoor, Concierge services, Computer rental, Suitable for children, Coffee in lobby, Library, Grocery, Parking (free) Multilingual staff, Complimentary newspapers in lobby, Front desk (limited hours), Free wireless Internet, Dry cleaning/laundry service, Fitness facilities.

★★★

Staybridge Suites Sorrento Mesa
6639 Mira Mesa Blvd
San Diego CA 92121
(858) 453-5343
$171 - $249
Bed & Pet Discount Offered

Pet Policy: Pets up to 80 lbs, $15 first night, $10 thereafter not to exceed $150. Must have vaccination records with you.

Features: Business center, Swimming pool - outdoor, Barbecue grill(s), Free breakfast, Braille or raised signage, Gift shops or newsstand, Number of suites: 131, Number of floors: 4, Suitable for children, Coffee in lobby, Grocery, Parking (free), Multilingual staff, Free wireless Internet, Accessible bathroom, Accessibility equipment for the deaf, Dry cleaning/laundry service, Fitness facilities.

★★★★★

The Grand Del Mar
5300 Grand Del Mar Court
San Diego CA 92130
(858) 314-1930
$383 - $3,900
Bed & Pet Discount Offered

Pet Policy: Pets welcome, $100 per stay fee.

Features: Business center, Full-service health spa, Swimming pool - outdoor, Babysitting or child care, Supervised child care/activities, Restaurant(s), Gift shops or newsstand, Number of rooms: 249, Number of floors: 3, Breakfast available (additional charge), Arcade/game room, Library, Room service (24 hours), Shoe shine, Multilingual staff, Nearby fitness center (free), Porter/bellhop, Doorman/doorwoman, Security guard, Limo or Town Car service available, Free wireless Internet, Beauty services, Concierge, Technology helpdesk, Children's club, Accessible bathroom, Accessibility equipment for the deaf, Braille or raised signage, Dry cleaning/laundry, Poolside bar, Bar/lounge, Shopping on site, Children's swimming pool, Golf course,, Tennis courts, Valet parking (additional charge).

★★★½

The Sofia Hotel
150 W Broadway
San Diego CA 92101
(800) 826-0009
$128 - $449
Bed & Pet Discount Offered

Pet Policy: Pets accepted, $25 per pet per night.

Features: Business center, Bar/lounge, Health club, Concierge, Free wireless Internet, Accessible bathroom, Accessibility equipment for the deaf, Braille or raised signage, Restaurant(s), Number of rooms: 212, Number of floors: 7, Multilingual staff, Massage - treatment room(s), Smoke-Free property, Parking (valet) $28 Per Day, Dry cleaning/laundry service.

The US Grant - A Luxury Collection Hotel
326 Broadway
San Diego CA 92101
(619) 232-3121
$175 - $3,500
Bed & Pet Discount Offered

Pet Policy: Dogs and cats up to 40 lbs are welcome, $150 per pet per stay. The US Grant is pleased to welcome pets with a bed, two bowls, a welcome kit including toys and cleaning supplies, and a Pet in Room sign. Our concierge will also be pleased to arrange pet sitting services for an additional fee.

Features: Shoe shine, Room service, Bar/Lounge, Concierge, Security guard, Number of rooms: 270, Number of floors: 11, Spa services on site, Parking (valet) $32/day, Nearby fitness center (free), Beauty services, Free wireless Internet, Accessible bathroom, 24-hour business center, Dry cleaning/laundry service, Restaurant(s), Gift shops or newsstand, Breakfast available (additional charge), Multilingual staff, Complimentary newspapers, Porter/bellhop, Doorman/doorwoman, Limo or Town Car service available, Smoke-Free property, Currency exchange, Coffee in lobby,

★★★★

The Westin Gaslamp Quarter, San Diego
910 Broadway Cir
San Diego CA 92101
(619) 239-2200
$158 - $1,489
Bed & Pet Discount Offered

Pet Policy: Dogs Welcome, no fee. Short waiver form must be filled out at check-in.

Features: Bar/Lounge, Swimming pool - outdoor, Elevator, Business center, Spa services on site, Accessible bathroom, Accessibility equipment for the deaf, Braille or raised signage, Babysitting or child care, Restaurant(s), Supervised child care/activities, Concierge services, Gift shops or newsstand, Number of rooms: 450, Number of floors: 16, Translation services, Computer rental, Room service (24 hours), Shoe shine, Multilingual staff, Complimentary newspapers in lobby, Free wireless Internet, Smoke-Free property, Parking (valet) $32 Per Day, Fitness facilities, Wheelchair accessible, Currency exchange, Dry cleaning/laundry service, Breakfast available (additional charge), Massage - treatment room(s), ATM/banking, Porter/bellhop.

★★

Travelodge Mission Valley
1201 Hotel Cir S
San Diego CA 92108
(619) 297-2271
$44 - $174
Bed & Pet Discount Offered

Pet Policy: Pets accepted, $10 per pet per night. We have rooms specifically for pets located near a grassy walking area to walk them

Features: Bar/lounge, Restaurant(s), Business services, Spa tub (outdoor), Free parking.

★★
Vagabond Inn Hotel Circle
625 Hotel Cir S
San Diego CA 92108
(619) 297-1691
$64 - $199
Bed & Pet Discount Offered

Pet Policy: Pets accepted, $20 per pet per night.

Features: Coffee in lobby, Business services, 2 Outdoor pools, Number of rooms: 88, Number of floors: 2, Free breakfast, Multilingual staff, Accessible bathroom, Accessibility equipment for the deaf, Braille or raised signage, Computer rental, Free Internet.

★★
Vagabond Inn Point Loma
1325 Scott St
San Diego CA 92106
(619) 224-3371
$55 - $84
Bed & Pet Discount Offered

Pet Policy: Small pets welcome, $10 per pet per night, limit 2 per room.

Features: Outdoor pool, Free Breakfast, Coffee in lobby, Number of rooms: 40, Number of suites: 3, Parking (free), Complimentary newspapers, Free wireless Internet, Multilingual staff, Business services.

★★★★
W San Diego
421 W B St
San Diego CA 92101
(619) 398-3100
$159 - $2,200
Bed & Pet Discount Offered

Pet Policy: Pets welcome, $25 per day plus $100 per stay cleaning fee.

Features: Bar/Lounge, Outdoor pool, Spa services, Concierge, Security guard, Video library, Computer rental, Business center, Restaurant(s), Gift shop, Number of rooms: 261, Number of floors: 19, Complimentary newspapers, Doorman/doorwoman, Porter/bellhop, Limo or Town Car service available, Free wireless Internet, Dry cleaning/laundry, Room service (limited hours), Smoke-Free property, Fitness facilities, Wheelchair accessible, Currency exchange, Multilingual staff, Valet parking (fee),

★★★★
Westin San Diego
400 W Broadway
San Diego CA 92101
(619) 239-4500
$178 - $319
Bed & Pet Discount Offered

Pet Policy: We welcome your canine companion, up to 45 lbs, with an amenity bag for the urban dog, as well as his or her very own Westin Heavenly dog bed and a polished food and water bowl.

Features: Concierge, Outdoor pool, Porter/bellhop, Doorman/doorwoman, Security guard, Dry cleaning/laundry service, Massage - spa treatment room(s), Wireless Internet (additional charge), 2 Restaurants,, 24-hour business center, Cruise terminal shuttle (free), Smoke-Free property, Spa services, Bar/lounge, Airport transportation (free), Complimentary newspapers, Shoe shine, Room service (24 hours), Wheelchair accessible, Gift shop, Number of rooms: 436, Number of floors: 26, Multilingual staff, Parking (valet) $32 Per Day, Accessible bathroom, Accessibility equipment for the deaf, Braille or raised signage, Fitness facilities

Woodfin Suite Hotel San Diego
10044 Pacific Mesa Blvd
San Diego CA 92121
(858) 597-0500
$109 - $309
Bed & Pet Discount Offered

Pet Policy: Pets accepted, $10 per night per pet, plus $200 refundable deposit.

Features: Outdoor pool, Guest laundry, Business center, Bar/lounge, Restaurant(s), Number of rooms: 155, Number of floors: 4, Video library, Parking (free), Nearby fitness center (free), Free wireless Internet, Accessible bathroom, Accessibility equipment for the deaf, Braille or raised signage, Fitness facilities.

San Dimas

Also see the following nearby communities that have pet friendly lodging: Pomona - 3 miles, Glendora - 4 miles, Claremont - 4 miles, Diamond Bar - 7 miles, Upland - 8 miles, Walnut - 8 miles, Chino - 9 miles, Chino Hills - 10 miles, City Of Industry - 10 miles

Extended Stay America Los Angeles - San Dimas
601 W Bonita Ave
San Dimas CA 91773
(909) 394-1022
$54 - $94
Bed & Pet Discount Offered

Pet Policy: One pet is allowed in each guest room. A $25 per day non-refundable cleaning fee (not to exceed $150) will be charged the first night of your stay.

Features: Elevator, Gift shops or newsstand, Number of rooms: 104, Number of floors: 3, Airport transportation (additional charge), Business services, Wireless Internet (additional charge), Nearby fitness center (free), Limo or Town Car service available.

★

Red Roof San Dimas
204 North Village Ct.
San Dimas CA 91773
(909) 599-2362
$53 - $73

Pet Policy: 1 well-behaved pet permitted without charge.

Features: Free wireless Internet, Outdoor swimming pool, Coffee in lobby, Cable TV, Data ports.

San Francisco

Also see the following nearby communities that have pet friendly lodging: Brisbane - 6 miles, Sausalito - 7 miles, South San Francisco - 8 miles, Alameda - 9 miles, San Bruno - 10 miles, Emeryville - 10 miles

Argonaut Hotel - a Kimpton Hotel
495 Jefferson St
San Francisco CA 94109
(415) 563-0800
$198 - $509
Bed & Pet Discount Offered

Pet Policy: Pets welcome. No size restriction. No Fees. Special pet amenities include treats, bowls, tags with hotel info, and even pet packages with special food, dog walking, and toys

Features: Concierge, Business Center, Room service , Security guard, Bar/lounge, Restaurant(s), Number of rooms: 252, Number of floors: 4, Translation services, Parking fee, Breakfast available (additional charge), Multilingual staff, Complimentary newspapers, Porter/bellhop, Doorman/doorwoman, Limo or Town Car service available, Smoke-Free, Dry cleaning/laundry, Free Internet, Fitness center.

Beresford Arms Hotel
701 Post At Jones
San Francisco CA 94109
(415) 673-2600
$108 - $159
Bed & Pet Discount Offered

Pet Policy: Pets accepted, $25 per pet per stay.

Features: Parking (valet) $24 or SUV $35/day, Concierge, Number of rooms: 95, Number of floors: 8, Coffee in lobby, Video library, Free breakfast, Porter/bellhop, Free wireless Internet, Nearby fitness center (discount), Accessible bathroom, Dry cleaning/laundry service, Year Built 1910.

Beresford Hotel
635 Sutter St
San Francisco CA 94102
(415) 673-9900
$88 - $100
Bed & Pet Discount Offered

Pet Policy: Pets allowed with a fee at check in. Limited to designated pet rooms.

Features: Bar/lounge, Restaurant, Concierge, Number of rooms: 114, Number of floors: 7, Video library, Complimentary newspapers, Free Internet, Nearby fitness center (discount), Free breakfast, Parking (valet) $24/Day SUV $35/Day, Dry cleaning/laundry service, Gift shops or newsstand, Porter/bellhop, Designated smoking areas, Business center.

Best Western Americania
121 7th St
San Francisco CA 94103
(415) 626-0200
$88 - $159
Bed & Pet Discount Offered

Pet Policy: Pets allowed with No Restrictions, well behaved dogs and cats welcomed $25 per stay

Features: Free wireless Internet, Business center, Bar/lounge, Parking (valet) $20/day, Restaurant(s), Outdoor pool, Number of rooms: 143, Complimentary newspapers, Security guard, Limo or Town Car service available, Concierge, Smoke-Free property, Dry cleaning/laundry service, Fitness facilities.

Best Western Hotel California
580 Geary St
San Francisco CA 94102
(415) 441-2700
$125 - $278

Pet Policy: Pets accepted on advance approval. Please contact hotel directly for reservations.

Features: Bar/lounge, Coffee in lobby, Business center, Concierge, Restaurant(s), Number of rooms: 83, Number of floors: 7, Breakfast available (additional charge), Complimentary newspapers in lobby, Free wireless Internet, Smoke-Free property, Dry cleaning/laundry service, Fitness facilities.

Best Western Tuscan Inn Fisherman's Wharf-Kimpton
425 North Point
San Francisco CA 94133
(800) 648-4626
$118 - $289
Bed & Pet Discount Offered

Pet Policy: Pets welcome. No size restriction. No Fees. Special pet amenities include treats, bowls, tags with hotel info, and even pet packages with special food, dog walking, and toys

Features: Concierge, Business services, Room service (limited hours), ***Continued on next page***

Best Western Tuscan Inn Fisherman's Wharf-Kimpton Continued from previous page

Parking garage, Nearby fitness center (discount), Restaurant(s), Number of rooms: 221, Number of floors: 4, Parking (fee), Coffee in lobby, Breakfast available (additional charge), Multilingual staff, Complimentary newspapers, Porter/bellhop, Limo or Town Car service available, Dry cleaning/laundry service.

★★★★½

Fairmont Heritage Place, Ghirardelli Square
900 N Point Street
San Francisco CA 94109
(415) 268-9900
$549 - $1,332
Bed & Pet Discount Offered

Pet Policy: Pets under 45 lbs, $20 per night per pet. Limit 2 per room. No aggressive breeds.

Features: Bar/lounge, Babysitting or child care, Number of suites: 53, Number of floors: 4, Video library, Complimentary newspapers, Room service, Porter/bellhop, Parking fee, Free breakfast, Multilingual staff, Doorman/doorwoman, Security guard, Dry cleaning/laundry service, Limo or Town Car service available, Billiards, Supervised child care/activities, Shopping on site, Coffee in lobby, Children's club, Free wireless Internet, Accessible bathroom, 24-hour business center, Concierge.

★★★★★

Four Seasons San Francisco
757 Market St
San Francisco CA 94103
(415) 633-3000
$394 - $1,000
Bed & Pet Discount Offered

Pet Policy: Pets up to 35 lbs accepted. Limit 1 pet per room.

Features: Babysitting or child care, Indoor pool, Restaurant(s), Hair salon, Gift shop, Breakfast available (additional charge), Health club, Room service, Shoe shine, Multilingual staff, Porter/bellhop, Doorman/doorwoman, Concierge, Full-service health spa, Dry cleaning/laundry, Wireless Internet (additional charge), Parking (valet), Business center,

★★★½

Galleria Park Hotel, a Joie de Vivre Boutique Hotel
191 Sutter St
San Francisco CA 94104
(415) 413-4718
$159 - $515
Bed & Pet Discount Offered

Pet Policy: Pet friendly hotel - an ideal city getaway hotel for you and your pet, complete with a private urban park located on the 3rd floor

Features: Business Center, Room service (limited hours), Parking (valet) $35/Day (SUVs $48), Restaurant(s), Concierge services, Number of rooms: 177, Number of floors: 8, Cell phone/mobile rental, Complimentary newspapers in lobby, Porter/bellhop, Doorman/doorwoman, Limo or Town Car service available, Free wireless Internet, Nearby fitness center (discount), Dry cleaning/laundry service.

Good Hotel
112 7th Street
San Francisco CA 94103
(415) 621-7001
$78 - $142
Bed & Pet Discount Offered

Pet Policy: Pet friendly hotel with treats and water/food bowls upon check in. $25 per pet, maximum 2 per room.

Features: Restaurant(s), Concierge services, Number of rooms: 117, Number of floors: 5, Airport transportation (additional charge), Complimentary newspapers in lobby, Use of nearby fitness center (free), Porter/bellhop, Security guard, Medical assistance available, Free wireless Internet, Parking $20 Per Day, Dry cleaning/laundry service, Smoke-Free property.

Grand Hyatt San Francisco Union Square
345 Stockton St
San Francisco CA 94108
(415) 398-1234
$199 - $409
Bed & Pet Discount Offered

Pet Policy: Pets are accepted with advanced approval. Please contact hotel directly for reservations and restrictions.

Features: Elevator, Bar/Lounge, ATM/Banking, Concierge desk, Business center, Restaurant(s), Number of rooms: 685, Number of floors: 36, Translation services, Wireless Internet (additional charge), Breakfast available (additional charge), Spa services on site, Shoe shine, Multilingual staff, Porter/bellhop, Doorman/doorwoman, Security guard, Limo or Town Car service available, Medical assistance available, Currency exchange, Room service (limited hours), Massage - treatment room(s), Smoke-Free property, Technology helpdesk, Accessible bathroom, Dry cleaning/laundry service, Fitness facilities.

Harbor Court Hotel - a Kimpton Hotel
165 Steuart St
San Francisco CA 94105
(415) 882-1300
$149 - $419
Bed & Pet Discount Offered

Pet Policy: Pets welcome. No size restriction. No Fees. Special pet amenities include treats, bowls, tags with hotel info, and even pet packages with special food, dog walking, and toys

Features: Bar/Lounge, Nearby fitness center (discount), Room service, Restaurant(s), Number of rooms: 131, Complimentary newspapers, Porter/bellhop, Limo or Town Car service available, Smoke-Free, Hair salon, Dry cleaning/laundry, Wireless Internet (fee), Valet parking (fee).

Hayes Valley Inn
417 Gough Street
San Francisco CA 94102
(415) 431-9131
From $76
Bed & Pet Discount Offered

Pet Policy: Pets welcome, $50 deposit. Deposit is non-refundable if stay 3 or more days.

Features: Business services, Guest laundry, Translation services, Smoke-Free property, Gift shops or newsstand, Number of rooms: 28, Number of floors: 3, Airport transportation (additional charge), Free wireless Internet, Free breakfast, Complimentary newspapers, Beauty services, Parking nearby (fee).

★★★★
Hilton San Francisco Downtown/Financial District
750 Kearny St
San Francisco CA 94108
(415) 433-6600
$127 - $304
Bed & Pet Discount Offered

Pet Policy: Dogs up to 200 pounds allowed. $100 fee per stay.

Features: Full-service health spa, Currency Exchange,, Wheelchair Accessible, Bar/Lounge, Concierge, Security guard, Room service, Shoe shine, Restaurant(s), Gift shop, Number of rooms: 544, Number of floors: 27, Airport transportation (additional charge), Translation services, Breakfast available (additional charge), Health club, Multilingual staff, Complimentary newspapers, Porter/bellhop, Doorman/doorwoman, Limo or Town Car service available, Massage available, Parking – fee, Dry cleaning/laundry, Business center, Wireless Internet (fee).

★★★★
Hilton San Francisco Union Square
333 O'Farrell St.
San Francisco CA 94102
(415) 771-1400
$135 - $334
Bed & Pet Discount Offered

Pet Policy: Pets up to 75 lbs accepted, $50 per stay.

Features: Business center, Sauna, Outdoor pool. Security guard, Parking (valet) $56/day No SUVs, Translation services, Shopping on site, Room service, Concierge, Number of rooms: 1,900, Computer rental, Wireless Internet (fee), Multilingual staff, Complimentary newspapers, Porter/bellhop, Doorman/doorwoman, Limo or Town Car service available, Dry cleaning/laundry, Fitness center (fee).

★★★
Holiday Inn Civic Center
50 8th St
San Francisco CA 94103
(415) 626-6103
$98 - $218
Bed & Pet Discount Offered

Pet Policy: Small pets under 20 lbs, or any Service Animals, $75 per stay.

Features: Currency Exchange, Outdoor pool, Accessibility equipment for the deaf, Braille or raised signage, Accessible bathroom, Bar/lounge, Restaurant(s), Gift shop, Number of suites: 3, Number of floors: 14, Health club, Multilingual staff, Complimentary newspapers, Room service, Porter/bellhop, Wireless Internet, Business center.

★★★
Holiday Inn Golden Gateway
1500 Van Ness Ave
San Francisco CA 94109
(888) 465-4329
$122 - $349
Bed & Pet Discount Offered

Pet Policy: Pets up to 75 lbs allowed, $35 per stay. Limited to standard guest rooms only.

Features: Smoke-Free property, Bar/lounge, Concierge desk, Swimming pool - outdoor, Accessible bathroom, Accessibility equipment for the deaf, Braille or raised signage, Business center, ATM/banking, Room service (limited hours), Restaurant(s), Gift shops or newsstand, Number of suites: 5, Number of floors: 26, Breakfast available (additional charge), Currency exchange, Multilingual staff, Complimentary newspapers in lobby, Porter/bellhop, Wireless Internet, Dry cleaning/laundry service, Fitness facilities, Self-parking (additional charge).

★★★:
Holiday Inn San Francisco-Fisherman's Wharf
1300 Columbus Ave
San Francisco CA 94133
(415) 771-9000
$132 - $255
Bed & Pet Discount Offered

Pet Policy: Dogs and cats, up t0 50 lbs, $85 per stay cleaning fee.

Features: Currency Exchange, ATM/Banking, Business center, Guest laundry, Concierge desk, Accessible bathroom, Accessibility equipment for the deaf, Braille or raised signage, Bar/lounge, Restaurant(s), Gift shops or newsstand, Number of floors: 5, Health club Multilingual staff, Room service, Porter/bellhop, Free wireless Internet, Self-parking (additional charge).

★★★½
Hotel Abri - Union Square
127 Ellis Street
San Francisco CA 94102
(415) 392-8800
$158 - $339
Bed & Pet Discount Offered

Pet Policy: Pets up to 75 lbs accepted, No extra charge.

Features: Room service (limited hours), Business center, Porter/bellhop, Doorman/doorwoman, Limo or Town Car service available, Smoke-Free property, Parking (valet) $43 Daily/ $58 (SUV), Dry cleaning/laundry service, Free wireless Internet.

★★½
Hotel Bijou
111 Mason St
San Francisco CA 94102
(415) 771-1200
$80 - $219
Bed & Pet Discount Offered

Pet Policy: Pets under 20 lbs accepted with fee.

Features: Concierge services, Coffee in lobby, Breakfast available (additional charge), Number of rooms: 65, Number of floors: 6, Parking (additional charge), Wireless Internet (additional charge), Multilingual staff, Complimentary newspapers in lobby, Limo or Town Car service available, Smoke-Free property, Parking (valet) $28/Day SUV $35/Day, Dry cleaning/laundry service, Airport transportation (additional charge)..

★★★
Hotel Carlton, a Joie de Vivre Boutique Hotel
1075 Sutter St
San Francisco CA 94109
(800) 738-7477
$111 - $309
Bed & Pet Discount Offered

Pet Policy: Pets welcome, $35 per night. Offers special pet bed made of organic material .

Features: Elevator, Nearby fitness center (discount), Business services, Medical assistance available, Concierge services, Parking (valet) $30/Day No SUVs, Restaurant(s), Number of rooms: 161, Number of floors: 9, Breakfast available (additional charge), Multilingual staff, Complimentary newspapers in lobby, Porter/bellhop, Limo or Town Car service available, Wireless Internet, Accessible bathroom, Accessibility equipment for the deaf, Braille or raised signage, Dry cleaning/laundry service.

★★½
Hotel Del Sol, a Joie de Vivre Boutique Hotel
3100 Webster St
San Francisco CA 94123
(415) 921-5520
$134 - $209
Bed & Pet Discount Offered

Pet Policy: Joie de Vivre has 14 pet-friendly properties in California, with Fido-friendly packages, amenities and a progressive pet policy designed to make hotel stays hospitable for dogs and their owners alike. Unlike many hotels, Joie de Vivre's properties do not impose weight restrictions on dogs and typically do not charge pet fees (provided there is no damage to a guestroom and dog owners abide by pet policy rules).

Features: Swimming pool - outdoor, Concierge, Complimentary newspapers in lobby, Limo or Town Car service available, Nearby fitness center (discount), Elevator, Number of rooms: 57, Video library, Free breakfast, Parking (free), Multilingual staff, Porter/bellhop, Smoke-Free property, Accessible bathroom, Accessibility equipment for the deaf, Braille or raised signage, Dry cleaning/laundry service, Room service (limited hours), Computer rental, Library, Business center, Medical assistance available, Creche (nursery), Smoke-Free property, Suitable for children, Grocery/convenience store, Coffee in lobby, Free wireless Internet.

★★★
Hotel Diva
440 Geary St
San Francisco CA 94102
(415) 885-0200
$168 - $274
Bed & Pet Discount Offered

Pet Policy: Dogs allowed, up to 40 lbs in standard rooms, up to 60 lbs in upgraded rooms. 2 dogs allowed provided combined weight within those limits. An additional cleaning fee of $25 is charge.

Features: Business Center, Computer rental, Coffee in lobby, Complimentary newspapers, Porter/bellhop, Doorman/doorwoman, Limo or Town Car service available, Free wireless Internet, Smoke-Free property, Restaurant(s), Room service, Concierge, Number of rooms: 114, Dry cleaning/laundry, Fitness facilities, Valet parking (fee).

★★★½

Hotel Frank
386 Geary Street
San Francisco CA 94102
(415) 986-2000
$159 - $269
Bed & Pet Discount Offered

Pet Policy: Pets under 50 lbs, $25 cleaning fee.

Features: Bar/lounge, Room service, Coffee in lobby, Porter/bellhop, Limo or Town Car service available, Free wireless Internet, Smoke-Free, Nearby fitness center (discount), Parking $28/Day Offsite, Concierge, Business center, Restaurant(s), Number of rooms: 153, Number of floors: 13, Breakfast available (additional charge), Multilingual staff, Complimentary newspapers, Dry cleaning/laundry, Year Built 1908.

★★★½

Hotel Kabuki - a Joie de Vivre Boutique Hotel
1625 Post St
San Francisco CA 94115
(415) 922-3200
$159 - $289
Bed & Pet Discount Offered

Pet Policy: Joie de Vivre has 14 pet-friendly properties in California, with Fido-friendly packages, amenities and a progressive pet policy designed to make hotel stays hospitable for dogs and their owners alike. This property has a 50 lbs size limit but pet fees (provided there is no damage to a guestroom and dog owners abide by pet policy rules).

Features: Business Center, Concierge, Nearby fitness center (discount), Restaurant(s), Number of rooms: 218, Breakfast available (additional charge), Porter/bellhop, Doorman/doorwoman, Multilingual staff, Wireless Internet, Accessible bathroom, Accessibility equipment for the deaf, Braille or raised signage, Dry cleaning/laundry, Valet parking (additional charge).

★★★★

Hotel Monaco San Francisco - a Kimpton Hotel
501 Geary St
San Francisco CA 94102
(415) 292-0100
$198 - $669
Bed & Pet Discount Offered

Pet Policy: Pets welcome. No size restriction. No Fees. Special pet amenities include treats, bowls, tags with hotel info, and even pet packages with special food, dog walking, and toys

Features: Elevator, Security guard, Full-service health spa, Business center, Bar/lounge, Restaurant(s), Concierge services, Number of rooms: 201, Number of floors: 7, Parking (additional charge), Coffee in lobby, Breakfast available (additional charge), Room service (24 hours), Shoe shine, Multilingual staff, Complimentary newspapers in lobby, Porter/bellhop, Limo or Town Car service available, Wireless Internet, Technology helpdesk, Dry cleaning/laundry service, Fitness facilities, Smoke-Free property.

Hotel Nikko San Francisco
222 Mason St
San Francisco CA 94102
(415) 394-1111
$161 - $950
Bed & Pet Discount Offered

Pet Policy: Pets allowed. $50 per stay. Must register pets at check-in.

Features: Currency Exchange, Sauna, Bar/Lounge, Swimming pool - indoor, Health club, Business center, On-site car rental, Shoe shine, Wireless Internet (additional charge), Elevator, Room service (24 hours), ATM/Banking, Restaurant(s), Concierge services, Gift shops or newsstand, Number of rooms: 532, Number of floors: 25, Parking (additional charge), Spa services on site, Multilingual staff, Complimentary newspapers in lobby, Porter/bellhop, Doorman/doorwoman, Security guard, Limo or Town Car service available, Massage - treatment room(s), Smoke-Free property, Accessible bathroom, Braille or raised signage, Dry cleaning/laundry service, Nightclub, Beauty services.

Hotel Palomar San Francisco - a Kimpton Hotel
12 4th St
San Francisco CA 94103
(415) 348-1111
$240 - $520
Bed & Pet Discount Offered

Pet Policy: Pets welcome. No size restriction. No Fees. Special pet amenities include treats, bowls, tags with hotel info, and even pet packages with special food, dog walking, and toys

Features: Business services, Elevator, Bar/lounge, Shoe shine, Room service (limited hours), Technology helpdesk, Coffee in lobby, Spa services on site, Security guard, Medical assistance available, Concierge services, Parking (valet) $42/Day Hybrids $10, Restaurant(s), Number of rooms: 9, Number of suites: 198, Parking (additional charge), Breakfast available (additional charge), Multilingual staff, Complimentary newspapers in lobby, Porter/bellhop, Doorman/doorwoman, Limo or Town Car service available, Free wireless Internet, Smoke-Free property, Nearby fitness center (discount), Dry cleaning/laundry service.

Hotel Rex, a Joie de Vivre Boutique Hotel
562 Sutter St
San Francisco CA 94102
(415) 433-4434
$149 - $399
Bed & Pet Discount Offered

Pet Policy: Joie de Vivre has 14 pet-friendly properties in California, with Fido-friendly packages, amenities and a progressive pet policy designed to make hotel stays hospitable for dogs and their owners alike. Unlike many hotels, Joie de Vivre's properties do not impose weight restrictions on dogs and typically do not charge pet fees (provided there is no damage to a guestroom and dog owners abide by pet policy rules).

Continued on next page

Hotel Rex
Continued from previous page

Features: Bar/Lounge, Business Center, Elevator, Restaurant(s), Room service (limited hours), Concierge services, Number of rooms: 94, Number of floors: 7, Breakfast available (additional charge), Spa services on site, Shoe shine, Multilingual staff, Complimentary newspapers in lobby, Porter/bellhop, Limo or Town Car service available, Medical assistance available, Free wireless Internet, Smoke-Free property, Nearby fitness center (discount), Dry cleaning/laundry service, Valet parking (additional charge).

★★★
Hotel Triton - a Kimpton Hotel
342 Grant Ave
San Francisco CA 94108
(415) 394-0500
$178 - $449
Bed & Pet Discount Offered

Pet Policy: Pets welcome. No size restriction. No Fees. Special pet amenities include treats, bowls, tags with hotel info, and even pet packages with special food, dog walking, and toys

Features: Concierge services, Room service (limited hours), Restaurant(s), Number of rooms: 140, Computer rental, Multilingual staff, Complimentary newspapers in lobby, Business center, Limo or Town Car service available (Mon - Fri), Free wireless Internet, Parking garage (additional charge), Smoke-Free property, Fitness facilities.

★★★½
Hotel Union Square
114 Powell St
San Francisco CA 94102
(415) 397-3000
$128 - $300
Bed & Pet Discount Offered

Pet Policy: Dogs allowed, up to 40 lbs in standard rooms, up to 60 lbs in upgraded rooms. 2 dogs allowed provided combined weight within those limits. An additional cleaning fee of $25 is charge.

Features: Parking (valet) $30/Day SUV $36/Day, Nearby fitness center (discount), Free wireless Internet, 24-hour business center, Free reception, Coffee in lobby, Room service (limited hours), Elevator, Concierge services, Number of rooms: 131, Parking (additional charge), Multilingual staff, Complimentary newspapers in lobby, Smoke-Free property, Currency Exchange, Dry cleaning/laundry service, Year Built 1913, Restaurant.

★★½
Hotel Vertigo
940 Sutter Street
San Francisco CA 94109
(415) 885-6800
$79 - $179
Bed & Pet Discount Offered

Pet Policy: Dogs only, under 50 lbs welcome, $25 cleaning fee.

Features: Business services, Elevator, Concierge services, Number of rooms: 102, Number of floors: 7, Complimentary newspapers in lobby, Porter/bellhop, Wireless Internet, Smoke-Free property, Parking (valet) $35/day, Dry cleaning/laundry.

Hotel Vitale-a Joie de Vivre Hotel
8 Mission St
San Francisco CA 94105
(415) 278-3700
$219 - $799
Bed & Pet Discount Offered

Pet Policy: Dogs welcome, no size limit or fees. Many pet amenities.

Features: Business Center, Bar/Lounge, Elevator, Coffee in lobby, Video library, Room service (24 hours), Use of nearby fitness center (free), Medical assistance available, Shoe shine, Dry cleaning/laundry service, Restaurant(s), Concierge services, Number of rooms: 199, Number of floors: 8, Parking (additional charge), Breakfast available (additional charge), Multilingual staff, Complimentary newspapers, Porter/bellhop, Doorman/doorwoman, Limo or Town Car service available, Free wireless Internet, Massage - treatment room(s), Smoke-Free property, Technology helpdesk, Wheelchair accessible, Suitable for children, Pool table, Media library, Accessible bathroom, Accessibility equipment for the deaf, Braille or raised signage, Full-service health spa.

InterContinental Mark Hopkins
1 Nob Hl
San Francisco CA 94108
(800) 496-7621
$159 - $369
Bed & Pet Discount Offered

Pet Policy: Pets allowed, $50 per night. Pet designated rooms only. Must not leave in room alone.

Features: Business Center, Babysitting or child care, Concierge, Business services, Year Built 1926, Bar/lounge, Accessible bathroom, Accessibility equipment for the deaf, Braille or raised signage, Currency Exchange, Restaurant(s), Room service , Gift shop, Number of rooms: 382, Number of suites: 33, Number of floors: 16, Cell phone/mobile rental, Computer rental, Parking (additional charge), Wireless Internet (additional charge), Complimentary newspapers, Porter/bellhop, Fitness facilities.

InterContinental San Francisco
888 Howard St
San Francisco CA 94103
(415) 616-6500
$170 - $398
Bed & Pet Discount Offered

Pet Policy: Pets accepted, $50 per night. Must not leave pets unattended in room.

Features: Bar/lounge, Health club, Security guard, Room service (24 hours), Accessible bathroom, Accessibility equipment for the deaf, Braille or raised signage, Indoor pool, Restaurant(s), Gift shop, Number of rooms: 550, Number of floors: 32, Parking (fee), Breakfast available (additional charge), Porter/bellhop, Doorman/doorwoman, Limo or Town Car service available, Full-service health spa, Smoke-Free property, Multilingual staff, Dry cleaning/laundry, Wireless Internet (additional charge), Business center, Concierge.

★★★★

JW Marriott San Francisco Union Square
500 Post St
San Francisco CA 94102
(415) 771-8600
$188 - $299
Bed & Pet Discount Offered

Pet Policy: Pets allowed, $75 per stay cleaning fee.

Features: Business center, Shoe Shine, Bar/Lounge, Restaurant(s), Number of floors: 21, Breakfast available (additional charge), Spa services, Complimentary newspapers, Porter/bellhop, Doorman/doorwoman, Security guard, Limo or Town Car service available, Wireless Internet (additional charge), Parking (fee), Smoke-Free, Nearby fitness center (discount), Room service, Dry cleaning/laundry.

★★★

Kensington Park Hotel
450 Post St
San Francisco CA 94102
(415) 788-6400
$149 - $299
Bed & Pet Discount Offered

Pet Policy: Dogs allowed, up to 40 lbs in standard rooms, up to 60 lbs in upgraded rooms. 2 dogs allowed provided combined weight within those limits. An additional cleaning fee of $25 is charged.

Features: Nearby fitness center (free), Parking (valet) $35/Day SUVs $45/Day, Business center, Number of rooms: 92, Airport transportation (additional charge), Coffee in lobby, Multilingual staff, Complimentary newspapers, Free wireless Internet, Concierge, Smoke-Free, Dry cleaning/laundry, Fitness facilities.

★★★

Larkspur Hotel Union Square
524 Sutter St
San Francisco CA 94102
(415) 421-2865
$119 - $189
Bed & Pet Discount Offered

Pet Policy: Pets up to 50 lbs welcome, no extra charge.

Features: Business Services, Concierge, Coffee in lobby, Parking (valet) $40/Day, SUV $50/Day, Nearby fitness center (discount), Gift shops or newsstand, Number of rooms: 114, Number of floors: 8, Library Multilingual staff, Complimentary newspapers, Porter/bellhop, Free wireless Internet, Smoke-Free, Business center, Bar/lounge, Dry cleaning/laundry.

Laurel Inn, a Joie de Vivre Boutique Hotel
444 Presidio Ave
San Francisco CA 94115
(415) 567-8467
$129 - $228
Bed & Pet Discount Offered

Pet Policy: Joie de Vivre has 14 pet-friendly properties in California, with Fido-friendly packages, amenities and a progressive pet policy designed to make hotel stays hospitable for dogs and their owners alike. Joie de Vivre's properties do not impose weight restrictions on dogs and do not charge pet fees (provided there is no damage to a guestroom and owners abide by pet policy rules).

Features: Bar/Lounge, Concierge, Number of rooms: 49, Number of floors: 3, Business services, Wireless Internet (additional charge), Video library, Free breakfast, ***Continued on next page***

Laurel Inn
Continued from previous page

Multilingual staff, Complimentary newspapers, Limo or Town Car service available, Nearby fitness center (discount), Parking $18/day, Accessible bathroom, Accessibility equipment for the deaf, Braille or raised signage, Dry cleaning/laundry.

★★★★
Le Meridien San Francisco
333 Battery St
San Francisco CA 94111
(415) 296-2900
$148 - $4,500
Bed & Pet Discount Offered

Pet Policy: Dogs up to 40 lbs and cats allowed, 9th floor rooms only, $90 per stay. Pet amenities include a dog treat, dog bed, food bowls and a mat, dog toy, and a "Dog in Room" sign. Must not leave alone in room.

Features: Bar/Lounge, Concierge , Business center, Currency exchange, Technology helpdesk, Nearby fitness center (discount), Medical assistance available, Room service (24 hours), Security guard, Restaurant(s), Number of rooms: 360, Number of floors: 24, Breakfast available (additional charge), Multilingual staff, Complimentary newspapers, Porter/bellhop, Doorman/doorwoman, Wireless Internet, Coffee in lobby, Shoe shine, Cell phone/mobile rental, Parking (valet) $49/Day, SUVs $59, Smoke-Free, Dry cleaning/laundry service.

Not rated
Marines Memorial Hotel
609 Sutter Street
San Francisco CA 94102
(415) 673-6672
$199 - $200

Pet Policy: Pets up to 20 lbs accepted, $12 per day

Features: Fitness center with lap swimming pool, Restaurant.

Not rated
Marriott Exeustay Corinthian Suites
512 Van Ness Avenue
San Francisco CA 94102
(800) 500-5110
$109 - $152

Pet Policy: Pets accepted, $500 refundable deposit per pet. Limit 2 pets.

Features: Furnished apartments, 30 day minimum stay may be required.

★★★½

Marriott San Francisco Fisherman's Wharf
1250 Columbus Ave
San Francisco CA 94133
(415) 775-7555
$129 - $269
Bed & Pet Discount Offered

Pet Policy: Dogs up to 50 lbs. $100 cleaning fee.

Features: Concierge, Business Center, Technology helpdesk, Currency exchange, Bar/lounge, Room service, Restaurant(s), Number of rooms: 285, Number of floors: 5, Translation services, Breakfast available (additional charge), Spa services, Multilingual staff, Complimentary newspapers, Porter/bellhop, Doorman/doorwoman, Limo or Town Car service available, Medical assistance available, Wireless Internet, Massage - treatment room(s), Parking (fee), Smoke-Free, Accessible bathroom, Accessibility equipment for the deaf, Braille or raised signage, Dry cleaning/laundry, Fitness center..

★★

Motel 6 San Francisco Downtown
895 Geary St
San Francisco CA 94109
(415) 441-8220
$99 - $100
Bed & Pet Discount Offered

Pet Policy: Well-behaved pets stay Free. Animals that pose a health or safety risk may not remain onsite, and include those that, in our manager's discretion, are too numerous for any one room, cause damage to our property or that of other guests, are too disruptive, are not properly attended, or demonstrate undue aggression. All pets must be declared at check-in. Pets must be attended to and under control at all times. If unavoidable circumstances require a pet to remain in a room while the owner is offsite, the pet must be secured in a crate or travel carrier. Pets must be on a leash or securely carried outside of rooms.

Features: Number of rooms: 69, Number of suites: 4, Number of floors: 3, Airport transportation (additional charge), Business services, Coffee in lobby, Parking (free), Multilingual staff, Security guard, Nearby fitness center (discount).

★★★★

Palace Hotel - Luxury Collection
2 New Montgomery St
San Francisco CA 94105
(415) 512-1111
$179- $399
Bed & Pet Discount Offered

Pet Policy Pets up to 80 lbs accepted, $100 per stay fee.

Features: Indoor pool, Bar/Lounge, Shoe shine, Concierge, Translation services, Currency exchange, Medical assistance available, Business center, Room service, Shopping on site, Coffee in lobby, Restaurant(s), Number of rooms: 552, Number of floors: 8, Parking (fee), Breakfast available (additional charge), Health club, Spa services, Multilingual staff, , Porter/bellhop, Doorman/doorwoman, Security guard, Wireless Internet (additional charge), Massage - treatment room(s), Complimentary newspapers Smoke-Free, Dry cleaning/laundry.

Parc 55 Wyndham San Francisco - Union Square
55 Cyril Magnin St
San Francisco CA 94102
(415) 392-8000
$109 - $319
Bed & Pet Discount Offered

Pet Policy The Wyndham Parc 55 Hotel welcomes our guests to bring their pets to stay in our guestrooms. Service animals accompanying persons with disabilities are always welcomed at the Wyndham Parc 55 Hotel. Service animals need to be registered at the front desk, however, are not required to pay the one-time pet charge, nor have a weight limit. A one-time pet charge of $50 will be applied to your account per stay. No more than two pets per room are allowed at any one time. Pets must be no more than 50 lbs in weight. When in public areas of the Hotel, pets must be kept on a leash or in a carrier. Pets are not allowed in Cityhouse restaurant or in the health club. This exclusion does not apply to service animals. Pets must not be left unattended in the guestrooms. Pets must be house-trained and clean. An additional $250 cleaning charge may apply if pets create excessive mess. Dogs barking or cats meowing can disturb other guests. If your pet is left unattended and making noise, housekeeping will remove your pet from the room and you will be charged a minimum fee of $90. You will be charged an additional $30 per hour after the third hour. Housekeeping will NOT clean your room if your pet is left unattended. If both you and your pet are in the room while the housekeeper is present, your pet must be leashed or caged. Please contact housekeeping regarding the cleaning time you prefer for your room. Guests are responsible for all property damages and/or personal injuries resulting from their pet. Please contact housekeeping at extension 57 for bowls, leashes or pet treats. You agree to release, defend and indemnify the Wyndham Parc 55 Hotel, from any and all claims or damages related to your pet's stay at the hotel.

Features: Number of rooms: 1,010, Number of floors: 32, Wireless Internet- additional charge, Breakfast available (additional charge), Pool table, Health club, Spa services, Multilingual staff, Business center, Doorman/doorwoman, Security guard, Porter/bellhop, Limo or Town Car service available, Massage - treatment room(s), Smoke-Free, Concierge, Currency exchange, Bar/lounge, Restaurant(s), Gift shop, Parking (valet) $42/Day $47 SUVs/Day, Accessible bathroom, Accessibility equipment for the deaf, Braille or raised signage, Dry cleaning/laundry, Room service.

Prescott Hotel - a Kimpton Hotel
545 Post St
San Francisco CA 94102
(415) 563-0303
$178 - $399
Bed & Pet Discount Offered

Pet Policy Pets welcome. No size restriction. No Fees. Special pet amenities include treats, bowls, tags with hotel info, and even pet packages with special food, dog walking, and toys

Features: Coffee in lobby, Business services, Bar/lounge, Shoe shine, Restaurant(s), Room service, Number of rooms: 164, Number of floors: 7, Breakfast available (additional charge), Multilingual staff, Complimentary newspapers, Porter/bellhop, Doorman/doorwoman, Limo or Town Car service available, Wireless Internet, Smoke-Free property, Concierge, Dry cleaning/laundry service, Fitness facilities, Valet parking (additional charge).

★★★
Radisson Hotel Fisherman's Wharf
250 Beach St
San Francisco CA 94133
(415) 392-6700
$169 - $189
Bed & Pet Discount Offered

Pet Policy Pets welcome, $75 per pet per stay cleaning fee charged.

Features: Business services, Security guard, 24-hour business center, Dry cleaning/laundry service, Accessible bathroom, Accessibility equipment for the deaf, Braille or raised signage, Free wireless Internet, Fitness facilities, Parking fee, Wheelchair accessible, Swimming pool - outdoor, Concierge, Shopping on site, Number of rooms: 355, Number of floors: 4, Multilingual staff, Complimentary newspapers, Porter/bellhop, Smoke-Free property.

★★
Rodeway Inn Civic Center
860 Eddy St
San Francisco CA 94109
(415) 474-4374
$53 - $88
Bed & Pet Discount Offered

Pet Policy Rodeway Inns charge a fee of $10 per night per pet and require a $50 damage deposit, which is refunded if the room is in order at check out. Max of 2 pets per room. A veterinarian certificate that the pet is on a flea and parasite program and that they are Free from parasites is required. Pets may not be left alone in the room unless in a cage.

Features: Guest laundry, Number of rooms: 34, Number of floors: 2, Airport transportation (additional charge), Business services, Parking (free), Complimentary newspapers in lobby.

★★
Rodeway Inn Downtown
101 9th St
San Francisco CA 94103
(415) 621-3655
$65 - $92
Bed & Pet Discount Offered

Pet Policy: Rodeway Inns charge a fee of $10 per night per pet and require a $50 damage deposit, which is refunded if the room is in order at check out. Max of 2 pets per room. A veterinarian certificate that the pet is on a flea and parasite is required. Pets may not be left alone in the room unless in a cage.
Continued on next page

Rodeway Inn Downtown
Continued from previous page

Features: Parking (free), Coffee in lobby, Number of rooms: 34, Number of floors: 3, Free breakfast, Complimentary newspapers, Free wireless Internet, Accessible bathroom, Accessibility equipment for the deaf, Braille or raised signage.

★★★★½

Serrano Hotel - a Kimpton Hotel
405 Taylor St
San Francisco CA 94102
(415) 885-2500
$144 - $519
Bed & Pet Discount Offered

Pet Policy Pets welcome. No size restriction. No Fees. Special pet amenities include treats, bowls, tags with hotel info, and even pet packages with special food, dog walking, and toys

Features: Security guard, Bar/lounge, Sauna, Coffee in lobby, Concierge services, Room service (limited hours), Shoe shine,, Restaurant(s), Number of rooms: 236, Number of floors: 17, Breakfast available (additional charge), Multilingual staff, Complimentary newspapers, Business center, Porter/bellhop, Doorman/doorwoman, Limo or Town Car service available, Free wireless Internet, Massage - treatment room(s), Parking fee, Smoke-Free property, Technology helpdesk, Dry cleaning/laundry, Fitness facilities.

★★★★

Sheraton Fisherman's Wharf
2500 Mason St
San Francisco CA 94133
(415) 362-5500
$148 - $299
Bed & Pet Discount Offered

Pet Policy 1 pet up to 75 pounds, no fee. Damage waiver must be signed and pets should not be left unattended in room.

Features: Room service (limited hours), Restaurant(s), Swimming pool - outdoor, Number of rooms: 531, Number of floors: 4, Suitable for children, Breakfast available (additional charge), Multilingual staff, Porter/bellhop, Doorman/doorwoman, Security guard, Limo or Town Car service available, Parking (valet) $43/Day, SUVs $60, Business center, Currency exchange, Concierge desk, Smoke-Free property, Accessible bathroom, Accessibility equipment for the deaf, Braille or raised signage, Dry cleaning/laundry service, Free wireless Internet, Fitness facilities.

★★★½

Sir Francis Drake - a Kimpton Hotel
450 Powell Street
San Francisco CA 94102
(800) 795-7129
$149 - $349
Bed & Pet Discount Offered

Pet Policy Pets welcome. No size restriction. No Fees. Special pet amenities include treats, bowls, tags with hotel info, and even pet packages with special food, dog walking, and toys

Features: Parking garage (additional charge), Medical assistance available, Concierge services, Nightclub, Shopping on site, Elevator, Bar/lounge, Technology helpdesk, Security guard, *Continued on next page*

Sir Francis Drake
Continued from previous page

Room service (limited hours), Babysitting or child care, Business center, Restaurant(s), Number of rooms: 417, Number of floors: 21, Breakfast available (additional charge), Multilingual staff, Complimentary newspapers in lobby, Porter/bellhop, Doorman/doorwoman, Limo or Town Car service available (Mon - Fri), Dry cleaning/laundry service, Fitness facilities, Free wireless Internet, Limo or Town Car service available, Free Internet.

★★★

Steinhart Hotel and Apartments
952 Sutter Street
San Francisco CA 94109
(800) 553-1900
$299 - $300
Bed & Pet Discount Offered

Pet Policy Dogs allowed, up to 40 lbs in standard rooms, up to 60 lbs in upgraded rooms. 2 dogs allowed provided combined weight within those limits. An additional cleaning fee of $25 is charge.

Features: Business services, Elevator, Number of rooms: 57, Number of floors: 6, Barbecue grill(s), Guest laundry, Use of nearby fitness center (free), Front desk (limited hours), Free wireless Internet, Dry cleaning/laundry service, Concierge services.

★★★★½

Taj Campton Place
340 Stockton St
San Francisco CA 94108
(415) 781-5555
$213- $640
Bed & Pet Discount Offered

Pet Policy Pets accepted, $100 pet per stay.

Features: Concierge desk, Room service (24 hours), Shoe shine, Bar/lounge, Elevator, Restaurant(s), Number of rooms: 110, Number of floors: 15, Breakfast available (additional charge), Health club, Complimentary newspapers in lobby, Porter/bellhop, Doorman/doorwoman, Wireless Internet (additional charge), Parking (valet) $45 Per Day, Accessible bathroom, Braille or raised signage, Dry cleaning/laundry service.

★★★★♥

The Fairmont San Francisco
950 Mason Street Atop Nob Hill
San Francisco CA 94108
(415) 772-5000
$178 - $798
Bed & Pet Discount Offered

Pet Policy Pets under 20 pounds are permitted in the hotel. The animal must be on a leash at all times and must not be left unattended in the room. Seeing-eye dogs are always welcome and exempt of restrictions.

Features: Business Center, Concierge desk, Elevator, Translation services, Sauna, Bar/lounge, Steam room, Hair salon, Full-service health spa, Wireless Internet (additional charge), Breakfast available (additional charge), Currency exchange, Nightclub, Shoe shine, Multilingual staff, Complimentary newspapers in lobby, Porter/bellhop, Doorman/doorwoman, Security guard, Limo or Town Car service available, Medical assistance available, Massage - treatment room(s),

Continued on next page

The Fairmont San Francisco
Continued from previous page

Technology helpdesk, Parking (valet) $50/Day $50 SUVs/Day, Restaurant(s), Shopping on site, Number of rooms: 591, Cell phone/mobile rental, Computer rental, Coffee in lobby, Accessible bathroom, Accessibility equipment for the deaf, Braille or raised signage, Dry cleaning/laundry service, Health club, Room service (24 hours), ATM/banking.

★★½

The Inn San Francisco
943 South Van Ness Avenue
San Francisco CA 94110
(415) 641-0188
$175 - $227

Pet Policy Dogs allowed on advanced approval, no fee. You must contact the property directly for pet approval.

Features: Number of rooms: 21, Number of floors: 3, Year Built 1872, Library, Free breakfast, Free wireless Internet, Smoke-Free property, Parking $15/Day, Dry cleaning/laundry service.

★★★★★♥

The Ritz-Carlton, San Francisco
600 Stockton St
San Francisco CA 94108
(415) 773-6168
$298- $809

Pet Policy There is a 10 lb. weight limit for dogs. Reservations must be made through the Executive Offices. All dogs must be leashed when riding hotel Elevators and be carried by their owners through the lobby of the hotel. All public areas, including The Lobby Lounge and The Dining Room are reserved for owners only, with the exception of service dogs. Pet fee is $125.

Features: Business center, Bar/lounge, Restaurant(s), Concierge, Breakfast available (additional charge), Spa services on site, Limo or Town Car service available, Smoke-Free property, Coffee in lobby, Steam room, Accessible bathroom, Braille or raised signage, Fitness center, Valet parking (fee).

★★★★★

The St. Regis San Francisco
125 3rd St
San Francisco CA 94103
(415) 284-4000
$358 - $1,249
Bed & Pet Discount Offered

Pet Policy Pets less than 30 lbs, fully trained, restrained and in compliance with local laws are permitted in the hotel. Pets are not permitted in the St. Regis lobby bar, Vitrine, Spa, pool and fitness center. Upon arrival a cleaning fee of $150 will be charged to your account. Pets are only allowed on the 12th and 13th floors. Associates will not enter any guestroom while a dog is present (with or without the handler). Pet-sitters and walkers can be arranged upon request.

Features: Shoe shine, Steam room, Swimming pool - indoor, Room service (24 hours), Floor butler, Beauty services, Concierge desk, Elevator, Full-service health spa, Bar/lounge, Business center, Restaurant(s),
Continued on next page

The St. Regis San Francisco
Continued from previous page

Number of rooms: 260, Number of floors: 20, Business services, Parking (additional charge), Wireless Internet (additional charge), Breakfast available (additional charge), Multilingual staff, Porter/bellhop, Doorman/doorwoman, Limo or Town Car service available, Massage - treatment room(s), Dry cleaning/laundry service, Security guard, Sauna, Fitness facilities.

★★★★
The Westin San Francisco Market Street
50 3rd St
San Francisco CA 94103
(415) 974-6400
$139 - $649
Bed & Pet Discount Offered

Pet Policy Dogs, 40 lbs or less welcome. No fee. Limit 2 per room. Your pampered pooch will enjoy a Heavenly Dog Bed, food and water bowls and a special floor mat, while owners will receive clean-up supplies and their own welcome kit. If you need assistance locating groomers, dog parks, pet supply stores, simply ask our concierge. Introduce yourself to the most elegant choice of San Francisco dog friendly hotels, and revel in the convenience of our special pet amenities.

Features: Business Center, Coffee in lobby, Room service, Concierge, Computer rental, Bar/lounge, Currency exchange, Translation services, Cell phone/mobile rental, Shoe shine, Complimentary newspapers, Porter/bellhop, Doorman/doorwoman, Security guard, Medical assistance available, Wireless Internet (additional charge), Smoke-Free property, Technology helpdesk, Accessible bathroom, Accessibility equipment for the deaf, Braille or raised signage, Dry cleaning/laundry, Restaurant(s), Number of rooms: 676, Number of floors: 36, Breakfast available (additional charge), Multilingual staff, Fitness facilities, Valet parking (additional charge).

★★★★
The Westin St Francis on Union Square
335 Powell Street
San Francisco CA 94102
(415) 397-7000
$151 - $379
Bed & Pet Discount Offered

Pet Policy: One pet under 40 pounds. No Fee. Pet beds and other pet amenities available on request.

Features:, Shoe Shine, Bar/Lounge, Full-service health spa, Number of rooms: 1,195, Number of floors: 31, Parking fee, Wireless Internet (additional charge), Breakfast available (additional charge), Health club, Multilingual staff, Complimentary newspapers, Porter/bellhop, Doorman/doorwoman, Security guard, Massage - treatment room(s), Smoke-Free property, Business center, Shopping on site, Room service, Translation services, Concierge, Restaurant(s), Dry cleaning/laundry.

★★
Travelodge at the Presidio
2755 Lombard St
San Francisco CA 94123
(415) 931-8581
$88 - $139
Bed & Pet Discount Offered

Pet Policy: Only small dogs allowed, $20 per pet per day.

Features: Business services, Coffee in lobby, Free breakfast, Parking (free), Accessible bathroom, Accessibility equipment for the deaf, Business center, Smoke-Free property, Free wireless Internet.

★★
Travelodge By The Bay
1450 Lombard St
San Francisco CA 94123
(415) 673-0691
$93 - $129
Bed & Pet Discount Offered

Pet Policy: Dogs Allowed In 6 Pet Friendly Rooms, $23 Fee Per Pet Per Night, - must reserve in advance. Crate required If pets are left unattended in room.

Features: Guest laundry, Elevator, Parking $12 Per Day, Restaurant(s), Concierge, Smoke-Free property, Free wireless Internet, Number of rooms: 71.

★★
Travelodge Golden Gate
2230 Lombard St
San Francisco CA 94123
(415) 922-3900
$59 - $248
Bed & Pet Discount Offered

Pet Policy: Pets accepted, $20 per pet per day.

Features: Business services, Wireless Internet, Smoke-Free property, Number of rooms: 29, Number of floors: 3, Airport transportation (additional charge), Parking (free), Multilingual staff, Complimentary newspapers in lobby

★★★½
Villa Florence, a Larkspur Hotel
225 Powell St
San Francisco CA 94102
(415) 397-7700
$139 - $338
Bed & Pet Discount Offered

Pet Policy: Pets accepted, $75 per pet per stay fee.

Features: Bar/Lounge, Concierge, Complimentary newspapers, Porter/bellhop, Free wireless Internet, Nearby fitness center (discount), Elevator, Business center, Restaurant(s), Number of rooms: 182, Number of floors: 7, Room service (limited hours), Dry cleaning/laundry service, Valet parking (fee).

W Hotel San Francisco
181 3rd St
San Francisco CA 94103
(415) 777-5300
$189 - $498
Bed & Pet Discount Offered

Pet Policy: Pets up to 50 lbs welcome. $100 per stay cleaning fee.

Features: Indoor pool, Currency exchange, Concierge, Business center, Bar/lounge, Video library, Technology helpdesk, Translation services, Nearby fitness center (discount), Spa services, Security guard, Shoe shine, Room service, Parking fee, Breakfast available (additional charge), Multilingual staff, Complimentary newspapers, Porter/bellhop, Doorman/doorwoman, Limo or Town Car service available, Free wireless Internet, Restaurant(s), Number of rooms: 410, Number of floors: 31, Dry cleaning/laundry service, Smoke-Free property.

San Gabriel

Also see the following nearby communities that have pet friendly lodging: Rosemead - 2 miles, Monterey Park - 3 miles, South Pasadena - 4 miles, Pasadena - 4 miles, El Monte - 5 miles, South El Monte - 5 miles, Arcadia - 5 miles, Commerce - 7 miles, Monrovia - 7 miles, Pico Rivera - 7 miles, Bell Gardens - 9 miles, Whittier - 10 miles

★★★½
Hilton Los Angeles San Gabriel
225 W Valley Blvd
San Gabriel CA 91776
(626) 270-2700
$116 - $289
Bed & Pet Discount Offered

Pet Policy: Pets up to 75 lbs accepted, $50 per stay fee. Limit 2 pets per room.

Features: Business center, Bar/lounge, Parking (fee), Room service (24 hours), Concierge, Coffee in lobby, Translation services, Restaurant(s), Outdoor pool, Gift shops or newsstand, Number of rooms: 222, Number of floors: 6, Breakfast available (additional charge), Multilingual staff, Porter/bellhop, Limo or Town Car service available, Massage - treatment room(s), Dry cleaning/laundry service, Fitness facilities.

San Jose

Also see the following nearby communities that have pet friendly lodging: Campbell - 5 miles, Milpitas - 8 miles, Santa Clara - 8 miles, Cupertino - 8 miles, Los Gatos - 8 miles, Sunnyvale - 10 miles

★★★½
Crowne Plaza San Jose Downtown
282 Almaden Blvd
San Jose CA 95113
(408) 998 0400
$98 - $209
Bed & Pet Discount Offered

Pet Policy: Dogs and cats welcome. $50 per stay.

Features: Sauna, Accessible bathroom, Accessibility equipment for the deaf, Braille or raised signage, Bar/lounge, Restaurant(s), Gift shops or newsstand, Number of floors: 9, Multilingual staff, Complimentary newspapers, Room service, Business center, Concierge, Wireless Internet, Smoke-Free property, Parking (fee), Fitness facilities.

★★
Days Inn Airport
1280 N 4th St
San Jose CA 95112
(408) 437-9100
$51 - $89
Bed & Pet Discount Offered

Pet Policy: Dogs only, $10 per stay.

Features: Coffee in lobby, Free breakfast, Parking (free), Multilingual staff, Complimentary newspapers in lobby, Business center.

★★★★
Doubletree Hotel San Jose
2050 Gateway Pl
San Jose CA 95110
(408) 453-4000
$89 - $289
Bed & Pet Discount Offered

Pet Policy: Pets up to 100 lbs accepted, $50 fee. Registered guests are responsible for any damage caused by pets. Housekeeping personnel will inspect accommodations upon departure. In consideration of other guests, we ask pet owners to ensure guest room noise levels are kept to a minimum. Refunds to guests inconvenienced by noisy pets (up to $100) will be charged ***Continued on next page***

Doubletree Hotel San Jose
Continued from next page

to the registered pet owners. Housekeepers are prohibited from entering rooms occupied by pets unless guests are present or unless pets are crated.

Features: Business center, Dry cleaning/laundry service, Bar/lounge, Airport transportation (free), Restaurant(s), Swimming pool - outdoor, Gift shops or newsstand, Number of rooms: 505, Pool table, Nightclub, Multilingual staff, Porter/bellhop, Free wireless Internet, Concierge desk, Fitness facilities, Room service, Parking (additional charge).

★★

ESD San Jose Downtown
55 East Brokaw Rd
San Jose CA 95112
(408) 453-3000
$99 - $144

Pet Policy: One pet is allowed in each guest room. A $25 per day non-refundable cleaning fee (not to exceed $150) will be charged the first night of your stay. Weight, size and breed restrictions may apply. Please contact the hotel directly with inquiries. Please Note: "Signature" rooms do not currently accommodate pets, with the exception of handicap accessible rooms.

Features: Fully equipped kitchens, Refrigerator, Microwave, Stovetop, Workspace with computer data port, Free local phone calls, Iron and ironing board, Guest laundry, Free wireless Internet, Number of rooms 138.

★★

Extended Stay America San Jose - Santa Clara
2131 Gold St
San Jose CA 95002
(408) 262-0401
$84 - $109
Bed & Pet Discount Offered

Pet Policy: One medium-size pet is allowed in each guest room. A $25 per day non-refundable Cleaning fee (not to exceed $150) will be charged the first night of your stay.

Features: Guest laundry, Elevator, Number of rooms: 101, Number of floors: 3, Suitable for children, Wireless Internet (additional charge), Parking (free).

Extended Stay America San Jose - South - Edenvale
6199 San Ignacio Ave
San Jose CA 95119
(408) 226-4499
$59 - $104
Bed & Pet Discount Offered

Pet Policy: One medium-size pet is allowed in each guest room. A $25 per day non-refundable cleaning fee (not to exceed $150) will be charged the first night of your stay.

Features: Guest laundry, Elevator, Swimming pool - outdoor, Number of rooms: 121, Number of floors: 3, Wireless Internet (additional charge), Parking (free), Multilingual staff.

Extended Stay Deluxe San Jose - Airport
55 E Brokaw Rd
San Jose CA 95112
(408) 453-3000
$79 - $134
Bed & Pet Discount Offered

Pet Policy: One medium-size pet is allowed in each guest room. A $25 per day cleaning fee (not to exceed $150) will be charged the first night.

Features: Dry cleaning/laundry service, Outdoor pool, Coffee in lobby, Airport transportation (free), Number of rooms: 138, Number of floors: 4, Barbecue grill(s), Wireless Internet (additional charge), Free breakfast, Complimentary newspapers in lobby, Business center, Fitness facilities.

Extended Stay Deluxe San Jose - South - Edenvale
6189 San Ignacio Ave
San Jose CA 95119
(408) 226-4499
$69 - $119
Bed & Pet Discount Offered

Pet Policy: One medium-size pet is allowed in each guest room. A $25 per day non-refundable cleaning fee (not to exceed $150) will be charged the first night of your stay.

Features: Guest laundry, Number of rooms: 98, Number of floors: 3, Business services, Wireless Internet (additional charge), Parking (free), Multilingual staff, Swimming pool - outdoor seasonal, Use of nearby fitness center (discount).

Fairfield Inn & Suites by Marriott - San Jose Airp
1755 N 1st St
San Jose CA 95112
(408) 453-3133
$83 - $174
Bed & Pet Discount Offered

Pet Policy: Pets allowed with $75 per stay cleaning fee.

Features: Swimming pool - outdoor, Business Center, Coffee in lobby, Elevator, Multilingual staff, RV and truck parking, Airport transportation (free), Number of rooms: 186, Number of floors: 3, Free breakfast, Parking (free), Complimentary newspapers in lobby, Accessible bathroom, Accessibility equipment for the deaf, Dry cleaning/laundry service, Free wireless Internet, Fitness facilities.

Hilton San Jose
300 Almaden Blvd
San Jose CA 95110
(408) 287-2100
$118 - $259
Bed & Pet Discount Offered

Pet Policy: Pets up to 75 lbs accepted, $75 per stay.

Features: Shoe Shine, Business Center, Currency Exchange, Outdoor pool, Bar/lounge, Restaurant(s), Room service (limited hours), Concierge services, Gift shops or newsstand, Number of rooms: 355, Number of floors: 18, Translation services, Suitable for children, Breakfast available (additional charge), Multilingual staff, Complimentary newspapers in lobby, Porter/bellhop, Doorman/doorwoman, Security guard, Free wireless Internet, Self-parking $19/Day, Accessible bathroom, Accessibility equipment for the deaf, Braille or raised signage, Dry cleaning/laundry service, Fitness facilities.

Homestead San Jose-
1560 N 1st St
San Jose CA 95112
(408) 573-0648
$64 - $114
Bed & Pet Discount Offered

Pet Policy: Pets allowed, no size restriction, $25 per day to a maximum of $150 per stay. Limit of 1 pet per room.

Features: Elevator, Number of rooms: 152, Number of floors: 3, Barbecue grill(s), Wireless Internet (additional charge), Parking (free).

Howard Johnson Express Inn San Jose Convention Cen
1215 S 1st St
San Jose CA 95110
(408) 280-5300
$67 - $83
Bed & Pet Discount Offered

Pet Policy: Pets allowed. $10 per night per pet plus $40 refundable deposit.

Features: Number of rooms: 58, Number of floors: 2, Free breakfast, Parking (free), Use of nearby fitness center (free), Free wireless Internet, Accessible bathroom, Braille or raised signage, Dry cleaning/laundry service, Business center

La Quinta Inn San Jose Airport
2585 Seaboard Ave
San Jose CA 95131
(408) 435-8800
$55 - $74
Bed & Pet Discount Offered

Pet Policy: Cats and dogs up to 50 pounds are accepted in all guest rooms. Housekeeping services for rooms with pets require pet owner be present or pet must be crated. No fees or deposits are required.

Features: Accessible bathroom, Airport transportation (free), Swimming pool - outdoor, Number of rooms: 150, Number of floors: 2, Free breakfast, Free parking, Multilingual staff, Dry cleaning/laundry, Fitness center, Business center, Smoke-Free property, Free wireless Internet.

Motel 6 San Jose Airport Central
1440 N 1st Street
San Jose CA 95112
(408) 453-7750
$59 - $62
Bed & Pet Discount Offered

Pet Policy: Well-behaved pets stay Free. Animals that pose a health or safety risk may not remain onsite, and include those that, in our manager's discretion, are too numerous for any one room, cause damage to our property or that of other guests, are too disruptive, are not properly attended, or demonstrate undue aggression. All pets must be declared at check-in. In consideration of all guests, pets must be attended to and under control at all times. If unavoidable circumstances require a pet to remain in a room while the owner is offsite, the pet must be secured in a crate or travel carrier. Pets must be on a leash or securely carried outside of guest rooms.

Features: Free wireless Internet, Multilingual staff, Outdoor pool - seasonal, Wheelchair accessible, Number of rooms: 75, Number of floors: 2, Business services, Accessible bathroom, Braille or raised signage, RV and truck parking, Coffee in lobby.

Not rated:

Oakwood 101 San Fernando
101 E San Fernando Street
San Jose CA 95112
(602) 427-2752
$143 - $150

Pet Policy: Pets welcome, $10 per day, plus repair of any damages.

Features: Full kitchen, Fitness center, Parking, Guest laundry. 30 day minimum stay may be required.

Not rated

Oakwood San Jose South
700 S. Saratoga Ave.
San Jose CA 95129
(602) 427-2752
$100 - $156

Pet Policy: Pets accepted with limitations and fee. Contact hotel directly for more information and to make reservations.

Features: Furnished apartments, Onsite massage therapist, Dry cleaning. 30 day minimum stay may be required.

★★

Quality Inn Silicon Valley
2390 Harris Way
San Jose CA 95131
(408) 434-9330
$69 - $89
Bed & Pet Discount Offered

Pet Policy: Pets up to 25 lbs, $20 per night per pet. Limit 2 per room.

Features: Elevator, Number of rooms: 49, Number of floors: 3, Coffee in lobby, Parking (free), Complimentary newspapers in lobby, Sauna, Dry cleaning/laundry, Airport transportation (free), Wireless Internet, Free Breakfast, Fitness facilities.

★★★

Residence Inn by Marriott San Jose South
6111 San Ignacio Ave
San Jose CA 95119
(408) 226-7676
$115 - $209
Bed & Pet Discount Offered

Pet Policy: Pets allowed, $100 per stay cleaning fee.

Features: Free Breakfast, Swimming pool - outdoor, Elevator, Number of rooms: 150, Number of floors: 3, Business services, Barbecue grill(s), Coffee in lobby, Parking (free) Complimentary newspapers in lobby, Free wireless Internet, Dry cleaning/laundry service, Tennis on site, Fitness facilities

San Jose Airport Garden Hotel
1740 N 1st Street
San Jose CA 95112
(408) 793-3300
$70- $173
Bed & Pet Discount Offered

Pet Policy: Dogs up to 25 lbs accepted, $50 per pet per stay.

Features: Parking (free), Concierge, Swimming pool - outdoor, Airport transportation (free), Restaurant(s), Room service, Number of rooms: 512, Number of suites: 12, Number of floors: 3, Multilingual staff, Porter/bellhop, Bar/lounge, Accessible bathroom, Accessibility equipment for the deaf, Braille or raised signage, Dry cleaning/laundry, Wheelchair accessible, Security guard, Limo or Town Car service available, Smoke-Free property, Technology support staff, Free wireless Internet, Business center, RV and truck parking, Smoke-Free property, Fitness center.

Staybridge Suites by Holiday Inn - San Jose
1602 Crane Ct
San Jose CA 95112
(408) 436-1600
$220 - $221
Bed & Pet Discount Offered

Pet Policy: Pets allowed with nonrefundable fee. Up to $75 for 1-6 nights and up to $150 for 7+ nights. Each pet must weigh less than 80 lbs. Pet agreement must be signed at check-in. Record of complete and up-to-date vaccinations required.

Features: Accessible bathroom, Accessibility equipment for the deaf, Braille or raised signage

★★★★

The Fairmont San Jose
170 S Market Street
San Jose CA 95113
(408) 998-1900
$128 - $339
Bed & Pet Discount Offered

Pet Policy: Pets under up to 70 pounds are permitted in the Hotel at an additional cost of $75 per stay. Your pet must be on a leash at all times and must not be left unattended in the room. Any damage incurred to the room by the pet is the responsibility of the guest. Service dogs are always welcome and exempt of charges.

Features: Business center, Babysitting or child care, Hair salon, Bar/lounge, Parking fee, Outdoor pool, Currency exchange, Room service, Sauna, Restaurant(s), Concierge, Gift shops or newsstand, Number of rooms: 808, Number of floors: 20, Business services, Wireless Internet (additional charge), Breakfast available (additional charge), Spa services, Multilingual staff, Complimentary newspapers, Porter/bellhop, Doorman/doorwoman, Security guard, Limo or Town Car service available, Massage - treatment room(s), Fitness center.

★★★★

The Sainte Claire, a Larkspur Collection Hotel
302 S Market St
San Jose CA 95113
(408) 295-2000
$118 - $119
Bed & Pet Discount Offered

Pet Policy: Pets up to 60 lbs accepted, $75 per stay.

Features: Bar/Lounge, Room service, ATM/banking, Number of rooms: 171, Breakfast available (additional charge), Restaurant, Health club, Complimentary newspapers, Nearby fitness center (free), Porter/bellhop, Security guard, Smoke-Free, Concierge, Business center, Computer rental, Parking (valet) $21 Per Day, Accessible bathroom, Accessibility equipment for the deaf, Braille or raised signage, Dry cleaning/laundry, Free wireless Internet, Year built:1926.

TownePlace Suites by Marriott San Jose Cupertino
440 Saratoga Ave
San Jose CA 95129
(408) 984-5903
$71 - $199
Bed & Pet Discount Offered

Pet Policy: Pets allowed, $100 per stay.

Features: Business Center, Coffee in Lobby, Outdoor pool, Number of rooms: 101, Number of floors: 3, BBQ area, Free breakfast, Parking (free), Complimentary newspaper, Smoke-Free, Grocery/convenience store, Dry cleaning/laundry, Free wireless Internet, Fitness center.

Vagabond Inn San Jose Airport
1488 N 1st St
San Jose CA 95112
(408) 453-8822
$68 - $80
Bed & Pet Discount Offered

Pet Policy: Pet friendly rooms, $20 per night.

Features: Business center, Free wireless Internet, Swimming pool - outdoor, Number of rooms: 76, Coffee in lobby, Guest laundry, Free breakfast, Free parking.

Not rated:
Valley Inn San Jose
2155 The Alemeda
San Jose CA 95126
(408) 241-8500
$53 - $69

Pet Policy: Small pets allowed, $10 per pet per night.

Features: 26 rooms, Coffee/tea makers, Video players, Modem/data port connections, Refrigerators, Whirlpool baths in suites.

San Juan Capistrano

Also see the following nearby communities that have pet friendly lodging: Dana Point - 4 miles, Capistrano Beach - 5 miles, Laguna Hills - 6 miles, San Clemente - 7 miles, Laguna Beach - 7 miles, Lake Forest - 8 miles.

Best Western Capistrano Inn
27174 Ortega Hwy
San Juan Capistrano CA 92675
(949) 493-5661
$99 - $129
Bed & Pet Discount Offered

Pet Policy: Small pets allowed with $25 fee.

Features: Outdoor pool, Business center, Gift shops or newsstand, Number of rooms: 108, Number of floors: 2, Airport transportation (additional charge), Coffee in lobby, Complimentary newspapers, Nearby fitness center (free), Porter/bellhop, Free wireless Internet, Smoke-Free property, Dry cleaning/laundry service, Wheelchair accessible.

San Luis Obispo

Also see the following nearby communities that have pet friendly lodging: Pismo Beach - 7 miles, Los Osos - 9 miles

Best Western Royal Oak Hotel
214 Madonna Rd
San Luis Obispo CA 93405
(805) 544-4410
$89 - $149
Bed & Pet Discount Offered

Pet Policy: Pets allowed.

Features: Swimming pool - outdoor, Business center, Concierge, Number of rooms: 99, Number of floors: 2, Coffee in lobby, Free breakfast, Complimentary newspapers, Porter/bellhop, Free wireless Internet, Dry cleaning/laundry, Fitness center.

Days Inn San Luis Obispo
2050 Garfield St
San Luis Obispo CA 93401
(805) 549-9911
$63 - $139

Pet Policy: Hotel accepts pets. Please contact the property directly to book a pet room. Additional pet fee of $15 per day per pet.

Features: Elevator, Business services, BBQ area, Coffee in lobby, Free wireless Internet, Free breakfast, Parking (free), Complimentary newspapers, Swimming pool - outdoor seasonal, Security guard

Embassy Suites Hotel - San Luis Obispo
333 Madonna Rd
San Luis Obispo CA 93405
(805) 549-0800
$124 - $219
Bed & Pet Discount Offered

Pet Policy: Pets up to 50 lbs, $25 per day.

Features: Indoor pool, Airport transportation (free), Wireless Internet (additional charge), Bar/lounge, Room service, Number of suites: 196, Number of floors: 4, Coffee in lobby, Multilingual staff, Free breakfast, Complimentary newspapers, Business center, Accessible bathroom, Accessibility equipment for the deaf, Braille or raised signage, Dry cleaning/laundry, Fitness center, Shopping.

Holiday Inn Express San Luis Obispo
1800 Monterey St
San Luis Obispo CA 93401
(805) 544-8600
$124 - $229
Bed & Pet Discount Offered

Pet Policy: Pets allowed, $30 per night.

Features: Gift shops or newsstand, Number of rooms: 100, Number of floors: 3, Free breakfast, Multilingual staff, Business center, Free wireless Internet, Accessible bathroom, Accessibility equipment for the deaf, Braille or raised signage, Outdoor pool, Dry cleaning/laundry, Fitness facilities.

Rodeway Inn San Luis Obispo
1001 Olive St
San Luis Obispo CA 93405
(805) 544-0400
$41- $104
Bed & Pet Discount Offered

Rodeway Inns charge a fee of $10 per night per pet and require a $50 damage deposit, which is refunded if the room is in order at check out. Max of 2 pets per room. A veterinarian certificate that the pet is on a flea and parasite program is required. Pets may not be left alone in the room unless in a cage.

Features: Business services, Coffee in lobby, Number of rooms: 27, Number of floors: 1.

San Luis Inn And Suites
404 Santa Rosa St
San Luis Obispo CA 93405
(805) 544-0881
$39 - $125
Bed & Pet Discount Offered

Pet Policy: Welcomes all well-behaved pets, $25 per pet per stay. With surrounding walking trails and nearby fields the Sands Suites & Motel is the most pet-friendly lodging establishment on the Central Coast of California. Limited to pet friendly rooms.
Continued on next page

San Luis Inn And Suites
Continued from previous page

Features: Guest laundry, Swimming pool - outdoor, Free breakfast, Business services, Number of rooms: 35, Number of floors: 2, Parking (free), Free wireless Internet, Smoke-Free property.

★★
Super 8 Motel - San Luis Obispo
1951 Monterey St
San Luis Obispo CA 93401
(805) 544-6888
$54 - $79
Bed & Pet Discount Offered

Pet Policy: Pets welcome, $10 per night per pet.

Features: Business services, Free breakfast, Multilingual staff, Complimentary newspapers, Wireless Internet, Swimming pool - outdoor seasonal, Free Parking,.

★★
Vagabond Inn San Luis Obispo
210 Madonna Rd
San Luis Obispo CA 93405
(805) 544-4710
$58 - $116
Bed & Pet Discount Offered

Pet Policy: Pets allowed, $10 per pet per night. No size restrictions.

Features: Coffee in lobby, Swimming pool - outdoor, Number of rooms: 60, Number of floors: 2, Free breakfast, Parking (free) Complimentary newspapers in lobby, Smoke-Free property.

San Marcos

Also see the following nearby communities that have pet friendly lodging: Vista - 4 miles, Escondido - 5 miles, Carlsbad - 7 miles, Encinitas - 8 miles, Rancho Santa Fe - 9 miles

★★★
Lake San Marcos Resort
1025 La Bonita Dr
San Marcos CA 92078
(760) 744-0120
$68 - $139
Bed & Pet Discount Offered

Pet Policy: Pets up to 50 lbs accepted, $75 per stay.

Features: Concierge, Billiards, Elevator, Bar/lounge, Restaurant(s), Room service, Gift shops or newsstand, Number of rooms: 140, Number of floors: 2, Coffee in lobby, Parking (free), Multilingual staff, Complimentary newspapers, Limo or Town Car service available, Free wireless Internet, Dry cleaning/laundry, Swimming pool - outdoor, Golf course on site, Tennis on site, Fitness facilities

★★
Ramada Limited San Marcos
517 W San Marcos Blvd
San Marcos CA 92069
(760) 471-2800
$47 - $99
Bed & Pet Discount Offered

Pet Policy: Small pets welcome with a fee.

Features: Number of rooms: 85, Number of floors: 2, Coffee in lobby, Guest laundry, Free breakfast, Parking (free), Multilingual staff, Complimentary newspapers. Free wireless Internet, Swimming pool - outdoor seasonal, Business services.

Residence Inn by Marriott San Diego North San Marcos
1245 Los Vallecitos Blvd
San Marcos CA 92069
(760) 591-9828
$109 - $229
Bed & Pet Discount Offered

Pet Policy: Pets allowed, $50 per stay cleaning fee.

Features: Fitness facilities, Heated swimming, Wheelchair accessible, Concierge services, Gift shops or newsstand, Number of rooms: 112, Number of suites: 112, Number of floors: 4, Suitable for children, Barbecue grill(s), Coffee in lobby, Pool table, Free breakfast, Grocery, Health club, Parking (free) Multilingual staff, Complimentary newspapers in lobby, Dry cleaning/laundry, Limo or Town Car service available, Smoke-Free property, Technology helpdesk, Nearby fitness center (discount), Technology support staff, Designated smoking areas, Billiards or pool table, Free wireless Internet, Accessible bathroom, Accessibility equipment for the deaf, Braille or raised signage, 24-hour business center, Free reception, RV and truck parking

San Martin

Also see the following nearby communities that have pet friendly lodging: Gilroy - 5 miles, Morgan Hill - 6 miles

Cordevalle A Rosewood Resort
1 Cordevalle Club Drive
San Martin CA 95046
(408) 695-4500
$325 - $450
Bed & Pet Discount Offered

Pet Policy: Pets welcome, $100 per pet per stay. From the moment one arrives on property with their pet, a heartwarming welcome is felt. Upon entering your guest room, your pet will discover CordeValle bedding as well as custom amenities that includes food and water dishes and doggy treats. Be sure to schedule your Free one-hour dog walking service (per stay) with the front desk before arrival. Keep leashed when outside. There are two pet friendly outside dining areas.

Features: Bar/lounge, Steam room, Business center, Full-service health spa, Concierge desk, Babysitting or child care, Restaurant(s), Swimming pool - outdoor, Gift shops or newsstand, Number of rooms: 45, Number of floors: 1, Room service, Breakfast available (additional charge), Doorman/doorwoman, Massage - treatment room(s), Accessible bathroom, Accessibility equipment for the deaf, Braille or raised signage, Free wireless Internet, Golf course on site, Tennis on site, Fitness facilities.

San Mateo

Also see the following nearby communities that have pet friendly lodging: Belmont - 3 miles, Burlingame - 3 miles, San Carlos - 5 miles, Millbrae - 5 miles, Redwood City - 7 miles, San Bruno - 7 miles, South San Francisco - 8 miles

Comfort Inn Airport South
350 N Bayshore Blvd
San Mateo CA 94401
(650) 344-6376
$55 - $93
Bed & Pet Discount Offered

Pet Policy: Pet accommodation: $35 Per Stay Per Pet Limit: 2 Pets Per room

Features: Free Breakfast, Concierge desk, Elevator, Airport transportation (free), Business services, Number of rooms: 110, Number of suites: 3, Number of floors: 4, Coffee in lobby, Wireless Internet (additional charge), Parking (free), Multilingual staff, Complimentary newspapers in lobby, Limo or Town Car service available, Dry cleaning/laundry service, Health Club.

★★

Homestead San Francisco - San Mateo - SFO
1830 Gateway Dr
San Mateo CA 94404
(650) 574-1744
$84 - $114
Bed & Pet Discount Offered

Pet Policy: Pets allowed, no size restriction, $25 per day to a maximum of $150 per stay. Limit of 1 pet per room.

Features: Guest laundry, Number of rooms: 137, Number of floors: 2, BBQ area, Wireless Internet (additional charge), Free parking, Front desk (limited hours), Use of nearby fitness center (discount).

Not rated

Marriott Execustay Bridgepoint
1987 Bridgepointe Circle
San Mateo CA 94404
(510) 576-4100
$161 - $209

Pet Policy: Cat friendly, nightly fees and deposit required.

Features: Fully furnished apartments, Business center, Fitness center, Full kitchens, In unit washers and dryers.
Minimum stay of 30 days may be required

Not rated

Oakwood at Archstone at San Mateo
1101 Park Place
San Mateo CA 94403
(602) 427-2752
$144 - $197

Pet Policy: Accepts up to 2 pets. Additional fees.

Features: Furnished apartments with fully equipped kitchens, Fitness center. Minimum say of 30 days may be required.

Not rated

Oakwood at Bridgepointe
1927 Bridgepointe Circle
San Mateo CA 94403
(602) 427-2752
$144 - $197

Pet Policy: Pets accepted with limitations and fee. Contact hotel directly for more information and to make reservations.

Features: Furnished apartments, Free wireless Internet, Fitness Center, Business Center, Washers & Dryers in room, Fireplaces in some units

Residence Inn by Marriott
2000 Windward Way
San Mateo CA 94404
(650) 574-4700
$109 - $110
Bed & Pet Discount Offered

Pet Policy: Pets allowed, $75 per stay cleaning fee.

Features: Free Breakfast, Guest laundry, Business Services, Room service, Number of suites: 159, Number of floors: 2, Complimentary newspapers, Swimming pool, Smoke-Free, Fitness facilities.

San Pedro

Also see the following nearby communities that have pet friendly lodging: Harbor City - 5 miles, Torrance - 7 miles, Carson - 8 miles, Long Beach - 9 miles, Redondo Beach - 9 miles, Signal Hill - 9 mile

Doubletree Hotel San Pedro
2800 Via Cabrillo Marina
San Pedro CA 90731
(310) 514-3344
$108 - $204
Bed & Pet Discount Offered

Pet Policy: Pets up to 25 lbs accepted, $50 fee.

Features: Sauna, Outdoor pool, Bar/lounge, Restaurant(s), Room service , Concierge, Gift shop, Number of rooms: 226, Coffee in lobby, Breakfast available (additional charge), Health club, Parking (free), Multilingual staff, Complimentary newspapers, Business center, Porter/bellhop, Wireless Internet, Beauty services, Marina, Smoke-Free property Dry cleaning/laundry, Tennis courts.

Vagabond Inn San Pedro
215 S Gaffey St
San Pedro CA 90731
(310) 831-8911
$74 - $120
Bed & Pet Discount Offered

Pet Policy: Pets up to 50 lbs accepted, $25 fee per stay. Limit 2 per room.

Features: Business services, Parking fee, Outdoor pool, Number of rooms: 73, Number of floors: 3, Airport transportation (additional charge), Ski storage, Guest laundry, Free breakfast, Multilingual staff, Complimentary newspapers, Free wireless Internet, Accessible bathroom, Braille or raised signage, Elevator, Coffee in lobby

San Rafael

Also see the following nearby communities that have pet friendly lodging: Corte Madera - 4 miles, Mill Valley - 6 miles, Novato - 8 miles, Sausalito - 9 miles, Richmond - 10 miles

Extended Stay Deluxe
1775 Francisco Blvd
San Rafael CA 94901
(415) 451-1887
$94 - $124
Bed & Pet Discount Offered

Pet Policy: One pet is accepted per guest room. The General Manager may allow additional pets, based on his or her own discretion. Guests with a pet are charged a minimum $75 pet fee upon check-in

Features: Guest laundry, Coffee in lobby, Indoor pool, Number of rooms: 112, Number of floors: 4, BBQ area, Wireless Internet (additional charge), Multilingual staff, Nearby fitness center (free), Business center.

Not rated 
Gerstile Park Inn
34 Grove Street
San Rafael CA 64901
(415) 721-7611
$189 - $275

Pet Policy: Dogs of any size, $10 per night per dog, limit of 2 per room.

Features: Year built: 1895, Free wireless Internet, Full breakfast (free), King suites with Jacuzzi tubs, Decks, Kitchens in some suites.

San Ramon

Also see the following nearby communities that have pet friendly lodging: Danville - 4 miles, Dublin - 5 miles, Castro Valley - 8 miles, Pleasanton - 9 miles

★★
Extended Stay America San Ramon - Bishop Ranch
2100 Camino Ramon
San Ramon CA 94583
(925) 242-0991
$59 - $104
Bed & Pet Discount Offered

Pet Policy: One small pet is allowed in each guest room. A $25 per day non-refundable cleaning fee (not to exceed $150) will be charged the first night of your stay.

Features: Swimming pool - outdoor, Guest laundry, Elevator, Number of rooms: 128, Number of floors: 3, Coffee in lobby, Wireless Internet (additional charge), Parking (free), Front desk (limited hours), Use of nearby fitness center (discount).

★★
Homestead San Ramon - Bishop Ranch
18000 San Ramon Valley Blvd
San Ramon CA 94583
(925) 277-0833
$59- $94
Bed & Pet Discount Offered

Pet Policy: Pets allowed, no size restriction, $25 per day to a maximum of $150 per stay. Limit of 1 pet per room.

Features: Elevator, Number of rooms: 148, Number of floors: 3, Barbecue grill(s), Coffee in lobby, Wireless Internet (additional charge), Parking (free), Front desk (limited hours), Nearby fitness center (discount), Dry cleaning/laundry service.

★★★½
Marriott San Ramon
2600 Bishop Dr
San Ramon CA 94583
(925) 867-9200
$99 - $199
Bed & Pet Discount Offered

Pet Policy: Pets accepted, $100 fee per stay.

Features: Wireless Internet, Sauna, Business Center, Bar/lounge, Elevator, Restaurant(s), Swimming pool - outdoor, ATM/banking, Concierge services, Gift shops or newsstand, Number of rooms: 330, Number of floors: 6, Airport transportation (additional charge), Computer rental, Parking (additional charge), Coffee in lobby, Breakfast available (additional charge) Multilingual staff, Complimentary newspapers in lobby, Porter/bellhop, Security guard, Accessible bathroom, Braille or raised signage, Dry cleaning/laundry service, Room service (limited hours), Fitness facilities.

Residence Inn By Marriott
1071 Market Pl
San Ramon CA 94583
(925) 277-9292
$109 - $199
Bed & Pet Discount Offered

Pet Policy: Pets allowed, $100 per stay cleaning fee.

Features: Free Breakfast, Business services, Swimming pool - outdoor, Number of rooms: 106, Number of floors: 2, Barbecue grill(s), Coffee in lobby, Parking (free), Complimentary newspapers in lobby. Free wireless Internet, Dry cleaning/laundry service, Tennis on site, Fitness facilities

San Simeon

Also see the following nearby communities that have pet friendly lodging: Cambria - 4 miles

Best Western Plus Cavalier Ocienfront
9415 Hearst Drive
San Simeon CA 93452
(805) 927-4688
$104 - $299

Pet Policy: Pets allowed. Must be attended at all times.

Features: Non-smoking property, Television with VCR, Hair dryer, Iron and ironing board, Voice mail, Data port, Mini bar, Coffee maker.

Not rated
Courtesy Inn San Simeon
9450 Castillo Drive
San Simeon CA 93452
(805) 927-4691
$59 - $89

Pet Policy: Pets allowed, $20 per night per pet, limited to pet friendly rooms. All Pets must be on a leash at all times when outside of the room. Pets cannot be left unattended.

Features: Indoor pool & spa, Wireless Internet.

San Simeon Lodge
9520 Castillo Dr
San Simeon CA 93452
(805) 927-4601
$49 - $85
Bed & Pet Discount Offered

Pet Policy: Allows dogs only up to 25 pounds for $10 per night per dog, limit 2 per room. Pets allowed in 10 1st floor rooms only. Pets cannot be left alone in room. Has pet friendly outdoor dining patio.

Features: Bar/lounge, Sauna, Grocery, Restaurant(s), Gift shops or newsstand, Number of rooms: 62, Number of floors: 2, Business services, Breakfast available (additional charge), Pool table, Parking (free), Front desk (limited hours), Swimming pool - outdoor seasonal, Poolside bar, Guest laundry, Fitness facilities, Free wireless Internet.

Silver Surf Motel
9390 Castillo Dr
San Simeon CA 93452
(805) 927-4661
$49 - $119
Bed & Pet Discount Offered

Pet Policy: Pets accepted, $10 per night per pet. Limit of 3 pets per room.

Features: Swimming pool - indoor, Number of rooms: 72, Business services, Multilingual staff, Shopping on site, Suitable for children, Guest laundry, Free wireless Internet.

The Morgan Hotel San Simeon
9135 Hearst Drive
San Simeon CA 93452
(805) 927-3878
$89 - $129
Bed & Pet Discount Offered

Pet Policy: Pets accepted, $25 per pet per night.

Features: Concierge, Outdoor pool, Bar/lounge, Business services, Coffee in lobby, Number of rooms: 55, Number of floors: 2, Free breakfast, Spa services, Multilingual staff, Complimentary newspapers, Free wireless Internet, Smoke-Free property, Nearby fitness center (discount).

Not rated
The Morgan San Simeon
9135 Hearst Drive
San Simeon CA 93452
(805) 927-3878
$84 - $179

Pet Policy: Pets accepted, $25 per pet per night.

Features: Free wireless Internet, Coffee makers in room, Hair dryer, Iron and ironing board, Continental breakfast (free), non-smoking property.

San Ysidro

Also see the following nearby communities that have pet friendly lodging: Chula Vista - 5 miles, National City - 9 miles, Coronado - 10 miles

Best Western Americana Inn
815 W San Ysidro Blvd
San Ysidro CA 92173
(619) 428-5521
$78 - $79
Bed & Pet Discount Offered

Pet Policy: Pets up to 80 lbs accepted, $20 per night plus $50 refundable deposit.

Features: Outdoor heated pool, Wheelchair accessible, Number of rooms: 120, Number of floors: 2, Airport transportation (additional charge), BBQ area, Guest laundry, Free breakfast, Multilingual staff, Complimentary newspapers, Business center, Free wireless Internet, Accessible bathroom, Accessibility equipment for the deaf.

Rodeway Inn - San Ysidro
643 E San Ysidro Blvd
San Ysidro CA 92173
(619) 428-2800
$49 - $69
Bed & Pet Discount Offered

Pet Policy: Pets up to 25 lbs, $1JO per night, $100 refundable deposit. Limit 1 pet per room.

Features: Number of rooms: 69, Guest laundry, Free breakfast, Free wireless Internet, Accessibility equipment for the deaf, Braille or raised signage.

Santa Ana

Also see the following nearby communities that have pet friendly lodging: Garden Grove - 4 miles, Orange - 5 miles, Fountain Valley - 5 miles, Costa Mesa - 5 miles, Anaheim - 7 miles, Huntington Beach - 7 miles, Newport Beach - 8 miles, Irvine - 10 miles

Candlewood Suites OC Airport-
2600 Red Hill Avenue
Santa Ana CA 92705
(949) 250-0404
$96 - $130

Pet Policy: Pets up to 80 lbs accepted, $!0 per night, not to exceed $150. Must have current vaccination records.

Continued on next page

Candlewood Suites OC Airport
Continued from previous page

Bed & Pet Discount Offered

Features: BBQ area, Business services, Accessible bathroom, Accessibility equipment for the deaf, Braille or raised signage, Number of floors: 3, Coffee in lobby, Guest laundry, Multilingual staff, Free wireless Internet, Fitness facilities.

Embassy Suites Santa Ana - Orange County Airport N
1325 E. Dyer Rd.
Santa Ana CA 92705
(714) 241-3800
$109 - $170
Bed & Pet Discount Offered

Pet Policy: Pets up to 35 lbs allowed, $50 per stay fee.

Features: Bar/lounge, Airport transportation (free), Restaurant(s), Room service, Concierge, Gift shops or newsstand, Number of rooms: 300, Number of floors: 10, Computer rental, Free breakfast, Multilingual staff, Business center, Porter/bellhop, Security guard, Wireless Internet, Accessible bathroom, Accessibility equipment for the deaf, Dry cleaning/laundry, Indoor pool, Fitness center.

La Quinta Inn & Suites Orange County-Santa Ana
2721 Hotel Ter
Santa Ana CA 92705
(714) 540-1111
$75 - $85
Bed & Pet Discount Offered

Pet Policy: Cats and dogs up to 50 pounds are accepted in all guest rooms. Housekeeping services for rooms with pets require pet owner be present or pet must be crated. No fees or deposits are required.

Features: Free breakfast, Airport transportation (free), Accessible bathroom, Outdoor pool, Number of rooms: 183, Number of floors: 3, Complimentary newspapers, Guest laundry, Free wireless Internet, Business center, Fitness facilities.

Motel 6 Irvine
1717 E Dyer Rd
Santa Ana CA 92705
(949) 261-1515
$53- $65
Bed & Pet Discount Offered

Pet Policy: Well-behaved pets stay Free. Animals that pose a health or safety risk may not remain onsite, and include those that, in our manager's discretion, are too numerous for any one room, cause damage to our property or that of other guests, are too disruptive, are not properly attended, or demonstrate undue aggression. All pets must be declared at check-in. Pets must be attended to and under control at all times. If unavoidable circumstances require a pet to remain in a room while the owner is offsite, the pet must be secured in a crate or travel carrier. Pets must be on a leash or securely carried outside of guest rooms.

Features: Outdoor pool, Guest laundry, RV and truck parking.

Red Roof Santa Ana
2600 North Main Street
Santa Ana CA 92705
(714) 542-0311
$53 - $65

Pet Policy: 1 well-behaved pet permitted without charge.

Features: Restaurant on site.

Santa Barbara

Canary Hotel
31 W Carrillo St
Santa Barbara CA 93101
(805) 884-0300
$255 - $2,000
Bed & Pet Discount Offered

Pet Policy: Pets welcome - $35 per night. Canine Club Menu The name "Canary Islands" is said to be derived from the Latin "Insula Canaria" meaning "Island of Dogs". When the ancient Romans established contact with the islands they found a dense population of large dogs, such as the impressive Presa Canario. Therefore we have named Canary Hotel's services for your pooch "Club Canario." As part of our canine club, your four legged friend will receive: A comfy bed with hotel linens to rest weary paws Bowls for the all-important daily "feeding and watering" ritual An organic treat to whet any canine appetite A Canary Hotel Frisbee to help keep in shape A limited edition Canary Hotel collar tag A personal grooming kit especially for the travelling dog.

Features: Swimming pool - outdoor, Parking (valet) $20 Per Night, Bar/lounge, Restaurant(s), Concierge services, Number of rooms: 97, Number of floors: 6, Coffee in lobby, Breakfast available (additional charge), Room service (24 hours), Spa services on site, Multilingual staff, Complimentary newspapers in lobby, Business center, Porter/bellhop, Security guard, Free wireless Internet, Parking garage – additional charge, Smoke-Free property, Nearby fitness center (discount), Dry cleaning/laundry service.

Casa Del Mar Inn B&B
18 Bath Street
Santa Barbara CA 93101
(805) 963-4418
$134 - $219
Bed & Pet Discount Offered

Pet Policy: Limited to 1 large pet or 2 small pets. Pet charge is $15/night for each pet. Pet must be accompanied at all times. DO NOT leave pet alone in room at any time. Dogs should be on a leash when walking on property. Pets are NOT allowed to enter into the breakfast room during breakfast and wine & cheese hours.

Features: Free Breakfast, Suitable for children, Number of rooms: 21, Smoke-Free property.

★★
Extended Stay America Santa Barbara - Calle Real
4870 Calle Real
Santa Barbara CA 93111
(805) 692-1882
$97 - $159
Bed & Pet Discount Offered

Pet Policy: One pet is allowed in each guest room. A $25 per day non-refundable cleaning fee (not to exceed $150) will be charged the first night of your stay.

Features: Room service (limited hours), Number of rooms: 104, Number of floors: 3, Coffee in lobby, Wireless Internet (additional charge), Guest laundry, Parking (free), Nearby fitness center (discount).

★★★★
Fess Parker's Doubletree Resort
633 E Cabrillo Blvd
Santa Barbara CA 93103
(805) 564-4333
$245 - $415
Bed & Pet Discount Offered

Pet Policy: All pets welcome, $25 per night. Step outside your door of this Santa Barbara pet-friendly hotel, where you both can enjoy miles of landscaped walking paths along the beachfront and parks. Want to go for a swim? Take your dogs with you. There are dog-friendly beaches a short drive away!! Our concierge can assist with directions to dog-friendly beaches and off-leash parks as well as hiking trails in the local mountains. Delight in all the services available within our impressive Santa Barbara pet-friendly lodging. In addition to the spacious rooms and special treat bag for our furry friends, we also offer: Acres of landscaped grounds; Pet menus for in-room dining; All sizes welcome.

Features: Business Center, Bar/Lounge, Security guard, Swimming pool - outdoor, Tennis on site, Airport transportation (free), Elevator, Restaurant(s), Hair salon, ATM/banking, Concierge services, Gift shops or newsstand, Number of rooms: 360, Suitable for children, Parking (additional charge), Wireless Internet (additional charge), Poolside bar, Room service (24 hours), Spa services on site, Complimentary newspapers in lobby, Porter/bellhop, Doorman/doorwoman, Limo or Town Car service available, Accessible bathroom, Accessibility equipment for the deaf, Braille or raised signage, Dry cleaning/laundry service, Fitness facilities.

★★★★★
Four Seasons Santa Barbara
1260 Channel Dr
Santa Barbara CA 93108
(805) 969-2261
$495 - $1,975
Bed & Pet Discount Offered

Pet Policy: Dogs up to 50 lbs, no fee. Must not leave unattended in room.

Features: Year Built 1928, 2 Outdoor pools, Bar/lounge, Babysitting or child care, Elevator, Wheelchair accessible, Supervised child care/activities, Shopping on site, Number of rooms: 181, Number of suites: 26, Number of floors: 2, Computer rental, Parking (additional charge), Coffee in lobby, Poolside bar, ***Continued on next page***

Four Seasons Santa Barbara
Continued from previous page

Currency exchange, Room service (24 hours), Multilingual staff, Complimentary newspapers, Porter/bellhop, Doorman/doorwoman, Security guard, Dry cleaning/laundry service, Concierge, Full-service health spa, Massage - treatment room(s), Smoke-Free property, Children's club, Technology support staff, Wireless Internet (additional charge), Accessible bathroom, 24-hour business center, 3 Restaurants, Tennis on site, Fitness facilities.

Hotel Mar Monte
1111 E Cabrillo Blvd
Santa Barbara CA 93103
(805) 963-0744
$149 - $319
Bed & Pet Discount Offered

Pet Policy: Dogs only, $75 per stay. Must stay in designated pet rooms.

Features: Beauty services, Bar/Lounge, Outdoor pool, Concierge, Spa services, Parking (additional charge), Room service , Restaurant(s), Gift shops or newsstand, Number of rooms: 173, Breakfast available (additional charge), Multilingual staff, Complimentary newspapers, Doorman/doorwoman, Porter/bellhop, Security guard, Wireless Internet, Massage - treatment room(s), Smoke-Free property, Dry cleaning/laundry service, Business center, Accessible bathroom.

Not rated
Oasis Inn & Suites
3344 State Street
Santa Barbara CA 93105
(805) 687-6611
$71 - $149

Pet Policy: Small pets allowed, $15 per pet per night plus $50 refundable deposit.

Features: Formerly the Guesthouse Inn & Suites, Number of rooms: 33, Kitchens in some rooms, Swimming pool, Wireless Internet, HBO.

★★★★½

Pacifica Suites
5490 Hollister Ave
Santa Barbara CA 93111
(805) 683-6722
$189 - $190
Bed & Pet Discount Offered
e

Pet Policy: Pets up to 40 lbs accepted, $20 per night per pet. Limit 2 per room. Pit Bulls and Rottweiler are not accepted. Limited to ground floor pet designated rooms only.

Features: Free Breakfast, Swimming pool - outdoor, Airport transportation (free), Number of suites: 87, Number of floors: 2, Business services, Parking (free), Spa services on site, Free wireless Internet, Nearby fitness center (discount), Accessible bathroom, Accessibility equipment for the deaf, Braille or raised signage, Dry cleaning/laundry service.

San Ysidro Ranch, A Rosewood Resort
900 San Ysidro Lane
Santa Barbara CA 93108
(805) 565-1700
$750 - $1,900
Bed & Pet Discount Offered

Pet Policy: Pets welcome, $100 per pet per stay. A warm welcome from the staff who offer a welcome treat from the cookie jar on the front counter and then have pets sign in alongside their "parents" - in a "Privileged Pets" registration book, with their very own paw print Signature San Ysidro Ranch bedding, and a selection of amenities that includes Ty Bow Wow Beanies chew toys and doggie treats

Features: Bar/lounge, Fitness facilities, Restaurant(s), Heated outdoor pool, Concierge, Number of rooms: 41, Guest laundry, Spa services.

Secret Garden Inn
1908 Bath St
Santa Barbara CA 93101
(805) 687-2300
From $220
Bed & Pet Discount Offered

Pet Policy: Pets are welcome with advance notice in the cottages with private deck (Garden, Hummingbird, Oriole, Kingfisher, Nightingale, Wood Thrush) with an extra $20 fee per night.

Features: Romantic gardens, Hidden pathways, Full breakfast (free), Parking (free), Spa services on site, Smoke-Free property, Free wireless Internet.

The Parkside Inn
424 Por La Mar
Santa Barbara CA 93103
(805) 963-0744
$89 - $158
Bed & Pet Discount Offered

Pet Policy: Pets accepted, $75 per stay.

Features: Elevator, Room service, Number of rooms: 24, Breakfast available (additional charge), Parking (free), Multilingual staff, Porter/bellhop, Security guard, Limo or Town Car service available, Medical assistance available, Free wireless Internet, Smoke-Free property, Dry cleaning/laundry service.

Santa Clara

Also see the following nearby communities that have pet friendly lodging: Sunnyvale - 2 miles, Cupertino - 5 miles, Milpitas - 5 miles, Mountain View - 6 miles, Campbell - 8 miles, San Jose - 8 miles, Los Altos - 8 miles, Palo Alto - 9 miles, Fremont - 9 miles, Newark - 10 miles

Biltmore Hotel and Suites
2151 Laurelwood Rd
Santa Clara CA 95054
(408) 988-8411
$81- $189
Bed & Pet Discount Offered

Pet Policy: Pets welcome with one-time fee of $50. At the Biltmore Hotel and Suites in Santa Clara, pets are guests too! We're pleased to offer the leading pet-friendly lodging in the Santa Clara/San Jose, California area. Our dog-friendly Santa Clara, California vacation hotel is a place where your four-legged companions are treated like guests. Pet-designated accommodations are located on the ground floor near our garden and outdoor walking space. Our hotel is also nearby several pet-friendly parks, beaches and campuses to frolic with your pet.
Continued on next page

Biltmore Hotel and Suites
Continued from previous page

Features: Business Center, Swimming pool - outdoor, Airport transportation (free), Restaurant(s), Room service, Gift shops or newsstand, Number of rooms: 262, Number of floors: 9, Suitable for children, Parking (free), Multilingual staff, Complimentary newspapers, Doorman/doorwoman, Security guard, Smoke-Free property, Accessible bathroom, Accessibility equipment for the deaf, Braille or raised signage, Dry cleaning/laundry, Fitness facilities, Wireless Internet (additional charge).

★★
Candlewood Suites Silicon Valley
481 El Camino Real
Santa Clara CA 95050
(408) 241-9305
$98 - $109
Bed & Pet Discount Offered

Pet Policy: Pets allowed with nonrefundable fee of $15 for the first night and $10 for every additional night up to a total of $150. Each pet must be less than 80 lbs. Pet agreement must be signed at check-in. Record of complete/current vaccinations may be required.

Features: Business services, Accessible bathroom, Accessibility equipment for the deaf, Braille or raised signage, Gift shops or newsstand, Number of suites: 122, Number of floors: 3, Barbecue grill(s), Coffee in lobby, Parking (free) Multilingual staff, Wireless Internet, Dry cleaning/laundry service, Fitness facilities.

★★★★
Hilton Santa Clara
4949 Great America Pkwy
Santa Clara CA 95054
(408) 330-0001
$103 - $158
Bed & Pet Discount Offered

Pet Policy: Pets up to 75 lbs, $75 per stay.

Features: Bar/Lounge, Outdoor pool, Room service, Concierge, Number of rooms: 280, Free wireless Internet, Multilingual staff, Complimentary newspapers, Porter/bellhop, Security guard, Restaurant, Dry cleaning/laundry service, Fitness facilities, Braille or raised signage, Accessibility equipment for the deaf, Wheelchair accessible, Accessible bathroom, 24-hour business center

★★
Hotel Stratford
2499 El Camino Real, Hwy 101 ex San Tomas
Santa Clara CA 95051
(408) 244-9610
$59 - $118
Bed & Pet Discount Offered

Pet Policy: Small pets accepted, $25 per day per pet to a maximum of $300 per stay, plus $25 refundable deposit.

Features: Free wireless Internet, Number of rooms: 31, Number of floors: 2, Free breakfast, Parking (free), Complimentary newspapers in lobby, Business center, Designated smoking areas.

Marriott Santa Clara-Silicon Valley
2700 Mission College Blvd
Santa Clara CA 95054
(408) 988-1500
$99 - $129
Bed & Pet Discount Offered

Pet Policy: Pets allowed. $75 cleaning fee.

Features: Security guard, Restaurant(s), Swimming pool - outdoor, Concierge, Gift shop, Number of rooms: 759, Number of floors: 13, Computer rental, Breakfast available (additional charge), Shoe shine, Multilingual staff, Complimentary newspapers, Business center, Porter/bellhop, Wireless Internet, Massage - treatment room(s), Sauna, Smoke-Free property, Technology helpdesk, Bar/lounge, Room service, Dry cleaning/laundry, Tennis courts, Fitness center, Parking fee.

Not rated
Oakwood at Bella Vista
1500 Vista Club circle
Santa Clara CA 95054
(602) 427-2752
$130 - $176

Pet Policy: Pets accepted with limitations and fee. Contact hotel directly for more information and to make reservations.

Features: Furnished extended stay apartments, Heated swimming pool, Fitness center, Kitchens, Patio or Balcony. Minimum stay of 30 days may be required.

Not rated
Oakwood Nantucket
1600 Nantucket Circle
Santa Clara CA 95054
(602) 427-2752
$138 - $139

Pet Policy: Pets accepted with limitations and fee. Contact hotel directly for more information and to make reservations.

Features: Furnished extended stay apartments. Minimum stay of 30 days may be required.

Not rated
Oakwood Golden Triangle
1650 Hope Drive
Santa Clara CA 95054
(602) 427-2752
$135 - $176

Pet Policy: Pets accepted with limitations and fee. Contact hotel directly for more information and to make reservations.

Features: Fully furnished apartments, Wireless Internet, Swimming pool, Spa and Hot tub. Minimum stay of 30 days may be required.

★★½

Quality Inn & Suites Silicon Valley
2930 El Camino Real
Santa Clara CA 95051
(408) 241-3010
$79 - $89
Bed & Pet Discount Offered

Pet Policy: Pets up to 25 lbs, $20 per night. Limit of 2 per room.

Features: Swimming pool - outdoor, Number of rooms: 69, Number of suites: 16, Number of floors: 2, Business services, Coffee in lobby, Free breakfast, Parking (free). Free wireless Internet, Accessible bathroom, Accessibility equipment for the deaf, Braille or raised signage, Dry cleaning/laundry.

Not rated
Synergy Bella Vista
1500 Club Cirtle
Santa Clara CA 95054
(925) 807-1155
$101 - $125

Pet Policy: Pets Allowed. Please confirm with hotel via phone or email reservations@synergyrelo.com to confirm your pet will be accommodated before you arrive.

Features: Furnished apartments, Free wireless Internet, Flat screen TV, Washer & Dryer in each unit, Concierge services, Swimming pools: 2, Fitness Center, Billiards, Business Center. 30 day minimum stay may be required.

Not rated
Synergy Carlyle
4515 Carlyle Court
Santa Clara CA 95054
(925) 807-1155
$114 - $133

Pet Policy: Pets accepted. Please call the number shown prior to arrival to make sure your pet can be accommodated.

Features: Furnished apartments, Swimming pool, Sauna & spa, Fitness center, Wireless Internet, Flat screen TV, Washer & Dryer in each unit, Concierge services, Billiards, Business Center. 30 day minimum stay may be required.

Not rated
Synergy River Terrace
700 Agnew Road
Santa Clara CA 95054
(925) 807-1155
$85 - $86

Pet Policy: Dogs and Cats accepted, $500 refundable deposit plus $35 per month fee for cats, $50 for dogs.

Features: Furnished apartments, swimming pool. 30 day minimum stay may be required.

★★
Vagabond Inn Santa Clara
3580 El Camino Real
Santa Clara CA 95051
(408) 241-0771
$69 - $79
Bed & Pet Discount Offered

Pet Policy: Pets accepted, $20 per pet per night.

Features: Guest laundry Free wireless Internet, Swimming pool - outdoor, Number of rooms: 70, Number of floors: 2, Coffee in lobby, Free breakfast with hot waffles, Parking (free).

Santa Clarita

Also see the following nearby communities that have pet friendly lodging: Valencia - 3 miles, Stevenson Ranch - 3 miles, Castaic - 8 miles

Super 8 Santa Clarita Valencia
17901 Sierra Hwy
Santa Clarita CA 91351
(661) 252-1722
$62 - $117
Bed & Pet Discount Offered

Pet Policy: Dogs only, $20 per stay. Limit 1 dog per room.

Features: Number of floors: 2, Free continental breakfast, swimming pool, Coffee in lobby, Wireless Internet, Restaurant, Parking Free.

Santa Cruz

Also see the following nearby communities that have pet friendly lodging: Scotts Valley - 5 miles, Ben Lomond - 8 miles

Bay Front Inn – Santa Cruz
325 Pacific Ave
Santa Cruz CA 95060
(831) 423-8564
$64 - $119
Bed & Pet Discount Offered

Pet Policy: Pet friendly, $15 per night per pet

Features: Swimming pool - outdoor, Number of rooms: 38, Number of floors: 3, Free breakfast, Parking (free), Smoke-Free property, Front desk (limited hours), Free wireless Internet.

Inn At Pasatiempo
555 Highway 17
Santa Cruz CA 95060
(800) 230-2892
$80 - $265
Bed & Pet Discount Offered

Pet Policy: Dogs only, up to 40 lbs, $25 per night. Limit 1 dog per room.

Features: Bar/Lounge, Smoke-Free, Business services, Room service, Number of rooms: 54, Free breakfast, Free wireless Internet, Restaurant, Dry cleaning/laundry, Outdoor pool - seasonal.

Motel Santa Cruz
370 Ocean St
Santa Cruz CA 95060
(831) 458-9220
$85 - $99
Bed & Pet Discount Offered

Pet Policy: Pet friendly rooms available with additional fee.

Features: Guest laundry, Number of rooms: 62, Number of floors: 3, Parking (free), Multilingual staff, Complimentary newspapers, Wireless Internet.

Not rated
Ocean Echo Inn
401 Johans Beach Drive
Santa Cruz CA 955062
(877) 747-8713
$130 - $145

Pet Policy: Pets accepted in limited pet designated rooms only, additional fee.

Features: Beach front, Some rooms include Kitchens with full size refrigerator.

Pacific Inn Santa Cruz
330 Ocean St
Santa Cruz CA 95060
(831) 425-3722
$65 - $200
Bed & Pet Discount Offered

Pet Policy: Pets up to 30 lbs accepted, $15 per pet per night. Limit 2 pets per room.

Features: Number of rooms: 36, Number of floors: 3, Accessible bathroom, Free wireless Internet, Heated indoor pool, Parking (free), Guest laundry, Coffee in lobby, Wheelchair accessible, Free breakfast.

Paradise Inn by the Beach
311 2nd St
Santa Cruz CA 95060
(831) 426-7123
$55 - $199
Bed & Pet Discount Offered

Pet Policy: Pets welcome, $15 per pet per night.

Features: Room service (limited hours), Number of rooms: 25, Number of floors: 2, Coffee in lobby, Wireless Internet, Swimming pool - outdoor seasonal, Self-parking (free)

Santa Cruz Beach Inn
600 Riverside Ave
Santa Cruz CA 95060
(831) 458-9660
$63 - $263
Bed & Pet Discount Offered

Pet Policy: Pets welcome, $15 per pet per night.

Features: Number of rooms: 79, Number of floors: 3, Complimentary newspapers, Smoke-Free property, Free wireless Internet, Accessible bathroom, RV and truck parking, Outdoor pool, Business services, Coffee in lobby, Free breakfast, Parking (free).

West Cliff Inn - A Four Sisters Inn
174 W Cliff Dr
Santa Cruz CA 95060
(831) 457-2200
$275 - $325
Bed & Pet Discount Offered

Pet Policy: Dogs only, up to 40 lbs, $65 additional fee, limit 2 per room. Pet owners will be liable for any additional cleaning bills or repairs, should they be required. All pets must be vaccinated and licensed and you agree to obtain and provide current records from a licensed veterinarian regarding this. The inn may request this information from you at any time.

Features: Number of rooms: 9, Number of floors: 3, Coffee in lobby, Parking (free), Smoke-Free property, Free wireless Internet, Free breakfast, Wheelchair accessible, Year Built 1877, Free reception.

Santa Maria

Best Western Plus Big America
1725 N Broadway
Santa Maria CA 93454
(800) 426-3213
$97 - $117
Bed & Pet Discount Offered

Pet Policy: Allows small pets. May not leave in room alone.

Features: Number of rooms: 106, Number of floors: 2, Business services, Elevator, Airport transportation (free), Swimming pool - outdoor, Wheelchair accessible, Free breakfast, Parking (free) Multilingual staff, Accessible bathroom, Accessibility equipment for the deaf, Braille or raised signage, Free wireless Internet, Restaurant(s), Piano, Complimentary newspapers, Nearby fitness center (free), Security guard, Area shuttle (free), 24-hour front desk.

Candlewood Suites Santa Maria
2079 Roemer Court
Santa Maria CA 93454
(805) 928-4155
$89 - $114
Bed & Pet Discount Offered

Pet Policy: Pets up to 80 lbs, $75 for up to 6 nights, $150 for more. $150 deposit required.

Features: Gift shops or newsstand, Number of rooms: 72, Barbecue grill(s), Multilingual staff, Fitness facilities, Accessible bathroom, Accessibility equipment for the deaf, Braille or raised signage, Dry cleaning/laundry service, Business center.

Historic Santa Maria Inn
801 S Broadway
Santa Maria CA 93454
(805) 928-7777
$104 - $129
Bed & Pet Discount Offered

Pet Policy: Dogs, any size, $50 per stay. Limit of 2 dogs per room.

Features: Room service (limited hours), Outdoor pool, Airport transportation (free), Parking garage (free), Bar/lounge, Shopping on site, Restaurant(s), Hair salon, ATM/banking, Concierge, Number of rooms: 164, Number of floors: 6, Breakfast available (additional charge), Nightclub, Spa services, Multilingual staff, Complimentary newspapers, Nearby fitness center (free), Porter/bellhop, Security guard, Free wireless Internet, Massage - treatment room(s), Dry cleaning/laundry service.

Holiday Inn Hotel and Suites Santa Maria
2100 N Broadway
Santa Maria CA 93454
(805) 928-6000
$84 - $165
Bed & Pet Discount Offered

Pet Policy: Pets welcome, $25 per night per pet.

Features: Fitness facilities, Accessible bathroom, Accessibility equipment for the deaf, Braille or raised signage, Outdoor pool, Business services, Bar/lounge, Restaurant, Gift shop, Number of suites: 207, Multilingual staff, Complimentary newspapers, Room service, Concierge, Wireless Internet, Sauna.

Quality Inn & Suites Santa Maria
210 Nicholson Avenue
Santa Maria CA 93454
(805) 922-5891
$105 - $106
Bed & Pet Discount Offered

Pet Policy: Well-behaved pets welcome, $25 per night per pet. Limit of two pets per room.

Coffee in lobby, Children's pool, Outdoor adult pool, Business services, Free Breakfast, BBQ area, Number of rooms: 64, Guest laundry, Restaurant, Complimentary newspapers, Wireless Internet.

★★

Rodeway Inn Santa Maria
1995 S Broadway
Santa Maria CA 93454
(805) 614-7062
$60 - $110
Bed & Pet Discount Offered

Pet Policy: Rodeway Inns charge a fee of $10 per night per pet plus a $50 damage deposit. Max of 2 pets per room. A veterinarian certificate that the pet is on a flea and parasite program is required. Pets may not be left alone in the room unless in a cage.

Features: Multilingual staff, On-site medical assistance available, Number of rooms: 23

Santa Monica

Also see the following nearby communities that have pet friendly lodging: Venice - 3 miles, Marina Del Rey - 4 miles, Culver City - 5 miles, Beverly Hills - 6 miles, Los Angeles - 7 miles, Topanga - 7 miles, West Hollywood - 8 miles, Inglewood - 8 miles, El Segundo - 9 miles, Sherman Oaks - 9 miles, Studio City - 10 miles

★★★★
Ambrose, The
1255 20 Street at Arizona
Santa Monica CA 90404
(310) 315-1555
$199- $269

Pet Policy: Pets up to 30 lbs accepted, $30 per night.

Organic continental breakfast - Free, Parking (free), Free wireless Internet, Local shuttle, Fitness facilities access.

★★
Bayside Hotel
2001 Ocean Ave
Santa Monica CA 90405
(310) 396-6000
$159 - $999
Bed & Pet Discount Offered

Pet Policy: Pets welcome. $50 per stay fee.

Features: Parking (additional charge), Free wireless Internet, Number of rooms: 45, Number of floors: 2, Smoke-Free property.

★★★★
Channel Road Inn, A Four Sisters Inn
219 W Channel Rd
Santa Monica CA 90402
(310) 459-1920
$175 - $371
Bed & Pet Discount Offered

Pet Policy: Dogs only, up to 40 lbs, $65 additional fee, limit 2 per room. Pet owners will be liable for any additional cleaning bills or repairs, should they be required. All pets must be vaccinated and licensed and you agree to obtain and provide current records from a licensed veterinarian regarding this. The inn may request this information from you at any time.

Features: Concierge services, Free breakfast, Business services, Suitable for children, Library, Number of rooms: 14, Number of floors: 3, Parking (free), Free wireless Internet, Coffee in lobby, Complimentary newspapers in lobby, Front desk (limited hours), Video library, Piano, Massage - treatment room(s), Smoke-Free property, Free reception.

★★★½
Georgian Hotel
1415 Ocean Ave
Santa Monica CA 90401
(310) 395-9945
$216 - $300
Bed & Pet Discount Offered

Pet Policy: Dogs and cats up to 25 pounds are welcome for a $100 fee per stay of seven nights or less. Single pets 26 pounds to 50 pounds, or two pets, up to a combined weight total of 50 pounds are accepted for a $150 fee per stay of seven nights or less. For stays longer than seven nights, our pet charge shifts from a one-time charge to a weekly charge. The Georgian Hotel is pleased to offer Pet Turndown Service. This service includes a pet mat, a water bowl, a toy and a treat (treat is replenished each night at turndown).

Continued on next page

Georgian Hotel
Continued from previous page

Features: Room service (24 hours), Concierge services, Business center, Bar/lounge, Restaurant(s), Number of rooms: 84, Number of floors: 8, Parking (additional charge), Multilingual staff, Complimentary newspapers in lobby, Porter/bellhop, Free wireless Internet, Smoke-Free property, Nearby fitness center (discount), Shoe shine, Accessible bathroom, Accessibility equipment for the deaf, Braille or raised signage, Dry cleaning/laundry service, Year Built 1933, Breakfast available (additional charge).

★★★★
JW Marriott Santa Monica Le Merigot
1740 Ocean Ave
Santa Monica CA 90401
(310) 395-9700
$349 - $419
Bed & Pet Discount Offered

Pet Policy: Pets allowed, $150 per stay cleaning fee plus $100 refundable deposit.

Features: Fitness facilities, Business center, Swimming pool - outdoor, Bar/lounge, Full-service health spa, Concierge desk, Parking (valet) $32/day, Babysitting or child care, Restaurant(s), Gift shops or newsstand, Number of rooms, Video library, Room service (24 hours), Shoe shine, Multilingual staff, Complimentary newspapers, Wireless Internet.

★★★★
Loews Santa Monica Beach Hotel
1700 Ocean Ave
Santa Monica CA 90401
(310) 458-6700
$349 - $3,600
Bed & Pet Discount Offered

Pet Policy: No Restrictions. Loews Hotels offers a standardized *Loews Loves Pets* program at the chain's 16 hotels across the US and in Canada. Well behaved pets of all types (except some aggressive breeds) are welcome. The Loews program offers specialized services and first-class amenities designed to make pets and their owners feel at home when traveling together. Amenities: Personal welcoming note from the hotel general manager with a listing of pet services available at the hotel, including dog-walking routes, veterinarian information, pet shop and grooming locations, pet attractions, pet-sitters, pet-friendly restaurants, and other resources Specialized bedding for dogs and cats. Free bag of pet treats and a pet toy. Special pet place mats with food and water bowls, and a special *Do Not Disturb*: sign. Room Service Menu: Menu items include dishes such as grilled lamb or chicken with rice for dogs, grilled liver or salmon with rice for cats, and for health conscious cats and dogs Loews also offers a vegetarian entree Additional Pet Services: Pet-walking and sitting services can be arranged through the concierge desk the Loews *Did You Forget Closet* includes: dog and cat beds in different sizes, leashes and collars, and pet videos;
Continued on next page

Loews Santa Monica Beach Hotel Continued from previous page

guests can also purchase essential items through the *Did You Forget Closet* including: kitty litter boxes, pooper-scoopers, and pet toys rooms for guests staying with pets undergo special cleaning procedures including the use of specially-filtered vacuums to remove pet allergens in preparation for subsequent guests.

Features: Outdoor pool, Beauty services, Concierge, Business center, Room service (24 hours), Health club, Parking garage – additional charge, Bar/lounge, Security guard, Full-service health spa, Accessible bathroom, Accessibility equipment for the deaf, Gift shop, Number of rooms: 342, Number of floors: 8, Breakfast available (additional charge), Multilingual staff, Complimentary newspapers, Porter/bellhop, Doorman/doorwoman, Wireless Internet, Dry cleaning/laundry, 2 Restaurants.

Not rated
Oakwood at the Plaza Arboretum
2200 Colorado Ave
Santa Monica CA 90404
(602) 427-2752
$139 - $208

Pet Policy: Pets accepted with limitations and fee. Contact hotel directly for more information and to make reservations.

Features: Furnished apartments, Swimming pools, Outdoor spa, Fitness center, Business center, Restaurants on site. Minimum stays may be required.

★★
Santa Monica Travelodge Pico Boulevard
3102 Pico Blvd
Santa Monica CA 90405
(310) 450-5766
$115 - $139

Pet Policy: Pets under 20 lbs accepted, fee. Must book directly with hotel.

Features: Business services, Barbecue grill(s), Free breakfast, Parking (free), Complimentary newspapers in lobby, Accessible bathroom, Free wireless Internet.

★★★★
Sheraton Delfina
530 Pico Blvd
Santa Monica CA 90405
(310) 399-9344
$199 - $399
Bed & Pet Discount Offered

Pet Policy: One dog up to 40 pounds is allowed per room. A $75 non-refundable deposit is required per stay. The traditional lower floor rooms have been designated for easy in and out access

Features: Wheelchair accessible, Security guard, Outdoor pool, Room service, Bar/lounge, Parking $30/Day, Concierge, Smoke-Free, 2 Restaurants, Number of rooms: 310, Number of floors: 9 Multilingual staff, Free newspapers, Porter/bellhop, Wireless Internet, Accessible bathroom, Accessibility equipment for the deaf, Braille or raised signage, Dry cleaning/laundry, Fitness center.

The Fairmont Miramar Hotel & Bungalows
101 Wilshire Blvd
Santa Monica CA 90401
(310) 576-7777
$329 - $519
Bed & Pet Discount Offered

Pet Policy: Pets welcome, no fee. Must have current vaccination records with you. Fairmont offers the widest range of pet services available while staying in the Santa Monica area. Upon check in, your pet will receive his/her own bed, bowls, and complementary treats. If your dog has an allergy of any kind, please notify the front desk, and we will make every attempt to arrange a special treat just for your pet! If you left Fido's favorite ball at home, no worries, our exclusive partner Healthy Spot of Santa Monica offers Fairmont guests 10% off.

Features: Hair salon, Full-service health spa, Bar/lounge, Concierge desk, Swimming pool - outdoor, Multilingual staff, Complimentary newspapers in lobby, Porter/bellhop, Doorman/doorwoman, Limo or Town Car service available, Wireless Internet (additional charge), Massage - treatment room(s), Smoke-Free property, Parking (valet) $30/Day (Hybrids park Free), Dry cleaning/laundry service, Room service (24 hours), Security guard, Business center, Poolside bar, Shoe shine, Restaurant(s), Gift shops or newsstand, Number of rooms: 302, Number of floors: 10, Computer rental, Breakfast available (additional charge), Currency exchange, Health club, Year Built 1914.

Santa Nella

Also see the following nearby communities that have pet friendly lodging: Los Banos - 10 miles

Holiday Inn Express Santa Nella
28976 Plaza Dr
Santa Nella CA 95322
(209) 826-8282
$76 - $99
Bed & Pet Discount Offered

Pet Policy: Pets allowed only in rooms with 2 Queen beds. $10 per night per pet.

Features: Number of rooms: 100, Business services, Guest laundry, Free breakfast, Multilingual staff, Free wireless Internet, Outdoor pool, Accessible bathroom, Accessibility equipment for the deaf, Braille or raised signage, Dry cleaning/laundry service, Fitness facilities.

Hotel deo Oro
13070 State Highway 33
Santa Nella CA 95322
(209) 826-4444
$75 - $100
Bed & Pet Discount Offered

Pet Policy: Pets welcome, $10 per pet per night.

Features: Arcade/game room, Multilingual staff, Complimentary newspapers, Business center, Free wireless Internet Outdoor pool - seasonal, Bar/lounge, Room service (limited hours), Dry cleaning/laundry service, RV and truck parking.

Santa Paula

Also see the following nearby communities that have pet friendly lodging: Camarillo - 9 miles, Fillmore - 10 mile

Glen Tavern Inn
134 North Mill St
Santa Paula CA 93060
(805) 933-5550
$132 - $185
Bed & Pet Discount Offered

Pet Policy: Pets under 35 lbs accepted, $10 per pet per night. Upon arrival, your pet will be given a bag of treats and two bowls for food and water. The hotel grounds offer plenty of walking and green space for your pets to roam. Walk over to Santa Paula's Steckel Park, which offers many pet friendly areas for hiking, frolicking and afternoons of fetch. Or head over to the beautiful pet friendly Ventura beaches.

Features: Room service, Guest laundry, Outdoor pool, Airport transportation (additional charge), Bar/lounge, Business services, Coffee in lobby, Nearby fitness center (discount), Restaurant, Number of rooms: 41, Number of suites: 2, Complimentary newspapers, Limo or Town Car service available, Free Internet, Smoke-Free, Year Built 1911, Wheelchair accessible, Multilingual staff.

Santa Rosa

Also see the following nearby communities that have pet friendly lodging: Rohnert Park - 8 miles, Windsor - 8 miles, Sebastopol - 9 miles

Americas Best Value Inn
1800 Santa Rosa Avenue
Santa Rosa CA 95407
(707) 523-3480
$57 - $70

Pet Policy: Pets, any size, welcome with $15 per stay.

Features: Number of rooms - 43, Number of floors – 2, Free Internet, Cable TV, Mini fridge, Hairdryer.

Best Western Garden Inn
1500 Santa Rosa Avenue
Santa Rosa CA 95404
(888) 256-8004
$99 - $119
Bed & Pet Discount Offered

Pet Policy: Dogs up to 50 lbs. are welcome for a $15/ night fee for each pet. Limit of 2 per room.

Features: Number of rooms: 78, Business services, Breakfast available (additional charge), Guest laundry, Restaurant, Free Internet, Outdoor pool – seasonal.

Best Western Wine Country Inn
870 Hopper Ave
Santa Rosa CA 95403
(707) 545-9000
$109 - $110
Bed & Pet Discount Offered

Pet Policy: Dogs only, $20 per pet per stay.

Features: Accessible bathroom, Accessibility equipment for the deaf, Braille or raised signage, Number of rooms: 90, Number of floors: 2, Outdoor pool - seasonal, Business services, Coffee in lobby, Free breakfast, Parking (free) Multilingual staff, Complimentary newspapers, Free wireless Internet, Dry cleaning/laundry, Fitness facilities.

2632 Cleveland Ave
Santa Rosa CA 95403
(707) 542-5544
$59 - $74
Bed & Pet Discount Offered

Pet Policy: Pet accommodation: $15/night per pet. Pet Deposit: $25/stay

Features: Elevator, Number of rooms: 100, Number of floors: 3, Business services, Free breakfast, Parking (free) Complimentary newspapers in lobby, Free wireless Internet, Swimming pool - outdoor

Courtyard by Marriott Santa Rosa
175 Railroad St
Santa Rosa CA 95401
(707) 573-9000
$110 - $229
Bed & Pet Discount Offered

Pet Policy: Pets accepted. Contact hotel directly.

Features: Fitness facilities, Restaurant(s), Number of rooms: 138, Number of floors: 5, Business services, Coffee in lobby, Grocery, Complimentary newspapers, Free wireless Internet, Smoke-Free property, Accessible bathroom, Accessibility equipment for the deaf, Braille or raised signage, Dry cleaning/laundry, Swimming pool – outdoor.

Days Inn Santa Rosa CA
3345 Santa Rosa Ave
Santa Rosa CA 95407
(707) 568-1011
$55 - $94
Bed & Pet Discount Offered

Pet Policy: Pets allowed, $10 per pet per night

Features: Restaurant(s), Hair salon, Gift shops or newsstand, Business services, Coffee in lobby, Health club, Parking (free), Complimentary newspapers in lobby, Sauna, Swimming pool - outdoor seasonal, Free wireless Internet.

Extended Stay America Santa Rosa - North
100 Fountain Grove Pkwy
Santa Rosa CA 95403
(707) 541-0959
$74 - $99
Bed & Pet Discount Offered

Pet Policy: One pet is allowed in each guest room. A $25 per day non-refundable cleaning fee (not to exceed $150) will be charged the first night of your stay.

Features: Guest laundry, Number of rooms: 94, Number of floors: 3, Wireless Internet (additional charge), Parking (free), Use of nearby fitness center (free).

Extended Stay America Santa Rosa - South
2600 Corby Ave
Santa Rosa CA 95407
(707) 546-4808
$59 - $79
Bed & Pet Discount Offered

Pet Policy: Pets of any size are welcome for an additional $25 per night, up to $75.

Features: Guest laundry, Elevator, Number of rooms: 114, Number of floors: 3, Airport transportation (additional charge), Business services, Suitable for children, Wireless Internet (additional charge), Parking (free) Multilingual staff, Front desk (limited hours), Security guard, Use of nearby fitness center (discount).

★★★½
Fountaingrove Inn Hotel
101 Fountain Grove Pkwy
Santa Rosa CA 95403
(707) 578-6101
$95 - $450
Bed & Pet Discount Offered

Pet Policy: Accepts up to two pets under 50 lbs for $25 per pet per night plus a $50 deposit. Pets are not allowed in the pool or the restaurant, pets should not be left unattended and pets should always be leashed.

Features: Business Center, Bar/Lounge, Restaurant(s), Room service (limited hours), Concierge services, Number of rooms: 124, Number of floors: 2, Breakfast available (additional charge), Parking (free), Multilingual staff, Complimentary newspapers in lobby, Porter/bellhop, Free wireless Internet, Smoke-Free property, Swimming pool - outdoor seasonal, Dry cleaning/laundry service, Year Built 1899, Fitness facilities.

★★★½
Hilton Sonoma Wine Country
3555 Round Barn Blvd
Santa Rosa CA 95403
(707) 523-7555
$89 - $189
Bed & Pet Discount Offered

Pet Policy: Allows pets up to 75 lbs, $50 per stay.

Features: Outdoor pool, Bar/lounge, Restaurant, Room service, Concierge, Gift shop, Number of rooms: 246, Number of floors: 3, Wireless Internet (additional charge), Multilingual staff, Business center, Security guard, Accessible bathroom, Accessibility equipment for the deaf, Braille or raised signage, Dry cleaning/laundry, Fitness facilities.

★★½
Quality Inn & Suites Wine Country
3000 Santa Rosa Ave
Santa Rosa CA 95407
(707) 521-2100
$69 - $89
Bed & Pet Discount Offered

Pet Policy: Quality Inns charge a fee of $10 per night per pet and may require a $50 damage deposit, which is refunded if the room is in order at check out. Quality Inns accept any well-behaved pets with a maximum of 3 per room, but dogs are limited to 50 pounds. Pets may not be left alone in the room unless in a cage.

Features: Business services, Coffee in lobby, Number of rooms: 63, Number of floors: 2, Free breakfast, Complimentary newspapers, Free wireless Internet, Accessible bathroom, Accessibility equipment for the deaf, Braille or raised signage, Fitness facilities.

★★
Travelodge Santa Rosa
1815 Santa Rosa Ave
Santa Rosa CA 95407
(707) 542-3472
$50 - $76
Bed & Pet Discount Offered

Pet Policy: Pets accepted, $10 per night per pet.

Features: Multilingual staff, Complimentary newspaper, Outdoor pool - seasonal, Business services, Free breakfast.

Travelodge Santa Rosa Downtown
635 Healdsburg Ave
Santa Rosa CA 95401
(707) 544-4141
$55 - $99
Bed & Pet Discount Offered

Pet Policy: Pets up to 40 lbs, $10 per night per pet. Limit of 2 pets per room.

Features: Elevator, Business services, Free breakfast, Parking (free), Multilingual staff, Complimentary newspapers in lobby, Swimming pool - outdoor seasonal.

Sausalito

Also see the following nearby communities that have pet friendly lodging: Mill Valley - 4 miles, Corte Madera - 5 miles, San Francisco - 7 miles, San Rafael - 9 miles

Cavallo Point
601 Murray Cir
Fort Baker
Sausalito CA 94965
(415) 339-4700
$279 - $675
Bed & Pet Discount Offered

Pet Policy: Cavallo Point Lodge is pleased to welcome you and your dog. When booking, please indicate if you are bringing one or two dogs. We can accept a maximum of two friendly dogs per room. Dogs must be leashed at all times while on property, including the center parade ground. Owners must be present or the pet removed from the room for housekeeping to freshen your room. Please do not leave pets unattended in guest rooms out of respect for other guests around you. Please refrain from tying your pet to trees and other objects on property. Dogs are restricted from entering the Healing Arts Center & Spa as well as Farley Bar and Murray Circle restaurant with the exception of the terrace in front of the restaurant and bar. A $75 one-time fee will be automatically charged to your account. If there is any damage to the room due to your pet, the cost of repair will be charged to your account. The owner hereby represents Cavallo Point Lodge that their pet is not inclined to bite, and that in the event that their dog bites causing injury while on the Lodge premises, the owner hereby agrees to fully and hold harmless and indemnify Cavallo Point Lodge from any liability.

Features: Room service, Security guard, Full-service health spa, Concierge, Bar/lounge, Elevator, Parking fee, Business center, Restaurant(s), Gift shops or newsstand, Number of rooms: 142, Number of floors: 2, Breakfast available (additional charge), Health club, Porter/bellhop, Wireless Internet, Massage - treatment room(s), Smoke-Free property, Accessible bathroom, Accessibility equipment for the deaf, Braille or raised signage, Dry cleaning/laundry.

Scotts Valley

Also see the following nearby communities that have pet friendly lodging: Ben Lomond - 5 miles, Santa Cruz - 5 miles

Not rated.
Best Western Inn – Scotts Valley
6020 Scotts Valley Drive
Scotts Valley CA 95066
(831) 438-6666
$102 - $199

Pet Policy: Pets accepted with small fee at check-in.

Features: Coffee in lobby, Continental breakfast (free), Heated pool and spa, Fitness center nearby (discount), Guest laundry, Business center.

★★★
Hilton Santa Cruz/Scotts Valley
6001 La Madrona Drive
Scotts Valley CA 95060
(831) 440-1000
$122 - $249
Bed & Pet Discount Offered

Pet Policy: Pets up to 75 lbs accepted, $50 per stay.

Features: Swimming pool - outdoor, Bar/Lounge, Elevator, Restaurant(s), Room service, Number of rooms: 160, Business center, Limo or Town Car service available, Free wireless Internet, Smoke-Free property, Concierge, Accessible bathroom, Accessibility equipment for the deaf, Braille or raised signage, Dry cleaning/laundry, Fitness center.

Seal Beach

Also see the following nearby communities that have pet friendly lodging: Los Alamitos - 4 miles, Signal Hill - 5 miles, Long Beach - 5 miles, Cypress - 6 miles, Hawaiian Gardens - 6 miles, Huntington Beach - 7 miles, La Palma - 7 miles, Buena Park - 8 miles, Cerritos - 8 miles, Fountain Valley - 8 miles, Garden Grove - 10 miles

Not rated
Oakwood Long Beach Marina
333 First Street
Seal Beach CA 90740
(602) 427-2752
$99 - $198

Pet Policy: Pets accepted with limitations and fee. Contact hotel directly to make reservations.

Features: Newly renovated furnished apartments, Wireless Internet, Swimming pool, Outdoor spa, Tennis, Fitness center. Cable TV, Full, Breakfast (free). Minimum stay of 30 days may be required.

★★½
Pacific Inn
600 Marina Dr
Seal Beach CA 90740
(866) 466-0300
$119 - $246
Bed & Pet Discount Offered

Pet Policy: Pets up to 35 lbs accepted, $50 per stay cleaning fee. Dogs can play on the nearby dog beach while enjoying their stay at our Pet Friendly Hotel.

Features: Swimming pool - indoor, Business services, Concierge, Number of rooms: 71, Number of suites: 2, Number of floors: 3, Coffee in lobby, Guest laundry, Complimentary newspapers, Accessible bathroom, Accessibility equipment for the deaf, Braille or raised signage, Airport transportation (free), Restaurant, Free wireless Internet, Area shuttle (free), Fitness facilities, Business Center, Free Breakfast.

Seaside

Also see the following nearby communities that have pet friendly lodging: Monterey - 3 miles, Marina - 5 miles, Pacific Grove - 5 miles, Carmel - 7 miles

Gateway Thunderbird Motel
1909 Fremont Blvd
Seaside CA 93955
(831) 394-6606
$50 - $80
Bed & Pet Discount Offered

Pet Policy: Pets allowed, $50 cash pet fee at check-in.

Features: Guest laundry, Free wireless Internet, Free breakfast Number of rooms: 66, Number of floors: 2, Parking (free), Front desk (limited hours).

Sebastopol

Also see the following nearby communities that have pet friendly lodging: Occidental - 5 miles, Valley Ford - 7 miles, Bodega - 8 miles, Rohnert Park - 8 miles, Santa Rosa - 9 miles

Vine Hill Inn B&B
3949 Vine Hill Road
Sebastopol CA 95472
(707) 823-8832
From $172
Bed & Pet Discount Offered

Pet Policy: 1 pet permitted in each room, no fee.

Features: Swimming pool - outdoor, Number of rooms: 4, Barbecue grill(s), Free breakfast.

Selma

Also see the following nearby communities that have pet friendly lodging: Fowler - 4 miles, Kingsburg - 8 miles

Super 8 Selma Fresno Area
3142 Highland Ave
Selma CA 93662
(559) 896-2800
$58 - $89
Bed & Pet Discount Offered

Pet Policy: Pets under 20 lbs accepted, $10 per night per pet.

Features: Shopping on site, Number of floors: 2, Free breakfast, Parking (free), Swimming pool - outdoor seasonal, Internet (free).

Sherman Oaks

Also see the following nearby communities that have pet friendly lodging: Van Nuys - 3 miles, Studio City - 4 miles, Tarzana - 5 miles, Universal City - 6 miles, West Hollywood - 7 miles, Northridge - 7 miles, Beverly Hills - 7 miles, Burbank - 7 miles, Woodland Hills - 8 miles, Canoga Park - 9 miles, Hollywood - 9 miles, Topanga - 9 miles, Santa Monica - 9 miles

Best Western Carriage Inn
5525 Sepulveda Blvd
Sherman Oaks CA 91411
(818) 787-2300
$84 - $161
Bed & Pet Discount Offered

Pet Policy: Pets allowed. Limited availability.

Features: Guest laundry, Room service, Bar/lounge, Business services, Restaurant(s), Number of rooms: 181, Number of floors: 2, Parking (free), Multilingual staff, Free wireless Internet, Dry cleaning/laundry service, Fitness facilities, Outdoor pool.

Shoshone

Not rated
Amargosa Opera House
CA-127 and State Line Road
Shoshone CA 92384
(760) 852-4441
$65 - $80

Pet Policy: Pets are allowed on a case by case basis. You must call the property directly and make your reservations to see if a room is available.

Features: Historical Inn near Death Valley, Built 1923, Private baths.

Signal Hill

Also see the following nearby communities that have pet friendly lodging: Long Beach - 0 miles, Seal Beach - 5 miles, Hawaiian Gardens - 6 miles, Los Alamitos - 6 miles, Carson - 7 miles, Cypress - 8 miles, La Palma - 8 miles, Cerritos - 8 miles, Harbor City - 8 miles, San Pedro - 9 miles, Norwalk - 9 miles, Buena Park - 9 miles, Downey - 10 miles, Torrance - 10 miles

Rodeway Inn Signal Hill
3555 E Pacific Coast
Signal Hill CA 90755
(562) 597-4455
$59 - $90
Bed & Pet Discount Offered

Pet Policy: Rodeway Inns charge a fee of $10 per night per pet and require a $50 damage deposit, which is refunded if the room is in order at check out. Max of 2 pets per room. A veterinarian certificate that the pet is on a flea and parasite program and that they are Free from parasites is required. Pets may not be left alone in the room unless in a cage.

Features: Elevator, Number of rooms: 44, Number of floors: 3, Free breakfast, Parking (free), Free wireless Internet, Swimming pool - outdoor seasonal, Business services.

Simi Valley

Also see the following nearby communities that have pet friendly lodging: Chatsworth - 7 miles, Calabasas - 9 miles, Canoga Park - 9 miles

Extended Stay America Los Angeles - Simi Valley
2498 Stearns St
Simi Valley CA 93063
(805) 584-8880
$66 - $101

Pet Policy: One pet is allowed in each guest room. A $25 per day non-refundable cleaning fee (not to exceed $150) will be charged the first night of your stay.

Features: Guest laundry, Elevator, Number of rooms: 104, Number of floors: 3, Parking (free).

Solvang

Also see the following nearby communities that have pet friendly lodging: Buellton - 4 miles

Meadowlark Inn
2644 Mission Drive
Solvang CA 93463
(805) 688-4631
From $150
Bed & Pet Discount Offered

Pet Policy: Well behaved, quiet and friendly dogs only are allowed with reservation only in some of our kitchen rooms. We do not allow cats or other animals at any time. The fee per dog per day is $25 plus tax and there is a maximum of 2 dogs per room. A $100 deposit per dog is charged and refunded within 24 hours of check out after housekeeping inspection and if there are no damages. Dogs may not sit on the bedding or furniture unless covered with a sheet and dogs may not sleep in the beds. Dogs may not be left alone in a room at any time. Doggie dishes are available at the front desk. Please do not let dogs use people dishes from our kitchens. Dogs must be leashed at all times on the property and kept quiet. Dogs are not allowed in the breakfast room, the center lawn or in the pool area. The right front lawn is the designated doggy potty area, owners must pick up after their dogs and dispose in designated trash receptacles.

Features: Barbecue grill(s), Arcade/game room, Free breakfast, Business center, Media library.

Wine Valley Inn
1564 Copenhagen Dr
Solvang CA 93463
(805) 688-2111
$80 - $319
Bed & Pet Discount Offered

Pet Policy: Pets accepted, $25 per pet per night, to a maximum of $500 per stay, plus $200 refundable deposit.

Features: Free wireless Internet, Number of floors: 3, Free breakfast, Spa services on site, Year Built 1804, Fitness facilities.

Sonoma

Also see the following nearby communities that have pet friendly lodging: Boyes Hot Springs - 6 miles, Napa - 9 miles

Best Western Sonoma Valley Inn
550 2nd St W
Sonoma CA 95476
(707) 938-9200
$149 - $299
Bed & Pet Discount Offered

Pet Policy: Pets under 50 pounds. $10. Limited Pet Rooms.

Features: Free wireless Internet, Steam Room, Coffee in lobby, Business services, Swimming pool - outdoor, Guest laundry, Free breakfast, Complimentary newspapers, Dry cleaning/laundry, Fitness facilities.

Inn At Sonoma - A Four Sisters Inn
630 Broadway
Sonoma CA 95476
(707) 939-1340
From $157
Bed & Pet Discount Offered

Pet Policy: Dogs only, up to 40 lbs, $65 additional fee, limit 2 per room. Pet owners will be liable for any additional cleaning bills or repairs, should they be required. All pets must be vaccinated and licensed and you agree to obtain and provide current records from a licensed veterinarian regarding this. The inn may request this information from you at any time.

Features: Wheelchair accessible, Parking (free), Concierge, Number of rooms: 19,, Number of floors: 3, Elevator, Coffee in lobby, Video library, Complimentary newspapers in lobby, Front desk (limited hours), Smoke-Free property, Free wireless Internet., Free breakfast, Accessible bathroom, Free reception.

★★★★
Renaissance Lodge at Sonoma Resort and Spa
1325 Broadway
at Leveroni & Napa Roads
Sonoma CA 95476
(707) 935-6600
$199 - $419
Bed & Pet Discount Offered

Pet Policy: Pets up to 30 lbs allowed, $75 per stay cleaning fee. Limit 1 per room. Must not leave unattended.

Features: Sauna, Concierge desk, Swimming pool - outdoor, Coffee in lobby, Business center, Bar/lounge, Elevator, Restaurant(s), Room service (limited hours), Gift shops or newsstand, Number of rooms: 182, Number of floors: 2, Breakfast available (additional charge), Poolside bar, Parking (free), Multilingual staff, Porter/bellhop, Doorman/doorwoman, Security guard, Wireless Internet, Full-service health spa, Massage - treatment room(s), Accessible bathroom, Accessibility equipment for the deaf, Braille or raised signage, Dry cleaning/laundry service, Fitness facilities

★★
Sonoma Creek Inn
239 Boyes Boulevard
Sonoma CA 95476
(707) 939-9463
$89 - $159
Bed & Pet Discount Offered

Pet Policy: Pets up to 60 lbs accepted, $20 per stay. Limit 2 per room.

Features: Number of rooms: 16, Number of floors: 2, Business services, Parking (free), Front desk (limited hours), Smoke-Free property, Coffee shop or cafe, Free wireless Internet, Coffee in lobby, Complimentary newspapers in lobby.

The Fairmont Sonoma Mission Inn & Spa
100 Boyes Boulevard
Sonoma CA 95416
(707) 938-9000
$168 - $489
Bed & Pet Discount Offered

Pet Policy: Pets welcome, maximum of 2 per room, $25 per room per night. Any pet at the resort must be on a leash at all times and must not be left unattended in the guest room. Pets are not permitted in the Food & Beverage outlets and are not permitted in the Pool due to health regulations. The Housekeeping Department will have beds, bowls, food (treats) and toys for dogs and cats, and these will be placed in the guest room prior to arrival. Free biodegradable pet waste pick up bags are available at the Front Desk.

Features: Wheelchair accessible, Piano, Outdoor pool – seasonal, Technology support staff, Babysitting or child care, Bar/lounge, Full-service health spa, Restaurant(s), Room service (limited hours), ATM/banking, Shopping on site, Number of rooms: 226, Number of floors: 3, Parking (additional charge), Breakfast available (additional charge), Poolside bar, Health club, Shoe shine, Multilingual staff, Complimentary newspapers in lobby, Porter/bellhop, Doorman/doorwoman, Security guard, Limo or Town Car service available, Beauty services, Concierge, Massage - treatment room(s), Steam room, Sauna, Accessible bathroom, Accessibility equipment for the deaf, Braille or raised signage, Dry cleaning/laundry service, Airport transportation (additional charge), Wireless Internet (additional charge), 24-hour business center, Area shuttle (free), Golf course, Tennis courts, Year Built 1927, Free reception.

Sonora

Also see the following nearby communities that have pet friendly lodging: Jamestown - 4 miles, Twain Harte - 9 miles

★★★

Best Western Sonora Oaks
19551 Hess Ave
Sonora CA 95370
(209) 533-4400
$129 - $149
Bed & Pet Discount Offered

Pet Policy: Pets allowed limit of 1 per rm, $25 daily. Ground level rooms only. May never leave in room alone.

Features: Bar/lounge, Room service, Swimming pool - outdoor, Barbecue grill(s) Restaurant(s), Number of rooms: 101, Number of floors: 2, Free breakfast, Free wireless Internet, Business center.

★★
Inns Of California Sonora
350 S Washington Street
Sonora CA 95370
(209) 532-3633
$70 - $100
Bed & Pet Discount Offered

Pet Policy: Pets accepted, $25 per day plus $100 deposit.

Features: Outdoor pool, Guest laundry, Free breakfast, Business center, Technology helpdesk, Free wireless Internet, Accessible bathroom, Accessibility equipment for the deaf.

Not rated
Quail Hollow One
20230 Grouse Way
Sonora CA 95370
(209) 533-1310
$75 - $100

Pet Policy: Pets allowed with $300 refundable deposit. Limit 2 pets.

Features: Furnished apartments, minimum stay may be required.

Sonora Days Inn
160 S Washington St
Sonora CA 95370
(209) 532-2400
$55 - $69
Bed & Pet Discount Offered

Pet Policy: Pets accepted, $10 per day. Pet reservations must be confirmed in advance directly with property for availability. Historic room types are not pet rooms.

Features: Free Breakfast, Restaurant(s), Coffee in lobby, Wireless Internet (additional charge), Swimming pool - outdoor seasonal, Complimentary newspapers, RV and truck parking, Year Built 1896

South El Monte

Also see the following nearby communities that have pet friendly lodging: El Monte - 2 miles, Rosemead - 3 miles, San Gabriel - 5 miles, City Of Industry - 6 miles, Pico Rivera - 6 miles, Whittier - 6 miles, Monterey Park - 6 miles, Arcadia - 7 miles, Monrovia - 7 miles, Commerce - 8 miles, Pasadena - 8 miles, Bell Gardens - 9 miles, South Pasadena - 9 miles, Norwalk - 10 miles, Downey - 10 miles, La Mirada - 10 miles

Rodeway Inn City of Industry
1228 N. Durfee Ave
South El Monte CA 91733
(626) 579-4490
$60- $84
Bed & Pet Discount Offered

Pet Policy: Rodeway Inns charge a fee of $10 per night per pet and require a $50 damage deposit, which is refunded if the room is in order at check out. Max of 2 pets per room. A veterinarian certificate that the pet is on a flea and parasite program and that they are Free from parasites is required. Pets may not be left alone in the room unless in a cage.

Features: RV and truck parking, Number of rooms: 56, Number of floors: 2, Guest laundry, Free breakfast, Parking (free), Free wireless Internet.

South Lake Tahoe

★★★
3 Peaks Resort & Beach Club
931 Park Ave
South Lake Tahoe CA 96150
(530) 544-4131
$42 - $279
Bed & Pet Discount Offered

Pet Policy: Pets up to 60 lbs, $25 per night. Limit 2 per room. Pets must be quiet or you may be asked to leave and forfeit remaining nights.

Features: BBQ area, Guest laundry, Number of rooms: 56, Suitable for children, Coffee in lobby, Pool table, Free wireless Internet, Smoke-Free property, Swimming pool - outdoor seasonal.

★★★
3 Peaks Resort and Beach Club
931 Park Avenue
South Lake Tahoe CA 96150
(530) 544-4131
$89 - $431

Pet Policy: Pets allowed.

Features: Walking distance to Heavenly Ski Resort and Lake Tahoe, Private beach, Swimming pool & Jacuzzi– outdoor – heated – seasonal,

Not rated
7 Seas Inn
4145 Manzanita Avenue
South Lake Tahoe CA 96150
(530) 544-7031
$79 - $120

Pet Policy: Friendly pets are welcome and must be registered at time of check-in. There is a $10 fee per pet per night. We reserve the right to ask you to leave if your pet is in any way aggressive and in any way makes our other guests uncomfortable. Pets must be crated if left alone in the room. Pet Sitting is available at Tahoe Tails and Trails.

Features: Walking to casinos, Heavenly Gondola and Lake Tahoe, Private Beach, Hot spa, Free breakfast, Wireless Internet, Refrigerator, Microwave, Ski boat.

★★
Alder Inn
1072 Ski Run Blvd
South Lake Tahoe CA 96150
(530) 544-4485
$69 - $109
Bed & Pet Discount Offered

Pet Policy: Great pet friendly place .Dogs receive own bed, towel and a treat. $20 fee.

Features: Number of rooms: 24, Number of floors: 2, Free breakfast, Ski shuttle, Swimming pool - outdoor, Barbecue grill(s), Coffee in lobby, Ski storage, Guest laundry, Parking (free), Smoke-Free property, Beach/pool umbrellas, Free wireless .

Not rated
Alpine Inn and Spa
920 State Line
South Lake Tahoe CA 96150
(530) 544-3340
$65 - $70

Pet Policy: Pets accepted, $10 per pet per night.

Walking distance to Stateline casinos, close to Heavenly Ski Resort and Lake Tahoe Beaches

Best Western Plus Timber Cove Lodge
3411 Lake Tahoe Blvd
South Lake Tahoe CA 96150
(530) 541-6722
$106 - $121
Bed & Pet Discount Offered

Pet Policy: Pets allowed, $25 per night, $100 deposit, designated ground floor rooms only.

Features: Concierge, Marina on site, Massage - treatment room(s), Swimming pool - outdoor seasonal, Accessible bathroom, Dry cleaning/laundry service, Free wireless Internet, Bar/lounge, Restaurant(s), Wheelchair accessible, Number of rooms: 262, Number of floors: 3, Guest laundry, Free breakfast, Suitable for children, Coffee in lobby, Accessibility equipment for the deaf, Braille or raised signage, Fitness facilities.

★★

Big Pines Mountain House
4083 Cedar Ave
South Lake Tahoe CA 96150
(530) 541-5155
$42 - $124
Bed & Pet Discount Offered

Pet Policy: Pet Friendly.

Features: Technology helpdesk, Private beach, Ski shuttle, Guest laundry, Suitable for children, BBQ area, Coffee in lobby, Number of rooms: 70, Number of floors: 2, Airport transportation (additional charge), Free breakfast, Multilingual staff, Ski-in/ski-out, Free wireless Internet, Concierge, Smoke-Free property, Swimming pool - outdoor seasonal, Accessible bathroom, Accessibility equipment for the deaf, Braille or raised signage, Business center.

★½

Econo Lodge South Lake Tahoe
2659 Lake Tahoe Blvd
South Lake Tahoe CA 96150
(530) 544-3959
$34 - $119
Bed & Pet Discount Offered

Pet Policy: Pets up to 45 lbs, $25 per stay. Limit 1 pet per room.

Features: Number of rooms: 62, Free continental breakfast, Free wireless Internet.

★★

Heavenly Inn
930 Park Avenue
South Lake Tahoe CA 96150
(530) 544-2400
$84 - $96

Pet Policy: We welcome your dog to Heavenly Inn and expect he will have a wonderful stay. There is an area just north of the hotel where it will be convenient to walk your dog. Only domesticated, common household dogs will be allowed. Dogs of vicious or aggressive disposition deemed by management to be potentially harmful to the Health and safety of others are prohibited. Maximum weight: 25 lbs. Dogs must be crate trained and housebroken. Pets must be inside crate if left alone in your room. Pet fee is $25 per night, per pet up to 2 pets. The guest shall keep the unit and surrounding areas free of pet odors, insect infestation, ***Continued on next page***

Heavenly Inn
Continued from previous page

pet waste and litter and maintain the unit in sanitary condition at all times. The guest shall be responsible to clean up after their pet anywhere on Heavenly Inn or Secrets Inn property including carrying a pooper scooper and disposable plastic bag any time the pet is outside the unit. Pet waste shall be bagged and disposed of in appropriate trash receptacles. Pet waste or pet litter shall not be deposited in the toilet. The guest shall keep his/her pet inside the unit at all times except for transportation on and off Heavenly Inn property and daily walks for dogs. When outside the unit, dogs must be controlled on a leash. Dogs shall wear a collar with a tag identifying the pet and its owner, with name, address and telephone number. The guest must leave a contact number with the office so they may be reached at any time if there should be an issue with their pet causing a disturbance in the room; the guest may be asked to leave if the pet becomes a disturbance issue with no refund of monies paid. No excessive barking!

Features: Flat screen TVs, DVD players, Wireless, Kitchenettes.

★★½
Highland Inn
3979 Lake Tahoe Blvd
South Lake Tahoe CA 96150
(530) 544-3862
$49 - $249
Bed & Pet Discount Offered

Pet Policy: Pet friendly, $20 per pet per night plus $100 deposit.

Features: Babysitting or child care, Shopping on site, Gift shops or newsstand, Number of rooms: 30, Number of floors: 2, Multilingual staff, Complimentary newspapers in lobby, Free wireless Internet.

Not rated
Lake Tahoe Ambassador Lodge
4130 Manzanita Ave South
South Lake Tahoe CA 96150
(530) 544-6461
$35 - $102

Pet Policy: Pets accepted, $15 per night.

Features: Swimming pool - outdoor, Wheelchair accessible, Business services, Wireless Internet, Barbecue grill(s), Number of rooms: 56, Number of floors: 2, Coffee in lobby, Children's swimming pool, Multilingual staff, Complimentary newspapers, Front desk (limited hours), Private beach, Smoke-Free property, Swimming pool - outdoor seasonal.

Not rated
National 9 Inn South Lake Tahoe
3901 Pioneer Trail
South Lake Tahoe CA 96150
(530) 541-2119
$36 - $50

Pet Policy: Pets accepted. Details of pet policy have not been made available. Please contact the property directly for more information.

Features: Swimming pool available June 1 – August 30, Jacuzzi available December 1 – April 1.

Park Tahoe Inn
4011 Lake Tahoe Blvd
South Lake Tahoe CA 96150
(530) 544-6000
$99 - $214
Bed & Pet Discount Offered

Pet Policy: Pet friendly. $25 per night

Features: Number of rooms: 116, Number of floors: 2, Suitable for children, Coffee maker, Mini fridge, Complimentary newspapers in lobby, Ski shuttle, Smoke-Free property, Swimming pool - outdoor seasonal, Jacuzzi – outdoor year-round, Accessible bathroom, 24-hour business center, Wheelchair accessible, Free wireless Internet, Concierge desk.

Not rated
Pinewood Inn
3818 Lake Tahoe Blvd
South Lake Tahoe CA 96150
(530) 544-3319
$30 - $70

Pet Policy: Pets up to 50 lbs allowed, $25 per night per pet.

Features: Free Internet, Microwave, Refrigerator.

Rodeway Inn Casino Center
4127 Pine Blvd
South Lake Tahoe CA 96150
(530) 541-7150
$35 - $99
Bed & Pet Discount Offered

Pet Policy: Rodeway Inns charge a fee of $10 per night per pet and require a $50 damage deposit, which is refunded if the room is in order at check out. Max of 2 pets per room. A veterinarian certificate that the pet is on a flea and parasite program and that they are Free from parasites is required. Pets may not be left alone in the room unless in a cage.

Features: Coffee in lobby, Private beach, Swimming pool – outdoor, Number of rooms: 120, Number of floors: 3, Business services, Guest laundry, Free breakfast, Multilingual staff, Complimentary newspapers, Free wireless Internet, Smoke-Free.

Super 8 Lake Tahoe
3600 Lake Tahoe Blvd
South Lake Tahoe CA 96151
(530) 544-3476
$32 - $89
Bed & Pet Discount Offered

Pet Policy: A nonrefundable $10 pet deposit is charged per stay. Pets may not be left unattended in the guestrooms. We ask that you clean up after your pets when walking them on hotel property.

Features: Accessible bathroom, Accessibility equipment for the deaf, Braille or raised signage, Restaurant(s), Parking (free), Wireless Internet.

Not Rated
Travelers Inn and Suites South
3930 Pioneer Trail
South Lake Tahoe CA 96150
(877) 747-8713
$37 - $110

Pet Policy: Pets allowed, $10 per pet per night.

Features: Basic motel within walking distance to Heavenly Ski Resort.

Vagabond Inn Lake Tahoe
3892 Lake Tahoe Blvd
South Lake Tahoe CA 96150
(530) 544-3642
$35 - $99

Pet Policy: Service animals accompanying persons with disabilities are always accepted. Pets must be declared during guest registration. Pets must not be left unattended in the hotel room or suite. A pet fee can be required for each pet. Contact the property directly as pet friendly rooms may not be available all the time. Pet owner will be responsible for any damage caused by their pets.

Features: Airport transportation (free), Number of rooms: 36, Number of floors: 2, Free breakfast, Wireless Internet, Outdoor swimming pool, Designated smoking areas, Coffee in lobby.

South Pasadena

Also see the following nearby communities that have pet friendly lodging: Pasadena - 3 miles, San Gabriel - 4 miles, Monterey Park - 4 miles, Rosemead - 5 miles, Arcadia - 7 miles, Glendale - 7 miles, El Monte - 8 miles, South El Monte - 9 miles, Commerce - 9 miles, Monrovia - 9 miles, Hollywood - 10 miles

Arroyo Vista Inn
335 Monterey Road
South Pasadena CA 91030
(323) 478-7300
$175 - $215
Bed & Pet Discount Offered

Pet Policy: Pets under 25 lbs, $25 per pet per night. Limit 2 per room. Pets must not be left unattended in room.

Features: Free breakfast, Number of rooms: 10, Free wireless Internet.

South San Francisco

Also see the following nearby communities that have pet friendly lodging: San Bruno - 2 miles, Brisbane - 2 miles, Millbrae - 4 miles, Burlingame - 5 miles, San Francisco - 8 miles, San Mateo - 8 miles, Montara - 10 miles, Moss Beach - 10 miles

★★★½

Embassy Suites San Francisco Airport - South San Francisco
250 Gateway Blvd
South San Francisco CA 94080
(650) 589-3400
$129 - $229
Bed & Pet Discount Offered

Pet Policy: Pets up to 50 lbs, $50 per stay, per pet.

Features: Swimming pool - indoor, Security guard, Bar/lounge, Airport transportation (free), Restaurant(s), Room service, Gift shops or newsstand, Number of suites: 312, Number of floors: 10, Business services, Wireless Internet (additional charge), Free breakfast, Multilingual staff, Complimentary newspapers, Porter/bellhop, Limo or Town Car service available, Dry cleaning/laundry, Parking fee.

La Quinta Inn San Francisco Airport North
20 Airport Blvd
South San Francisco CA 94080
(650) 583-2223
$71 - $82
Bed & Pet Discount Offered

Pet Policy: Cats and dogs up to 50 pounds are accepted in all guest rooms. Housekeeping services for rooms with pets require pet owner be present or pet must be crated. No fees or deposits are required.

Features: Elevator, Guest laundry, Bar/lounge, Airport transportation (free), Number of rooms: 171, Number of floors: 4, Free breakfast, Parking (free) Multilingual staff, Free wireless Internet, Swimming pool - outdoor seasonal, Accessible bathroom, Dry cleaning/laundry service, Fitness facilities.

★★★

Larkspur Landing South San Francisco
690 Gateway Blvd
South San Francisco CA 94080
(650) 827-1515
$109 - $189
Bed & Pet Discount Offered

Pet Policy: Pets welcome, $75 per pet per stay.

Features: Business Center, Airport transportation (free), Concierge, Number of suites: 111, BBQ area, Coffee in lobby, Video library, Free breakfast, Free parking, Complimentary newspapers, Porter/bellhop, Free wireless Internet, Dry cleaning/laundry, Fitness center.

Motel 6 San Francisco Airport
111 Mitchell Ave
South San Francisco CA 94080
(650) 877-0770
$55 - $56
Bed & Pet Discount Offered

Pet Policy: Well-behaved pets stay Free. Animals that pose a health or safety risk may not remain onsite, and include those that, in our manager's discretion, are too numerous for any one room, cause damage to our property or that of other guests, are too disruptive, are not properly attended, or demonstrate undue aggression. All pets must be declared at check-in. Pets must be attended to and under control at all times. If unavoidable circumstances require a pet to remain in a room while the owner is offsite, the pet must be secured in a crate or travel carrier. Pets must be on a leash or securely carried outside of guest rooms.

Features: Coffee in lobby, Elevator, Number of rooms: 117, Number of floors: 3, Suitable for children, Parking (free).

★★★

Residence Inn by Marriott San Francisco Airport at
1350 Veterans Way
South San Francisco CA 94080
(650) 871-4100
$139 - $179
Bed & Pet Discount Offered

Pet Policy: Pets allowed, $100 per stay cleaning fee.

Features: Business services, Grocery/convenience store, Airport transportation (free), Swimming pool - outdoor, Number of rooms: 152, Number of floors: 4, Barbecue grill(s), Coffee in lobby, Free breakfast, Parking (free) Multilingual staff, Complimentary newspapers in lobby, Use of nearby fitness center (free), Dry cleaning/laundry service.

St Helena

Also see the following nearby communities that have pet friendly lodging: Calistoga - 7 miles, Yountville - 9 miles

Harvest Inn
1 Main St
St Helena CA 94574
(707) 963-9463
$268 - $549
Bed & Pet Discount Offered

Pet Policy: Pets welcome, $100 per visit, limit 2 per room. Please do not leave unattended in room. The Harvest Inn is the most pet friendly Napa Valley hotel, and we promise to pamper your pet from the moment of check-in. Harvest Inn special treatment includes a luxurious bed of their own, custom pet bowls, doggy bags and delicious (so Fido has told us) treats to make your pet's vacation a happy memory. In addition, we'll provide you with a list of pet friendly restaurants and wineries in the area, and a discount coupon for our local partner pet store, Fideaux.

Features: Free Breakfast, Business Center, Bar/Lounge, Free wireless Internet, Number of rooms: 74, Coffee in lobby, Spa services on site, Multilingual staff, Complimentary newspapers in lobby, Porter/bellhop, Security guard, Limo or Town Car service available, Massage - treatment room(s), Smoke-Free property, Concierge desk, Swimming pool - outdoor, Dry cleaning/laundry service.

Stevenson Ranch

Also see the following nearby communities that have pet friendly lodging: Valencia - 3 miles, Santa Clarita - 3 miles, Castaic - 8 miles, Chatsworth - 9 miles

Comfort Suites Stevenson Ranch
25380 The Old Rd
Stevenson Ranch CA 91381
(661) 254-7700
$89 - $105
Bed & Pet Discount Offered

Pet Policy: Pet charge: $25 pet/stay. Pet Limit: 2 pets/room. Maximum 50 pounds/pet.

Features: Elevator, Free breakfast, Swimming pool - outdoor, Business services, Guest laundry, Number of rooms: 101, Number of floors: 3, Parking (free), Complimentary newspapers in lobby, Free wireless Internet, Fitness facilities.

Extended Stay America Los Angeles - Valencia
24940 Pico Canyon Rd
Stevenson Ranch CA 91381
(661) 255-1044
$71 - $89
Bed & Pet Discount Offered

Pet Policy: One pet is allowed in each guest room. A $25 per day non-refundable cleaning fee (not to exceed $150) will be charged the first night of your stay.

Features: Elevator, Number of rooms: 104, Number of floors: 3, Business services, Wireless Internet (additional charge), Guest laundry, Parking (free), Multilingual staff.

Fairfield Inn By Marriott Santa Clarita
25340 The Old Rd
Stevenson Ranch CA 91381
(661) 290-2828
$89 - $99
Bed & Pet Discount Offered

Pet Policy: Pets accepted, $75 per stay cleaning fee.

Features: Swimming pool - outdoor, Business services, Elevator, Number of rooms: 66, Number of floors: 3, Coffee in lobby, Guest laundry, Free breakfast, Parking (free), Complimentary newspapers in lobby, Use of nearby fitness center (free), Accessible bathroom, Accessibility equipment for the deaf, Braille or raised signage, Dry cleaning/laundry service.

La Quinta Inn & Suites Santa Clarita-Valencia
25201 The Old Rd
Stevenson Ranch CA 91381
(661) 286-1111
$89 - $139
Bed & Pet Discount Offered

Pet Policy: Cats and dogs up to 50 pounds are accepted in all guest rooms. Housekeeping services for rooms with pets require pet owner be present or pet must be crated. No fees or deposits are required.

Features: Elevator, Business center, Coffee in lobby, Swimming pool - outdoor, Accessible bathroom, Number of rooms: 112, Number of floors: 4, Free breakfast, Parking (free), Complimentary newspapers in lobby, Free wireless Internet, Smoke-Free property, Dry cleaning/laundry service, Fitness facilities.

Residence Inn By Marriott Santa Clarita
25320 The Old Rd
Stevenson Ranch CA 91381
(661) 290-2800
$129 - $189
Bed & Pet Discount Offered

Pet Policy: Pets allowed, $75 per stay cleaning fee.

Features: Elevator, Swimming pool - outdoor, Number of suites: 90, Number of floors: 3, Coffee in lobby, Guest laundry, Free breakfast, Parking (free) Complimentary newspapers in lobby, Dry cleaning/laundry service, Fitness facilities.

Stockton

Also see the following nearby communities that have pet friendly lodging: Lodi - 9 miles

★★★:

Best Western Heritage Inn
111 E March Lane
Stockton CA 95207
(209) 474-3301
$62 - $99
Bed & Pet Discount Offered

Pet Policy: Small pets allowed. $20 per stay.

Features: Swimming pool - outdoor, Free reception, Bar/lounge, Restaurant(s), ATM/banking, Number of rooms: 200, Number of suites: 7, Number of floors: 3, Business services, Coffee in lobby, Free breakfast, Parking (free), Multilingual staff, Complimentary newspapers in lobby, Wireless Internet, Dry cleaning/laundry service, Fitness facilities.

Clarion Inn & Suites
4219 E Waterloo Road
Stockton CA 95215
(209) 931-3131
$69 - $78
Bed & Pet Discount Offered

Pet Policy: Pet charge: $25 per stay Pet limit: 1 pet maximum 10 pounds per room

Features: Business services, Bar/lounge, Swimming pool - outdoor, Restaurant(s), Number of rooms: 141, Number of floors: 2, Parking (free), Multilingual staff, Free wireless Internet.

Comfort Inn Stockton
3951 E Budweiser Ctr
Stockton CA 95205
(209) 931-9341
$75 - $85
Bed & Pet Discount Offered

Pet Policy: Small pets under 25 lbs, $15 per night.

Features: Number of rooms: 64, Free breakfast, Swimming pool - outdoor seasonal, Free wireless Internet, Guest laundry.

Comfort Inn Stockton
2654 W March Ln
Stockton CA 95207
(209) 478-4300
$72 - $99
Bed & Pet Discount Offered

Pet Policy: Small pets under 25 lbs, $15 per night.

Features: Elevator, Number of rooms: 122, Number of floors: 3, Coffee in lobby, Free breakfast, Parking (free) Complimentary newspapers in lobby, Free wireless Internet, Business services, Swimming pool - outdoor, Guest laundry.

Extended Stay America Stockton - March Lane
2844 W March Ln
Stockton CA 95219
(209) 472-7588
$59 - $79
Bed & Pet Discount Offered

Pet Policy: One pet up to 25 lbs is allowed in each guest room. A $25 per day non-refundable cleaning fee (not to exceed $150) will be charged the first night of your stay.

Features: Guest laundry, Elevator, Number of rooms: 92, Number of floors: 3, Wireless Internet (additional charge), Parking (free), Front desk (limited hours).

Hilton Stockton
2323 Grand Canal Blvd
Stockton CA 95207
(209) 957-9090
$98 - $169
Bed & Pet Discount Offered

Pet Policy: Pets up to 75 lbs, $75 per stay.

Features: Swimming pool - outdoor, Bar/lounge, Elevator, Restaurant(s), Room service (limited hours), ATM/banking, Number of rooms: 198, Number of floors: 5, Breakfast available (additional charge), Parking (free), Gift shops or newsstand, Coffee in lobby, Concierge desk, Smoke-Free property, Dry cleaning/laundry service, Free wireless Internet, 24-hour business center, Fitness facilities.

Howard Johnson Express Inn Stockton CA
33 N Center St
Stockton CA 95202
(209) 948-6151
$60 - $149
Bed & Pet Discount Offered

Pet Policy: Pets allowed, $10 per pet per night.

Features: Number of rooms: 90, Number of floors: 3, Guest laundry, Elevator, Shopping on site, Business services, Coffee in lobby, Wireless Internet (additional charge), Multilingual staff, Complimentary newspapers, Swimming pool - outdoor seasonal.

Knights Inn Stockton
4540 N El Dorado St
Stockton CA 95207
(209) 478-2944
$49 - $59
Bed & Pet Discount Offered

Pet Policy: Pet friendly rooms available with deposit.

Features: Number of rooms: 53, Number of floors: 3, Free breakfast, Parking (free), Smoke-Free property, Swimming pool - outdoor seasonal.

Knights Inn Stockton North
8009 N Highway 99
Stockton CA 95212
(209) 956-5200
$55 - $56
Bed & Pet Discount Offered

Pet Policy: Pet friendly rooms available.

Features: Free breakfast, Front desk (limited hours), Free wireless Internet, Barbecue grill(s), Coffee in lobby

La Quinta Inn Stockton
2710 W March Ln
Stockton CA 95219
(209) 952-7800
$44 - $89
Bed & Pet Discount Offered

Pet Policy: Cats and dogs up to 50 pounds are accepted in all guest rooms. Housekeeping services for rooms with pets require pet owner be present or pet must be crated. No fees or deposits are required.

Features: Accessible bathroom, Outdoor pool, Number of rooms: 152, Number of floors: 3, Business services, Guest laundry, Free breakfast, Multilingual staff, Nearby fitness center (free), Dry cleaning/laundry, Free Internet.

Lexington Plaza Waterfront
110 W Fremont St
Stockton CA 95202
(209) 944-1140
$77 - $239
Bed & Pet Discount Offered

Pet Policy: Dogs and cats welcome, $20 per night. Pet beds and dish provided.

Features: Elevator, Multilingual staff, Smoke-Free property, Dry cleaning/laundry service, Free wireless Internet, Fitness facilities, Restaurant(s), Business center, Self-parking (additional charge).

Red Roof Inn Stockton
1707 W Fremont St
Stockton CA 95203
(209) 466-7777
$52 - $62
Bed & Pet Discount Offered

Pet Policy: One well-behaved family pet is permitted. Pets must be declared during guest registration. In consideration of all Red Roof guests, pets must never be left unattended in the guestroom.

Features: Business center, Outdoor pool, Number of rooms: 62, Number of floors: 3, Free breakfast, Multilingual staff, Accessible bathroom, Accessibility equipment for the deaf, Braille or raised signage

★★★

Residence Inn By Marriott
3240 W March Ln
Stockton CA 95219
(209) 472-9800
$159 - $199
Bed & Pet Discount Offered

Pet Policy: Pets welcome, any size, $75 per stay.

Features: Coffee in lobby, Outdoor pool, Number of rooms: 104, Number of floors: 3, Business services, Barbecue grill(s), Free breakfast, Complimentary newspapers, Free wireless Internet, Dry cleaning/laundry service, Fitness facilities.

Rodeway Inn Stockton
339 S Wilson Way
Stockton CA 95205
(209) 466-2951
$49 - $54
Bed & Pet Discount Offered

Pet Policy: Rodeway Inns charge a fee of $10 per night per pet plus a $50 damage deposit, which is refunded if the room is in order at check out. Max of 2 pets per room. A veterinarian certificate that the pet is on a flea and parasite program is required. Pets may not be left alone in the room unless crated.

Features: Number of rooms: 23, Number of floors: 2, Business services, Free breakfast, Free wireless Internet.

Studio City

Also see the following nearby communities that have pet friendly lodging: Universal City - 3 miles, Sherman Oaks - 4 miles, West Hollywood - 4 miles, Burbank - 4 miles, Hollywood - 5 miles, Beverly Hills - 6 miles, Van Nuys - 6 miles, Glendale - 7 miles, Tarzana - 9 miles, Culver City - 9 miles, Santa Monica - 10 miles, Los Angeles - 10 mile

Not rated
Marriott Executay Apartments Windsor
4055 Lankershim Blvd
Studio City CA 91604
(888) 526-0566
$137 - $169

Pet Policy: Dogs and Cats, up to 40 lbs, allowed, $500 deposit, $250 refundable. Maximum 2 per apartment. Cats allowed on any floor, Dogs only in designated units. No aggressive breeds.

Features: Furnished apartments, near Weddington Park. Minimum stay of 30 days may be required.

Sportsmen's Lodge
12825 Ventura Blvd
Studio City CA 91604
(818) 755-5000
$107 - $164
Bed & Pet Discount Offered

Pet Policy: Small dogs under 25 lbs allowed. $75 nonrefundable cleaning fee required.

Features: ATM/banking, Room service , Concierge, Beauty services, Bar/lounge, Swimming pool - outdoor, RV and truck parking, Parking $10 Per Night, Poolside bar, Nearby fitness center (discount), Restaurant(s), Gift shops or newsstand, Number of rooms: 200, Number of floors: 5, Complimentary newspapers, Roll-in shower, Accessibility equipment for the deaf, Dry cleaning/laundry, Wireless Internet (additional charge).

Suisun City

Also see the following nearby communities that have pet friendly lodging: Fairfield - 1 mile, Vacaville - 9 mile

Hampton Inn and Suites Suisun City Waterfront
2 Harbor Ctr
Suisun City CA 94585
(707) 429-0900
$80 - $138
Bed & Pet Discount Offered

Pet Policy: Dogs only, up to 40 lbs.

Features: Bar/lounge, Babysitting or child care, Elevator, Swimming pool - outdoor, Wheelchair accessible, Concierge services, Number of rooms: 102, Number of suites: 29, Number of floors: 4, Suitable for children, Coffee in lobby, Free breakfast, Parking (free), Multilingual staff, Complimentary newspapers in lobby, Dry cleaning/laundry service, Limo or Town Car service available, Smoke-Free property, Beach/pool umbrellas, Accessible bathroom, Accessibility equipment for the deaf, Braille or raised signage, 24-hour business center, Fitness facilities,

Sun City

Also see the following nearby communities that have pet friendly lodging: Canyon Lake - 4 miles, Lake Elsinore - 10 miles

Americas Best Value Inn
27680 ENCANTO DRIVE
Sun City CA 92586
(951) 672-1861
$53 - $59

Pet Policy: Pets under 50 lbs, $10 per night per pet. Limit 2 per room.

Features: Minutes from Temecula wine country, Continental breakfast (free), Coffee in lobby, Guest laundry, Free wireless Internet, Swimming pool – outdoor, Microwave, Mini fridge, Cable TV with HBO, Hair dryer.

Sunnyvale

Also see the following nearby communities that have pet friendly lodging: Santa Clara - 2 miles, Cupertino - 4 miles, Mountain View - 4 miles, Los Altos - 6 miles, Palo Alto - 7 miles, Milpitas - 7 miles, Campbell - 8 miles, San Jose - 10 miles, Newark - 10 mile

★★

Comfort Inn Silicon Valley
1071 E El Camino Real
Sunnyvale CA 94087
(408) 244-9000
$69 - $99
Bed & Pet Discount Offered

Pet Policy: Pets up to 40 lbs, $25 per night. Limit 2 per room. Please indicate bringing pets in reservation request.

Features: Coffee in lobby, Swimming pool - outdoor, Elevator, Room service (limited hours), Gift shops or newsstand, Number of rooms: 64, Number of floors: 3, Free breakfast, Parking (free) Complimentary newspapers in lobby, Use of nearby fitness center (free), Business center, Wireless Internet.

★★

Homestead Studio Suites San Jose - Sunnyvale
1255 Orleans Dr
Sunnyvale CA 94089
(408) 734-3431
$94 - $104
Bed & Pet Discount Offered

Pet Policy: All pets are welcome except certain aggressive breeds A non-refundable $25/day. For extended stay guests (4 nights or more), there is a one-time non-refundable $75 charge.

Features: Guest laundry, Number of rooms: 145, Number of floors: 2, Business services, Barbecue grill(s), Wireless Internet (additional charge), Parking (free), Use of nearby fitness center (discount).

Larkspur Landing Sunnyvale
748 N Mathilda Ave
Sunnyvale CA 94085
(408) 733-1212
$80 - $129
Bed & Pet Discount Offered

Pet Policy: Pets welcome, $75 per pet per stay.

Features: Business Center, Coffee in lobby, Library, Elevator, Concierge, Number of suites: 126, Number of floors: 4, Video library, Free breakfast, Grocery, Parking (free), Multilingual staff, Complimentary newspapers in lobby, Porter/bellhop, Limo or Town Car service available, Free wireless Internet, Dry cleaning/laundry service, Fitness facilities.

Quality Inn Silicon Valley
1280 Persian Dr
Sunnyvale CA 94089
(408) 744-1100
$79 - $109
Bed & Pet Discount Offered

Pet Policy: Quality Inns charge a fee of $10 per night per pet but do not charge any other fees. They may require a $50 damage deposit, which is refunded if the room is in order at check out. Quality Inns accept any well-behaved pets with a maximum of 3 per room, but dogs are limited to 50 pounds. Pets may not be left alone in the room unless in a cage.

Features: Business Center, Swimming pool - outdoor heated, Concierge, Number of rooms: 72, Number of floors: 2, Coffee in lobby, Guest laundry, Free breakfast, Video library, Parking (free), Complimentary newspapers, Free wireless Internet, Dry cleaning/laundry service, Fitness facilities.

★★½

Ramada Inn - Silicon Valley
1217 Wildwood Ave
Sunnyvale CA 94089
(408) 245-5330
$55 - $109
Bed & Pet Discount Offered

Pet Policy: Pets allowed, $15 per pet per night Plus refundable deposit.

Features: Free breakfast, Swimming pool - outdoor, Bar/lounge, Restaurant(s), ATM/banking, Number of rooms: 172, Number of floors: 2, Business services, Parking (free), Multilingual staff, Free wireless Internet, Nearby fitness center (discount), Dry cleaning/laundry service.

★★★

Residence Inn by Marriott Silicon Valley Sunnyvale
1080 Stewart Dr
Sunnyvale CA 94086
(408) 720-8893
$119 - $189
Bed & Pet Discount Offered

Pet Policy: Pets allowed, $100 per stay cleaning fee.

Features: Free Breakfast, Swimming pool - outdoor, Airport transportation (free), Number of rooms: 247, Number of floors: 2, Barbecue grill(s), Coffee in lobby, Parking (free), Complimentary newspapers in lobby, Business center, Free wireless Internet, Smoke-Free property, Dry cleaning/laundry service, Tennis on site, Fitness facilities

★★★

Residence Inn by Marriott Silicon Valley Sunnyvale
750 Lakeway Dr
Sunnyvale CA 94085
(408) 720-1000
$119 - $210
Bed & Pet Discount Offered

Pet Policy: Pets allowed. $100 per stay cleaning fee.

Features: Free Breakfast, Outdoor pool, Tennis courts, Airport transportation (free), Number of rooms: 231, Number of floors: 2, BBQ area, Coffee in lobby, Grocery, Complimentary newspapers, Business center, Free wireless Internet, Beauty services, Dry cleaning/laundry, Fitness facilities.

★★★½

Sheraton Sunnyvale Hotel
1100 N Mathilda Ave
Sunnyvale CA 94089
(408) 745-6000
$109 - $119
Bed & Pet Discount Offered

Pet Policy: Pets are allowed. Guest must sign a Pet Waiver upon check-in. Pets must be accompanied by owner at all times on leash or in a crate. Guests will be responsible for costs if excess damage or deep cleaning is required. If damage is discovered after checkout, the credit card on record will be charged.

Features: Airport transportation (free), Bar/lounge, Restaurant(s), Room service, Number of rooms: 173, Number of floors: 2, Breakfast available (additional charge), Complimentary newspapers, Concierge, Accessibility equipment for the deaf, Dry cleaning/laundry, Multilingual staff, Accessible bathroom, Outdoor pool, Fitness facilities, Technology support staff, Nearby fitness center (free), Gift shop, Area shuttle (free), 24-hour business center, Porter/bellhop, Free wireless Internet, BBQ area, Smoke-Free, Security guard, Coffee in lobby, Technology helpdesk.

Staybridge Suites Sunnyvale
900 Hamlin Court
Sunnyvale CA 94089
(408) 745-1515
$176 - $200
Bed & Pet Discount Offered

Pet Policy: Pets up to 80 lbs, $15 first night, $10 thereafter not to exceed $150. Must have vaccination records with you.

Swimming pool - outdoor, Business services, Accessible bathroom, Accessibility equipment for the deaf, Braille or raised signage, Fitness center, Concierge, Gift shop, Number of rooms: 138, Number of floors: 3, Dry cleaning/laundry.

TownePlace Suites by Marriott San Jose Sunnyvale
606 S Bernardo Ave
Sunnyvale CA 94087
(408) 733-4200
From $169
Bed & Pet Discount Offered

Pet Policy: Pets allowed, $75 per stay.

Features: Free Breakfast, Coffee in Lobby, Number of rooms: 95, Number of floors: 4, Barbecue grill(s), Complimentary newspapers, Business center, Nearby fitness center (free), Smoke-Free property, Grocery/convenience store, Roll-in shower, Accessibility equipment for the deaf, Dry cleaning/laundry, Free Internet, Fitness facilities.

Vagabond Inn Sunnyvale
816 West Ahwanee Avenue
Sunnyvale CA 94085
(408) 734-4607
$70 - $86
Bed & Pet Discount Offered

Pet Policy: Pets accepted, $10 per pet per night.

Features: Business services, Outdoor pool, Restaurant, Number of rooms: 60, Number of floors: 2, Coffee in lobby, Guest laundry, Free breakfast, Complimentary newspapers, Nearby fitness center (free), Free wireless Internet.

Susanville

Super 8 Susanville CA
3975 Johnstonville Rd
Susanville CA 96130
(530) 257-2782
$65 - $77

Pet Policy: Pets permitted, $10 per pet per night. Please make reservation directly with hotel as number of pet rooms very limited.

Features: Business services, Free breakfast, Swimming pool - outdoor seasonal.

Sutter Creek

Also see the following nearby communities that have pet friendly lodging: Amador City - 2 miles, Jackson - 3 mile

★★

Days Inn Sutter Creek Ca
271 Hanford St
On Hwy 49
Sutter Creek CA 95685
(209) 267-9177
$63 - $114
Bed & Pet Discount Offered

Pet Policy: Pets accepted, $15 per night.

Features: Elevator, Business services, Coffee in lobby, Free breakfast, Parking (free), Complimentary newspapers in lobby, Business center, Free wireless Internet, Poolside bar

Tahoe Vista

Also see the following nearby communities that have pet friendly lodging: Truckee - 9 miles, Olympic Valley - 9 mile

Not rated
Tahoe Vistana Inn
6549 North Lake Blvd
Tahoe Vista CA 96148
(530) 546-2529
$74 - $170

Pet Policy; Pets up to 80 pounds accepted. $15 per night per pet plus $100 refundable damage deposit. All pets must be on a treatment plan to prevent fleas. All pets must be on a leash at all times when not inside your assigned room. All pets must be crated/caged when left alone in the room. Any violation of this policy will result in an additional $100 charge. We reserve the right to refuse housekeeping to any room where the pet is not crated/caged. Pets must be walked in the designated areas only. All pets being walked in designated areas must be cleaned up after. Plastic bags are available from the front desk in the lobby, and must be placed in the dumpster outside – please do not use your in-room trash can. Any noise or behavior complaints concerning your pet will be addressed immediately. If you are unable to alleviate the issue, then you and your pet will be asked to leave, and will be financially responsible for any time remaining on your stay.

Features: Heated Spa, Microwave, Refrigerator, Coffee maker, boat parking.

Tarzana

Also see the following nearby communities that have pet friendly lodging: Woodland Hills - 3 miles, Canoga Park - 4 miles, Northridge - 5 miles, Van Nuys - 5 miles, Sherman Oaks - 5 miles, Topanga - 6 miles, Chatsworth - 7 miles, Calabasas - 8 miles, Studio City - 9 miles

Tarzana Inn
19170 Ventura Blvd.
Tarzana CA 91356
(818) 345-9410
$89 - $99

Pet Policy; Pets allowed, $10 per pet per day. Reservations must be made directly with hotel.

Features: Free continental breakfast, Swimming pool – heated, Parking (free), Free wireless Internet, Refrigerators, Coffee makers, Cable TV with HBO, Hair dryers, Irons and ironing boards, Complimentary daily newspaper.

Tehachapi

Best Western Mountain Inn
416 W TEHACHAPI BLVD
Tehachapi CA 93561
(661) 822-5591
$72 - $89

Pet Policy; Pets accepted on advanced approval directly from hotel.

Features: Hair dryer, Refrigerator, Microwave, HBO.

Holiday Inn Express Hotel & Suites Tehachapi
901 Capital Hills Pkwy
Tehachapi CA 93561
(661) 822-9837
$88 - $121
Bed & Pet Discount Offered

Pet Policy; Pets are allowed with a non-refundable charge of $25 per stay and pet must be less than 50 lbs. Pet rooms are request only and cannot be guaranteed. Pet rooms are only available on first floor and prior reservation is recommended.

Features: Swimming pool - outdoor, Accessible bathroom, Accessibility equipment for the deaf, Braille or raised signage, Gift shops or newsstand, Number of rooms: 80, Number of suites: 17, Number of floors: 3, Free breakfast, Parking (free), Multilingual staff, Complimentary newspapers in lobby, Business center, Free wireless Internet, Fitness facilities.

★★

La Quinta Inn Tehachapi
500 E Steuber Rd
Tehachapi CA 93561
(661) 823-8000
$85 - $86
Bed & Pet Discount Offered

Pet Policy; Cats and dogs up to 50 pounds are accepted in all guest rooms. Housekeeping services for rooms with pets require pet owner be present or pet must be crated. No fees or deposits are required.

Features: Bar/lounge, Restaurant, Wireless Internet (additional charge), Complimentary newspapers, Security guard, Swimming pool - outdoor seasonal, Accessible bathroom, Free breakfast, Business center, Fitness facilities, Smoke-Free property.

Temecula

Also see the following nearby communities that have pet friendly lodging: Fallbrook - 9 miles

Embassy Suites Hotel Temecula Valley Wine Country
29345 Rancho California Rd
Temecula CA 92591
(951) 676-5656
$101 - $169
Bed & Pet Discount Offered

Pet Policy; Pets up to 30 lbs accepted, $25 per day per pet. Limit of 2 pets per room.

Features: Bar/Lounge, Outdoor pool, Free breakfast, Room service, Restaurant, Gift shop, Number of rooms: 176, Number of floors: 5, Complimentary newspaper, Accessible bathroom, Accessibility equipment for the deaf, Braille or raised signage, Dry cleaning/laundry service, Wheelchair accessible, Technology support staff, Free wireless Internet, Business center, Free reception, Fitness facilities.

★★

Extended Stay America Temecula - Wine Country
27622 Jefferson Avenue
Temecula CA 92590
(909) 587-8881
$64 - $124
Bed & Pet Discount Offered

Pet Policy; One pet is allowed in each guest room. A $25 per day non-refundable cleaning fee (not to exceed $150) will be charged the first night

Features: Number of rooms: 107, Number of floors: 3, Nearby fitness center (free), Front desk (limited hours), Wireless Internet, Guest laundry.

La Quinta Inn & Suites Temecula
27330 Jefferson Ave
Temecula CA 92590
(951) 296-1003
$79 - $139
Bed & Pet Discount Offered

Pet Policy; Cats and dogs up to 50 pounds are accepted in all guest rooms. Housekeeping services for rooms with pets require pet owner be present or pet must be crated. No fees or deposits are required.

Features: Business center, Concierge, Coffee in lobby, Translation services, Accessible bathroom, Swimming pool - outdoor, Number of rooms: 54, Number of floors: 3, Suitable for children, Free breakfast, Complimentary newspapers, Free wireless Internet, Smoke-Free property, Fitness facilities.

Quality Inn Wine Country
27338 Jefferson Ave
Temecula CA 92590
(951) 296-3788
$63 - $129
Bed & Pet Discount Offered

Pet Policy; Quality Inns charge a fee of $10 per night per pet and may require a $50 refundable damage deposit. Quality Inns accept any well-behaved pets with a maximum of 3 per room, but dogs are limited to 50 pounds. Pets may not be left alone in the room unless in a cage.

Features: Coffee in lobby, Outdoor pool, Number of rooms: 71, Number of floors: 3, Free breakfast, Smoke-Free, Guest laundry.

★★

Rodeway Inn Temecula
28718 Front St
Temecula CA 92590
(951) 676-4833
$52 - $149
Bed & Pet Discount Offered

Pet Policy: Rodeway Inns charge a fee of $10 per night per pet plus a $50 damage deposit, which is refunded if the room is in order at check out. Max of 2 pets per room. A veterinarian certificate that the pet is on a flea and parasite program is required. Pets may not be left alone in the room unless crated.

Features: Business services, Number of rooms: 39, Number of floors: 2, Guest laundry, Free breakfast, Complimentary newspapers, Outdoor pool - seasonal, Free wireless Internet.

The Sea Ranch

Also see the following nearby communities that have pet friendly lodging: Gualala - 9 miles

The Sea Ranch Lodge
60 Sea Walk Drive
The Sea Ranch CA 95497
(800) 732-7262
$295 - $395

Pet Policy: We are a dog friendly hotel. Maximum of two dogs per room. When making your reservation, please indicate whether you will be bringing one or two dogs. There is a charge of $50 per dog for the entire visit (fee subject to change).

Features: Ocean view accommodations, Restaurant, Number of rooms: 20, Fireplaces in some rooms, Free breakfast, Complimentary newspapers, Free wireless Internet.

Thousand Oaks

Also see the following nearby communities that have pet friendly lodging: Westlake Village - 6 miles, Camarillo - 9 miles

La Quinta Inn & Suites Thousand Oaks Newbury Park
1320 Newbury Rd
Thousand Oaks CA 91320
(805) 499-5910
$79 - $85
Bed & Pet Discount Offered

Pet Policy: Cats and dogs up to 50 pounds are accepted in all guest rooms. Housekeeping services for rooms with pets require pet owner be present or pet must be crated. No fees or deposits are required.

Features: Free breakfast, Guest laundry, Outdoor pool, Accessible bathroom, Number of rooms: 121, Number of floors: 3, Complimentary newspapers, Business center, Free wireless Internet, Fitness center..

Palm Garden Hotel
495 N Ventu Park Rd
Thousand Oaks CA 91320
(805) 716-4200
$99 - $119
Bed & Pet Discount Offered

Pet Policy: Pets accepted, $30 per stay. Must book in advance and indicate bringing pet.

Features: Bar/Lounge, Restaurant, Room service, Outdoor pool, Number of rooms: 154, Number of floors: 3, Business services, Guest laundry, Free breakfast, Complimentary newspapers, Accessible bathroom, Free wireless Internet, Fitness facilities.

TownePlace Suites by Marriott Thousand Oaks
1712 Newbury Road
Thousand Oaks CA 91320
(805) 499-3111
$89 - $94
Bed & Pet Discount Offered

Pet Policy: Pets allowed, $75 per stay.

Features: Coffee in lobby, BBQ area, Business center, Suitable for children, Multilingual staff, Complimentary newspapers, Free wireless Internet, Elevator, Swimming pool - outdoor, Number of rooms: 93, Number of floors: 3, Accessible bathroom, Accessibility equipment for the deaf, Braille or raised signage, Dry cleaning/laundry, Smoke-Free property, Fitness facilities.

Thousand Palms

Also see the following nearby communities that have pet friendly lodging: Rancho Mirage - 4 miles, Palm Desert - 5 miles, Cathedral City - 6 miles, Palm Springs - 9 miles

Red Roof Inn Palm Springs - Thousand Palms
72215 Varner Rd
Thousand Palms CA 92276
(760) 343-1381
$64 - $171
Bed & Pet Discount Offered

Pet Policy: Red Roof's Pet Policy: One well-behaved family pet is permitted. Service animals are always welcome. Pets must be declared during guest registration. Pets must never be left unattended in the guestroom.

Features: Number of rooms: 116, Number of floors: 2, Coffee in lobby, Complimentary newspapers, Accessible bathroom, Outdoor pool, Guest laundry, Free breakfast, Multilingual staff, Free Internet.

Three Rivers

Americas Best Value Inn
39625 Sierra Drive
Three Rivers CA 93271
(559) 561-4449
$68 - $96

Pet Policy: Small pets allowed, $5 per pet per night.

Features: All ground floor units, Housekeeping units available, Fireplaces in some rooms, Continental breakfast (free), Guest laundry, Cable TV.

Comfort Inn & Suites Sequoia/Kings Canyon
40820 Sierra Dr
Three Rivers CA 93271
(559) 561-9000
$69 - $139
Bed & Pet Discount Offered

Pet Policy: Pets up to 25 lbs, $35 per stay. Limit 2 per room. Pets not allowed in food or pool areas.

Features: Guest laundry, Swimming pool - outdoor, Gift shops or newsstand, Number of rooms: 103, Number of floors: 1, Free breakfast, Multilingual staff, Free wireless Internet, Accessibility equipment for the deaf, Fitness facilities.

Sequoia River Dance B & B
40534 Cherokee Oaks Drive
Three Rivers CA 93271
(559) 561-4411
From $136
Bed & Pet Discount Offered

Pet Policy: Well-behaved cats and dogs of any size are accepted, $15 per night.

Features: Number of rooms: 5, Suitable for children, BBQ area, Library, Video library, Free breakfast, Dry cleaning/laundry, Free Internet access.

Sierra Lodge Three Rivers
43175 Sierra Dr
Three Rivers CA 93291
(559) 561-3681
$51 - $159
Bed & Pet Discount Offered

Pet Policy: Well-behaved pets accepted, $10 per pet per night plus $20 refundable deposit. Limit 2 per room.

Features: Barbecue grill(s), Suitable for children, Free breakfast, Gift shops or newsstand, Multilingual staff, Swimming pool - outdoor seasonal, Library, Free reception, Concierge services, Free wireless Internet, Business center, Smoke-Free property.

Western Holiday Lodge
40105 Sierra Drive
Highway 198
Three Rivers CA 93271
(559) 561-4119
$53- $129

Pet Policy: Pets accepted with fee at check-in.

Features: Breakfast (free), Free wireless Internet, Non-smoking property.

Topanga

Also see the following nearby communities that have pet friendly lodging: Woodland Hills - 6 miles, Tarzana - 6 miles, Calabasas - 7 miles, Santa Monica - 7 miles, Canoga Park - 8 miles, Sherman Oaks - 9 miles, Venice - 10 miles

Topanga Canyon Inn Bed and Breakfast
20310 Callon Drive
Topanga CA 90290
(310) 600-1325
$151 - $299
Bed & Pet Discount Offered

Pet Policy: Pets are not permitted inside the property, however, you can reserve the Clark and Carole Room and keep your animal in a crate on the private patio. Alternatively, you can keep your animal in a crate in a protected, outside location at the Inn. We can loan you a crate. We can also provide you with names and numbers of nearby pet care facilities.

Features: Free breakfast, Parking (free), Smoke-Free property, Free wireless Internet.

Torrance

Also see the following nearby communities that have pet friendly lodging: Harbor City - 2 miles, Redondo Beach - 3 miles, Carson - 4 miles, Gardena - 4 miles, Hermosa Beach - 5 miles, Manhattan Beach - 6 miles, Hawthorne - 7 miles, San Pedro - 7 miles, El Segundo - 8 miles, Long Beach - 9 miles, Inglewood - 10 miles, Signal Hill - 10 miles

Days Inn Torrance
4111 Pacific Coast Hwy
Torrance CA 90505
(310) 378-8511
$55 - $99
Bed & Pet Discount Offered

Pet Policy: Pets allowed, $10 per pet per day.

Features: Swimming pool - outdoor, Restaurant, Number of rooms: 92, Number of floors: 4, Coffee in lobby, Free breakfast, Parking (free), Wireless Internet

ESA LAX-Torrance Harbor
19200 Harbor Gateway
Torrance CA 90301
(310) 328-6000
$74 - $107

Pet Policy: One pet is allowed in each guest room. A $25 per day cleaning fee (not to exceed $150) will be charged the first night of your stay.

Features: Fully furnished apartments, Recliner work desk, Kitchen, Movie channels, Two line phone with data port, Laundry facility, Weekly housekeeping. Minimum 30 day stay may be required.

Extended Stay America Los Angeles - Torrance Harbor
19200 Harborgate Way
Torrance CA 90501
(310) 328-6000
$74 - $95
Bed & Pet Discount Offered

Pet Policy: One pet under 25 lbs is allowed in each guest room. A $25 per day cleaning fee (not to exceed $150) will be charged the first night of stay.

Features: Guest laundry, Elevator, Number of rooms: 122, Number of floors: 3, Parking (free), Front desk (limited hours), Security guard, Wireless Internet.

Extended Stay America Los Angeles -Torrance
3525 Torrance Blvd
Torrance CA 90503
(310) 540-5442
$69 - $97
Bed & Pet Discount Offered

Pet Policy: One pet is allowed in each guest room. A $25 per day cleaning fee (not to exceed $150) will be charged the first night of your stay.

Features: Guest laundry, Business services, Wireless Internet (additional charge), Front desk (limited hours), Use of nearby fitness center (discount).

Holiday Inn Torrance
19800 S Vermont Ave
Torrance CA 90502
(310) 781-9100
$85 - $163
Bed & Pet Discount Offered

Pet Policy: Well-mannered pets allowed, $50 per stay.

Features: Sauna, Swimming pool - outdoor, ATM/banking, Guest laundry, Bar/lounge, Restaurant, Gift shops or newsstand, Parking (free), Multilingual staff, Room service, Business center, Porter/bellhop, Free wireless Internet, Concierge desk, Accessible bathroom, Accessibility equipment for the deaf, Braille or raised signage, Dry cleaning/laundry service, Fitness facilities.

Homestead - Torrance
3995 W Carson St
Torrance CA 90503
(310) 543-0048
$69 - $114
Bed & Pet Discount Offered

Pet Policy: Pets allowed, no size restriction, $25 per day to a maximum of $150 per stay. Limit of 1 pet per room.

Features: Guest laundry, Number of rooms: 139, Number of floors: 3, Business services, Wireless Internet, Nearby fitness center (discount)

Ramada Inn Torrance
2880 Pacific Coast Hwy
Torrance CA 90505
(310) 325-0660
$57 - $129
Bed & Pet Discount Offered

Pet Policy: Pets welcome, $10 per pet per night plus $50 refundable deposit.

Features: Free breakfast, Coffee in lobby, Currency exchange, Parking (free), Multilingual staff, Business center, Swimming pool - outdoor seasonal, Dry cleaning/laundry service.

Residence Inn By Marriott
3701 Torrance Blvd
Torrance CA 90503
(310) 543-4566
$95 - $179
Bed & Pet Discount Offered

Pet Policy: Pets allowed, $100 per stay cleaning fee.

Features: Outdoor pool, ATM/banking, Number of rooms: 247, Barbecue grill(s), Guest laundry, Poolside bar, Free breakfast, Restaurant, Parking (free), Multilingual staff, Use of nearby fitness center (free), Wireless Internet, Smoke-Free property.

Staybridge Suites Torrance
19901 Prairie Ave
Torrance CA 90503
(310) 371-8525
$94 - $215
Bed & Pet Discount Offered

Pet Policy: Pets allowed with nonrefundable fee of $15 for the first night and $10 for each additional night not to exceed $150. Each pet (2 max per room) must weigh less than 80 lbs. Pet agreement must be signed at check-in.

Features: Free Breakfast, Outdoor pool, BBQ area, Accessible bathroom, Accessibility equipment for the deaf, Braille or raised signage, Gift shops or newsstand, Business services, Grocery, Health club, Multilingual staff, Free wireless Internet, Dry cleaning/laundry service, Fitness facilities.

Tracy

Also see the following nearby communities that have pet friendly lodging: Lathrop - 9 miles

Best Western Luxury Inn
811 W Clover Rd
Tracy CA 95376
(209) 832-0271
$59 - $69
Bed & Pet Discount Offered

Pet Policy: Pets accepted with small fee at check in.

Features: Free wireless Internet, Outdoor pool, Number of floors: 3, Free breakfast, Complimentary newspapers, Bar/lounge, Restaurant, Wheelchair accessible, Shopping on site, Smoke-Free property.

★★

Extended Stay America
2526 Pavilion Pwky
Tracy CA 95304
(209) 832-4700
$59 - $74
Bed & Pet Discount Offered

Pet Policy: One medium-size pet is allowed in each guest room. A $25 per day cleaning fee (not to exceed $150) will be charged the first night of stay.

Features: Guest laundry, Number of rooms: 101, Number of floors: 3, Wireless Internet (fee), Multilingual staff, Complimentary newspapers..

★★

Microtel Tracy
861 W Clover Rd
Tracy CA 95376
(209) 229-1201
$63 - $149
Bed & Pet Discount Offered

Pet Policy: Pets accepted, $10 per night per room.

Features: Business center, Number of rooms: 69, Number of floors: 3, Computer rental, Suitable for children, Coffee in lobby, Free breakfast, Multilingual staff, Complimentary newspapers, Free wireless Internet, Dry cleaning/laundry, Fitness facilities.

Quality Inn Tracy
3511 N Tracy Blvd
Tracy CA 95376
(209) 835-1335
$59 - $69
Bed & Pet Discount Offered

Pet Policy: Pets accepted, $10 per night plus $50 deposit. Limit 1 pet per room.

Features: Outdoor pool - seasonal, Free breakfast, Coffee in lobby, Business services, Gift shops or newsstand, Number of rooms: 59, Number of floors: 3, Multilingual staff, Guest laundry.

Truckee

Also see the following nearby communities that have pet friendly lodging: Olympic Valley - 8 miles, Tahoe Vista - 9 miles

The Inn at Truckee
11506 Deerfield Dr
Truckee CA 96161
(530) 587-8888
$80 - $155
Bed & Pet Discount Offered

Pet Policy: Pets are welcome for an additional $15 per night. Please note that pets CANNOT be left unattended in rooms.

Features: Accessible bathroom, Free wireless Internet, Wheelchair accessible, Number of rooms: 42, Number of floors: 3, Guest laundry, Free breakfast, Multilingual staff, Sauna, Ski shuttle, Smoke-Free property.

The Ritz-Carlton, Lake Tahoe
13031 Ritz Carlton Highland Ct
Truckee CA 96161
(530) 562-3000
$425 - $1,675
Bed & Pet Discount Offered

Pet Policy: Pet-friendly rooms are available upon request. A one-time $125 pet cleaning fee will be charged upon check-in. With the exception of documented service animals, pets are not allowed in any public area where food and beverage is served. Please note this includes The Living Room which is the hotel's main lobby.

Features: Valet parking (fee), Babysitting or child care, Outdoor pool, Wheelchair accessible, Supervised child care/activities, Hair salon, Concierge, Shopping on site, Number of rooms: 170, Number of suites: 17, Number of floors: 6, Ski storage, Arcade/game room, Health club, Children's swimming pool, Multilingual staff, Porter/bellhop, Doorman/doorwoman, Limo or Town Car service available, Ski-in/ski-out, Full-service health spa, Massage - treatment room(s), Smoke-Free property, Technology helpdesk, Children's club, Accessible bathroom, Accessibility equipment for the deaf, Dry cleaning/laundry service, Free wireless Internet, 24-hour business center, 3 Restaurants.

Tulare

Also see the following nearby communities that have pet friendly lodging: Visalia - 9 miles

★★★

Best Western Plus Town & Country Lodge
1051 N Blackstone St
Tulare CA 93274
(559) 688-7537
$71 - $89
Bed & Pet Discount Offered

Pet Policy: Two pet maximum, 40 pounds & under, $20 per stay.

Features: Outdoor pool, Number of rooms: 93, Number of floors: 2, Business center, Fitness facilities, Free breakfast, RV and truck parking, Barbecue grill(s), Accessible bathroom, Dry cleaning/laundry service, Wheelchair accessible, Accessibility equipment for the deaf, Bar/lounge.

Charter Inn & Suites
1016 E Prosperity Ave
Tulare CA 93274
(559) 685-9500
$65 - $125
Bed & Pet Discount Offered

Pet Policy: Your four-legged traveling companion is a welcome guest at Charter Inn & Suites. Ask about our special blanket and water bowl for our four-legged guests Our pet friendly policy includes dogs and cats. Pet deposit applies.

Features: Free Breakfast, Coffee in lobby, Swimming pool - outdoor, Number of rooms: 70, Number of suites: 9, Number of floors: 3, Complimentary newspapers, Security guard, Dry cleaning/laundry service, Bar/lounge, Translation services, Barbecue grill(s), Parking (free), Multilingual staff, Nearby fitness center (discount), Technology support staff, Free wireless Internet, 24-hour business center, Free reception, Fitness facilities

Days Inn Tulare
1183 N Blackstone St
Tulare CA 93274
(559) 686-0985
$48 - $90
Bed & Pet Discount Offered

Pet Policy: We are delighted to welcome you and your pet as our guests. Upon check in at the hotel you will receive a pet welcome package containing: Dog treats (2), Disposal bags (2), Map with directions to pet friendly parks, Pet in room" do not disturb sign

Features: Free Breakfast, Outdoor pool, Number of rooms: 90, Number of floors: 3, Business services, Coffee in lobby, Parking (free), Multilingual staff, Complimentary newspapers, Free wireless Internet.

La Quinta Inn & Suites Tulare
1500 N Cherry Ct
Tulare CA 93274
(559) 685-8900
$75 - $88
Bed & Pet Discount Offered

Pet Policy: Pets allowed without fee. Must not leave unattended in room.

Features: Free breakfast, Coffee in lobby, Number of rooms: 69, Number of floors: 3, Multilingual staff, Complimentary newspapers, Smoke-Free, Accessible bathroom, Outdoor pool, Dry cleaning/laundry, Fitness facilities, Business center, Free Internet.

Quality Inn Tulare
1010 E Prosperity Ave
Tulare CA 93274
(559) 686-3432
From $69
Bed & Pet Discount Offered

Pet Policy: Dogs only, under 25 lbs. Fee $15 per dog per night

Features: Sauna, Free breakfast, Coffee in lobby, Elevator, Outdoor pool, Number of rooms: 58, Number of floors: 3, Guest laundry, Multilingual staff, Complimentary newspapers, Free wireless Internet, Accessible bathroom, Fitness facilities.

Turlock

Also see the following nearby communities that have pet friendly lodging: Ceres - 9 miles

Not rated
Americas Best Value Inn
701 20th Century Blvd
Turlock CA 95380
(209) 634-3111
$58 - $75

Pet Policy: Pets allowed, $10 per pet per night plus $25 refundable deposit. Limit 2 pets per room.

Features: Number of rooms: 19, Free wireless Internet, HBO, Microwave, Refrigerator, Coffee maker, Hair dryer, Free continental breakfast, Area shuttle (free).

Best Western Orchard Inn
5025 N Golden State Blvd
Turlock CA 95380
(209) 667-2827
From $75
Bed & Pet Discount Offered

Pet Policy: Small pets allowed.

Features: Number of rooms: 71, Number of floors: 2, Business center, Swimming pool - outdoor, Free breakfast, Parking (free), Complimentary newspapers in lobby, Wireless Internet.

★★
Candlewood Suites Turlock
1000 Powers Ct
Turlock CA 95380
(209) 250-1501
$81 - $99
Bed & Pet Discount Offered

Pet Policy: Pets up to 80 lbs accepted. Fee $75 per stay for up to 6 nights, $150 for longer. Must have current vaccination record.

Features: Accessible bathroom, Accessibility equipment for the deaf, Braille or raised signage, Number of rooms: 89, Number of floors: 3, Barbecue grill(s), Dry cleaning/laundry, Free wireless Internet, Grocery/convenience store, Business services, Complimentary newspapers, Fitness facilities.

Comfort Suites Turlock
191 N Tully Rd
Turlock CA 95380
(209) 667-7777
$74 - $79
Bed & Pet Discount Offered

Pet Policy: Pet Accommodations: $20 per pet per day. Pet Limit: 2 pets per room, 50 pounds and under.

Features: Free breakfast, Swimming pool - outdoor seasonal, Free wireless Internet, Number of floors: 3, Number of rooms: 71

Days Inn Turlock
185 N Tully Rd
Turlock CA 95380
(209) 634-2944
$41 - $60
Bed & Pet Discount Offered

Pet Policy: Pets allowed, $10 per night.

Features: Coffee in lobby, Number of floors: 2, Free breakfast, Complimentary newspapers in lobby, Security guard, Free wireless Internet

Not rated
Sunrise Inn
1350 N Golden State Blvd
Turlock CA 95380
(209) 216-5586
$39 - $110

Pet Policy: Pets up to 25 lbs accepted. Pets are required to have all their vaccination shots and must be Free of fleas and ticks. Current up-to-date vet documentation must be supplied to the Sunrise Inn Front Desk upon check-in. Pit bulls are forbidden at Sunrise Inn. Must be leashed when outside of room.

Features: Number of rooms: 42, refrigerators, microwaves, Nintendo Sports (additional charge), Internet (free), Free continental breakfast.

★★
Travelodge Turlock CA
201 W Glenwood Ave
Turlock CA 95380
(209) 668-3400
$59 - $80
Bed & Pet Discount Offered

Pet Policy: Pets any size welcome, $25.

Features: Business services, Coffee in lobby, Free breakfast, Multilingual staff, Complimentary newspapers, Wireless Internet, Swimming pool - outdoor seasonal, Guest laundry.

Twain Harte

Also see the following nearby communities that have pet friendly lodging: Sonora - 9 mile

Not rated
El Dorado Motel
22678 Twain Harte Drive
Twain Harte CA 95383
(209) 586-4479
$69 - $99

Pet Policy: Pets allowed, $25 per night. Limited to one of 3 pet friendly rooms, all having only outside entrances.

Features: Family oriented motel in the Sierra Foothills.

★★★½
McCaffrey House Bed & Breakfast
23251 State Highway 108
Twain Harte CA 95383
(209) 586-0757
From $171
Bed & Pet Discount Offered

Pet Policy: Dogs welcome, $25 per dog per night. Your dog may not be left alone in guest rooms. Please keep your dog on a leash in public areas. We will provide a sheet to cover the comforter should your dog sleep on the bed with you. When breakfast is served on the deck, your dog is welcome to join you. We ask that your dog be clean, well groomed, and have current shots and flea & tick care. An aggressive dog is not welcome, nor are young pups. A dog must be good around other people and like other dogs.

Features: Library, Free Breakfast, Video library, Suitable for children, Number of rooms: 8, Parking (free), Free wireless Internet.

Ukiah

Not rated
Best Western Plus Orchard Inn
555 South Orchard Avenue
Ukiah CA 95482
(707) 462-1514
$66 - $159

Pet Policy: Up to 2 dogs per room with a 80 pound weight limit. Additional pet types (cats, birds, etc.) may be accepted at the hotel's discretion. Pet rate is $20 per day with a $100 per week maximum

Features: HBO, Refrigerator, Microwave, Free wireless Internet, Free hot breakfast, Outdoor pool & hot tub, Business services.

★★½
Comfort Inn & Suites
1220 Airport Park Blvd
Ukiah CA 95482
(707) 462-3442
$89 - $124
Bed & Pet Discount Offered

Pet Policy: Pets up to 30 lbs accepted - $20/night. Maximum of 1 pet, per room allowed.

Features: Outdoor pool, Guest laundry, Business services, Free breakfast, Gift shops or newsstand, Number of rooms: 61, Number of floors: 2, Coffee in lobby, Free wireless Internet.

★★
Days Inn Ukiah
950 N State St
Ukiah CA 95482
(707) 462-7584
$41 - $122
Bed & Pet Discount Offered

Pet Policy: Pets allowed, $10 per night per pet

Features: Swimming pool - outdoor, Number of rooms: 54, Number of floors: 2, Business services, Coffee in lobby, Free breakfast, Complimentary newspapers in lobby, Free wireless Internet.

Discovery Inn Ukiah
1340 N State St
Ukiah CA 95482
(707) 462-8873
$59 - $129
Bed & Pet Discount Offered

Pet Policy: Pets welcome with fee. We can provide special hotel lodgings in our "pet wing," where your best friend will be truly pampered.

Features: Free wireless Internet, Free breakfast, Fitness facilities, Restaurant(s), Gift shops or newsstand, Number of rooms: 172, Number of floors: 2, Coffee in lobby, Guest laundry, Grocery, Swimming pool - outdoor seasonal, Business center.

Quality Inn Ukiah
1050 S State St
Ukiah CA 95482
(707) 462-2906
From $54
Bed & Pet Discount Offered

Pet Policy: Quality Inns charge a fee of $10 per night per pet and may require a $50 damage deposit, which is refunded if the room is in order at check out. Quality Inns accept any well-behaved pets with a maximum of 3 per room, but dogs are limited to 50 pounds. Most properties have designated rooms for people traveling with their pet. Pets may not be left alone in the room unless in a cage.

Features: Swimming pool - outdoor, Number of rooms: 43, Number of floors: 2, Business services.

Super 8 Ukiah
693 S Orchard Ave
Ukiah CA 95482
(707) 468-8181
$50 - $68
Bed & Pet Discount Offered

Pet Policy: Pets welcome, $5 per night per pet.

Features: Concierge desk, Free breakfast, Room service (limited hours), Business services, Guest laundry, Full-service health spa, Swimming pool - outdoor seasonal, Free wireless Internet.

Travelodge Ukiah
1720 N State St
Ukiah CA 95482
(707) 462-5745
$67 - $149
Bed & Pet Discount Offered

Pet Policy: Pets accepted, $10 per pet per day.

Features: Swimming pool - outdoor, Accessible bathroom, Accessibility equipment for the deaf, Braille or raised signage, Number of rooms: 55, Number of suites: 8, Number of floors: 2, Guest laundry, Business center, Gift shops or newsstand, Free breakfast, Dry cleaning/laundry service.

Union City

Also see the following nearby communities that have pet friendly lodging: Hayward - 4 miles, Newark - 5 miles, Fremont - 6 miles, Castro Valley - 8 miles.

Crowne Plaza Union City
32083 Alvarado Niles Rd
Union City CA 94587
(510) 489-2200
$90 - $128
Bed & Pet Discount Offered

Pet Policy: Pets accepted, $50 first night, $100 for more than 1 night.

Features: Swimming pool - outdoor, Bar/lounge, Airport transportation (free), Restaurant(s), ATM/banking, Gift shops or newsstand, Number of floors: 6, Business services, Multilingual staff, Complimentary newspapers in lobby, Room service, Business center, Porter/bellhop, Wireless Internet, Accessible bathroom, Accessibility equipment for the deaf, Braille or raised signage, Concierge desk, Fitness facilities.

Extended Stay America Union City - Dyer Street
31950 Dyer Street
Union City CA 94587
(510) 441-9616
$74 - $89
Bed & Pet Discount Offered

Pet Policy: One pet is allowed in each guest room. A $25 per day non-refundable cleaning fee (not to exceed $150) will be charged the first night stay.

Features: Guest laundry, Swimming pool – outdoor, Elevator, Number of rooms: 121, Number of floors: 4, Wireless Internet (additional charge), Parking (free), Front desk (limited hours).

Universal City

Also see the following nearby communities that have pet friendly lodging: Studio City - 3 miles, Hollywood - 3 miles, West Hollywood - 3 miles, Burbank - 4 miles, Beverly Hills - 5 miles, Glendale - 5 miles, Sherman Oaks - 6 miles, Van Nuys - 8 miles, Culver City - 9 miles, Los Angeles - 9 miles

★★★½
Hilton Los Angeles/Universal City
555 Universal Hollywood Dr
Universal City CA 91608
(818) 506-2500
$143 - $364
Bed & Pet Discount Offered

Pet Policy: Pets up to 75 lbs accepted, $50 per stay fee. Limit 2 pets per room.

Features: Swimming pool - outdoor, Bar/lounge, Elevator, Restaurant(s), Number of rooms: 483, Number of suites: 23, Number of floors: 24, Wireless Internet (additional charge), Breakfast available (additional charge), Multilingual staff, Business center, Porter/bellhop, Doorman/doorwoman, Security guard, Parking (valet) $22.00, Accessible bathroom, Accessibility equipment for the deaf, Dry cleaning/laundry, Smoke-Free property, Poolside bar, Concierge, Fitness facilities, Room service.

★★★½
Sheraton Universal Hotel
333 Universal Hollywood Dr
Universal City CA 91608
(818) 980-1212
$165 - $309
Bed & Pet Discount Offered

Pet Policy: Cats and dogs up to 80 pounds are allowed, with a maximum of two per room. Proof of vaccinations is required. Pets must be accompanied by owner at all times on a leash or in a crate or enclosed pet carrier. No pet deposit is required. A cleaning fee may be added if necessary.

Features: Bar/Lounge, Outdoor pool, Poolside bar, Business services, Concierge, Parking fee, Room service, Security guard, Restaurant(s), Gift shops, Number of rooms: 451, Number of floors: 20, Wireless Internet (additional charge), Currency exchange, Multilingual staff, Porter/bellhop, Limo or Town Car service available, Smoke-Free property, Dry cleaning/laundry, Fitness facilities.

Upland

Also see the following nearby communities that have pet friendly lodging: Claremont - 4 miles, Rancho Cucamonga - 5 miles, Ontario - 5 miles, Chino - 7 miles, Pomona - 7 miles, San Dimas - 8 miles, Chino Hills - 9 miles

★★
Guesthouse International Inn & Suites
1191 E Foothill Blvd
Upland CA 91786
(909) 949-4800
$69 - $99

Pet Policy: Pets accepted, contact hotel directly for details and reservations.

Features: Swimming pool - outdoor, Business center, Number of rooms: 114, Number of floors: 2, Business services, Guest laundry, Free breakfast, Complimentary newspapers, Accessible bathroom, Free wireless Internet, Fitness facilities.

Upper Lake

Also see the following nearby communities that have pet friendly lodging: Nice - 4 miles, Lakeport - 8 miles

Super 8 Motel - Upper Lake
450 E Highway 20
Upper Lake CA 95485
(707) 275-0888
$51 - $109
Bed & Pet Discount Offered

Pet Policy: Pets permitted, $10 per pet per night. Very limited number of pet rooms. Please confirm reservation directly with hotel before arriving.

Features: Free breakfast, Business services, Barbecue grill(s), Swimming pool - outdoor seasonal

Not rated:
Tallman Hotel
9550 Main Street
Upper Lake CA 95485
(707) 275-2244
$125 - $239

Pet Policy: We make every effort to accommodate well-trained pets under 20 pounds but availability can only be confirmed when booking by phone and an additional pet fee will apply.

Features: Year built: 1890, Swimming pool, Wireless Internet.

The Lodge At Blue Lakes
5135 W Highway 20
Upper Lake CA 95485
(707) 275-2181
$100 - $200
Bed & Pet Discount Offered

Pet Policy: Dogs only are allowed, up to 35 lbs, $25 per night. We do not accept the following breeds: Akita, Bull Dogs, Cane Corso, Chow, Doberman Pinscher, German Shephard, Mastiffs, Pit Bull, Presa Canario, Rottweiler. Dogs should not be left unattended in room for more than 2 hours, are not permitted in pool area and must be leashed when outside the room. Excessive noise is not permitted.

Features: Number of rooms: 20, Number of floors: 1, Barbecue grill(s), Free breakfast, Parking (free), Business center, Concierge desk, Marina on site, Smoke-Free property, Swimming pool - outdoor seasonal, Designated smoking areas, Free wireless Internet, RV and truck parking

Vacaville

Also see the following nearby communities that have pet friendly lodging: Fairfield - 9 miles, Suisun City - 9 miles, Dixon - 10 miles

Not rated
Americas Best Value Inn
1571 E Monte Vista Ave
Vacaville CA 95688
(707) 448-6482
$49 - $65

Pet Policy: Small pets welcome, no additional fee.

Features: Free continental breakfast, Outdoor swimming pool and Jacuzzi, Free wireless Internet, Microwave, Mini fridge, Cable TV, Iron and ironing board.

Courtyard by Marriott Vacaville
120 Nut Tree Pkwy
Vacaville CA 95687
(707) 451-9000
$89 - $119
Bed & Pet Discount Offered

Pet Policy: Now a Pet-Friendly Hotel, with designated rooms for easy access & convenience

Features: Restaurant(s), Swimming pool - outdoor, Number of rooms: 127, Number of floors: 2, Coffee in lobby, Parking (free), Complimentary newspapers in lobby, Free wireless Internet, Bar/lounge, Wheelchair accessible, Suitable for children, Barbecue grill(s), Health club, Multilingual staff, Use of nearby fitness center (free), Dry cleaning/laundry service, Smoke-Free property, 24-hour business center, Smoke-Free property, Snack bar/deli.

★★

Extended Stay America Sacramento - Vacaville
799 Orange Dr
Vacaville CA 95687
(707) 469-1371
$69 - $86
Bed & Pet Discount Offered

Pet Policy: Pets any size welcome, $25 per night, to maximum of $75.

Features: Elevator, Number of rooms: 92, Number of floors: 3, Wireless Internet (additional charge), Complimentary newspapers in lobby, Front desk (limited hours), Guest laundry.

★★½

Quality Inn And Suites
1050 Orange Dr
Vacaville CA 95687
(707) 446-8888
$62 - $74
Bed & Pet Discount Offered

Pet Policy: Pets allowed in pet friendly rooms. $95 per night. $150 refundable pet deposit required upon check in.

Features: Free breakfast, Swimming pool - outdoor, Restaurant, Number of rooms: 114, Number of floors: 2, Multilingual staff, Business center, Fitness facilities.

★★★

Residence Inn by Marriott Vacaville
360 Orange Dr
Vacaville CA 95687
(707) 469-0300
$113 - $190
Bed & Pet Discount Offered

Pet Policy: Pets up to 35 lbs accepted with $75 per stay. Limit of 2 per room.

Features: Grocery, Free breakfast, Gift shops or newsstand, Elevator, Swimming pool - indoor, Wheelchair accessible, Hair salon, Parking (free), Complimentary newspapers, Concierge, Smoke-Free property, Free wireless Internet, Fitness facilities.

★★

Super 8 Vacaville
101 Allison Ct
Vacaville CA 95688
(707) 449-8884
$48 - $79
Bed & Pet Discount Offered

Pet Policy: Dogs only, up to 50 lbs accepted, $10 per night per pet.

Features: Free breakfast, Parking (free), Swimming pool - outdoor seasonal

Valencia

Also see the following nearby communities that have pet friendly lodging: Stevenson Ranch - 3 miles, Santa Clarita - 3 miles, Castaic - 6 miles

Best Western Valencia Inn
27413 Wayne Mills Place
Valencia CA 91355
(661) 255-0555
$71 - $109

Pet Policy: Pets allowed. $10 per pet per night.

Features: HBO, Free wireless Internet, Outdoor swimming pool and hot tub, Free parking.

★★★

Hilton Garden Inn Valencia Six Flags
27710 The Old Rd
Valencia CA 91355
(661) 254-8800
$104 - $144
Bed & Pet Discount Offered

Pet Policy: Pets up to 75 lbs accepted, $50 per stay.

Features: Bar/lounge, , Restaurant(s), Room service, Outdoor pool, Wheelchair accessible, Parking (valet), Number of rooms: 152, Number of floors: 2, Computer rental, Business center, Smoke-Free property, Fitness facilities, Accessible bathroom, Accessibility equipment for the deaf.

Vallejo

Also see the following nearby communities that have pet friendly lodging: American Canyon - 5 miles, Martinez - 10 miles

Best Western Inn & Suites
1596 Fairgrounds Dr
Vallejo CA 94589
(707) 554-9655
$71 - $109
Bed & Pet Discount Offered

Pet Policy: Pets accepted with small fee at check-in.

Features: Nearby fitness center (free), Outdoor pool, Number of rooms: 117, Number of floors: 3, Free breakfast, Parking (free), Multilingual staff, Security guard, Free wireless Internet, Smoke-Free property

★★★

Courtyard by Marriott Vallejo Napa Valley
1000 Fairgrounds Dr
Vallejo CA 94589
(707) 644-1200
$109 - $159
Bed & Pet Discount Offered

Pet Policy: 1 pet up to 35 lbs, $25 per stay.

Features: Business center, Bar/lounge, Coffee in lobby, Room service, Security guard, Restaurant(s), Outdoor pool, Gift shops or newsstand, Number of rooms: 172, Number of floors: 5, Multilingual staff, Complimentary newspapers, Free wireless Internet, Smoke-Free, Dry cleaning/laundry, Fitness facilities.

★★

Howard Johnson Inn and Suites Vallejo
44 Admiral Callaghan Lane
Vallejo CA 94591
(707) 643-1061
$51 - $99

Pet Policy: Pet friendly with fee. Contact hotel directly for details and reservations.

Features: Business center, Nearby fitness center (free), Number of rooms: 78, Guest laundry, Free breakfast, Multilingual staff, Complimentary newspapers, Restaurant, Outdoor pool - seasonal, Grocery/convenience store, Free wireless Internet.

Ramada Inn Vallejo/Napa Valley Area
1000 Admiral Callaghan Ln
Vallejo CA 94591
(707) 643-2700
$80 - $99
Bed & Pet Discount Offered

Pet Policy: Pets up to 20 lbs allowed, $50 per stay. Limit 2 pets per room.

Features: Outdoor pool, BBQ area, Multilingual staff, Complimentary newspapers, Dry cleaning/laundry service, Free Breakfast, Free wireless Internet, Accessibility equipment for the deaf, Restaurant(s), Accessible bathroom, Nearby fitness center (free).

Travel Inn Vallejo
160 Lincoln Rd E
Vallejo CA 94591
(707) 552-7220
From $60
Bed & Pet Discount Offered

Pet Policy: Pets accepted with nominal fee.

Features: Coffee in lobby, Barbecue Grill(s), Number of rooms: 60, Number of floors: 2, Airport transportation (additional charge), Nearby fitness center (free), Free Internet, Dry cleaning/laundry.

Valley Ford

Also see the following nearby communities that have pet friendly lodging: Bodega - 1 mile, Occidental - 6 miles, Sebastopol - 7 miles

Valley Ford Hotel
14115 Coast Highway 1
Valley Ford CA 94972
(707) 876-1983
$115 - $116
Bed & Pet Discount Offered

Pet Policy: 1 medium size pet accepted in 1 designated room, $25 per stay.

Features: Suitable for children, Restaurant(s), Number of rooms: 6, Year Built 1864

Van Nuys

Also see the following nearby communities that have pet friendly lodging: Sherman Oaks - 3 miles, Northridge - 5 miles, Tarzana - 5 miles, Studio City - 6 miles, Canoga Park - 7 miles, Woodland Hills - 8 miles, Burbank - 8 miles, Universal City - 8 miles, Chatsworth - 8 miles, West Hollywood - 9 miles

Motel 6 Van Nuys
6909 Sepulveda Blvd
Van Nuys CA 91405
(818) 787-5400
$65 - $98
Bed & Pet Discount Offered

Pet Policy: Well-behaved pets stay Free. Animals that pose a health or safety risk may not remain onsite, and include those that, in our manager's discretion, are too numerous for any one room, cause damage to our property or that of other guests, are too disruptive, are not properly attended, or demonstrate undue aggression. All pets must be declared at check-in. Pets must be attended to and under control at all times. If unavoidable circumstances require a pet to remain in a room while the owner is offsite, the pet must be secured in a crate or travel carrier. Pets must be on a leash or securely carried outside of guest rooms.

Features: Outdoor pool, Elevator, Coffee in lobby.

Venice

Also see the following nearby communities that have pet friendly lodging: Marina Del Rey - 2 miles, Santa Monica - 3 miles, Culver City - 4 miles, Los Angeles - 6 miles, Inglewood - 6 miles, El Segundo - 7 miles, Beverly Hills - 7 miles, Hawthorne - 8 miles, Manhattan Beach - 9 miles, West Hollywood - 9 miles, Topanga - 10 miles

Cadillac Hotel
8 Dudley Avenue
Venice CA 90291
(310) 399-8876
$105 - $1,065
Bed & Pet Discount Offered

Pet Policy: Dogs and Cats accepted, $25 per pet per stay.

Features: Concierge desk, Elevator, Guest laundry, Parking $10/Day, Number of rooms: 47, Number of floors: 4, Arcade/game room, Pool table, Multilingual staff, Smoke-Free property, Bar/lounge, Wireless Internet (additional charge), Year Built 1914.

Su Casa at Venice Beach
431 Ocean Front Walk
Venice CA 90291
(310) 452-9700
$158 - $159

Pet Policy: We do not generally accept pets, but sometimes make exceptions. Please call directly to discuss your pet.

Features: Number of rooms: 12, Free wireless Internet, Free breakfast, Guest laundry, Suitable for children, Smoke-Free property, Restaurant(s).

Ventura

Also see the following nearby communities that have pet friendly lodging: Ojai - 10 miles

Cliff House Inn
6602 Pacific Coast Hwy
Ventura CA 93001
(800) 892-5433
$119 - $124
Bed & Pet Discount Offered

Pet Policy: Small pets accepted, with security deposit.

Features: Restaurant(s), Room service (limited hours), Swimming pool - outdoor, Suitable for children, Poolside bar, Free breakfast, Parking (free), Multilingual staff, Picnic area, Front desk (limited hours), Private beach, Free wireless Internet.

Crowne Plaza Ventura Beach
450 E Harbor Blvd
Ventura CA 93001
(805) 648-2100
$108 - $221
Bed & Pet Discount Offered

Pet Policy: Dogs only, $50. Allowed only in 4th floor non-ocean view rooms. Dogs may be allowed on beach if on leash.

Features: Outdoor pool, Free wireless Internet, Bar/lounge, Restaurant(s), Room service (limited hours), Concierge, Gift shops or newsstand, Number of rooms: 258, Number of floors: 12, Business services, Parking (fee), Guest laundry, Multilingual staff, Complimentary newspapers, Business center, Porter/bellhop, Accessible bathroom, Accessibility equipment for the deaf, Braille or raised signage, Dry cleaning/laundry service, Fitness facilities.

Four Points by Sheraton Ventura Harbor
1050 Schooner Dr
Ventura CA 93001
(805) 658-1212
$125 - $236
Bed & Pet Discount Offered

Pet Policy: Pets welcome, $75 per stay per pet. Limit of 2 per room. Pets must not be left unattended.

Features: Bar/lounge,, Restaurant(s), Room service , Outdoor pool, Number of rooms: 175, Number of floors: 3, Airport transportation (additional charge), Coffee in lobby, Breakfast available (additional charge),Complimentary newspapers, Business center, Security guard, Smoke-Free, Gift shop, Multilingual staff, Pick up service from train station, Accessible bathroom, Accessibility equipment for the deaf, Braille or raised signage, Dry cleaning/laundry, Free wireless Internet, Fitness facilities.

★★
La Quinta Inn Ventura
5818 Valentine Rd
Ventura CA 93003
(805) 658-6200
$52 - $85
Bed & Pet Discount Offered

Pet Policy: Cats and dogs up to 50 pounds are accepted in all guest rooms. Housekeeping services for rooms with pets require pet owner be present or pet must be crated. No fees or deposits are required.

Features: Swimming pool - outdoor, Accessible bathroom, Elevator, Number of rooms: 142, Number of floors: 3, Free breakfast, Parking (free), Multilingual staff, Dry cleaning/laundry service, Free Internet.

★★★½
Marriott Ventura Hotel
2055 Harbor Blvd
Ventura CA 93001
(805) 643-6000
$149 - $209
Bed & Pet Discount Offered

Pet Policy: Dogs up to 75 lbs accepted, $75 per stay.

Room service (limited hours), Elevator, Restaurant(s), Swimming pool - outdoor, Gift shops or newsstand, Number of rooms: 285, Number of floors: 4, Computer rental, Coffee in lobby, Breakfast available (additional charge), Shoe shine, Complimentary newspapers in lobby, Business center, Porter/bellhop, Security guard, Wireless Internet, Concierge desk, Parking garage (additional charge), Smoke-Free property, Dry cleaning/laundry service, Bar/lounge, Fitness facilities.

★★
Vagabond Inn Ventura
756 E Thompson Blvd
Ventura CA 93001
(805) 648-5371
$71 - $94
Bed & Pet Discount Offered

Pet Policy: Pets, any size accepted, $10 per night per pet.

Features: Free wireless Internet, Free Breakfast, Swimming pool - outdoor, Restaurant(s), Number of rooms: 82, Number of floors: 2, Coffee in lobby, Parking (free), Multilingual staff, Complimentary newspapers in lobby, Suitable for children

Victorville

Also see the following nearby communities that have pet friendly lodging: Hesperia - 8 miles, Adelanto - 8 miles

Ambassador Hotel Victorville
15494 Palmdale Rd
Victorville CA 92392
(760) 245-6565
$79 - $80
Bed & Pet Discount Offered

Pet Policy: Pets accepted, $25 per day.

Features: Poolside bar, Business center, Free breakfast, Suitable for children, Bar/lounge, Elevator, Number of rooms: 162, Number of floors: 6, Parking (free), Complimentary newspapers in lobby, Swimming pool - outdoor seasonal, Fitness facilities, Free wireless Internet.

Comfort Suites Victorville
12281 Mariposa Rd
Victorville CA 92395
(760) 245-6777
$84 - $89
Bed & Pet Discount Offered

Pet Policy: Pet Accommodations: $15 per night, non-refundable cleaning fee. Pets under 40 lbs, limit 2 per room.

Features: Business services, Coffee in lobby, Guest laundry, Number of rooms: 77, Number of floors: 3, Free breakfast, Parking (free), Complimentary newspapers in lobby, Free wireless Internet, Swimming pool - outdoor (heated), Fitness facilities.

Days Inn Suites Victorville
14865 Bear Valley Rd
Victorville CA 92392
(760) 948-0600
$58 - $99
Bed & Pet Discount Offered

Pet Policy: Pets allowed, $10 per pet per night

Free breakfast, Complimentary newspapers in lobby, Cable TV with HBO, Outdoor swimming pool, Guest laundry, Free wireless Internet, Microwave and fridges available.

Days Inn Victorville
15401 Park Ave E
Victorville CA 92392
(760) 241-7516
$43 - $61
Bed & Pet Discount Offered

Pet Policy: Pets Allowed.

Features: Swimming pool - outdoor, Free breakfast, Number of floors: 2, Free wireless Internet.

Hawthorn Suites by Wyndham Victorville
11750 Dunia Road
Victorville CA 92392
(760) 949-4700
$129 - $179
Bed & Pet Discount Offered

Pet Policy: Pets accepted, $5 per day per pet

Features: Free breakfast, Business center, Barbecue grill(s), Coffee in lobby, Swimming pool - outdoor, Elevator, Gift shops or newsstand, Number of rooms: 75, Number of floors: 3, Airport transportation (additional charge), Complimentary newspapers in lobby, Limo or Town Car service available, Free wireless Internet, Dry cleaning/laundry service, Self-parking (free), Fitness facilities.

Howard Johnson Express Victorville
16868 Stoddard Wells Rd
Victorville CA 92394
(760) 951-5958
$47 - $74

Pet Policy: Pet friendly with fee. Contact hotel directly for details and reservations.

Features: Free breakfast, Swimming pool – outdoor, Complimentary newspapers in lobby, Coffee maker, Iron and ironing board.

Quality Inn & Suites
14173 Green Tree Blvd
Victorville CA 92392
(760) 245-3461
$79 - $95
Bed & Pet Discount Offered

Pet Policy: Pets under 40 lbs, $15 per night. Limit 2 pets per room.

Features: Business services, Elevator, Bar/lounge, Restaurant(s), Swimming pool - outdoor, Gift shops or newsstand, Number of rooms: 168, Number of floors: 3, Coffee in lobby, Beauty services.

Red Roof Inn Victorville
13409 Mariposa Rd
Victorville CA 92395
(760) 241-1577
$44 - $89
Bed & Pet Discount Offered

Pet Policy: Pets Accepted. No Fee.

Outdoor pool, Wheelchair accessible, Number of rooms: 94, Number of suites: 14, Number of floors: 3, Coffee in lobby, Guest laundry, Free wireless Internet, Accessible bathroom, RV and truck parking.

★★

Victorville Travelodge
12175 Mariposa Rd
Victorville CA 92392
(760) 241-7200
$38 - $65
Bed & Pet Discount Offered

Pet Policy: Dog only, $6 per night.

Features: Free breakfast, Business services, Guest laundry, Parking (free), Wireless Internet, Swimming pool - outdoor seasonal.

Visalia

Also see the following nearby communities that have pet friendly lodging: Tulare - 9 miles

Holiday Inn Plaza - Visalia
9000 W Airport Drive
Visalia CA 93277
(559) 651-5000
$89 - $169
Bed & Pet Discount Offered

Pet Policy: Pet allowed with a non-refundable $25 fee per night. Specific ground-floor rooms only. Pet may not be left unattended in guest room. Leash Free Bark Park + Dog Run across street from hotel.

Features: Accessible bathroom, Accessibility equipment for the deaf, Braille or raised signage, Bar/lounge, Business center, Indoor & Outdoor pools, Restaurant, Room service Gift shop, Number of rooms: 256, Number of suites: 14, Number of floors: 5, Coffee in lobby, Multilingual staff, Complimentary newspapers, Porter/bellhop, Free wireless Internet, Dry cleaning/laundry service, Airport transportation (free), Fitness facilities.

La Quinta Inn & Suites Visalia/Sequoia Gateway
5438 W Cypress Ave
Visalia CA 93277
(559) 739-9800
$89 - $104
Bed & Pet Discount Offered

Pet Policy: Cats and dogs up to 50 pounds are accepted in all guest rooms. Housekeeping services for rooms with pets require pet owner be present or pet must be crated. No fees or deposits are required.

Features: Business center, Free wireless Internet, Smoke-Free, Indoor pool, Number of rooms: 65, Number of floors: 3, Coffee in lobby, Guest laundry, Free breakfast, Complimentary newspapers, Concierge, Accessible bathroom, Fitness facilities

Motel 6 - Visalia
4645 W. Noble Ave
Visalia CA 93277
(559) 732-5611
$55 - $75
Bed & Pet Discount Offered

Pet Policy: Well-behaved pets stay Free. Animals that pose a health or safety risk may not remain onsite, and include those that, in our manager's discretion, are too numerous for any one room, cause damage to our property or that of other guests, are too disruptive, are not properly attended, or demonstrate undue aggression. All pets must be declared at check-in. Pets must be attended to and under control at all times. If unavoidable circumstances require a pet to remain in a room while the owner is offsite, the pet must be secured in a crate or travel carrier. Pets must be on a leash or securely carried outside of guest rooms.

Features: Business services, Coffee in lobby, Free wireless Internet, Free breakfast, Complimentary newspapers, Business center, Outdoor pool.

Super 8 Visalia
4801 W Noble Ave
Visalia CA 93277
(559) 627-2885
$63 - $75
Bed & Pet Discount Offered

Pet Policy: Pets welcome, $20 per night per pet.

Features: Business services, Swimming pool - outdoor, Number of floors: 2, Parking (free)

Vista

Also see the following nearby communities that have pet friendly lodging: San Marcos - 4 miles, Carlsbad - 6 miles, Escondido - 7 miles, Oceanside - 8 miles, Encinitas - 9 miles

★★

Americas Best Value Inn Vista
330 Mar Vista Dr
Vista CA 92083
(760) 726-2900
$65 - $75
Bed & Pet Discount Offered

Pet Policy: Accepts small pets.

Features: Guest laundry, Business services, Number of floors: 2, Free breakfast, Parking (free), Free wireless Internet, Swimming pool - outdoor seasonal.

Casa Blanca Retreat
3215 Vista Pacifica
Vista CA 92084
(760) 599-9991
From $249

Pet Policy: Pets are not permitted inside the property, however they may stay, crated, outside the property with advanced approval.

Features: Swimming pool - outdoor, Barbecue grill(s), Guest laundry, Designated smoking areas.

★★

La Quinta Inn San Diego Vista
630 Sycamore Ave
Vista CA 92083
(760) 727-8180
$48 - $71
Bed & Pet Discount Offered

Pet Policy: Cats and dogs up to 50 pounds are accepted in all guest rooms. Housekeeping services for rooms with pets require pet owner be present or pet must be crated. No fees or deposits are required.

Features: Elevator, Swimming pool - outdoor, Accessible bathroom, Restaurant(s), Number of rooms: 106, Free breakfast, Parking (free), Multilingual staff, Internet (free).

TownePlace Suites by Marriott San Diego Vista
2201 S Melrose Dr
Vista CA 92081
(760) 216-6010
$139 - $179
Bed & Pet Discount Offered

Pet Policy: Pets accepted, $100 cleaning fee per stay.

Features: Barbecue grill(s), Coffee in lobby, Free breakfast, Parking (free), Complimentary newspapers in lobby, Dry cleaning/laundry service, Smoke-Free property, Free wireless Internet, Accessible bathroom, Accessibility equipment for the deaf, Braille or raised signage, 24-hour business center, Elevator, Swimming pool - outdoor heated, Wheelchair accessible, Concierge services, Number of rooms: 94, Number of floors: 3.

Walnut

Also see the following nearby communities that have pet friendly lodging: Diamond Bar - 2 miles, City Of Industry - 4 miles, Pomona - 6 miles, Brea - 7 miles, Chino Hills - 8 miles, San Dimas - 8 miles, Glendora - 8 miles, Chino - 9 miles, Placentia - 9 miles, Fullerton - 9 miles, Yorba Linda - 10 miles, Claremont - 10 miles

★★

Quality Inn And Suites Walnut
1170 Fairway Dr
Walnut CA 91789
(909) 594-9999
$74 - $99
Bed & Pet Discount Offered

Pet Policy: Pets up to 15 lbs, $35 per night plus $200 deposit. Limit of 2 pets per room. Available in designated pet rooms only.

Features: Guest laundry, Business services, Elevator, Arcade/game room, Swimming pool - outdoor, Number of rooms: 92, Number of floors: 2, Parking (free), Multilingual staff, Complimentary newspapers in lobby, Free wireless Internet.

Walnut Creek

Also see the following nearby communities that have pet friendly lodging: Pleasant Hill - 3 miles, Concord - 6 miles, Danville - 6 miles, Martinez - 7 miles

Holiday Inn Express Walnut Creek
2730 N Main St
Walnut Creek CA 94596
(925) 932-3332
$79 - $99
Bed & Pet Discount Offered

Pet Policy: Our hotel only accepts dogs, up to 20 lbs, for $25 per stay. Dogs cannot be left unattended in room at any time and are not permitted in the breakfast dining room.

Features: Bar/lounge, Multilingual staff, Room service, Business center, Free wireless Internet, Concierge, Free breakfast, Pick up service from train station, Accessible bathroom, Accessibility equipment for the deaf, Braille or raised signage, Dry cleaning/laundry, Outdoor pool, Smoke-Free, Area shuttle (free), Fitness facilities, Gift shop.

Not rated
Oakwood At Archstone Walnut Creek
1445 TREAT BLVD
Walnut Creek CA 95496
(602) 427-2752
$180 - $238

Pet Policy: Pets accepted with restrictions and fee. Contact hotel for more information reservations.

Features: Furnished apartments, Kitchens, Dining Room, Full bathroom(s), 1 and 2 bedroom units. Minimum 30 day stay may be required.

Warner Springs

Warner Springs Ranch
31652 Highway 79
Warner Springs CA 92086
(760) 782-4200
$109 - $119
Bed & Pet Discount Offered

Pet Policy: Pets accepted, $20 per night. Limited number of pet rooms. Be sure to declare pet at check in or additional fees may be charged.

Features: Full-service health spa, Hair salon, Bar/lounge, Restaurant(s), Outdoor pool, Gift shops or newsstand, Number of rooms: 234, Breakfast available (additional charge), Security guard, Grocery/convenience store, Accessible bathroom, Free wireless Internet.

Watsonville

Also see the following nearby communities that have pet friendly lodging: Freedom - 2 miles

Best Western Plus Rose Garden Inn
740 Freedom Blvd
Watsonville CA 95076
(831) 724-3367
$99 - $129
Bed & Pet Discount Offered

Pet Policy: Dogs allowed, at least 1 year old. $15 per day.

Features: Free breakfast, Outdoor pool, Number of rooms: 45, Number of floors: 2, Business services, Coffee in lobby, Guest laundry, Complimentary newspapers, Free wireless Internet, Fitness facilities.

Red Roof Inn Watsonville
1620 W Beach St
Watsonville CA 95076
(831) 740-4520
$55 - $59
Bed & Pet Discount Offered

Pet Policy: Pets welcome, first pet Free, 2nd is $15.

Features: Heated pool, Wheelchair accessible, Concierge, Number of rooms: 95, Number of suites: 2, Number of floors: 3, Coffee in lobby, Multilingual staff, Complimentary newspaper, Free Wireless Internet, Dry cleaning/laundry, Accessible bathroom, Business center, RV and truck parking.

Weed

Also see the following nearby communities that have pet friendly lodging: Mount Shasta - 8 miles

Comfort Inn Central
1844 Shastina Dr
Weed CA 96094
(530) 938-1982
$79 - $89
Bed & Pet Discount Offered

Pet Policy: Pets allowed with $100 refundable deposit plus $10 per night

Features: Guest laundry, Business services, Number of rooms: 55, Number of floors: 3, Coffee in lobby, Free breakfast, Swimming pool - outdoor seasonal, Swimming pool - outdoor, Fitness facilities.

Quality Inn And Suites Weed
1830 Black Butte Dr
Weed CA 96094
(530) 938-1308
$74 - $84
Bed & Pet Discount Offered

Pet Policy: Pets accepted, $15 per pet per night. Limit 2 per room.

Features: Free breakfast, Business services, Number of rooms: 50, Number of floors: 2, Coffee in lobby, Multilingual staff, Free wireless Internet.

West Hollywood

Also see the following nearby communities that have pet friendly lodging: Beverly Hills - 2 miles, Universal City - 3 miles, Hollywood - 3 miles, Studio City - 4 miles, Culver City - 6 miles, Los Angeles - 6 miles, Burbank - 7 miles, Sherman Oaks - 7 miles, Glendale - 7 miles, Santa Monica - 8 miles, Venice - 9 miles, Marina Del Rey - 9 miles, Inglewood - 9 miles, Van Nuys - 9 miles

Andaz West Hollywood - a Hyatt Hotel
8401 W Sunset Blvd
West Hollywood CA 90069
(323) 656-1234
$233 - $1,675
Bed & Pet Discount Offered

Pet Policy: Pets accepted with additional fee at check-in

Features: Currency Exchange, Bar/Lounge, Business services, Health club, Computer rental, Room service (24 hours), Restaurant(s), Swimming pool - outdoor, Number of rooms: 257, Number of floors: 14, Breakfast available (additional charge), Multilingual staff, Complimentary newspapers in lobby, Doorman/doorwoman, Security guard, Parking garage (fee), Accessible bathroom, Accessibility equipment for the deaf, Braille or raised signage, Dry cleaning/laundry service, Free wireless Internet.

Chamberlain West Hollywood
1000 Westmount Dr
West Hollywood CA 90069
(310) 657-7400
$179 - $369
Bed & Pet Discount Offered

Pet Policy: We do allow pets up to 25 pounds and there is a one-time fee of $100 per pet per week. We have a waiver form that is required to be filled out at time of check in.

Features: Swimming pool - outdoor, Spa services on site, Bar/Lounge, Business Services, Security guard, Concierge , Room service (24 hours), Restaurant(s), Wireless Internet (additional charge), Multilingual staff, Doorman/doorwoman, Limo or Town Car service available, Medical assistance available, Massage - treatment room(s), Complimentary newspapers, Nearby fitness center (discount), Dry cleaning/laundry service, Smoke-Free property.

Le Montrose Suite Hotel
900 Hammond St
West Hollywood CA 90069
(310) 855-1115
$169 - $299
Bed & Pet Discount Offered

Pet Policy: Pets accepted, $100 per pet fee.

Features: Security guard, Babysitting or child care, Parking (valet) $26/day, Room service, Concierge, Bar/lounge, Swimming pool - outdoor, Restaurant(s), On-site car rental, Gift shops or newsstand, Number of rooms: 132, Cell phone/mobile rental, Business services, Computer rental, Suitable for children, Wireless Internet (additional charge), Pool table, Spa services on site, Multilingual staff, Complimentary newspapers, Porter/bellhop, Doorman/doorwoman, Limo or Town Car service available, Dry cleaning/laundry, Fitness facilities.

Le Parc Suite Hotel
733 NW Knoll Drive
West Hollywood CA 90069
(310) 855-8888
$199 - $369
Bed & Pet Discount Offered

Pet Policy: Pets welcome, one-time $75 fee. Pets should not be left unattended in room. If absolutely necessary, please put out do not disturb sign. Also pets must be leashed when outside the room, and are not permitted in restaurant, health club or sky deck.

Features: Sauna, Swimming pool - outdoor, Business center, Parking (valet – $28 per day), Bar/lounge, Elevator, Restaurant(s), Room service, Concierge, Number of rooms: 154, Number of floors: 4, Translation services, Coffee in lobby, Breakfast available (additional charge), Video library, Porter/bellhop, Doorman/doorwoman, Limo or Town Car service available, Medical assistance available, Free wireless Internet, Barbecue grill(s), Accessible bathroom, Accessibility equipment for the deaf, Braille or raised signage, Multilingual staff, Dry cleaning/laundry service, Tennis on site, Health club.

★★★★½
London West Hollywood
1020 N San Vicente Blvd
West Hollywood CA 90069
(310) 854-1111
$279 - $629
Bed & Pet Discount Offered

Pet Policy: Dogs only, under 20 lbs. $275 deposit, $150 refundable. Limit 1 per room. Hotel has its own English Bulldog as property mascot.

Features: Concierge, Currency Exchange, Wheelchair Accessible, Bar/Lounge, Swimming pool - outdoor, Poolside bar, Room service (24 hours), Security guard, Free breakfast, Gift shops or newsstand, Number of rooms: 200, Number of floors: 10, Porter/bellhop, Doorman/doorwoman, Beauty services, Parking (valet) $32/day, Dry cleaning/laundry service, Free wireless Internet, 3 Restaurants, Suitable for children, Limo or Town Car service available, Designated smoking areas, Accessible bathroom, Multilingual staff, Braille or raised signage, 24-hour business center, Spa services on site, Health club.

★★★★
Palihouse Holloway
8465 Holloway Dr
West Hollywood CA 90069
(323) 656-4100
$249 - $524
Bed & Pet Discount Offered

Pet Policy: Pets up to 40 lbs accepted with fee of $125 for each month.

Features: Bar/lounge, Business services, Nearby fitness center (discount), Room service (limited hours), Free wireless Internet, Elevator, Restaurant(s), ATM/banking, Concierge services, Number of rooms: 37, Number of floors: 4, Cell phone/mobile rental, Parking (additional charge), Breakfast available (additional charge), Complimentary newspapers in lobby, Front desk (limited hours), Dry cleaning/laundry service

★★★★
Petit Ermitage
8822 Cynthia St
West Hollywood CA 90069
(310) 854-1114
$300 - $425
Bed & Pet Discount Offered

Pet Policy: Pets up to 15 lbs allowed, first floor only. $150 per stay.

Features: Swimming pool – outdoor, Concierge, Wheelchair accessible, Room service (24 hours), Number of suites: 80, Number of floors: 4, Business services, Parking fee, Security guard, Breakfast available (additional charge), Fitness facilities, Restaurant(s), Doorman/doorwoman, Number of Porter/bellhop, Dry cleaning/Laundry, Multilingual staff, Bar/lounge, Piano, Free wireless Internet.

Sunset Tower Hotel
8358 W Sunset Blvd
West Hollywood CA 90069
(323) 654-7100
$294 - $495
Bed & Pet Discount Offered

Pet Policy: Pets welcome with $100 per stay fee. Your dog gets a mini bed, bowl, and treats, and can run around off-leash at the park next door.

Features: Business Center, Dry cleaning/laundry, Room service (24 hours), Bar/lounge, Babysitting or child care, 2 Restaurants, Swimming pool - outdoor, Concierge, Number of rooms: 64, Video library, Currency exchange, Shoe shine, Multilingual staff, Complimentary newspapers, Porter/bellhop, Doorman/doorwoman, Security guard, Limo or Town Car service available, Free wireless Internet, Parking (valet) $25 Per Day, Accessible bathroom, Accessibility equipment for the deaf, Braille or raised signage, Year Built 1929, Fitness facilities.

West Sacramento

Also see the following nearby communities that have pet friendly lodging: Sacramento - 4 miles

Extended Stay America Sacramento - West Sacramento
795 Stillwater Rd
West Sacramento CA 95606
(916) 371-1270
$59 - $79
Bed & Pet Discount Offered

Pet Policy: One medium-size pet is allowed in each guest room. A $25 per day cleaning fee (not to exceed $150) will be charged the first night.

Features: Guest laundry, Number of rooms: 104, Number of floors: 3, Suitable for children, Coffee in lobby, Wireless Internet (additional charge), Parking (free), Nearby fitness center (discount).

★★★½

Ramada Inn & Plaza Harbor
1250 Halyard Dr
West Sacramento CA 95691
(916) 371-2100
$55 - $126
Bed & Pet Discount Offered

Pet Policy: Pets up to 25 lbs accepted, $25 per pet per day.

Features: Business center, Free breakfast, Outdoor pool, Gift shops or newsstand, Business services, Coffee in lobby, Porter/bellhop, Dry cleaning/laundry, Fitness facilities, Parking – fee.

Rodeway Inn Capitol
817 West Capitol Avenue
West Sacramento CA 95691
(916) 371-6983
$49 - $64
Bed & Pet Discount Offered

Pet Policy: Rodeway Inns charge a fee of $10 per night per pet plus a $50 damage deposit, which is refunded if the room is in order at check out. Max of 2 pets per room. A veterinarian certificate that the pet is on a flea and parasite program is required. Pets may not be left alone in the room unless crated.

Features: Business center, Number of rooms: 39, Number of floors: 2, Guest laundry, Free breakfast, Parking (free), Free wireless Internet, Airport transportation (additional charge)

Westlake Village

Also see the following nearby communities that have pet friendly lodging: Thousand Oaks - 6 miles, Calabasas - 8 miles

Four Seasons Westlake Village
2 Dole Dr
Westlake Village CA 91362
(818) 575-3000
$280 - $1,380
Bed & Pet Discount Offered

Pet Policy: Pets up to 15 lbs, no fee, limit of two per room. Must not leave unattended in room, and may not bring in food or pool areas.

Features: Bar/lounge, Babysitting or child care, Swimming pool - indoor, Swimming pool - outdoor, Wheelchair accessible, Parking (additional charge), ATM/banking, Gift shops or newsstand, Number of rooms: 269, Number of suites: 27, Number of floors: 5, Translation services, Computer rental, Suitable for children, Coffee in lobby, Poolside bar, Currency exchange, Health club, Room service (24 hours), Multilingual staff, Complimentary newspapers in lobby, Doorman/doorwoman, Security guard, Dry cleaning/laundry service, Beauty services, Concierge desk, Full-service health spa, Massage - treatment room(s), Smoke-Free property, Billiards, Technology support staff, Wireless Internet (additional charge), Porter/bellhop, Accessible bathroom, Accessibility equipment for the deaf, Braille or raised signage, 24-hour business center, 3 Restaurants.

★★★

Residence Inn Marriott Westlake
30950 Russell Ranch Rd
Westlake Village CA 91362
(818) 707-4411
From $114
Bed & Pet Discount Offered

Pet Policy: Pets allowed, $100 per stay cleaning fee

Features: Elevator, Free breakfast, Grocery, Parking (free), Multilingual staff, Business center, Limo or Town Car service available, Smoke-Free property, Billiards, Designated smoking areas, Accessible bathroom, Accessibility equipment for the deaf, Braille or raised signage, Dry cleaning/laundry service, Free wireless Internet, Swimming pool - outdoor, Guest laundry, Barbecue grill(s).

Westley

Also see the following nearby communities that have pet friendly lodging: Patterson - 4 miles

★★

Days Inn Westley
7144 Mccracken Rd I 5
Westley CA 95387
(209) 894-5500
$39 - $59
Bed & Pet Discount Offered

Pet Policy: Pets allowed, $10 per night per pet.

Features: Shopping on site, Coffee in lobby, Free breakfast, Wireless Internet, Swimming pool - outdoor seasonal, Guest laundry, Business center, RV and truck parking.

Econo Lodge Westley
7100 McCracken Rd
Westley CA 95387
(209) 894-3900
$54 - $64
Bed & Pet Discount Offered

Pet Policy: Pet Accommodation:$10/night, 1 pet up to 20 pounds

Features: Swimming pool - outdoor, Guest laundry, Free breakfast, Business services, Gift shops or newsstand, Number of rooms: 37, Number of floors: 2, Complimentary newspapers in lobby.

Westmorland

Americas Best Value Inn
351 West Main Street
Westmorland CA 92281
(760) 351-7100
$62 - $125

Pet Policy: Small pets, $20 per pet per night.

Features: Number of rooms: 47, Number of suites: 3, Free wireless Internet, Microwave, Mini fridge, Coffee maker, HBO, Free continental breakfast, Jacuzzi in 2 units, Swimming pool – indoor, Business services.

Whittier

Also see the following nearby communities that have pet friendly lodging: Pico Rivera - 4 miles, Norwalk - 4 miles, La Mirada - 4 miles, Downey - 6 miles, Cerritos - 6 miles, South El Monte - 6 miles, Bell Gardens - 6 miles, Commerce - 7 miles, City Of Industry - 8 miles, Buena Park - 8 miles, Fullerton - 8 miles, La Palma - 8 miles, Rosemead - 8 miles, Hawaiian Gardens - 8 miles, El Monte - 8 miles, Monterey Park - 9 miles, Brea - 9 miles, San Gabriel - 10 miles, Cypress - 10 miles

Not rated

Scottish Inns Whittier
11435 Whittier Boulevard
Whittier CA 90601
(562) 699-5199
$54 - $95

Pet Policy: Pets allowed.

Features: Number of rooms: 40, Free wireless Internet, Microwave and mini fridge.

★★

Vagabond Inn Whittier
14125 Whittier Blvd
Whittier CA 90605
(562) 698-9701
$64 - $65

Pet Policy: Pets accepted, $10 per pet per night. Limited number of pet friendly rooms, hotel requests booking directly.

Features: Free wireless Internet, Guest laundry, Free Breakfast, Outdoor pool, Number of rooms: 49, Number of floors: 3, Business services, Coffee in lobby, Multilingual staff, Complimentary newspapers.

Williams

Quality Inn Williams
400 C St
Williams CA 95987
(530) 473-2381
$74.- $84
Bed & Pet Discount Offered

Pet Policy: Quality Inns charge a fee of $10 per night per pet plus a $50 damage deposit, which is refunded if the room is in order at check out. Quality Inns accept any well-behaved pets with a maximum of 3 per room, but dogs are limited to 50 pounds. Pets may not be left alone in the room unless crated.
Continued on next page

Quality Inn Williams
Continued from previous page

Features: Gift shops or newsstand, Full-service health spa, Outdoor pool - seasonal, Free breakfast, Number of rooms: 60, Number of floors: 2.

Ramada Williams
374 Ruggeri Way
Williams CA 95987
(530) 473-5120
$63 - $79
Bed & Pet Discount Offered

Pet Policy: 1 pet per room up to 50 lbs, $25 per stay.

Features: Number of rooms: 51, Number of suites: 15, Number of floors: 2, Business services, Coffee in lobby, Guest laundry, Free breakfast, Multilingual staff, Complimentary newspapers, Wireless Internet, Fitness facilities.

Not Rated
Stage Stop Inn
330 7th Street
Williams CA 95987
(530) 473-2281
$36 - $54

Pet Policy: Pets welcome, $10 per night per pet additional fee.

Features: Continental Breakfast (free), Swimming pool, RV parking.

Willits

★★★
Baechtel Creek Inn & Spa, an Ascend Collection hot
101 Gregory Ln
Willits CA 95490
(707) 459-9063
$119 - $120
Bed & Pet Discount Offered

Pet Policy: Pet accommodation: 20.00 per night per pet. Pet limit: 2 pets per room, up to 25 lbs. If travelling with a pet, select pet-friendly room only.

Features: Business services, Health club, Outdoor pool, Gift shops or newsstand, Number of rooms: 43, Number of floors: 2, Free breakfast, Spa services on site, Free wireless Internet, Coffee in lobby, Smoke-Free property, Accessible bathroom, Complimentary newspapers, Nearby fitness center (discount).

Not rated
Old West Inn Willits
1221 South Main Street
Willits CA 95490
(707) 459-4201
$54 - $65

Pet Policy: Pets accepted, $15 per pet.

Features: Western themed rooms, Free continental breakfast, Free wireless Internet, Microwave, Refrigerator, Coffee maker.

Willows

Baymont Inn & Suites Willows
199 N Humboldt Ave
Willows CA 95988
(530) 934-9700
$63 - $139
Bed & Pet Discount Offered

Features: Pet Policy: Pets allowed, $10 per night per pet.

Free breakfast, Swimming pool - outdoor seasonal, Room service

Days Inn Willows Ca
475 N Humboldt Ave
Willows CA 95988
(530) 934-4444
$67 - $94
Bed & Pet Discount Offered

Pet Policy: Pets accepted, $10 per pet per night. No size restriction.

Features: RV and truck parking, Free breakfast, Business services, Coffee in lobby, Free wireless Internet, Swimming pool - outdoor seasonal.

Not rated:
Economy Inn Willows
435 North Tehama Street
Willows CA 95988
(530) 934-4224
$52 - $70

Pet Policy: Pets accepted, $10 per night per pet.

Features: Free wireless Internet, Smoking rooms available on request.

Holiday Inn Express & Suites Willows
545 N Humboldt Avenue
Willows CA 95988
(530) 934-8900
$108 - $124
Bed & Pet Discount Offered

Pet Policy: Pets accepted, $20 per pet per night.

Features: Accessible bathroom, Accessibility equipment for the deaf, Braille or raised signage, Swimming pool - outdoor, Number of floors: 3, Business center, Fitness facilities

Safari Motel
251 S Tehama St
Willows CA 95988
(530) 934-5923
$48 - $72
Bed & Pet Discount Offered

Pet Policy: Pets accepted. Please contact hotel directly for pet policy details.

Features: Wheelchair accessible, Number of rooms: 15, Guest laundry, Multilingual staff, Designated smoking areas, Free wireless Internet, Braille or raised signage, RV and truck parking.

Super 8 Willows
457 Humboldt Ave
Willows CA 95988
(530) 934-2871
$50 - $69
Bed & Pet Discount Offered

Pet Policy: Pets permitted, $10 per night per pet. Pets must remain quiet at all times.

Features: Business services, Free breakfast, Parking (free), Swimming pool - outdoor seasonal

Willows Travelodge
249 N Humboldt Ave
Willows CA 95988
(530) 934-4603
$48 - $115
Bed & Pet Discount Offered

Pet Policy: Pets allowed, $10 per night per pet

Features: Swimming pool - outdoor, Free breakfast, Parking (free)

Windsor

Also see the following nearby communities that have pet friendly lodging: Healdsburg - 6 miles, Santa Rosa - 8 miles

Hampton Inn & Suites Windsor/Sonoma Wine Country
8937 Brooks Road South
Windsor CA 95492
(707) 837-9355
$107 - $184
Bed & Pet Discount Offered

Pet Policy: Pets up to 25 lbs. $25 fee.

Features: Dry cleaning/laundry service, Swimming pool - outdoor, Number of rooms: 116, Number of floors: 3, Coffee in lobby, Free breakfast, Multilingual staff, Grocery/convenience store, Parking (free), Accessible bathroom, Accessibility equipment for the deaf, Braille or raised signage, Free wireless Internet, Wheelchair accessible, Suitable for children, Complimentary newspapers in lobby, Smoke-Free property, 24-hour business center, RV and truck parking, Fitness facilities.

Woodland

Days Inn Woodland
1524 E Main St
Woodland CA 95776
(530) 666-3800
$51 - $70
Bed & Pet Discount Offered

Pet Policy: Pets allowed, $10 per night per pet.

Features: Business services, Coffee in lobby, Free wireless Internet, Free breakfast, Parking (free), Complimentary newspapers in lobby, Swimming pool - outdoor seasonal

Holiday Inn Express Sacramento Airport Woodland
2070 Freeway Dr
Woodland CA 95776
(530) 662-7750
$133 - $162
Bed & Pet Discount Offered

Pet Policy: Pets allowed, $20 per night for first two pets, $20 per additional pet per night. Also a $20 deposit per pet per stay. Pets must never be left alone in the room.

Features: Accessible bathroom, Accessibility equipment for the deaf, Braille or raised signage, Free breakfast, Parking (free), Multilingual staff, Business center, Free wireless Internet, Smoke-Free property, Nearby fitness center (discount), Airport transportation (free), Swimming pool - indoor, Number of rooms: 69, Number of floors: 3, Dry cleaning/laundry service, Fitness facilities.

Woodland Hills

Also see the following nearby communities that have pet friendly lodging: Canoga Park - 2 miles, Tarzana - 3 miles, Calabasas - 5 miles, Topanga - 6 miles, Northridge - 6 miles, Chatsworth - 6 miles, Van Nuys - 8 miles, Sherman Oaks - 8 miles

Extended Stay America Los Angeles - Woodland Hills
20205 Ventura Blvd
Woodland Hills CA 91364
(818) 710-1170
$67 - $87
Bed & Pet Discount Offered

Pet Policy: One pet up to 40 lbs is allowed in each guest room. A $25 per cleaning fee (not to exceed $150) will be charged the first night of your stay.

Features: Guest laundry, Business services, Number of rooms: 146, Number of floors: 3, Coffee in lobby, Wireless Internet (additional charge), Parking (free), Use of nearby fitness center (discount).

Hilton Woodland Hills / Los Angeles
6360 Canoga Ave
Woodland Hills CA 91367
(818) 595-1000
$189 - $239
Bed & Pet Discount Offered

Pet Policy: Pets up to 75 lbs, $50 per stay fee, allowed on designated pet floor. Standard Rms Only.

Features: Technology helpdesk, Shoe shine, Coffee in lobby, Nearby fitness center (free), Pool table, Room service, Security guard, Bar/Lounge, Concierge, Business Center, Restaurant(s), Gift shops or newsstand, Number of rooms: 326, Number of floors: 16, Breakfast available (additional charge), Multilingual staff, Porter/bellhop, Wireless Internet, Smoke-Free property, Airport transportation (free), Dry cleaning/laundry, Fitness facilities, Parking fee.

Holiday Inn Woodland Hills-Warner Center
21101 Ventura Blvd
Woodland Hills CA 91364
(818) 883-6110
$89 - $154
Bed & Pet Discount Offered

Pet Policy: Pets accepted, $75 per stay cleaning fee.

Features: Swimming pool - outdoor, Business center, Bar/lounge, Elevator, Restaurant(s), Room service (limited hours), Concierge, Gift shops or newsstand, Number of rooms: 120, Number of floors: 6, Breakfast available (additional charge), Parking (free), Multilingual staff, Front desk (limited hours), Porter/bellhop, Free wireless Internet, Accessible bathroom, Accessibility equipment for the deaf, Braille or raised signage, Dry cleaning/laundry service, Fitness facilities.

★★★

Oakwood Woodland Hills East
22122 Victory Blvd.
Woodland Hills CA 91367
(602) 427-2752
$107 - $182

Pet Policy: Pets accepted with limitations and fee. Contact hotel directly for more information and to make reservations.

Features: Furnished apartments, Fireplaces available, Kitchens, Studios – 2 bedroom units. Minimum 30 stay may be required.

Yermo

Also see the following nearby communities that have pet friendly lodging: Barstow - 10 miles

Oak Tree Inn Yermo
35450 Yermo Rd
Yermo CA 92365
(760) 254-1148
$53 - $74
Bed & Pet Discount Offered

Pet Policy: Pets welcome, $10 per pet per night.

Features: Parking (free), Guest laundry, Swimming pool - outdoor heated, Fitness facilities, RV and truck parking, Restaurant(s)

Yorba Linda

Also see the following nearby communities that have pet friendly lodging: Placentia - 5 miles, Brea - 7 miles, Chino Hills - 7 miles, Orange - 8 miles, Diamond Bar - 9 miles, Fullerton - 9 miles, Anaheim - 9 miles, Walnut - 10 miles, Chino - 10 miles

Extended Stay America Orange County - Yorba Linda
22711 Oakcrest Cir
Yorba Linda CA 92887
(714) 998-9060
$56 - $78
Bed & Pet Discount Offered

Pet Policy: One pet is allowed in each guest room. A $25 per day non-refundable cleaning fee (not to exceed $150) will be charged the first night of your stay.

Features: Guest laundry, Elevator, Number of rooms: 117, Number of floors: 4, Business services, Wireless Internet (additional charge), Parking (free), Multilingual staff, Front desk (limited hours).

Yountville

Also see the following nearby communities that have pet friendly lodging: Napa - 8 miles, St Helena - 9 miles, Boyes Hot Springs - 9 miles

Bardessono
6526 Yount Street
Yountville CA 94599
(707) 204-6000
$399 - $650
Bed & Pet Discount Offered

Pet Policy: Pets welcome, $125 per pet per stay.

Features: Bar/lounge, Babysitting or child care, Restaurant(s), Swimming pool - outdoor, Wheelchair accessible, Gift shops or newsstand, Shopping on site, Parking (free), Multilingual staff, Number of rooms: 62, Number of floors: 2, Free wireless Internet, Porter/bellhop, Doorman/doorwoman, Concierge desk, Full-service health spa, Massage - treatment room(s), Smoke-Free property, Technology helpdesk, Dry cleaning/laundry service.

Lavender, A Four Sisters Inn
2020 Webber Ave
Yountville CA 94599
(707) 944-1388
$275 - $276
Bed & Pet Discount Offered

Pet Policy: Dogs only, up to 40 lbs, $65 additional fee, limit 2 per room. Pet owners will be liable for any additional cleaning bills or repairs, should they be required. All pets must be vaccinated and licensed and you agree to obtain and provide current records from a licensed veterinarian regarding this. The inn may request this information from you at any time.

Features: Concierge, Number of rooms: 8, Coffee in lobby, Free breakfast, Parking (free), Smoke-Free property, Free wireless Internet, Wheelchair accessible, Garden, Free reception.

Yreka

Baymont Inn & Suites
148 Moonlit Oaks Ave
Yreka CA 96097
(530) 841-1300
$54 - $98
Bed & Pet Discount Offered

Pet Policy: Pet friendly, $10 per pet per night

Features: Free breakfast, Free wireless Internet, Fitness facilities

Best Western Miners Inn
122 E Miner St
Yreka CA 96097
(530) 842-4355
$84 - $144

Pet Policy: Pets allowed, Pets 20 lbs. and under have a $5 fee; pets 21 lbs. and over have a fee of$10 fee

Features: Number of rooms: 130, Two bedroom suites available with kitchenettes.

Comfort Inn Yreka
1804b Fort Jones Rd
Yreka CA 96097
(530) 842-1612
$69 - $104
Bed & Pet Discount Offered

Pet Policy: Pets up to 35 lbs, $10 per night per pet plus $20 deposit.

Features: Coffee in lobby, Swimming pool - outdoor, Shopping on site, Business services, Free breakfast, Free wireless Internet, Number of rooms: 50.

★½

Econo Lodge Inn Suites Yreka
526 S Main St
Yreka CA 96097
(530) 842-4404
$53 - $61
Bed & Pet Discount Offered

Pet Policy: Pet Accommodation: $10/per night Pet Deposit: $20/per stay (Refundable). Maximum 2 pets per room up to 50 lbs.

Features: Number of rooms: 44, Number of floors: 2, Coffee in lobby, Free breakfast, Parking (free), Multilingual staff, Free wireless Internet, Swimming pool - outdoor seasonal, Airport transportation (additional charge), Fitness facilities.

Klamath Motor Lodge
1111 S Main St
Yreka CA 96097
(530) 842-2751
$49 - $61
Bed & Pet Discount Offered

Pet Policy: Dogs only with nightly fee.

Features: Swimming pool - outdoor, Number of rooms: 28, Number of floors: 2, Free breakfast, Concierge desk, Free wireless Internet.

Not rated:
Relax Inn of Yreka
1210 South Main Street
Yreka CA 96097
(530) 842-2791
$44 - $57

Pet Policy: Pets welcome, $5 per night per pet, limit of 3 per room. Pets are not allowed in the lobby.

Features: Coffee maker, Microwave, Mini fridge, Hair dryer, Free continental breakfast, Swimming pool, Kids under 12 stay Free.

Rodeway Inn Yreka
1235 S Main St
Yreka CA 96097
(530) 842-4412
$52 - $54
Bed & Pet Discount Offered

Pet Policy: Rodeway Inns charge a fee of $10 per night per pet and require a $50 damage deposit, which is refunded if the room is in order at check out. Max of 2 pets per room. A veterinarian certificate that the pet is on a flea and parasite program and that they are Free from parasites is required. Pets may not be left alone in the room unless in a cage.

Features: Number of rooms: 41, Number of floors: 1, Free breakfast, Swimming RV and truck parking, Swimming pool - outdoor, Health club.

Super 8 Yreka Ca
136 Montague Rd
Yreka CA 96097
(530) 842-5781
$48 - $69
Bed & Pet Discount Offered

Pet Policy: Pets welcome, any size, $10 per night per pet.

Features: Business services, Free breakfast, Parking (free), Swimming pool - outdoor seasonal, RV and truck parking

Yuba City

Also see the following nearby communities that have pet friendly lodging: Marysville - 3 miles

Days Inn Yuba City
700 N Palora Ave
Yuba City CA 95991
(530) 674-1711
$42 - $65
Bed & Pet Discount Offered

Pet Policy: Pet Accommodations:$50 refundable deposit and$10 per night, per pet, up to 2 pets, limit of 60 lbs.

Features: Number of floors: 2 – no Elevator, Swimming pool - outdoor, Business services, Free breakfast, Parking (free), Complimentary newspapers in lobby.

Econo Lodge Inn And Suites Yuba City
730 N Palora Avenue
Yuba City CA 95991
(530) 674-1592
$49 - $68
Bed & Pet Discount Offered

Pet Policy: Pets up to 60 lbs, $10 per pet per night. Limit 2 per room.

Features: Business services, Guest laundry, Free breakfast, Coffee in lobby, Number of rooms: 52, Number of floors: 3, Parking (free), Complimentary newspapers in lobby, Wireless Internet (free), Swimming pool - outdoor seasonal.

Yucca Valley

Super 8 Motel Yucca Valley Joshua Tree National Pa
57096 29 Palms Hwy
Yucca Valley CA 92284
(760) 228-1773
$44 - $60
Bed & Pet Discount Offered

Pet Policy: Pets welcome, $10 per pet per night.

Features: Business services, Coffee in lobby, Free breakfast, Parking (free), Swimming pool - outdoor seasonal

www.ingramcontent.com/pod-product-compliance
Lightning Source LLC
Chambersburg PA
CBHW070337090426
42733CB00009B/1216
* 9 7 8 0 6 1 5 4 9 9 0 4 8 *